Brief Contents

the Bedford Book of Genres

a guide & reader

Amy Braziller
Red Rocks Community College

Elizabeth Kleinfeld
Metropolitan State College of Denver

BEDFORD / ST. MARTIN'S
Boston ◆ New York

For Bedford/St. Martin's

Publisher for Composition: Leasa Burton
Executive Editor: Ellen Thibault
Senior Production Editor: Deborah Baker
Assistant Production Manager: Joe Ford
Executive Marketing Manager: Molly Parke, Emily Rowin
Editorial Assistant: Amanda Legee
Copyeditor: Jennifer Greenstein
Indexer: Mary White
Permissions: Susan Doheny, Caryn Burtt
Senior Art Director: Anna Palchik
Text Design: Emily F. Friel
Cover Design: Marine Miller, Donna Dennison
Composition: Integra
Printing and Binding: RR Donnelley and Sons

President, Bedford/St. Martin's: Denise B. Wydra
Editorial Director, English and Music: Karen S. Henry
Director of Marketing: Karen R. Soeltz
Production Director: Susan W. Brown
Director of Rights and Permissions: Hilary Newman

Manufactured in the United States of America.
9 8 7 6 5 4
f e d c b a

For information, write: Bedford/St. Martin's, 75 Arlington Street, Boston, MA 02116
  (617-399-4000)

ISBN 978-0-312-38656-6

Acknowledgments

Acknowledgments and copyrights appear on the same page as the text and art selections they cover; these acknowledgments and copyrights constitute an extension of the copyright page. It is a violation of the law to reproduce these selections by any means whatsoever without the written permission of the copyright holder.

Preface for Instructors

It's a beautiful, multimodal world. It's a gorgeous stream of videos, blogs, ads, radio essays, graphic novels, PowerPoint presentations, editorials, artifacts, profiles, and infographics. It's colorful, chaotic, and fascinating. With so many genres in the world, why limit our students to the written essay (as wonderful a genre as it is)? Why not use multiple genres to teach students how to read and respond to any rhetorical situation?

The Bedford Book of Genres grew out of our wish to help our students with rhetorical analysis—to help them see its value and learn how to apply it in any setting. We hope that students using this book will recognize rhetorical analysis as the foundation for reading any kind of text critically and for composing any kind of text persuasively. We hope they'll experiment and take risks while learning to think through their research, composing, and reflecting processes in terms of purpose, audience, and other considerations. We hope they'll create smart, interesting work that's fun and thought-provoking for them to compose—and for you to grade (not to be underrated!).

So why a book about genres? Because working in a variety of genres and modes gets students to invest in what they do in first-year writing. When we began to experiment with multigenre/modal assignments in our own classrooms, we saw that happen. Now our students are excited, curious, and really "into" their projects. They bring fun, imagination, and personality into their academic work. And they see what they do in terms of skills they can travel with, and work they can showcase in their portfolios.

A Rhetorical Road Map for Reading & Composing—in Any Genre

We set out to make this book do two things, mainly. First, to provide the basics that students need to read any text, follow any author's rhetorical moves, and recognize the elements at work in any genre. Second, to offer a framework for analysis and composition to help students understand their *own* rhetorical situations, to make smart choices as composers themselves, and to select and work in genres that are best for their purposes.

No one is an expert on every genre. But we, you, and our students don't have to be. We can all start from different places, and with any level, or lack, of technical skills. With these factors in mind, we do not cover every genre there is (though our editor did make us try!). Instead, we've put together a compendium of common genres. And we present them for students to read and analyze, and for them to use as models or jumping-off points for their own creations.

How This Book Is Organized

THE GUIDE

This is the heart of the book, where we introduce students to the concept of genres, then move them from analyzing the work of others to composing their own texts. The Guide is divided into two parts.

Part 1: Experimenting with Genres

1. Understanding Genres • 2. Narrative Genres • 3. Informative Genres • 4. Persuasive Genres

In Part 1, students explore the world of genres based on three primary purposes: narrating, informing, and persuading. Here they learn to apply a rhetorical lens for analyzing a variety of genre texts so that they can understand authors' choices (with a focus on purpose, audience, rhetorical appeals, modes, and media). At the same time, they learn to identify what makes a genre a genre. Students learn to analyze conventions, to examine the common elements of a given genre and the typical use of style, design, and sources. The Guided Readings, dozens of texts that we've annotated to point out composers' rhetorical situations and how they work with their chosen genre (explained in detail on p. ix), are a big part of how this all happens. Also in Part 1, we nudge students toward experimentation and sketching out their own genre compositions.

Part 2: Composing in Genres

5. Exploring Topics & Creating a Research Proposal • 6. Evaluating & Choosing Sources • 7. Integrating & Documenting Sources • 8. Composing in Genres • 9. Revising & Remixing Your Work • 10. Assembling a Multigenre Project

In Part 2, students move from exploring a topic to creating and finishing a project. They follow six student authors and artists through every step of the research and composing processes. Jasmine Huerta takes us with her as she explores her topic (diabetes) and drafts a research plan (Chapter 5); Emily Kahn shows us how she evaluates a specific source for her project on women in comic books; and Calvin Sweet chooses one out of three possible sources on the subject of race and

Hurricane Katrina (Chapter 6). Paul Pierre shows us how to quote from a source, paraphrase, and summarize as he fleshes out his work on nonviolent protest (Chapter 7), and in Chapters 8 and 9, Gwen Ganow takes us through her entire process, from drafting to her final work on the social value of superheroes.

THE READER

11. Identity • 12. The Body • 13. The Environment • 14. Heroes & Villains

In the Reader, we offer a thematic approach to a variety of topics and genres. The readings offer models for composing, sources to draw upon, and hopefully some moments that are thought-provoking, entertaining, and inspiring, too. (For more on this, see pp. xiii–xiv.)

Guided Readings—Help Students Analyze Various Genres, in Print and Online

Annotated Guided Readings throughout the Guide and e-pages highlight the rhetorical moves that writers and composers make in different genres and modes, and point out common genre conventions. We've designed the annotations—presented in the margins of twenty-seven texts—to help students see what choices authors make, and what the consequences of those choices are. As students notice what professional writers and composers do, they become more aware of what they can and should do in their own work.

These Guided Readings demystify genres and help students recognize familiar strategies composers make across genres, such as appealing to readers' sense of pathos or logos. They also help students understand aspects of composing in genres and modes they might not be familiar with, and to look at features such as design.

How to Find and Use a Guided Reading

The Guided Readings are clearly listed in the book's table of contents and in chapter menus; they are designed with large headings and framed with annotations, and the genre of the reading is named in a color-coded navigational bar at the top of the page.

The annotations in the margins of the Guided Readings are structured around two main ideas: (1), the composer's specific rhetorical situation (purpose, audience, rhetorical appeals, modes/media); and (2), the typical conventions of the genre (common elements, style, design, and sources). We see this as a kind of "grid" that

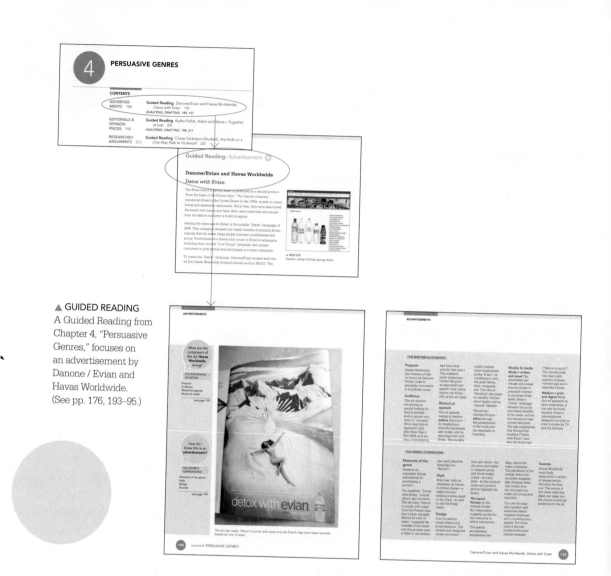

▲ GUIDED READING
A Guided Reading from Chapter 4, "Persuasive Genres," focuses on an advertisement by Danone / Evian and Havas Worldwide. (See pp. 176, 193–95.)

students might apply whenever they read or compose any kind of text, in their composition course and beyond.

As your students begin to learn about reading genres critically, you may ask them to annotate texts that you or they bring to class (texts not included in the book); they might want to model their analyses on the structure of the annotations that appear in the margins of our Guided Readings. You'll find Guided Readings in Chapters 1–4 and in Chapters 8 and 10.

GUIDED READINGS

Guided Processes—Show How Other Students Compose

As mentioned above, we follow several of our former students throughout the book, showing work they did in our classes in various stages, from brainstorming to finished project. Allowing students to see how other real students approach composing in genres lets students see that there is no one-size-fits-all way to compose. Seeing, for example, how Gwen Ganow, featured in Chapters 8–10, moves from a very early rough draft through a variety of later drafts shows how important revision is and, more importantly, what revision looks like for a real student writer.

Kristen LaCroix's three-dimensional collage, featured in Chapter 1, "Understanding Genres," inspires students to think creatively about how they can present their own ideas. More multigenre projects are showcased in Chapter 10, where you'll find Gwen Ganow's complete project, Dawson Swan's project on nature deficit disorder, and Neil Carr's project on video games and violence.

Presenting real students' work also gives us a chance to show that we envision the students who will use this book as interesting and complex, and as desiring a challenge to compose using various techniques for a variety of outcomes.

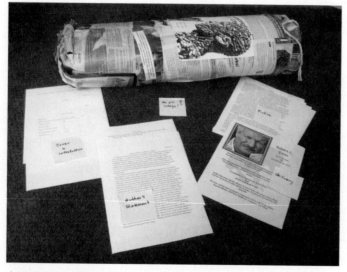

▲ MULTIGENRE PROJECT   One of the multigenre projects in the book is by student Kristen LaCroix, who created and assembled a variety of genre compositions critiquing direct-to-consumer prescription drug advertising. (See Chapter 1, p. 23.)

How to Find and Use a Guided Process

Like the Guided Readings, the Guided Processes (found in Chapters 5–9) are easy to locate in the table of contents, in the chapter menus, and on the page. Guided Processes walk your students through the steps other students have taken to research, compose, and revise, working in genres that were in some cases new and unfamiliar to them. They show that students don't have to begin as experts to research a topic and make a point about it in a new and interesting way.

The Guided Processes also work as reference materials that students can refer back to as they work through their own projects.

GUIDED PROCESSES ▶
Part of two Guided Processes, from Chapter 8 (see pp. 436, 444–45, 451). In Chapters 8, 9, and 10, we follow one student, Gwen Ganow, as she moves from a brainstorm and exploratory draft, through her research, composing, revising, and remixing processes.

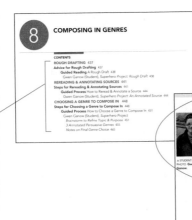

8

COMPOSING IN GENRES

CONTENTS

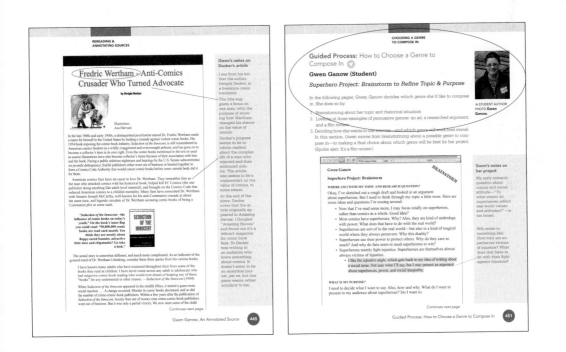

REREADING & ANNOTATING SOURCES

Guided Process: How to Reread & Annotate a Source ▼

Gwen Ganow (Student)

Superhero Project: An Annotated Source

A STUDENT AUTHOR PHOTO Gwen Ganow.

Gwen decided to return to her sources, which included Dwight Decker's essay "Fredric Wertham: Anti-Comics Crusader Who Turned Advocate" (see p. 445), Brandford Wright's book *Comic Book Nation*, and various comic books by Alex Ross. She focused on the Dwight Decker essay, which she had found through a simple Google search on the history of comics. She especially liked how the author of the piece approached comics as a subject worthy of serious study. She also liked the author's tone and thought she might want to use a similar tone in her own writing. In this way, Gwen read this piece as both a source of information and a source of inspiration for *how* to write about her topic.

Gwen found Dwight Decker's article at *The Art Bin*, a magazine published by Karl-Erik Tallmo of Slowtox Press and archived at the press's blog. Decker notes at the end of his article: "This is a re-written version of an article that appeared in the magazine *Amazing Heroes* in 1987. Also available in Swedish. © Dwight Decker, 1987, 1997." *Amazing Heroes* (1981–1992, published by Fantagraphics Books) was a magazine about comics for comic book fans. The article is reprinted here.

By permission of the author, © Dwight Decker.

REREADING & ANNOTATING SOURCES

Fredric Wertham—Anti-Comics Crusader Who Turned Advocate

by Dwight Decker

Illustration: Asa Harvard.

In the late 1940s and early 1950s, a distinguished psychiatrist named Dr. Fredric Wertham made a name for himself in the United States by leading a crusade against violent comic books. His 1954 book exposing the comic-book industry, *Seduction of the Innocent*, is still remembered in American comics fandom as a wildly exaggerated and overwrought polemic and has gone on to become a collector's item in its own right. Even the comic books mentioned in the text or used as source illustrations have also become collector's items because of their association with him and the book. Facing a public relations nightmare and hearings by the U.S. Senate subcommittee on juvenile delinquency, fearful publishers either went out of business or banded together to form a Comics Code Authority that would censor comic books before some outside body did it for them.

American comics fans have no cause to love Dr. Wertham. They remember him as the man who attacked comics with his hysterical book, helped kill EC Comics (the one publisher doing anything like adult-level material), and brought on the Comics Code that reduced American comics to a childish mentality. Many fans have associated Dr. Wertham with Senator Joseph McCarthy, well-known for his anti-Communist crusade at about the same time, and legends circulate of Dr. Wertham accusing comic books of being a Communist plot or some such.

"*Seduction of the Innocent*—the influence of comic books on today's youth." On the book's inner flap you could read: "90,000,000 comic books are read each month. You think they are mostly about floppy-eared bunnies, attractive little mice and chipmunks? Go take a look."

SEDUCTION OF THE INNOCENT

The actual story is somewhat different, and much more complicated. As an indicator of the general trend of Dr. Wertham's thinking, consider these three quotes from his various books:

I have known many adults who have treasured throughout their lives some of the books they read as children. I have never come across any adult or adolescents who had outgrown comic-book reading who would ever dream of keeping any of these "books" for any sentimental or other reason. — *Seduction of the Innocent* (1954)

When *Seduction of the Innocent* appeared in the middle fifties, it started a grass-roots social reaction. . . . A change occurred. In comic books decreased, and so did the number of crime-comic-book publishers. Within a few years after the publication of *Seduction of the Innocent*, twenty-four out of twenty-nine crime-comic-book publishers went out of business. But it was only a partial victory. We now meet some of the child

Continues next page

Gwen Ganow, An Annotated Source **445**

Gwen's notes on Decker's article

I see from his bio that the author, Dwight Decker, is a freelance comic translator.

The title suggests a focus on one man, with the purpose of showing how Wertham changed his stance on the value of comics.

Decker's purpose seems to be to inform readers about the complex life of a man who rejected and then embraced comics. The article also seems to be a commentary on the value of comics, to some extent.

At the end of the piece, Decker notes that the article originally appeared in *Amazing Heroes*. I Googled "*Amazing Heroes*" and found out it's a defunct magazine for comic book fans. So Decker was writing to an audience who knew something about comics. It doesn't seem to be an analytical journal, per se, but this piece seems rather scholarly to me.

CHOOSING A GENRE TO COMPOSE IN

Guided Process: How to Choose a Genre to Compose In ▼

Gwen Ganow (Student)

Superhero Project: Brainstorm to Refine Topic & Purpose

A STUDENT AUTHOR PHOTO Gwen Ganow.

In the following pages, Gwen Ganow decides which genre she'd like to compose in. She does so by:

1. Brainstorming about her topic and rhetorical situation
2. Looking at three examples of persuasive genres: an ad, a researched argument, and a film review.
3. Deciding how she wants to use sources—and which genre will work best overall. In this section, Gwen moves from brainstorming about a possible genre to compose in—to making a final choice about which genre will be best for her project. (Spoiler alert: It's a film review.)

Print Layout View   Size: 1   100%

Gwen Ganow

Superhero Project: Brainstorm   BRAINSTORM

WHERE AM I WITH MY TOPIC AND RESEARCH QUESTION?

Okay, I've sketched out a rough draft and looked at an argument about superheroes. But I need to think through my topic a little more. Here are some ideas and questions I'm tossing around:

• Now that I've read some more, I may focus totally on superheroes, rather than comics as a whole. Good idea?
• Most comics have superheroes. Why? Also, they are kind of underdogs with power. What does that have to do with the real world?
• Superheroes are sort of in the real world—but also in a kind of magical world where they always persevere. Why this duality?
• Superheroes use their power to protect others. Why do they care so much? And why do fans seem to need superheroes to win?
• Superheroes mainly fight injustice. Superheroes are themselves almost always victims of injustice.
   • I like the injustice angle, which gets back to my idea of writing about a social issue. Not sure what I'll say, but I may present an argument about superheroes, power, and social inequality.

WHAT IS MY PURPOSE?

I need to decide what I want to say. Also, how and why. What do I want to present to my audience about superheroes? Do I want to

Continues next page

Guided Process: How to Choose a Genre to Compose In **451**

Gwen's notes on her project

My early research question about comics and social attitude—"To what extent do superheroes reflect real-world values and attitudes?"—is too broad.

Will revise to something like: How/why are superheroes victims of injustice? What does that have to do with their fight against injustice?

GUIDED PROCESSES

Chapter 5
Sharon Freeman (Student), *How to Choose a Topic*
Jasmine Huerta (Student), *How to Create a Bibliography*

Chapter 6
Emily Kahn (Student), *How to Preview a Source*
Calvin Sweet (Student), *How to Evaluate Sources*

Chapter 7
Paul Pierre (Student), *How to Quote from a Source*
Paul Pierre (Student), *How to Paraphrase a Source*
Paul Pierre (Student), *How to Summarize a Source*

Chapter 8
Gwen Ganow (Student), *How to Reread & Annotate a Source*
Gwen Ganow (Student), *How to Choose a Genre to Compose In*
Gwen Ganow (Student), *How to Compose a Genre Piece*
Gwen Ganow (Student), *How to Compose an Author's Statement*

Clear Guidance on the Author's/Artist's Statements Students Write to Accompany Their Work

We believe that the Author's/Artist's Statements that students compose—in which they explain how and why they created their specific genre composition(s)—are crucial. And we've found, through our review programs, conference panels, hands-on workshops, and conversations with many of you, that you think the same. These Statements give students a venue in which to discuss their work in terms of choices and intentions and even to make a case for the sources they drew on (we ask our students to include Works Cited pages with their Statements). Most significantly, these reflective pieces give students a place to think critically about their composing processes, about how they worked with (or outside of) a genre's typical conventions, and how they positioned themselves rhetorically, in terms of their audience and purpose. Even if, say, a student is not pleased with her genre composition (maybe her collage is less than perfect, or her brief documentary or her video ad is not exactly what she'd hoped, or she didn't plan her time well, or she didn't have ample resources), she can still do the thoughtful work in her Statement that we want to see in a first-year writing course. Because being able to reflect on and constructively critique one's own work is a lifelong skill that will serve our students well beyond our classrooms.

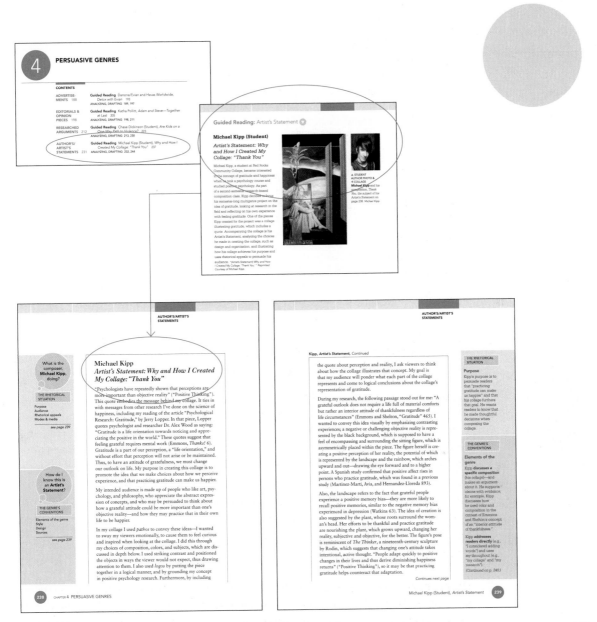

A Collection of Thematic Readings—with a Great Mix of Genres and Modes—for Students to Draw On

While some themes in our Reader (identity, the body, the environment, heroes and villains) are found in other textbooks, the readings themselves take an unusual approach to the topic. For example, in Chapter 12, "The Body," we include a medical history of Ronald Reagan and a provocative fat studies essay. And Chapter 14, "Heroes & Villains," is not your typical textbook fare. When we chose the readings,

▲ ARTIST'S STATEMENT
This Artist's Statement by student Michael Kipp, presented as a Guided Reading in Chapter 4, shows Kipp's analysis of and reflection on his own work. (Excerpted here. See pp. 238–42.)

we made sure to offer a variety of voices and genres, including research-based essays, blog entries, instructions, advertisements, and photographs.

Students can use these chapters to help them hone their critical reading skills, study the rhetorical choices composers make in various genres, and integrate different pieces for research-based writing on these topics. Each chapter begins with an introduction to the theme followed by a selection of starter projects that help students generate ideas related to the topic and anticipate some of the ideas the chapter explores. Clusters of readings are followed by a group of rhetorical analysis questions and a variety of activities geared toward composing in genres. Each chapter ends with more lengthy composing assignments that we've named research experiments.

Navigable and Flexible

We've designed this book to work both as a guide that supports students as they analyze and compose their own multimodal texts and as a reference that they can easily refer to as they work on their own or with peers. Color-coded labeling of genres, easy-to-find annotated readings, and bands at the top of each page clearly indicate where you are in each chapter. In Chapter 7, "Integrating & Documenting Sources," blue and green framing set off the MLA and APA coverage, and visual examples of sources reinforce many of the entries.

In addition to the reference features, we wanted to make this book flexible enough to support a variety of approaches to first-year composition. Whether you ask your students to compose in different genres or not, we hope you will take advantage of the guidelines provided for applying rhetorical analysis, as well as the variety of texts and genres that students can use for practicing rhetorical analysis.

For those of you who like to emphasize visual rhetoric in your class, you might focus on the many visual examples in the book, including maps, photo essays, and infographics.

If your primary focus is on interesting topics and themes, you might want to teach the book through a thematic lens. In addition to the thematic chapters and clusters in the Reader, we have provided an Index of Themes that sorts the rich contents of the book into plenty of relevant and exciting categories that will spark student attention and imagination.

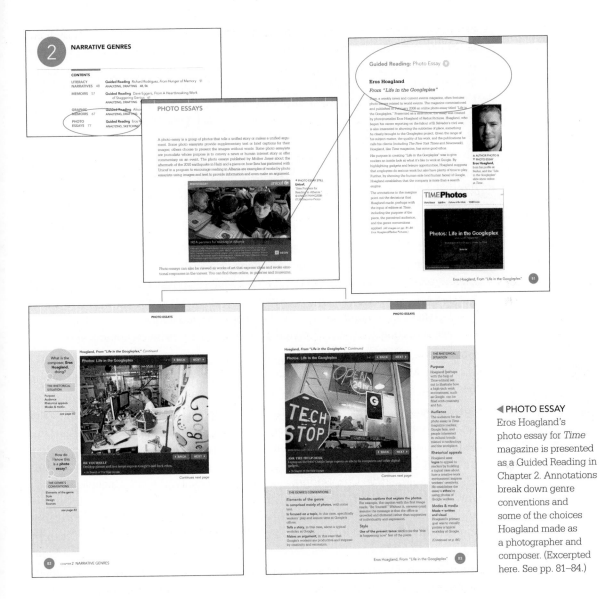

▲ PHOTO ESSAY
Eros Hoagland's photo essay for *Time* magazine is presented as a Guided Reading in Chapter 2. Annotations break down genre conventions and some of the choices Hoagland made as a photographer and composer. (Excerpted here. See pp. 81–84.)

Acknowledgments

We could not have written this book without the support and good cheer of many people. Obviously, if our own students hadn't gamely agreed to work on projects in multiple genres and modes, our teaching, and thus the book, would have stalled immediately, and so our first and heartiest thanks go to all the students who have taken our first-year writing classes. We are grateful to all the students whose work appears in these pages, especially to Gwen Ganow, whose work is featured in Chapters 8–10.

Once we had the idea to write a book, Rory Baruth, a sales manager with Bedford/ St. Martin's, patiently listened to us ramble on about our idea and helped us figure out how to channel our energy into a cogent proposal. Much like a relay race, Rory handed off our early ideas to Leasa Burton, who saw the possibility we envisioned. Not only did Leasa understand our vision, but she also knew that our work needed the deft and creative hands of the ultimate animal lover Ellen Thibault. An editor reigns supreme, and we are forever grateful to the directive attention and shaping the masterful Thibault brought to this project. She somehow knew when to reel in our ridiculousness and when to spur it on. Additionally, we would be remiss if we did not thank all the great minds at Bedford, but especially Joan Feinberg, Denise Wydra, Karen Henry, Molly Parke, Karita dos Santos, and Deb Baker. Our thanks, too, to Mallory Ladd and Amanda Legee for their splendid work on the instructor's manual.

This book has been a six-plus-year journey of endless hours attached to each other and our computers. We could not have done this without the support of our loved ones. Amy is so thankful for her partner Nan Walker's constant encouragement and surrender of the kitchen to numerous writing sessions. Liz is grateful to her husband, Tom DeBlaker, and daughter, Lily, for their patience and support during this lengthy process; additionally, Travitt Hamilton's encouragement is much appreciated.

We'd like to thank our reviewers, many of whom generously offered comments through the entire development of the book—and who have become part of the community surrounding this project: Eric James Abbey, Oakland Community College; Gerald Adair, Bluegrass Community & Technical College; Sonja Andrus, Collin County Community College; Jane Blakelock, Wright State; Ashley Bourgeois, University of Kentucky; Amber Buck, College of Staten Island, City University of New York; Carrie Cook, Georgetown College; Gretchen M. Coulter, Whatcom Community College; Michelle Cox, Bridgewater State University; the late Genevieve Critel, Ohio State University; Erica Deiters, Moraine Valley Community College; Loren Eason, University of California, Irvine; Michelle Eble, East Carolina University; Christine Garbett, Bowling Green State University; Melissa Goldthwaite, St. Joseph's University; John Gooch, University of Texas at Dallas; Judy Holiday, Arizona State University; Ashley Holmes, Elon University; Deborah Kellner, University of Cincinnati; Tammie Kennedy, University of Nebraska, Omaha; Juliette Kitchens, Nova Southeastern University; Tamara Kuzmenkov, Tacoma Community College; Lynn Lewis, Oklahoma State University; Chris Mays, Illinois State University; Melissa Graham Meeks, formerly of Georgia Institute of Technology; Susan Meyers, Oregon State University; Jayne Moneysmith, Kent State University at Stark; Anthony Mulholland, College of Southern Nevada; Thomas Nicholas, Prairie State College; Allison Palumbo, University of Kentucky; James Purdy, Duquesne University; Martine Courant Rife, Lansing Community College; David Seitz, Wright State University; Jeremy Shermak, Moraine Valley Community College; Marti Singer, Georgia State University;

Jacqueline Smilack, University of Colorado, Denver; Amy Ferdinandt Stolley, St. Xavier University; Huatong Sun, University of Washington, Tacoma; Katherine Tirabassi, Keene State College; Ryan Trauman, University of Louisville; Quinn Warnick, St. Edward's University; Suzanne Webb, Washington State University, Tri-Cities; Jamie White-Farnham, University of Wisconsin-Superior; and Christy Zink, George Washington–University.

We want to thank our enthusiastic colleagues who have encouraged us throughout the project. Their belief in our vision and excitement at the prospect of a finished text helped spur us on. Many local independent coffee shops contributed the java jolt needed when composing and revising—Pajama Baking Company, Pablo's, St. Mark's, Rooster & Moon, and Michelangelo's.

And most importantly, we'd like to thank each other for sharing a brain, food, cocktails, and the good fortune to collaborate on this journey.

—Amy Braziller
Elizabeth Kleinfeld

You Get More Choices for *The Bedford Book of Genres*

Bedford/St. Martin's offers resources and format choices that help you and your students get even more out of the book and your course. To learn more about or order any of the following products, contact your Bedford/St. Martin's sales representative, e-mail sales support (sales_support@bfwpub.com), or visit the Web site at bedfordstmartins.com/bookofgenres/catalog.

Choose from Alternative Formats of *The Bedford Book of Genres*

Bedford/St. Martin's offers a range of affordable formats, allowing students to choose the one that works for them. For details, visit bedfordstmartins.com /bookofgenres/formats.

» **Guide** (paperback, 592 pages). The Guide edition introduces students to a range of genres and walks them through analyzing and composing in them. To order this book, use ISBN 978-1-4576-5413-8.

» **Guide (pdf e-Book).** *The Bedford e-Book to Go for The Bedford Book of Genres: A Guide* is a portable, downloadable e-Book at about half the price of the print book. For other popular e-Book formats, visit bedfordstmartins.com/ebooks.

Choose the Flexible *Bedford e-Portfolio*

Students can collect, select, and reflect on their coursework and personalize and share their e-Portfolio for any audience—instructors, peers, potential employers, or family and friends. Instructors can provide as much or as little structure as they see fit. Rubrics and learning outcomes can be aligned to student work, so instructors and programs can gather reliable and useful assessment data. Every *Bedford e-Portfolio* comes preloaded with *Portfolio Keeping* and *Portfolio Teaching*, by Nedra Reynolds and Elizabeth Davis. *Bedford e-Portfolio* can be purchased separately or packaged with the print book at a significant discount. An activation code is required. To order the *Bedford e-Portfolio* with the print book, use ISBN 978-1-4576-7627-7. Visit bedfordstmartins.com/eportfolio.

Select Value Packages

Add value to your text by packaging one of the following resources with *The Bedford Book of Genres*. To learn more about package options for any of the following products, contact your Bedford/St. Martin's sales representative or visit bedfordstmartins.com/bookofgenres/catalog.

LearningCurve for Readers and Writers, Bedford/St. Martin's adaptive quizzing program, quickly learns what students already know and helps them practice what they don't yet understand. Game-like quizzing motivates students to engage with their course, and reporting tools help teachers discern their students' needs. *LearningCurve for Readers and Writers* can be packaged with *The Bedford Book of Genres* at a significant discount. An activation code is required. To order LearningCurve packaged with the print book, use ISBN 978-1-4576-7648-2. For details, visit bedfordstmartins.com/englishlearningcurve.

VideoCentral is a growing collection of videos for the writing class that captures real-world, academic, and student writers talking about how and why they write. Writer and teacher Peter Berkow interviewed hundreds of people—from Michael Moore to Cynthia Selfe—to produce fifty brief videos about topics such as revising and getting feedback. VideoCentral can be packaged with *The Bedford Book of Genres* at a significant discount. An activation code is required. To order VideoCentral packaged with the print book, use ISBN 978-1-4576-7591-1.

i-series is a popular series that presents multimedia tutorials in a flexible format—because there are things you can't do in a book.

> » *ix visualizing composition 2.0* helps students put into practice key rhetorical and visual concepts. To order *ix visualizing composition 2.0* packaged with the print book, use ISBN 978-1-4576-7595-9.

> » *i-claim: visualizing argument* offers a new way to see argument—with six multimedia tutorials, an illustrated glossary, and a wide array of multimedia

arguments. To order *i-claim: visualizing argument* packaged with the print book, use ISBN 978-1-4576-7636-9.

Portfolio Keeping, Third Edition, by Nedra Reynolds and Elizabeth Davis, provides all the information students need to use the portfolio method successfully in a writing course. *Portfolio Teaching*, a companion guide for instructors, provides the practical information instructors and writing program administrators need to use the portfolio method successfully in a writing course. To order *Portfolio Keeping* packaged with the print book, use ISBN 978-1-4576-7574-4.

Try *Re:Writing 2* for Fun

bedfordstmartins.com/rewriting

What's the fun of teaching writing if you can't try something new? The best collection of free writing resources on the Web, *Re:Writing 2* gives you and your students even more ways to think, watch, practice, and learn about writing concepts. Listen to Nancy Sommers on using a teacher's comments to revise. Try a logic puzzle. Consult our resources for writing centers. All free for the fun of trying it. Visit bedfordstmartins.com/rewriting.

Instructor Resources

bedfordstmartins.com/bookofgenres/catalog

You have a lot to do in your course. Bedford/St. Martin's wants to make it easy for you to find the support you need—and to get it quickly.

Teaching with The Bedford Book of Genres is available as a PDF that can be downloaded from the Bedford/St. Martin's online catalog. In addition to chapter overviews and teaching tips, this instructor's manual includes sample syllabi, correlations to the Council of Writing Program Administrators' Outcomes Statement, and classroom activities. Visit bedfordstmartins.com/bookofgenres/catalog.

Teaching Central offers the entire list of Bedford/St. Martin's print and online professional resources in one place. You'll find landmark reference works, sourcebooks on pedagogical issues, award-winning collections, and practical advice for the classroom—all free for instructors. Visit bedfordfordstmartins.com/teachingcentral.

Bits collects creative ideas for teaching a range of composition topics in an easily searchable blog format. A community of teachers—leading scholars, authors, and editors—discuss revision, research, grammar and style, technology, peer review, and much more. Take, use, adapt, and pass the ideas around. Then, come back to the site to comment or share your own suggestion. Visit bedfordstmartins.com/bits.

Bedford Coursepacks for the most common course management systems—Blackboard, Angel, Desire2Learn, Moodle, or Sakai—allow you to easily download digital materials from Bedford/St. Martin's for your course. To see what's available for *The Bedford Book of Genres*, visit bedfordstmartins.com/coursepacks.

Brief Contents

Contents

For e-Pages content, visit **bedfordstmartins.com/bookofgenres**.

3   Informative Genres   87

For e-Pages content, visit **bedfordstmartins.com/bookofgenres**.

Integrating & Documenting Sources 366

For e-Pages content, visit **bedfordstmartins.com/bookofgenres**.

For e-Pages content, visit **bedfordstmartins.com/bookofgenres**.

Guide

PART 1

EXPERIMENTING WITH GENRES
FROM ANALYSIS TO DRAFT

UNDERSTANDING GENRES

CONTENTS

MEMOIR ▶
Marjane Satrapi, Persepolis. *Everett Collection.*

What is a *genre*, anyway? A *genre* is a composition's kind, category, or sort. Genres give us a way to categorize or describe types of compositions. For example, a song is a musical composition—but individual songs fall into specific genre categories, including punk, rap, R&B, soul, indie, and death metal.

Why bother thinking about genres? Because they represent possibilities. We wrote this book to acknowledge that in college and beyond there are *way* more genres available to us besides the five-paragraph essay or the traditional term paper. As respectable and time-honored as those genres are, there are a whole lot of other options out there. We wrote this book to help you understand and create in a variety of genres—and we invite you to produce works that matter to you and enjoy doing so. As an added bonus, paying attention to genre will make you a better writer and artist. Why? Because you'll be focused on the needs of your audiences and your own purposes as a composer. ▶

What do you need to know about genres? First, genres change according to the ways people use them. Before digital composing, writers who wanted to record their thoughts wrote with a pen in a journal or diary, in a physical notebook. Then blogs were created.

Second, genres are flexible: They overlap and don't fall neatly into the categories and primary purposes we've outlined in this book. For example, we present graphic memoirs in Chapter 2, "Narrative Genres," but this genre could also work in Chapter 4, "Persuasive Genres." That's because while memoirists tell the stories of their own lives, they also persuade readers to empathize with them and to see the world in a certain way. Remember that as a writer, you define your use of a genre based on your purposes and audiences, and you can do more than one thing at a time. Your ad can do more than persuade; your literacy narrative can do more than tell a story.

What do you already know about genres? Think for a minute about the different genres you compose in each day. As a student, you write research papers and presentations; these are two examples of academic genres. In each case, you know what is expected of you as a writer, because you understand certain features of the genre. You know that to write a research

What kinds of composing have you done so far as a student? What are some of the features that define the works you've composed?

▼ BLOG
The Dragonfly Woman Blog. *Christine L. Goforth.*

HOME   GALLERY   EDUCATIONAL MATERIALS   GLOSSARY   SCIENTIFIC NAMES   DW ARCHIVE   ABOUT DW   CONTACT ME
THE DRAGONFLY SWARM PROJECT

The Dragonfly Woman

Well-Nigh Wordless Wednesday: Itty Bitty Wasp

Posted on November 14, 2012 | 6 Comments

I was walking past my back door about a month ago and caught sight of something out of the corner of my eye. I went to inspect and discovered this:

© C. L. Goforth

Itty bitty wasp

A very tiny wasp! I'm betting it's one of the parasitic wasps based on the diminutive size and enormous hind legs. I grabbed my iPhone and my "macro" lens and snapped a few photos because it was simply too adorable to pass up. Apparently my glass could do with a bit of cleaning though...

e For an Index of Sources & Contexts for material referenced in this chapter, see the e-Pages at **bedfordstmartins.com /bookofgenres**.

What do you already know about advertising? What qualities make an ad successful?

PHOTO ▶
Annie L. Burton
author of the memoir *Memories of Childhood's Slavery Days* (1909). Images courtesy of *Documenting the American South, The University of North Carolina at Chapel Hill Libraries.*

paper, you must gather and interpret a variety of reliable sources and cite them in a specific way.

In other situations, you choose your own genre to compose in, depending on what you want to say, who you want to say it to, and how you want to say it. Your choice of genre also depends on your own skills and interests, as well as the materials available to you. For example, your band is playing next week and you need to advertise the event. Your purpose is to persuade your potential audience to come to your show. You might choose to present your ad as a poster. Depending on your supplies and desired effect, you could create a handmade poster to tape up at school or design one on your computer to post on Facebook. Alternatively, you might choose to advertise by creating and posting a short music video.

One of the best ways to become a better writer/composer is to read like one—to pay attention to what other writers/composers do, how and why they work in a particular genre, and how they make that genre work for them.

Let's look at an example from history. Annie L. Burton (ca. 1858–unknown) was born a slave and as an adult decided

Memories of Childhood's
Slavery Days

By
Annie L. Burton

BOSTON
ROSS PUBLISHING COMPANY
1909

to write about her experiences; her 1909 memoir is titled *Memories of Childhood's Slavery Days*. Why did she choose to write a memoir instead of poetry or editorials or technical manuals? Most likely, Burton chose the memoir because it was a popular genre in her day that allowed her to tell the story she wanted to tell, suited her interests and skills, and reached the audience she wanted to reach. Maybe if she had been trained in music, she would have written operas, or if she had been born a little later, she would have told her story as a documentary film.

> Our clothes were little homespun cotton slips, with short sleeves. I never knew what shoes were until I got big enough to earn them myself. If a slave man and woman wished to marry, a party would be arranged some Saturday night among the slaves. The marriage ceremony consisted of the pair jumping over a stick. If no children were born within a year or so, the wife was sold. At New Year's, if there was any debt or mortgage on the plantation, the extra slaves were taken to Clayton and sold at the court house. In this way families were separated.   —**Annie L. Burton**

What we do know is that Burton wrote a memoir (a genre), specifically one that detailed her life as a slave. In her memoir, Burton wrote in the first person, portrayed real people, described settings, conveyed conflict, and told stories from her own life. These elements are features of the memoir genre and of any autobiography. Burton's purpose as a memoirist would have been to inform readers about what life as a slave—and later as a free person—was like; another purpose might have been to connect with women readers about what it was like to be a woman and a slave; yet another might have been to engage the imagination of readers. Her audience would have been literate former slaves and white readers, most likely in the North because her book was published in Boston. Her current readers might include students, scholars, and historians who want to read a firsthand account of slave life.

Do you read memoirs? What other observations can you make about the memoir as a genre?

The Rhetorical Situation

What is *rhetoric*? *Rhetoric* refers to the ability to communicate effectively and with a purpose. So what is a *rhetorical situation*? It's the context in which you create a composition. To put it simply, as a writer, you have a specific purpose and an audi-

For examples of **literacy narratives** and **memoirs**, see the Index of Genres on page G-1.

ence. You need to know what you want to say; you also need to know your readers' expectations and accommodate them in some way. For example, when you write a review of a restaurant on yelp.com, you know that Yelp readers want to know your opinion of the meal; they also expect specific details about the individual dishes, service, and ambience you experienced.

Purpose: Why are you composing?

Every time you write—or compose anything, in any genre—you do so for a reason. In this book, we've identified three main purposes for composing:

» To present a narrative / to tell a story (Chapter 2)

» To inform (Chapter 3)

» To persuade (Chapter 4)

There are many reasons to write and sometimes these reasons overlap. As writers, we often have several purposes for creating a single text. Let's look at a possible example. Let's assume that you love farmers' markets and want to establish one in your town.

Your purpose   You want to start up a weekly local farmers' market. To make this happen, you need to (1) present your idea to others and (2) persuade them that it's worth acting upon. You expect that some people will object.

Your rhetorical situation   In this context, you have more than one purpose. In order to persuade others, you need to explain your idea, say what's great about it, provide supporting statistics, and tell a persuasive story about how a similar plan succeeded in a neighboring town. You also have more than one audience. Some people will agree with you 100 per-

---

CHECKLIST Composing with a Purpose

As you begin to compose, ask yourself:

☐ Why am I writing? What do I want to communicate? And to whom?

☐ What do I want my audience to believe or do after reading my composition?

☐ Is what I'm communicating objectionable or controversial to anyone? If so, how will I address this?

☐ If I'm telling a story, why is it significant, and how will I make it compelling?

☐ If I'm sharing information, why is it important, and how will I communicate its authority?

☐ If I'm trying to persuade others, what are the best ways to do so, for my particular readers?

cent; others won't be so sure; still others, maybe grocery store owners or city planners, will reject your idea altogether.

Your plan and genre choice After considering your purpose and audience, you decide to write an editorial on your local newspaper's blog. You also plan to present your idea in person at the next town meeting.

As you begin writing your editorial, you may shift your purpose slightly—away from simply proposing and arguing for your plan—and toward focusing on the success of neighboring towns' farmers' markets and how they benefited local grocery stores. This will boost your persuasiveness with your resistant grocery store owners.

However, you may decide that rather than an editorial or a presentation, some other genre might better serve your purpose. For example, you may find that the best way to establish a farmers' market is to take a more personal approach by writing a letter to the mayor. You might also survey local citizens to see whether they'd like the opportunity to buy produce from local farmers. The point here is to see how your purpose affects your choice of genre, and how you can work in your genre to impact your audience.

Audience: Who are you composing for?

Every time you compose, you do so for an audience. Audiences are made up of people—and people can be easily bored, pressed for time, or generally disinterested. You need to grab their attention and keep it.

Let's look at an example: Imagine you are traveling across the country and want to tell stories of your adventures (your purpose) to your friends, family, and even strangers interested in travel (your audience). You decide that the best way to reach your audience is to create a blog where you can write about your experiences, show maps and photos, and connect to other social media sites. That is what the world-traveling blogger who calls himself Giladhiz decided to do (see p. 10).

Giladhiz clearly understands his audience and wants them to stick with him. To this end, he:

» Provides a photo of himself and an "About the Author" section so that readers can make a personal connection with him.

What genres have you written in today? Why? And who were your audiences?

CHECKLIST Composing for an Audience

As you begin to compose, ask yourself:

☐ Who is my audience in terms of demographics? Are they mostly male or mostly female? What is their age range? Where do they live? What do they like? Do they have particular religious beliefs? Are they from a particular social class? Are they of a particular race or ethnic background?

☐ What is my audience's stake in the issue I'm presenting? Do they care? Why or why not?

☐ What does my audience value? Will my message be in line with—or contradictory to—their values? How can I present my message so that my audience will consider it? And perhaps even be persuaded by it?

☐ What level of education does my audience have? What kind of language will best reach them?

» Addresses his readers directly: "So, dear friends and accidental surfers, allow me to begin with the reasons that brought me to plan and go on that trip."

» Writes in a casual, readable, and humorous style, meant to hook his readers and keep them interested in his ongoing adventures.

INFORMATIVE ▶
TRAVEL BLOG
Blogger Giladhiz,
from *Gilad Is Doing
South America.* Gilad H.

When you write, do you think of who will read your writing? When you compose a song, a video, or even a status update, do you think of who will experience what you've created?

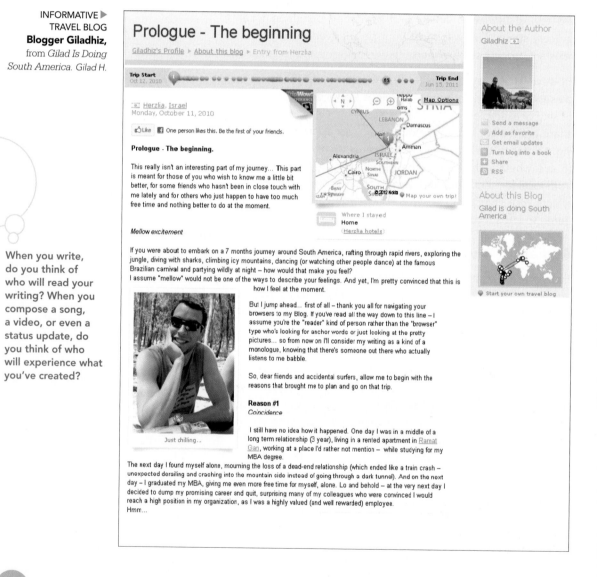

Prologue - The beginning

Giladhiz's Profile ▶ About this blog ▶ Entry from Herzlia

Trip Start
Oct 12, 2010

Trip End
Jun 15, 2011

Herzlia, Israel
Monday, October 11, 2010

👍 Like One person likes this. Be the first of your friends.

Prologue - The beginning.

This really isn't an interesting part of my journey... This part is meant for those of you who wish to know me a little bit better, for some friends who hasn't been in close touch with me lately and for others who just happen to have too much free time and nothing better to do at the moment.

Where I stayed
Home
(Herzlia hotels)

Mellow excitement

If you were about to embark on a 7 months journey around South America, rafting through rapid rivers, exploring the jungle, diving with sharks, climbing icy mountains, dancing (or watching other people dance) at the famous Brazilian carnival and partying wildly at night – how would that make you feel?
I assume "mellow" would not be one of the ways to describe your feelings. And yet, I'm pretty convinced that this is how I feel at the moment.

But I jump ahead... first of all – thank you all for navigating your browsers to my Blog. If you've read all the way down to this line – I assume you're the "reader" kind of person rather than the "browser" type who's looking for anchor words or just looking at the pretty pictures... so from now on I'll consider my writing as a kind of a monologue, knowing that there's someone out there who actually listens to me babble.

So, dear fiends and accidental surfers, allow me to begin with the reasons that brought me to plan and go on that trip.

Reason #1
Coincidence

I still have no idea how it happened. One day I was in a middle of a long term relationship (3 year), living in a rented apartment in Ramat Gan, working at a place I'd rather not mention – while studying for my MBA degree.

Just chilling...

The next day I found myself alone, mourning the loss of a dead-end relationship (which ended like a train crash – unexpected derailing and crashing into the mountain side instead of going through a dark tunnel). And on the next day – I graduated my MBA, giving me even more free time for myself, alone. Lo and behold – at the very next day I decided to dump my promising career and quit, surprising many of my colleagues who were convinced I would reach a high position in my organization, as I was a highly valued (and well rewarded) employee.
Hmm...

About the Author
Giladhiz

📧 Send a message
💗 Add as favorite
✉ Get email updates
📖 Turn blog into a book
➕ Share
📡 RSS

About this Blog
Gilad is doing South America

📍 Start your own travel blog

» Structures his post with subheadings to guide readers, and provides options for navigating content and for e-mailing or connecting by social media.

For examples of **blogs** and **blog posts,** see the Index of Genres on page G-1.

Rhetorical Appeals: Ethos, pathos, and logos

Whether your purpose is to tell a story, report information, or persuade, you need to get your audience on board. Even when persuasion is not your primary goal, it is always part of what you're doing, no matter what. We persuade our audiences by using what are called rhetorical appeals. There are three types of these, and they are often used in combination:

» *Ethos* is the credibility, authority, and trustworthiness the writer/composer conveys to the audience.

» *Pathos* is an appeal to an audience's emotions or values.

» *Logos* is the logic and connection of facts and evidence to the point being made.

As a writer/composer, you get to decide which appeals to use, depending on your audience, purposes, and choice of genre. For example:

» You're creating a memoir or an encyclopedia entry; you need to get readers to see you as an expert and accept your information as credible. In this case, you rely on *ethos*.

» You're creating an ad to persuade your audience to buy a product (especially something without tangible benefits, such as potato chips or a vacation package). In this case, you might appeal to their emotions and desires, relying on *pathos*.

» You're writing an editorial or an argumentative essay; you need to get your readers to agree with your conclusions. In this case, you might take them logically through the different elements of the arguments you're analyzing, relying on *logos*.

Modes & Media

What is a *mode*? What does it have to do with *media*? *Mode* is how a composition is experienced by readers/viewers/listeners.

For the purposes of this book, we work with three modes: writer or text-based, visual, and audio.

Media is the delivery mechanism of the composition, including the following:

» Print

» Digital

» Face-to-face

A particular mode can be delivered in multiple media; for example, an audio essay could be recorded either on an old-fashioned tape recorder or digitally. We've broken out the modes and media of some of the genres in this chapter.

NARRATIVE GENRES	Mode	Medium
MEMOIR Marjane Satrapi, *Persepolis* (p. 4)	**WRITTEN** **AND VISUAL**	**PRINT** **AND FILM**
MEMOIR Annie L. Burton, *Memories of Childhood's Slavery Days* (p. 6)	**WRITTEN**	**PRINT**
TRAVEL BLOG Giladhiz, *Gilad Is Doing South America* (p. 10)	**WRITTEN AND VISUAL**	**DIGITAL**
ARTIST'S STATEMENT Kristen LaCroix, *Prescription for Change* (p. 33)	**WRITTEN (BUT** **ACCOMPANIES** **A COLLAGE/SCULPTURE**	**DIGITAL**

For examples of **graphic works,** see the Index of Genres on page G-1.

Genre Conventions

Do you want to be a great writer or composer? If so, you need to know something about the genre you're composing in; you need to know its basic qualities and agreed-upon rules, and you need to be familiar with some examples. As Scott McCloud shows in his book *Understanding Comics*, writers ▶ and artists who work on comics use visual images and text to convey ideas, balloons to indicate dialogue, and simple but dynamic drawings and design to hold the reader's attention. Let's say you want to tell a story and you want to convey it graphically. You don't need to be McCloud or Picasso or Art Spiegelman, but you do need to understand how artists, graphic novelists, and memoirists work with visuals and text to tell stories. It helps to have some familiarity with the genre (read a few examples!) and perhaps have one example in mind as a model (see p. G-1 for some ideas). Or let's say you want to draw an annotated map of your neighborhood. It would help to know some of the established conventions of map-makers, such as using color to represent specific geography, or symbols to identify features or places. If your blog posts give your opinions on the editorials published on *Slate* or *The Huffington Post*, for example, you will have more authority if you link directly to the material you're responding to. Hyperlinking is a convention of the blog genre.

How much do you need to know? Keep an open mind as you choose genres to compose in. Consider collaborating with classmates who have more detailed knowledge of the genres that you're less familiar with. Often students in our writing

◀ COMIC
Scott McCloud,
from his book
*Understanding Comics:
The Invisible Art.*
HarperCollins.

classes will discuss and figure out together the conventions of specific genres and media (e.g., video or PowerPoint) and go from there. Other times they keep it simple but thoughtful, creating scrapbooks, print-based texts, or audio essays.

Elements of the Genre

In this book, we ask you to pay attention to the main features of a given genre: the specific elements that are common to most examples of the genre. For instance, most press release writers try to be as brief and objective as possible, and aim at answering the questions who, what, why, where, and when. For those reasons, we consider brevity, objectivity, and thoroughness to be elements of the press release genre. (For an example, see Paul Henderson's press release on p. 18 about the Wall Arch collapse.)

Style

Style refers to the particular ways we communicate. In this book, we pay attention to the techniques that individual writers use—and to what extent these techniques reflect the style of others composing in the same genre. We look at how much detail writers include, and how precise that detail is. We listen for tone (seriousness, humor, etc.) and voice (the presence of the author) and analyze how these qualities affect the overall composition. How a writer uses sources is part of style, as well. A writer who has cultivated a serious, academic style will probably use serious, academic sources as evidence. On the other hand, a writer with a more casual, chatty style might depend more on conversations with friends for evidence.

As a writer, you use style when you compose. The trick is to make sure that the style you're using is appropriate to your purpose and accessible and persuasive to your audience. For example, the writer and traveler Giladhiz uses a particular style on his blog. Because he is interested in attracting "accidental surfers" to his blog—that is, people who stumble upon his blog accidentally—he takes a casual and funny approach to his travels rather than a serious, scholarly tone. A serious, scholarly tone would probably appeal to an audience interested in the economics or politics of his travels, but because Giladhiz's purpose is to share his quirky, funny adventures, his casual, humorous style makes more sense.

Design

Design describes the visual features of a composition, including the use of headings, format, color, and illustration. Design is aesthetic but also functional. As we discuss throughout the book, the design features you and other writers choose can play an important role in the level of success in achieving purposes and reaching audiences. Take a look at how Giladhiz uses images in his blog. Maps show readers exactly where this traveler is, and the photos of Giladhiz help readers connect with him personally. Giladhiz's photos documenting his travels let readers see what he saw. Because one of his purposes is to allow others to share in his travels vicariously, the photos are particularly important.

Sources

Sources are the people, conversations, documents, books, journal articles, movies, and other works that we refer to for facts, perspectives, and models as we compose. For example, sources Giladhiz drew on for his travel blog (see p. 10) include Google Maps, the people he meets, and tourist information, such as brochures from historical sites. In this book, we consider sources because sources shape what writers create.

When you compose in certain genres, such as academic and research essays, you need to document the sources you refer to. In other cases, such as novels, comics, and music lyrics, while you've read and used sources, you're not required to document them formally. Whether or not sources need to be documented depends on the rhetorical situation. Sources referred to in a research essay aimed at academic readers should be documented because readers will want to know where ideas and information came from; the purposes of song lyrics are different, though. Listeners of a song aren't listening for information, so the sources of information are less important. Throughout the book we look at the conventions of specific genres in this regard, and in Chapter 7, we provide specific guidelines for using documentation styles.

In order to compose in different genres, you first should be able to identify them, see how other writers use them to achieve purposes and reach audiences, and learn some of the basic features so you can experiment.

How might the use of sources help boost—or undermine—your ethos as a composer?

CHECKLIST: Identifying Genres

Are you looking at a particular composition and wondering what genre it is? Keep the following questions in mind.

THE RHETORICAL SITUATION

☐ **Purpose.** Is the author telling a story? (See Chapter 2, "Narrative Genres.") Is the author reporting information? (See Chapter 3, "Informative Genres.") Is the author persuading? (See Chapter 4, "Persuasive Genres.") Is the writer telling a story, reporting, writing creatively, and persuading all at the same time? Don't worry. Sometimes purposes for writing/composing—and the genres we use—overlap.

☐ **Audience.** Who seems to be the author's primary audience? Secondary audience? How do you know? Why do you think someone would read (view, listen to, etc.) the text? How does the author capture and sustain audience attention?

☐ **Rhetorical appeals.** How does the author use the rhetorical appeals—ethos, pathos, and logos—to reach his or her audience? How does the author convey credibility? What kinds of evidence does the author offer to support the point of the piece?

☐ **Modes & media.** What choices has the writer made about mode? If multiple modes are used, how do they interact with each other? For example, if the piece includes both visuals and writing, is meaning conveyed by both the visuals and the writing, or does one mode convey more meaning than the other? What choices has the writer made about media? How do the writer's choices about modes and media reflect his or her purposes and audiences?

THE GENRE'S CONVENTIONS

☐ **Elements of the genre.** What do you know about this genre already? What are some of the typical features of this genre? How is the content organized? How does the author use words, images, or other media to convey a purpose and reach an audience?

☐ **Style.** What is the author's tone? How would you describe the language of the piece? How much detail does the author use?

☐ **Design.** What does the composition look (sound, feel, smell, etc.) like? How do words and visuals and other media work together in the genre, physically? How would you describe the format of the composition? Would the format change if the mode were changed? For example, if a newspaper editorial moves from a print medium to an online medium, what changes occur in the genre?

☐ **Sources.** What sources does the author draw on for research? How do you know? How does the author incorporate and give credit to sources? Is there documentation? Hyperlinking?

CASE STUDY:
ONE EVENT, TWO GENRES

Arch Collapse at a National Park

In this case study, two writers report on a single event. One writes a press release, the other a blog post.

The event: In August 2008, a rock formation in Utah's famous Arches National Park collapses.

The writers:

» **Paul Henderson**, a ranger at the park who also wrote press releases

» **Shaan Hurley**, a blogger and fan of the park who had hiked and photographed it

The compositions:

» "Wall Arch Collapses," a press release by Paul Henderson

» "The Wall Arch Collapses in Arches National Park," a blog post by Shaan Hurley

As you'll see, Henderson and Hurley provide much of the same information about the arch collapse, but they write in different genres, and with different purposes and audiences in mind. The notes in the margins of each piece explain their rhetorical situations and how they work within the conventions of the press release and the blog post.

Think of a current issue. How is the issue covered in different genres—for example, in a news report, an editorial, documentary footage, and a comic strip?

Guided Reading: Press Release ▼

Paul Henderson

Wall Arch Collapses

At the time of the collapse, Paul Henderson was chief of Interpretation and Visitor Services for Arches National Park, which is managed by the National Park Service, part of the U.S. Department of the Interior. When the arch collapsed, Henderson was interviewed by news outlets, including MSNBC, which also quoted from the press release on page 18.

(Image on page 18 courtesy of National Park Service.)

What is the composer, **Paul Henderson,** doing?

THE RHETORICAL SITUATION

Purpose
Audience
Rhetorical appeals
Modes & media

see page 19

How do I know this is a **press release?**

THE GENRE'S CONVENTIONS

Elements of the genre
Style
Design
Sources

see page 19

National Park Service

Find a Park   Discover History   Explore Nature   Get Involved   Working with Communities   Teachers   Kids   About Us

Arches | National Park
Utah

Wall Arch Collapses

Date: August 8, 2008
Contact: Paul Henderson, 435-719-2140

Subscribe 🔊 | What is RSS

Wall Arch, located along the popular Devils Garden Trail at Arches National Park collapsed sometime during the night of August 4, 2008. Rock has continued to fall from the arms of the remaining portion of the arch necessitating the closure of the Devils Garden Trail just beyond Landscape Arch.

On August 7, 2008, representatives from both the National Park Service Geologic Resources Division and the Utah Geological Survey visited the site and noted obvious stress fractures in the remaining formation. Rock debris has completely blocked this section of the trail. The closure will remain in effect until visitor safety issues can be resolved.

First reported and named by Lewis T. McKinney in 1948, Wall Arch was a free standing arch in the Slickrock member of the Entrada sandstone. The opening beneath the span was 71-feet wide and 33-1/2 feet high. It ranked 12th in size among the over 2,000 known arches in the park.

All arches are but temporary features and all will eventually succumb to the forces of gravity and erosion. While the geologic forces that created the arches are still very much underway, in human terms it's rare to observe such dramatic changes.

No one has reported observing the arch collapse and there were no visitor injuries.

THE RHETORICAL SITUATION

Purpose

Henderson, who works for the National Park Service, a government agency, writes **to inform** readers about the collapse. He reports that there were no injuries and that the area is temporarily closed. He reassures readers that the event is normal, that arches are temporary and "eventually succumb to the forces of gravity and erosion."

Audience

Henderson's readers want an **official statement** from park management, rather than one by an outside observer. Readers are mainly members of news organizations—but also park patrons, including hikers and nature photographers, looking for details.

Rhetorical appeals

For Henderson and other press release writers, **ethos** is crucial. Readers need to trust the authority of the writer and his information, especially because Henderson represents a government agency.

Henderson establishes **logos** by presenting information in a sensible order, beginning with the event and ending with its effects.

Modes & media

Henderson **uses text to inform and visuals to show the effect** of the collapse. His press release was posted digitally on the National Park Service's site and was probably also distributed by e-mail to various news organizations.

THE GENRE'S CONVENTIONS

Elements of the genre

Addresses who, what, when, where, why, and how. Henderson does so as follows:

Who = readers who care about the environment and park

What = the arch collapse

When = 8/4/08

Where = specific location of the collapse

Why = gravity and erosion

How = falling debris

Is brief and timely. Like most press releases, this is concisely worded, just a few paragraphs long. Henderson wrote it just four days after the event.

Begins with most important content. Henderson begins with the most crucial information and follows it with significant details.

Includes contact info for media.

Henderson wants readers, especially the news media (the target audience for press releases), to be able to get in touch.

Style

Conveys an objective tone. Henderson doesn't give his opinion; he also writes in the neutral third person.

Is clear, direct writing. Henderson provides facts simply and details concisely (e.g., "Rock debris has completely blocked this section of the trail").

Design

Presents a simple, clean layout. Henderson uses a standard press release design, with a headline to summarize and get attention, a dateline, and contact information. There are just two images to support the text.

The Web page itself includes the name of the park, an image, and a menu bar for easy navigation.

Sources

Draws on official information. Henderson uses facts from the National Park Service and from the Utah Geological Survey, which he credits in the body of his press release.

Guided Reading: Blog Post ⊽

Shaan Hurley

The Wall Arch Collapses in Arches National Park

Blogger Shaan Hurley has a background in mechanical design and works in the field of technology. *All Things Autodesk & Technology* is Hurley's personal blog; he also posts on Twitter. He posted the following entry in August 2008. *(Image courtesy of Shaan Hurley at Autodesk.)*

What is the composer, Shaan Hurley, doing?

THE RHETORICAL SITUATION

Purpose
Audience
Rhetorical appeals
Modes & media

see page 21

How do I know this is a blog post?

THE GENRE'S CONVENTIONS

Elements of the genre
Style
Design
Sources

see page 21

All Things Autodesk & Technology

Shaan Hurley
Autodesk Technologist for the Office of the CTO

The Wall Arch Collapses in Arches National Park

Almost one year ago to the week I was in the beautiful and world famous Arches National Park which is little more than 4 hours drive from my home in Utah. Just this week perhaps Tuesday one of the famous sandstone arches fell, Wall Arch is now Wall Pile. While Wall Arch was not the most spectacular or stunning, it was a beautiful arch.

Arches are formed by an ever changing nature and erosion and leave us with only a small window of geological time in which to marvel at the arches before they succumb to gravity. Who knows, perhaps another arch was born that we have not seen in the past year as well. Last year while I was photographing many of the arches and absolutely enjoying the natural beauty and silence in between the tourist buses,

I hiked back to Landscape arch which itself had suffered a partial collapse in1991. Since it was so hot that day and I figured I would get back there again soon I did not hike the remaining quarter mile to photograph Wall Arch by the Devils Garden. Now I will not have the opportunity to photograph Wall Arch except the remnants on the ground. It is another example of how things you take for granted may disappear.

If you ever have the chance to Visit the Moab Utah region or Southern Utah you should do so as it is beyond words and one of the reasons I know call this state home. This is photography heaven for color and so many varied landscape and rare geography. One of the other things I love about the area is the history of the Fremont people from thousands of years ago leaving their art on the rock walls and then last but not least Green River Utah having the worlds best watermelon when hiking in 100+ deg F. weather. If you are ever in Utah let me know as I am always happy to get an excuse to head to Moab and love showing the hidden gems beyond the tourist trails.

Here are a couple of my photos from the hike back on August 4th 2007 in Arches National Park. I still have hundreds of photos yet to publish, It may sound odd for someone to see some sense of loss in what to some may just be a sandstone structure born of erosion but if you have ever been there in the silence and the vibrant glow of red at twilight you would understand the magic of the area. This is natures art and landscape at it's finest.

http://www.flickr.com/photos/bti/

Never take for granted who or what you can see today, you may not have the opportunity tomorrow.

Have a great weekend,

Shaan

THE RHETORICAL SITUATION

Purpose

Hurley has a few reasons for writing: **to inform** readers about the collapse, **to share** his own experiences and photos of the park, and **to persuade** readers to enjoy nature now, rather than later, when the opportunity may not exist. He writes: "Now I will not have the opportunity to photograph Wall Arch except the remnants on the ground. It is another example of how things you take for granted may disappear."

Audience

His readers are fans of the park, other hikers and photographers, and even potential park visitors. His readers are looking for a **personal take** (rather than an official statement) on the arch collapse.

Rhetorical appeals

Because Hurley's main goal is to urge readers to seize an opportunity, he relies largely on **pathos** to appeal to emotion. Notice how he describes the beauty and "magic" of the park.

He also establishes **ethos**, or his authority to write on this topic, by sharing his firsthand experiences and photos of the park.

Modes & media

Hurley **uses text and visuals to inform**. His blog is digital and embedded with hyperlinks that bring readers to additional information. Readers can also share the link so others can read Hurley's post.

THE GENRE'S CONVENTIONS

Elements of the genre

Presents brief, visual, hyperlinked content. Like most effective blog posts, Hurley's is just a few paragraphs long, visually interesting, and embedded with links that offer more information without adding length.

Written in short paragraphs. Hurley's concise, chunked text keeps digital readers interested.

Includes relevant photos. Hurley's images provide context, attract readers, and offer his perspective on the event.

Provides an "about" page and a comments area (not shown here). Hurley gives biographical information and a space for readers to offer feedback and share their own views on the park.

Style

Conveys a conversational voice/tone. Hurley, like many bloggers, offers his own reflections and is present in his writing. He writes in the first person, addressing readers directly.

Design

Clear layout; user-friendly navigation. Like other blogs, Hurley's is designed so users can easily find additional content; they can also access his page on flickr.com.

Sources

Draws on official and firsthand information. Hurley credits the National Park Service for some of the photos; he also draws on his own experience (his trip of 2007) and external sources such as *Wikipedia*.

Shaan Hurley, *The Wall Arch Collapses in Arches National Park*

Questions: Analyzing Paul Henderson's press release and Shaan Hurley's blog post

1. Purpose. Reread Henderson's press release and Hurley's blog post. What are the writers' purposes? How can you tell? How do these purposes differ? How might they overlap?

2. Audience. Who do you imagine is the primary reader for Henderson's press release? For Hurley's blog post? Explain.

3. Rhetorical appeals. How effective are Henderson and Hurley in using ethos, pathos, or logos to reach their audiences? Which appeals do they rely on most effectively, and why?

4. Rhetorical appeals. Consider how hyperlinks, photos, and other information can contribute to a composer's ethos. Why do you think Hurley used the National Park Service as a source for information and images? How did this choice affect his ethos?

5. Modes & media. Both Henderson and Hurley use a combination of text and visuals. If you were to add audio or video to either piece, what would you add? What meaning or information would the audio or video add?

6. Elements of the genre. As a reader interested in the arch collapse, would you be likely to consult a press release? A blog? Both? Neither? Explain. To what extent is genre important? And in what contexts? When might it not matter?

7. Elements of the genre. What are the most significant differences between the press release and blog post as genres? Based on these examples, what conventions of these genres can you identify? How do these conventions affect what the writers say and how they convey it?

8. Style. Analyze the language Henderson and Hurley use. What do their words and tone suggest about their different purposes and audiences?

9. Design. How does the design of each piece enable readers to quickly find information they want or need?

10. Design. Look again at the photos included in the blog post and press release. What purposes do they serve in each? How effectively do the authors use them?

11. Sources. How does Hurley use the National Park Service's press release as a source? How does that source contribute to his success in achieving his purpose and reaching his audience?

For examples of **informative genres,** see Chapter 2 and the Index of Genres on page G-1.

Kristen LaCroix's Project on Drug Advertising

Let's look at a project by student writer Kristen LaCroix. Kristen is a former student of Liz Kleinfeld (coauthor of this textbook); Kristen was enrolled in Liz's composition class at Red Rocks Community College.

Kristen reflects on what she's doing now:

> Following my time at Red Rocks, I attended Colorado State University and graduated in the summer of 2010 with a degree in biological sciences. I am an intern with the Rocky Mountain Raptor Program and volunteering at the Denver Aquarium to pursue a career working with exotic wildlife. I hope to end up working as a medical director of a sanctuary or rehabilitation clinic for exotic animals.

Kristen reflects on her project:

> Looking back at this project, I remember wanting to choose a topic that I could find a lot of information on—I also wanted to be able to conduct interviews with experts. My grandfather worked in the pharmaceutical industry, and it's an area that has always interested me. It's a topic I care about and could easily take a stance on, largely because of my grandfather's experience. I found that the most challenging portion of this project was connecting all of the information together and getting it to flow. This project ultimately got me to see that there are lots of ways to present information and to persuade other people about your ideas.

For more examples of **student projects,** see Chapters 8, 9, and 10.

Kristen created her project in response to an assignment Liz gave the class. Liz asked students to:

» Research a specific issue or topic of interest to them.

» Present an argument about that topic to their audience (their primary audience would be Liz and the rest of the class).

◄ STUDENT AUTHOR PHOTO
Kristen LaCroix.
Kristen LaCroix.

» Choose three genres to compose in, being sure to pick those that would work well for their topics and arguments.

» Persuade their audience to agree with their perspective—and/or to take action on the issue.

Students were also asked to submit the following with their genre pieces:

» An Author's/Artist's Statement for each piece, in which they explain their rhetorical choices and include an MLA-style Works Cited list

» An Introduction to the project that states the overall objective and unifies the genre pieces into a whole

What issues are most important to you? How do you figure out which issues make the best topics for research and writing projects?

Researching a Topic

Kristen thought she'd like to write about the pharmaceutical industry because her grandfather had spent his career in that field and his stories about it fascinated her. She had no idea how she would focus her topic, so she started by doing some research. In addition to interviewing her grandfather, she also began her research

PEER-REVIEWED ▶
JOURNAL ARTICLE
Julie M. Donohue, PhD, et al.,
from *The New England Journal of Medicine (NEJM).*
Courtesy of the New England Journal of Medicine.

The **NEW ENGLAND JOURNAL of MEDICINE**

| HOME | ARTICLES & MULTIMEDIA ▾ | ISSUES ▾ | SPECIALTIES & TOPICS ▾ | FOR AUTHORS ▾ | CME ▸ |

SPECIAL ARTICLE

A Decade of Direct-to-Consumer Advertising of Prescription Drugs

Julie M. Donohue, Ph.D., Marisa Cevasco, B.A., and Meredith B. Rosenthal, Ph.D.
N Engl J Med 2007; 357:673-681 | August 16, 2007 | DOI: 10.1056/NEJMsa070502

Share:

| Abstract | **Article** | References | Citing Articles (89) |

It has been 10 years since a change in a policy of the Food and Drug Administration (FDA) allowed direct-to-consumer advertising of prescription drugs on television. Such advertising has been criticized for encouraging inappropriate use of medications and driving up drug spending.[1,2] Concern that such advertising may lead to increased use of expensive medications was amplified by the introduction of a prescription-drug benefit in Medicare in 2006 (Part D). Studies of the effect of advertising on prescribing practices have shown that such advertising increases classwide sales, helps to avert underuse of medicines to treat chronic conditions, and leads to some overuse of prescription drugs.[3-5]

with some copies of *Health* magazine and *Good Housekeeping,* which contained ads and articles related to the drug industry, geared toward a general audience. As her research deepened, she looked into more scholarly professional resources, too, such as an article (by Julie M. Donohue, PhD, et al.) on advertising prescription drugs from *The New England Journal of Medicine* (*NEJM*). (For complete guidelines on research and working with sources, see Chapter 5, "Exploring Topics & Creating a Research Proposal," Chapter 6, "Evaluating & Choosing Sources," and Chapter 7, "Integrating & Documenting Sources.")

Choosing a Topic

Kristen reflected on the conversations she'd had with her grandfather and the articles she'd read in *Health, NEJM*, and other periodicals. She was particularly struck by the number of direct-to-consumer drug ads she'd found in *Health* magazine and at the Food and Drug Administration Web site. She did more research and found that this type of advertising by drug companies is pervasive in popular magazines and media. Kristen felt these ads might also be dangerous and decided to explore further.

Determining a Purpose

As she focused her topic and conducted more research, Kristen was further persuaded that direct-to-consumer drug ads could be harmful. She decided that she would use her project to persuade others as well. With this purpose in mind, she thought about her audience of classmates. They might not be aware of the extent of direct-to-consumer drug ads; she realized that she would first need to inform her readers of the ads' pervasiveness before she could build her main argument about their possible impact on consumers.

Considering Audience

In order to connect with her audience, Kristen knew she needed to first consider what her potential readers might already know and think about pharmaceutical companies and the ads they produced. She figured her classmates were probably a lot like her: interested in staying healthy and somewhat ignorant about how drug companies market their products and spend their money. She knew they would not want to read a dry report about advertising trends, so she began thinking about genres that might grab and hold their attention.

Who are the main audiences for the compositions you create as a student? Your classmates? Instructor? Anyone with an Internet connection? How do you negotiate and appeal to your audiences?

Using Rhetorical Appeals

Kristen knew that she would need to use ethos, pathos, and logos to her advantage in order to persuade her audience. She could establish her ethos as an author by taking her subject seriously and by drawing upon authoritative sources. She could appeal to her readers' pathos by including sad stories of consumers who suffered or even died as the result of the aggressive marketing of a drug. And while she didn't want to bog down her audience with excessive detail, she did want to provide major facts about how drug companies advertise—and the figures related to the money they make as a result. This information, presented in an order that made sense and accompanied by an Author's Statement explaining her choices, would appeal to her readers' sense of logos.

Choosing a Genre(s)

Taking into account her purpose, audience, and the ways she planned to persuade her audience, Kristen decided to create a series of compositions:

A collage/sculpture Kristen created a giant capsule and covered it with a collage of prescription drug ads pulled from *Health* magazine and *Good Housekeeping*. She thought this creative and visual genre would get her classmates' attention and give them a sense of the hefty volume of direct-to-consumer ads created by drug companies. Kristen hoped that once readers saw in a visually graphic way exactly how many direct-to-consumer ads by drug companies appeared in two mainstream magazines, they would be persuaded that there was a problem. Kristen chose drug ads for her collage that appeal to the emotions (pathos) of her readers through scary stories of untreated illness; the ads also feature statistics, which appeal to readers'

ARTIFACT ▶
Kristen LaCroix,
pill capsule collage/
sculpture. *This and all
images on pages 27–31
courtesy of Kristen
LaCroix.*

sense of logic (logos) and draw on the authority (ethos) of doctors. She also used the capsule in a creative and functional way—as a container for her other genre pieces, described below.

A biographical profile   Kristen wrote a profile of her grandfather, Charles, who worked in the pharmaceutical industry. She used this genre as a way to convey facts and information about the drug industry. She thought that this information, coming through her grandfather's perspective, would be more interesting to her audience than if she presented it in a different genre, such as a report. She hoped that because her grandfather worked in the pharmaceutical industry, his observations about how it had changed over time would help persuade readers to question some industry practices. Kristen used her profile of her grandfather—which is based on her own primary research and his recollections—to appeal to readers' sense of logic (logos) and draw on her grandfather's authority (ethos) as a professional in the field.

LaCroix 7

Charles

He appeared weathered with thousands of memories and emotions; consequently, he sat serenely in his chair inhaling the calm air around him. This skillful man, Charles Fortin, had cared for and supported three beautiful daughters and an amazing wife. Charles presented himself with pride due mainly to his great success during his younger years. However, after retiring from a lifetime spent traveling while working for growing companies, he had suffered greatly through many medical tribulations. His outfit this day, a gray sweat suit, illustrated his need for comfortable settings and less movement. His bulbous glasses encompassed his face, demanding attention. A man of eighty-five years, his movements were gradual and his responses defined tranquility.

Gently, Charles began, "After finishing college, I paid a visit to my student advisor in hopes that I would be able to find a suitable career to support my wife and three-month-old daughter." His statement, coupled with perfect presentation, depicted Charles as the man who worked relentlessly to accomplish his goals. His advisor organized an interview with Lederle Laboratories where Charles was first introduced to the pros and cons of the drug industry. Slightly tipping back his frail head, Charles explained, "I worked for Lederle for fifteen years, promoting their products to doctors and pharmacies around the globe before I switched companies and gained the title of Sales Manager of Pharmaceuticals for all countries except the U.S." Charles paused shortly to collect his thoughts, illustrating his irrefutable abilities as a well-spoken gentleman.

Charles's pale complexion began to glow as he described the fulfillment he gained during his career. His grin spread across his face as he explained that through his profession he was able to help people because he assisted in the distribution of life-saving products to individuals all over the world. Charles's smile defended his achievements as he slowly leaned back in the black chair, reminiscing about his past. Inhaling deeply, he continued, "Back in those days, prescriptions were so successful in healing people, they were only used when they were needed."

His face bloomed with frustration as he considered the different advertising campaigns utilized throughout the pharmaceutical industry today. Pausing for a short break, Charles went into the kitchen. He came back with several pills of different colors and sizes, explaining, "Each of these medications I take for many reasons, whether for my heart, arthritis, or my cold, each of these came from my doctor and are the only things stopping the pain that I would be forced to deal with on an everyday basis." His assorted prescriptions all seemed necessary. Charles inhaled deeply while looking down at his medications, revealing the different purposes each pill served. None of the pills, he divulged, were medications he'd asked for after seeing them in advertisements; they'd all been prescribed by his physician. "I wouldn't know what I wanted if I needed medication, that is a decision best left in the hands of a trained professional," he explained.

▲ BIOGRAPHICAL PROFILE
Kristen LaCroix, the first page of her biographical profile of her grandfather, Charles.

▲ PHOTO
Kristen LaCroix's grandmother and grandfather.

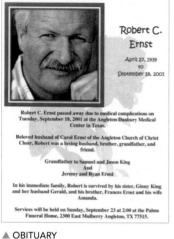

Robert C.
Ernst

April 27, 1939
to
September 18, 2001

Robert C. Ernst passed away due to medical complications on
Tuesday, September 18, 2001 at the Angleton Danbury Medical
Center in Texas.

Beloved husband of Carol Ernst of the Angleton Church of Christ
Choir, Robert was a loving husband, brother, grandfather, and
friend.

Grandfather to Samuel and Jason King
And
Jeremy and Ryan Ernst

In his immediate family, Robert is survived by his sister, Ginny King
and her husband Gerald, and his brother, Frances Ernst and his wife
Amanda.

Services will be held on Sunday, September 23 at 2:00 at the Palms
Funeral Home, 2300 East Mulberry Angleton, TX 77515.

▲ OBITUARY
Kristen LaCroix, remembrance
of Robert C. Ernst.

An obituary   Kristen also created an obituary for a man named Robert C. Ernst, who died from a prescription drug–induced heart attack. She drew on an article that she'd read about Ernst's death, and also listed it in her Works Cited list. Kristen created the obit to help bring home to her audience the life-and-death seriousness of the topic; here she was able to convey facts to inform her readers, and also appeal to her readers' pathos. She thought that once readers learned that prescription drugs themselves can be lethal, they would be persuaded to take the issue seriously. Kristen uses the genre of the obituary to appeal to readers' emotions (pathos) by building sympathy for the man who died and the family left behind.

An Artist's Statement and Introduction   To accompany each of her three compositions (her capsule, profile, and obituary), Kristen also wrote an Artist's Statement in which she explained her rhetorical choices. Kristen's primary audience for these Statements is her instructor, Liz, but she also knew some of her classmates would be interested in knowing more about the decisions she made as she worked on her project. Kristen used a serious tone to convey to Liz that she approached the entire project in a scholarly, serious way (ethos). She also talked methodically about the choices she made, to show that she had thought through her decisions and their consequences (logos). Kristen composed an Introduction that addressed her project as a whole; in it, she discussed how her genre compositions work together to form a unified argument about direct-to-consumer drug advertising—and also prepared her audience to experience her project in a coherent way.

Working with Modes & Media

Have you ever
created a project
that you wish
you'd had more
time to complete?
Reflecting on that
experience, what
would you have
done differently or
better to make your
point? What would
you revise, and why?

Kristen was comfortable working in written modes, but she also wanted to use visuals to stimulate her readers' imaginations and keep their attention. Her pill capsule collage/sculpture is the most visual composition she created and the only one that is three-dimensional; Kristen assumed her readers would be seeing it face-to-face (you are seeing it in print because the collage has been photographed and reprinted in this book). She wrote the biographical profile and it appears in print. She also wrote the obituary and included visuals; this piece also appears in print. However, if she'd had more time, she might have included these pieces on a blog or Web site. When considering her audience—her classmates and instructor—Kristen decided to create print pieces that could be passed around and read in class. Kristen composed her Artist's Statements as print documents; however, if she had decided to present her genre pieces digitally on a Web site or blog, she

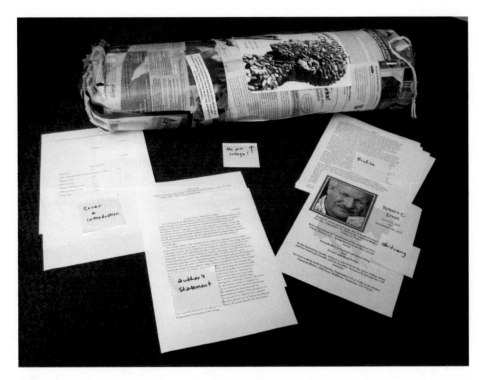

might have chosen to incorporate different media into her Statements, or recorded
them as audio or video essays, for example.

Working with Style

Kristen observed the conventions of the genres she chose: She also chose to compose in a style that would be very accessible to her readers. She did not want to
bore her readers with technical language, or alienate readers she hoped to persuade. She anticipated that many of her readers might not see direct-to-consumer
advertising by pharmaceutical companies as a serious enough problem for them
to spend time and energy worrying about. Kristen knew that she had to provide
enough details to convince readers to take her argument seriously, but not so many
that readers would feel overwhelmed.

Working with Design

To catch her readers' attention, Kristen included visuals (see the obituary) and
color (see her collage). Further, while a collage is normally flat and two-dimensional,

Kristen decided to present hers in sculpture form. She also hoped that by composing her collage out of prescription drug ads, she'd spark her audience's curiosity so that they'd want to know more about her project and main point.

Drawing from Sources

Kristen used a variety of sources for her project, including interviews with her grandfather, the advertisements she found in *Good Housekeeping* and *Health* magazine, and several articles from peer-reviewed journals. When she selected her sources, she thought about how her choices would reflect upon her ethos. She wanted to come across as authoritative, thoughtful, and intelligent, so she chose sources that struck her as authoritative, thoughtful, and intelligent. She found articles in journals she knew were respected, such as *The New England Journal of Medicine*. She wrote an Artist's Statement for each genre piece she created, and in those Statements she spoke directly about how the sources she used affected her thinking about her subject. She also provided a Works Cited list with each Statement.

Guided Reading: Collage/Sculpture ▼

Kristen LaCroix (Student)

Prescription for Change:
The Impact of Direct-to-Consumer
Drug Advertising

Following is a photo of Kristen's collage capsule. The annotations on page 32 show how she addressed her rhetorical situation and connected with her audience through the genre she chose.

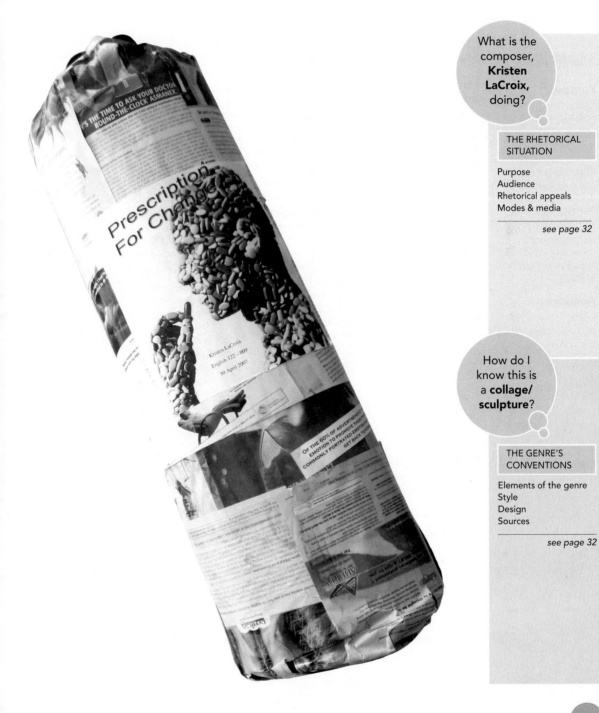

Prescription For Change

Kristen LaCroix
English 122 – 009
30 April 2007

What is the composer, **Kristen LaCroix,** doing?

THE RHETORICAL SITUATION

Purpose
Audience
Rhetorical appeals
Modes & media

see page 32

How do I know this is a **collage/ sculpture**?

THE GENRE'S CONVENTIONS

Elements of the genre
Style
Design
Sources

see page 32

Kristen LaCroix, *Prescription for Change*

LaCroix, *Collage/Sculpture*, Continued

THE RHETORICAL SITUATION

Purpose

Kristen's main purpose—for her project as a whole—is **to persuade** her audience that direct-to-consumer ads are potentially dangerous; she must also first inform her audience about the pervasiveness of these ads, which she does by creating this capsule.

Audience

Kristen's instructor and classmates are her primary readers.

Rhetorical appeals

Kristen appeals to **pathos** by presenting viewers with an imaginative object, and to **logos** and **ethos** by providing her sources as part of that sculpture.

Modes & media

Mode = visual
Medium = face-to-face

THE GENRE'S CONVENTIONS

Elements of the genre

As a piece of sculpture, it is **three-dimensional**, and in this case, handmade out of everyday materials.

As a collage, it features **layered texts and images,** which convey a main theme. Color directs attention to different content.

A DIY feel invites viewers to interact with and explore the object.

Style

Kristen conveys a **playful tone, but also makes an argument** with this piece. The numerous ads from two mainstream magazines reinforce her argument that they are pervasive and potentially dangerous. Her title, "Prescription for Change," and the image of the pill-covered face on the cover sheet further telegraph her argument.

Design

While most collages are two-dimensional, Kristen's piece is a **3-D sculpture** made from plastic bottles and **covered with a collage.** The two halves fit together in the middle and open up, capsule-like, to reveal not medicine, but her individual genre pieces.

Sources

Kristen draws on ads from *Good Housekeeping* and *Health* magazine.

Kristen submitted her project with an Author's/Artist's Statement for each genre piece in which she explains and supports the rhetorical choices she made as she created her project. On page 33 is her Statement for the capsule collage/sculpture part of her project. Sometimes an instructor will specify that students write one Author's/Artist's Statement that encompasses an entire project instead of individual Statements for each piece. For this particular class, Liz asked students to provide individual Statements for each genre piece, as well as an Introduction to provide a kind of project-wide Statement.

Kristen LaCroix (Student)

Artist's Statement

What is the composer, Kristen LaCroix, doing?

LaCroix 4

Artist's Statement:

How and Why I Created My Collage/Sculpture

It is necessary for all individuals to realize the amount of drug advertisements in all forms of media, to recognize the problem with our current drug industry. I created a collage to allow people to see the immense amount of marketing found merely throughout common magazines. Using only two magazines, I created a collage that couldn't even hold all the full-page advertisements that I found. Furthermore, oddly enough, the two magazines that included such an intense amount of advertising were *Health* and *Good Housekeeping*. The drug advertisements throughout these magazines included anything from sleeping pills to medication to ease the aftereffects of chemotherapy.

The collage displays a few examples of the marketing campaigns for prescription drugs and is in turn the best genre to present the obvious problem. The collage represents a message to simply acknowledge the ways companies advertise in an attempt to gain consumers' trust while marketing a product. A massive amount of pharmaceutical companies' income is turned around to be used for advertising. One CBS News article I found listed the top twenty drugs advertised in 2000. The drug with the largest advertising campaign, Vioxx, had approximately $161 million spent on advertising that year (Lee). Soon thereafter, in 2004, the drug Vioxx was pulled off the market after causing the death of many patients using it. Many prescriptions that are on the collage, such as Flonase and Celebrex, were listed in this article as well. The company that produced the nasal spray Flonase spent $78 million advertising their product in 2000 (Lee). There have been no adverse implications for this drug thus far; nevertheless, similar to several other drugs that are heavily advertised, there are other products available for consumers that are not as pricey and work as well if not even better.

Drug companies create their advertisements to be directed at specific target audiences in an effort to gain the most profit during their campaigns; however, this genre piece is not intended for any specific audience and instead is meant to heighten the awareness of all individuals because we will all at some point be victims of advertising schemes. This genre piece functions as both the packaging for the project and the introduction to the project. It highlights the overwhelming number of advertisements for prescription medications the average person is exposed to on a regular basis. Another way I incorporated information throughout the entire project was by displaying different facts scattered around my collage as well. I believe this helps describe the information being portrayed throughout the collage.

THE RHETORICAL SITUATION

Purpose
Audience
Rhetorical appeals
Modes & media

see page 34

How do I know this is an **Artist's Statement?**

THE GENRE'S CONVENTIONS

Elements of the genre
Style
Design
Sources

see page 35

Continues next page

LaCroix, *Artist's Statement*, *Continued*

THE RHETORICAL SITUATION

Purpose

In her Statement, Kristen **describes the rhetorical choices** she made while creating the collage/sculpture piece of her project. She also **discusses the sources** she drew on.

Audience

Kristen's audience for her collage and Statement is the same as that for the rest of her project: her instructor and classmates.

Rhetorical appeals

Kristen clearly articulates her intentions and shows her credibility (**ethos**) by noting and documenting her sources. She supports her argument logically (**logos**) by drawing on research and providing her sources in her Statement. She informs readers about drug ads, and supports her claims with specific ads.

Modes & media

Mode = written
Medium = print

The next step to rising above the pharmaceutical companies' control is to recognize the trend with drugs that are being advertised as well as their current usage. The drug industry defends their promotional advertising, suggesting that it "helps educate consumers of potential conditions and encourages them to see their doctor for diagnosis and treatment" ("Direct-to-Consumer"). However, critics argue that this advertising is primarily emotional and commonly understates the side effects, causing misleading information to be fed to consumers. According to SourceWatch, a report conducted by the U.S. Government Accountability Office in November 2006 explained:

> "Studies we reviewed found that increases in [direct-to-consumer] advertising have contributed to overall increases in spending on both the advertised drug itself and on other drugs that treat the same condition . . . one study of 64 drugs found a median increase in sales of $2.20 for every $1 spent on [direct-to-consumer] advertising" ("Direct-to-Consumer").
>
> Moreover, it was also found that 86% of consumers who had seen promotional advertisements for prescription drugs requested and ultimately received a prescription for the drug they wanted (Graham).

Although this genre piece doesn't directly convey information gathered from the advertisements themselves, different sources pointed out the common characteristics throughout each advertisement. Almost all of the advertisements use the same techniques to persuade the consumer to relate health, well-being, and happiness with the use of the prescription medication. In one analysis, it was found that 67% of advertisements collected used emotional appeals to gain the reader's attention. Of the 60% of advertisements that were using emotion to promote their product, the most commonly portrayed emotion was the aspiration to get back to normal (Woloshin). This is evident in advertisements on the collage in which individuals with allergies run through fields with flowers because they're "Claritin clear" and elderly arthritis sufferers can convey their happiness hugging a child because of Celebrex. Overall, this genre shows the common characteristics of drug advertisements presenting the ways they induce a reader to believe that the answer to their problem lies within being prescribed the medication.

LaCroix, *Artist's Statement*, Continued

LaCroix 6

Works Cited

"Direct-to-Consumer Advertising." *SourceWatch.org*. SourceWatch, 7 Mar. 2007. Web.
19 Apr. 2007. <http://www.sourcewatch.org/
index.php?title=Direct-to-consumer_advertising>.

Graham, John R. "Direct-to-Consumer Pharmaceutical Advertising: What Does
the Literature (Not) Say?" *Health Policy Prescriptions* 3.4 (2005): n. pag.
27 Apr. 2007. <http://www.pacificresearch.org/pub/hpp/2005/hpp_11-5.html>.

Lee, Kent. "Drug Advertising Skyrockets." *CBS News*. CBS News, n.d. Web.
25 Apr. 2007. <http://www.cbsnews.com/2100-204_162-329293.html>.

Woloshin, Steven, Lisa M. Schwartz, and H. Gilbert Welch. "The Value of Benefit Data
in Direct-to-Consumer Drug Ads." *Health Affairs*. Project HOPE, 28 Apr. 2004.
Web. 25 Apr. 2007. <http://content.healthaffairs.org/content/suppl/2004/04/28/
hlthaff.w4.234v1.DC1>.

THE GENRE'S CONVENTIONS

Elements of the genre

Composers use Statements to **explain how and why they created a work.** Kristen explains why she created her collage: to give viewers a sense of the quantity of drug ads in mainstream magazines.

Style

A Statement can be written in different styles: Kristen chose an **academic style and tone.** She makes a case for how she reached her audience through appeals and discusses how she used sources.

Design

Kristen designed this document using **MLA format.** (For more on MLA guidelines, see pp. 395–414.)

Sources

Kristen draws on research of a variety of sources. She explains and analyzes her decisions in this Statement. She also documents her sources in a Works Cited list.

Questions: Analyzing Kristen LaCroix's project

1. Purpose. Kristen's overall purpose is to persuade her audience that direct-to-consumer drug ads are dangerous. How persuasive are her individual genre compositions (capsule, profile, obituary, and Artist's Statement)? Explain.

2. Audience. Kristen, who was writing for her instructor and classmates, made some assumptions during her composing process about how to reach them. What are some of her assumptions? And how accurately do you think she assessed her audience?

3. Audience. As a student, do you feel you are included in the audience for these pieces? Why or why not?

4. Rhetorical appeals. How effectively does Kristen work with the appeals of logos, pathos, and ethos? Does she seem to favor one over the others? Explain.

5. Modes & media. Kristen created her biographical profile and obituary in print form; do you think they would be more effective in digital form? Why or why not? How might her pill capsule collage/sculpture be conveyed digitally? How might she make her compositions more interactive?

6. Elements of the genre. How does Kristen use the conventions of each genre to help her make her point? For example, how does the image of the deceased man make the obituary more powerful? How does the overlapping of images in the collage help to make her point?

7. Style. Kristen wanted to write the biographical profile in a tone that would appeal to her classmates. Did the tone she used appeal to you? Why or why not? And how effective is her use of detail in the obituary? Explain.

8. Design. How does the shape of the collage contribute to its appeal and persuasiveness? Look again at the obituary and think of some related genres. For example, at some memorial services, small brochure-type documents that include memories about the deceased are distributed. How might Kristen's obituary message have changed (or not) if she had chosen a different genre?

9. Sources. After reviewing Kristen's Artist's Statement for her collage/sculpture, are you surprised to see how her sources informed her work? Why or why not?

CHECKLIST: Choosing a Genre
Do you need to decide on a genre to compose in? Ask yourself the following questions.

WHAT'S YOUR RHETORICAL SITUATION?

☐ **Purpose.** Is my purpose to tell a story, inform, or persuade? Do I have several purposes, and if so, which is my primary purpose?

☐ **Audience.** How would I describe my primary audience? Whose attention do I want most? Who are the people I want to persuade? Do I have another, secondary audience? How will I entice this audience?

☐ **Rhetorical appeals.** How will I establish my credibility (ethos)? Will appealing to my audience's emotions help me persuade them (pathos)? How might logic (logos) help me convince others?

☐ **Modes & media.** Do I want to work with written words? Will I present my ideas in person, orally? Will I use visuals? How about audio? Does my idea lend itself to video? Do I want my piece to be available digitally or in print? Will I use some combination of these modes and media?

WHAT GENRE CONVENTIONS MATTER?

☐ **Elements of the genre.** How will I structure my composition? What is the best way to combine elements to convey my purpose—and make my case to my audience?

☐ **Style.** Whatever form my composition takes (visual, verbal, etc.), what is the best tone to use to reach my audience? What voice will I use? How present will I be in my composition? What kind of language will I use? What level of detail will I need to convey my purpose?

☐ **Design.** How do I want my composition to look? How will the layout help me achieve my purpose?

☐ **Sources.** What sources will I draw on for my composition? Do I need to conduct interviews? Do I need to research online or in the library? How will I attribute my sources?

2 NARRATIVE GENRES

CONTENTS

FAIRY TALE ▶
Gustave Doré
illustration from "Le Petit Chaperon Rouge."

e For e-Pages content, visit **bedfordstmartins .com/bookofgenres**.

We share stories every day: on the bus, in the checkout line, at home. We experience them through social media, memoirs (p. 57), history books, comics, movies, and the evening news. We remember them from the fairy tales of childhood. Constructing narratives is a universal impulse; stories help us make sense of our lives and connect with others. Regardless of the specific genres our stories take—and whether they're fact or fiction, comedies or tragedies, or something in between—they generally include real people or made-up characters, a setting, a conflict, and action.

In your composition course, you may be asked to write a literacy narrative: a story about how you learned to read and write. But there are other, less formal ways to share stories. For example, even a single page from a photo album or scrapbook, such as the one below, suggests part of the story of someone's life. Enikö DeLisle, a blogger in Edgartown, Massachusetts, created an online scrapbook page dedicated to the story of Peter Farkas and Edith Nanay. ▼

For an Index of Sources & Contexts for material referenced in this chapter, see the e-Pages at **bedfordstmartins.com /bookofgenres.**

◄ SCRAPBOOK PAGE
Enikö DeLisle,
"Peter and Edith." The caption for this couple, Peter Farkas, and Edith Nanay, reads: "Like the story of the country mouse and the city mouse, Peter and Edith were from very different worlds, brought together by fate and circumstance—Or was it destiny? They met at a photographer friend's studio on the day this photo was taken of Edith at age 20—it was love at 1st sight." Above the photos of Peter and Edith are images of their parents. *Enikö DeLisle Design.*

Creating narratives goes back to ancient times: Early aboriginal people painted cave walls with symbols and pictures of animals to convey meaning. Ancient Greeks told stories of gods and heroes, and Native Americans created and passed down legends to warn about tricksters and celebrate heroes. Today's oral histories function similarly, preserving stories that might otherwise be forgotten. For example, the StoryCorps project, archived at the Library of Congress, records the life stories of everyday people. ▼

ORAL HISTORY ▶
StoryCorps project.
StoryCorps.

▼ OBITUARY
Elizabeth A. Niles,
from the National Archives and Records Administration.
Old Records Division Reference File, Record Group 94, Records of the Adjutant General's Office, National Archives.

Woman Who Fought In Civil War Beside Hubby Dies, Aged Ninety-Two

RARITAN, N.J., Oct. 4.—Mrs. Elizabeth A. Niles, 92, who, with close-cropped hair and a uniform, concealed her sex and is said to have fought beside her husband through the civil war is dead here today, aged ninety-two.

The war call found the couple on their honeymoon. The husband, Martin Niles, joined the ranks of the Fourth New Jersey Infantry, and when the regiment left Elizabeth Niles marched beside him. She fought through many engagements, it is said, and was mustered out, her sex undiscovered. Her husband died several years after the war.

Another narrative genre is the obituary. Sound morbid? Check ◀ out the obituaries shown here for Elizabeth A. Niles and Harvey Phillips (on p. 47). Don't these sound like people you wish you'd met? Writers of obituaries, sometimes the deceased himself or herself (some people write them well in advance), sometimes a friend or family member, tell the story of the deceased through key biographical details. A related genre, the eulogy, is a speech delivered at the funeral or memorial, usually written by friends or family members. Through eulogies, writers share stories about the deceased's life, character, and accomplishments. Even an epitaph, the inscription on a gravestone, can tell a story about a life.

The Rhetorical Situation

There are a lot of ways to tell a story—and countless genres for telling them. However, as a composer you always make specific rhetorical choices. These choices have to do with your purpose and audience, the strategies you use to reach your readers, the media you create in, the style and design of your story, and the sources you draw on to create it.

Purpose: Why tell stories?

As we worked on this book, we always began our sessions with an exchange of stories about what happened during the course of the day. It helped us reconnect. Our students do this before class, talking about what happened in other classes or at their jobs; no doubt, they do the same at home.

We also use narrative genres to chronicle events. A story may be just a few sentences or it may be epically long, such as *The Odyssey* or *War and Peace*. A story can be true (such as an autobiography) or it can be made up (such as a short story, novel, or other work of fiction). Some stories change history, such as the *Narrative of the Life of Frederick Douglass, an American Slave, Written by Himself*. Douglass's autobiography, which he published in 1845 while living in the North as an escaped slave, helped spark the abolitionist movement in ▼ the United States.

e For coverage of **fairy tales** and a sample tale, see e-Pages at bedfordstmartins.com /bookofgenres.

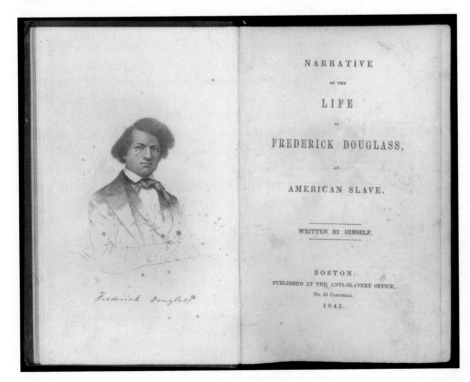

◀ MEMOIR
Frederick Douglass (1818–95).
Narrative frontispiece and title page. *Newberry Library, Chicago, Illinois, USA / The Bridgeman Art Library.*

NARRATIVE

OF THE

LIFE

OF

FREDERICK DOUGLASS,

AN

AMERICAN SLAVE.

WRITTEN BY HIMSELF.

BOSTON:
PUBLISHED AT THE ANTI-SLAVERY OFFICE,
No. 25 CORNHILL.
1845.

We also use stories to entertain—and instruct. For example, while most well-known fairy tales are pretty good reads, they were actually created to teach children some kind of lesson. Following is the text of "The Shepherd's Boy and the Wolf," commonly known as "The Boy Who Cried Wolf." This fable is attributed to Aesop (ca. 620–564 BCE), a (possibly mythical) storyteller who lived in Ancient Greece. Note the final line, which explicitly states the moral of the story.

FABLE ▶
Aesop,
"The Shepherd's Boy and the Wolf," from the digital collections of the University of Virginia Library.

UNIVERSITY *of* VIRGINIA LIBRARY

The Shepherd's Boy and the Wolf

A SHEPHERD-BOY, who watched a flock of sheep near a village, brought out the villagers three or four times by crying out, "Wolf! Wolf!" and when his neighbors came to help him, laughed at them for their pains. The Wolf, however, did truly come at last. The Shepherd-boy, now really alarmed, shouted in an agony of terror: "Pray, do come and help me; the Wolf is killing the sheep"; but no one paid any heed to his cries, nor rendered any assistance. The Wolf, having no cause of fear, at his leisure lacerated or destroyed the whole flock.

There is no believing a liar, even when he speaks the truth.

Have you ever read a story and wondered about its authenticity? How much does a story's validity have to do with its author? Can you think of examples of an author (or speaker) who seems unreliable?

Why else do we tell stories? To persuade others—or even to sell something. For example, in a job interview, you might tell relevant stories about your previous experience that show you're qualified for the position you're discussing. In terms of selling, think of the many TV ads that use a narrative to make a case about a product, such as car commercials that go something like this: A well-dressed young couple walks through the woods with their kids and golden retriever and then they all pile into their shiny new SUV. The creators of the ad, hired by the SUV manufacturer, are selling you not only the shiny vehicle, but an entire conceptual package including luxury, romance, the American dream, and even environmentalism. In this case, the brief story (couple, kids, dog, woods, car) is used to convince you to buy a large automobile.

Audience: How do we get others to connect with our stories?

We write stories in order to explore our experiences and share them with others. For a story to resonate, readers must be able to connect with it personally. As writers, we strive for ways to make that happen. For example, in his memoir, *Dreams from My Father*, Barack Obama shares his experiences growing up as a black American and the struggles he faced as he traced his origins, something many readers can relate to. He tells his story through a series of anecdotes that read like a conversation, beginning with how he heard of his father's death. By beginning with such a universal situation and using an informal tone, Obama gets readers invested in his story. Alison Bechdel's *Fun Home* (p. 70) is a graphic memoir about her family's sometimes comedic, sometimes tragic, dysfunction. To reach her audience, she tells a series of stories through images and text written in the first person. She uses humor and her strong writer's voice to invite readers into her story.

There are many reasons for sharing stories—and many ways of reaching readers or listeners. For example, Erna Anolik tells of her experience at Auschwitz through the University of Southern California's Shoah Foundation. Anolik appeals directly to her audience by appearing on video. (To view her testimony, select "Camps" from the topics menu at Shoah.) ▼

What are the stories that make up your life? What are your earliest memories? How did you learn to read and write?

Camps

"Concentration Camps" or "Labor Camps" were facilities in which people were incarcerated on the basis of their political and/or religious beliefs or ethnicity, usually without regard to due process.

◄ ORAL HISTORY/ TESTIMONIAL **Erna Anolik,** "On Surviving a Concentration Camp," from the Shoah Foundation. *Image of Erna Anolik, "On the Topic of Camps," provided by the USC Shoah Foundation— The Institute for Visual History and Education, http://sfi.usc.edu/.*

Rhetorical Appeals: How do we use ethos, logos, and pathos to tell stories?

Whether your favorite narrative genre is the Facebook status line or the memoir, you'll be most effective if you tap into the rhetorical appeals: ethos, logos, and pathos.

▲ VIDEO MEMOIR
Amy Braziller,
from *Writing the Music Train.*

Ethos—How you, as an author or composer, are perceived by your audience is crucial when you tell a story. For example, if you write an autobiography, deliver a eulogy, or share an oral history, your readers and listeners assume that what you are telling them is true, that the stories have actually taken place. If you create a photo essay, such as the one included in this chapter (p. 81), your viewers assume that you have accurately depicted real events. If you create a work of fiction (a short story, a novel, etc.), your ethos as an author is also important. Readers want to trust that you're going to tell them an interesting, worthwhile story, perhaps with a solid, interesting plot and relatable characters they can care about.

◄ In her video memoir, *Writing the Music Train*, Amy documents her days as a punk rocker. She presents herself as a writer who was stunted by a teacher's comments on her early writing; she tells how she succeeded as a writer by composing songs and lyrics in a punk rock band. Here, Amy establishes her ethos as a memoirist by presenting original lyrics, a piece of writing "corrected" by her teacher, and a series of punk-inspired self-portraits.

Logos—The logic you use as an author or composer is also significant when you tell a story. For example, a short story, even if it is not told chronologically, usually follows a pattern in which the plot and characters unfold in a logical manner to the reader.

Pathos—Your appeal to readers' emotions can go a long way in bringing your story home. For example, when you write a memoir, you identify a moment in your life that has emotional significance, and convey it in a way that gets readers to identify emotionally with that experience.

The Tyler Clementi Foundation was created in memory of Tyler Clementi, a Rutgers University student who was bullied for being gay and who ultimately committed suicide in 2010. The language on the page titled "Tyler's Story" reflects love, pride, and grief. The foundation briefly described at the bottom of the screen was created in Tyler's honor and to provide anti-bullying resources for gay teens.

◄ WEB SITE
The Tyler Clementi Foundation,
"Tyler's Story."
The Tyler Clementi Foundation.

Modes & Media: What are the best choices? How will they affect your story?

A story's *mode* is how the story is communicated—text, audio, video, or a combination of these modes. A story's *medium* can be print, digital, or face-to-face.

NARRATIVE GENRES	Mode	Medium
MEMOIR Frederick Douglass, *Narrative of the Life of Frederick Douglass* (p. 41)	**WRITTEN**	**PRINT**
FABLE Aesop, "The Shepherd's Boy and the Wolf" (p. 42)	**WRITTEN**	**DIGITAL**
ORAL HISTORY/TESTIMONIAL Erna Anolik, "On Surviving a Concentration Camp" (p. 43)	**VISUAL AND AUDIO**	**DIGITAL**

The Genre's Conventions

Elements of the Genre: What do all stories have in common?

Writers rely on certain techniques and conventions to tell a story. You might start with a premise and think about how to convey the story in terms of exposition (the basic information you need to share), tension, rising action, conflict, climax, and resolution (also known as plot, if you're writing creatively). You need to think about your viewpoint, tone, and voice as a storyteller, and how that will affect your reader or listener. You also need to make sure the people involved (or characters, if you're writing creatively) are as interesting and dynamic as possible. Use every sentence to move your story forward to its resolution.

Style: How does it contribute to your story?

What is your individual style? Individual writers use different styles, have different voices, and include different kinds of details. The following paragraph is by the fiction author Junot Díaz. This is his character Yunior speaking in a short story called "Fiesta, 1980." Pay attention to how he works with the short story genre.

> **EXCERPT FROM A SHORT STORY**
> Mami's youngest sister—my Tia Yrma—finally made it to the United States that year. She and Tio Miguel got themselves an apartment in the Bronx, off the Grand Concourse, and everybody decided that we should have a party. Actually, my dad decided, but everybody—meaning Mami, Tia Yrma, Tio Miguel, and their neighbors—thought it a dope idea. On the Friday of the party Papi got back from work around six. Right on time. We were all dressed by then, which was a smart move on our part. If Papi had walked in and caught us lounging around in our underwear, man, he would have kicked our asses something serious.
> —**Junot Díaz**, from "Fiesta, 1980" (*Drown*)

Díaz uses style and voice to convey a narrator who is young and hip within the context of 1980. His narrator, Yunior—who Díaz has acknowledged in interviews is an alter ego—uses language such as "dope idea" and "man, he would have kicked our asses something serious." He creates a narrator who is observant, who has an eye for detail. Díaz writes from the first-person (I) point of view, inviting readers to identify with his main character/narrator. He hints at a conflict between the narrator and his father; Díaz uses the technique of foreshadowing to suggest a future struggle, telling readers that the father's response to laziness ("lounging around in our underwear") would have been to "have kicked our asses." Díaz assures us, as readers, that we'll get the whole story: His choices contribute to his ethos as an author, and to the ethos of his narrator as a central character and storyteller.

What stories (or other kind of writing) have you read that have a strong, memorable "voice"—whether in terms of the author or a character? How does voice affect your experience as a reader?

e For more on **short stories**, see the e-Pages for this chapter at **bedfordstmartins.com /bookofgenres**.

Design: What is the best format for your story?

How we design a narrative contributes to our readers' experience. The obituary shown here for Harvey Phillips, for example, was designed by editors and designers at *The New York Times*, who made careful decisions about what to emphasize through images, typeface, and interactive features. The photo of Harvey Phillips playing the tuba reinforces his career as "Titan of the Tuba." The large font size used for the title and the second color used for the hyperlinks add emphasis, making essential information clear to the reader. Hyperlinks in the obituary connect readers to related content. For example, the phrase "to play carols and other festive fare" links to a YouTube video of Harvey Phillips playing at Rockefeller Center's skating rink in 2008. Clearly, the editors and designers anticipated that readers might want to see and hear one of Phillips's performances, and so they added that link and presented it in the first paragraph.

Sources: What information should you draw on to tell stories?

When we tell or write stories, we often draw on our own experiences. For example, Liz may tell a story about something funny that happened to her this morning, in which case her own life is the source. In other situations, we draw on other sources. Take, for example, the obituary of Elizabeth A. Niles (p. 40). The author interviewed Niles's family to learn details about her life and death. Another example is Amy's video memoir (p. 44); sources she used include photographs, video recordings of her musical performances, and a poster from the club where she performed. Other works, such as fairy tales (see "The Shepherd's Boy and the Wolf," p. 42, and "Little Red Riding Hood," in the e-Pages for this chapter), movies such as *Star Wars*, and books such as *The Lord of the Rings*, draw on tales and legends of the past, including Greek mythology, European folklore, and Icelandic epic poetry.

Music

Harvey Phillips, a Titan of the Tuba, Dies at 80

By DANIEL J. WAKIN
Published: October 24, 2010

The tuba players mass by the hundreds every year on the Rockefeller Center ice-skating rink to play carols and other festive fare, a holiday ritual now ingrained in the consciousness of New York.

The tradition began in 1974, the brainchild of Harvey Phillips, a musician called the Heifetz of the tuba. In his time he was the instrument's chief evangelist, the inspirer of a vast solo repertory, a mentor to generations of players and, more simply, Mr. Tuba.

Most tuba players agree that if their unwieldy instrument has shed any of the bad associations that have clung to it — orchestral clown, herald of grim news, poorly respected back-bencher best when not noticed, good for little more than the "oom" in the oom-pah-pah — it is largely thanks to Mr. Phillips's efforts. He waged a lifelong campaign to improve the tuba's image.

▲ OBITUARY
Daniel J. Wakin, "Harvey Phillips, a Titan of the Tuba, Dies at 80." *From The New York Times, October 24, 2010 © 2010 The New York Times. All rights reserved.*

LITERACY NARRATIVES

A literacy narrative tells a story of remembering. In this sense, it is similar to the memoir (p. 57) and the graphic memoir (p. 67). Like memoirists, when the writers of literacy narratives tell their own stories, they relate events and also analyze how these events have shaped their identities. However, there is an important difference between the memoir and the literacy narrative: The writers of literacy narratives tell a story specifically about how they learned to read and/or write.

You may be familiar with literacy narratives already; many memoirs include sections about how the author learned to read or write or important moments in the development of their literacy. Examples include Jimmy Santiago Baca's *Working in the Dark* and Eudora Welty's *One Writer's Beginnings*. Other memoirs focus more on the development of the author's literacy, such as Stephen King's *On Writing* and Anne Lamott's *Bird by Bird*. Sometimes memoirists will use the story of the development of their reading and writing as a context in which other stories are woven, as Azar Nafisi does in *Reading Lolita in Tehran: A Memoir in Books*, in which she tells the story of a secret women's book group in Iran and how the books they read reflected and affected the lives of the women in the group.

> What was the first book (or sentence or word) you read? What was the context? Where were you, and who was present? What was the experience like for you?

Analyzing Literacy Narratives: What to Look For

THE RHETORICAL SITUATION

Purpose People write literacy narratives because their formative experiences with reading and writing are important to them; they want to share their stories with others, especially if their literacy histories involve obstacles or challenges. Some may also want to make an argument about the importance of literacy.

Audience Literacy narratives are often written in composition classes and other college courses. Instructors assign this genre to help students understand what influences their speaking, reading, and writing. In this case, a writer's main audience is his or her instructor and classmates. Outside of the classroom, writers create literacy narratives to help educators, librarians, and other people involved in literacy fields better understand how literacy practices and histories manifest themselves in people's lives. (For examples of narratives in various media—text, audio, and video—see the Digital Archive of Literacy Narratives at Ohio State University.)

Literacy narratives are often published for a wider, popular audience; they may appear in a magazine or journal, or as part of a larger collection of essays, as is the case for the narrative that appears later in this section (the excerpt from Richard Rodriguez's *Hunger of Memory* on p. 51).

Rhetorical appeals   Writers of literacy narratives use direct language and real details from their lives to establish credibility (ethos). They also make logical connections (logos) between their narratives and the larger issues of literacy; oftentimes, these authors write to emphasize and argue about the importance of literacy, which makes the use of logos especially important.

Modes & media   Many writers of literacy narratives use the traditional essay or book form; for example, Helen Keller includes her memoir of learning to understand Braille in her autobiography, *The Story of My Life*. Other literacy narratives appear on the Internet as blog entries or YouTube videos, or are presented in online archives.

THE GENRE'S CONVENTIONS

Elements of the genre   Literacy narratives can take the form of memoirs, in which writers reflect on moments in their lives that show how reading and writing have affected their experiences and sense of self. Authors of literacy narratives convey their experiences, framing their interactions with the world in terms of reading and writing. They also use personal anecdotes and autobiographical details to re-create their experiences for the reader.

Like memoirs, most literacy narratives are written in the first person. Authors of literacy narratives tell stories not just for the sake of recounting events; rather, their goal is for the narrative to culminate in a larger idea or theme that drives the essay. Writers also use literary elements such as setting, character development, dialogue, vivid descriptions and details, symbols, and metaphors.

Style   Authors use detail to re-create their literacy experiences for readers. For example, in her literacy narrative, Helen Keller shows readers, through specific examples, what it was like to be a blind and deaf child:

EXCERPT FROM A LITERACY NARRATIVE
My aunt made me a big doll out of towels. It was the most comical, shapeless thing, this improvised doll, with no nose, mouth, ears or eyes—nothing that even the imagination of a child could convert into a face. Curiously enough, the absence of eyes struck me more than all the other defects put together. I pointed this out to everybody with provoking

persistency, but no one seemed equal to the task of providing the doll with eyes. A bright idea, however, shot into my mind, and the problem was solved. I tumbled off the seat and searched under it until I found my aunt's cape, which was trimmed with large beads. I pulled two beads off and indicated to her that I wanted her to sew them on my doll. She raised my hand to her eyes in a questioning way, and I nodded energetically. The beads were sewed in the right place and I could not contain myself for joy.

—**Helen Keller,** from *The Story of My Life*

Think of the stories, memoirs, and other narratives you've read, viewed, or listened to in your life. What details stand out from these stories? How do they affect the ways you think about and remember each story?

Most authors of this genre take literacy seriously, which is why they want to write about it and share their experiences with readers; however, each author of a literacy narrative conveys his or her story in a unique voice. Keller's voice emphasizes that in many ways, she was just like any other child, playing with dolls, for example. Her matter-of-fact tone helps readers identify with and understand her childhood experiences.

Design   The literacy narrative usually takes an essay format: It has an introduction, body paragraphs, and a conclusion. However, literacy narratives can take different forms, including audio essay and documentary. In their written form, literacy narratives use typography to emphasize certain points or language.

Sources   Like print and graphic memoirs, literacy narratives seldom cite outside sources, because the source of information is almost always just the writer's memories of his or her own life.

Richard Rodriguez

From Hunger of Memory:
The Education of Richard Rodriguez

Richard Rodriguez's *Hunger of Memory* is a collection of autobiographical essays. In the following excerpt, which he calls a memoir, and which is also a literacy narrative (see how genres overlap!), Rodriguez focuses on the power of language as he explores his childhood experiences in a bilingual world. Rodriguez relates the struggles he faced living in between a Spanish-speaking world and an English-speaking world.

The notes in the margins point out Rodriguez's goals as a writer and his strategies for connecting with his readers. They also show how he works with the genre's conventions to tell a compelling story about literacy. *(Excerpt on pp. 52-53 reprinted by permission of David R. Godine, Publisher, Inc. Copyright © 1982 by Richard Rodriguez.)*

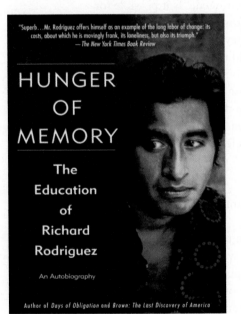

◄ BOOK COVER
Richard Rodriguez
on the cover of his autobiography.
Used by permission of Bantam Books, a division of Random House, Inc. Any third party use of this material, outside of this production, is prohibited. Interested parties must apply directly to Random House, Inc., for permission.

What is the composer, Richard Rodriguez, doing?

THE RHETORICAL SITUATION

Purpose
Audience
Rhetorical appeals
Modes & media

see page 53

How do I know this is a literacy narrative?

THE GENRE'S CONVENTIONS

Elements of the genre
Style
Design
Sources

see page 54

Richard Rodriguez
From *Hunger of Memory*

Three months. Five. Half a year passed. Unsmiling, ever watchful, my teachers noted my silence. They began to connect my behavior with the difficult progress my older sister and brother were making. Until one Saturday morning three nuns arrived at the house to talk to our parents. Stiffly, they sat on the blue living room sofa. From the doorway of another room, spying the visitors, I noted the incongruity—the clash of two worlds, the faces and voices of school intruding upon the familiar setting of home. I overheard one voice gently wondering, "Do your children speak only Spanish at home, Mrs. Rodriguez?" While another voice added, "That Richard especially seems so timid and shy."

That Rich-heard!

With great tact the visitors continued, "Is it possible for you and your husband to encourage your children to practice their English when they are home?" Of course, my parents complied. What would they not do for their children's well-being? And how could they have questioned the Church's authority which those women represented? In an instant, they agreed to give up the language (the sounds) that had revealed and accentuated our family's closeness. The moment after the visitors left, the change was observed. "*Ahora*, speak to us *en inglés*," my father and mother united to tell us.

At first, it seemed a kind of game. After dinner each night, the family gathered to practice "our" English. (It was still then *inglés*, a language foreign to us, so we felt drawn as strangers to it.) Laughing, we would try to define words we could not pronounce. We played with strange English sounds, often over-anglicizing our pronunciations. And we filled the smiling gaps of our sentences with familiar

Rodriguez, From *Hunger of Memory*, *Continued*

Spanish sounds. But that was cheating, somebody shouted. Everyone laughed. In school, meanwhile, like my brother and sister, I was required to attend a daily tutoring session. I needed a full year of special attention. I also needed my teachers to keep my attention from straying in class by calling out, Rich-heard—their English voices slowly prying loose my ties to my other name, its three notes, Ri-car-do. Most of all I needed to hear my mother and father speak to me in a moment of seriousness in broken—suddenly heartbreaking—English. The scene was inevitable: One Saturday morning I entered the kitchen where my parents were talking in Spanish. I did not realize that they were talking in Spanish, however, until at the moment they saw me, I heard their voices change to speak English. Those gringo sounds they uttered startled me. Pushed me away. In that moment of trivial misunderstanding and profound insight, I felt my throat twisted by unsounded grief. I turned quickly and left the room. But I had no place to escape to with Spanish. (The spell was broken.) My brother and sisters were speaking English in another part of the house.

Again and again in the days following, increasingly angry, I was obliged to hear my mother and father: "*Speak to us en inglés*" (*Speak*). Only then did I determine to learn classroom English. Weeks afterward, it happened: One day in school I raised my hand to volunteer an answer. I spoke out in a loud voice. And I did not think it remarkable when the entire class understood. That day, I moved very far from the disadvantaged child I had been only days earlier. The belief, the calming assurance that I belonged in public, had at last taken hold.

THE RHETORICAL SITUATION

Purpose

Rodriguez aims to share the story of how he came to speak both English and Spanish.

Audience

The author knows his primary readers care about language and identity. They are bilingual or native English speakers interested in themes of education, family, and coming-of-age.

Rhetorical appeals

Rodriguez begins with a brief story about his parents being willing to do anything for their children, an appeal to **pathos**. The teachers' connecting of Rodriguez's behavior to his lack of English is an example of **logos**.

Rodriguez, From *Hunger of Memory,* Continued

THE RHETORICAL SITUATION

Modes & media

Mode = written This literacy narrative is written. Because Rodriguez's topic is language, his choice to convey his story in written words makes sense. If he were to adapt this narrative using digital technology, he might embed audio so his readers could hear what he experienced.

Medium = print Rodriguez's book is intended to be read in hard-copy format or as an e-book. In either case, it's intended to be read from beginning to end, one page at a time, unlike online literacy narratives, which can be read in a non-linear fashion.

THE GENRE'S CONVENTIONS

Elements of the genre

This is an **autobiographical account about literacy.** Rodriguez shares childhood experiences of learning to speak, read, and write.

He uses **anecdotes** to advance a central idea; e.g., with the brief, personal story in paragraph 1, Rodriguez prepares readers for his ideas about language and identity, and his argument about bilingual education.

He writes in the **first person** and **describes settings** to connect readers with his experience. He contrasts his home setting with his classroom (where he is an outsider) to emphasize the difference in his private and public encounters with literacy.

Style

Rodriguez **uses rich detail** to re-create his experience for readers. Because his essay centers on how he hears language, he focuses on bringing the dialogue alive and uses **phonetic spelling** so that readers hear exactly what he hears.

His **tone and voice reflect his personality and speech.** He quotes the nuns to emphasize how they enunciate and "Americanize" words.

Design

Rodriguez uses italics to highlight Spanish and English words, and also to emphasize certain passages and sounds (*"That Rich-heard!"*).

Sources

Rodriguez does not cite outside sources because he is the source of his story.

Questions: Analyzing Rodriguez's literacy narrative

1. Purpose. Rodriguez not only tells a story about his experiences with language, but also makes an argument regarding bilingual education. What is his argument? How persuasive is he?

2. Purpose. Reread the final paragraph of the essay. Why do you think Rodriguez chose to conclude this way?

3. Audience. What techniques does Rodriguez use to connect with his audience? Is an audience that has experienced bilingual education his target audience? Why or why not?

4. Rhetorical appeals. How does Rodriguez develop his ethos as someone who speaks about education with authority? How does his phonetic spelling of "Rich-heard" contribute to the pathos of the piece?

5. Modes & media. Imagine Rodriguez's literacy narrative as a digital text online. Which words of the excerpt could be linked to other Web sites? For example, perhaps the word "Rich-heard" could be linked to a YouTube video in which someone says the name as Rodriguez's family would say it; this might emphasize how strange the Americanized pronunciation sounded to Rodriguez.

6. Elements of the genre. What are some similarities between Rodriguez's literacy narrative and memoirs that you may be familiar with (e.g., see Dave Eggers's memoir on p. 61)?

7. Style. Given that writers of literacy narratives tell stories about how they learned to speak, read, or write, why might many of them include dialogue? What role does dialogue play in Rodriguez's literacy narrative?

8. Style. Rodriguez includes some Spanish words in his narrative. How do the Spanish words contribute to the essay's effect?

9. Design. Rodriguez italicizes bits of dialogue. What do you think is his purpose for doing so?

10. Sources. The source for this literacy narrative excerpt is Rodriguez's own memory. Do you think a narrative written by one of the nuns would differ significantly from Rodriguez's? Why or why not?

Drafting a Literacy Narrative

CHECKLIST: Drafting a Literacy Narrative
Thinking of writing about how you learned to speak, read, and write? Ask yourself the following questions.

WHAT'S MY RHETORICAL SITUATION?

☐ **Purpose.** What specific moment in my life as a reader or writer do I want to write about? Why? What questions do I have about that moment? How might I interpret that moment? What insights do I want to share with others? How did that moment shape me as a reader or writer?

☐ **Audience.** How would I describe my readers? Why will my experience with reading or writing matter to my readers? What do I want them to get out of my story? And how will I reach them?

☐ **Rhetorical appeals.** How will I establish my authority as a writer? How reliable will I be as a narrator? To what extent will I appeal to my readers' emotions? To what extent will I rely on logic to support my interpretations of my experiences?

☐ **Modes & media.** Do I want readers to experience my story in written, audio, or visual form? Do I want my literacy narrative to be print, electronic, or presented face-to-face?

WHAT GENRE CONVENTIONS MATTER?

☐ **Elements of the genre.** I'm writing about my own life: How will I keep my writing true and accurate? How much will I disclose about myself (and others) in my literacy memoir? Will I write in the first person? What anecdotes will I use to tell the story of myself as a reader or writer, and why? Also, what literary elements might I use? For example, will I use dialogue (as Rodriguez does) or a metaphor to help readers compare my experience to something else?

☐ **Style.** What tone will I take in my writing? Will my literacy narrative be serious or funny? Academic or down-to-earth? What kind of language will I use? How much detail will I include?

☐ **Design.** What format will my literacy narrative take? Do I want to compose a standard literacy narrative, focusing on words, or do I want to create a graphic literacy narrative that includes illustrations?

☐ **Sources.** What memories will I draw on? Will I need to check my story with others from my life, or will I rely on my own recollections and interpretations?

PRACTICE
Want to experiment? Draft your own literacy narrative.

Do some freewriting about an early memory of reading or speaking and how that early event shaped your attitudes and experiences with language. Draft a narrative in which you tell the story of your early experience; be sure to make specific points about how that experience shaped you as a reader, writer, and/or speaker. Include anecdotes, details, and quotations from conversations, as Rodriguez does.

MEMOIRS

The word *memoir* comes from the Old French *memoire* and Latin *memoria*, both meaning "memory." A memoir is a written (or graphic, film-based, etc.) and true account about one's own life and experience. Often, memoirists' works focus on a specific and significant moment in their lives—one that has specific meaning and importance.

A memoir is like a personal essay, except that memoirists tend to focus on looking at their past, asking questions, analyzing, and attempting to make sense of their lives. Memoirists also tend to use literary techniques, including dialogue. Some memoirs are funny, like David Sedaris's *Me Talk Pretty One Day*, which includes essays about his life as an American in France. Other memoirs are more serious, such as Joan Didion's *The Year of Magical Thinking*, about her loss of her husband and daughter, and Frank McCourt's *Angela's Ashes*, about his impoverished childhood in Ireland.

Some memoirists are famous; some are infamous. For example, former president Bill Clinton, in his memoir, *My Life*, discusses his two presidential terms with a focus on his successes and failures, as well as the life that brought him to the White House, and even his intimate life, including his affair with an intern. In the category of infamous, French art thief Stéphane Breitwieser wrote a memoir, *Confessions of an Art Thief*, about how he stole a billion dollars' worth of art. Another infamous example is author James Frey, who came under fire for fabricating his struggles with addiction in *A Million Little Pieces,* a book that he and his publisher originally presented as a memoir.

> What moment(s) in your life would you most want to write about in a memoir? Why?

Analyzing Memoirs: What to Look For

THE RHETORICAL SITUATION

Purpose Memoirists share their stories because they believe they can offer insights to others, as does Mitch Albom in his memoir, *Tuesdays with Morrie*, in which he writes about how people develop values. Memoirists write because they want to share lessons learned in difficult times, as Isabel Allende does in *Paula*, her memoir of watching her adult daughter die. Sometimes they write because they want to explain themselves, or "tell their side of the story," as rapper Eminem's mother, Debbie Nelson, does in her memoir, *My Son Marshall, My Son Eminem*. Many memoirists (like Sedaris) also aim to entertain their readers, but for most, the goal is to share their experiences.

Audience   Memoirists (such as Albom and Allende, mentioned above) often write for a wide readership and publish their works in books and magazines such as *The New Yorker* and *O: The Oprah Magazine*. Some write for popular audiences (such as Nelson, especially). However, some write for narrower audiences, such as fans of poetry: Donald Hall, in his memoir *The Best Day the Worst Day*, writes about his life with poet Jane Kenyon. This book appeals to Liz, for example, because she is a fan of both of these poets, and is interested in learning about them as writers and partners too. Memoirists can offer insights and information about what they are most famous for (in Hall's case, poetry).

Rhetorical appeals   To earn their readers' trust, memoirists must be reliable narrators of their own stories. They develop their ethos through the anecdotes they share, but also through the language and tone they use. Isabel Allende, in another memoir, entitled *Aphrodite: A Memoir of the Senses*, uses sophisticated yet playful language to establish herself as—you guessed it—sophisticated and playful: "I repent of my diets, the delicious dishes rejected out of vanity, as much as I lament the opportunities for making love that I let go by because of pressing tasks or puritanical virtue." Sensationalist or overly dramatic language, such as the use of many superlatives (*biggest, grandest, smartest*), or an overreliance on exclamation points (*I was so scared!!*) could compromise the ethos of the memoirist.

Modes & media   Traditionally, memoirs are written in book or essay form. A memoir will sometimes include photos of the memoirist to supplement the text, giving the reader a visual image to associate with an anecdote or bit of personal history. Memoirs are occasionally adapted into films or television movies, as in the case of *Persepolis*, Marjane Satrapi's graphic memoir, which was made into an animated film in 2007.

THE GENRE'S CONVENTIONS

Elements of the genre   Because memoirs are based on writers' memories, most are naturally written in the first person. Memoirs feel intimate not only because of their first-person perspective, but because their authors reveal personal thoughts and feelings to the reader. Self-disclosure, the sharing of emotion, personal ideas, facts, and other information, invites readers into a bond with the author, drawing them into a shared sense of trust.

How would you describe your life— in six words? *SMITH* magazine invites you to publish your mini-memoir at their site.

Memoirists use many of the same techniques fiction writers use, such as dialogue, vivid descriptions of settings, imagery, and metaphor. Instead of inventing *characters*, memoirists include other real people in their work. For example, in David Sedaris's memoirs, his boyfriend Hugh is a frequent presence, as are members of Sedaris's family.

Memoirists present anecdotes to illustrate specific moments or points. An anecdote is usually just a few sentences long and is usually amusing rather than sad, such as this anecdote from Donald Hall's *The Best Day the Worst Day*:

> One morning when I tried to start the Plymouth, it barely turned over and wouldn't catch. I was puzzled until I checked the thermometer on the porch. It was minus twenty-one degrees—and I had not noticed: New Hampshire's cold is drier than Michigan's and less painful.

Memoirs are true, or at least represent the truth as the author honestly remembers it. Sometimes others who have a stake in the stories in someone else's memoir challenge the accuracy of those stories. For example, some of Frank McCourt's neighbors from his hometown in Ireland have different memories of the degree of misery McCourt suffered. McCourt writes in his memoir *Angela's Ashes*:

> People everywhere brag and whimper about the woes of their early years, but nothing can compare with the Irish version: the poverty; the shiftless loquacious alcoholic father; the pious defeated mother moaning by the fire; pompous priests; bullying schoolmasters; the English and the terrible things they did to us for 800 long years.
>
> Above all—we were wet.

But is *Angela's Ashes* a totally factual story? asks *Los Angeles Times* writer Tim Rutten, upon McCourt's death. Rutten explores the answer:

> [S]ome outraged Limerick residents insisted not, and the local newspaper dredged up old photos of Frank and [McCourt's brother] Malachy well dressed and their long-suffering mother sleek and fed. Still, if the McCourt family misery was neither as unrelieved nor as perfect as the author recalled it, his account "was no less true for all of that."

How "true" or accurate a memoir is has to do with the nature of memory; memory is subjective and imperfect. Memory, and how we write about it, also has to do with our personalities, our sense of others—and of justice and injustice, our hopes and wishes. As readers and writers, we need to take these factors into account when we approach the memoir. However, there is a big difference between lapses and other imperfections of the memory—and the purposeful invention of things that never happened. In extreme cases, when an author's work is more fiction than truth, the memoirist loses all credibility (see the discussion of James Frey on p. 57).

Style   Memoirists use a lot of detail to tell their stories. In fact, Bill Clinton's memoir was criticized for being too richly detailed. (One Amazon.com review asks, "Do we really need to know the name of his childhood barber?")

For more **memoirs** and other biographical genres, see the Index of Genres on page G-1.

Memoirists also use a great range of tones to tell a story. For example, even Frank McCourt's memoir about misery is not without wit and charm ("Above all—we were wet"). The style of a memoir can vary considerably depending on who the author is. Bill Clinton, known as charismatic and talkative as governor of Arkansas and president of the United States, comes across as charming and garrulous in his memoir. His vocabulary reflects his worldliness and education, and his sentences are often long and detailed. Consider the first sentence in Clinton's *My Life*:

> Early on the morning of August 19, 1946, I was born under a clear sky after a violent summer storm to a widowed mother in the Julia Chester Hospital in Hope, a town of about six thousand in southwest Arkansas, thirty-three miles east of the Texas border at Texarkana.

At forty-nine words long, this sentence is three times the length of the average written sentence. A much shorter but very powerful sentence begins Isabel Allende's memoir *Paula*:

> Listen, Paula.

These words instantly indicate that the memoir is part letter to Paula, Allende's dying daughter.

Design   Most memoirs are print texts published in book form (however, see also "Graphic Memoirs," p. 67). Although the text-based memoir focuses on words (not images), some memoirs feature a gallery of photos and documents from the writer's life. The book cover usually presents a flattering photo of the writer. For example, on the cover of his memoir, Bill Clinton does not look beleaguered (as he may have felt during the Whitewater hearings or impeachment proceedings of his second term); rather, he is smiling and looks healthy and at ease.

Sources   Most memoirs are based on personal observation and experience. For this reason, memoirists seldom cite outside sources. However, if someone were to write a memoir of a group or an organization, that person would, no doubt, draw on historical documents, interviews, and other sources of information.

Guided Reading: Memoir ▼

Dave Eggers

From A Heartbreaking Work of Staggering Genius

The following excerpt is from Dave Eggers's memoir, *A Heartbreaking Work of Staggering Genius*. In it, Eggers tells the true story of how, at the age of twenty-two, he became the guardian fully responsible for raising his younger brother after both his parents died within a few weeks of each other. This excerpt is from the beginning of the book, when his mother is dying. Eggers has since made a name for himself as an author and editor, writing several highly praised novels and running McSweeney's, an independent publisher. Eggers also cofounded 826 Valencia, a literacy tutoring center for kids.

Annotations in the margins of the excerpt on pages 62–63 show the choices Eggers made in terms of his purpose, sense of audience, and use of rhetorical appeals. You'll also see notes on how this work reflects the conventions of the memoir genre—in terms of its real-life content and specific techniques. *(Excerpt on pp. 62–63 reprinted with the permission of Simon & Schuster, Inc.)*

PHOTO ▶
Dave Eggers.
Courtesy of McSweeney's Publishing.

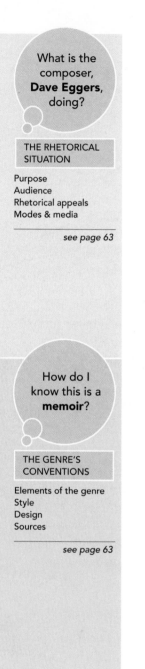

What is the composer, **Dave Eggers**, doing?

THE RHETORICAL SITUATION

Purpose
Audience
Rhetorical appeals
Modes & media

see page 63

How do I know this is a **memoir**?

THE GENRE'S CONVENTIONS

Elements of the genre
Style
Design
Sources

see page 63

Dave Eggers
From *A Heartbreaking Work of Staggering Genius*

I am holding the nose. As the nose bleeds and we try to stop it, we watch TV. On the TV an accountant from Denver is trying to climb up a wall before a bodybuilder named Striker catches him and pulls him off the wall. The other segments of the show can be tense—there is an obstacle course segment, where the contestants are racing against each other and also the clock, and another segment where they hit each other with sponge-ended paddles, both of which can be extremely exciting, especially if the contest is a close one, evenly matched and with much at stake—but this part, with the wall climbing, is too disturbing. The idea of the accountant being chased while climbing a wall . . . no one wants to be chased while climbing a wall, chased by anything, by people, hands grabbing at their ankles as they reach for the bell at the top. Striker wants to grab and pull the accountant down—he lunges every so often at the accountant's legs—all he needs is a good grip, a lunge and a grip and a good yank—and if Striker and his hands do that before the accountant gets to ring the bell . . . it's a horrible part of the show. The accountant climbs quickly, feverishly, nailing foothold after foothold, and for a second it looks like he'll make it, because Striker is so far below, two people-lengths easily, but then the accountant pauses. He cannot see his next move. The next grip is too far to reach from where he is. So then he actually *backs up*, goes down a notch to set out on a different path and when he steps down it is unbearable, the suspense. The accountant steps down and then starts up the left side of the wall, but suddenly Striker is there, out of nowhere—*he wasn't even in the screen!*—and he has the accountant's leg, at the calf, and he yanks and it's over. The accountant flies from the wall (attached by rope of course)

Eggers, From *A Heartbreaking Work of Staggering Genius,* Continued

and descends slowly to the floor. It's terrible. I won't watch this show again.

Mom prefers the show where three young women sit on a pastel-colored couch and recount blind dates that they have all enjoyed or suffered through with the same man. For months, Beth and Mom have watched the show, every night. Sometimes the show's participants have had sex with one another, but use funny words to describe it. And there is the funny host with the big nose and the black curly hair. He is a funny man, and has fun with the show, keeps everything buoyant. At the end of the show, the bachelor picks one of the three with whom he wants to go on another date. The host then does something pretty incredible: even though he's already paid for the three dates previously described, and even though he has nothing to gain from doing anything more, *he still gives the bachelor and bachelorette money for their next date.*

Mom watches it every night; it's the only thing she can watch without falling asleep, which she does a lot, dozing on and off during the day. But she does not sleep at night.

"Of course you sleep at night," I say.

"I don't," she says.

THE RHETORICAL SITUATION

Purpose

As a memoirist, Eggers's overall purpose is to tell a story about his life. In this case, the story is also about the lives of his family members.

Audience

Eggers's audience is adults who appreciate creative, innovative, and literary memoirs.

Rhetorical appeals

Eggers establishes his **ethos** as an author, writing directly to readers and setting up the story of his mother's illness. He details the chase scene on TV, building tension and appealing to the **pathos** (emotions) of his readers, inviting us to identify with his experience.

THE GENRE'S CONVENTIONS

Elements of the genre

Is written in first person ("I am holding . . .").

Is a true story about the writer's real life. The narrative

represents Eggers's memory of this time in his life; however, his sister Beth objected to this account because Dave did not portray her as an equal parent to their

brother Toph, though she claims to have been.

Mentions actual people in the writer's life. Here Eggers writes about his mother and mentions

his sister Beth; elsewhere he writes about his younger brother, Toph; other siblings; friends; and acquaintances.

Eggers, From *A Heartbreaking Work of Staggering Genius,* Continued

THE RHETORICAL SITUATION

Modes & media

Mode = written
Author Dave Eggers probably assumed that his readers would be adults reading his memoir alone to themselves because that is the conventional way that books are read. Although some memoirs include photographs of the author, Eggers did not include any images beyond artwork for the cover.

Medium = print *A Heartbreaking Work of Staggering Genius* is available in print and as an audiobook. It is presented here in print, and the assumption is that you will read it linearly, that is, from beginning to end. (Though in this case, you might be noticing the annotations in the margins as well.)

THE GENRE'S CONVENTIONS

Includes a personal anecdote. In this case, it's a serious one about his mother's illness, and how it shows itself one night in front of the TV.

Is written using literary techniques, including dialogue ("Of course you sleep at night.").

Style

Eggers's style and tone convey his personality.
"There is an obstacle course segment, where the contestants are racing against each other and also the clock, and another segment where they hit each other with sponge-ended paddles, both of which can be extremely exciting," for example, indicates his wry wit.

The writing is rich in details.
Instead of simply saying he is watching a physical contest on TV, he specifies, "On the TV an accountant from Denver is trying to climb up a wall before a bodybuilder named Striker catches him and pulls him off the wall."

Design

Text with little white space between paragraphs.

Sources

No footnotes or Works Cited list. The main source for the memoir is Eggers's life.

Questions: Analyzing Eggers's memoir

1. Purpose. Why might Eggers give so much detail about the shows he is watching on television?

2. Audience. Why would someone want to read Eggers's story, which is, in part, about his mother dying of cancer?

3. Audience. In this excerpt from his memoir, how does Eggers develop a sense of intimacy with his readers?

4. Rhetorical appeals. Most memoirists are themselves their main source of information. Based on this excerpt, are you convinced that Eggers has established his ethos? Is he a reliable narrator? Why or why not?

5. Modes & media. If you were in charge of selecting an actor to read the audio version of this book, whom would you select, and why?

6. Elements of the genre. Considering how fallible human memory is, how much accuracy do you expect in a memoir? Do you have higher or lower expectations of accuracy for autobiographies or histories? Why? And how does creativity figure into the memoir as a genre?

7. Style. Eggers wrote his memoir in the first person. Imagine that he rewrote this excerpt in the third person ("*Dave is holding his mother's nose. As the nose bleeds and they try to stop it, they watch TV.*"). How would you read the memoir differently?

8. Style. Based on the excerpt from *A Heartbreaking Work of Staggering Genius*, what is your impression of Eggers's personality? Which details in the excerpt lead you to feel this way?

9. Design. In this brief excerpt, Eggers uses a long, unbroken paragraph: What do you think this text style indicates about the tone and style of the book?

10. Sources. Because Eggers himself is the main source of the book, the story he tells is told from his perspective. His sister, Beth, claimed that he inflated his role in raising their little brother, Toph. Is there anything in this excerpt that you think might be seen differently by someone who was there?

Drafting a Memoir

CHECKLIST: Drafting a Memoir Thinking of composing a memoir? Ask yourself the following questions.

WHAT'S MY RHETORICAL SITUATION?

☐ **Purpose.** What specific moment in my life do I want to write about? Why? What questions do I have about that moment? How might I interpret that moment? What insights do I want to share with others?

☐ **Audience.** How would I describe my potential readers? Why will my memoir matter to them? What do I want them to get out of it? And how will I reach them?

☐ **Rhetorical appeals.** How will I establish my authority as a writer? How reliable will I be as a narrator? To what extent will I appeal to readers' emotions? How will I use logic to support my interpretations?

☐ **Modes & media.** Do I want readers to experience my story in written, audio, or visual form? Do I want my memoir to be print, electronic, or presented face-to-face?

WHAT GENRE CONVENTIONS MATTER?

☐ **Elements of the genre.** As a person writing about my own life, how will I keep my writing true and accurate? How much will I disclose about myself (and others) in my memoir? Will I write in the first person? What anecdotes will I use, and why? Also, what literary elements might I use? For example, will I use dialogue?

☐ **Style.** What tone will I take in my writing? Will my memoir be funny? Serious? Tragic? What kind of language will I use? How much detail will I provide?

☐ **Design.** What format will my memoir take? Will I compose a print memoir—and if so, will I include photographs and other images? Or will I compose a graphic memoir or other type of memoir?

☐ **Sources.** What memories will I draw on? Will I need to check my story with others from my life, or will I rely on my own recollections and interpretations?

PRACTICE Want to experiment? Draft your own memoir.

Think about a key event in your life. Draft a few paragraphs in which you begin telling the story of the event in the first person. Use specific details and language so that your readers will feel like they were there. Consider how you want your readers to feel as they read your draft: Do you want them to laugh, cry, be outraged, or something else?

GRAPHIC MEMOIRS

The graphic memoir is a memoir told through text and images, usually drawings. Sometimes there are more words than images, but usually it's the other way around. If you are interested in composing any kind of memoir (whether it's in graphic or comic book form, or a film, for example), we suggest that you read the "Memoirs" section of this chapter (p. 57).

The graphic memoirist Alison Bechdel (p. 70) has described her process in interviews: First she writes her text; then she inks the images. Other graphic memoirists use different techniques, foregrounding the images in the panels and writing the text in later. You may already be familiar with graphic memoirs, a genre first made popular by Art Spiegelman's *Maus*, a graphic memoir about surviving the Holocaust. Graphic narratives now have a place as respected literary texts: They're the focus of college courses; they've won Pulitzer Prizes; and they've inspired successful movies including *A History of Violence* and *Sin City*.

> What are your favorite graphic memoirs or novels? What aspects of the story are most memorable? Why?

Analyzing Graphic Memoirs: What to Look For

THE RHETORICAL SITUATION

Purpose   Like other memoirists, graphic memoirists tell the story of (or a story from) a writer's life. Using such literary devices as character (in this case, real people rather than fictional ones), dialogue, and setting, graphic memoirists connect their readers with their work. Graphic memoirs, which look something like extended comic strips, focus on transporting the reader to a world that is very different from everyday reality. Sometimes a graphic narrative, such as Marjane Satrapi's *Persepolis*, discloses elements of a culture—Satrapi's life growing up in Iran and later as an expatriate—showing readers a world that may be outside their own experience.

Audience   Graphic memoirists know that their audiences want a look into someone else's life, as told by that person. Graphic memoirists know their audiences are particularly drawn toward the visual, and perhaps grew up reading comic books, or really like illustrated texts or alternative narrative forms.

As graphic memoirs are becoming more popular in academic settings, with instructors assigning them as part of their reading lists—or as an alternative to the print memoir in composition classes—more students are creating and reading them.

Rhetorical appeals   The play between visuals and text helps graphic memoirists emphasize certain aspects of the narrative to readers. Because memoirists want their readers to empathize with their experiences, they often use appeals to emotion to draw readers into their world. For example, when a story is meant to elicit shock, the shape of the letters and the use of bold graphics, along with the expressions on the character's face, can guide the reader's emotional response, emphasizing pathos. In a graphic memoir, ethos is a central concern, because the audience must trust that the writer is accurately representing experience and events.

Modes & media   Graphic memoirs usually take print form but are sometimes digitized for the Web. Graphic memoirs and novels are often adapted for film, reimagined as animated stories, as is the case with *Persepolis*.

Consider Art Spiegelman's graphic memoir *Maus*, which is a Holocaust narrative (the story of Spiegelman's father). To what extent is the graphic memoir an appropriate genre for dealing with traumatic experiences?

THE GENRE'S CONVENTIONS

Elements of the genre   Like all memoirs, the graphic memoir has a real-life plot that revolves around a series of events, or a storyline. The storyline hinges on a central conflict driven by real people who function as characters do in fiction. The central conflict of Marjane Satrapi's *Persepolis*, for example, is her (and her family's) struggle to survive the Iranian Revolution (of 1979, also known as the Islamic Revolution); at that time, the country's monarchy was overthrown and Iran became an Islamic republic with an increasingly repressive government.

To tell their stories, graphic memoirists use words—usually organized into short, simple sentences—that provide dialogue and move the plot along toward the conflict and its resolution. The visuals (usually inked drawings) move the plot, too, but also assist in creating the setting, atmosphere, and emotion of the memoir.

The written content of the graphic memoir often appears in boxes or in sentences interspersed among the visuals. Dialogue is usually placed in a bubble or box linked to the character's mouth. Most graphic composers do not present words and sentences in traditional paragraphs. The advantage is that by isolating a sentence in a box, the author creates a snapshot of a moment, or of a series of moments, adding to the power of the story. Further, though the graphic narrative may not provide traditional transitions between ideas and scenes, there are some transitional expressions that help the visual memoirist move from one idea to the next. For example, the words "only four months earlier" show a jump back in time.

Just as in comic strips, the visuals of a graphic memoir do a lot to relate the story and reinforce aspects of the written narrative. The visuals, which can focus in on a detail and pan out like a movie camera, for example, emphasize certain moments and allow readers to see what is happening. See the "Design" section below for more on how drawings function in a graphic memoir.

Style The reader's experience depends on the written and visual style of the graphic memoirist—how much (and what kind of) detail and specific techniques he or she uses, and the quality of the visual story's voice and tone.

Tone and voice. Graphic memoirists communicate the tone of their stories and their voices as storytellers through word choice, diction, visuals, and the choice of typeface and other graphics. For example, if a character is feeling exasperated, the writer might choose a font (such as **Impact**) to illustrate that mood.

Detail. Depending on their target audience, graphic memoirists may use intricate, almost lifelike detail, as in Bechdel's *Fun Home* (p. 70). Other times, graphic memoirists might take a more cartoon/superhero approach, such as that of DC Comics' *Watchmen*. Typically, graphic memoirists limit their reliance on text, using it primarily to keep the plot moving. Sentences in a given panel tend to be short, without much embellishment. In Satrapi's *Persepolis*, the narrative detail is written in a journalistic style, giving readers a sense of watching a revolution unfold.

Design Like comic strips, graphic memoirs are organized into visual panels, usually squares or rectangles that essentially freeze a moment in its own individual space. Like all graphic composers, graphic memoirists make choices about where to place panels, how large to make them, and what words from the written narrative to emphasize. They also decide how and where to place figures and objects within a panel, in order to direct the reader. The size of one object next to another (scale), the direction an object is facing in relation to the page, and the cutting off of part of an object in a frame are all careful choices that create meaning for readers.

For more **graphic memoirs** and other biographical genres, see the Index of Genres on page G-1.

Other design choices include whether to use a font, real handwriting or lettering, or a font that mimics handwriting. Many graphic composers use block lettering, boldface, and italics when they want to show emphasis, and use different graphical styles when needed (such as `Courier` or other distinctive fonts). Graphic memoirists also need to make decisions about the style, shape, and size of boxes, balloons, or other word-framing devices. Sometimes they assign specific shapes for specific speakers in the story. They also make choices about white space from panel to panel, and within a frame of text. White space is used for aesthetic reasons, but also to call attention to certain parts of the text, to provide a visual pause, or to represent the absence of something or someone.

Sources See "Memoirs" (p. 57).

Alison Bechdel

From Fun Home: A Family Tragicomic

Alison Bechdel gained notoriety in the comics scene in 1983 with her syndicated strip *Dykes to Watch Out For*. In her comic strip, Bechdel combined political commentary with the daily lives of mostly lesbian characters, narrating their love affairs, breakups, and adventures as attendees at such lesbian festivals as the Michigan Womyn's Music Festival.

After years of working on this comic strip, Bechdel wrote a graphic memoir, *Fun Home: A Family Tragicomic,* published in 2006. In *Fun Home*, she tells the story of growing up with a closeted father who ran a funeral parlor and taught English. In this work, Bechdel conveys the importance of her father in her life. The section that we've excerpted is from the book's first chapter. In it, Bechdel's own coming-out story is overshadowed by the death of her father.

As a graphic memoirist, Bechdel makes plenty of decisions about her purposes and how she will draw in her readers. She also works with many of the conventions of the graphic narrative, while using a style that is all her own. The annotations in the margins of the work draw your attention to these choices, inviting you to think critically about their impact on you as a reader and composer.

(All images and cover: From FUN HOME: A FAMILY TRAGICOMIC by Alison Bechdel. Copyright © 2006. Reprinted by permission of Houghton Mifflin Harcourt Publishing Company. All rights reserved.)

▲ BOOK COVER
& AUTHOR PHOTO ▶
Alison Bechdel,
*Fun Home: A Family
Tragicomic.* Author
photo: Liza Cowan.

Bechdel, From *Fun Home*, *Continued*

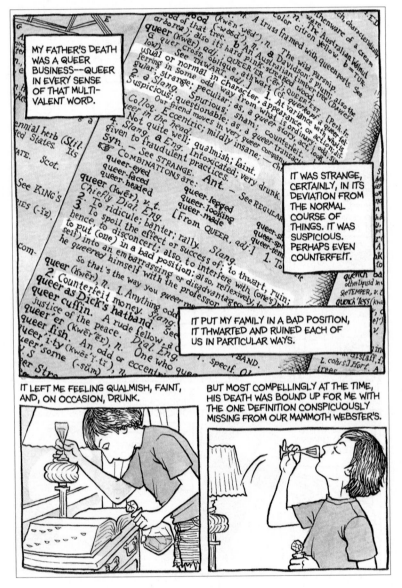

MY FATHER'S DEATH WAS A QUEER BUSINESS--QUEER IN EVERY SENSE OF THAT MULTI-VALENT WORD.

IT WAS STRANGE, CERTAINLY, IN ITS DEVIATION FROM THE NORMAL COURSE OF THINGS. IT WAS SUSPICIOUS. PERHAPS EVEN COUNTERFEIT.

IT PUT MY FAMILY IN A BAD POSITION, IT THWARTED AND RUINED EACH OF US IN PARTICULAR WAYS.

IT LEFT ME FEELING QUALMISH, FAINT, AND, ON OCCASION, DRUNK.

BUT MOST COMPELLINGLY AT THE TIME, HIS DEATH WAS BOUND UP FOR ME WITH THE ONE DEFINITION CONSPICUOUSLY MISSING FROM OUR MAMMOTH WEBSTER'S.

Continues next page

What is the composer, **Alison Bechdel**, doing?

THE RHETORICAL SITUATION

Purpose
Audience
Rhetorical appeals
Modes & media

see page 72

How do I know this is a **graphic memoir**?

THE GENRE'S CONVENTIONS

Elements of the genre
Style
Design
Sources

see page 73

Bechdel, From *Fun Home*, *Continued*

THE RHETORICAL SITUATION

Purpose

Bechdel's goal is to tell a story about her life, which includes childhood, coming out, and coming to terms with her father's identity and death.

Audience

Bechdel knows her readers enjoy memoirs and are especially drawn to comics and graphic novels. They are also interested in the coming-of-age and sexual identity themes in *Fun Home*.

Rhetorical appeals

Bechdel appeals to readers' emotions (**pathos**) by showing how her father's "queer death" caused her to feel "qualmish, faint, and, on occasion, drunk." The author uses events from her life to establish her **ethos**. Announcing "I am a lesbian" helps establish her ethos in what is partly a coming-out story.

(Continued on p. 74)

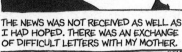

Bechdel, From *Fun Home*, *Continued*

THE GENRE'S
CONVENTIONS

Elements of the genre

Bechdel **tells a real-life story** in a form that **looks like a comic strip.**

The author **focuses on a central conflict**: her attempt to understand a childhood surrounded in secrets. (Elsewhere in the work, she moves back and forth between her own coming-out story and her father's inability to come out as a gay man.)

Her plot and conflict are driven by real people: Bechdel, the narrator; her mother; and her father. Sometimes she presents characters visually (narrator and father), other times through dialogue (mother).

(Continued on p. 74.)

Bechdel, From *Fun Home*, *Continued*

THE RHETORICAL SITUATION

Modes & media

Mode = written and visual Bechdel uses both the written and visual texts to communicate her story about coming out. Bechdel's use of visuals—such as when she mails a letter to her parents or talks on the phone with her mother—shows readers how Bechdel wants us to view her at that moment.

Medium = print Just like traditional memoirs, graphic memoirs are available in both print and digital media. Bookstores, these days, have sections devoted to graphic novels, where you can also find graphic memoirs such as Bechdel's. There are, however, digital graphic novels and memoirs that are often created online.

Web sites such as Comic Master allow you to create your own short graphic novel/memoir online using their free software.

THE GENRE'S CONVENTIONS

The visuals don't just represent the text—they highlight specific aspects and create emphasis. E.g., Bechdel presents the dictionary definition of the word *queer*. By blowing up the dictionary page, she shows her narrator-self coming to grips with ways to read her father's identity and death.

The visuals move the action along by showing it. E.g., we know Bechdel mails the letter not because the text says so, but because she shows herself licking the envelope and putting it in the mailbox.

Bechdel's **drawings take up more space than her words**; her words convey the weight of the narrative while the images convey the emotion.

Text is not presented in paragraphs. E.g., the isolated sentences in the top frame create a snapshot of moments. Combined, they would create a traditional paragraph but would have a very different effect.

Style

Bechdel uses **diction and word choice** to portray an educated, articulate character. E.g., she says she "imagined my confession as an emancipation. . . ."

The distance Bechdel's narrative voice has from her story gives the reader a lens through which she sees her past from an adult perspective. E.g., when she tells how others responded to her coming-out letter, she states, "The news was not received as well as I had hoped."

Design

Bechdel's text font mimics handwriting and she uses bold, italics, and other type effects to convey emotion.

She also **varies her layout;** e.g., some panels are parallel to each other, while others are not aligned evenly.

The **shapes of frames** around the text indicate what is thought, spoken, or narrated. Different shapes indicate who is speaking. In the bottom right frame, the mother's dialogue appears in a jagged box that comes out of the phone.

Bechdel uses **graphical style** to approximate reality. E.g., when the narrator types out, "I am a lesbian," Bechdel switches to Courier to approximate typing. On the third page shown here, Bechdel uses a lot of **white space** to call attention to the text and to represent the absence of her father.

Sources

Bechdel's source is her own memory, so there are no citations to outside materials.

Questions: Analyzing Bechdel's graphic memoir

1. Purpose. What parallels does Bechdel draw between her father's homosexuality and her own coming out?

2. Audience. Based on the short excerpt, who would you say is the audience for this graphic memoir? Why?

3. Rhetorical appeals. How do the visuals emphasize the main character's emotional state?

4. Modes & media. What different elements of the plot do the text and visuals emphasize?

5. Elements of the genre. Are there any places where the visuals and words seem to contradict each other or seem to be in tension with each other? If so, why do you think there is a contradiction or tension?

6. Elements of the genre. How much time is covered in the pages shown? How does Bechdel show the passage of time?

7. Elements of the genre. Only three pages of the graphic memoir are represented here. Even though it is a small snapshot of the book, what sense do you get of Bechdel as the narrator of her own story? How do the different graphic elements, combined with words, give you that sense of her?

8. Style. How would you describe the level of detail Bechdel uses in her visuals? In her text? Does the level of detail serve different purposes? If so, how?

9. Design. Sometimes Bechdel chooses to sandwich the narrative text between the visual panels. Other times, she places the narrative text within its own box. What reasons might she have for this? Are the narrative pieces that are in a box more significant? Why?

10. Sources. The main source for the graphic memoir is Alison Bechdel's life and experience. How does this influence your reading of the work?

Drafting a Graphic Memoir

CHECKLIST: Drafting a Graphic Memoir
Thinking of composing a graphic memoir? Ask yourself the following questions.

WHAT'S MY RHETORICAL SITUATION?

☐ **Purpose.** What specific moment in my life do I want to write about? Why? What questions do I have about that moment? How might I interpret that moment? What insights do I want to share with others? How would visuals illustrate the moment and make my experience more tangible for my reader?

☐ **Audience.** Who are my potential readers? Why will my memoir matter to them? What do I want them to get out of it? How old are they and how will I reach them? How will I use visuals to do that?

☐ **Rhetorical appeals.** How will I establish my authority as a writer? How reliable will I be as a narrator? To what extent will I appeal to my readers' emotions? How might I use logic?

☐ **Modes & media.** Do I want to create my story first with graphics or text? What aspects will I represent visually, and what aspects will I represent in written form? Would my graphic memoir be appropriate to translate into a film? Do I want to create my story using ink on paper or using a digital program?

WHAT GENRE CONVENTIONS MATTER?

☐ **Elements of the genre.** How will I keep my writing true and accurate? How much will I disclose about myself (and others) in my graphic memoir? Will I write in the first person? What anecdotes will I use to tell my story, and why? How will I visually represent my characters? Will they be true to life or exaggerated? How will I balance the narrative with dialogue?

☐ **Style.** What tone will I take in my writing? Will my graphic memoir be funny? Serious? Tragic? What kind of language will I use? How much detail will I provide? How will I use the visuals to convey my tone?

☐ **Design.** What fonts will I use? How might I use shapes of boxes to indicate specific character voices? Will I vary the shapes of my panels?

☐ **Sources.** What specific memories will I draw on? Will I need to check my story with others from my life, or will I rely on my own recollections and interpretations? Will I need to research historical and cultural events related to the time period of my story?

PRACTICE Want to experiment? Draft and sketch out your own graphic memoir.

Identify a pivotal moment in your life. Sketch out a few panels of a graphic memoir that convey the moment and its importance. Think about how you want the key people who participated in the event to come across to readers and how you can convey those characteristics with visual details. Think about what you want to convey through dialogue and what you want to convey through internal reflection.

PHOTO ESSAYS

A photo essay is a group of photos that tells a unified story or makes a unified argument. Some photo essayists provide supplementary text or brief captions for their images; others choose to present the images without words. Some photo essayists are journalists whose purpose is to convey a news or human interest story or offer commentary on an event. The photo essays published by *Mother Jones* about the aftermath of the 2010 earthquake in Haiti and a piece on how Ikea has partnered with UNICEF in a program to encourage reading in Albania are examples of works by photo essayists using images and text to provide information and even make an argument.

◄ PHOTO ESSAY STILL
UNICEF,
"Ikea Partners for Reading in Albania."
© *UNICEF/NYHQ2008-0133/Giacomo Pirozzi.*

Photo essays can also be viewed as works of art that express ideas and evoke emotional responses in the viewer. You can find them online, in galleries and museums, and also in magazines such as *Life*, *Time*, and *National Geographic*. Photo essayists generally aim to make a particular point or argument; some make specific social commentaries. For example, photographer Walker Evans (1903–75) and writer James Agee (1909–55) collaborated on a book-length photo essay about the hardships of tenant farmers in the American South in the 1930s. *Let Us Now Praise Famous Men* is a very word-heavy photo essay.

TEXT FROM PHOTO ESSAY
During July and August 1936 Walker Evans and I were traveling in the middle south of this nation, and were engaged in what, even from the first, has seemed to me rather a curious piece of work. It was our business to prepare, for a New York magazine, an article on cotton tenantry in the United States, in the form of a photographic and verbal record

PHOTO FROM ▶
PHOTO ESSAY
Walker Evans, "Lily
Rogers Fields." This
photo appeared in
*Let Us Now Praise
Famous Men.* Shown
here is Lily Rogers
Fields, the wife of
sharecropper Bud
Fields, and their
two children. Evans
took this photo in
1936 in Hale County,
Alabama. *Library of
Congress.*

of the daily living and environment of an average white family of tenant farmers. We had
first to find and to live with such a family; and that was the object of our traveling.

—**James Agee,** from *Let Us Now Praise Famous Men*

Other photo essays involve fewer words, such as many of the photo essays available
online at the *Time* magazine site. See, for example, the photo essay titled
"Famous Couples."

Analyzing Photo Essays: What to Look For

THE RHETORICAL SITUATION

Purpose   Photo essayists have two main goals: to tell a story and/or to make a
point. Usually their work is focused on a specific theme. For example, the Agee and
Evans photo essay collaboration (p. 77) focuses on the experiences of sharecroppers

in the South, and in doing so, asks the viewer to look at the relationship of those who are privileged (those who read the book) and those who are less fortunate (the subjects of the book). Photo essayists usually seek to evoke an emotional response in the viewer. For example, the creators of the *Time* essay on famous couples emphasize the endurance of love in relationships by showing celebrity couples enjoying a happy moment.

Audience   Photo essayists know that their audiences are drawn to visual storytelling—and to the issues and themes of their works, which may be social and cultural, journalistic, and/or artistic. For example, photo essayist and documentarian Brenda Ann Kenneally, creator of an ongoing project called "Upstate Girls," aims her work at those interested in her intimate look at working-class women and their families. Norbert Wu targets his essay "Life beneath Antarctic Ice" at an audience interested in nature.

Rhetorical appeals   Depending on their subject matter and composition, photo essayists may emphasize logos, pathos, or ethos to make their point. For instance, Andrew Testa's disturbing photo essays of Bangladeshi women who were scarred by acid for refusing to accept marriage proposals emphasize pathos by showing the women's scars close up; ethos is also important because viewers must trust that Testa has not used lighting or perspective to distort reality.

Modes & media   While photo essayists usually combine visuals with some written text, some also incorporate bits of audio, such as in *The New York Times* photo essay "One in 8 Million," which highlights the lives of ordinary New Yorkers. Photo essays can be print based, but also offered digitally, as is *Let Us Now Praise Famous Men;* or they can be created mainly for online publication, such as *Time* magazine's photo essays.

When might it be more appropriate to create a photo essay rather than a written essay? To what extent do your purpose, audience, and subject affect your choice of whether to create in a visual mode?

THE GENRE'S CONVENTIONS

Elements of the genre   A photo essay can be used to tell a simple story, but the genre is often used to persuade viewers to sympathize with a point of view or to take a specific action. For example, through "Upstate Girls," Brenda Ann Kenneally, hopes that viewers connect with the subjects' struggles and triumphs.

Some photo essayists include captions to provide context; others include more text, with a 50:50 text-to-image ratio, such as in Suzanne Merkelson's "Keeping Up with the Qaddafis," published online in March 2011 in *Foreign Policy*. In this piece, Merkelson accompanies each photo with at least one paragraph of text.

Photo essayists make rhetorical choices about their purpose and audience, and they choose images carefully, in the same way a writer chooses words, paragraphs, and structure. The photo essayist chooses each image with the viewer's intellectual, emotional, or other responses in mind. Similarly, a photo essay can be structured much like any persuasive essay. For example, the introductory images, which function like a written essay's introduction, need to establish the subject matter and further the purposes of the piece—to push the narrative or argument forward.

Photo essayists use some techniques that narrative essayists, storytellers, and persuasive writers do (pp. 45–46 and 183). That is, they select and sequence their content in a way that will spark their readers' interest, keep them reading/viewing, and ultimately convince them of a particular point of view. Initial images may serve as an introduction, while those that follow may build in terms of intensity to support the argument the photo essayist wants to make. (See "Design," below.)

Style

Detail. Most photo essayists do not provide much detail in the text of their essays. For example, most captions give just enough information for readers to understand the story behind (and location of) the related photo. The photos themselves can show varying degrees of detail—in some cases, capturing one element up close, such as a person's face; in others, showing a panoramic view of a landscape.

Tone. Photo essayists choose images that reflect the mood they want to convey. For example, a photo essayist who wants to stir readers to take action in response to an environmental disaster such as an oil spill might feature an image of someone rescuing and rehabilitating an oil-soaked bird.

For more **visual genres**, see the Index of Genres on page G-1.

Design A good photo essayist usually presents a variety of images (from different perspectives) and arranges the images in an order that builds emotion, furthers an argument, or advances a story. For example, a photo essayist who wants to tell a story might sequence the images from one event to the next, much like a narrative essayist would. In other cases, the photo essayist might not choose a linear progression, but might instead order images for maximum impact, especially when presenting an argument.

Sources Photo essays always involve primary research, as the photographer is always witnessing the subject of the photos firsthand. Brenda Ann Kenneally's photo essay on working-class women, for example, is entirely informed by Kenneally's interviews with the women she photographed. Sometimes secondary research must be conducted as well, to fill in historical details or other information.

Guided Reading: Photo Essay ▼

Eros Hoagland

From "Life in the Googleplex"

Time, a weekly news and current events magazine, often features photo essays related to world events. The magazine commissioned and published in February 2006 an online photo essay titled "Life in the Googleplex." Presented as a slide show, the essay was created by photojournalist Eros Hoagland of Redux Pictures. Hoagland, who began his career reporting on the fallout of El Salvador's civil war, is also interested in showing the subtleties of place, something he clearly brought to the Googleplex project. Given the range of his subject matter, the quality of his work, and the publications he calls his clients (including *The New York Times* and *Newsweek*), Hoagland, like *Time* magazine, has some good ethos.

His purpose in creating "Life in the Googleplex" was to give readers an inside look at what it's like to work at Google. By highlighting gadgets and leisure opportunities, Hoagland suggests that employees do serious work but also have plenty of time to play. Further, by showing the human side (and human faces) of Google, Hoagland establishes that the company is more than a search engine.

▲ AUTHOR PHOTO &
▼ PHOTO ESSAY
Eros Hoagland, from his profile at Redux, and the "Life in the Googleplex" slide show online at *Time*.

The annotations in the margins point out the decisions that Hoagland made, perhaps with the input of editors at *Time*, including the purpose of the piece, the perceived audience, and the genre conventions applied. *(All images on pp. 81–84: Eros Hoagland/Redux Pictures.)*

TIME **Photos**

200

Photo Essays | LightBox | Pictures of the Week | TIME Covers

Photos: Life in the Googleplex

Inside Google Headquarters

Photographs by Eros Hoagland / Redux for TIME

Enter ▶

• In Search of The Real Google

Hoagland, *From "Life in the Googleplex,"* Continued

Photos: Life in the Googleplex   1 of 12   ◀ **BACK**   **NEXT** ▶

EROS HOAGLAND / REDUX FOR TIME

◀ **BACK**   **NEXT** ▶

BE YOURSELF
Desktop gizmos and lava lamps express Google's laid-back ethos.

• In Search of The Real Google

Continues next page

What is the composer, **Eros Hoagland**, doing?

THE RHETORICAL SITUATION

Purpose
Audience
Rhetorical appeals
Modes & media

see page 83

How do I know this is a **photo essay**?

THE GENRE'S CONVENTIONS

Elements of the genre
Style
Design
Sources

see page 83

**Hoagland, *From "Life in the Googleplex,"* ** *Continued*

Photos: Life in the Googleplex   2 of 12   ◀ BACK   NEXT ▶

EROS HOAGLAND / REDUX FOR TIME

◀ BACK   NEXT ▶

ASK THE HELP DESK
Laptop on the fritz? Google keeps experts on site to fix computers and other digital gadgets.

• In Search of The Real Google

Continues next page

THE RHETORICAL SITUATION

Purpose

Hoagland (perhaps with the help of *Time* editors) set out to illustrate how a high-tech work environment, such as Google, can be filled with creativity and fun.

Audience

The audience for the photo essay is *Time* magazine readers, Google fans, and people interested in cultural trends related to technology and the workplace.

Rhetorical appeals

Hoagland uses **logos** to appeal to readers by building a logical case about how a creative work environment inspires workers' creativity. He establishes the essay's **ethos** by using photos of Google workers.

Modes & media

Mode = written and visual
Hoagland's primary goal was to visually portray a typical workday at Google.

(Continued on p. 84.)

THE GENRE'S CONVENTIONS

Elements of the genre

Is comprised mainly of photos, with some text.

Is focused on a topic, in this case, specifically workers' play and leisure time at Google's offices.

Tells a story, in this case, about a typical workday at Google.

Makes an argument, in this case that Google's workers are productive and inspired by creativity and recreation.

Includes captions that explain the photos.
For example, the caption with the first image reads, "Be Yourself." Without it, viewers could assume the message is that the office is crowded and cluttered rather than supportive of individuality and expression.

Style

Use of the present tense reinforces the "this is happening now" feel of the piece.

Hoagland, *From "Life in the Googleplex,"* Continued

Adding written
details tells a more
complete story;
it also provides a
commentary about
what is taking place,
to persuade viewers
that the workplace
atmosphere is
pleasant.

Medium = digital
Although *Time*
publishes photo
essays in their print
edition, "Life in the
Googleplex" was
published digitally
at *Time's* Web site.
Publishing this essay
online is especially
appropriate because
Google is a digital
company; further,
the advantages of
publishing online
are obvious. As long
as viewers have an
Internet connection,
they can see and
share the essay; if
it were only in print
form, they would
need to locate a copy
of that edition of the
magazine.

Photos: Life in the Googleplex   3 of 12   ◄ BACK   NEXT ►

EROS HOAGLAND / REDUX FOR TIME

◄ BACK   NEXT ►

GOOGLER WITH GOGGLES
A lifeguard sits on duty as an employee works out in one of two swim-in-place pools at
Google's headquarters.

• In Search of The Real Google

A **playful tone** emphasizes that Google is a
fun place to work. For example, the swimmer
is referred to as a "Googler with Goggles."

Design

The variety of the photos suggests the
breadth of activities that can take place in
the Googleplex. Elements of the text are
highlighted by typeface choice and color.

Captions consistently appear below the
photos and each caption has a pithy heading.

Sources

Hoagland conducted primary research—
spending time at Google, following around
employees, trying to capture the elements of
a typical day and different aspects of work
and play.

Questions: Analyzing Hoagland's photo essay

1. Purpose. What is the unifying message of the three photos shown? Explain in one sentence.

2. Purpose. Do the photos tend to focus more on people or objects? Why do you think Hoagland chose that emphasis?

3. Audience. What techniques did Hoagland use so that viewers would see the playful nature of working at Google?

4. Rhetorical appeals. Based on the three photos shown, what is your impression of the ethos of Hoagland and the *Time* editors he most likely worked with?

5. Modes & media. If there were no captions, what assumptions might you make about life at Google? Are there places where the image is able to fully convey its message without the text? Where and how? Why is this essay best viewed digitally, rather than in print?

6. Elements of the genre. In "Life in the Googleplex," do the photos illustrate the captions or do the captions describe the photos? Explain your answer.

7. Elements of the genre. View the entire "Googleplex" slide show. Now that you've seen the whole thing, would you say that this essay is primarily telling a story or making an argument? Why?

8. Style. How does the tone and voice of the writing emphasize the working environment at Google? How does the selection and presentation of photographs contribute to that tone? Use specific examples to illustrate your answer.

9. Design. View the entire "Googleplex" slide show again. Pay attention to how Hoagland and *Time* ordered the images. How might a different ordering of images impact the narrative? How do Hoagland and *Time* use organization of the images to build logic?

10. Sources. The photos were taken by Eros Hoagland, a professional photographer commissioned by *Time* magazine (Hoagland is the source of the images). Do you think someone working at Google would choose to highlight different aspects of working there? How?

Sketching Out a Photo Essay

CHECKLIST: Sketching Out a Photo Essay Thinking of composing a photo essay? Ask yourself the following questions.

WHAT'S MY RHETORICAL SITUATION?

☐ **Purpose.** What is my story, and why do I want to tell it? Or do I want to do more than tell a story? If so, what main point or argument do I want to make, and why?

☐ **Audience.** Who are my readers/viewers that I want to attract to my photo essay? Why will my photo essay matter to them? What do I want them to get out of it? And how will I reach them?

☐ **Rhetorical appeals.** How will I use ethos, pathos, and logos to reach my audience? How will I establish my authority as a photographer and writer? Will I rely more on pathos or logos? How will my photos and text work together to appeal to my readers' sense of ethos, pathos, and/or logos?

☐ **Modes & media.** Do I want to present my photo essay in hard-copy format, as in a photo album; or electronically, as on a Web site; or in some other way? How will these choices impact how my viewers experience my photo essay? For example, would it be better to present it online or as a collection of large photos matted and framed on the wall?

WHAT GENRE CONVENTIONS MATTER?

☐ **Elements of the genre.** I know that the best photo essays tell a story but also put forth some type of argument. For example, in his "Googleplex" essay, Eros Hoagland asks viewers to see Google as a successful company in part because the workplace itself encourages creativity. How does this compare to what I want to do? What argument will I make in my photo essay—and how will I do it?

☐ **Style.** What tone do I want to strike? Playful, like in "Life in the Googleplex"? Or more serious, like in Kenneally's photo essay?

☐ **Design.** What order will I arrange the photos in, and how will the order affect how my viewers understand my story?

☐ **Sources.** Where will I need to go to take my photos? Will I want to photograph individuals and their possessions? Or perhaps historical sites? Will I need to request special permission to do so?

PRACTICE Want to experiment? Draft your own photo essay.

Just as Hoagland and *Time* convey a sense of work life at Google in their photo essay, you might want to do something similar. What do you have to say about your own workplace, campus, or residence? Brainstorm about how people at one or more of those locations feel about that place; then take three to five photos of the place that convey that feeling. Your draft photo essay should offer some kind of commentary on the place you've chosen as your subject; it should not simply show it. Add brief captions similar to the ones in the "Googleplex" essay that help tell a story and offer perspective.

3 INFORMATIVE GENRES

CONTENTS

◀ CHART/INFOGRAPHIC

e For e-Pages content, visit **bedfordstmartins** .com/bookofgenres.

e For an Index of
Sources & Contexts for
material referenced in this
chapter, see the e-Pages
at **bedfordstmartins.com
/bookofgenres.**

Information is everywhere, all the time: online, on your phone, in e-mail, on social networking sites, on TV, and on radio. It's on billboards, road signs, and menus. But not all information is equal: Some is reliable; some is not. How do we make sense of it all? The trick is to (1) figure out which *sources* of information are the best, and (2) analyze, use, and share that information according to your needs as a reader or writer.

In daily life, you draw on a variety of sources for information. When you don't know the meaning of a word, you might go to *Dictionary.com.*

DICTIONARY ENTRY ▶
Dictionary.com,
"Vertiginous."
© Dictionary.com, LLC
vertiginous. Dictionary
.com. Collins English
Dictionary—Complete
& Unabridged 10th
Edition. HarperCollins
Publishers, http://
dictionary.reference
.com/browse/
vertiginous.

Dictionary.com | vertiginous

ver·tig·i·nous 🔊 [ver-**tij**-*uh*-n*uh* s] ? Show IPA
adjective
1. whirling; spinning; rotary: *vertiginous currents of air.*
2. affected with <u>vertigo</u>; dizzy.
3. liable or threatening to cause <u>vertigo</u>: *a vertiginous climb.*
4. apt to change quickly; unstable: *a vertiginous economy.*

Origin:
1600–10; < Latin *vertīginōsus* dizzy, equivalent to *vertigin-* (stem of *vertīgō*) <u>vertigo</u> + *-ōsus* <u>-ous</u>

How else do you use sources? A few more scenarios:

» You're curious about Prohibition after watching a movie set in the 1920s, so you check out the History Channel site, a trusted encyclopedia, or a PBS documentary for a better sense of that period.

» You want to plant tomatoes on your back porch, so you consult a reference book or online guide by the American Horticultural Society on varieties that grow best in your region.

» You want to avoid the flu, so you read the U.S. Department of Health and Human Services' latest recommendations online or stop in at your pharmacy for information about the flu vaccine.

» You need to create a presentation using software you don't know how to use, so you refer to a Microsoft PowerPoint tutorial or ask an experienced colleague for a quick lesson.

How do you deal
with the information
you encounter
online every day?
How do you know
what's fact and
what's not?

» There's something wrong with your car and you don't know what the flashing light on your dashboard means, so you flip through your owner's manual or call a knowledgeable mechanic.

In each of these cases, you've found convenient but also authoritative sources.

Authoritative sources of information   Here's another scenario. Let's say you want to prepare for a disaster. You do a quick search on YouTube, and turn up a video by a guy in a gas mask who is part of a survivalist fringe group living in a desert bunker. His instructions in the video are rambling, confusing, and possibly paranoid (to take the example to an extreme). Though the video may be riveting, this is a poor source of information because the author lacks credibility (or ethos) and logic (logos). A better, if less colorful, source would be a government organization such as Homeland Security, FEMA (Federal Emergency Management Agency), or the American Red Cross. These are considered excellent sources of information because these organizations are long established and made up of experts. The material they publish is researched, written, and reviewed by authorities in the field of emergency preparation; approved by the government; and tested out in actual emergencies. For example, Homeland Security's "Preventing Terrorism" advice has been vetted by a major government organization (see p. 90).

Author bias   No author is purely objective, including Homeland Security. Personal viewpoints, inclinations, and prejudices can creep into any communication, whether it's a recipe or a government document. Bias can show up in the language that writers use. For example, Homeland Security's use of the terms *Counterterrorism* and *Border Security* indicate a specific point of view. No matter its source, information is never 100 percent unbiased.

Bias can also be apparent in the tone a writer uses. Let's say an article appears in your local newspaper about a family lost during a snowmobiling trip. You might expect the reporter to simply present the facts of what happened. However, after reading closely, you see the reporter's opinion has subtly found its way onto the page: The family's lack of preparation and

▼ PHOTO
John W. Gertz, "Man Wearing Gas Mask Using Cell Phone." Beware of information from unreliable sources. *John W. Gertz/Corbis.*

INSTRUCTIONS ▶
Homeland Security, "Preventing Terrorism." *Department of Homeland Security.*

Homeland Security

| Home | Topics | How Do I? | Get Involved | News | About DHS |

Preventing Terrorism

Preventing Terrorism Overview
Protecting the American people from terrorist threats is the reason the Department of Homeland Security was created, and remains our highest priority.

Biological Security
We protect the nation's health security by providing early detection and early warning of bioterrorist attacks.

Chemical Security
Some chemical facilities possess materials that could be stolen and used to make weapons. A successful attack on certain high-risk facilities could cause a significant number of deaths and injuries.

Countering Violent Extremism
The threat posed by violent extremism is neither constrained by international borders nor limited to any single ideology.

Critical Infrastructure Security
Critical infrastructure is the physical and cyber systems and assets so vital to the United States that their incapacity or destruction would have a debilitating impact on our physical or economic security or public health or safety.

Explosives
DHS works to enhance the nation's counter-IED capabilities and reduce the threat of explosive attack against critical infrastructure, the private sector, and federal, state, local, tribal, and territorial entities.

if you SEE something SAY something

If You See Something, Say Something
A program to raise public awareness of indicators of terrorism and terrorism-related crime, and to emphasize the importance of reporting suspicious activity to the proper state and local law enforcement authorities.

National Terrorism Advisory System
NTAS alerts communicate information about terrorist threats by providing timely, detailed information to the public, government agencies, first responders, public sector organizations, airports and other transportation hubs.

When was the last time you noticed a sign in an airport, train station, or bus stop? Make a point to examine one and ask yourself: Who created the sign? Whose point of view does it convey? What assumptions does it convey about travelers?

---

ignorance about avalanche safety influenced the writer and affected his or her tone and the use (or omission) of details. On the other hand, imagine that the reporter thinks the family did the best they could have—they were as prepared as possible, but no one could have survived that avalanche. In that case, the writer would use a more sympathetic tone.

Even a nutritional label reflects the biases, assumptions, and values of its authors. For example, the creators of the label here ▶ assume that calories and fat are more important than other nutritional information, and so calories, calories from fat, and total fat grams are presented first. Protein, vitamins, and minerals appear toward the bottom of the chart. The author, in this case, is a government organization, the National Heart, Lung, and Blood Institute (NHLBI) at the National Institutes of Health.

Presenting information is not a neutral activity. All writing has a persuasive quality, and informative writing is no exception. This is not a bad thing, just something to keep in mind as you read and compose.

The Rhetorical Situation

Purpose: Why share information?

When we write to inform, we share facts and details with our readers. One type of informative writing is instructions. If you've ever purchased a piece of furniture that required assembly, you've probably worked with a set of instructions. The instructions were likely designed by an engineer or technical writer with two goals: (1) to help you put together parts of an object, and (2) to persuade and assure you that through simple language and design that the task would be easy.

Sharing information, according to *Merriam-Webster*, is sharing "knowledge obtained from investigation, study, or instruction." A set of instructions certainly gives information "obtained from investigation": Most instructions undergo usability testing and are revised for clarity and accuracy before publication.

Another example of informative writing is the informational brochure. You've probably seen these at your doctor's or dentist's office—brochures about how to control asthma or whiten your teeth. Consider the teeth whitening brochure: It may provide facts about various methods; however, it might also offer reasons for whitening, pricing information, and a photo of an attractive model with sparkling-white teeth. Is the material in the brochure presented *only* to inform, or is there another motive at work? Could the brochure creators also be trying to convince you to whiten your teeth?

What instructions have you referred to lately? How helpful were they? Were they written for someone like you? How could you tell?

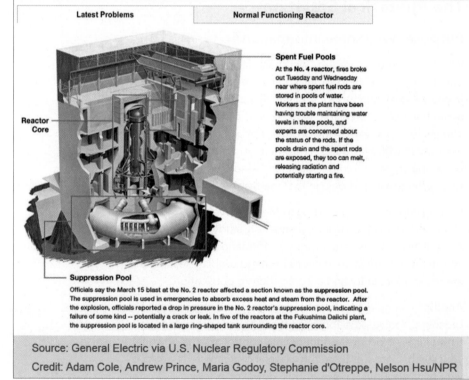

SPECIAL SERIES

the science of japan's nuclear crisi

Explainer: What Are Spent Fuel Rods?

by JOE PALCA

March 15, 2011   2:28 PM

Inside The Nuclear Reactors

Latest Problems	Normal Functioning Reactor

Reactor Core

Spent Fuel Pools

At the No. 4 reactor, fires broke out Tuesday and Wednesday near where spent fuel rods are stored in pools of water. Workers at the plant have been having trouble maintaining water levels in these pools, and experts are concerned about the status of the rods. If the pools drain and the spent rods are exposed, they too can melt, releasing radiation and potentially starting a fire.

Suppression Pool

Officials say the March 15 blast at the No. 2 reactor affected a section known as the suppression pool. The suppression pool is used in emergencies to absorb excess heat and steam from the reactor. After the explosion, officials reported a drop in pressure in the No. 2 reactor's suppression pool, indicating a failure of some kind -- potentially a crack or leak. In five of the reactors at the Fukushima Daiichi plant, the suppression pool is located in a large ring-shaped tank surrounding the reactor core.

Source: General Electric via U.S. Nuclear Regulatory Commission

Credit: Adam Cole, Andrew Prince, Maria Godoy, Stephanie d'Otreppe, Nelson Hsu/NPR

When you read informative genres, keep an eye out for what *else* is going on. An author of a scientific report, for example, may present facts, but as a way to influence you to share an opinion or take an action.

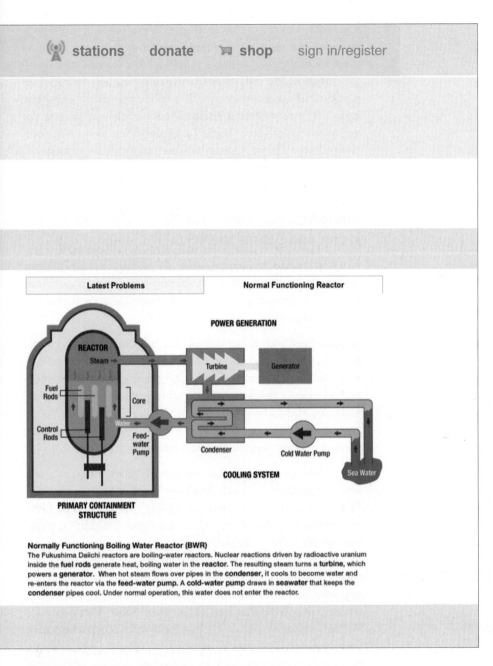

| Latest Problems | Normal Functioning Reactor |

POWER GENERATION

REACTOR

Steam →

Turbine

Generator

Fuel
Rods

Core

Control
Rods

Water ←

Feed-
water
Pump

Condenser

Cold Water Pump

Sea Water

COOLING SYSTEM

**PRIMARY CONTAINMENT
STRUCTURE**

Normally Functioning Boiling Water Reactor (BWR)
The Fukushima Daiichi reactors are boiling-water reactors. Nuclear reactions driven by radioactive uranium inside the **fuel rods** generate heat, boiling water in the **reactor**. The resulting steam turns a **turbine**, which powers a **generator**. When hot steam flows over pipes in the **condenser**, it cools to become water and re-enters the reactor via the **feed-water pump**. A cold-water pump draws in **seawater** that keeps the **condenser** pipes cool. Under normal operation, this water does not enter the reactor.

Audience: How do we inform others?

As writers, we need to know our audiences—who they are and what they want. For example, in the piece above an "Explainer" feature created for National Public Radio, writer

For more examples of **news articles** and **charts/infographics,** see the Index of Genres on page G-1.

Joe Palca, along with the illustrators listed below the images, provides the facts of a recent news event (Japan's nuclear reactor problems following the March 2011 tsunami) and visuals that show the differences between a normally functioning reactor and a damaged one. The NPR writer and illustrators know that most of their readers are not nuclear experts and do not want tons of text or technical jargon; general readers want clear information (in "layman's terms") so they can understand the basics of a complex system.

Rhetorical Appeals: How do we use ethos, logos, and pathos to inform?

When we write to inform, how do we get our audiences invested? Whether you're composing a research paper, fact sheet, or flowchart, you will use the rhetorical appeals: ethos, logos, and pathos.

Ethos—how you, as an author, are perceived by your audience—is extremely important when reporting information. That's why it's essential to draw on reliable sources of information in your research, and to convey that knowledge with authority, and as neutrally as possible. If your audience thinks you are unreliable, or that you have some unstated motive, then you will not have established your ethos.

The article on page 95 was written by Mireya Navarro, an environmental reporter for *The New York Times*. In her article, "E.P.A. Rejects City Timeline on PCBs," she covers the facts of how the Environmental Protection Agency is putting pressure on New York City public schools to speed up their plan to replace toxic and potentially hazardous fluorescent light fixtures. Navarro establishes her ethos by stating facts, quoting from authoritative sources, and keeping her tone neutral and her writing as free of her own opinion as possible. Further, her position as a writer for a renowned newspaper contributes to her ethos, as does her profile, which notes her experience and links to her other articles about the environment.

◀ NEWS ARTICLE

Mireya Navarro, "E.P.A. Rejects City Timeline on PCBs." Navarro's ethos as a reporter helps readers see her as a reliable, informative source. *From The New York Times, March 11, 2011 © 2011 The New York Times. All rights reserved.*

▲ AUTHOR BIO
Mireya Navarro, author page at *The New York Times.* From The New York Times, *March 11, 2011, © 2011 The New York Times. All rights reserved.*

Logos—or your use of logic as an author—is also significant. "How to" or instructional genres, such as recipes, make heavy use of logos. When cooks create recipes, they direct the reader in what to do, in a specific order. Chopping ingredients, mixing them, and cooking them must be presented to readers as logical steps. In the example on page 96, the chef, Lora Guillotte of *Saucie.com*, presents her recipe for Louisiana Pork Chops in a logical manner, listing the ingredients and measures clearly, outlining the steps, and illustrating them with helpful images.

Pathos—your appeal to your readers' emotions—is generally not a priority when you're writing to inform. On the other hand, if you want to inform but also persuade your readers, you can appeal to their emotions. For example, in the *Saucie .com* recipe for Louisiana Pork Chops, the author appeals to readers' pathos by suggesting that like her, they are busy preparing for holidays, and therefore want an uncomplicated

recipe. Lora also posts two final images under her recipe that reflect her sense of humor and show that she enjoyed her own "fine" creation. Use your judgment about when to use humor when writing to inform; generally it is appropriate for less formal informational genres, but you also have to consider this in terms of your specific purposes and audiences.

Modes & Media: How can they help you inform?

A composition's *mode* is how the content itself is communicated—whether in writing, by voice, through images, through sounds, or in some combination. A composition's *medium* is the final form or mechanism that it's delivered in, such as print, digital, or face-to-face. Following is a breakdown of the modes and media of some of the compositions presented in this chapter:

INFORMATIVE GENRES	Mode	Medium
ILLUSTRATION, ONLINE Harvard School of Public Health, "Food Pyramid" (p. 117)	**VISUAL**	**DIGITAL**
INSTRUCTIONS, ONLINE Homeland Security, "Preventing Terrorism" (p. 90)	**WRITTEN**	**DIGITAL**
DICTIONARY ENTRY, ONLINE *Dictionary.com*, "vertiginous" (p. 88)	**WRITTEN** **AND AUDIO**	**DIGITAL**
RECIPE, ONLINE Lora Guillotte, "Louisiana Pork Chops" (p. 96)	**WRITTEN** **AND VISUAL**	**DIGITAL**
INSTRUCTIONS, ONLINE Ann Pizer, "Downward Facing Dog" (p. 99)	**WRITTEN,** **VISUAL, AND** **VIDEO**	**DIGITAL**

A Word about Modes

Visuals are crucial when we're learning something new, such as the pork chop recipe (p. 96) and the yoga pose (p. 99), which is provided in three modes—through text, an image, and video. For the yoga pose, without the visual, readers would need much more text to understand what they should be doing. Even better is the video, which shows viewers all the steps required to achieve the pose.

The pork chop recipe also benefits from accompanying visuals. When people are cooking, they usually want text that describes the ingredients they need and steps they need to follow—as well as images of what the food should look like as they prepare it, and when it's done. Still images might be best in this case. While a video might show a reader how the actual steps are performed, it's difficult to cook and watch a video at the same time.

Think about your favorite ads or commercials (or even the ones you find most annoying). Do you find yourself identifying with the people featured in them? Why or why not?

Audio is also useful in certain situations. For example, *Dictionary.com* presents information about the word *vertiginous* in two modes—as text (for readers and writers), and as an audio file (for speakers) so users of the site can learn the correct pronunciation of the word.

What informative texts have you read today? Think of street signs, recipes, product labels, news articles, and course assignments. What traits do they share? How do these texts function to inform you?

The Genre's Conventions

Elements of the Genre: What does all informative writing have in common?

Two essential qualities of the best informative writing are accuracy and clarity. Whether you are writing a news report in which you provide straight facts, or are creating a set of instructions in which you detail the steps for performing a certain task, you need to be accurate, clear, and direct. Informative writing should also be presented in an order that will make sense to readers. For example, when providing instructions, it's a good idea to present information in small, digestible units—and to move from simple to complex.

Let's examine the choices Ann Pizer makes in her instructions for doing a yoga pose, shown on page 99. In this example, Pizer starts with basic information about a yoga pose known as "downward facing dog," including the benefits of the pose. She then breaks it down into a series of numbered tasks; each step represents a single move, so that viewers can take their time. The order of the steps is very important too. While an experienced yogi may go into the pose in what appears to be one fluid motion, a new practitioner needs to consciously move each body part into place and do so in a particular order to avoid injury. Because alignment is important in yoga, Pizer carefully specifies how body parts should line up, as in step 1, where she notes that the wrists should be "underneath the shoulders" and the knees should be "underneath the hips." Barry Stone's photo of a woman in the pose shows readers how wrists and knees should be aligned. Pizer follows her directions with notes tailored for beginners and more advanced practitioners to allow for some customization of the directions.

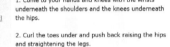
▲ INSTRUCTIONS
Ann Pizer,
"Downward Facing Dog," About.com: Yoga. © 2012 Ann Pizer About.com. Reprinted with permission.

Style: How does it help you inform?

When you're writing to inform, it's important to present content in a style that's accessible to your audience. You'll also want to consider the voice and tone you will use. Is a strong writer's presence appropriate for your composition, or should you be more neutral? And how much detail will you need to provide to get your ideas across? For most informative genres, you will probably use a neutral tone to convey information. Because your primary goal is to inform your readers about something, you'll probably want to avoid wild flourishes of language. For example, in the pork chop recipe, the writer instructs readers to "mix spices together"; she does not say "merge all the aromatic flavors of world cuisines." Attention to detail is also crucial in genres that inform. For example, in step 8 of Ann Pizer's yoga pose instructions, she gives enough detail so beginners understand how the pose will change for them over time as they become more practiced.

For more examples of **instructions,** see the Index of Genres on page G-1.

Design: What is the best format for informing?

Design helps readers (and viewers, listeners, etc.) navigate information. In the instructions below, the designers at Tieknots.org show readers where to begin, what steps to follow, and where to end. The number next to each step shows readers where they are in the process. The simple design and limited detail allow readers to focus in on each move. Further, the design is scaled so that it can fit on a business card, making the instructions both concise and portable.

INSTRUCTIONS ▶
"How to Tie a Tie."
Who needs words
when a clear "how to"
diagram can do the
trick? *Shutterstock.*

What colors grab your attention? Do these colors change depending on what you're looking at? For example, what colors might attract your attention in a textbook design, or an advertisement, or online instructions?

Sources: What research should you draw on to inform your readers?

When you write to inform, you need to be informed yourself: You need to draw on the best sources possible (see "Authoritative sources of information," p. 89). For example, journalist Mireya Navarro, author of "E.P.A. Rejects City Timeline on PCBs" (p. 95), interviews EPA administrator Judith Enck for her article. We can assume that Enck is an expert in her field and a reliable source. To take another example, imagine that it's an election year, and you're creating a chart about voting trends. You might use information from the U.S. Census Bureau.

ENCYCLOPEDIA ENTRIES

Collecting facts has been a human pursuit for a long time. In the first century CE, a Roman author, naturalist, and military man named Pliny the Elder tried to record everything known about the natural world in his thirty-seven-volume *Naturalis Historia*, the world's first encyclopedia-like document. (You can read it at the Perseus Digital Library, in English or the original Latin.)

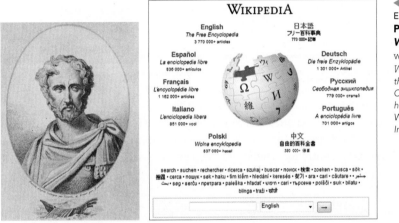

◀ PORTRAIT & WIKI ENCYCLOPEDIA
Pliny the Elder and Wikipedia. What would Pliny say about *Wikipedia*? *Pliny the Elder: Library of Congress. Wikipedia homepage: Courtesy of Wikimedia Foundation, Inc. All rights reserved.*

Pliny, like all encyclopedists, aimed to provide what was known about a specific or general topic in a way that worked best for his target audience. The *Encyclopaedia Britannica* is a source of general information on many topics; it's geared toward readers who want to gain a broad understanding of a given subject. More specialized encyclopedias, such as *The Encyclopedia of Women's History in America* by Kathryn Cullen-DuPont, may cover topics in more depth, assuming readers already have some understanding of the topic.

Encyclopedias share several characteristics:

» They serve as a general (or sometimes specialized) reference.

» They provide information that is considered true (meaning it is agreed upon by experts on the topic).

» They are compilations and syntheses of what others have said, rather than original research (that is, they are tertiary sources).

» They are organized into individual articles that are well researched and written by content experts, typically people with an academic degree related to the subject they're writing about.

How often do you refer to encyclopedias? What are the benefits—and limitations—of using an encyclopedia as a source?

Analyzing Encyclopedia Entries: What to Look For

Purpose Encyclopedists provide an overview of a subject so that readers can gain a general understanding of it. For example, here is how editors of *The Columbia Encyclopedia* describe their reference book (accessed at *Encyclopedia.com*):

▼ ENCYCLOPEDIA ENTRY *Gale Encyclopedia of Medicine,* via Encyclopedia.com, "Psychosis." *From Gale Encyclopedia of Medicine V4,3E. © 2006 Gale, a part of Cengage Learning, Inc. Reproduced by permission. www. cengage.com/ permissions.*

Encyclopedias available in our online research library

The Columbia Encyclopedia (Sixth Edition): An authoritative, English-language dictionary containing more than 51,000 topics, The Columbia Encyclopedia provides trusted facts and information you can count on. Because more than 200 editors and academic advisors strive for depth and accuracy in each edition of the oldest, most venerable English-language encyclopedia in the world, this encyclopedia's topics are thorough and clear.

◄ ONLINE ENCYCLOPEDIA *Columbia Encyclopedia. Reproduced by permission. www.cengage .com/permissions.*

Other encyclopedias are more specialized; they tend to be aimed at readers interested in a particular field. The *Gale Encyclopedia of Medicine* is an example of a specialized resource. Below is the entry for "Psychosis," written by Paula Ford-Martin and Rebecca Frey.

International Encyclopedia...	Gale Encyclopedia of...	The Oxford Companion to the...	Gale Encyclopedia of Psychology	Further reading

Psychosis

Gale Encyclopedia of Medicine, 3rd ed. | 2006 | Ford-Martin, Paula; Frey, Rebecca | Copyright

Psychosis
Definition
Psychosis is a symptom or feature of mental illness typically characterized by radical changes in personality, impaired functioning, and a distorted or nonexistent sense of objective reality.

Description
Patients suffering from psychosis have impaired reality testing; that is, they are unable to distinguish personal subjective experience from the reality of the external world. They experience **hallucinations** and/or **delusions** that they believe are real, and may behave and communicate in an inappropriate and incoherent fashion. Psychosis may appear as a symptom of a number of mental disorders, including mood and **personality disorders.** It is also the defining feature of **schizophrenia,** schizophreniform disorder, **schizoaffective disorder,** delusional disorder, and the psychotic disorders (i.e., brief psychotic disorder, shared psychotic disorder, psychotic disorder due to a general medical condition, and substance-induced psychotic disorder).

Causes and symptoms
Psychosis may be caused by the interaction of biological and psychosocial factors depending on the disorder in which it presents; psychosis can also be caused by purely social factors, with no biological component.

Biological factors that are regarded as contributing to the development of psychosis include genetic abnormalities and substance use. With regard to chromosomal abnormalities, studies indicate that 30% of patients diagnosed with a psychotic disorder have a microdeletion at chromosome 22q11. Another group of researchers has identified the gene G72/G30 at chromosome 13q33.2 as a susceptibility gene for child-hood-onset schizophrenia and psychosis not otherwise specified.

With regard to **substance abuse,** several different research groups reported in 2004 that cannabis (**marijuana**) use is a risk factor for the onset of psychosis.

Migration is a social factor that influences people's susceptibility to psychotic disorders. Psychiatrists in Europe have noted the increasing rate of schizophrenia and other psychotic disorders among immigrants to almost all Western European countries. Black immigrants from Africa or the Caribbean appear to be especially vulnerable. The stresses involved in migration include family breakup, the need to adjust to living in large urban areas, and social inequalities in the new country.

Audience Encyclopedists know that their primary audience is general readers looking for a reliable but quick snapshot of a topic. For example, writers for the online encyclopedia *MedlinePlus* know their readers are mainly nonprofessionals consulting *Medline* for basic information about symptoms, causes, and treatment. The writers know they must be accurate and fairly brief; they can link to additional resources with more in-depth information. On the other hand, encyclopedists who write for more specialized reference works aimed at specific professional audiences, such as *Medpedia*—an open resource geared toward doctors and associated with major medical schools including Harvard and Stanford—provide a deeper level of information in their entries.

A Word about *Wikipedia*

Wikipedia is the most popular reference site on the Internet. As an encyclopedia, *Wikipedia* has all the features of that genre, with one important exception: Instead of entries being written by scholars, entries can be written by anyone. Indeed, that's what the *wiki* part of the name means: A wiki is a Web site that can be edited by users. *Wikipedia* is open-access, meaning almost all of its entries can be edited by anyone who registers with the site.

Because anyone can edit an entry, many people have concerns about the reliability of the information found on *Wikipedia*. However, others argue that because anyone who finds an error can correct it, *Wikipedia* is actually as reliable as any other reference source. In fact, a 2005 study by the science journal *Nature* found that *Wikipedia* entries had no more errors than entries in *Encyclopaedia Britannica*.

Tip: Most entries on *Wikipedia* include a list of (often linked) sources drawn on by the entry authors. These sources are often worth checking out, so even if you (or your instructor) decide that *Wikipedia* is not an appropriate source for your research, you might find an entry's reference list useful.

Rhetorical appeals   Encyclopedists appeal to readers through ethos—as content experts presenting accurate information. In turn, readers can assume that an encyclopedia entry is authoritative and trustworthy. Encyclopedists also appeal through logos, presenting content in a logical manner, often moving from general to more specific information. Writers begin an entry by defining the topic and often then break it out into subtopics, bringing up associated terms, people, and places. You can see this at work in the "Psychosis" entry from the *Gale Encyclopedia of Medicine* (p. 102). Further, in an online encyclopedia, keywords and subtopics are hyperlinked, which contributes to the logos of the entry.

What are your thoughts on digital encyclopedias—specifically on open-source reference works such as *Wikipedia*? How do you use these sources? And to what extent do you consider them trustworthy?

Modes & media   Encyclopedia entries are written texts that can appear in print or digital formats. Before the digital age, a family would purchase an entire set of print encyclopedias; it's now more common to purchase an encyclopedia on DVD, or to use free online resources such as *Encyclopedia.com* or *Wikipedia*.

Elements of the genre

Well researched and accurate. Entries are completely fact based. Encyclopedists gather, scrutinize, and synthesize information from many reliable sources to create an entry on a given topic. They convey proven information as objectively as possible (without the interference of opinion).

Written by experts. Most encyclopedias enlist professionals who have a deep level of knowledge on the topic of the entry to be written. This can also be true of wiki-platform encyclopedias that have a peer-review policy.

Clear. Encyclopedists provide basic information in a direct and straightforward manner.

Brief. Entries are not exhaustive; rather, they are intended as jumping-off points for further research. While some entries can be relatively long—for example, the complete entry on "Global Warming" from *Encyclopaedia Britannica* (p. 108) prints out at thirty-four pages long—they are still extremely short compared with the length of a book on the subject. The top three books on global warming at this moment— *Climate of Extremes* by Patrick J. Michaels and Robert Balling Jr., *Climate of Corruption* by Larry Bell, and *Climate Change* by Edmond A. Mathez—average 303 pages long.

Style

Just enough detail. Encyclopedists provide just enough detail to inform general readers. However, in a given entry, they mention related topics, concepts, and keywords that readers may want to pursue with further research. For example, *Wikipedia*'s "Motivation" entry (approximately seven printed pages) includes a one-paragraph summary of self-determination theory as well as links to a separate entry on that topic, one of the developers of the theory, and the topic of intrinsic motivation (see p. 105).

In contrast, Daniel H. Pink's book on motivation, *Drive: The Surprising Truth about What Motivates Us*, offers a deeper level of information on the theory, devoting five pages to who originally posed it, how it's been applied, and how it's held up through cultural and societal changes.

Precise language/word choice. Encyclopedists are specific and exact writers. For example, the *Wikipedia* entry on "Motivation" refers not just to "researchers" but

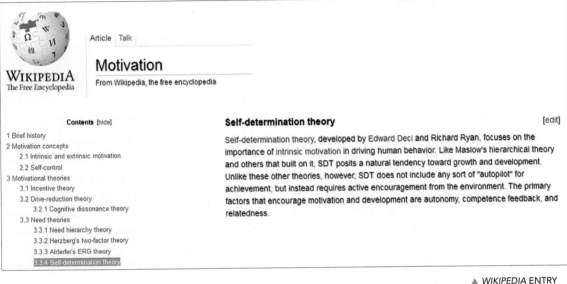

WIKIPEDIA
The Free Encyclopedia

Article Talk

Motivation

From Wikipedia, the free encyclopedia

Contents [hide]

1 Brief history
2 Motivation concepts
  2.1 Intrinsic and extrinsic motivation
  2.2 Self-control
3 Motivational theories
  3.1 Incentive theory
  3.2 Drive-reduction theory
    3.2.1 Cognitive dissonance theory
  3.3 Need theories
    3.3.1 Need hierarchy theory
    3.3.2 Herzberg's two-factor theory
    3.3.3 Alderfer's ERG theory
    3.3.4 Self-determination theory

Self-determination theory   [edit]

Self-determination theory, developed by Edward Deci and Richard Ryan, focuses on the importance of intrinsic motivation in driving human behavior. Like Maslow's hierarchical theory and others that built on it, SDT posits a natural tendency toward growth and development. Unlike these other theories, however, SDT does not include any sort of "autopilot" for achievement, but instead requires active encouragement from the environment. The primary factors that encourage motivation and development are autonomy, competence feedback, and relatedness.

▲ *WIKIPEDIA* ENTRY
Wikipedia,
"Motivation."
Shown here is the
"self-determination
theory" section
of the main entry,
"Motivation." The
writers of this entry
use clear language
and specifically name
the researchers who
developed self-
determination theory.
*Courtesy of Wikimedia
Foundation, Inc. All
rights reserved.*

to three specific researchers: Deci, Ryan, and Maslow. Imagine how you might question the authority of a reference work if the writers used ambiguous terms and generalizations, rather than specifics.

Encyclopedists often use formal, academic language to bolster their authority and emphasize their seriousness. That means they avoid contractions, slang, and abbreviated forms such as "info" for "information."

Use of the third person and a serious tone. Encyclopedists write in the third person, which reinforces their ethos and reminds readers that the entries are based on shared knowledge amongst an expert group, not just the perspective of one person. They use a serious tone to project credibility (ethos) to readers. If you were creating an encyclopedia entry, you probably wouldn't write it in the sarcastic tone of Jon Stewart, for example. Although the information in an entry might be informative *and* funny, using humor as a rhetorical strategy in an encyclopedia entry might undermine your authority and trustworthiness as an encyclopedist.

Design

Accessible. Encyclopedia entries need to be designed so that readers can quickly identify and use information on a particular page. Hard-copy reference works often use descriptive headers or footers so readers can navigate easily.

Consistent. Encyclopedias and other reference works follow a consistent format. In a dictionary, for example, each entry might begin with the name of the entry, followed by the part of speech, followed by a phonetic spelling. Every entry in the dictionary would follow that format.

Clearly titled. The name or title of the entry is in large, bold letters at the top of the entry, in order to clearly indicate the topic. In the case of a longer entry, the repetition of the title words orients the reader back to the original search term.

Hyperlinked to other entries (in online editions). The use of hyperlinks in an entry allows encyclopedists to provide more information without lengthening the entry itself. These links identify terminology (see "Just enough detail" above) and provide additional search terms to assist readers in narrowing their investigation of a broad subject. For example, the *Gale Encyclopedia of Medicine* entry on "Psychosis" (p. 102) connects that topic with schizophrenia and other specific disorders, helping narrow the broad initial term. As a researcher, you might then go to *EBSCOhost* or another rich database to explore the connection between psychosis and schizophrenia.

Sources

Variation in attribution of sources. Encyclopedia entries may not contain any documentation attributing the information to particular sources. While this might appear to be plagiarism, it is not. Encyclopedia entries are usually composed by experts in the field; therefore, the encyclopedists have firsthand knowledge of the information through their extensive research background.

Encyclopaedia Britannica entries, for example, are written and overseen by an editorial board of advisors. Board members often include Nobel Prize winners, scholars, and scientists who are well-known in their respective fields.

On the other hand, *Wikipedia* entries and many other encyclopedia entries do include footnotes as well as extensive reference lists. For example, here is the bibliography section of the entry for "Psychosis" by Paula Ford-Martin and Rebecca Frey, from the *Gale Encyclopedia of Medicine*:

When you refer to an encyclopedia entry, do you think about the people who composed it? About their expertise? Their biases? To what extent do these factors affect your trust in the source itself?

For coverage and more examples of **reference works entries,** see the Index of Genres on page G-1.

International Encyclopedia...	Gale Encyclopedia of...	The Oxford Companion to the...	Gale Encyclopedia of Psychology	Further reading

Psychosis

⊕ Tools

Gale Encyclopedia of Medicine, 3rd ed. | 2006 | Ford-Martin, Paula; Frey, Rebecca | Copyright

Resources

BOOKS

American Psychiatric Association. *Diagnostic and Statistical Manual of Mental Disorders.* 4th ed., revised. Washington, D.C.: American Psychiatric Association, 2000.

Beers, Mark H., MD, and Robert Berkow, MD., editors. "Psychiatric Emergencies." In *The Merck Manual of Diagnosis and Therapy*. Whitehouse Station, NJ: Merck Research Laboratories, 2004.

Beers, Mark H., MD, and Robert Berkow, MD., editors. "Schizophrenia and Related Disorders." In *The Merck Manual of Diagnosis and Therapy*. Whitehouse Station, NJ: Merck Research Laboratories, 2004.

PERIODICALS

Addington, A. M., M. Gornick, A. L. Sporn, et al. "Polymorphisms in the 13q33.2 Gene G72/G30 Are Associated with Childhood-Onset Schizophrenia and Psychosis Not Otherwise Specified." *Biological Psychiatry* 55 (May 15, 2004): 976-980.

Hutchinson, G., and C. Haasen. "Migration and Schizophrenia: The Challenges for European Psychiatry and Implications for the Future." *Social Psychiatry and Psychiatric Epidemiology* 39 (May 2004): 350-357.

Sharon, Idan, MD, and Roni Sharon. "Shared Psychotic Disorder." *eMedicine* June 4, 2004. ☐http://www.emedicine.com/med/topic3352.htm☐.

Sim, M. G., E. Khong, and G. Hulse. "Cannabis and Psychosis." *Australian Family Physician* 33 (April 2004): 229-232.

Tolmac, J., and M. Hodes. "Ethnic Variation among Adolescent Psychiatric In-Patients with Psychotic Disorders." *British Journal of Psychiatry* 184 (May 2004): 428-431.

Verdoux, H., and M. Tournier. "Cannabis Use and Risk of Psychosis: An Etiological Link?" *Epidemiologia e psichiatria sociale* 13 (April-June 2004): 113-119.

Williams, N. M., and M. J. Owen. "Genetic Abnormalities of Chromosome 22 and the Development of Psychosis." *Current Psychiatry Reports* 6 (June 2004): 176-182.

◀ ENCYCLOPEDIA ENTRY *Gale Encyclopedia of Medicine,* via *Encyclopedia.com,* "Psychosis." The bibliography for the "Psychosis" entry by Paula Ford-Martin and Rebecca Frey lists solid sources, such as the American Psychiatric Association's diagnostic manual and *The Merck Manual of Diagnosis and Therapy*. Both are considered to be authoritative texts. From Gale Encyclopedia of Medicine *V4, 3E*. © *2006 Gale, a part of Cengage Learning, Inc. Reproduced by permission.* www.cengage.com/ permissions.

Michael E. Mann, Henrik Selin, et al., for *Encyclopaedia Britannica*

Global Warming

Encyclopaedia Britannica has been publishing for nearly 250 years, giving it a level of credibility and authority that other, newer encyclopedia brands can't compete with. This status is further bolstered by the fame of some of its recent contributors, who include Albert Einstein, Marie Curie, Sigmund Freud, and Carl Sagan.

The primary contributors for the entry below on "Global Warming" are Michael E. Mann and Henrik Selin. Mann is a professor of meteorology at Pennsylvania State University and the director of the Earth System Science Center. He has published many journal articles and received numerous awards for his research. Selin is a professor in the international relations department at Boston University and an affiliated researcher at the Center for Climate Science and Policy Research at Linköping University in Sweden. He has authored books, book chapters, and articles on energy and climate. These authors and *Encyclopaedia Britannica* have some serious ethos.

The following example from the online edition of *Britannica* is typical of an entry in a general encyclopedia. Note: Reprinted here are short excerpts from the much longer entry for "Global Warming." *(Illustrations on pages 108–113: Reprinted with permission from Encyclopaedia Britannica, © 2012 by Encyclopaedia Britannica Inc.)*

ENCYCLOPÆDIA **Britannica**

About the Editorial Board

Current Members
Wendy Doniger
Richard Fishman
Benjamin M. Friedman
Leslie H. Gelb
David Gelernter
Murray Gell-Mann
Vartan Gregorian
Lord Sutherland of Houndwood
Lord Weidenfeld of Chelsea

Recent Members
Rosalia Arteaga
David Baltimore
Nicholas Carr
Zaha Hadid

The Encyclopædia Britannica Editorial Board of Advisors

For any organization that aspires to take all human knowledge, organize it, summarize it, and publish it in a form that people find useful, the challenges and opportunities have never been greater than they are today. The volume of information is exploding, the world is shrinking, and digital media are changing the way we read, think, and learn.

To meet these challenges and opportunities, Britannica has done what we have always done throughout our 240-year history: sought the very best minds in the world to help us.

In the past, they had names like Albert Einstein, Sigmund Freud, Marie Curie, Bertrand Russell, T.H. Huxley, and George Bernard Shaw, all of whom were Britannica contributors in their day.

Today they are the men and women of Britannica's Editorial Board of Advisors—the Nobel laureates and Pulitzer Prize winners, the leading scholars, writers, artists, public servants, and activists who are at the top of their fields. They meet regularly to share ideas, to debate, and to argue, in a unique collegium whose purpose is to understand today's world so that the resulting encyclopedia can be the best there is. We are proud to be associated with these exceptional people, and we are deeply grateful for their contributions, not only to our own publishing objectives but to the larger cause of promoting knowledge in the world today.

ENCYCLOPÆDIA
Britannica
Facts matter

Search Articles

global warming

Contributors

Primary Contributors

Michael E. Mann

Henrik Selin

Other Contributors

The Editors of *Encyclopaedia Britannica*

Heather Campbell

Swati Chopra

Darshana Das

John Higgins

Gloria Lotha

J. E. Luebering

Richard Pallardy

Dutta Promeet

John P. Rafferty

Marco Sampaolo

Veenu Setia

Gaurav Shukla

Shiveta Singh

What are the composers, **Mann, Selin, et al.**, doing?

THE RHETORICAL SITUATION

Purpose
Audience
Rhetorical appeals
Modes & media

see page 110

How do I know this is an **encyclopedia entry**?

THE GENRE'S CONVENTIONS

Elements of the genre
Style
Design
Sources

see page 110

(Continued on p. 112.)

ENCYCLOPÆDIA
Britannica
Facts matter

Search Articles

global warming, the phenomenon of increasing average air temperatures near the surface of Earth over the past one to two centuries. Since the mid-20th century, climate scientists have gathered detailed observations of various weather phenomena (such as temperature, precipitation, and storms) and of related influences on climate (such as ocean currents and the atmosphere's chemical composition). These data indicate that Earth's climate has changed over almost every conceivable timescale since the beginning of geologic time and that, since at least the beginning of the Industrial Revolution, the influence of human activities has been deeply woven into the very fabric of climate change.

Giving voice to a growing conviction of most of the scientific community, the Intergovernmental Panel on Climate Change (IPCC) reported that the 20th century saw an increase in global average surface temperature of approximately 0.6 °C (1.1 °F). The IPCC went on to state that most of the warming observed over the second half of the 20th century could be attributed to human activities, and it predicted that by the end of the 21st century the average surface temperature would increase by another 1.8 to 4.0 °C (3.2 to 7.2 °F), depending on a range of possible scenarios. Many climate scientists agree that significant economic and ecological damage would result if global average temperatures rose by more than 2 °C [3.6 °F] in such a short time. Such damage might include increased extinction of many plant and animal species, shifts in patterns of agriculture, and rising sea levels. The IPCC reported that the global average sea level rose by some 17 cm (6.7 inches) during the 20th century, that sea levels rose faster in the second half of that century than in the first half, and that—again depending on a wide range of possible scenarios. Many climate scientists agree that significant economic and ecological damage would result if global average temperatures rose by more than 2 °C [3.6 °F] in such a short time. Such damage might include increased extinction of many plant and animal species, shifts in patterns of agriculture, and rising sea levels. The IPCC reported that the global average sea level rose by some 17 cm (6.7 inches) during the 20th century, that sea levels rose faster in the second half of that century than in the first half, and that—again depending on a wide range of scenarios—the global average sea level could rise by another 18 to 59 cm (7 to 23 inches) by the end of the 21st century. Furthermore, he IPCC reported that average snow cover in the Northern Hemisphere declined by 4 percent, or 1.5 million square km (580,000 square miles), between 1920 niles), between 1920 and 2005.

The scenarios referred to above depend mainly on future concentrations of certain trace gases, called greenhouse gases, that have been injected into the lower atmosphere in increasing amounts through the burning of fossil fuels for industry, transportation, and residential uses. Modern global warming is the result of an increase in magnitude of the so-called greenhouse effect, a warming of Earth's surface and lower atmosphere caused by the presence of water vapour, carbon dioxide, methane, and other greenhouse gases. Of all these gases, carbon dioxide is the most important, both for its role in the greenhouse effect and for its role in the human economy. It has been estimated that, at the beginning of the industrial age in the mid-18th century, carbon dioxide concentrations in the atmosphere were roughly 280 parts per million (ppm). By the end of the 20th century, carbon dioxide concentrations had reached 369 ppm (possibly the highest concentrations in at least 650,000 years), and, if fossil fuels continue to be burned at current rates, they are projected

ENCYCLOPÆDIA
Britannica
Facts matter

Search Articles

to reach 560 ppm by the mid-21st century—essentially, a doubling of carbon dioxide concentrations in 300 years. It has been calculated that an increase of this magnitude alone (that is, not accounting for possible effects of other greenhouse gases) would be responsible for adding 2 to 5 °C (3.6 to 9 °F) to the global average surface temperatures that existed at the beginning of the industrial age.

A vigorous debate is in progress over the extent and seriousness of rising surface temperatures, the effects of past and future warming on human life, and the need for action to reduce future warming and deal with its consequences. This article provides an overview of the scientific background and public policy debate related to the subject of global warming. It considers the causes of rising near-surface air temperatures, the influencing factors, the process of climate research and forecasting, the possible ecological and social impacts of rising temperatures, and the public policy developments since the mid-20th century.

Climatic variation since the last glaciation

Global warming is related to the more general phenomenon of climate change, which refers to changes in the totality of attributes that define climate. In addition to changes in air temperature, climate change involves changes to precipitation patterns, winds, ocean currents, and other measures of Earth's climate. Normally, climate change can be viewed as the combination of various natural forces occurring over diverse timescales. Since the advent of human civilization, climate change has involved an "anthropogenic," or exclusively human caused, element, and this anthropogenic element has become more important in the industrial period of the past two centuries. The term *global warming* is used specifically to refer to any warming of near-surface air during the past two centuries that can be traced to anthropogenic causes.

To define the concepts of global warming and climate change properly, it is first necessary to recognize that the climate of Earth has varied across many timescales, ranging from an individual human life span to billions of years. This variable climate history is typically classified in terms of "regimes" or "epochs." For instance, the Pleistocene glacial epoch (about 2,600,000 to 11,700 years ago) was marked by substantial variations in the global extent of glaciers and ice sheets. These variations took place on timescales of tens to hundreds of millennia and ere driven by changes in the distribution of solar radiation across Earth's surface. The distribution of solar radiation is known as the insolation pattern, and it is strongly affected by the geometry of Earth's orbit around the Sun and by the orientation, or tilt, of Earth's axis relative to the direct rays of the Sun.

Worldwide, the most recent glacial period, or ice age, culminated about 21,000 years ago in what is often called the Last Glacial Maximum. During this time, continental ice sheets extended well into the middle latitude regions of Europe and North America, reaching as far south as present-day London and New York City. Global annual mean temperature appears to have been about 4–5 °C (7–9 °F) colder than in the mid-20th century. It is important to remember that these figures are a global average. In fact, during the height of this last ice age, Earth's climate was characterized by greater cooling at higher latitudes (that is, toward the poles) and relatively little cooling over large parts of the tropical oceans (near the Equator). This glacial interval terminated abruptly about 11,700 years ago and was followed by the subsequent relatively ice-free period known as the Holocene Epoch. The modern period of Earth's history is conventionally defined as residing within . . .

Continues next page

THE RHETORICAL SITUATION

Audience

The audience for *Britannica* and this entry is readers who want an overview on a topic, in this case global warming. Readers are most likely from a general rather than an expert audience. They may use this entry as a jumping-off point for further research.

Rhetorical appeals

Mann and Selin establish their **ethos** as experts through their clear writing, authoritative tone, and bibliography of sources. Readers can also click on their names to see their qualifications to write on this topic.

The other contributors are "content editors" that *Britannica* uses for their subject knowledge and analytical abilities, to ensure the accuracy and currency of the article.

(Continued on p.113.)

Michael E. Mann, Henrik Selin, et al., for *Encyclopaedia Britannica, Global Warming*

ENCYCLOPÆDIA
Britannica
Facts matter

Search Articles

Bibliography

Documentaries
Of the several productions describing the scientific concepts behind the global warming phenomenon, *An Inconvenient Truth* (2006), produced by LAURIE DAVID, LAWRENCE BENDER, and SCOTT Z. BURNS and narrated by ALBERT GORE, JR., is the most lauded. A feature placing special emphasis on solutions that reduce carbon dioxide production is *Global Warming: What You Need to Know* (2006), produced by the Discovery Channel, the BBC, and NBC News Productions and narrated by TOM BROKAW. Other noted documentaries on global warming include two originally aired on PBS-TV: *What's Up with the Weather?* (2007), produced by JON PALFREMAN; and *Global Warming: The Signs and the Science* (2005), produced by DAVID KENNARD and narrated by ALANIS MORISSETTE.

Michael E. Mann

Scientific Background
An excellent general overview of the factors governing Earth's climate over all timescales is presented in WILLIAM RUDDIMAN, *Earth's Climate: Past and Future* (2000). In addition, RICHARD C.J. SOMERVILLE, *The Forgiving Air: Understanding Environmental Change* (1996, reissued 1998), is a readable introduction to the science of climate and global environmental change. JOHN HOUGHTON, *Global Warming: The Complete Briefing* (1997), also offers an accessible treatment of the science of climate change as well as a discussion of the policy and ethical overtones of climate change as an issue confronting society. SPENCER WEART, *Discovery of Global Warming* (2003), provides a reasoned account of the history of climate change science.

A number of books present thoughtful discussions of global warming as an environmental and societal issue. Still prescient is an early account provided in BILL MCKIBBEN, *The End of Nature* (1989). Other good treatments include STEPHEN SCHNEIDER, *Laboratory Earth* (2001); ALBERT GORE, *An Inconvenient Truth* (2006); ELIZABETH KOLBERT, *Field Notes from a Catastrophe* (2006); EUGENE LINDEN, *The Winds of Change* (2006); TIM FLANNERY, *The Weather Makers* (2006); and MIKE HULME, *Why We Disagree About Climate Change: Understanding Controversy, Inaction and Opportunity* (2009). An excellent exposition for younger readers is found in ANDREW REVKIN, *The North Pole Was Here* (2007).

Public Policy Background
STEPHEN H. SCHNEIDER, ARMIN ROSENCRANZ, and JOHN O. NILES (eds.), *Climate Change Policy: A Survey* (2002), is a primer on various aspects of the policy debate that explains alternatives for dealing with climate change. A broad analysis of the climate change debate is imparted in ANDREW E. DESSLER and EDWARD A. PARSON, *The Science and Politics of Global Climate Change: A Guide to the Debate* (2006). A summary of the quantitative aspects of greenhouse gas emissions designed to assist stakeholders and policy makers is provided in KEVIN A. BAUMERT, TIMOTHY HERZOG, and JONATHAN PERSHING, *Navigating the Numbers: Greenhouse Gas Data and International Climate Policy* (2005).

ENCYCLOPÆDIA
Britannica
Facts matter

Search Articles

A somewhat more technical introduction to the science of climate change is provided in DAVID ARCHER, *Global Warming: Understanding the Forecast* (2006). More advanced treatments of the science of global warming and climate change are included in INTERGOVERNMENTAL PANEL ON CLIMATE CHANGE: WORKING GROUP I, *Climate Change 2007: The Physical Science Basis: Summary for Policymakers: Fourth Assessment Report* (2007); and INTERGOVERNMENTAL PANEL ON CLIMATE CHANGE: WORKING GROUP II, *Climate Change 2007: Climate Change Impacts, Adaptations, and Vulnerability: Fourth Assessment Report* (2007). Possible solutions to the challenges of global warming and climate change are detailed in INTERGOVERNMENTAL PANEL ON CLIMATE CHANGE: WORKING GROUP III, *Climate Change 2007: Mitigation of Climate Change: Fourth Assessment Report* (2007).

JOHN T. HOUGHTON, *Global Warming: The Complete Briefing*, 3rd ed. (2004), offers a perspective on climate change from one of the leading participants in the IPCC process. DANIEL SAREWITZ and ROGER PIELKE, JR., "Breaking the Global-Warming Gridlock," *The Atlantic Monthly*, 286(1):55–64 (2000), presents an alternative view on how to make progress on climate policy by focusing on reducing vulnerability to climate impacts.

Thoughtful discussions of the politics underlying the issue of climate change are provided in ROSS GELBSPAN, *Boiling Point* (2004); MARK LYNAS, *High Tide* (2004); and ROSS GELBSPAN, *The Heat Is On* (1998). The social justice implications involved in adapting the human population to changing climatic conditions are presented in W. NEIL ADGER et al. (eds.), *Fairness in Adaptation to Climate Change* (2006).

Henrik Selin

THE RHETORICAL SITUATION

Mann and Selin appeal to readers' sense of **logos** (logic) by presenting the information in an accessible way; further, they provide specific data in relation to the topic, such as temperatures.

Modes & media

Mode = written and visual The authors convey information in words, but also with charts and graphs. For example, they use a chart to explain temperature changes, and a video to illustrate greenhouse gases, showing how fossil fuels get released into the environment. These modes, along with animations, show readers the impact of pollutants on the environment.

Medium = digital There are pros and cons to providing information digitally. The pros are the many options for providing information. Digital encyclopedias also allow readers to connect through social media. For example, in the *Britannica* "Global Warming" entry, a share button allows readers to share the link on such sites as Twitter, Facebook, and LinkedIn, and to add the link to a social bookmarking site such as del.icio.us or Google. The cons are the ads. Because the entry is part of the free online resources *Britannica* provides, it is surrounded by ads. A printed encyclopedia would not include ads.

Michael E. Mann, Henrik Selin, et al., for *Encyclopaedia Britannica Global Warming*

THE GENRE'S
CONVENTIONS

Sources

Mann and Selin,
who themselves
are sources of
information, do not
provide footnotes,
in-text citations, or
a Works Cited list,
but they do provide
a bibliography and
a list of links to
external sites that
connect readers to
other sources that
they recommend as
authoritative.

ENCYCLOPÆDIA
Britannica
Facts matter

Search Articles

Websites

External Websites

- Common Questions About Climate Change - United Nations Environment
  Programme - World Meteorological Organization
- StopGlobalWarming.org
- A Paleo Perspective on Global Warming
  Discussion on paleoclimate research and global warming, and other issues regarding
  climate variability and change.
- U. S. Enviornmental Protection Agency - Global Warming
  Educational information on global warming and climate change, from the U.S.
  Environmental Protection Agency. Includes a primer on the greenhouse effect and
  recent trends in global climate; a glossary of climate change terms; material on the
  potential global warming impacts on health, water resources, and different
  ecosystems; and notes on local, national, and global actions to reduce climate
  change. Offers the contents of the quarterly newsletter "Inside the Greenhouse," a
  presentation on the impacts of climate change, and an inventory of U.S. emissions of
  carbon dioxide, methane, nitrous oxide, and other greenhouse gases.
- Environmental Education For Kids - Global Warming is Hot Stuff!
- Fact Monster - Global Warming
- How Stuff Works - Science - Global Warming
- NeoK12 - Educational Videos, Lessons and Games - Global Warming
- Science and Society - Global Warming
- National Geographic - Environment - What Is Global Warming?
- Think Quest - Global Warming
- National Aeronautics and Space Administration - Global Warming
- PBS Online - Savage Seas
- The Electronic Universe - Greenhouse Effect
- The Official Site of "An Inconvenient Truth"
- How Stuff Works - Science - How Does Global Warming Affect Hunting Season?
- How Stuff Works - Science - How Will Global Warming Affect Autumn?
- How Stuff Works - Science - Is Global Warming Destroying Mount Everest?
- How Stuff Works - Science - The Top 10 Worst Effects of Global Warming

Questions: Analyzing *Britannica*'s encyclopedia entry

1. Purpose. Although the topic of global warming is somewhat controversial, encyclopedists aim to inform—to take a neutral stance rather than try to persuade. What are some of the strategies the authors of the "Global Warming" entry use in order to avoid taking a position?

2. Audience. Who do you imagine is most likely to look up "global warming" in an online encyclopedia: a student, a businessperson, a teacher, or a scientist? What do you imagine his or her purpose might be?

3. Rhetorical appeals. Read an entry on a topic of your choice in *Wikipedia* and then read an entry on the same topic in another online encyclopedia. Compare the authors' techniques in the two entries. Do you notice them using similar methods to develop their ethos? What differences do you notice? Which entry sounds more authoritative, in your opinion? Why?

4. Modes & media. In what modes and media have you used encyclopedias? Do you have a preference for one mode or medium over another? Why?

5. Elements of the genre. As pointed out in the "Global Warming" annotations, encyclopedia entries serve as starting points for research. After reading the entry, what questions do you have about the topic? What are you curious about that you might want to research through other, more in-depth sources?

6. Elements of the genre. An encyclopedia entry about global warming is briefer than a book on the topic. As you read the *Britannica* entry excerpt, was there information you wished had been expanded upon? Why?

7. Style. Notice the neutral, third-person voice. How might your reading of this entry be different if the authors had written it in the first person?

8. Design. The entry is consistently formatted and designed so readers stay oriented. How important is it to you that information be easy to find in a reference work? Why? Can you think of examples of reference works that are not well designed?

9. Sources. In the *Britannica* entry, the authors rarely use attribution phrases such as "according to." How does this affect your reading of the entry? How might your experience as a reader be different if the entry were peppered with parenthetical notes and attribution phrases?

Drafting an Encyclopedia Entry

CHECKLIST: Drafting an Encyclopedia Entry
Thinking of drafting an encyclopedia entry? Ask yourself the following questions.

WHAT'S MY RHETORICAL SITUATION?

☐ **Purpose.** What specific topic do I want to write about? Which subtopics do I want to write about? How will I define my topic and subtopics? Writing an entry about "fashion" implies that I will cover fashion over the course of history. Writing about "street fashion," however, significantly narrows the time period I would need to cover.

☐ **Audience.** Who are my readers? How many of them are experts on my topic? Nonexperts who have a mild interest in my topic? What questions will they expect my entry to answer? Are there technical terms I may need to define (or hyperlink to definitions)? What kinds of examples will my readers relate to?

☐ **Rhetorical appeals.** How will I establish my authority as a writer? What kinds of vocabulary, diction, and examples will I use to convey authority?

☐ **Modes & media.** Do I want readers to experience my entry in print or digital format? Do I want to include images or videos?

WHAT GENRE CONVENTIONS MATTER?

☐ **Elements of the genre.** To keep my entry relatively brief, I will need to summarize other, longer works on the topic. Which works will I summarize? How will I make sure my writing is extremely precise? What terms might I need to carefully define?

☐ **Style.** How much do I want to develop my discussion of the topic? An entry geared toward a general audience (as in *Wikipedia*) will be less developed than one geared toward experts (as in *Medpedia*). Should I outline all the topics and subtopics I plan to cover? Then I can consider whether I'm over- or underdeveloping any of the subtopics, given who I imagine my audience to be.

☐ **Design.** How can I use titles and subtitles to make my entry easy to access for readers? If I create a digital entry, how will I use hyperlinks to direct readers to other entries?

☐ **Sources.** In addition to a list of sources, will I want to include a list of "additional resources" for readers who want to do their own research?

PRACTICE Want to experiment? Draft your own encyclopedia entry.

Are you an expert on a particular subject? Choose one that you're well versed in, and draft an encyclopedia entry on that topic based on what you already know and what you can learn by doing some research (that does not involve *Wikipedia* or any encyclopedia). Remember to include only facts and information that are largely uncontested by others who are well versed in the subject. You may want to include visual features to illustrate key concepts.

CHARTS/INFOGRAPHICS

As writers, students, and professionals, we create charts—or any type of info-graphic, such as tables, graphs, and diagrams—to present information simply and visually. Anyone can create a chart, especially with software such as Microsoft Excel or shareware such as iCharts.

Analyzing Charts/Infographics: What to Look For

THE RHETORICAL SITUATION

Purpose   Writers create charts to give a snapshot of complex information—and to draw attention to relationships among the items presented. If you are creating a chart, you might want to keep it simple. An effective way of achieving your pur-pose through an infographic is to create a chart with x- and y-axes.

When might you create a chart? Let's say you're thinking about majoring in engi-neering, but you're not sure which branch would be most lucrative. Because you are an excellent but rather obsessive student, you decide that the best way to represent this information is to create a bar chart (also known as a bar graph). In the PayScale example on page 118, the x-axis represents the range of salaries (in dollars); the y-axis represents the range of types of engineering. In this format, the data—which is clearly labeled—is easy to understand. Clearly, petroleum engineering majors have the high-est earning potential, at least as of 2012, when PayScale created the graph. Note that in digital form, the graph links to PayScale's full methodology for creating it.

Another reason to create a chart is to use it as a persuasive tool. A chart showing that incomes rise as education levels rise can be used to persuade lawmakers to invest more money in education, for example.

Audience   Graph creators know that their readers want information in a concise, easy-to-read format. They know readers might consult their chart for data that will help them make a decision, as in the salaries graph. To take another example, someone creating a chart that compares test scores of students admitted to graduate schools knows that readers are probably students choosing graduate schools to apply to.

▲ CHART
The x and y axes.

CHART/INFOGRAPHIC ▶
Harvard University, Food Pyramid. © 2008 Harvard University. For more information about The Healthy Eating Pyramid, please see The Nutrition Source, Department of Nutrition, Harvard School of Public Health, http://www.thenutritionsource.org, and Eat, Drink, and Be Healthy, by Walter C. Willett, M.D., and Patrick J. Skerrett (2005), Free Press/Simon & Schuster Inc.

BAR GRAPH ▶
PayScale, Inc.,
"Majors That Pay You
Back." The left column
(or *y* axis) lists specific
majors; the bottom
row (or *x* axis) shows
salaries, making
this chart clear and
effective. Petroleum
engineering, anyone?
PayScale.com.

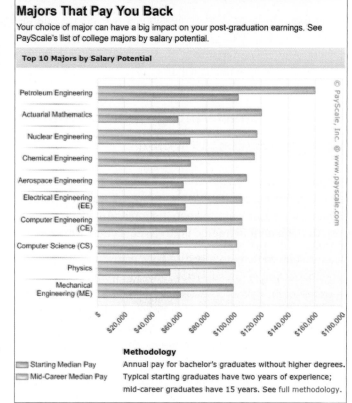

What types of
information are
best presented
visually? Are there
certain types of
infographics (pie
charts, graphs, etc.)
that you prefer over
others? Why?

Rhetorical appeals   Chart authors need to establish ethos by conducting research and presenting correct information in their infographics, in order to gain readers' confidence in the content. They can also appeal to audiences through logos, by using logical organization and smart, digestible design. In the example on page 119, job seeker Christopher Perkins appeals to readers' logic and pathos (in this case, through humor) by reimagining how to connect with his potential readers/employers with a visual resume.

Modes & media   Chart authors use visuals and text to share data. Often the visual content dominates and text is used mainly for labels. In terms of media, charts are communicated in print and digitally. Digital charts have the benefit of including hyperlinks to the chart's sources of information (as in the PayScale chart on engineering salaries above).

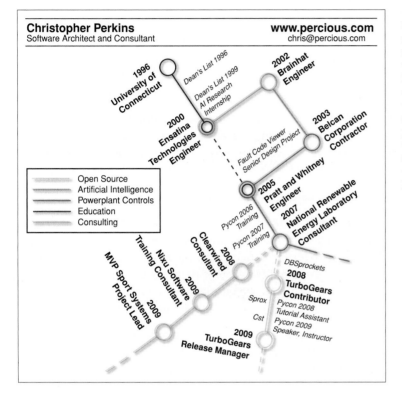

Christopher Perkins
Software Architect and Consultant

www.percious.com
chris@percious.com

◄ RESUME
Christopher Perkins,
resume designed as a
subway map. Perkins
takes a chance
by presenting his
employment history
this way, but chances
are good that his
potential employers
(software companies)
may value his creative
visual thinking and
humor.
*Courtesy of Christopher
Perkins.*

Elements of the genre Chart makers compose works that are:

Based on facts/data. The information that writers present in charts is based on research that the writer draws on (such as existing statistics from a government Web site), or collects personally (through primary research such as interviews).

Precise; clearly labeled and titled. Chart makers provide specific values for each item they address and show readers exactly how items relate to each other. Chart makers choose titles that define the scope of the chart's content, convey purpose, or summarize their findings. For example, the chart on page 122 is titled "Why Does a Salad Cost More Than a Big Mac?" Within the chart, labels further clarify. For example, in a chart with *x*- and *y*-axes, both axes are labeled so readers/viewers know if numerical amounts are billions or thousands.

Have you ever seen
a resume or other
business document
presented in a way
that surprised you?
What was it? Was it
as informative as the
more conventional
version would have
been?

Analyzing Charts/Infographics: What to Look For

Illustrated with symbols that convey information. Visual devices such as bars, lines, and sections or slices (of a pie chart) represent specific values and convey data clearly. Writers need to decide which type of chart works best for the information they're presenting. For example, line charts are best used when time is involved, because they can show trends over the course of a particular period.

Supplemented with a key or footnotes when needed. Chart makers sometimes provide a key (or legend) to let readers know what certain features of the visual mean. A key for a map defines each symbol; for example, tents might represent campgrounds. Footnotes connect readers to the sources of the chart's information.

Style   Chart makers make careful choices about style, including:

What details to present. Most chart makers don't include much detail; they usually provide a clear visual accompanied by brief text. The goal of chart writers is to make it easy for readers to absorb data quickly. Too much detail, especially for a general audience, might make it difficult for readers to see what's most important. However, if your audience is a group of specialists in a particular field who would like detail, then more in-depth data would be appropriate.

What techniques, tone, and voice to use. The best charts use simple, direct language, and the less the better. Chart makers use text judiciously, to provide a title, convey facts, label axes, and concisely explain symbols and colors in accompanying keys or legends. Their tone is neutral and objective.

Design   When chart makers lay out their work, they keep the following in mind:

Simple is best. The whole point is to make information accessible and digestible.

Color is key. Chart makers use color and shading to separate and highlight different pieces of information.

The parts need to be arranged logically/spatially. Chart makers lay out information and visuals in a way that shows readers what is most important to glean. In charts where there are multiple elements, or even multiple visuals that form one infographic, designers add white space between the elements to show separation, or place the elements near each other to show connections.

Sources   Charts are based on composers' knowledge or research. Readers assume that the chart maker is presenting reliable data based on specific sources. Many charts include a source or list of sources, which adds to their credibility and authority.

When it comes to charts, what is the happy medium between providing too many details and not enough?

For more coverage and examples of **infographics** and **maps,** see the Index of Genres on page G-1.

Physicians Committee for Responsible Medicine

Why Does a Salad Cost More Than a Big Mac?

The Physicians Committee for Responsible Medicine (PCRM) is a nonprofit organization focused on promoting nutrition and good health. The editors at PCRM created the chart on page 122 to compare the cost of a salad with that of a Big Mac, and to determine why a salad is more expensive. PCRM's choice of a pyramid allows them to make an easy-to-digest comparison of data; it also brings to mind the food pyramid chart created by the U.S. Department of Agriculture, whose purpose is to direct people to eat healthier diets. (See the new and old pyramids online at *The Washington Post*.) *(Illustration on page 122: Courtesy of Physicians Committee for Responsible Medicine.)*

◄ WEB SITE
PCRM,
homepage.
Courtesy of Physicians Committee for Responsible Medicine.

What is **PCRM**, the composer of the chart, doing?

THE RHETORICAL SITUATION

Purpose
Audience
Rhetorical appeals
Modes & media

see page 123

How do I know this is a **chart**?

THE GENRE'S CONVENTIONS

Elements of the genre
Style
Design
Sources

see page 123

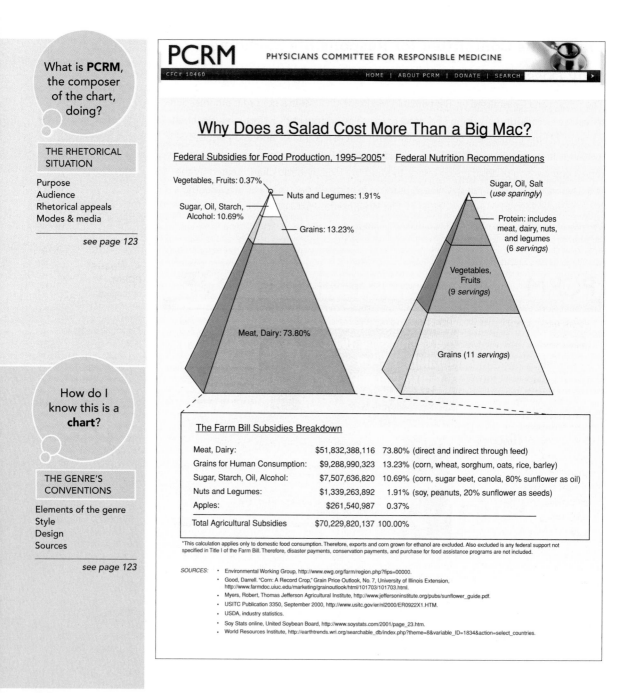

PCRM

PHYSICIANS COMMITTEE FOR RESPONSIBLE MEDICINE

CFC# 10460

HOME | ABOUT PCRM | DONATE | SEARCH

Why Does a Salad Cost More Than a Big Mac?

Federal Subsidies for Food Production, 1995–2005*

Vegetables, Fruits: 0.37%
Nuts and Legumes: 1.91%
Sugar, Oil, Starch, Alcohol: 10.69%
Grains: 13.23%
Meat, Dairy: 73.80%

Federal Nutrition Recommendations

Sugar, Oil, Salt (*use sparingly*)
Protein: includes meat, dairy, nuts, and legumes (6 *servings*)
Vegetables, Fruits (9 *servings*)
Grains (11 *servings*)

The Farm Bill Subsidies Breakdown

Meat, Dairy:	$51,832,388,116	73.80% (direct and indirect through feed)
Grains for Human Consumption:	$9,288,990,323	13.23% (corn, wheat, sorghum, oats, rice, barley)
Sugar, Starch, Oil, Alcohol:	$7,507,636,820	10.69% (corn, sugar beet, canola, 80% sunflower as oil)
Nuts and Legumes:	$1,339,263,892	1.91% (soy, peanuts, 20% sunflower as seeds)
Apples:	$261,540,987	0.37%
Total Agricultural Subsidies	$70,229,820,137	100.00%

*This calculation applies only to domestic food consumption. Therefore, exports and corn grown for ethanol are excluded. Also excluded is any federal support not specified in Title I of the Farm Bill. Therefore, disaster payments, conservation payments, and purchase for food assistance programs are not included.

SOURCES:
- Environmental Working Group, http://www.ewg.org/farm/region.php?fips=00000.
- Good, Darrell. "Corn: A Record Crop," Grain Price Outlook, No. 7, University of Illinois Extension, http://www.farmdoc.uiuc.edu/marketing/grainoutlook/html/101703/101703.html.
- Myers, Robert, Thomas Jefferson Agricultural Institute, http://www.jeffersoninstitute.org/pubs/sunflower_guide.pdf.
- USITC Publication 3350, September 2000, http://www.usitc.gov/er/nl2000/ER0922X1.HTM.
- USDA, industry statistics.
- Soy Stats online, United Soybean Board, http://www.soystats.com/2001/page_23.htm.
- World Resources Institute, http://earthtrends.wri.org/searchable_db/index.php?theme=8&variable_ID=1834&action=select_countries.

Purpose

PCRM's purpose is to present complex information in a simple, digestible format. They also seek to persuade readers of a problem in terms of foods the U.S. government subsidizes (left pyramid) versus the foods Americans should be eating (right pyramid).

Audience

Readers of this infographic want facts, and they want them efficiently presented. They may be general readers, healthcare professionals, lawmakers, voters, or anyone with a specific interest in food subsidies, nutrition, and government.

Rhetorical appeals

The authors establish their **ethos** by identifying themselves as physicians, and therefore as health and nutrition experts. They further support that ethos with the precision of the information, their choice of sources, and the careful citing of sources.

The authors use logic (**logos**) by presenting the data in the pyramid charts, and also in the table below.

Modes & media

Mode = written and visual The editors at PCRM use a combination of visuals and text to convey information and make an argument about federal subsidies and nutritional costs levied on consumers. At the top of the chart, they rely on the visual, juxtaposing two food pyramids (one of federal subsidies and one of nutrition recommendations). Below the food subsidies pyramid is a table that breaks down exact dollar amounts. Combining the table, graphic, and sources (at the bottom) provides rich information, boosting the persuasive power of the piece.

Medium = digital This information is geared toward a general online audience (anyone searching online for nutritional information, or even the cost of a Big Mac, might find this chart). If PCRM created the chart to be published in their own newsletter, the audience would be limited to physicians or other healthcare professionals. Though this infographic isn't interactive, many online charts like this are, allowing audiences to plug in certain information; can you imagine how the PCRM chart might be made interactive?

Elements of the genre

Based on data. The PCRM authors draw on seven sources, including the USDA.

Precise. Percentages and numbers of items are precise (down to the decimal point); e.g., vegetables and fruits are listed as .37%, rather than rounded up to .4%.

Clearly titled. The words in the title convey the main point of the chart.

Clearly labeled. The labels clarify what each item is and its specific value (e.g., labels convey that grains make up 13.23% of subsidies).

Uses symbols. The two pyramids represent items and values related to federal subsidies versus those related to federal nutrition recommendations.

Style

Minimal detail is used—but enough to make the information clear and authoritative. The two pyramids convey the essence of the information; the text provides concise information about subsidies.

PCRM's tone is **objective**. All information is presented as fact.

Design

Color indicates the separation of categories (e.g., vegetables and fruits are green in the right-hand pyramid). Leader lines make clear how text and visuals relate. Information below the visuals is provided in list form and as a bulleted list for easy reading.

Sources

PCRM's research draws on seven sources, which are listed at the bottom of the chart.

Questions: Analyzing PCRM's chart/infographic

1. Purpose. How do the PCRM editors inform their readers about why a salad costs more than a Big Mac? To what extent are they presenting an argument?

2. Audience. Describe the audience that PCRM targets with this infographic. Is the target audience consumers? People interested in economics? Dieters? Vegetarians? Provide support for your answer.

3. Rhetorical appeals. One way the PCRM editors establish ethos is by listing the sources they used. How else is ethos established?

4. Modes & media. What are the advantages of making the chart available digitally? How might the PCRM editors revise the chart to take better advantage of a digital medium?

5. Elements of the genre. How does the title of the chart help shape the way you understand the information presented? Describe the tone of the title. To what extent does it reflect the conventions of the genre?

6. Elements of the genre. The chart has two visuals. What is the impact of the side-by-side presentation of these visuals?

7. Style. Describe the level of detail in this chart. Why do you think the PCRM editors chose to add another layer of detail with the table underneath the first graphic?

8. Design. How does the use of color relate to the information presented in the chart?

9. Design. Why is a pyramid an appropriate chart for presenting this information? What would be different if the PCRM editors had used a bar chart or a pie chart?

10. Sources. Why do you think the PCRM editors omitted any data from McDonald's in the chart?

Drafting a Chart/Infographic

CHECKLIST: Drafting a Chart/Infographic

Thinking of creating a chart or other infographic? Ask yourself the following questions.

WHAT'S MY RHETORICAL SITUATION?

☐ **Purpose.** What financial experience that I've encountered might be interesting to represent in a chart? Why? Do I want to look at it from a personal angle or a more global perspective? What are all the considerations I need to take into account to represent the data that correspond to that experience?

☐ **Audience.** Who are my readers? Why should/will my chart matter to them? What do I want them to get out of it? And how will I reach them? Does my audience consist of general readers or specialists in the field? What level of detail will my chart need?

☐ **Rhetorical appeals.** How will I establish my authority and reliability as a writer? How will I convey my information so my readers believe my data? To what extent will I rely on logic to support my interpretations? How will I organize the information to convey the logic?

☐ **Modes & media.** Do I want readers to experience my chart primarily as a visual? How much text will accompany my chart? Do I want readers to access my chart digitally or in print? Why?

WHAT GENRE CONVENTIONS MATTER?

☐ **Elements of the genre.** What types of data will I use to create my chart? Will I use colors or symbols in the chart? How will I represent those in my legend? Have I used sources based on research? Will I use footnotes to attribute those sources? Do I want my title to indicate my ultimate findings or present a question?

☐ **Style.** How will I keep my tone objective? What level of detail will I include in my chart?

☐ **Design.** How do I want to organize my chart spatially? Are there multiple visuals? Does each visual have accompanying text? Are colors appropriate for my chart? If so, what colors will help me convey my information? Is a bar chart or a line graph better for conveying my information?

☐ **Sources.** Is my chart based on my own knowledge or do I need to do research to gather data and statistics? How many sources do I need to draw on in order to present the information effectively?

PRACTICE   Want to experiment? Draft your own chart or other infographic.

Think about how you spent time over the last week: doing homework, attending class, working, socializing, sleeping, eating, exercising, and so on. Then choose a visual way to represent this information, taking into account your data, what you want to convey and why, how you can best establish your ethos—and also your choices of text, images, color, and design.

The first newspapers were handwritten pages that reported on economic and social issues in Europe in the 1400s. The first successful English-language paper was *The Weekly Newes*, established in the 1620s; a little later, *The London Gazette* became the official newspaper of Great Britain (1666). In 1704, a bookseller and postmaster named John Campbell kicked off newspapers in America with *The Boston News-Letter*, an effort that was followed up more successfully in 1728 by Benjamin Franklin, who published *The Pennsylvania Gazette*, a paper considered to be *The New York Times* of the eighteenth century.

▲ PORTRAIT &
NEWSPAPER ▶

An issue of *The Pennsylvania Gazette,* personally managed by Benjamin Franklin. What would Franklin think about the Internet? Where would he get his news? *Both images: Library of Congress.*

Today, most cities have at least one local daily newspaper; Chicago, for example, has the *Chicago Sun-Times* and the *Chicago Tribune*. Daily newspapers are divided into sections on world, domestic, and local news; sports; business; science; health;

obituaries; and weather. Many have sections dedicated to editorials/opinions, food, travel, education, entertainment, and fashion, along with advice columns, comics, puzzles, and horoscopes. Smaller communities and organizations also publish newspapers on topics of interest to more specific audiences (such as the Boston area's *Wicked Local*, a consortium of local/community newspapers). Many publications are available online and include links to related stories and topics, as well as social media features that allow readers to post reactions to published stories.

Before the Internet, major newspapers were published once or twice a day. However, now that readers can check news headlines and follow stories online throughout the day, they expect constant updates. News reporting and publishing is now a 24/7 occupation; this makes us all better-informed citizens, but it also means that news agencies focused on breaking news are more vulnerable to misreporting and error. (For example, in 2011, in their zeal to break and update the story of the shooting of Arizona congresswoman Gabrielle Giffords, several news agencies reported that she was shot dead, though she survived the shooting. See the *Columbia Journalism Review*.)

While newspapers publish many kinds of writing—persuasive editorials, letters to the editor, advice columns, ads—at their core are factual news articles written by reporters. Reporters research their writing: They gather information for a story by conducting interviews, serving as eyewitnesses (reporting from the scene, for example), checking public records, and working with library and online sources. News journalists need to be able to back up the accuracy of their writing with facts from several reliable sources.

In news articles, writers present facts. In editorials, they present opinions. That said, the line between fact and opinion can blur, especially on broadcast news programs. Can you think of examples where a news report feels too much like an opinion piece? If so, how do you account for this?

Analyzing News Articles: What to Look For

THE RHETORICAL SITUATION

Purpose   Journalists research and write news articles to inform readers of facts and events. Their purpose is to present true and fair accounts of issues and happenings, and to do so while adhering to ethical standards, such as those outlined by the Society of Professional Journalists.

Among the largest news providers are CNN, ABC, MSNBC, Fox News, the Associated Press, *The New York Times*, and *The Washington Post*. (For more news providers, see "Modes & media" below.) Depending on a news organization's size and scope, it might cover a range of world, national, and perhaps local news, and specific subject areas such as business, culture, science, and entertainment. Like any organization, each news provider has its own policies, agenda, and built-in biases. That said, ideally, the news articles that they publish or air are as fact based and objective as possible.

Keep in mind that news articles can appear in the context of other genres. In an online newspaper, for example, a news article might appear near an advertisement or an editorial or other opinion piece. It's a good practice to clarify for yourself what is informative fact-based reporting and what is editorial writing (see also Chapter 4).

Audience Journalists who write news articles know readers want to be informed about world events and issues, and to be kept up-to-date, especially online. They know that some readers will scan the first few paragraphs to get the main idea, so they need to include the most important material up front. Some readers who are especially interested—personally or professionally—in a given topic, however, will read for depth. They will read the entire article and also turn to related articles. Journalists keep that audience in mind as well.

Rhetorical appeals Journalists use ethos and logos to reach their audiences. A news publisher's reputation for "getting the story right" is crucial, as are the reputations of reporters associated with the publisher. If a reporter's credibility is seriously tarnished, his or her career in journalism will quickly end. In 2003, for example, promising *New York Times* reporter Jayson Blair was fired for plagiarizing parts of several news reports he had written. The *Times* called it "a low point in the 152-year history of the newspaper" and apologized profusely to its readers.

There is debate, both within the news industry itself and among readers and commentators, of what constitutes "news." The impact of reality television, which is cheaper to produce than dramas or news programs, is a factor, as is the mainstream appeal of celebrity and reality-star gossip. Whatever your opinion of the entertainment news published by *Gawker*, *TMZ*, and others, it's clear that the writers and editors at these organizations know how to appeal to their readers' pathos (emotions) with sensational headlines and stories about affairs, addictions, and arrests.

Modes & media   News articles can take many forms. Here, we're highlighting written news articles, because text can appear in print or digital formats. With the rise of digital news sites such as *The Huffington Post*, many print newspapers have moved online (see also "Purpose" on p. 127). Most traditional print newspapers have companion Web sites; for example, you can read many of the same stories in both the print and online versions of *The New York Times*, the *Wall Street Journal, The Washington Post*, and the *Los Angeles Times*, although some online content requires a subscription. The advantages of the online news article are that it can be updated instantly, can link to related articles and sources, and can be accompanied by video. Online publications also allow readers to post comments, making these sources much more interactive than print newspapers.

Traditional news outlets, such as those just mentioned, are not the only sources of news reports. News reports also commonly appear in news magazines, such as *Time, Newsweek/The Daily Beast, Slate, Salon*, and *Harper's*, and on blogs. Some news blogs, such as *This Just In*, are associated with a particular news outlet, in this case CNN. Others, such as the *Renewable Energy Law Blog*, report on news relevant to their readers; in the case of the *Renewable Energy Law Blog*, readers are clients and potential clients of the law firm that hosts the blog. In still other news blogs, writers report or comment on news, but they're not affiliated with a news outlet. Rather, these are individual blogs, such as *Not a Sheep*, *Jezebel*, and *Buzzfeed*, where bloggers present news snippets and then comment on them.

In addition to appearing in print and in digital formats, news stories can also take the form of audio and video reports. National Public Radio covers all the top stories that print and digital news outlets cover, but they of course do it in audio form. Many digital news outlets, such as MSNBC, also make videos of news coverage available online.

THE GENRE'S CONVENTIONS

Elements of the genre
Well researched and fact-checked. As discussed above, the authority (or ethos) of the reporter, publisher, and content is crucial. Writers must be scrupulous in their research and fact-checking. A rule of thumb in journalism is to verify a report with at least three reliable sources. When an error is discovered in an article, journalists

and publishers are usually quick to make a correction and apologize. For example, CNET News, a technology publication affiliated with CBS News, states their corrections policy on their Web site.

Corrections

CNET strives to meet the highest standards for accuracy and completeness in our editorial coverage; it is our policy to always correct errors when they occur and to notify readers of changes to our content. We classify editorial changes as *corrections, clarifications,* or *updates.*
• A correction rights a factual error.
• A clarification adjusts statements that were not factually incorrect but may have been unclear or misleading.
• An update revises content with information not available when the story was originally published.
To report possible errors in content, please email our editorial department. Include the URL of the page where the error occurs. Our editors will review all reports of errors to determine if a correction is warranted.

Please note: This page pertains to text corrections and factual errors on existing editorial product reviews only. For help with pricing errors, CNET Download.com descriptions, broken links, passwords, and registration, please visit CNET Customer Help Center.

Usually aimed at a broad audience. Most newspapers, news magazines, and news sites have a very broad readership with varying degrees of education, so the level of vocabulary in a news article must be appropriate for all. Most are written with a vocabulary considered to be ninth or tenth grade. *The New York Times,* however, is written at a twelfth-grade level of vocabulary and comprehension.

Think of the sources where you get your news. How would you characterize the writing? The vocabulary level? How do a journalist's style and word choice contribute to your reading experience?

Opens with a concise summary in a lead (or lede) paragraph. Most journalists begin their news articles with a paragraph that states the most important aspects of their story and grabs the reader's attention. In the rest of the article, reporters elaborate on what was presented in the opening paragraph. Because many readers skim rather than read a full article, the content of the lead paragraph is especially important.

Presents information in order of importance. Paragraphs that follow the lead and make up the body of the article provide details and supporting evidence from sources. Paragraphs closer to the beginning of the story provide details that are more important in understanding the essence of the story; those closer to the end, however, provide information that is less essential, given that some readers may not read the whole article to the end.

As explained in the "Style" section below, news journalists tend to structure their articles with an overview of the important information at the beginning, so readers can get information quickly.

Includes quotations. Journalists often quote sources directly to add flavor to their articles and to maintain the feel of "just the facts, ma'am." No one can accuse a reporter of misinterpreting what someone said if the reporter includes direct quotations.

Written in short paragraphs. Journalists often write in short paragraphs because they're easier to read than long ones. They're also easier on the eyes, especially considering the formats news articles are generally published in—either in narrow columns in print newspapers or online.

Style

Neutral tone/absence of personal opinion. The goal of writing a news article is to report information. It's appropriate for news journalists to use a serious and fairly formal tone in their writing; of course, "formal" doesn't have to mean dry. It's also appropriate for journalists to refrain from editorializing, unless they are writing an editorial or hosting an opinion column, for example.

Objective, third-person voice. An objective stance conveys the cut-and-dry, fact-based nature of news articles. News journalists also use precise language in order to clearly communicate facts and details, and use the third person (*he/she/they*) rather than the first person (*I/we*).

Just enough detail for the general reader. Journalists use specific details to support their generalizations. In the annotated article by Nicholas Wade (p. 137), you'll notice that the writer is very specific about how cats lap water. However, Wade gives only the level of detail that a general reader can understand. For example, he explains that "the cat darts its tongue, curving the upper side downward so that the tip lightly touches the surface of the water. The tongue is then pulled upward at high speed, drawing a column of water behind it." A general reader can grasp this level of detail easily. A scientist or veterinarian may want more detail, but that level of detail would only be appropriate for a specialized audience of scientists or veterinarians.

Design

Attention-grabbing title/headline. The title of a news article is called a headline. It is usually presented in much larger or bolder type than the story itself, and is brief and descriptive. Headlines are used to attract readers and are sometimes provocative; see, for example, the front page of the *New York Post*, a paper that is notorious for its over-the-top headlines. Compare that to the longer, more serious headline used by the BBC News on page 132.

Usually reporters write in the third person (*he/she/they*) because it is a neutral way to present facts. However, sometimes they use the first person (*I/we*). How might a journalist's use of *I* affect your reading of an article? What strategies might that writer use to persuade you that he or she is being objective?

▲ NEWSPAPER ***New York Post,*** front page. When it comes to unrestrained headlines, the *Post* rarely disppoints. *From the New York Post © 4/15/1983 NYP Holdings, Inc. All rights reserved.*

Byline. A byline is the presentation of the author's name, usually below the headline and above the text of the article. Sometimes the byline notes that the author is a correspondent or staff writer. Below, BBC News correspondent James Reynolds is credited for his report from Cairo.

NEWS ARTICLE ▶
James Reynolds, byline at BBC News (bbc.co.uk). Reynolds, who has been with the BBC since 1996, is the group's Tehran Correspondent. Note also the headline for Reynolds's report: descriptive and serious. Compare it to the *Post* headline on page 131.

The BBC's James Reynolds near the Rabaa al-Adawiya mosque encampment, says the air is thick with smoke from burning tyres

At four o'clock in the morning, at one of the entrances to the Rabaa al-Adawiya mosque encampment, a dozen guards stood behind a row of sandbags.

The men carried sticks and wore small gas masks around their necks. Some leaned back against the sandbags. Beyond the barricade, I could just make out the heads of a group of men standing for pre-dawn prayers. No-one appeared to want to leave.

Serif typeface. A serif font has a very small flare at the stroke ends and corners of letters, while a sans serif font lacks these strokes. Print articles are often presented in serif fonts (such as in the print edition of *The New York Times*), while sans serif fonts, such as those used by BBC News (below) are a good choice for the readability of digital content. Compare a serif **A** to a sans serif **A**.

Use of columns or chunking. News sites such as the BBC's (see below) present articles in chunked sections that have their own headings. Digital content may be presented in multiple columns or on different sections of the grid with various ways to navigate the content. Print newspapers are limited to columns of no more than fifty-two characters wide.

Images: photos, graphs, and multimedia components. Many news articles, especially breaking news on a Web site, or a front-page story in a print paper, are con-

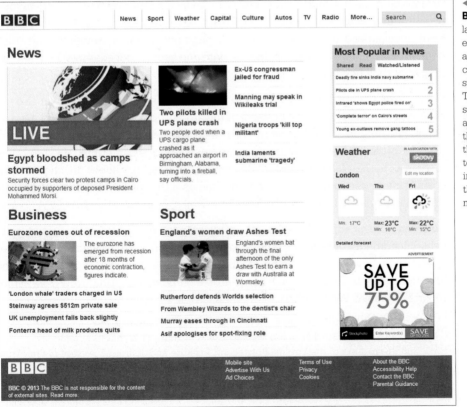

◀ NEWS SITE
BBC News. The layout chosen by the editors and designers at the BBC presents content in a clean, streamlined format. The consistent sans serif font for text and headings, the three-column grid, the chunking of text, and the use of images contribute to the readability and modern aesthetic.

textualized with photos, charts, graphs, and, in the case of the online source, video and other multimedia. This is true of the BBC News site (p. 133), where the main story (of August 14, 2013, about Egypt) features prominently and leads readers to plenty of related content and live video. A piece with a video or audio component usually includes an arrow icon or other visual element to indicate this; sometimes the video or audio itself is the news story.

News publishers use visual and multimedia to grab readers' attention, provide context, and enrich the content of print articles. For example, the article on page 134 reports on the civil-union ceremonies that took place after Colorado's civil-union law went into effect. The article features a large photo; a few paragraphs down are links to related stories. The featured photo and photo gallery give readers context for the event.

Headers, footers, and tabs. Designers of online news sites provide tabs and navigational menus and search boxes to keep readers oriented. The designers use repeated design features to reinforce the agency's identity. For example, a print newspaper's title appears on every page and in other elements, and titles, headers, and footers (which include the date and section, for example) help readers find what they need on the page.

Use of color. Online news sites include color images and video. Designers also use color typographically to direct attention toward particular content. Blue is used for hyperlinks (which turn a different color once you select them), red is sometimes used for breaking news headlines, and gray shading is sometimes used to orient readers as to their location within the content. Images and videos are shown in full color. Print newspapers, which are published on a thin paper called newsprint, are printed in black ink (such as *The New York Times*) or in color (such as *USA Today*).

Sources   News reports are based on eyewitness accounts, authoritative published documents, interviews, and records. Most journalists indicate their sources within their news articles, using attribution phrases such as "according to" and linking directly to their sources. In his article on how cats drink, *New York Times* reporter Nicholas Wade writes:

> Cats, both big and little, are so much classier, according to new research by Pedro M. Reis and Roman Stocker of the Massachusetts Institute of Technology, joined by Sunghwan Jung of the Virginia Polytechnic Institute and Jeffrey M. Aristoff of Princeton. Writing in the Thursday issue of Science, the four engineers report. . . .

◄ ONLINE NEWS ARTICLE
A *Denver Post* article with color photos, videos, and links to related stories. The multimedia—and how it's laid out—enriches the reader's experience and provides supporting evidence and context.
Story: Joey Bunch. Photos: Craig F. Walker. The Denver Post 5/2/2013.

Analyzing News Articles: What to Look For

For more examples of **news articles** see the Index of Genres on page G-1.

Wade makes it clear that the information he draws on is a researched article from the journal *Science* and from the four researchers he names. Journalists, unlike the authors of peer-reviewed journal articles (p. 143), do not use academic documentation styles such as MLA or APA (pp. 395 and 415). Because news journalism is a popular genre and not a scholarly genre, it has a different set of conventions for documenting sources, such as the phrasing that Wade uses on page 134. In news journalism, the thinking is that the reader doesn't need the same level of detail about sources that scholarly audiences need. That said, online news providers and journalists can boost their ethos by linking to their sources.

Nicholas Wade

For Cats, a Big Gulp with a Touch of the Tongue

The New York Times, which has been publishing since 1851, is considered highly accurate and is regarded as one of the most authoritative newspapers available. Its Web site and print circulation make it one of the most widely read newspapers in the world. It has won over one hundred Pulitzer Prizes, the most prestigious reporting award given. Nicholas Wade is a science reporter for *The New York Times*. He has written several science books, including 2009's *The Faith Instinct*, about the scientific basis of religious faith. The following article appeared in the Science section of the *Times*; the online version includes links to sources, infographics, and video that support the text. *(Text and images on pp. 138–39, From* The New York Times, *November 11, 2010 © 2010* The New York Times. *All rights reserved.)*

▲ AUTHOR PHOTO
Nicholas Wade, *New York Times* reporter. *Nicholas Wade.com, Naum Kazhdan/The New York Times/Redux.*

What is the composer, **Nicholas Wade**, doing?

THE RHETORICAL SITUATION

Purpose
Audience
Rhetorical appeals
Modes & media

see page 139

How do I know this is a **newspaper article**?

THE GENRE'S CONVENTIONS

Elements of the genre
Style
Design
Sources

see page 140

The New York Times

Science
For Cats, a Big Gulp With a Touch of the Tongue

By NICHOLAS WADE
Published: November 11, 2010

It has taken four highly qualified engineers and a bunch of integral equations to figure it out, but we now know how cats drink. The answer is: very elegantly, and not at all the way you might suppose.

⊕ Enlarge This Image

Pedro Reis

Cutta Cutta, who inspired the study, belongs to a researcher at M.I.T.

Multimedia

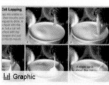

il Graphic
A Study of Cat Lapping

Connect With Us on Social Media
@nytimesscience on Twitter.
· Science Reporters and Editors on Twitter
Like the science desk on Facebook.

RECOMMEND
TWITTER
LINKEDIN
SIGN IN TO E-MAIL
PRINT
REPRINTS
SHARE

Cats lap water so fast that the human eye cannot follow what is happening, which is why the trick had apparently escaped attention until now. With the use of high-speed photography, the neatness of the feline solution has been captured.

The act of drinking may seem like no big deal for anyone who can fully close his mouth to create suction, as people can. But the various species that cannot do so — and that includes most adult carnivores — must resort to some other mechanism.

Dog owners are familiar with the unseemly lapping noises that ensue when their thirsty pet meets a bowl of water.

The dog is thrusting its tongue into the water, forming a crude cup with it and hauling the liquid back into the muzzle.

Cats, both big and little, are so much classier, according to new research by Pedro M. Reis and Roman Stocker of the Massachusetts Institute of Technology, joined by Sunghwan Jung of the Virginia Polytechnic Institute and Jeffrey M. Aristoff of Princeton.

Writing in the Thursday issue of Science, the four engineers report that the cat's lapping method depends on its instinctive ability to calculate the point at which gravitational force would overcome inertia and cause the water to fall.

What happens is that the cat darts its tongue, curving the upper side downward so that the tip lightly touches the surface of the water.

The tongue is then pulled upward at high speed, drawing a column of water behind it.

Continues next page

The New York Times

VIDEO »

More Video | Multimedia »

00:50   04:45
▶ PLAY   ✕ ◀)) ⚙ MENU

SCIENCE   ⊞ SHARE
How Cats Lap
The Biomechanics of Feline Water Uptake

Just at the moment that gravity finally overcomes the rush of the water and starts to pull the column down — snap! The cat's jaws have closed over the jet of water and swallowed it.

The cat laps four times a second — too fast for the human eye to see anything but a blur — and its tongue moves at a speed of one meter per second.

Being engineers, the cat-lapping team next tested its findings with a machine that mimicked a cat's tongue, using a glass disk at the end of a piston to serve as the tip. After calculating things like the Froude number and the aspect ratio, they were able to figure out how fast a cat should lap to get the greatest amount of water into its mouth. The cats, it turns out, were way ahead of them — they lap at just that speed.

To the scientific mind, the next obvious question is whether bigger cats should lap at different speeds.

The engineers worked out a formula: the lapping frequency should be the weight of the cat species, raised to the power of minus one-sixth and multiplied by 4.6. They then made friends with a curator at Zoo New England, the nonprofit group that operates the Franklin Park Zoo in Boston and the Stone Zoo in Stoneham, Mass., who let them videotape his big cats. Lions, leopards, jaguars and ocelots turned out to lap at the speeds predicted by the engineers.

The animal who inspired this exercise of the engineer's art is a black cat named Cutta Cutta, who belongs to Dr. Stocker and his family. Cutta Cutta's name comes from the word for "many stars" in Jawoyn, a language of the Australian aborigines.

Dr. Stocker's day job at M.I.T. is applying physics to biological problems, like how plankton move in the ocean. "Three and a half years ago, I was watching Cutta Cutta lap over breakfast," Dr. Stocker said. Naturally, he wondered what hydrodynamic problems the cat might be solving. He consulted Dr. Reis, an expert in fluid mechanics, and the study was under way.

At first, Dr. Stocker and his colleagues assumed that the raspy hairs on a cat's tongue, so useful for grooming, must also be involved in drawing water into its mouth. But the tip of the tongue, which is smooth, turned out to be all that was needed.

The project required no financing. The robot that mimicked the cat's tongue was built for an experiment on the International Space Station, and the engineers simply borrowed it from a neighboring lab.

THE RHETORICAL SITUATION

Purpose

As a science news reporter, Wade's purpose as author of this article is to explain recent findings about how cats drink.

Audience

Wade's audience includes general news readers, online readers, *Times* fans, animal lovers, and science enthusiasts.

Also, as a science journalist, Wade may have his own following, so some readers may be his fans.

Rhetorical appeals

Wade appeals to readers' sense of **ethos** through specific references to the work of four scientists who published an article in the journal *Science*.

He appeals to **pathos** by using humor, especially at the start of the article. He begins with a tongue-in-cheek statement: "It has taken four highly qualified engineers and a bunch of integral equations to figure it out."

He also appeals to readers' sense of logic (**logos**) by beginning with general statements about cats drinking water and then continuing with more specific details.

Modes & media
Mode = written, visual, and video
Wade shares most information in words, but the photos of Cutta Cutta and the video illustrate his most important points (note: scroll down to the video box on the *Times* page). Some news sites, such as *The Huffington Post*, present articles as videos that are introduced by a small amount of text.

Medium = digital
Wade's article was published at *The New York Times* online and also in print. Among the advantages of the digital version of the article are the addition of video and the links to other information, including the researched article that was Wade's source.

Elements of the genre
Well researched and accurate. Wade read a research report in *Science* and talked to the scientists who wrote it. He found out how the research was inspired, funded, and conducted.

Opens with a lead paragraph that sets up the article's subject: "[W]e now know how cats drink."

Presents information in order of importance. Wade begins with the researchers' findings: They discovered how cats drink, something previously unknown. "Cats lap water so fast that the human eye cannot follow what is happening, which is why the trick had apparently escaped attention until now."

Wade ends with information on how the research was funded, something fewer readers will be interested in.

Includes quotations to personalize the experience or information for the reader. The quote from Dr. Stocker shows what inspired his research: "Three and a half years ago, I was watching Cutta Cutta lap over breakfast."

Short paragraphs hold readers' attention.

Style
Neutral/no opinions. Wade doesn't indicate his personal opinion about how cats drink.

Objective, third-person voice. Wade reports what researchers

discovered, leaving himself out of the article. E.g., though he may be a dog owner himself, instead of writing "My dog," he writes "Dog owners are familiar" with the sounds dogs make when they drink.

Just enough detail for the general reader. Wade relates relevant details precisely, such as the formula used to calculate the drinking speed of cats: "The lapping frequency should be the weight of the cat species, raised to the power of minus one-sixth and multiplied by 4.6."

Design
Appealing headline. The title interests readers and conveys the gist of the article in a few words. Also,

the page presents the newspaper's title, the name of the section, and the date of publication.

Byline. Wade's name (rather than "staff writer") appears under the headline, which adds to his ethos.

Friendly typeface. *The New York Times* online uses a clean Georgia serif font designed specifically for easy screen reading.

Columns and chunking. The *Times* divides its Web page into columns—in this case the content and images are in one area; advertising (not shown here) is on the right.

Images and multimedia. A photo of Cutta Cutta gives readers a visual of the cat that inspired

the research, and a series of photos shows how cats drink. A video features the researchers explaining why they decided to study cats drinking.

Sources
Sources are acknowledged. Wade and the *Times* use hyperlinks to acknowledge sources. The names of the four engineers who wrote the report on cats are linked so readers can learn more about them. Linking to sources further conveys Wade's reliability and objectivity.

Questions: Analyzing Wade's news article

1. Purpose. What is Wade's main purpose in writing this article? What are some of his secondary purposes? Identify passages in the article where these purposes are apparent.

2. Purpose. Notice how Wade uses a slightly humorous title for his science- and research-based article. Why does he do this?

3. Audience. How does Wade appeal to people who are not cat lovers?

4. Rhetorical appeals. The online version of Wade's article includes hyperlinks that connect readers with additional information, including a researched article in *Science* and the biographical profiles of the scientists who wrote it, which contributes to the ethos of Wade and his article. How else does Wade convey a sense of ethos?

5. Rhetorical appeals. Cats and kittens can be extremely cute and there are many online videos devoted to celebrating how adorable they can be. How does Wade approach the subject from a different angle? Are there any spots where Wade emphasizes their cuteness? If so, where— and to what end?

6. Modes & media. Do you read news primarily online or do you read print newspapers? Why?

7. Elements of the genre. How does the lead paragraph set the stage for the rest of the article?

8. Style. How does Wade convey scientific information in a way that a general audience can understand? If possible, watch the video embedded in the article. How does its content connect with Wade's article? What stylistic differences, if any, do you see between Wade's writing and the voice-over of the video?

9. Design. Notice that the images and video are neatly lined up on the left side of the article rather than interspersed within the article where they are mentioned. Why did the designers at *The New York Times* lay it out this way?

10. Sources. Make a list of all the sources Nicholas Wade consulted while writing this article. Are there any sources that surprise you? How can you categorize the sources? Are they primary? Secondary? Tertiary? (See Chapter 6.)

Drafting a News Article

CHECKLIST: Drafting a News Article
Thinking of drafting a news article? Ask yourself the following questions.

WHAT'S MY RHETORICAL SITUATION?

☐ **Purpose.** What newsworthy event or issue do I want to report? Of all the people involved with the story, which person will be my focus? How can I bring the story and people to life for my readers?

☐ **Audience.** Who will read my article? How carefully will they read it? Why will they read it? What will they do with the information?

☐ **Rhetorical appeals.** How will I establish my authority as a writer? How will I logically connect ideas and details? How will I make sure that my use of pathos does not undercut my ethos?

☐ **Modes & media.** Will readers experience my article in print form or online? Do I want to include images or videos?

WHAT GENRE CONVENTIONS MATTER?

☐ **Elements of the genre.** Which information is important enough to my readers that I should present it first? Which information is interesting but not as important?

☐ **Style.** How will I keep my tone objective and neutral? What level of detail will I include in my article?

☐ **Design.** How will I use headers and footers, titles, headlines, tabs, and other design features to keep my readers oriented? Will my article appear online? If so, what information will I hyperlink? How might I embed photos or videos into the layout?

☐ **Sources.** How much research will I need to do to compose this article? Are there people I'll need to talk to? Where will I need to go? Will I need to locate documents or records in a library or online?

PRACTICE Want to experiment? Draft your own news article.

Think of an event or issue on your campus that you'd like to report on. Who are the people associated with the event or issue? Arrange to interview at least two of those involved so you can include their voices and perspectives in your article. How will you quote them? What quotes will do the most to bring your article to life? Next, draft a short article for an online newspaper that conveys the big picture of the topic, as well as relevant details that will interest your readers. Be sure to create a catchy headline and to hyperlink to any sources you use (including the people you interview).

PEER-REVIEWED JOURNAL ARTICLES

As a student, you've probably written a research paper or two. When you write research papers in the academic setting, your purpose is to investigate a specific topic, usually by examining what others have already said about it. You begin by drawing on a variety of sources, for example, articles from *EBSCOhost*. The articles from these journals are secondary sources. Once you've gathered your sources, you don't merely report what you've found: You also synthesize, compare, and analyze what has been said. You incorporate the voices of your sources in a systematic way, using quotations, citing sources in the body of your paper (or other composition), and listing them at the end. For some assignments, you might also respond to the sources you've researched by presenting and supporting your own argument. Like most writing, researched writing can also be persuasive. (For more on researched writing, see Chapter 5. For more on persuasive writing, see Chapter 4.)

Research papers do exist outside of the classroom, but they're not usually called "research papers"—and they are usually informed by primary research (that is, research conducted by the writer himself or herself). These papers may be called "articles," "professional researched reports," "scholarly journal articles," or "peer-reviewed journal articles." When we say a work has been "peer-reviewed," we mean that it has been read, critiqued, and approved by other experts/scholars.

Authors of peer-reviewed articles are scholars; they are recognized by other scholars as experts on the subject they're writing about. Many scholars are employed as professors at colleges and universities; others work in research laboratories. Research laboratories can be associated with universities, medical facilities (such as the Mayo Clinic), the government (such as the U.S. Naval Research Laboratory), for-profit organizations (such as Pfizer and other pharmaceutical companies), or nonprofit organizations (such as the Pew Research Center). Research laboratories and centers are sometimes referred to as "think tanks."

The organizations that publish peer-reviewed articles usually do so for a professional audience (rather than general readers). Two examples include *Nature*, a weekly science journal, and the Web site of the American Psychological Association, which compiles scholarly articles. Peer-reviewed articles are often presented at academic conferences, usually to audiences of peers and other experts on the subject.

In these forums, scholars must cite their sources rigorously; a charge of plagiarism can easily end an academic career. The readers of peer-reviewed journal articles are usually other experts in a given field, but might sometimes include more general readers, such as students or other nonexpert readers interested in the topics covered.

> What is the purpose of peer-reviewing? What makes a text authentically peer-reviewed?

> Should a wiki—where content is read and edited by peers—be considered a peer-reviewed source in the same way that a scholarly journal is? Why or why not?

Analyzing Peer-Reviewed Journal Articles: What to Look For

THE RHETORICAL SITUATION

Purpose   Scholars write articles for peer-reviewed journals in order to share their research results with others in the same field. Sometimes scholarly writers present groundbreaking new research, such as a new drug or an alternative energy source. Other times, they present more subtle findings, such as a different way of looking at existing data.

Another purpose of scholarly writers is to persuade readers to see things the way they do. For example, when presenting data, a scholar may want to argue for his or her own particular interpretation of the data. Most scholarly articles are meant to both inform and persuade.

What scholarly journals are related to your major? To what extent do you relate to them as a reader?

Audience   Authors of scholarly articles usually write for a fairly narrow primary audience that includes researchers, professors, and other scholars who want to stay up-to-date in their fields. However, they also have secondary audiences in mind. For example, as a student, you might refer to a scholarly journal article as a source for a research paper. Peer-reviewed journals exist in every academic field, including the sciences, humanities, and social sciences. For example, Amy and Liz both read academic journals such as *College Composition and Communication*, which focuses on teaching and composition; they use *CCC's* journal articles to deepen their own understanding of writing and teaching research. Another example, this one in science, is ▼ *Nature*, the most widely read journal of its kind. For academics needing to keep abreast of major stories in the sciences, reading *Nature* is crucial, as it keeps them informed about new discoveries, developments, and research by other professionals.

ONLINE JOURNAL ▶
***Nature* Homepage.**
Nature is cited by more scientists than any other science journal. *Macmillan.*

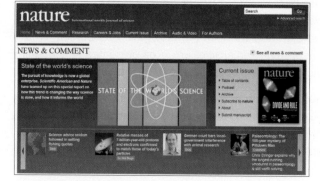

Rhetorical appeals   Scholars who write articles for peer-reviewed journals need to establish ethos by describing their research methods, explaining the data they collected and how they analyzed that information, and discussing their findings and conclusions in detail. They must also cite sources appropriately, taking into account the findings of others. And, because logic is important to scholarship and the writers' audience, writers must appeal to logos by building arguments that rest on tightly organized pieces of evidence and scrupulously researched data. Scholars must keep in mind that their readers will need to be convinced of the legitimacy of their research methods, the accuracy of their data collection, and the logic of their data analysis.

Modes & media   Scholarly articles are text based and may include visuals such as charts, graphs, and images to support and illustrate points. Journals are available in print and, increasingly, online; many articles that originate in print-based journals are available through subscription databases such as *EBSCOhost*, *JSTOR*, and *Project MUSE*. There are also a few scholarly journals that are only available digitally.

THE GENRE'S CONVENTIONS

Elements of the genre

Based on original research—or research of another expert or peer. In a peer-reviewed journal article, scholars usually write about their own original research.

» First, they identify a question that needs to be answered (such as "How does living near a nuclear reactor affect birthrates?").

» Next, they design an experiment or research plan that will allow that question to be studied (for example, identifying nuclear reactors, collecting data on birthrates in the surrounding communities over time, interviewing obstetricians who practice in the surrounding communities, etc.).

» Then, they perform the research, analyze the data gathered in the research, and offer their interpretations in writing. Authors usually refer to related research by other scholars to contextualize their own work.

Reviewed by others in the field for accuracy and reliability. Scholarly articles are written by scholars, for scholars. During a process known as "peer review," other experts in the field review the article to check for clarity and style, but even more important, to make sure the research conducted is a legitimate means of measuring or studying the subject of the article. Peer reviewers might question, for instance, the validity of studying birthrates near nuclear reactors by merely interviewing people who live in the community. They would probably want more rigorous, objective data, such as hospital records documenting pregnancies, fertility rates, and births.

Is thesis-driven. Scholarly authors write to make a point about the research they've conducted—a point that usually has both informative and persuasive elements to it. For example, if an author's point is "drugs X, Y, and Z alleviate symptoms of condition A," she will go on to inform readers of how she drew that conclusion (how she conducted the research and analyzed the data) and will also—if the article is well researched and written—persuade readers that the drugs discussed in the article should be prescribed more often.

Attributes sources/work of others. Scholars who write articles for peer-reviewed journals summarize, paraphrase, and quote from their sources. When writers use other sources (outside of their own original research), they properly document the work/voices of others through in-text citations and Works Cited lists.

Synthesizes sources. Like a student writing a research paper, scholars must synthesize their sources in journal articles. That is, they pull together information across multiple sources to make their points.

Uses formal and precise language. Scholarly writers use formal language to convey the seriousness of their ideas and research. They also use precise language to communicate complex information accurately and in detail. In a scientific research study, the difference between .1 and .01 can be crucial.

Style

Descriptive title. The title of a scholarly article needs to make clear what the article is about. In scientific fields, the more descriptive the better, such as "Hospital Mortality, Length of Stay, and Preventable Complications among Critically Ill Patients before and after Tele-ICU Reengineering of Critical Care Processes" (from *JAMA*). In the humanities, titles often have two parts: an imaginative or creative phrase, followed by a colon, and then a more descriptive phrase, such as "Black, White, and Blue: Racial Politics in B. B. King's Music from the 1960s" (an article by Ulrich Adelt, from *The Journal of Popular Culture*).

Strong, authoritative voice and tone. Authors of scholarly journal articles tend to use an authoritative voice and tone in their scholarly writing, which helps establish their ethos. For example, in "Status Struggles: Network Centrality and Gender Segregation in Same- and Cross-Gender Aggression," an article in *American*

Why do authors of scholarly articles tend to use long, descriptive titles? What are the benefits and drawbacks of such titles?

Sociological Review, authors Robert Faris and Diane Felmlee begin their article in a way that reinforces their expertise and authority:

> Aggression is commonplace in U.S. schools: bullying and other forms of proactive aggression adversely affect 30 percent, or 5.7 million, American youth each school year (Nansel et al. 2001). The National Education Association (1995) estimates that each weekday, 160,000 students skip school to avoid being bullied. This aggression has important consequences. Being victimized by bullies positively relates to a host of mental health problems, including depression (Baldry 2004), anxiety (Sharp, Thompson, and Arora 2000), and suicidal ideation (Carney 2000). —**Robert Faris and Diane Felmlee,** from "Status Struggles: Network Centrality and Gender Segregation in Same- and Cross-Gender Aggression," *American Sociological Review*, February 2011

Use of detail. Authors of scholarly articles use specific details to develop complex ideas. They also use details as evidence to back up their assertions. For example, in the article discussed above, Faris and Felmlee support general statements ("Aggression is commonplace in U.S. schools") with examples and evidence (bullying "affect[s] 30 percent, or 5.7 million, American youth each school year").

Design

Subheadings. Many peer-reviewed journal articles are divided into sections by subheadings that make a long, complex article accessible. Subheadings also signal to the reader when the writer is about to turn his or her focus to another example or another aspect of the topic.

Images. Many scholarly articles include images, such as photos, charts, and illustrations, to convey complex information visually. Those that are published digitally can include hyperlinks to sources and other materials.

Sources

Types of sources used. Scholarly writers must use sources that are authoritative and are appropriate to the topic and approach they've taken. For example, in the peer-reviewed article on page 148, the author draws heavily on movie reviews. This is appropriate because she discusses many films and their popular reception. Movie reviews would not be used for an article on molecular science, unless, for instance, the essay focuses on how molecular science is portrayed in films.

Works Cited list. Scholarly writers include a bibliography at the end of their articles. They list sources in the format dictated by the journal they're publishing in, or according to the format favored in their discipline's professional organization, such as the Modern Language Association (MLA style) and the American Psychological Association (APA style). For more on documentation, see Chapter 7.

For more examples
of **academic writing,**
including student work,
see the Index of Genres on
page G-1.

Sika Dagbovie-Mullins

Mixed-Race Superstars

Sika Dagbovie-Mullins is an assistant professor of English at Florida Atlantic University, where she teaches literature and researches the representation of mixed-race identity in literature and culture. Her article, originally titled "Star-Light, Star-Bright, Star Damn Near White: Mixed-Race Superstars," first appeared in 2007 in *The Journal of Popular Culture*, a scholarly, peer-reviewed journal. The journal, based at Michigan State University and published by the Popular Culture Association, presents the works of scholars in the field as well as in the related areas of literature, film studies, and African American studies. Dagbovie-Mullins's book *Crossing Black: Mixed-Race Identity in Modern American Fiction and Culture* was published in 2013.

ONLINE JOURNAL ▲

The Journal of Popular Culture, where Sika Dagbovie-Mullins published her article. *Courtesy of The Journal of Popular Culture.*

THE JOURNAL OF POPULAR CULTURE

Submissions | Recent Articles | Editorial Board | FAQs | Subscribe | Advertise | Awards

Star-Light, Star-Bright, Star Damn Near White: Mixed-Race Superstars

SIKA DAGBOVIE-MULLINS

In an episode of *The Chris Rock Show*, comedian Chris Rock searches the streets of Harlem to find out what people think of Tiger Woods.[1] When he asks three Asian storekeepers if they consider Woods Asian, one replies, "Not even this much," pressing two of his fingers together to show no space. This comic scene and the jokes that surround Woods's self-proclaimed identity reveal a cultural contradiction that I explore in this essay, namely the simultaneous acceptance and rejection of blackness within a biracial discourse in American popular culture. Though Woods's self-identification may not fit neatly into the black/white mixed-race identity explored in this project, he still falls into a black/white dichotomy prevalent in the United States. The Asian storekeepers agree with Rock's tongue-in-cheek suggestion that Tiger Woods is as black as James Brown, opposing sentiments like "The dude's more Asian than he is anything else" on an Asian American college Internet magazine ("Wang and Woods"). Woods cannot escape blackness (a stereotypical fried-chicken-and-collard-green-eating blackness according to Fuzzy Zoeller), and yet he also represents a multicultural poster boy, one whose blackness pales next to his much-celebrated multi-otherness.[2]

Through advertising, interviews, and publicity, biracial celebrities encode a distinct connection to blackness despite their projected (and sometimes preferred) self-identification. Drawing from Richard Dyer's *Stars*, I read biracial celebrities Halle Berry, Vin

Continues next page

What is the composer, **Sika Dagbovie-Mullins**, doing?

THE RHETORICAL SITUATION

Purpose
Audience
Rhetorical appeals
Modes & media

see page 150

How do I know this is a **peer-reviewed journal** article?

THE GENRE'S CONVENTIONS

Elements of the genre
Style
Design
Sources

see page 150

THE RHETORICAL
SITUATION

Purpose

As the author of
a peer-reviewed
journal article,
Dagbovie-Mullins
aims to inform her
readers of how
biracial celebrities
present their
"blackness." She also
makes an argument
about how American
popular culture both
accepts and rejects
"blackness."

THE GENRE'S
CONVENTIONS

**Elements of the
genre**
**Based on original
research and
research by other
scholars.** Dagbovie-
Mullins examines
the publicity and
representations of
three celebrities. She
acknowledges that
she uses some of the
ideas from another
scholar, Richard
Dyer, as models for
her ideas.

(Continued on p. 152.)

THE JOURNAL OF POPULAR CULTURE

Diesel, and Mariah Carey by analyzing autobiographical representations, celebrity statuses, public reception, and the publicity surrounding each of the representations.[3] Dyer writes, "Stars are, like characters in stories, representations of people. Thus they relate to ideas about what people are (or are supposed to be) like" (*Stars* 22). Recognizing that we can never know how much agency stars have in their image, I acknowledge that biographies or interviews are not necessarily "truths." However, the interviews, career moves (e.g., movie roles or music), public reception, and publicity that I examine all play a part in creating a star's image. I argue that the reception of mixed-race celebrities in popular culture reflects a national inclination to define blackness. While laws have historically defined who is black, social laws also attempted to regulate blackness, ensuring that blacks "kept their place." Similarly, in contemporary popular culture, advertisers and media attempt to define blackness. For mixed-race celebrities, this means blackness is deemed acceptable only when it upholds stereotypical white preconceptions and desires.

During and after slavery, many whites thought that mulattos were intellectually superior to "pure" blacks, a notion that confirmed white supremacy. At the same time, some whites believed mulattos were psychologically unstable, suggesting that even one drop of black blood could lead to mental and other deficiencies. Though mixed-race men were often labeled rapists and murderers, mixed-race women were seen as lascivious seductresses. Some of these same stereotypes reappeared in nineteenth and twentieth century American literature. Sterling Brown was the first to name the literary stereotype the "tragic mulatto." In "Negro Character as Seen by White Authors" he describes the archetype as "a victim of divided inheritance and therefore miserable" (162). The persistence of this stereotype has continued in contemporary popular culture, revealing America's obsession with race mixing and mixed-race bodies. Like census statisticians, America does not know what to do with "mulattos." Historically and today, mixed-race individuals are used to explore, praise, or condemn the "racial unknown."

THE JOURNAL OF POPULAR CULTURE

Though multiracial identity has become a modish identity that white Americans seek, desire, and fetishize, Americans still fear and loathe blackness, marginalizing and criminalizing black bodies. The fascination with mixed-race bodies is metaphorically synonymous to racial slumming in the late 1920s. Kevin Mumford explains, "the influx of white mainstream urbanites . . . temporarily participated in the interzones [black/white sex districts], usually for pleasure, and then returned to their homes and lives apart from the black/white vice districts" (133). Similarly, whites' obsession with black/white mixed-race bodies permits "consumption" of a more palatable form of blackness while allowing whites to return "home" or stay distanced from the supposedly less "attractive" aspects of black identity.

Some mixed-race celebrities are read as black, even when they distance themselves from blackness. Conversely, mixed-race celebrities who claim a black heritage often get labeled as multiracial, not black. In short, the contradictory desires of the American public and media, manifested in a simultaneous disavowal and celebration of mixed race, show both our discomfort and fascination with mixed-race people and their bodies in particular. In the entertainment industry, a star's biracial identity may fade, be tucked away, or even disappear according to audience perceptions and star construction. On the other hand, a mixed-race identity never satisfies. Berry may self-identify as black, yet the media often holds onto her multiracial background. Diesel's desire not to talk about his racial background unsurprisingly fuels more interest. Carey proudly asserts a biracial identity while alternately encoding blackness and "otherness" in the media. Although Berry is distinct from the two other celebrities in her constant embracing of and identification with blackness, the reception of all these celebrities groups them together. The hype surrounding Berry, Diesel, and Carey shows the inconsistencies of America's racial desires over whether to control blackness on the one hand or encourage racial harmony on the other, or perhaps to abandon race altogether. *Continues next page*

THE RHETORICAL SITUATION

Audience

Readers are most likely to be educators, scholars, and/or researchers interested in race, identity, and celebrity. As readers of *The Journal of Popular Culture*, they are already interested in the topics that title suggests—such as film, television, and other areas of pop culture.

Rhetorical appeals

One way the author establishes her **ethos** is by providing a careful cultural analysis of the anecdote from *The Chris Rock Show*.

Dagbovie-Mullins appeals to readers' **logos** by reviewing historical aspects of her topic and using the quotations and source summaries she chooses to logically build toward her conclusion.

Sika Dagbovie-Mullins, *Mixed-Race Superstars*

THE GENRE'S CONVENTIONS

Reviewed by peers.
The Journal of Popular Culture, where the article was published, is a scholarly, peer-reviewed journal based at Michigan State University.

Is thesis-driven.
Dagbovie-Mullins begins by stating the central issue she will address. Her thesis (spread over several sentences) provides her main argument and its consequences.

Identifies and synthesizes sources. The author goes beyond summarizing, paraphrasing, and quoting from sources; she synthesizes them to make a point. E.g., when discussing Halle Berry's role in *Monster's Ball,* she pulls together several sources to make her point.

(Continued on p. 154.)

THE JOURNAL OF POPULAR CULTURE

Claiming Halle Berry: Biracial or Black?

When Halle Berry won the Oscar for Best Actress in 2002, she became more widely recognized as an accomplished black actress. Berry's acceptance speech confirms her racial allegiance: "The moment is so much bigger than me. . . . It's [the Oscar] for every nameless, faceless woman of color that now has a chance because this door tonight has been opened." Despite Berry's claim, competing discourses on her ethnicity consume popular cultural discussions of her. In a 1994 interview with Lisa Jones, Berry makes clear, "I never once announced that I am interracial. I was never the one to bring it up. . . . Yet reporters constantly ask what childhood was like to an interracial person" (Jones "Blacker," 60). Berry consistently identifies as African American, evoking an identity grounded in a black politics. Jones asks Berry if mixed-race children should choose a race. Berry replies, "You've got to identify with one group or the other. It is a political choice" (60). Berry learned this, she claims, from her white mother who advised her to "accept being black, embrace it" (Kennedy 28). Berry's biracial background follows her in her movie roles and public persona, evidenced perhaps in the approval she seems to give to stereotypes of mulatta women. The media's investment in reading Halle Berry within a biracial narrative assures a biracial script both within the movies and in pseudo-liberal discussions of race. She is more easily accepted in a "role," both cinematic and stereotypic, that is familiar to Americans—that of the exotic mixed-race woman.[4]

Donald Bogle's discussion of Dorothy Dandridge is particularly helpful in thinking about Halle Berry. Bogle describes Dandridge as having "the rich golden skin tone that had always fascinated movie audiences, black and white." He continues, "she was a destructive personality, schizophrenic, maddening, euphoric, and self-destructive," all characteristics that define what the tragic mulatta has become: a beautiful, licentious, yet confused and unhappy woman (166). Dandridge's roles in films like *Carmen Jones* (1954), *Island in the Sun* (1957), and *Tamango* (1957)

THE JOURNAL OF POPULAR CULTURE

perpetuated the tragic mulatto stereotype around which her career became centered. Bogle asserts that Dandridge "epitomized the confused, unsatisfied movie star dominated by the publicity and lifestyle that informed her screen image" (174–75). Similarly, *Ego Trip's Big Book of Racism!*, a biting collection of satiric essays and lists, places Berry as number five in its "Top Ten Tragic Mulattos." The media unnecessarily emphasize her biraciality in any description of her misfortunes, including an abusive father and ex-boyfriend, two divorces, and a suicide attempt. The authors of *Ego Trip's* cite Berry's "emotionally wrenching turn as her troubled role model, Dorothy Dandridge" as partial evidence of her "tragic mulatto" status (Jenkins 81).

In an interview with Entertainment Television, Warren Beatty says, "She's a beautiful woman and she's the essence of that biracial thing in America that is so beautiful" ("Halle Berry"). Beatty, who acted with Berry in *Bulworth* (1998), romanticizes mixed-race identity as an American ideal, reducing Berry to the essence of a biracial "thing," no longer an individual but a notion or concept. Praising Berry as a national ideal inadvertently summons the history of black/white mixing in America, namely the sexual abuse of black women by white men during slavery. However, Beatty's comment also suggests a desire to interpret Berry within a "melting pot" framework, one that depoliticizes identity. This rhetoric abounds in multiracial literary interpretations, such as in Maria P. P. Root's assertion that "the accomplishment of complex identities by racially mixed persons gives us the hope that if individuals have been able to resolve conflicting values, claim identities, synthesize multiple heritages, and retain respect for individual heritages . . . perhaps it is possible for us eventually to do this as a nation" (347). Multiracial activists see a mixed-race Berry in the same way they view Tiger Woods, as an indication of racial harmony or what David L. Andrews and C. L. Cole describe as "racially coded celebrations which deny social problems and promote the idea that America has achieved

Continues next page

THE RHETORICAL SITUATION

Modes & media
Mode = written The author's scholarly article is text based (it appears in print and as a PDF online) and includes no images or graphics. Some journals encourage authors to use images and graphics; this is especially true for business and economics journals that publish articles that analyze relationships among factors, and as you might expect, art journals make heavy use of images of the art being discussed. (See "Charts/infographics" on p. 117.)

(Continued on p. 155.)

THE JOURNAL OF POPULAR CULTURE

THE GENRE'S
CONVENTIONS

Documents sources.
The author provides
in-text citations
when drawing on
outside sources.

**Uses formal
language.** The
author's choice
of terms such as
self-proclaimed and
discourse adds to
the serious feel of the
writing.

**Uses precise
language.** For
example, Dagbovie-
Mullins specifies
that *Monster's Ball*
"recycles nineteenth-
century" images,
clarifying that she
sees the film in a
particular historical
context.

Style

Descriptive title.
The author uses the
title to grab attention
and present the gist
of her argument.

**Strong author's
voice.** Dagbovie-
Mullins refers to
many sources but
her voice stays in
control; her voice
doesn't get lost
in the midst of
quotations.

(Continued on p.156.)

its multicultural ideal" (70).[5] Reading Berry in a biracial frame-work falls in line with historical and cinematic representations of mixed-race women and allows a white patriarchal system to prevail under the guise of politically correct rhetoric. In other words, other people define Berry and place her in a category that best satisfies white perceptions of race and mixed race.

The titles of articles on Berry reveal a tendency to read her as a modern day tragic mulatto. "Halle Berry, Bruised and Beautiful, Is on a Mission," "The Beautiful and Damned," "Am I Going to Be Happy or Not?" and even an unauthorized biography entitled *Halle Berry: A Stormy Life* all highlight Berry's troubled personal life, recalling mixed race literary characters whose beauty was rivaled only by their ugly misfortunes. Though the media extol Berry's beauty, their accolades always urge references to her tragic life. Films including *The Flintstones* (1994), *Introducing Dorothy Dandridge* (1999), *X-Men* (2000), *Die Another Day* (2002), and *Monster's Ball* (2002) also subtly accentuate Berry's image as tragic or exotic. In the miniseries *Queen* (1993), Berry plays Alex Haley's grandmother, daughter of a white master and a black slave. The producers stayed "true" to Queen's racial background by choosing Berry for the part and remained loyal to the "tragic mulatress text: Not only does *Queen* drag out mulatto clichés from every B movie and paperback, it luxuriates in them with eerie aplomb" (Jones, *Bulletproof Diva* 50). Yet even Berry's decidedly "monoracial" characters, like the role of Nina (a pro-black "fly girl") in *Bulworth*, repeat a tragic motif. Patricia Williams writes that Berry's role "never rises above the most ancient of clichés" by bordering "black and white," "hope and despair, good and bad, sane and insane; the positive and nega-tive divided by two, multiplied by sex" (11). In the sci-fi comic-book-turned-movie *X-Men*, Berry's character again occupies an "in-between" space. Lynne D. Johnson asserts that Berry's role as Storm in *X-Men* did not surprise, given her mixed racial back-ground: "Though not a tragic mulatto in the classic sense of the myth, being mixed in both the racial and genetic mutation sense

THE JOURNAL OF POPULAR CULTURE

THE RHETORICAL
SITUATION

**Medium = print
and digital** This
piece originally
appeared in both
the print and digital
versions of *The
Journal of Popular
Culture*. Subscribers
to the print journal
automatically get
online access to the
digital version of the
journal, enabling
readers to choose
which medium
they'd prefer to
read an article in
(there are no content
differences between
the versions).
Some journals have
developed apps
for iPads and other
mobile devices that
allow readers to
access the online
version of an article
on the go.

of the word, Storm is representative of this idea." In 2004, Berry played another mutant woman, *Catwoman*, first made famous by biracial actress Eartha Kitt in a 1960s television show. Like Berry's other films, *Catwoman* capitalizes on Berry's reputation as exotic, liminal, and hypersexual.[6]

Berry's casting as Leticia Musgrove in *Monster's Ball* prompted diverse reviews from moviegoers and critics. The reaction from the black community was mixed, mostly due to Berry's casting as a stereotypical black woman in a film that "unfolds like something that was written by Simon Legree, the slave owner in *Uncle Tom's Cabin*. Just hours after they meet, the black woman lustfully seduces the startled white man" (Wickham 15A).[7] While many reviews mention the clichés in *Monster's Ball*, most fail to mention the stereotypical image of black women.[8] Actress Angela Bassett declined the role, she claims, because "I wasn't going to be a prostitute on film. . . . I couldn't do that because it's such a stereotype about black women and sexuality" (Samuels 54). Bassett does not mention the stereotypes of mixed-race women implicit in Berry's portrayal of Leticia, a woman who wants Hank to "heal" her through sex. Here the movie recycles nineteenth-century images of black and mixed-race women as oversexual.[9] More specifically, the movie encourages the myth of mixed-race women "as lewd and lascivious as the men are idle, sensual, and dishonest" (Mencke 102). Though the film does not specifically label Leticia mixed race, her characterization urges such readings. Symbolically, the movie recalls the history of miscegenation yet, more specifically, the movie reinforces general perceptions of Halle Berry as biracial. One reviewer sarcastically claims that the film suggests blacks and whites will get along only when "black women are already half white, already measure up to the white beauty standard," like Halle Berry ("Monster Balls"). Berry's role in *Monster's Ball* speaks to Berry's own tragic mulatto image, and her image never strays far from the "biracial" characters she plays.

Continues next page

THE GENRE'S CONVENTIONS

Authoritative and declarative tone. The author states her case with confidence. She sometimes uses first person to present her ideas as a researcher and scholar.

Use of detail. The author follows her generalizations with specific examples to back up her claims. E.g., she states that "The titles of articles on Berry reveal a tendency to read her as a modern day tragic mulatto" and then provides evidence: "'Halle Berry, Bruised and Beautiful, Is on a Mission,' 'The Beautiful and Damned,' 'Am I Going to Be Happy or Not?' and even an unauthorized biography entitled *Halle Berry: A Stormy Life* all highlight Berry's troubled personal life, recalling mixed race literary characters whose beauty was rivaled only by their ugly misfortunes."

(Continued on p. 158.)

THE JOURNAL OF POPULAR CULTURE

As so many viewers and audiences have lamented, Hollywood representations of blackness have been limited and narrow. Movies have historically slighted actors who are "too black" and, simultaneously, shunned those who are "not black enough." Like Dorothy Dandridge and Lena Horne, Berry has been hindered by her lighter complexion, and sometimes deprived of movie auditions and offers for "black" roles. Berry's manager, Vincent Cirrincione, claims that when Berry auditioned for *Strictly Business* (1991), they told her to "get a tan" (Kennedy 28). Conversely, Cirrincione says other executives have told him "milk is milk until you add a little Hershey. It doesn't matter if you add a little Hershey or a lot" (Kennedy 28). More often than not, Berry does not signify real "blackness." Philip Kerr remarks that in *Monster's Ball*:

> I didn't see a black woman who looked, well, black. Am I the only one to have noticed? Halle Berry—who let's face it, is half-white—made a lachrymose, Oscar-winning thing about being a woman of colour, and yet the reality is that she looks no more like a person of colour than I do. Is it just me, or do most of the black women cast in Hollywood films, with their straight hair, thin lips and cappuccino-coloured skins, look just a little bit white? (Kerr 44)

Kerr's offensive statement uses biology to classify Berry, relying on crude physical descriptions like "straight hair" and "thin lips" to declare Berry "not black." Though Kerr's criticism rightly addresses the prejudice against darker actresses, his critique also suggests a restrictive and monolithic view of blackness. Such physical stereotypes of African Americans neglect the wide array of physical characteristics and skin color within black communities. Berry cannot pass and does not "look" white as Kerr suggests; her physical markings represent those commonly associated with a person of color. That Berry self-identifies as black makes Kerr's statement particularly insulting in terms of his desire to read her as "half-white." The media criminalizes dark skin, associating darkness with poverty, ignorance, and physical ugliness. Cannot Leticia be poor, desperate, downtrodden, and still light skinned? Aside

THE JOURNAL OF POPULAR CULTURE

from presenting narrow-minded views on race, Kerr's description shows that the public and critics invest in Berry's "whiteness."

Public discourses about Berry belabor her looks when referring to her celebrity allure. Charlie Kanganis, who directed Berry in *Race the Sun* (1996), compares Berry with "a double espresso machiatto, a dollop of shapely foam, a shower of cinnamon and cocoa." No other actress in "Cinema and the Female Star," a collection of reflections and tributes to actresses, is so objectified. Warren Beatty claims that people laugh when they first see Berry because "they don't know how else to react. They're not used to someone that beautiful." Literary descriptions of mixed-race women in early American fiction suggest a similar exceptional, almost unreal beauty. In Charles Chesnutt's *The House Behind the Cedars* (1900), John, not yet recognizing Rena as his sister, describes her as "strikingly handsome, with a stately beauty seldom encountered" (7). These characterizations imply a uniqueness associated with mixed race that persists in popular culture. Lynn Hirschberg claims that Berry's beauty is "actually distracting; the perfection of her face would not seem to allow anything less than a perfect life" (26). Would people review Berry's beauty in the same way if she were "just black" (and not "biracial")? She represents the supposed mystique of mixed-race people, alluring because they symbolize a social taboo. Her image represents "black" and "not black," which unsettles and entices. A *Time* article begins, "Is it a curse to be beautiful?" continuing a familiar rhetoric about Berry's looks, one that intensified after *Monster's Ball*. Descriptions of Berry's beauty intimate what has become a common boasting on numerous multiracial Web sites—that mixed-race people are "prettier." This notion gets directly and indirectly repeated in advertisements and magazines that use models who physically represent racial mixture. The point here is not to judge or critique Berry's beauty, but rather to examine why it attracts so much attention. Berry cannot be taken out of a historical context of mixed-race beauty images. Her image reflects back the fantasy that makes Americans both anxious and envious.

Continues next page

THE GENRE'S
CONVENTIONS

Details help readers
understand her
research and
evaluate the validity
of her conclusions.

Design

The author's name
and article title
appear at the top of
the page. The author
uses subheadings
to organize her
article into digestible
chunks. In addition
to a Works Cited list,
the author provides
notes to give readers
more details.

Sources

Dagbovie-Mullins
uses sources
appropriate to her
topic and audience,
including movie
reviews, because
she discusses
representations
in film. She cites
sources (as in-text
citations) in the body
of the paper and lists
these sources in the
Works Cited list at
the end. She uses
MLA documentation
style, which is the
style favored by *The
Journal of Popular
Culture*, where her
article appears.

THE JOURNAL OF POPULAR CULTURE

Multiracial to the Rescue: Vin Diesel

When Tiger Woods gained notoriety, he was proclaimed the new
multiracial face of America. Andrews and Cole maintain that
Woods represents the "latest in America's imagined realization
of its ideals (agency, equality, responsibility, and freedom) and its
imagined transformed sense of national self (America has become
the world that came to it)" (73). Yet Vin Diesel's recent explosion in Hollywood has introduced an even "better" Tiger Woods,
because unlike Woods, Diesel refuses to name himself racially.
Diesel, a self-described "mystery man," represents an amalgama-
tion of all races, literally in his racial ambiguity and symbolically
in his equally racially vague movie roles. In short, he is "everyman." His image enacts America's desired "other": multiracial,
de-politicized, and lacking any serious racial allegiance.

When asked about his background, Diesel firmly describes himself
as "multicultural." Diesel's name change from Mark Vincent
to Vin Diesel seems to corroborate his racial ambiguity or at
least encourage a multiracial reading of this ethnicity as "Vin"
is a stereotypical Italian American name. ("Diesel" refers to the
slang term, "cock diesel," describing a man's muscular physique.)
Diesel explains that this nickname emerged when he worked as
a bouncer: "We all had nicknames. It was wonderful to detach
a little bit" (Tesoriero 61). As an actor, Diesel appears to detach
from any racial group. Rumors abound about his Italian mother
and African American father, but he maintains, "I want to keep
my mystery" (Kirkland). Diesel denies "hiding anything": "It's not
that I don't want people to know anything. It's just that I would
rather spend more time talking about more productive things
that relate to the film [*XXX*]" (Kirkland). Diesel's silence seems a
strategic response not just to advertisers but also to the broader
cultural pattern that advertisers respond to, namely multiculturalism. One advertising executive asserts, "Both in the mainstream
and at the high end of the marketplace, what is perceived as good,
desirable, successful is often a face whose heritage is hard to pin

THE JOURNAL OF POPULAR CULTURE

down" (La Ferla). Diesel confirms what Danzy Senna jokingly calls "mulatto fever," telling one reporter that his "ambiguous, chameleon-like ethnicity" is "cool" (Thrupkaew). His production company, One Race, enforces his raceless image, reminiscent of Jean Toomer's early twentieth century proclamation, "I am at once no one of the races, and I am all of them." Diesel's explanation of his racial background captures how his image reflects America's desire for ethnic homogeneity. He presents no controversy and gives no reminders of black/white miscegenation.

Diesel's relationship with the black community seems dubious considering his reticence to claim any identity. Samuel Jackson, who stars with Diesel in *XXX*, tells *People Weekly*, "There's an air of mystery and danger about Vin, but he also has a little bit of the just-like-us quality" ("XXX Appeal" 87). Perhaps "just-like-us" speaks to the African American colloquial belief, "we know our own." Jackson's comments imply Diesel's blackness ("just-like-us") but also suggest his multiracial background ("air of mystery"). Despite claiming a nebulous "multicultural" description, Diesel has been somewhat accepted by the black community, at least superficially in terms of his appearances as a presenter at the 2002 NAACP Image Awards and his inclusion in *Ebony*'s 2003 top Black moneymakers list. This acceptance is, however, limited. A forum on bet.com (Black Entertainment Television) which posed the following question, "If Vin Diesel has any Black heritage, should he claim it publicly?" and articles such as "Outing Diesel" repeat a familiar resentment with celebrities who do not outwardly claim the black community (Hill). Still, that Diesel's refusal to acknowledge (or disclaim) blackness (or any race) has incited less anger and uproar than Tiger Woods's self-termed "Cablinasian" perhaps speaks to America's desire to forget about racial divisions. Similarly, publicity surrounding Vin Diesel exposes America's desires to be like Diesel, "of no particular place, and at the same time, able to be anywhere and be anything" (Iverem).

Continues next page

THE JOURNAL OF POPULAR CULTURE

Diesel's recent movies, with their over-the-top action and "heroes" of superhuman strength, seem geared toward teenagers. Diesel says he claims a "multicultural" identity because of his young audience: "I support the idea of being multicultural primarily for all the invisible kids, the ones who don't fit into one ethnic category and then find themselves lost in some limbo" (Iverem). Homi Bhabha contends that "the multicultural has itself become a 'floating signifier' whose enigma lies less in itself than in the discursive uses of it to mark social processes where differentiation and condensation seem to happen almost synchronically" (31). Diesel represents Bhabha's explication of the multicultural. The celebration over his fame both depends upon his difference as "Hollywood's new superhero: a self-made man unconfined by racial categories" (Thrupkaew) and his ability to relate to Americans as "multiethnic Everyman, a movie star virtually every demographic can claim as its own" (Svetkey). Diesel is a floating signifier, and, as *Boiler Room* director Ben Younger claims, "People seem to make him into whatever they want him to be" (Svetkey). Unlike Berry who cannot "pass," Diesel's racially uncertain physical characteristics allow him to pass as various ethnicities in his movies. For example, he plays an Italian in *Saving Private Ryan* (1998) and in *The Fast and the Furious* (2001), and a racially ambiguous person in *Boiler Room* (2000), *Pitch Black* (2000), and *The Chronicles of Riddick* (2004). While critics have charged Diesel with passing, others applaud his savvy marketing skills. Diesel admits, "Being multicultural has gone from the Achilles' heel of my career to my strength." He describes the world as a "big melting pot," deducing that "people are ready for a hero who is more ambiguous" (Thrupkaew).

XXX's advertising refers to its main character, Xander Cage, as "a new breed of secret agent," a seemingly intentional though oblique reference to Diesel's mixed-race background and his emergence in a genre once dominated by now outdated white action stars like Arnold Schwarzenegger, Sylvester Stallone, and Bruce Willis (White). Similar descriptions follow Diesel, naming him a new

THE JOURNAL OF POPULAR CULTURE

"multicultural hero" (Mora) and the "first truly All-American action hero" (White). Director Rob Cohen (*XXX* and *The Fast and the Furious*) maintains, "It has taken America a long time to acknowledge the new face of America . . . and to some degree, Vinny is that new face" (Kirkland). Such descriptions recall *Time*'s 1993 special issue cover, "The New Face of America," featuring a future mixed race, computer-made American woman. Suzanne Bost argues that *Time*'s female creation "charms . . . and yet she is taboo, bloodless, impure" (1). Lauren Berlant suggests that "new faces" like the *Time* cover respond to "problems of immigration, multiculturalism, sexuality, gender, and trans(national) identity that haunt the U.S." (398). What does it mean that this new representative (noncomputerized) face is a man, a "He-man" no less? Diesel's image, in part created through his movie roles, represents America's assimilation and capitalist impulses. In other words, his image encourages the idea that race is a commodity that people can trade, buy, or sell, virtually "e-racing" national histories of racialization. Henry Giroux writes, "National identity in the service of a common culture recognizes cultural differences only to flatten them out in the conservative discourse of assimilation and the liberal appeal to tolerance" (182). The suggestion that Diesel stands for "everyman" attempts to create a national identity that eliminates difference. Santiago Pozo, CEO of Arenas Entertainment, tells *Time*, "In the past, John Wayne and Jimmy Stewart were the face of America. . . . Today it's The Rock or Vin Diesel" (Tesoriero 61). Such a comparison suggests that biracial celebrities like The Rock or Diesel evoke a "multiracial sameness," a sugar pill oxymoron that ends up surreptitiously recentering white normative American identity.

Mariah Carey as Biracial Fantasy

If Halle Berry is America's prized mulatta, then Mariah Carey is her lascivious tragic sister. Carey's image depends on her exploitation of the mulatta stereotype.[10] On the one hand, she represents

Continues next page

THE JOURNAL OF POPULAR CULTURE

the alienated racial outsider in songs such as "Outside" (from the *Butterfly* album) where she bemoans the difficulties of not belonging. On the other hand, she exploits the notion of the racially ambiguous seductress, wearing next to nothing in music videos and publicity photos. Since Carey's self-titled debut album in 1990, she has publicly performed various "roles" including white ingenue, biracial outsider, black hiphopper, and erotic/exotic "other." Kate Lanier, a script-writer for Carey's film, *Glitter* (2002), asserts that "a lot of mixed-race girls and young women . . . hold Mariah up as a hero." Lanier claims this makes Carey "proud" because "for a long time she was encouraged to play up her white side. Since she has been allowed creative freedom, she has related more to black culture" (Beller 13). Carey's image both deflects and confirms blackness, creating an "in-between" status she teases in terms of her racialized sexuality. She wears biracial stereotypes like a black-face "costume," allowing audiences to explore racial and sexual fantasies while maintaining racial stereotypes.

Music reviews and articles have paid close attention to Carey's overt sexuality and racial shifts in a popular culture context. Vincent Stephens observes: "Along with genre changes, Carey has taken on a more sexualized visual persona and has become more outspoken about her multiracial heritage and struggles for artistic freedom" (234). Caroline Streeter sees Carey "transform[ing] from white to black before our very eyes" (311). Indeed, Carey's album covers trace her shifting racial movements from what Lisa Jones calls "a rainbow body of African descent, skin toasted almond and hair light brown" to her current whitewashed blond pin-up look (*Bulletproof Diva* 200). While other ethnic stars such as Jennifer Lopez or Beyoncé sport blond hair, Carey's hair transformation seems particularly racially motivated considering the initial marketing of Carey that concealed her blackness. In 1990, music critics labeled Carey a "white Whitney Houston" until outside pressures prompted her record company to make a statement. Carey cleared up misconceptions at a press confer-

THE JOURNAL OF POPULAR CULTURE

ence where she declared, "My father is black and Venezuelan. My mother is Irish and an opera singer. I am me" (Jones *Bulletproof Diva* 197). Following Carey's public disclosure, black publications ran articles such as "Mariah Carey Tells Why She Looks White but Sings Black" and "Mariah Carey: Not Another White Girl Trying to Sing Black," seemingly attempting to assure black audiences that Carey was not trying to pass or disregard her black ancestry. However, Carey's later physical transformation suggests an effort to depart visually from "black" and to reflect white standards of beauty.

Despite publicly claiming a multiracial heritage, Carey admits that her physical hints of blackness made her self-conscious. Recalling her *Butterfly* (1997) album cover, Carey shares that she felt pressured to cover up her face "because I had been told I looked horrible and too ethnic with my face showing" (Grigoriadis 194). As Carey's hair turns straighter and blonder, she increasingly signifies "whiteness" while contradictorily maintaining a position as ethnic "other" vis-a-vis her public assertions of biracialism. Richard Dyer suggests that "blondeness is racially unambiguous" and "the ultimate sign of whiteness" (*Heavenly Bodies* 44, 43). Carey represents a racial anomaly because her image simultaneously projects different racial tropes. These competing discourses establish Carey in a biracial narrative that depends upon her liminality.

Musically, Carey has moved from pop to hip-hop, in some ways a symbolic shift from white to black. After Carey divorced then Sony Music president Tommy Mottola, her music and image changed drastically. Carey claims that her *Butterfly* album symbolizes her feelings of personal and professional freedom impelled by her divorce. As she explained it in 1997, "I feel more free to put more of myself into my music" (Thigpen 113). With *Butterfly*, Carey has worked with more hip-hop artists and producers to tap into her "broad demographic." As she observes, "I have an audience that's urban and one that's Middle America." She continues, "So I have to really be a little bit conscious of the fact that

Continues next page

THE JOURNAL OF POPULAR CULTURE

it's broad, and also it's diverse in terms of the racial thing. I am anyway, being a mixed person racially" (Carey, Interview with Dimitri Ehrlich 338). On *Rainbow* (1999), Carey collaborated with hip-hop artists and rappers including Jay-Z, Usher, Da Brat, Missy Elliott, and Snoop Dogg. Carey's earlier albums *Mariah Carey* (1990), *Emotions* (1991), and *Daydream* (1995) demonstrated her penchant for love ballads and cross-over pop songs, save for Carey's "Dreamlover" remix with Ol' Dirty Bastard on *Daydream*. Earlier albums also feature Carey in her pre-blonde days, suggesting that Carey's physical transformation heightened after she professionally embraced black culture. In a 2002 MTV interview Carey revealed, "Most of my friends and most of the music I listen to and most of my influences are R&B and hip-hop" ("Mariah Carey: Shining Through the Rain"). Still, Carey's most hip-hop albums visually emphasize her whiteness, such as *Charmbracelet* which shows her with platinum streaks.

Carey constructs a stereotypical mulatta trope in public discussions of her biraciality. Inside the *Rainbow* CD liner Carey's message to fans expresses her desire for people of all races and hues to live with one another happily and without conflict. Her words both reveal her vision of racial unity and explain why multiracial organizations herald her as an ideal biracial "spokesperson." In "My Saving Grace" Carey positions herself as tragic, discussing how during her childhood she felt confused and suffered from low self esteem due to her mixedness. In general, she laments over the media's and public's obsession with her racial identity yet openly discusses her feelings of racial alienation and isolation. She shares always feeling "so separate from everybody, even if I never talked about it" (Udovitch 34). She attributes this alienation to various reasons: "Because my father's black and my mother's white. Because I'm very ambiguous-looking." Carey has claimed multiple descriptors including "person of color" and the glib, "I view myself as a human being" (Farley 75). Yet despite Carey's supposed desires to put the issue of her racial

THE JOURNAL OF POPULAR CULTURE

background to rest, she often brings it up in interviews and has appeared on national shows like *Oprah* to discuss such issues. In an *Oprah* show entitled "Mariah Carey Talks to Biracial Teens," Carey announces herself as somewhat of a multiracial nationalist, claiming, "I bond with mixed people" (7). Yet, Carey frequently exploits biracial stereotypes, betraying her role model status.

Carey's hypersexuality intensifies as she encodes "whiteness" via her album covers and "blackness" via her music, symbolically evoking the "warring" racial divisions and libidinous nature of the mulatta stereotype. Magazine photos play up her sexuality so that her overall image combines multiple representations: mulatta sex kitten, black performer, and white pin-up. However, Carey and her music are not considered "black" in the same way, for example, that Mary J. Blige represents "blackness." And physically, Carey is too ethnic to be a white sex symbol. The result places Carey in an in-between, mixed-race seductress narrative. For example, the *Rainbow* CD liner opens up to reveal a photo which exploits Carey as a heterosexual male fantasy: she suggestively lies on a bed in white cotton underclothes, wearing stiletto heels and licking a heart-shaped lollipop. A nearby phone lying off the hook may suggest Carey's possible roles as phone sex operator or prostitute. Magazine photos of Carey (as in *Vibe* March 2003) (Ogunnaike) are not just revealing, but border on soft porn. In one photo she wears a trench coat, partly opened to reveal her naked body. Another frames Carey lying on a couch, one hand on her breast, the other suggestively positioned below her stomach. Still another shows Carey in an unzipped miniskirt and unzipped midriff top, suggestively looking downwards at her skirt. While many pop stars like Christina Aguilera and Britney Spears also wear skimpy and sexy clothing, Carey's provocative style of dress is coupled with a publicized troubled multiracial identity, making her sexuality fetishized and tragic. Tellingly, Carey cites Marilyn Monroe, a star whose name virtually equaled sex in the 1950s and who began her career as a pin-up, as the

Continues next page

THE JOURNAL OF POPULAR CULTURE

person she most admires.[11] Not surprisingly, Barbara Walters symbolically likens the two, calling Carey "a soldier's pin-up girl come to life" while describing her Kosovo trip to visit U.S. troops (Carey, "Surviving the Glare").

Carey's semi-autobiographical box office failure, *Glitter*, confirms her racialized sexuality despite its attempts to critique biracial clichés. In one scene the music video director explains his idea for the main character's video: "She is not black, she is not white, she is exotic, OK?" This same theme follows representations of Carey's public and private life. In July 2001, Carey appeared on MTV's *Total Request Live* (*TRL*) pushing an ice-cream cart in a "Loverboy" (the name of *Glitter*'s first single) T-shirt and heels. She proceeded to perform a pseudo striptease, taking off her T-shirt to reveal a hidden skimpy outfit. Entertainment reporters and tabloids ridiculed Carey for her bizarre behavior and incoherent ramblings to *TRL* host, Carson Daly. Accordingly, *Ego Trip's Big Book of Racism!* comically named Carey their number one "Tragic Mulatto" for, among other things, "a propensity for 'whorelike attire,' a nervous breakdown, a mocked and derided cinematic debut, and a failed soundtrack" (Jenkins 81). Such descriptions urge the question, what role does Carey have in sexualizing her image? Carey reports feeling "constantly amazed" regarding her portrayal as "very loose morally and sexually," an ironic statement considering that Carey invites such readings in nearly all recent publicity photos and public outings ("Mariah Carey Discusses" 58). Though we can never know how much agency stars exert over their image, Carey seems to perpetuate wittingly an oversexual public persona. She represents a historically comfortable vision of mixed race women. Carey poses little threat to racial hierarchy because she fits a mold that showcases just enough "blackness" to intrigue but not enough to appear definitive or political.

THE JOURNAL OF POPULAR CULTURE

New Faces, Old Masks

The media commodifies biracialism by using "new" celebrity faces: Diesel's movie posters that target a younger, more multicultural and multiracial generation and Carey's seemingly produced and packaged embodiment of the mulatta seductress in videos, albums, and magazines. Despite Berry publicly announcing a black identity, her image still "sells" biracialism through media representations of her life and less obviously via her stereotyped movie roles. In this sense, all three stars symbolically represent the "multiracial neutral" in that their images "sell" the idea of racial pluralism and freedom, and yet their images remain "Other," available for audiences and consumers of all racial backgrounds to "claim" or "own." The popularity of these stars does not reflect a more racially tolerant or progressive America. Like the cliché "some of my best friends are black," which attempts to prove a supposed lack of racism, the multiracial craze only superficially embraces the dark "Other." Liberals and conservatives alike have repeatedly placed idealistic expectations on mixed-race individuals in discussions of racism and multiculturalism. Though expectations differ, this pattern gets repeated in a popular culture context with mixed-race stars. Thus, Tiger Woods is not just a superb athlete of color, but an emblem of racial harmony, the Great Multiracial Hope. When stars' images do not fit our vision, we force them into familiar stereotypes that satisfy other expectations. Halle Berry's image may not represent racial unity, but at least it does not depart from what we have learned to expect from mixed-race women. In a popular culture context, biraciality "works" for people who do not really want to confront racial issues when it exploits difference under the guise of celebrating diversity. The "new" faces of America have no racial responsibilities, loyalties, or obligations. People admire them for their beauty, celebrate them as America's future, and envy their "cool" multiracial status. However, old masks lurk alongside interpretations of what new faces represent, namely racial stereotypes. Until power relations equalize, any celebration of mixed race needs to recognize those who are not celebrating or benefiting from

Continues next page

Sika Dagbovie-Mullins, *Mixed-Race Superstars*

THE JOURNAL OF POPULAR CULTURE

America's longtime fascination. Questioning what it means to be black or part-black allows one to be critical of traditional assumptions about racial identification and realize the urgency of racial responsibility in a society built upon racial inequality.

NOTES

1. See *Best of the Chris Rock Show*.

2. In 1997, golfer Fuzzy Zoeller made a racist joke during the 62nd Masters golf tournament in Augusta, Georgia. He reportedly joked that he hoped fried chicken and collard greens would not be served at the next year's tournament should Tiger win and choose the menu.

3. My essay focused on these particular celebrities because they have represented multiple racial tropes in popular culture and in their work. Their immense popularity, I argue, is also connected to their "otherness." These stars differ from other biracial stars, such as Alicia Keys, whose blackness often foregrounds their public image. This essay was written after Mariah Carey's 2002 album and after Vin Diesel's and Halle Berry's 2004 films.

4. In his classic book, *Toms, Coons, Mulattoes, Mammies, and Bucks*, Donald Bogle examines the persistence of these five common stereotypes of African Americans on film. Bogle cites *The Debt* (1912) as one of the earliest film representations of the tragic mulatto. Like the literary stereotype, the mulatta on film was often near white, exceedingly beautiful, exotic, and doomed as a result of her mixed race.

5. Such perceptions abound in Web sites and often show up in online discussions, particularly following Berry's Oscar speech, which angered many people who self identify as multiracial. For example, responding to a post in a "Moms of Biracial Children" forum, one woman writes, "I didn't watch the awards but it's pretty sad that she had to put a label on the [Black] community she was thanking. . . . It's comments like that continues the separatism of races." Another respondent writes, "My daughter a beautiful little girl loves Halle Berry and couldn't understand why she only said she was black. I think it was a very confusing statement." See "Did Halle Berry Forget Her Mom Is White?" for other postings.

6. Continuing her portrayal of "liminal" characters, Berry says she is preparing for a movie entitled *The Guide*, playing "a spiritual woman—half Native American, half African-American—who guides people through times of crisis" (Ritz 128). Most recently, she portrayed Zora Neale Hurston's mixed-race character, Janie, in Oprah Winfrey's television rendition of *Their Eyes Were Watching God*.

7. See, for example, the online discussion, "Bassett: 'Monster' Role Was Demeaning."

8. For a sample of reviews on *Monster's Ball*, see Roger Ebert, Leslie Felperin, Lisa Schwarzbaum, and Stephanie Zacharek.

THE JOURNAL OF POPULAR CULTURE

9. In *Ar'n't I a Woman?: Female Slaves in the Plantation South*, Deborah Gray White argues that the jezebel stereotype that emerged during slavery was used to justify the sexual exploitation of black women. The stereotype suggested that black women were promiscuous and invited rape and sexual abuse.

10. Ironically, an April 2005 *Essence* article on Mariah Carey begins, "This 'mulatto' is hardly tragic" (121). See Joan Morgan.

11. See "All Mariah" on Carey's homepage (http://www.mariahcarey.com).

Works Cited

"All Mariah." *Mariah*. Web. 19 Mar. 2004. <http://www.monarc.com/mariahcarey/allm/index.asp>.

Andrews, David L., and C. L. Cole. "America's New Son: Tiger Woods and America's Multiculturalism." *Sport Stars: The Cultural Politics of Sporting Celebrity*. Ed. David L. Andrews and Steven J. Jackson. New York: Routledge, 2001. 70–86. Print.

"Bassett: 'Monster' Role Was Demeaning." Online discussion forum. The Black Web Portal Forum. Web. 28 Mar. 2004. <http://www.blackwebportal.com/forums/viewmessages.cfm?Forum=5&Topic= 1872>.

Beller, Thomas. "The New M.C." *Elle* July 2001: 109+. Print.

Berlant, Lauren. "The Face of America and the State of Emergency." *Disciplinarity and Dissent in Cultural Studies*. Ed. Carey Nelson and Dilip Parameshwar Gaonkar. New York: Routledge, 1996. 397–439. Print.

Berry, Halle, as told to David A. Keeps. "Halle Berry Dishes the Dirt." *Marie Claire* Feb. 2002: 52–59. Print.

Best of the Chris Rock Show. HBO, 1999. DVD.

Bhabha, Homi K. "Culture's in Between." *Multicultural States: Rethinking Difference and Identity*. Ed. David Bennett. London: Routledge, 1998. 29–36. Print.

Bogle, Donald. *Toms, Coons, Mulattoes, Mammies, and Bucks*. New York: Continuum, 2003. Print.

Bost, Suzanne. *Mulattas and Mestizas: Representing Mixed Identities in the Americas, 1850–2000*. Athens, GA: University of Georgia Press, 2005. 1. Print.

Continues next page

THE JOURNAL OF POPULAR CULTURE

Brown, Sterling B. "Negro Character as Seen by White Authors." *Journal of Negro Education* 2 Apr. 1933: 201. Print.

Carey, Mariah. "Outside." *Butterfly*. Columbia, 1997.

———. *Rainbow*. Columbia, 1999. CD.

———. Interview with Dimitri Ehrlich. *Interview*. Oct. 1999. 338–39. Print.

———. "My Saving Grace." *Charmbracelet*. Island Def Jam, 2002. CD.

———. "Surviving the Glare: Celebrities Who Prevailed After Scandal." Interview with Barbara Walters. *20/20*. ABC. 9 May 2002. Television.

Chambers, Veronica. "Mariah on Fire." *Newsweek* 15 Nov. 1999: 80–81. Print.

Chesnutt, Charles W. *The House Behind the Cedars*. New York: Modern Library, 2003. 7. Print.

Corliss, Richard. "Halle Berry: Monster's Ball." *Time* 21 Jan. 2002: 124–25. Print.

"Did Halle Berry Forget Her Mom Is White?" Online posting. 11 Sept. 2000. "Moms of Biracial Children." Commitment.com. Web. 23 Feb. 2004. <http://www.commitment.com/boards/boardMB/MBbrmsgs/142.html>.

Dyer, Richard. *Stars*. London: British Film Institute, 1979. Print.

———. *Heavenly Bodies: Film Stars and Society*. New York: St. Martin's Press, 1986. Print.

Ebert, Roger. Rev. of *Monster's Ball*. Dir. Marc Forster. *Chicago Sun-Times* 1 Feb. 2002. Web. 1 Mar. 2004. <http://www.suntimes.com/ebert/ebert_reviews/2002/02/020101/html>.

Farley, Christopher John. "Pop's Princess Grows Up." *Time* 25 Sept. 1995: 75. Print.

Felperin, Leslie. Rev. of *Monster's Ball*. Dir. Marc Forster. *Sight and Sound* June 2002 sec. 12.6: 46. Print.

Giroux, Henry A. "The Politics of National Identity and the Pedagogy of Multiculturalism in the USA." *Multicultural States: Rethinking Difference and Identity*. Ed. David Bennett. London: Routledge, 1998. 178–94. Print.

THE JOURNAL OF POPULAR CULTURE

Glitter. Dir. Vondie Curtis-Hall. Twentieth Century Fox, 2001. Film.

Grigoriadis, Veronica. "The Money Honey." *Allure* Sept. 2001: 190+. Print.

"Halle Berry." *Road to the Red Carpet*. Entertainment Television. 3 May 2003. Television.

Haynes, Esther. "Am I Going to Be Happy or Not?" *Jane* Dec. 2003: 126–28. Print.

Hill, James. "'Outing' Diesel." Bet.com. 2 Aug. 2002. Web. 4 Mar. 2004. <http://www.bet.com.articles/o,,c3gb3453-4121,00.html>.

Hirschberg, Lynn. "The Beautiful and Damned." *New York Times Magazine* 23 Dec. 2001: 26. Print.

Iverem, Esther. "A Monster Love." Rev. of *Monster's Ball*. Dir. Marc Forster. 21 Feb. 2002. *Seeing Black*. Web. 26 Feb. 2004. <http://www.seeingblack.com/x022102/monstersball.shtml>.

Jenkins, Sacha, Elliott Wilson, Chairman Jefferson Mao, Gabriel Alvarez, and Brent Rollins. *Ego Trip's Big Book of Racism!* New York: Regan Books, 2002. Print.

Johnson, Lynne D. "Bearing the Black Female Body as Witness in Sci-Fi." 1 Dec. 2003. *Pop Matters*. Web. 1 Mar. 2004. <http://www.popmatters.com/columnsjohnson/031218.shtml>.

Jones, Lisa. "The Blacker the Berry." *Essence* June 1994: 60+. Print.

———. *Bulletproof Diva: Tales of Race, Sex, and Hair*. New York: Doubleday, 1994. Print.

Kanganis, Charlie. "Halle Berry." *Senses of Cinema*. 23 Nov./Dec. 2002. Web. 1 Mar. 2004. <http://www.sensesofcinema.com/contents/02/23/symposium1.html#berry>.

Kennedy, Dana. "Halle Berry, Bruised and Beautiful, Is on a Mission." *New York Times* 10 Mar. 2002: 2A+. Print.

Kerr, Philip. "A Shocking Cheek." *New Statesman* 17 June 2002: 44. Print.

Kirkland, Bruce. "Word's Out: Vin's In." *Toronto Sun*. 4 Aug. 2004. Web. 4 Mar. 2004. <http://www.canoe.ca/JamMoviesArtistsD/diesel_vin.html>.

La Ferla, Ruth. "Generation E.A.: Ethnically Ambiguous." *New York Times* 28 Dec. 2003, sec. 9: 1+. Print.

Continues next page

THE JOURNAL OF POPULAR CULTURE

"Mariah Carey Discusses Her Sex Life, Race, Career." *Jet* 31 May 2000: 56–60. Print.

"Mariah Carey: Shining Through the Rain." Interview with John Norris. MTV. 3 Dec. 2002.

"Mariah Carey Talks to Biracial Teens." *Oprah*. ABC. 27 Dec. 1999. Transcript.

"Mariah Carey Tells Why She Looks White but Sings Black." *Jet* 3 Apr. 1991: 56–57. Print.

Mencke, John G. *Mulattoes and Race Mixture: American Attitudes and Images, 1865–1918*. Ann Arbor: Umi Research Press, 1979. Print.

"Monster Balls." Rev. of *Monster's Ball*, dir. Marc Forster. Metaphilm. Web. 29 Feb. 2004 <http://www.metaphilm.com/philms/monstersball.html>.

Mora, Renee Scolaro. Rev. of *XXX*, dir. Rob Cohen. *Pop Matters* 9 Aug. 2002. Web. 16 Feb. 2004 <http://www.popmatters.com/film/reviews/x/xxx.shtml>.

Morgan, Joan. "Free at Last." *Essence* Apr. 2005: 118–24. Print.

Mumford, Kevin J. *Interzones: Black/White Sex Districts in Chicago and New York in the Early Twentieth Century*. New York: Columbia University Press, 1997. Print.

Norment, Lynn. "Mariah Carey: Not Another White Girl Trying to Sing Black." *Ebony* Mar. 1991: 54–58. Print.

Ogunnaike, Lola. "Through the Fire." *Vibe* Mar. 2003: 113–20. Print.

Pappademas, Alex. "Over the 'Rainbow': A Tale of Two Mariahs." *Boston Phoenix*. 22 Nov. 1999. Web. 24 Mar. 2004 <http://weeklywire.com/ww/11-22-99/boston_music_2.html>.

Prince. "Controversy." *Controversy*. Warner Bros., 1981. CD.

Ritz, David. "Heart to Heart." *Essence* Dec. 2002: 128+. Print.

Root, Maria P. P. "From Shortcuts to Solutions." *Racially Mixed People in America*. Ed. Maria P. P. Root. Newbury Park: Sage, 1992. 342–47. Print.

Samuels, Allison. "Angela's Fire." *Newsweek* 1 July 2002: 54. Print.

Sanello, Frank. *Halle Berry: A Stormy Life*. London: Virgin Books, 2003. Print.

THE JOURNAL OF POPULAR CULTURE

Schwarzbaum, Lisa. Rev. of *Monster's Ball*. *Entertainment Weekly* 25 Jan. 2002. 2 Mar. 2004. EBSCO.

Stephens, Vincent. Rev. of *Rainbow*. *Popular Music & Society* Summer 2003, sec. 26.2: 234–35. Print.

Streeter, Caroline A. "The Hazards of Visibility: 'Biracial Women,' Media Images, and Narratives of Identity." *New Faces in a Changing America: Multiracial Identity in the 21st Century*. Ed. Loretta I. Winters and Herman L. DeBose. Thousand Oaks: Sage, 2003. 301–22. Print.

Svetkey, Benjamin. "Vin at All Costs." *Entertainment Weekly* 2 Aug. 2002: 5. Print.

Tesoriero, Heather Won. "The Next Action Hero." *Time* 5 Aug. 2002: 61–62. Print.

Thigpen, David E. Rev. of *Butterfly*. *Time* 15 Sept. 1997: 113. Print.

Thrupkaew, Noy. "The Multicultural Mysteries of Vin Diesel." Alternet.org. 16 Aug. 2002. Web. 4 Mar. 2004 <http://www.alternet.org/story.html?StoryID=13863>.

Udovitch, Mim. "An Unmarried Woman." *Rolling Stone* 5 Feb. 1998: 30–32. Print.

"Wang and Woods." Asian American E-Zine at Stony Brook University. 11 Dec. 2002. Web. 1 Apr. 2004 <http://www.aa2sbu.org/aaezine/articles/sports/12-WangAndWoods.shtml>.

White, Armond. Rev. of *XXX*, dir. Rob Cohen. *New York Press* Web. 4 Mar. 2004 <http://www.nypress.com/15/33/film/film2.cfm>.

White, Deborah Gray. *Ar'n't I a Woman?: Female Slaves in the Plantation South*. New York: Norton, 1984. Print.

Wickham, DeWayne. "Bassett Criticism Has Its Merit." *USA Today* Section: News, 15A. Print.

Williams, Patricia. "Bulworth Agonistes." *The Nation* 7 June 1998: 11. Print.

"XXX Appeal." *People Weekly* 19 Aug. 2002: 87–88. Print.

Zacharek, Stephanie. Rev. of *Monster's Ball*. Dir. Marc Forster. Salon.com. Web. 28 Mar. 2004. <http://archive.salon.com/ent/movies/review/2002/01/04/monsters_ball/>.

Questions: Analyzing Dagbovie-Mullins's peer-reviewed journal article

1. Purpose. Dagbovie-Mullins discusses Halle Berry, Vin Diesel, and Mariah Carey, but how does she make it clear from the beginning that she's not writing about these actors as entertainers? What seems to be her main purpose? Does she seem to have secondary purposes?

2. Audience. What are some features of this paper that make it clear that she's writing for other scholars, rather than, say, general readers of *People* magazine, who might also be interested in reading about Halle Berry, Vin Diesel, and Mariah Carey? How would the author need to revise for a *People* magazine audience?

3. Rhetorical appeals. How does Dagbovie-Mullins establish her authority on the topic she writes about?

4. Rhetorical appeals. How does the author appeal to your sense of logic in presenting examples and details to support her points? What are some specific details she uses that appeal to your sense of logos?

5. Modes & media. This particular article does not include any images, although there are thousands of images of Halle Berry, Vin Diesel, and Mariah Carey available. Why do you think the author opted not to integrate images into her article?

6. Elements of the genre. What is Dagbovie-Mullins's thesis? How easy was it for you to locate her thesis? What cues does she use in her introduction to indicate that the thesis is coming?

7. Elements of the genre. Do you have to be familiar with the author's sources to understand her point? Explain.

8. Style. Celebrities are typically considered more appropriate subjects for gossip magazines than scholarly journals. How does the author present celebrities as appropriate subjects for a researched article?

9. Design. Dagbovie-Mullins uses subheadings to break the article up into chunks. Did you find these helpful? Did you want fewer or more of them? Why or why not? Also note that some subheadings are questions, while others could be considered thought-provoking statements ("Multiracial to the Rescue: Vin Diesel"). How did these subheadings work on you as a reader? Did they make you want to keep reading? Explain.

10. Sources. Note the extensive Works Cited list. Glance through the list of sources and note how many seem to be scholarly sources and how many seem to be other types of sources. How does the use of nonscholarly sources seem appropriate or inappropriate for this article?

Drafting a Peer-Reviewed Journal Article

CHECKLIST: Drafting a Peer-Reviewed Journal Article Thinking of drafting a peer-reviewed journal article? Ask yourself the following questions.

WHAT'S MY RHETORICAL SITUATION?

☐ **Purpose.** What topic have I researched that I could inform other experts about? Have I discovered something about the topic that others like me might find interesting or conducive to their own research? Do I want to persuade readers of something? To effectively persuade readers, what will I need to inform them about?

☐ **Audience.** My readers will be experts on my general topic, but they won't know as much as I do about the aspect I'm writing about. How much back-ground information will they need? What kind of terminology will they expect? How will my readers use the information I present?

☐ **Rhetorical appeals.** How will I establish my authority as a writer? How will I build a case for my conclusions using logic? Will I need to cite sources to establish myself as an expert? What kinds of sources will help me build my case?

☐ **Modes & media.** Can some of the information I present be shown with a chart or graphic? Do I want readers to access my article in print or digitally? Or do I want to make both options available?

WHAT GENRE CONVENTIONS MATTER?

☐ **Elements of the genre.** How can I make sure my thesis is clear and declarative? How will I refer to my sources? How can I synthesize my sources to show readers how they are in conversation with each other?

☐ **Style.** How can I project an authoritative voice? How much detail will I need to provide so that readers will understand the complexity and validity of my research?

☐ **Design.** How will I use subheadings to present my information in chunks? Will I use images to illustrate points?

☐ **Sources.** Will my readers expect sources to be cited in MLA style, APA style, or another format? Will my readers respect the types of sources I've referred to?

PRACTICE Want to experiment? Draft your own peer-reviewed journal article.

Think about a topic you are researching for this class or another class. What are some of the issues surrounding your topic? Draft an opening paragraph that establishes you as an authority and also makes it clear that you are writing for fellow students rather than a general audience.

4 PERSUASIVE GENRES

CONTENTS

e For e-Pages content, visit bedfordstmartins.com /bookofgenres.

TRY TO SEE THINGS FROM MY POINT OF VIEW.

POLITICAL CARTOON ▶
Rex F. May. *Reprinted by permission of Rex May.*

Open your Web browser, page through any magazine, or take a walk to the coffee shop, and you will be barraged by texts and media created to persuade you—to think something, do something, like something, or buy something. Depending on the source you look at, city-dwelling Americans see between three thousand and five thousand ads per day.*

Online, advertisers individualize their messages to you. For example, when you log on to Amazon.com you are greeted with a list of recommendations based on your previous purchases. On Facebook, the ads on your page are generated according to your likes and dislikes, and other information you provide in your profile and posts.

While advertising is probably the most pervasive of persuasive genres, there are lots of other kinds of texts that we create at home, work, and school in order to convince others to see things our way. In fact, you could argue that almost every communication—a text message to a friend about what movie to see, an online posting of a cute kitten or puppy, a Match.com profile, an editorial on Fox News about the economy, a joke made on *The Simpsons* about the editorial on Fox News, or even a chapter in a textbook—has persuasive elements built into it.

The Rhetorical Situation

Purpose: Why write to persuade?

When we write to persuade, we do so because we want to convince our readers of something—usually to agree with us about a topic, issue, or idea, or to take a specific action. As a student, when you write a paper in which you take a stance on an issue or you give a speech in which you ask your audience to do something, you are writing to persuade. As a professional, when you apply for a job, you craft a resume and cover

▲ AD
Match.com. Have ads like this popped up in your browser window? According to Match.com, "1 in 5 relationships start online." *Courtesy of Match.com.*

*According to a study done by the journal *Pediatrics*, "The average young person views more than 3,000 ads per day on television (TV), on the Internet, on billboards, and in magazines" (see "Children, Adolescents, and Advertising," December 1, 2006). According to an article by Walter Kirn, published in *The New York Times Magazine*, "[R]esearchers estimate that the average city dweller is exposed to 5,000 ads per day, up from 2,000 per day three decades ago" (see "Here, There, and Everywhere," February 11, 2007).

▲ BUMPER STICKER
Imagina Productions.

letter and make a convincing case for yourself during your interview in order to persuade the person hiring that you are the best candidate. A persuasive text can be as simple as a six-word slogan.

Audience: How do we persuade others?

As citizens of a democracy, we may read persuasive texts, such as editorials, to help us figure out our own positions on specific issues. For instance, during election season, you might pay close attention to the opinion pages of local and national newspapers. The editorial boards of these newspapers publish editorials in which they try to convince you who to vote for, how to think of specific issues, and why.

Like the editorial board of *The New York Times*, any time you want to persuade your audience, you need to lay out your ideas, anticipate possible objections, and support your argument with relevant information. As with reporting information (see Chapter 3), accuracy is important when it comes to persuading others. Backing up your ideas and claims with correct information, gathered from reliable sources, will make your argument stronger.

The *Times* editorial board was well aware of their audience—which tends to be liberal, Democratic, and educated—when they wrote the piece on page 179 during the 2008 presidential election. The editors wrote: "We believe [Barack Obama] has the will and ability to forge the broad political consensus that is essential to finding solutions to this nation's problems." They supported their argument by contrasting Obama with his opponent, John McCain, and by providing carefully chosen details of Obama's platform and the choices he made as a senator.

Rhetorical Appeals: How do we use ethos, logos, and pathos to persuade?

Whether you want to convince others to agree with you on an important issue, to date you, to vote for your candidate, or to

What texts in your immediate surroundings (billboards, ads, etc.) are meant to persuade you of something? What persuasive techniques are evident? Which texts are most convincing? Why?

ONLINE EDITORIAL ▶
The New York Times Editorial Board, "Barack Obama for President."
From The New York Times, *October 23, 2013 © 2013 The New York Times.*
All rights reserved.

EDITORIAL

Barack Obama for President

Published: October 23, 2008

Hyperbole is the currency of presidential campaigns, but this year the nation's future truly hangs in the balance.

Multimedia

⌕ Interactive Feature
New York Times Endorsements Through the Ages

Related

Times Topics: Barack Obama

TWITTER
LINKEDIN
COMMENTS (1712)
SIGN IN TO E-MAIL OR SAVE THIS
PRINT
SHARE

The United States is battered and drifting after eight years of President Bush's failed leadership. He is saddling his successor with two wars, a scarred global image and a government systematically stripped of its ability to protect and help its citizens — whether they are fleeing a hurricane's floodwaters, searching for affordable health care or struggling to hold on to their homes, jobs, savings and pensions in the midst of a financial crisis that was foretold and preventable.

As tough as the times are, the selection of a new president is easy. After nearly two years of a grueling and ugly campaign, Senator Barack Obama of Illinois has proved that he is the right choice to be the 44th president of the United States.

Mr. Obama has met challenge after challenge, growing as a leader and putting real flesh on his early promises of hope and change. He has shown a cool head and sound judgment. We believe he has the will and the ability to forge the broad political consensus that is essential to finding solutions to this nation's problems.

In the same time, Senator John McCain of Arizona has retreated farther and farther to the fringe of American politics, running a campaign on partisan division, class warfare and even hints of racism. His policies and worldview are mired in the past. His choice of a running mate so evidently unfit for the office was a final act of opportunism and bad judgment that eclipsed the accomplishments of 26 years in Congress.

Given the particularly ugly nature of Mr. McCain's campaign, the urge to choose on the basis of raw emotion is strong. But there is a greater value in looking closely at the facts of life in America today and at the prescriptions the candidates offer. The differences are profound.

Mr. McCain offers more of the Republican every-man-for-himself ideology, now lying in shards on Wall Street and in Americans' bank accounts. Mr. Obama has another vision of government's role and responsibilities.

In his convention speech in Denver, Mr. Obama said, "Government cannot solve all our problems, but what it should do is that which we cannot do for ourselves: protect us from harm and provide every child a decent education; keep our water clean and our toys safe; invest in new schools and new roads and new science and technology."

Since the financial crisis, he has correctly identified the abject failure of government regulation that has brought the markets to the brink of collapse.

The Economy

The American financial system is the victim of decades of Republican deregulatory and anti-tax policies. Those ideas have been proved wrong at an unfathomable price, but Mr. McCain — a self-proclaimed "foot soldier in the Reagan revolution" — is still a believer.

Mr. Obama sees that far-reaching reforms will be needed to protect Americans and American business.

Mr. McCain talks about reform a lot, but his vision is pinched. His answer to any economic question is to eliminate pork-barrel spending — about $18 billion in a $3 trillion budget — cut taxes and wait for unfettered markets to solve the problem.

Mr. Obama is clear that the nation's tax structure must be changed to make it fairer. That means the well-off Americans who have benefited disproportionately from Mr. Bush's tax cuts will have to pay some more. Working Americans, who have seen their standard of living fall and their children's options narrow, will benefit. Mr. Obama wants to raise the minimum wage and tie it to inflation, restore a climate in which workers are able to organize unions if they wish and expand educational opportunities.

Mr. McCain, who once opposed President Bush's tax cuts for the wealthy as fiscally irresponsible, now wants to make them permanent. And while he talks about keeping taxes low for everyone, his proposed cuts would overwhelmingly benefit the top 1 percent of Americans while digging the country into a deeper fiscal hole.

National Security

The American military — its people and equipment — is dangerously overstretched. Mr. Bush has neglected the necessary war in Afghanistan, which now threatens to spiral into defeat. The unnecessary and staggeringly costly war in Iraq must be ended as quickly and responsibly as possible.

While Iraq's leaders insist on a swift drawdown of American troops and a deadline for the end of the occupation, Mr. McCain is still talking about some ill-defined "victory." As a result, he has offered no real plan for extracting American troops and limiting any further damage to Iraq and its neighbors.

Mr. Obama was an early and thoughtful opponent of the war in Iraq, and he has presented a military and diplomatic plan for withdrawing American forces. Mr. Obama also has correctly warned that until the Pentagon starts pulling troops out of Iraq, there will not be enough troops to defeat the Taliban and Al Qaeda in Afghanistan.

Mr. McCain, like Mr. Bush, has only belatedly focused on Afghanistan's dangerous unraveling and the threat that neighboring Pakistan may quickly follow.

Mr. Obama would have a learning curve on foreign affairs, but he has already showed sounder judgment than his opponent on these critical issues. His choice of Senator Joseph Biden — who has deep foreign-policy expertise — as his running mate is another sign of that sound judgment. Mr. McCain's long interest in foreign policy and the many dangers this country now faces make his choice of Gov. Sarah Palin of Alaska more irresponsible.

Both presidential candidates talk about strengthening alliances in Europe and Asia, including NATO, and strongly support Israel. Both candidates talk about repairing America's image in the world. But is seems clear to us that Mr. Obama is far more likely to do that — and not just because the first black president would present a new American face to the world.

Mr. Obama wants to reform the United Nations, while Mr. McCain wants to create a new entity, the League of Democracies — a move that would incite even fiercer anti-American furies around the world.

Unfortunately, Mr. McCain, like Mr. Bush, sees the world as divided into friends (like Georgia) and adversaries (like Russia). He proposed kicking Russia out of the Group of 8 industrialized nations even before the invasion of Georgia. We have no sympathy for Moscow's bullying, but we also have no desire to replay the cold war. The United States must find a way to constrain the Russians' worst impulses, while preserving the ability to work with them on arms control and other vital initiatives.

Both candidates talk tough on terrorism, and neither has ruled out military action to end Iran's nuclear weapons program. But Mr. Obama has called for a serious effort to try to wean Tehran from its nuclear ambitions with more credible diplomatic overtures and tougher sanctions. Mr. McCain's willingness to joke about bombing Iran was frightening.

The Constitution and the Rule of Law

Under Mr. Bush and Vice President Dick Cheney, the Constitution, the Bill of Rights, the justice system and the separation of powers have come under relentless attack. Mr. Bush chose to exploit the tragedy of Sept. 11, 2001, the moment in which he looked like the president of a unified nation, to try to place himself above the law.

Mr. Bush has arrogated the power to imprison men without charges and browbeat Congress into granting an unfettered authority to spy on Americans. He has created untold number of "black" programs, including secret prisons and outsourced torture.

The president has issued hundreds, if not thousands, of secret orders. We fear it will take years of forensic research to discover how many basic rights have been violated.

Both candidates have renounced torture and are committed to closing the prison camp in Guantánamo Bay, Cuba.

But Mr. Obama has gone beyond that, promising to identify and correct Mr. Bush's attacks on the democratic system. Mr. McCain has been silent on the subject.

Mr. McCain improved protections for detainees. But then he helped the White House push through the appalling Military Commissions Act of 2006, which denied detainees the right to a hearing in a real court and put Washington in conflict with the Geneva Conventions, greatly increasing the risk to American troops.

The next president will have the chance to appoint one or more justices to a Supreme Court that is on the brink of being dominated by a radical right wing. Mr. Obama may appoint less liberal judges than some of his followers might like, but Mr. McCain is certain to pick rigid ideologues. He has said he would never appoint a judge who believes in women's reproductive rights.

The Candidates

It will be an enormous challenge just to get the nation back to where it was before Mr. Bush, to begin to mend its image in the world and to restore its self-confidence and its self-respect. Doing all of that, and leading America forward, will require strength of will, character and intellect, sober judgment and a cool, steady hand.

Mr. Obama has those qualities in abundance. Watching him being tested in the campaign has long since erased the reservations that led us to endorse Senator Hillary Rodham Clinton in the Democratic primaries. He has drawn in legions of new voters with powerful messages of hope and possibility and calls for shared sacrifice and social responsibility.

Mr. McCain, whom we chose as the best Republican nominee in the primaries, has spent the last coins of his reputation for principle and sound judgment to placate the limitless demands and narrow vision of the far-right wing. His righteous fury at being driven out of the 2000 primaries on a racist tide aimed at his adopted daughter has been replaced by a zealous embrace of those same win-at-all-costs tactics and tacticians.

He surrendered his standing as an independent thinker in his rush to embrace Mr. Bush's misbegotten tax policies and to abandon his leadership position on climate change and immigration reform.

Mr. McCain could have seized the high ground on energy and the environment. Earlier in his career, he offered the first plausible bill to control America's emissions of greenhouse gases. Now his positions are a caricature of that record: think Ms. Palin leading chants of "drill, baby, drill."

Mr. Obama has endorsed some offshore drilling, but as part of a comprehensive strategy including big investments in new, clean technologies.

Mr. Obama has withstood some of the toughest campaign attacks ever mounted against a candidate. He's been called un-American and accused of hiding a secret Islamic faith. The Republicans have linked him to domestic terrorists and questioned his wife's love of her country. Ms. Palin has also questioned millions of Americans' patriotism, calling Republican-leaning states "pro-America."

This politics of fear, division and character assassination helped Mr. Bush drive Mr. McCain from the 2000 Republican primaries and defeat Senator John Kerry in 2004. It has been the dominant theme of his failed presidency.

The nation's problems are simply too grave to be reduced to slashing "robo-calls" and negative ads. This country needs sensible leadership, compassionate leadership, honest leadership and strong leadership. Barack Obama has shown that he has all of those qualities.

buy your product, you will be most persuasive if you relate to your audience through the rhetorical appeals—ethos, logos, and pathos.

Ethos, the authority and trustworthiness that you establish as a writer, composer, or speaker, is crucial when you want to persuade others. For example, if your boss asks you to review several possible locations for an important fund-raising event and recommend one, you will want to establish yourself as dedicated to getting a high-quality venue for a reasonable price. To do this, you'll need to demonstrate that you've taken the assignment seriously, studied the options objectively, and weighed your company's needs and priorities carefully.

Here's another example. Way back in 1981, horror writer Stephen King wrote an essay about why horror films are popular. Because he was already established as a best-selling horror author with titles like *Carrie* (1974) and *The Shining* (1977), both of which had already been made into successful horror movies, he had instant credibility, with which he developed an ethos as an expert on his subject. He went further than that, however, citing many examples throughout the essay to establish that he knows more than just his own experience. Here is an excerpt from the essay:

> We also go to re-establish our feelings of essential normality; the horror movie is innately conservative, even reactionary. Freda Jackson as the horrible melting woman in *Die, Monster, Die!* confirms for us that no matter how far we may be removed from the beauty of a Robert Redford or a Diana Ross, we are still light-years from true ugliness.
> —**Stephen King,** from "Why We Crave Horror Movies"

King furthers his ethos by taking his subject seriously and speaking specifically about it.

Logos, the logical chain of reasoning that you provide for readers, is extremely important when you are making any kind of argument. Imagine you are taking a car for a test drive to decide whether you will buy it. You might mention to the salesperson that you are interested in a car that won't be too bad for the environment. The salesperson might then present you with some facts about the mileage the car gets, the measures the manufacturer has taken at the factory to protect the

Are there particular types of persuasive texts you automatically trust? Distrust? Why?

environment, and the paper-free policy the dealership has initiated by conducting as much business as possible electronically. By talking to you about these factors, the salesperson is creating a chain of reasoning that—she hopes—will lead you to conclude that the car you are driving is an environmentally responsible choice.

Let's look at an example of a verbal argument made by media scholar Johanna Blakley. She gave a presentation about social media that was videotaped and published online by TED, a nonprofit open-source site devoted to "ideas worth spreading." In her TED talk, Blakley makes a case for how people connect. She says:

> [People] don't aggregate around age, gender, income. They aggregate around the things they love, the things that they like. And if you think about it, shared interests and values are a far more powerful aggregator of human beings than demographic categories. I'd much rather know whether you like *Buffy the Vampire Slayer* rather than how old you are. That would tell me something more substantial about you.
> —**Johanna Blakley,** from "Social Media and the End of Gender"

Notice how—after making her claim that people aggregate around their interests—she gives a specific example about interest in *Buffy the Vampire Slayer* being a better indicator than age of how much people have in common with each other.

Pathos is the appeal that you use when you want to evoke your readers' emotions. This comes in handy when you are trying to persuade someone to do something. An appeal to pathos connects you with your audience, and vice versa. For example, when a salesperson asks you about yourself and then tells you a bit about himself and you find some commonalities, that salesperson is appealing to your pathos. When he later tells you that he loves the stereo you are looking at, you're more likely to buy it because you've already identified with him.

Advertisers often appeal to pathos. For example, a commercial for Tide Free & Gentle detergent begins with a little girl trying on pairs of tights as a motherly woman's voice says:

> "Picking the right tights isn't always easy. Picking a free detergent is."

As the commercial continues, the girl frolics around her room, posing in front of her mirror in different pairs of tights, as the motherly voice continues talking about how Tide Free & Gentle detergent will ensure that whichever tights the girl picks, they will be clean and free of anything that can irritate her skin.

By focusing on the cuteness and innocence of the little girl, the ad equates a mother's desire to keep her daughter safe with choosing Tide Free & Gentle detergent. The advertisers associate protectiveness and love with the detergent itself.

Modes & Media: How can they help you persuade?

Following is a breakdown of the modes and media of some of the compositions presented in this chapter:

PERSUASIVE GENRES	Mode	Medium
AD Match.com (p. 177)	VISUAL AND WRITTEN	DIGITAL
BUMPER STICKER Imagina Productions, "Don't Text & Drive" (p. 178)	WRITTEN	PRINT
ONLINE EDITORIAL *The New York Times* Editorial Board, "Barack Obama for President" (p. 179)	VISUAL AND WRITTEN	DIGITAL

ONLINE & TV AD	VISUAL AND AUDIO	DIGITAL
Tide Free & Gentle detergent commercial (p. 182)		(ONLINE AND ON TELEVISION)

The Genre's Conventions

Elements of the Genre: What does all persuasive writing have in common?

Persuasive writers aim to change the reader's or viewer's mind in some way. Different authors and artists may use different strategies for achieving this, but most effective persuasive communication has two elements in common:

1. *Makes an explicit argument/position statement.* When writers state exactly what they'd like readers or viewers to do or think, then there is no guesswork involved. Many persuasive writers present an explicit position statement, such as "Voters should support Proposition 2 because it will reduce taxes in the long run." Others may strongly imply, but not explicitly state, the case they're making. The text of an ad won't always say, "Buy this product," but you get that idea from the use of persuasive images and text; ad writers make clear what they're trying to persuade you of, often without using direct language.

2. *Taps into audiences' values and emotions.* Most persuasive writers appeal to their readers' or viewers' sensibilities in some way. While this is true of most writers, it's particularly true of writers who want to persuade; it's essential to tap into ethos, pathos, and/or logos. Ethos is especially important because most readers will not be convinced by an unreliable author.

Style: How does it help you persuade?

When you want to persuade others, present your ideas in a way that will hold your readers' (or listeners' or viewers') attention. You will need their attention before you can make your specific arguments. You can do this with certain stylistic techniques—as well as through the voice and tone you use.

Let's look at an example. On January 8, 2011, Congresswoman Gabrielle Giffords and eighteen others were shot in a supermarket parking lot in Tucson, Arizona. Six people died. A few days later, President Obama gave a speech in Tucson that paid tribute to the injured and killed; the speech was also designed to persuade Americans not to blame each other or a particular political party for the tragedy (though the gunman was later described as mentally ill by the judge at his sentencing, early reports had circulated that his politics had inspired his actions). He began with a greeting to those present, noted the occasion for the speech, and said something about each person killed in the shooting. Then Obama moved on:

> [A]t a time when our discourse has become so sharply polarized—at a time when we are far too eager to lay the blame for all that ails the world at the feet of those who happen to think differently than we do—it's important for us to pause for a moment and make sure that we're talking with each other in a way that heals, not in a way that wounds. . . .
>
> Yes, we have to examine all the facts behind this tragedy. We cannot and will not be passive in the face of such violence. We should be willing to challenge old assumptions in order to lessen the prospects of such violence in the future. But what we cannot do is use this tragedy as one more occasion to turn on each other. That we cannot do. That we cannot do.
>
> As we discuss these issues, let each of us do so with a good dose of humility. Rather than pointing fingers or assigning blame, let's use this occasion to expand our moral imaginations, to listen to each other more carefully, to sharpen our instincts for empathy and remind ourselves of all the ways that our hopes and dreams are bound together.
>
> —**Barack Obama,** from his speech "Together We Thrive: Tucson and America," University of Arizona, January 12, 2011

Notice the structure of the excerpt above. Obama moves from providing context to actively presenting an argument to his listeners. One of his techniques is to use repetition to reinforce what he says. For example, he uses the phrase "at a time when" twice in the first sentence to keep listeners engaged; he uses the line "we cannot do" three times in order to emphasize his case that we cannot "turn on each other" during a divisive moment. Notice, too, the mix of long and very short sentences that create variety for listeners.

In this speech, Obama's tone is friendly but also serious and presidential.

Design: What is the best format for persuading?

Consider the Nike logo. Ever wonder who designed it? As it happens, in 1971 a graphic arts student at Portland State University named Carolyn Davidson created the Nike swoosh symbol, which became one of the most successful logos of all time. Years later, the ad firm Wieden + Kennedy penned the slogan "Just Do It." The campaign is noted by *Advertising Age* as one of the Top 100 Advertising Campaigns of the twentieth century. Why? Because the swoosh design and the slogan are clear, simple, and memorable. These are the qualities that make the campaign persuasive.

The design of a piece can contribute to its persuasiveness or work against it. Consider someone trying to convince you that he is a calm and patient person. Imagine that he is wearing a bright red T-shirt with the slogan "Don't think! Just *act!*" Chances are that the design of this person's wardrobe would work against persuading you that he is calm and patient.

Sources: What research should you draw on to persuade others?

To be persuasive, use sources to develop your credibility, to draw on for facts, and to support your claims and objectives. For example, if Liz wants to persuade her dean to send her to a conference, she'll need to do some research about the conference and then make a case for how the conference and the dean's goals are related.

In the composition on page 186, artist Dominic Episcopo aims to persuade viewers that, figuratively, America is "made of meat." In creating this piece, which is part of his "Meat America" series, he may have had in mind any or all of the following factors: high U.S. obesity rates, high levels of cholesterol and heart disease, or the country's dependence on a system of raising cattle that is hard on the environment and animals.

To support the argument he makes in his sculpture, Episcopo could draw on sources of information on meat consumption in the United States and its effects. For example, he could draw on the data in the chart on page 187 that shows the rise of Americans' beef consumption—from 63 pounds per person per year in 1950 to 85.56 pounds per person in 2010 (with the greatest consumption in 1975). Published by the Humane Society, this chart uses government census and USDA data, which makes it a particularly solid source.

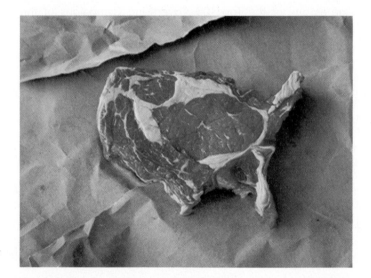

◀ PHOTO
▶ SCULPTURE &
▼ WEB SITE
Dominic Episcopo,
"United Steaks of America" (right), a work included at meatamerica.com (bottom). *Three images: Dominic Episcopo.*

MEAT AMERICA

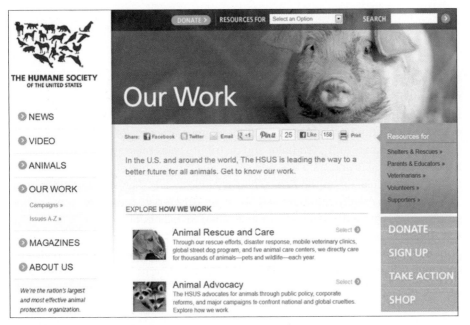

When you write to persuade, how do you use sources to support your argument? What types of sources are most persuasive? Why?

▲ WEB SITE & ▼ CHART

The Humane Society of the United States, "U.S. Per Capita Meat Consumption" and humanesociety.org. *The Humane Society of the United States homepage.*

ADVERTISEMENTS

An advertisement is any text created to persuade consumers to purchase a product or service. Print advertising is as old as the first newspapers, which appeared in England in the 1600s. Today, ads are everywhere and are presented in a variety of print and digital media. Advertisers spend large amounts of money to research potential customers and then tailor and distribute sales messages that will appeal to those consumers and translate into sales. The money they spend on Web advertising, in particular, is on the rise, especially display ads (banners and video ads). The Interactive Advertising Bureau (IAB), in its 2012 report, indicates record online ad revenues, with a 15 percent and more than $1 billion increase over 2011. The *Los Angeles Times* and eMarketer.com report that while advertisers still spend on print ads, they're spending more of their budgets on digital ads; by 2016 online ad spending is likely to nearly double ($62 billion), leaving print far behind ($32 billion).

How do you know when you are (or aren't) the target audience for an ad? Have you ever been offended or alienated by an ad? If so, why?

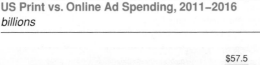

CHART ▶ **eMarketer.com/Los Angeles Times,** "U.S. Print vs. Online Ad Spending, 2011–2016." *eMarketer, Inc.*

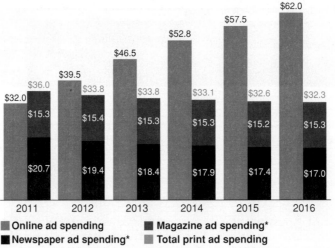

US Print vs. Online Ad Spending, 2011–2016
billions

	2011	2012	2013	2014	2015	2016
Total print ad spending	$36.0	$33.8	$33.8	$33.1	$32.6	$32.3
Online ad spending	$32.0	$39.5	$46.5	$52.8	$57.5	$62.0
Magazine ad spending*	$15.3	$15.4	$15.3	$15.3	$15.2	$15.3
Newspaper ad spending*	$20.7	$19.4	$18.4	$17.9	$17.4	$17.0

■ Online ad spending   ■ Magazine ad spending*
■ Newspaper ad spending*   ■ Total print ad spending

*Note: eMarketer benchmarks its US online ad spending projections against the IAB/PWC data, for which the last full year measured was 2010; eMarketer benchmarks its US newspaper ad spending projections against the NAA data, for which the last full year measured was 2010; *print only*
Source: eMarketer, Jan 2012

136019   www.eMarketer.com

Analyzing Advertisements: What to Look For

Purpose To sell their products and services, companies need to publicize information about what they're offering. They also need to win business from competitors. For example, the well-known Progressive auto insurance commercials advertise the company's "comparison shopping" feature, as shown below, to inform shoppers of their rates versus those of other carriers and support their claim that with Progressive, "You could save over $475 on car insurance."

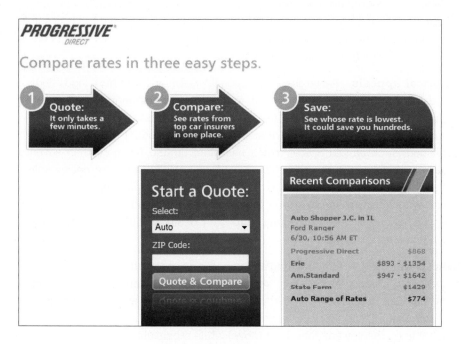

◄ ONLINE AD
Progressive,
"Compare Rates."
Courtesy of Progressive.

Audience When major advertising firms such as the Ad Agency, Arnold Worldwide, and Wieden + Kennedy create ads, they have a very clear picture of their target market, and they aim their branding, visuals, messages, and other persuasive tools squarely at that market. For example, the Old Spice commercials of 2010, featuring the actor Isaiah Mustafa, clearly target a young, tech-savvy, heterosexual female demographic. The creators of these quirky ads (Wieden + Kennedy) dusted off an old brand of men's cologne and made it more appealing to a new audience by using humor, personality, and a supersuave ladies' man. Originally released on YouTube and then as a Super Bowl commercial, the "Old Spice Guy" ad went viral within a few days, getting more than thirty-four million views in less than a week.

In the ad, Mustafa says: "Hello, ladies, look at your man, now back to me, now back at your man, now back to me. Sadly, he isn't me, but if he stopped using ladies' scented body wash and switched to Old Spice, he could smell like he's me. Look down, back up, where are you? You're on a boat with the man your man could smell like. What's in your hand, back at me. I have it, it's an oyster with two tickets to that thing you love. Look again, the tickets are now diamonds. Anything is possible when your man smells like Old Spice and not a lady. I'm on a horse." Then comes the voiceover: "*Smell like a man, man. Old Spice.*"

Rhetorical appeals Advertisers use appeals to ethos (authority), logos (logic), and pathos (emotion). Many ads that feature expert testimonials or celebrity endorsements, for example, make use of ethos; if you trust the expert giving the testimonial, you are more likely to trust the product. A product that has been long established, such as Old Spice, which has been around for more than seventy years, has its own built-in ethos. The advertisers of Old Spice further establish its ethos by emphasizing the macho quality of the product and choosing a super-fit actor with a deep voice to star in the commercial. The advertisers also appeal to viewers' sense of pathos—tapping into their desire to buy the product, even though it is a nonessential item.

Modes & media As more reading and viewing happen online, more advertising will happen there too. A digital ad, such as the Old Spice commercial mentioned above, has the potential to spread through social media and YouTube, giving advertisers more "bang for the buck." In terms of the medium, some online ads are static (e.g., display ads that don't move) while others are videos or animations that incorporate sound. There are even reports of a new medium called "smell-vertising": a product's scent is broadcast in an area with potential consumers of the product.

Think of an ad that features a visual image that doesn't directly relate to the product being promoted. What is the product? The visual? Why might the ad creators have made this choice?

Elements of the genre

Headlines. Advertisers use headlines to immediately attract the reader's attention. The headline often conveys the product's benefits through concise language. Additionally, advertisers pay special attention to the placement of the headline, ensuring that it is not obscured or overwhelmed by a visual element. In the case of some electronic ads, a headline may be read aloud by a narrator.

Visuals. Graphics work together with the headline to attract the reader. They also illustrate the point or provide visual evidence that supports the product's claim. In television commercials, advertisers edit the visuals to hold viewers' attention, maintaining a quick pace and not lingering for too long on one image.

Ad copy. Advertisers use the words of an advertisement, or ad copy, for specific purposes. They use a headline to get a consumer's attention and then draw the reader in further with an intriguing subheading. Copy that is not a headline or heading is called body text, and it tells about the benefits of the product or service and either implicitly or explicitly tells the consumer to make a purchase. Digital and TV ads also feature ad copy—it can be spoken and/or animated on the screen.

Advertising slogans. Advertisers often associate sayings or phrases with a product. For example, Nike's slogan is "Just Do It."

Signature. Usually found toward the bottom of a print ad, the signature includes the advertiser name and contact information. In digital and TV ads, contact information is not normally provided, but the brand and product name is made clear.

Style

Technique. The writing tends to be brief and directive. For example, in the original Smokey the Bear advertisements, Smokey addresses the reader: "Only YOU can prevent forest fires!" Words are usually secondary to visuals. Visuals are carefully selected as persuasive tools (see "Design" below). Because digital and TV ads are very short (usually thirty seconds or less), words are limited.

Details. Advertisers usually keep details (and words, in general) to a minimum.

Voice and tone. In a commercial, voice and tone can give the viewer an impression of the product's benefits. For example, if a company is promoting its product's ability to relieve stress, then the tone of the ad is usually soothing. If a financial company is advertising its services, then the tone is usually reassuring. Written ad copy conveys its tone through word choice and phrasing, while digital and TV ads convey tone through vocal intonation, pacing, and the qualities of the voice itself (male or female, deep or high, etc.).

Design

Visual of the product. Advertisers need to provide an image of what they're selling so consumers can identify and purchase it. If the product is less tangible (or not an object), such as an auto insurance policy, then some kind of visual emphasizes the message. For example, in some Geico ads, a caveman is the main visual, emphasizing how easy it is to purchase auto insurance.

Additional pathos-building images. Advertisers use visuals to convey ideas and tap into viewers' emotions. For example, in a commercial for Abilify (a drug used mainly to treat depression), the advertiser presents "before" and "after" images. The commercial begins with a series of people looking stressed, sad, and unable to do anything. The drug is introduced, followed by a series of visuals showing the same people engaged with life and smiling.

Color. Advertisers can further appeal to pathos by using images and colors associated with particular emotions.

For more examples of **advertisements,** see the Index of Genres on page G-1.

Product logos. Advertisers carefully design product logos to convey particular ideas and values about a product. For example, the Nike swoosh indicates speed and movement. All Nike products and advertisements feature the swoosh, which is instantly identifiable and long established.

Layout. In a print-based ad (or a static Web ad), the layout orients the reader and establishes the most important pieces of information. The main visual and headline are the most prominent in the advertisement; contact info and fine print are usually somewhere toward the bottom of the piece. Advertisers use similar principles in digital and TV commercials to make the featured product and message clear and conspicuous.

Sources   Advertising agencies conduct market research before creating ad campaigns so they can most efficiently identify and target their main audience and tailor their overall message accordingly. Once they've identified some possible directions for the content and design, they may ask a test audience to determine which ad will be most successful. Sources noted within an ad can include a company Web site where consumers can find more information about the product.

Guided Reading: Advertisement ▼

Danone/Evian and Havas Worldwide
Detox with Evian

The Evian brand of spring water is promoted as a natural product "from the heart of the French Alps." The Danone company introduced Evian to the United States in the 1970s, mostly in luxury hotels and expensive restaurants. Since then, they have associated the brand with luxury and have often used celebrities and people from the fashion industry to build its appeal.

Among the many ads for Evian is the notable "Detox" campaign of 2006. This campaign stressed the health benefits of drinking Evian, arguing that the water helps people maintain youthfulness and purity. Youthfulness is a theme that recurs in Evian's campaigns, including their current "Live Young" campaign that invites customers to post photos and participate in a video campaign.

To create the "Detox" campaign, Danone/Evian worked with the ad firm Havas Worldwide (formerly known as Euro RSCG). The firm also created Evian's popular "Live Young" campaign. Havas Worldwide creates ads and marketing plans for many major companies and is one of the largest advertising and marketing agencies in the world.

Danone/Evian also hired a firm called Codegent to create the digital marketing pieces for the "Detox" campaign. Copy on Codegent's site reads: "We've worked on Evian campaigns for a couple of years, now: the Detox with Evian campaign that was in conjunction with the on-pack promotion and the Evian Live Young campaign which also featured TV advertising. Bringing brands to life online, it's a great job."

Annotations in the margins of the Evian ad on page 194 point out the choices that Evian made in terms of their purpose, sense of audience, and use of rhetorical appeals. You'll also see notes on how this work reflects the conventions of the advertising genre—in terms of its persuasive appeal and specific techniques. *(Source for image on p. 194: various publications.)*

▲ WEB SITE
Danone, owner of Evian spring water.

What are the composers of the ad, **Havas Worldwide**, doing?

THE RHETORICAL SITUATION

Purpose
Audience
Rhetorical appeals
Modes & media

see page 195

How do I know this is an **advertisement**?

THE GENRE'S CONVENTIONS

Elements of the genre
Style
Design
Sources

see page 195

The ad copy reads: "Return to purity with water from the French Alps that's been naturally filtered for over 15 years."

Purpose

Havas Worldwide, the creators of this ad (hired by Danone/Evian), hope to persuade consumers to buy Evian water.

Audience

The ad creators are aiming at people looking for health benefits and/or people who want to "detoxify." (Note that this ad appeared right after New Year's Eve 2006, and the idea of detoxifying had been very popular that year.) The audience reads magazines (where the print ad appeared) and spends time online (notice the Evian URL in the ad copy).

Rhetorical appeals

The ad appeals mainly to readers' **pathos** (emotion)—by displaying a beautiful landscape and model, and by equating both with Evian. The model's nudity implies snow-angel-grade purity. It also—in combination with the giant falling drop—suggests sex. The idea of "detoxing" also plays on readers' worries about health and an "impure" lifestyle.

The ad also conveys Evian's **ethos** through the presentation of the bottle and the emphasis on branding.

Modes & media

Mode = written and visual The advertisers use visuals and a small amount of text to persuade viewers to purchase Evian water. Evian's "Detox" campaign stresses the purity and health benefits of the water, so both the visuals and text convey this point. The text emphasizes this through the headline ("Detox with Evian") and also the body copy ("Return to purity"). The visuals make the claim with pictures of snow-covered alps and a beautiful woman.

Medium = print and digital While this ad appeared in print magazines, it can also be found digitally. Evian's campaigns are designed not only for print, but also for TV and the Internet.

Elements of the genre

Presents an argument (visual and textual) for purchasing a product.

The headline, "Detox with Evian," is brief, direct, and directive. The ad copy, "Return to purity with water from the French Alps that's been naturally filtered for over 15 years," suggests the benefits of the water and the process used to filter it; the writers also used directive language (i.e., "Return").

Style

Brief text, with an emphasis on visuals. A central image—a naked woman making a snow angel in the Alps—is used to sell the Evian water.

Design

Color is used to create drama and focus attention. The writers and designers chose cool tones—blue and white—for the snow and water to suggest purity, and chose bright colors—red and pink—for the product name and product shot to highlight the brand.

The layout focuses on the woman's body; the composition suggests purity but also sexuality to entice consumers.

The spatial arrangement emphasizes the Alps, where the water originates. The placement of the woman below the mountain suggests that drinking water that comes from the mountain can make you young and beautiful.

The use of a sans serif typeface and lowercase letters suggests freshness and a contemporary quality. The clean lines of the font reinforce the pure/natural message.

Sources

Havas Worldwide most likely researched a variety of images before choosing the final one. The source of the water itself (the Alps) also plays into the choice of setting/backdrop for the ad.

Questions: Analyzing Danone/Evian and Havas Worldwide's advertisement

1. Purpose. What information did the creators of the ad provide (textually and visually) about Evian water? How interesting is the information? How persuasive is it? Explain.

2. Audience. How do the various images in the ad speak to its audience? Who is the primary target audience for this ad? Is there only one audience or are several audiences being addressed by the ad? Why do you think so?

3. Rhetorical appeals. How many different ways is the concept of "purity" conveyed in the ad? How is this used to persuade the audience?

4. Rhetorical appeals. Why do the ad's creators focus on Evian water's "detoxifying" properties? And what does this suggest about Evian's target audience?

5. Rhetorical appeals. Look up the word *detox* in a dictionary. Which of the definitions listed seems most appropriate in the case of the ad? Why?

6. Modes & media. The ad copy mentions the French Alps but does not mention the woman, although both are central visuals in the ad. Why do you think the creators chose not to include the woman in the ad copy?

7. Elements of the genre. The ad headline is very brief and directive. Does it have the same catchiness as the Nike slogan "Just Do It"? Why or why not?

8. Elements of the genre. What is the relationship between the visual images and the text? If the bottom portion of the ad with the text were eliminated, what would your reaction to the image be? How does your reaction change when you see the text?

9. Style. How would you characterize the tone of the ad copy? Does the tone fit the advertisement's purpose? Why or why not?

10. Design. Describe the visuals in the ad. What do the visuals suggest about what the advertisers want consumers to think/believe/feel about Evian?

11. Design. Water drops are used twice in the ad. What purpose do they serve?

12. Sources. Is it effective to use an image of the mountains where Evian water comes from as a backdrop in the ad? Why or why not?

Drafting an Advertisement

CHECKLIST: Drafting an Advertisement Thinking of creating an ad? Ask yourself the following questions.

WHAT'S MY RHETORICAL SITUATION?

☐ **Purpose.** What product do I use that I want to convince others to use? What are the reasons to use that product? Why would someone besides me want to use the product?

☐ **Audience.** Who are the people in my target audience? Who will use the product? When will they use the product? Where will they use the product? How will they use the product?

☐ **Rhetorical appeals.** How will I establish my credibility in my advertisement? How will I illustrate the product's reliability and ethos? How will I use emotions to persuade my reader to use the product? To what extent will I use logic to support my claim about the product?

☐ **Modes & media.** Will my ad be print-based or digital or made for TV? How will I use visual images to persuade? Will I use one primary image or others that are secondary? How will my text work with my images? Will text explain visuals? Complement them? Will I use animation?

WHAT GENRE CONVENTIONS MATTER?

☐ **Elements of the genre.** Will my visuals be literal or symbolic? What type of catchy slogan can I create to make my product memorable? Will I use the slogan as my headline or within the ad copy?

☐ **Style.** What tone will work best for selling my product? How will my intended audience respond to my tone?

☐ **Design.** What typeface should I use? What size type will work best with my visuals? How can I use layout in order to feature the most important elements and leave the least important for final viewing? How can I use color and other design elements to guide my viewers' experience?

☐ **Sources.** What kind of market research will I conduct? Will I test out my headline/slogan on a potential audience? Will I show them a series of visuals to see which is most persuasive?

PRACTICE Want to experiment? Draft your own advertisement.

Think of a product you consume or use, such as an energy drink, candy bar, computer, or article of clothing. Create a draft of a print advertisement that highlights a specific property/aspect of that product, such as the detoxifying properties of Evian. Use symbolic visuals to sell your product. Alternatively, create a digital or TV ad in which you use images, sound, and text.

EDITORIALS & OPINION PIECES

Editorials are related to **news articles**. Both types of writing are presented by news organizations (such as *The New York Times*, CNN, and your campus paper); however, editorials present opinions (which are subjective) and articles present facts (which are objective). For more on **news articles,** see the Index of Genres on page G-1.

Editorials and opinion pieces are texts that convey a writer's opinion on a particular topic, sometimes a controversial topic. This type of writing can be called by different names, such as *opinions, perspectives, commentaries,* and *viewpoints,* and can take the form of a letter to the editor or an online comment in response to an issue or other piece of writing.

Editorials appear in newspapers and magazines, on TV and radio, and in blogs and other online publications. Editorials also include editorial cartoons. An editorial represents the opinion of a news agency's editorial board, and therefore represents the opinion of the publisher. An opinion piece, on the other hand, could take the form of opinion columns by regular featured writers, and letters from readers in which they share their views. Many newspapers, such as the *Denver Post*, feature editorials and opinion pieces side by side; the *Denver Post* calls the page simply the Opinion Page. If your school publishes a newspaper, it probably also includes a section dedicated to editorials or opinions.

EDITORIAL PAGE ▶
The *Denver Post* Opinion page. *Printed with permission from The Denver Post.*

Analyzing Editorials & Opinion Pieces: What to Look For

THE RHETORICAL SITUATION

Purpose

Individual writers. An average citizen or student who writes an editorial or letter to the editor does so to convey his or her view on a specific issue, with the intent of persuading other readers. For example, in one issue of the *Oregon Daily Emerald*, a University of Oregon student wrote a column titled "Students Should Have Wider

Do you read editorials? What issues or events are most important to you? To what extent do we benefit from the opinions of others?

Gun Liberties," in response to an article discussing how the university campus prepares for a campus shooting. The student's purpose is clear—as is his opinion.

The same is true for an individual columnist—a staff or syndicated writer for a specific newspaper, magazine, or other news organization; that is, the columnist conveys his or her own opinion in the editorial and not the opinion of a publisher, though there is some gray area here because the writers are usually employed by the publisher.

Editorial board writers. Texts that are written by the editorial board of a newspaper or magazine convey the opinion of the publisher. These editorials are intended to educate and persuade readers to agree with a specific idea and/or to take a specific action. For example, in the *Denver Post* editorial "Trim Feds' Role in Policing Pot," the *Post* argues in support of a congressional measure that would eliminate marijuana from the federal government's list of controlled substances. The editorial boards of most newspapers reflect a conservative or liberal point of view through their editorials; for example, the editorial board of *The New York Times* has a reputation for being fairly liberal, while the editorial board of the *News-Gazette* of Champaign-Urbana, Illinois, has a reputation for being conservative.

Audience   Anyone with access to newspapers, magazines, television, radio, or the Internet can access editorials and opinion pieces. As a reader, you might scan the

▲ NEWSPAPER
EDITORIAL
**The Editorial Board
of the *Denver Post,***
"Trim Feds' Role in
Policing Pot." *Printed
with Permission from
The Denver Post.*

- Opinion

Opinion Home

Editorials and Debates

Columnists' Opinions

Readers' Opinions

E-mail | Print | RSS

When teachers cut class

Remember those days when your teacher unexpectedly called in sick? Some hapless substitute walked in, briefly struggled to teach a lesson and then surrendered class time to "study hall."

Despite anecdotal and academic evidence that students don't learn as much from substitutes, many school districts appear to have a problem with truant teachers, especially on sunny Fridays. An *Orlando Sentinel* reporter recently found that one district had 35% more teachers sick on Fridays than Wednesdays. A Minneapolis reporter found similar absentee problems there.

Besides hurting kids' education, these suspicious absences deplete school funds that could be spent on other education priorities. Substitutes generally cost districts $60 to $100 a day.

Academic and financial costs incurred when teachers skip class argue for tougher attendance measures. But a recent *Education Week* survey of superintendents found little taste for confronting teachers' unions. One Florida superintendent threw up her hands in helplessness. She had no choice but to accept the word of teachers that they were sick, she said, and challenging teachers on skipping school wasn't something she was going to make into an "issue."

That's not good enough, especially considering recent evidence from researchers at Duke and Harvard universities confirming what common sense already suggests: Teacher absences affect student performance. The Harvard study found that 10 days of teacher absence is equivalent to a student drawing a rookie teacher rather than a second-year teacher. The Duke University study of North Carolina schools found similar results.

A few superintendents have launched programs to reward teachers who take fewer sick days than the contract allows. Other programs pay bonuses to schools that reduce their overall absence rates.

None of this should be necessary. Most teachers work hard in demanding jobs for modest pay, but they get home for dinner, have plenty of school holidays and breaks, and get summers off. It's grossly unprofessional for those who aren't really ill to take long weekends during the school year.

Perhaps supervisors need to start treating truant teachers like children and demanding notes from their parents and doctors.

---

opinion pages of newspapers regularly, or mainly during an election or controversy, in order to read the opinions, analysis, and interpretations of others on these issues.

Writers of editorials keep their readers—primary and secondary audiences—in mind as they compose. For example, the editorial board of *USA Today* published an editorial titled "When Teachers Cut Class" (May 1, 2008), aimed primarily at a conservative audience of parents, taxpayers, and citizens opposed to teachers' unions; it is also aimed at the teachers they critiqued in the editorial. Among the responses

◀ LETTER TO
THE EDITOR
Myra Warne, "Time
to Show Respect to
America's Educators."
Text: © Myra White.

Time to show respect to America's educators

I take exception to USA TODAY's characterization of teachers in its editorial about high sick-leave rates in school districts on Fridays ("When teachers cut class," May 1).

After the terrorist attacks on Sept. 11, 2001, I pondered what I would do if my job situation changed. I went back to school and earned a master's degree in education.

Having spent nearly 30 years in business, where responsibilities are well-defined and employees are compensated for their work, I sometimes look at the options in teaching and wonder why such an important job is so poorly compensated yet receives more criticism than respect from the American public.

No one seems to consider that many teachers are the breadwinners in their families. Summers are often spent taking courses to keep up with licensure renewal or mandates.

Teachers don't exit school on the day students are released for the summer or return on the same day in the fall when students arrive. There are reports to complete, rooms to organize and lesson plans to write. Teachers spend hours writing lesson plans and aligning them to standards. I have done this, and it requires much effort.

Every teacher I know works hard to achieve success for his or her students. In business, we are expected to suffer failures in the pursuit of success. Teachers are held to a standard of 100%, and I cannot think of another profession, even medicine, that mandates 100% success, pays little and then harps when a person takes a day off — personal, sick or otherwise.

Myra Warne

Zanesville, Ohio

Do you listen to
editorials read on
the radio? What is
your experience as a
listener? As a writer,
how would you
decide on the best
mode and medium
for your editorial
message?

to the editorial was a letter to the editor from Myra Warne, an Ohio teacher who took exception to *USA Today*'s opinion.

Rhetorical appeals   Editorial and opinion piece writers rely most on ethos and logos to persuade readers of the validity of their positions. As shown on page 200, the editorial board at *USA Today*, for example, uses evidence to appeal to readers' sense of logic. If the reader accepts the results of the university studies about the ill effects of teacher absences on student learning, then the reader should make the logical leap that teacher absences need to be dealt with seriously. Myra Warne responds to the editorial using a variety of appeals, including pathos. She establishes her ethos by discussing all her years in business, establishing her expertise in the work world. Additionally, she appeals to readers' emotions by illustrating the amount of work teachers do during the summer when they are not working, hoping that her readers sympathize with the dedication of teachers.

Modes & media   Newspaper editorials and opinion pieces are usually presented as written texts; sometimes they're accompanied by a small photo of the writer to establish the writer's credibility. Some editorials include charts or other infographics. Some editorials are presented as audio texts, such as the commentaries offered by National Public Radio. Editorials and opinion pieces can be found both in print, such as in newspapers and magazines, and digitally, such as on the sites for *The New York Times* and NPR.

THE GENRE'S CONVENTIONS

Elements of the genre   Editorial and opinion piece writers do the following:

Clearly present their work as opinion writing. The distinction between an editorial or opinion piece and a news article is important: Editorials or opinion pieces are opinions based on research and analysis, whereas news articles are objective reporting based on research. That is, editorials reflect a personal view while news articles are supposed to be totally free of opinion. Editorials or opinion pieces are usually clearly labeled as *editorials* (or with another name such as *opinion, viewpoint, perspective,* or *commentary*).

Write concisely. An editorial or opinion piece is typically about five or so paragraphs long, which means the author needs to make his or her point quickly.

Begin with an introduction that gets readers' attention. For example, the authors of the *USA Today* piece on teachers' cutting class opens with a rhetorical question asking readers, "Remember those days when your teacher unexpectedly called in sick?" followed by a remark about the useless substitute. Immediately, readers are reminded of their own experiences and identify with the writers.

Identify and address counterarguments. Editorial and opinion piece writers make their strongest cases when they anticipate objections and opposition to their views. In the *Denver Post* editorial arguing for state control of marijuana (p. 199), the writers anticipate that readers might bring up the fact that state marijuana laws operate in conflict with federal laws. In response to this, the writers argue, "Those states may be operating outside of federal law, but it's with their citizens' consent."

Offer potential solutions. Often after explaining a problem, writers will examine potential solutions and suggest one over another. In the *USA Today* editorial, the writers mention some solutions but then conclude that the best one would be for teachers to simply stop taking sick days unless they are sick.

Close with a simple but memorable statement. For example, the final paragraph of the *USA Today* editorial is particularly memorable because of the writers' tone—and the sarcastic suggestion that, like absent children, absent teachers should provide a sick note from their parents.

Invite readers to respond. Many online editorials, such as the *USA Today* editorial, become discussion starters in which hundreds or even thousands of readers post replies to the original editorial and to other posts.

Style   Editorial and opinion piece writers do the following:

Include concise detail. Editorial and opinion piece writers use specific facts throughout their texts to support their position. Because they are making a case, they need to use enough evidence to convince readers, but they still need to keep the entire piece fairly brief.

Use a variety of techniques. To engage and persuade readers, editorial and opinion piece writers:

» Include quotations from experts to support their claims.

» Avoid errors in reasoning; such errors are known as logical fallacies. Here are some of the most common types:

>> *Red herring*: Distracting the reader from the real issue being argued; for example, "Global warming needs to be addressed, but people are struggling with gas prices."

>> *Ad hominem*: Attacking the person making an argument instead of addressing the argument; for example, "She says women should have equal rights, but look at how ugly she is."

>> *Hasty generalization*: Extrapolating unrealistically from one example; for example, "He lied; therefore all men are liars."

>> *Slippery slope*: Assuming that if one step is taken, then all sorts of catastrophic results will inevitably follow; for example, "If we increase taxes

by 1 percent today, tomorrow our children will be paying more in taxes than they take home."

» *Circular reasoning*: Defining a word by using the word, where the start is the same as the ending; for example, "The reason we should outlaw guns is that guns should be made illegal."

» *Post hoc*: Confusing chronology with causality; for example, "The cat peed on the bedspread because I just washed it."

» Use analogies and refer to cultural and historical events so that readers will identify with the issue.

» Avoid jargon and instead use language that will appeal to readers who may not be familiar with the issue.

» Use rhetorical questions to spark readers' attention.

Convey a clear, personable voice and tone. Writers use clear, persuasive language as they present their opinions and support them with facts. Editorial writers often write in the first person (*I*) and in a friendly and inviting tone to reach a wide readership.

Design   Editorial and opinion piece writers—and the designers they work with—do the following:

Write clear, interesting headlines. Whether they're published in print or online, editorials, like news articles, are presented with a headline designed to get readers' attention and to make it clear what the editorialist is writing about. Editorials and opinion pieces are also clearly labeled as such, or with other terms, such as *opinions* or *commentaries*, that denote subjective writing.

Repeat design features on the page. Whether you're reading an editorial or opinion piece in print or online, you'll see certain design elements on every page; these elements include the name of the newspaper, perhaps presented as a logo or otherwise branded, at the top and bottom of the page. This helps the writers and designers establish the news organization's identity. You might also find a heading indicating what part of the paper or site you've navigated to ("Editorial," "Opinion," etc.). The date also appears in these spots for easy reference.

How do editorial writers use sources to support their arguments? What sources are most persuasive? Can anecdotal evidence be as convincing as statistical data?

Note: Design features of editorials and opinion pieces are generally similar to those of newspaper articles. See Chapter 3, page 131, for more on news article design.

Sources   Editorial and opinion piece writers do the following:

Refer to specific examples. The editorial board of *USA Today* offers several specific pieces of evidence to make their point (p. 200), such as the actual cost of substitutes, the results of the *Education Week* survey, and the results of the Harvard and Duke studies. The writers make the case by offering a variety of support from credible sources.

Use attribution phrases. Editorialists present evidence to support their points, often using attribution phrases to let readers know where the data came from. For instance, in the *USA Today* editorial, "An *Orlando Sentinel* reporter recently found" cues readers that the source of the information on the most common sick days is an *Orlando Sentinel* article.

Guided Reading: Opinion Piece ▼

Katha Pollitt

Adam and Steve—Together at Last

Katha Pollitt is a regular columnist for *The Nation* magazine, where she writes an opinion column called "Subject to Debate," which has won the National Magazine Award for Columns and Commentary. *The Nation*, like Pollitt's column, tackles political and social issues, usually from a left-wing political perspective. Pollitt's work has appeared in other magazines including *Harper's* and *The New Yorker*. Her persuasive essay "Adam and Steve—Together at Last" first appeared in the December 15, 2003, issue of *The Nation*. The essay disputes the legitimacy of arguments against same-sex marriage. Although same-sex marriage is legal in many countries, such as Canada and South Africa, it has been a controversial issue in the United States, with supporters claiming that allowing same-sex unions extends basic rights to homosexuals, and opponents maintaining that legalizing same-sex unions would jeopardize all marriages. *(Pages 206–08: Text © Katha Pollitt. Art Courtesy of* The Nation.*)*

▲ AUTHOR PHOTO
Katha Pollitt.
Christina Pabst.

What is the composer, **Katha Pollitt**, doing?

**THE RHETORICAL
SITUATION**

Purpose
Audience
Rhetorical appeals
Modes & media

see page 207

How do I know this is an **opinion piece**?

**THE GENRE'S
CONVENTIONS**

Elements of the genre
Style
Design
Sources

see page 207

Adam and Steve--Together at Last

**Will someone please explain to me how permitting gays and lesbians to
marry threatens the institution of marriage?**

Katha Pollitt

Will someone please explain to me how permitting gays and lesbians to
marry threatens the institution of marriage? Now that the Massachusetts
Supreme Court has declared gay marriage a constitutional right, opponents really have to get their arguments in line. The most popular theory,
advanced by David Blankenhorn, Jean Bethke Elshtain, and other social
conservatives is that under the tulle and orange blossom, *marriage* is
all about procreation. There's some truth to this as a practical matter—
couples often live together and tie the knot only when baby's on the way.
But whether or not marriage is the best framework for child-rearing,
having children isn't a marital requirement. As many have pointed out, the
law permits marriage to the infertile, the elderly, the impotent, and those
with no wish to procreate; it allows married couples to use birth control,
to get sterilized, to be celibate. There's something creepily authoritarian and insulting about reducing marriage to procreation, as if intimacy
mattered less than biological fitness. It's not a view that anyone outside a
right-wing think tank, a Catholic marriage tribunal, or an ultra-Orthodox
rabbi's court is likely to find persuasive.

So scratch procreation. How about: Marriage is the way women domesticate
men. This theory, a favorite of right-wing writer George Gilder, has some
statistical support—married men are much less likely than singles to kill
people, crash the car, take drugs, commit suicide—although it overlooks such
husbandly failings as domestic violence, child abuse, infidelity, and abandon-
ment. If a man rapes his wife instead of his date, it probably won't show up
on a police blotter, but has civilization moved forward? Of course, this view

HOME | BLOGS | COLUMNISTS | CURRENT ISSUE | MAGAZINE ARCHIVE | MULTIMEDIA   COMMUNITY | NATION BUILDERS | STUDENTS

POLITICS   WORLD   BOOKS & ARTS   ECONOMY   ENVIRONMENT   ACTIVISM   SOCIETY   LIVED HISTORY   NEW YORK: THE GILDED CITY

of marriage as a barbarian-adoption program doesn't explain why women should undertake it—as is obvious from the state of the world, they haven't been too successful at it, anyway. (Maybe men should civilize men—bring on the Fab Five!) Nor does it explain why marriage should be restricted to heterosexual couples. The gay men and lesbians who want to marry don't impinge on the male-improvement project one way or the other. Surely not even Gilder believes that a heterosexual pothead with plans for murder and suicide would be reformed by marrying a lesbian?

What about the argument from history? According to this, marriage has been around forever and has stood the test of time. Actually, though, marriage as we understand it—voluntary, monogamous, legally egalitarian, based on love, involving adults only—is a pretty recent phenomenon. For much of human history, polygyny was the rule—read your Old Testament—and in much of Africa and the Muslim world, it still is. Arranged marriages, forced marriages, child marriages, marriages predicated on the subjugation of women—gay marriage is like a fairy tale romance compared with most chapters of the history of wedlock.

The trouble with these and other arguments against gay marriage is that they overlook how loose, flexible, individualized, and easily dissolved the bonds of marriage already are. Virtually any man and woman can marry, no matter how ill assorted or little acquainted. An eighty-year-old can marry an eighteen-year-old; a john can marry a prostitute; two terminally ill patients can marry each other from their hospital beds. You can get married by proxy, like medieval royalty, and not see each other in the flesh for years. Whatever may have been the case in the past, what undergirds marriage in most people's minds today is not some sociobiological theory about reproduction or male socialization. Nor is it the enormous bundle of privileges society awards to married people. It's love, commitment, stability. Speaking just for myself, I don't like marriage. I prefer the old-fashioned ideal of monogamous free love, not that it worked out particularly well in my case. As a social mechanism, moreover, marriage seems to me a deeply

Continues next page

Katha Pollitt, *Adam and Steve—Together at Last*   207

THE RHETORICAL
SITUATION

Purpose

Pollitt wants to convince readers that gay marriage should be accepted as a "constitutional right."

Audience

Pollitt's readers are interested in the gay marriage debate. They may be socially liberal or conservative; if they are regular readers of *The Nation*, they're probably socially liberal.

THE GENRE'S
CONVENTIONS

Elements of the genre

Pollitt makes it clear that this is an opinion piece, beginning with the tone of her title, a play on Adam and Eve, and her first sentence: "Will someone please explain to me. . . ." She goes on to **relate her opinions** on gay marriage.

Pollitt **grabs attention** by starting with a question and a reference to a court decision.

(Continued on p. 208.)

THE RHETORICAL SITUATION

Rhetorical appeals

By pointing out that "having children isn't a marital requirement," Pollitt appeals to **logos**; she shows that it isn't logical to disallow same-sex marriages on the basis that same-sex couples can't have children together.

(Continued on p. 209.)

THE GENRE'S CONVENTIONS

She strengthens her position when she identifies and critiques counterarguments.

She closes with a strong statement: "Gay marriage—it's not about sex, it's about separation of church and state." This simple line is likely to stick with readers long after they've forgotten Pollitt's specifics.

Nation.

| HOME | BLOGS | COLUMNISTS | CURRENT ISSUE | MAGAZINE ARCHIVE | MULTIMEDIA | | COMMUNITY | NATION BUILDERS | STUDENTS |

POLITICS   WORLD   BOOKS & ARTS   ECONOMY   ENVIRONMENT   ACTIVISM   SOCIETY   LIVED HISTORY   NEW YORK: THE GILDED CITY

unfair way of distributing social goods like health insurance and retirement checks, things everyone needs. Why should one's marital status determine how much you pay the doctor, or whether you eat cat food in old age, or whether a child gets a government check if a parent dies? It's outrageous that, for example, a working wife who pays Social Security all her life gets no more back from the system than if she had married a male worker earning the same amount and stayed home. Still, as long as marriage is here, how can it be right to deny it to those who want it? In fact, you would think that, given how many heterosexuals are happy to live in sin, social conservatives would welcome maritally minded gays with open arms. Gays already have the baby—they can adopt in many states, and lesbians can give birth in all of them—so why deprive them of the marital bathwater?

At bottom, the objections to gay marriage are based on religious prejudice: The marriage of man and woman is "sacred" and opening it to same-sexers violates its sacral nature. That is why so many people can live with civil unions but draw the line at marriage—spiritual union. In fact, polls show a striking correlation of religiosity, especially evangelical Protestantism, with opposition to gay marriage and with belief in homosexuality as a choice, the famous "gay lifestyle." For these people gay marriage is wrong because it lets gays and lesbians avoid turning themselves into the straights God wants them to be. As a matter of law, however, marriage is not about Adam and Eve versus Adam and Steve. It's not about what God blesses, it's about what the government permits. People may think *marriage* is a word wholly owned by religion, but actually it's wholly owned by the state. No matter how big your church wedding, you still have to get a marriage license from City Hall. And just as divorced people can marry even if the Catholic Church considers it bigamy, and Muslim and Mormon men can only marry one woman even if their holy books tell them they can wed all the girls in Apartment 3G, two men or two women should be able to marry, even if religions oppose it and it makes some heterosexuals, raised in those religions, uncomfortable.

Gay marriage—it's not about sex, it's about separation of church and state.

THE RHETORICAL SITUATION

Pollitt establishes her **ethos** by writing with authority and showing her familiarity with historical facts and theories (such as those put forth by Blankenhorn and Elshtain).

Modes & media

Mode = written The digital version also includes a visual, a small headshot of Pollitt. Most editorials and opinion pieces are written or audio. Words are vital to an editorialist making his or her point because the specificity and clarity of the editorialist's position is so important.

Medium = print and digital The content is the same in both versions, but the design and context are different. In the print version, the essay gets one complete page of the magazine. In the digital version, the column shares space with a menu bar at the top and several items that occupy the left-hand side of the screen, including a small headshot of Pollitt and links to related articles on *The Nation*'s Web site. These differences result from the varying needs and desires of print and digital editorial audiences.

THE GENRE'S CONVENTIONS

Style

Pollitt **uses specific facts** to back up her views; e.g., she provides details of aspects of George Gilder's theories and refers to other source texts, including the Bible.

She **uses rhetorical questions** effectively; for example, to hold the reader's interest, she asks, "Why should one's marital status determine how much you pay the doctor?"

Her tone is personal and informal. For example, she writes, "Speaking just for myself, I don't like marriage."

Design

The "Subject to Debate" **headline and its visual design draw readers in.** For easy reference, *The Nation*'s title appears at the top of the page. In the online version of this article, there are "About the Author," "Also by the Author," and "Related Topics" headings to orient readers within the site and expand their reading.

Sources

Pollitt **refers to several specific sources** (the voices of opposition), such as David Blankenhorn, the founder and president of the socially conservative Institute for American Values, and ethics professor Jean Bethke Elshtain, as well as the Old Testament. While sources are linked in some online editorials and opinion pieces, that's not the case here.

Questions: Analyzing Pollitt's opinion piece

1. Purpose. Does Pollitt convince you that gay marriage is "not about sex, it's about separation of church and state"? Why or why not?

2. Audience. How do you think a person opposed to gay marriage might respond to Pollitt's essay?

3. Rhetorical appeals. List the counterarguments Pollitt addresses. Do you think she's left out any? If so, why do you think she chose to focus on the ones she did?

4. Rhetorical appeals. How does Pollitt build her case? How does she appeal to her audience using logos?

5. Rhetorical appeals. To what extent does Pollitt come across as authoritative and knowledgeable? What does she do to convince you she is (1) authoritative and knowledgeable or (2) lacking in authority and knowledge? Explain.

6. Modes & media. Imagine that Pollitt had included a large black-and-white photo of two men kissing at the top of the essay. How would the addition of this image add to or detract from the effectiveness of the editorial?

7. Elements of the genre. Although Pollitt's essay doesn't feature a clearly stated position or thesis statement at the beginning, how does she make her position clear from the beginning? Where does Pollitt state her position most clearly?

8. Elements of the genre. How do the organization and paragraph structure help you pick out the specific counterarguments Pollitt addresses in her column?

9. Style. How would you characterize the tone of Pollitt's essay? How does it affect you as a reader? Do you think anyone would consider her language inflammatory? How does this work for or against her position?

10. Style. What does the title allude to? Why is that allusion appropriate for this essay?

11. Design. The final sentence is set off in its own paragraph. How does this add to the impact of Pollitt's conclusion?

12. Sources. Pollitt does not cite sources in every paragraph. How does she convince you that she is familiar with source material about, say, the history of marriage, without directly citing sources?

Drafting an Editorial or Opinion Piece

CHECKLIST: Drafting an Editorial or Opinion Piece Thinking of writing an editorial? Ask yourself the following questions.

WHAT'S MY RHETORICAL SITUATION?

☐ **Purpose.** What is my purpose? And what do I want to persuade others to think or do? Do I want readers to see things from a different perspective? To take action? Do I want them to completely change their minds on an issue? How feasible is it to try to change a person's mind?

☐ **Audience.** Who am I trying to persuade? What are my audience's concerns about the issue I'm writing about? What do they fear? What is their stake in the issue (what do they personally have to risk losing if they do what I want)?

☐ **Rhetorical appeals.** How will I establish myself as reasonable and authoritative on this issue? How can I use organization to appeal to my audience's sense of logos? Will my audience respond to emotional appeals or will I seem manipulative if I appeal to pathos?

☐ **Modes & media.** Will I use written words or audio or video to convey my point? Based on the audience I have in mind—are they more likely to read or listen to an editorial in print, on the radio, or on the Internet?

WHAT GENRE CONVENTIONS MATTER?

☐ **Elements of the genre.** How can I make it clear that I'm writing an opinion piece? How can I get my audience's attention immediately and show them how important and relevant this issue is to their lives? Which potential objections and counterarguments should I address? How can I make the closing of my editorial memorable?

☐ **Style.** Would it help to support my case by bringing in quotations from experts? Are there analogies that I could use that would appeal to my readers? What types of rhetorical questions would be most compelling for my editorial? How will I keep my language persuasive yet friendly?

☐ **Design.** Do I want to design a heading or logo for my column to identify myself as the author? How can I use a heading, logo, or other design element to develop my ethos?

☐ **Sources.** What kinds of sources will be most useful and most interesting and persuasive to my audience? How might I bring in sources to address potential objections and opposing arguments?

PRACTICE Want to experiment? Draft your own editorial or opinion piece.

Think about an issue you care deeply about. Think about what your position is on the issue. Then brainstorm a list of reasons/evidence that supports your position. What are some of the counterarguments? Do research so that you can provide some support, as Pollitt does with different theorists and their positions. Then combine your research and ideas into an editorial or opinion piece that convinces your audience that your position is a valid one.

RESEARCHED ARGUMENTS

A researched argument is any work in which a writer presents an argument and backs it up with solid sources. Most academic research papers are researched arguments (see also the peer-reviewed journal article discussed in Chapter 3, p. 148). Writers of researched arguments do the following:

» Investigate a topic and work with sources

» Make a specific and persuasive case about that topic

» Incorporate in their writing voices of their sources through summary, paraphrase, and quotation

» Cite those sources in the body of the composition

» List the sources at the end

When you read an argument text, are you more swayed by personal opinion and anecdote or research as support? Does it depend on the subject matter? Your expertise on the subject? The genre itself? Explain.

The main purpose of writing a researched argument is to persuade your readers of the merits of your argument. Drawing on and citing your sources builds a case for your argument.

Researched arguments appear in the same places that research papers do: in the classroom, in peer-reviewed journals, in magazines, and on the Internet in the form of blog entries and other argumentative pieces. Depending on the level of research they've conducted and where they publish their work, authors of this genre may be scholars, recognized by other scholars as experts on the subject they are writing about, or they may be reporters, bloggers, or other types of experts on their subject. For example, an experienced snowboarder who researches different snowboarding designs and blogs in favor of one would be considered an expert on the subject she's writing about.

For more examples of **researched compositions,** see the Index of Genres on page G-1.

At work, researched arguments often take the form of reports or memos. When an employee wants to persuade an organization to change a policy or procedure, he may write a memo or report in which he refers to specific research or to policies at similar organizations.

Analyzing Researched Arguments: What to Look For

THE RHETORICAL SITUATION

Purpose   We write researched arguments because we want to persuade others to share our point of view on a topic. We may be looking for readers to simply agree, or maybe to take a specific action. When you write a researched argument, you begin by conducting research in hopes that the quality and quantity of the data you present will convince readers. For example, Liz had the following experience: her department at Metro State recently considered whether or not to change the amount of credit students will receive for certain AP scores. Liz and a colleague argued their position on how much credit Metro State should give students in a memo to the department that cited the AP credit policies of several other similar universities and colleges. Their purpose was to get their colleagues to agree with them and to take action.

Henry Fong, host of the blog *FitBomb*, writes to persuade readers to adopt or at least consider the exercise and eating plans he favors. In the post on page 214, he argues for the Paleo Diet, citing research to back up his views on the benefits of "eating like a caveman." As you can see, he uses hyperlinks to cite his sources, furthering his ethos and logos. This is an example of a researched argument presented as a blog post.

Audience   Authors of researched arguments usually write for others who are interested in the topic being discussed. Readers may or may not agree with the argument the writer proposes, but they're generally curious enough to read about the perspectives of others. If you're an expert writing a researched argument for a peer-reviewed journal, then your audience is other experts. If you're writing a memo or report at work, then your audience is your colleagues. If you're writing a blog, such as Henry Fong does at *FitBomb*, you're writing for others who most likely share your enthusiasm for fitness—but who may or may not agree with everything you propose.

In the case of the *FitBomb* post on the Paleo Diet, it's clear the author is aware of his readers' potential skepticism. The Q&A format he adopts for the argument takes into account potential objections, and he addresses the reader directly: "What? Not good enough? I hear you. Frankly, I resisted going Paleo for quite a while."

> Do any of the blogs you read feature researched arguments? How persuasive do you find them? Have you ever changed your view on a topic because of a researched argument you read on a blog?

> ☞ **Attention, researchers & writers!**
>
> Poorly integrated and cited research casts doubt on you as an author and seriously compromises your ethos—while a smart use of sources does a lot to build it. See Chapter 7 for more on integrating and citing sources.

BLOG POST ▶

Henry Fong, "What
Is the Paleo Diet?," a
researched argument
at *FitBomb. All images
on pages 214–21: Henry
Fong/Fitbomb.com.*

START HERE   ABOUT   CROSSFIT   WHAT IS THE PALEO DIET?   MOST POPULAR   SHIRTS   NOM NOM PALEO APP

What Is The Paleo Diet?

INTRODUCTION

Even after eating this way for years, we still manage to catch
some of our dining companions off-guard. Their eyebrows
shoot up when we order our food sans bread, pasta, rice,
polenta or beans. The questions are always the same:

"Are you on Atkins or something?"

"Trying to lose weight?"

"You don't even eat *whole* grains?"

"What the hell is the matter with you?"

Well, here exactly is the matter with me: I EAT PALEO. As in
the Paleolithic (or "Paleo") Diet. You may have heard of it as
the Caveman Diet.

If you're feeling bookish, Loren Cordain's "The Paleo Diet" and Mark
Sisson's "The Primal Blueprint" introduced the concept of ancestral
eating approaches to tons of people. (Sisson, in particular, is an
excellent resource for tips and information on implementing this type of
nutritional template. Check out his massively popular site, Mark's Daily
Apple, for more.)

If you'd rather gaze into a computer screen, start with Cordain's Paleo
Diet FAQ, Sisson's how-to on living "Primally," and J. Stanton's "Eat
Like a Predator, Not Like Prey." This page on Melissa McEwen's site
also contains lots of useful resources for newbies. Hivelogic's Paleo
link primer is a great starting point, too. (And I'm not just saying that
'cause my wife's blog is listed as a Paleo cooking resource.)

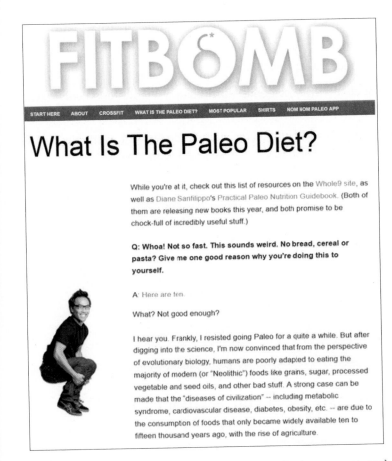

What Is The Paleo Diet?

While you're at it, check out this list of resources on the Whole9 site, as well as Diane Sanfilippo's Practical Paleo Nutrition Guidebook. (Both of them are releasing new books this year, and both promise to be chock-full of incredibly useful stuff.)

Q: Whoa! Not so fast. This sounds weird. No bread, cereal or pasta? Give me one good reason why you're doing this to yourself.

A: Here are ten.

What? Not good enough?

I hear you. Frankly, I resisted going Paleo for a quite a while. But after digging into the science, I'm now convinced that from the perspective of evolutionary biology, humans are poorly adapted to eating the majority of modern (or "Neolithic") foods like grains, sugar, processed vegetable and seed oils, and other bad stuff. A strong case can be made that the "diseases of civilization" -- including metabolic syndrome, cardiovascular disease, diabetes, obesity, etc. -- are due to the consumption of foods that only became widely available ten to fifteen thousand years ago, with the rise of agriculture.

Rhetorical appeals   When writing a researched argument, authors can establish ethos by:

» Describing their research methods

» Explaining the data they collected and how they analyzed it

» Discussing their findings and conclusions in detail

» Citing their sources appropriately

» Writing as directly and persuasively as possible

Writers can establish logos by:

» Stating their position clearly

» Stating each aspect of their argument clearly—and in an order that makes sense

» Anticipating and addressing objections

» Supporting their claims with evidence—including the views of others (drawn from their sources)

Do you prefer an author to sound like a know-it-all or would you rather an author admit that he or she doesn't know everything about the topic?

The author of the *FitBomb* post outlines his information and argument clearly. He explains what the diet is, and also makes a case for adopting the diet.

As this book goes to press, Henry Fong of *Fitbomb* presents his information on the Paleo Diet in the following parts, which are in turn broken out into a Q&A format:

Introduction

1. What to Eat and Why

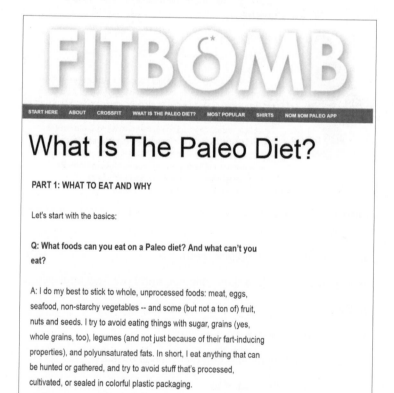

FITB⊙MB

START HERE   ABOUT   CROSSFIT   WHAT IS THE PALEO DIET?   MOST POPULAR   SHIRTS   NOM NOM PALEO APP

What Is The Paleo Diet?

PART 1: WHAT TO EAT AND WHY

Let's start with the basics:

Q: What foods can you eat on a Paleo diet? And what can't you eat?

A: I do my best to stick to whole, unprocessed foods: meat, eggs, seafood, non-starchy vegetables -- and some (but not a ton of) fruit, nuts and seeds. I try to avoid eating things with sugar, grains (yes, whole grains, too), legumes (and not just because of their fart-inducing properties), and polyunsaturated fats. In short, I eat anything that can be hunted or gathered, and try to avoid stuff that's processed, cultivated, or sealed in colorful plastic packaging.

2. What's Wrong with What We Eat?

3. You Aren't What You Eat (So Eat Some Fat)

4. Why I Eat Paleo

5. Mythbusting

6. Foods to Avoid and Why

7. Transitioning to Paleo

What voice and tone are appropriate for a researched argument? How might this vary, depending on context and medium?

Whether or not you agree with his take on "eating like a caveman," the author of the *FitBomb* post appeals to readers by doing much of what is described in the above section on ethos and logos. Further, he appeals to pathos through his use of humor, as in the excerpt that follows.

START HERE   ABOUT   CROSSFIT   WHAT IS THE PALEO DIET?   MOST POPULAR   SHIRTS   NOM NOM PALEO APP

What Is The Paleo Diet?

But wait – there's more! An excess of insulin in our blood isn't just bad because gives you an unsightly muffin-top. It's bad because it can make you very, very sick.

Let's say you're a carb junkie. You stock up on bread, pasta, rice and 100-calorie packs of Snackwells because they're low-fat. They know you by name at Jamba Juice and Auntie Anne's Pretzels. The

Modes & media   Researched arguments published as articles in peer-reviewed journals, as memos, and as reports are text based and may include visuals such as charts, graphs, and images to support and illustrate points. These types of pieces can be available in print or online. For example, the memo about AP scores that Liz wrote was circulated by e-mail. Blog entries, of course, are digital.

Elements of the genre

Author states a thesis or makes a clear claim. To make a position clear, a writer can (1) indicate the topic at hand and his or her position on it right in the title, (2) provide a clear thesis, doing so right at the beginning, or (3) combine both. In the *FitBomb* post on the Paleo Diet, the author uses clear subheadings for the various sections. In the section titled "What Really Causes Obesity?" he answers the question in a clear thesis in paragraph 1:

> The short answer: Excess carbohydrates. Especially sugar.

This clearly shows that the writer will argue against the commonly held belief that consuming too much fat leads to obesity; instead, he will argue that sugar causes us to be overweight.

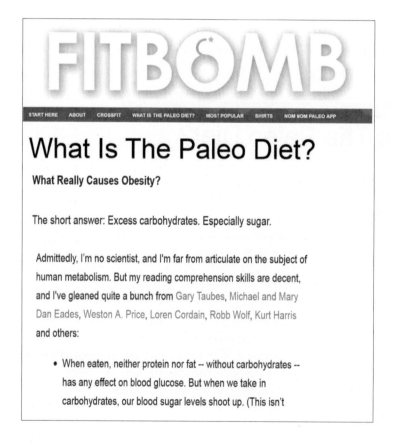

FITBOMB

START HERE   ABOUT   CROSSFIT   WHAT IS THE PALEO DIET?   MOST POPULAR   SHIRTS   NOM NOM PALEO APP

What Is The Paleo Diet?

What Really Causes Obesity?

The short answer: Excess carbohydrates. Especially sugar.

Admittedly, I'm no scientist, and I'm far from articulate on the subject of human metabolism. But my reading comprehension skills are decent, and I've gleaned quite a bunch from Gary Taubes, Michael and Mary Dan Eades, Weston A. Price, Loren Cordain, Robb Wolf, Kurt Harris and others:

- When eaten, neither protein nor fat -- without carbohydrates -- has any effect on blood glucose. But when we take in carbohydrates, our blood sugar levels shoot up. (This isn't

Authors present an argument. For example, the *FitBomb* blogger writes to explain the Paleo Diet—but mainly to persuade readers to adopt it. He supports his main argument with seven sections—moving from what the diet is, to what research shows about the diet, to why he likes it—and ends with advice on how readers can transition to it themselves. In each part of his argument, the writer supports himself with evidence.

Authors base their arguments on solid research. All researched writing relies on research of some kind. Most writers support their ideas by drawing on the research of others—of experts and leaders in the field. As a student, unless you do primary research (such as conducting interviews), you most likely draw on the research of others in your researched writing.

Some authors—mainly academics writing for peer-reviewed journals—draw on their own research, particularly if they've conducted a study or survey of some kind that brings in data. Arguments for peer-reviewed journals are usually written in a formal style using precise language. They are also reviewed by others in the field for accuracy and reliability. (For more on peer-reviewed journal articles, see Chapter 3.)

When Liz and Amy present papers at conferences, they draw on and cite specific research done by academic experts and colleagues to support their arguments. The *FitBomb* blogger cites more than two hundred sources, including research by established experts, such as the Weston A. Price Foundation, which focuses on nutrition education.

Authors address counterarguments. To build logos, writers need to acknowledge contrasting or opposing arguments and either (1) refute them by exposing their holes or presenting evidence that outweighs them or (2) concede that they are legitimate and then explain why, despite this legitimacy, the audience should take the author's position. In Liz's AP score memo, she conceded to the opposing argument that some students with AP scores of 3 in English might no longer apply to Metro State if they wouldn't receive credit for a composition class. However, she explained that in the long run, these students would actually be more successful if they were required to take a composition class at Metro State.

Authors synthesize and attribute the work of others. As noted above, citing sources—and specific examples—builds ethos. It's also a good idea to pull information from multiple sources and to synthesize it by showing readers how these sources align and differ. When a writer relies on only one source, it makes the argument look weak to readers, and therefore much less persuasive. (For more on synthesizing sources, see Chapter 7.)

Analyzing Researched Arguments: What to Look For

Style

Authors title their work to make their position clear. Authors of researched arguments title their work to make clear the topic they're writing about and what their position is. For example, for her memo subject line, which serves as the memo's title, Liz wrote: "Why we should raise AP scores for composition credit."

Authors write with authority. Writers use a strong voice and tone to convey expertise on a topic, support their ethos, and persuade their readers.

Authors get readers' attention with simple but memorable introductions and closing statements. For example, the *FitBomb* blogger starts with an anecdote.

Toward the end of his argument, the blogger concedes that the Paleo Diet isn't for everyone, but he does so with humor—subtly critiquing the "low-fat approach" and presenting a mental image of grass-fed beef, a central part of the Paleo Diet.

I have a number of friends who are committed to strict calorie-counting as a weight loss strategy, and I know plenty of others who've adopted the "everything in moderation" approach to eating. Some still look to egg-white omelets and low-fat (but high-sugar) cookies for weight loss purposes. If they're happy with those approaches, then that's their choice. I'm not going to force-feed them grass-fed beef. (I'm saving that stuff for me!)

Authors use detail. The more specific writers are—in terms of both the main point and the research they're drawing on—the better and more persuasive the argument.

Design

Authors use subheadings. Many writers divide their arguments into sections with subheadings that make a long, complex piece easier to navigate. (See p. 216.) Subheadings also signal readers that an author is shifting his or her focus.

Authors support their arguments with images. Photos, charts, and illustrations convey complex information visually—and can serve as sources. For example, the *FitBomb* blogger uses images to back up his argument about the Paleo Diet, such as the infographic on page 222, taken from a like-minded site, PaleolithicDiet.com.

Sources

Authors curate sources carefully. Authors of researched arguments use sources that their readers will respect. When Liz wrote the AP credit memo, she knew her audience—colleagues in the English department—would be swayed by what other English departments do. In the case of the *FitBomb* post, the author draws on sources by writers he identifies as experts on the Paleo Diet.

Authors cite sources—according to genre conventions. An author of a peer-reviewed journal article would include a bibliographic list at the end of the article and use parenthetical citations throughout. A blogger simply embeds links to his or her sources, as the *FitBomb* blogger does.

For more examples of **researched writing** and **academic writing,** including student work, see the Index of Genres on page G-1.

Analyzing Researched Arguments: What to Look For

INFOGRAPHIC ▶
PaleolithicDiet.com,
"The Paleolithic Diet
Explained," from the
FitBomb post.

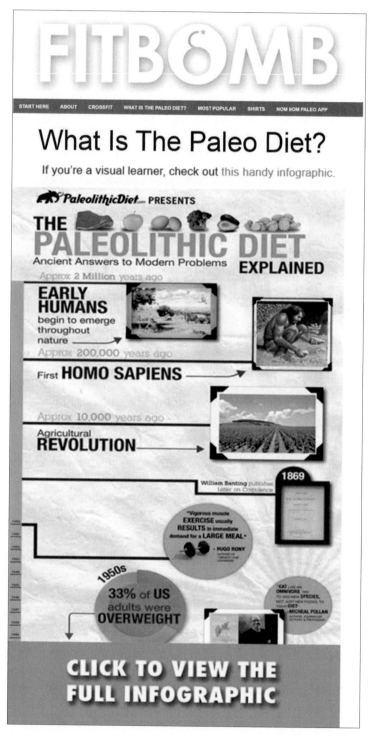

Chase Dickinson (Student)

Are Kids on a One-Way Path to Violence?

Chase Dickinson, a student from Herriman, Utah, wrote the following researched argument when he was a freshman at Weber State University, where he studied geoscience. As he mentions in the following essay, Dickinson worked for a video game vendor called Play N Trade, which factors into the argument he makes about video games in "Are Kids on a One-Way Path to Violence?" The essay, which he wrote for his English composition course, was also published in Weber State's journal of student work, called *Weber Writes*, edited in 2010 by Scott Rogers and Sylvia Newman.

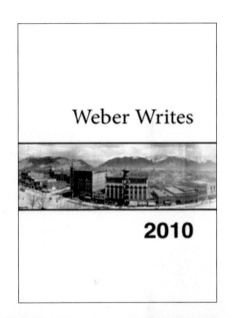

▼ STUDENT PHOTO, JOURNAL COVER, ▶ & UNIVERSITY WEB SITE ▼
Chase Dickinson; *Weber Writes*, the student journal that published Dickinson's researched essay; and Weber State University's site. *Author photo: Chase Dickinson. Journal cover: Weber State. Weber State homepage: Weber State.*

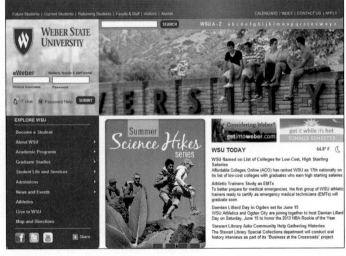

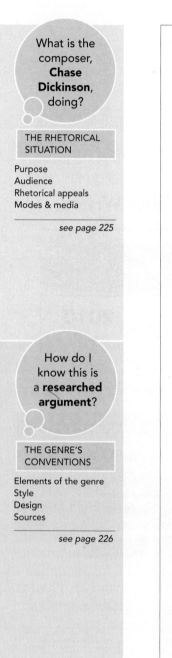

What is the composer, Chase Dickinson, doing?

THE RHETORICAL
SITUATION

Purpose
Audience
Rhetorical appeals
Modes & media

see page 225

How do I know this is a researched argument?

THE GENRE'S
CONVENTIONS

Elements of the genre
Style
Design
Sources

see page 226

Chase Dickinson
Are Kids on a One-Way Path to Violence?

In the popular video game *Grand Theft Auto* (GTA), players are thrust into a world without laws, free to do just about anything they want. Stealing cars, killing civilians, and causing general mayhem are common occurrences in the fictitious world of Liberty City. In fact, GTA is about as lawless as games get. But can a game such as *Grand Theft Auto* actually fuel real-world violence? There are many who believe so, and violent video games have therefore become a hotly debated topic in today's headlines.

If you were to listen to politicians and critics, the relationship between video games and crime is blatantly clear: children who play video games will either become more aggressive or actually commit real-world acts of violence. According to the lawyers of Lee Malvo, the young "DC Sniper," Malvo learned to shoot by playing "very realistic and gory" video games. These games were also said to have "desensitized (him) . . . to train him to shoot human forms over and over" (qtd. in Provan). Another popular argument against violent video games comes in the form of the infamous Columbine shootings in which Dylan Klebold and Eric Harris killed thirteen students and injured twenty-three more before killing themselves. During the investigation that followed, it was discovered that both teenagers enjoyed playing the bloody first-person shooter *Doom*, and that they went on the rampage shortly after their parents took the game away from them. It has also been speculated that the pair created a level in *Doom* with the same layout as their school in order to plan out their attack (Mikkelson). Yet another argument finds Jack Thompson, a leader in the fight against violent video games, blaming the Virginia Tech shooting on the first-person shooter *Counter-Strike*, saying that once again the shooter trained for his crime by playing the popular first-person shooter (qtd. in Benedetti).

Dickinson, *One-Way Path to Violence?* Continued

With video games rapidly gaining popularity, we have to ask ourselves if these crimes are actually caused by the increasing violence in games. While there are many who tend to think so, I believe that it is not the fault of the games themselves, but the lack of parental supervision and interaction with today's youth. Also, preexisting mental disorders have been found to play a huge role in how different people will react to video games.

Take, for example, the DC sniper shootings. *Halo*, the game that Malvo supposedly used to prepare for his crimes, employs the use of unrealistic guns to shoot giant alien bugs. Such actions are hardly effective ways to learn how to shoot a sniper rifle at human beings. Malvo even admitted that he trained by shooting a real gun at makeshift targets with paper plates for heads (Provan). Similarly, the claims that the Columbine shooters created a level with their school's layout were never found to be true. In fact, all of the levels they made were later found on their Web site, and all of them were based on fictitious locations on alien planets (Mikkelson). Lastly, no one was ever reported to have seen Seung-Hui Cho, the Virginia Tech shooter, playing any video games. His roommate told the New York Times that he would sometimes enter Cho's room and find Cho sitting at his desk, staring into nothingness (Biggs). He wasn't staring at a computer and playing *Counter-Strike*, but was rather staring at nothing at all.

In addition, Seung-Hui Cho had been diagnosed with selective mutism, a severe anxiety disorder, as well as major depressive disorder (Adams). The DC shooter had a long history of anti-social and criminal behavior, including the torturing of small animals (Kutner 8). Similarly, FBI investigations were able to conclude that Klebold was significantly depressed and suicidal, and Harris was a sociopath (Kutner 8).

Ultimately, it falls upon the parents to filter what gets to their kids, and, when a known mental problem exists, parents should

Continues next page

THE RHETORICAL SITUATION

Purpose

Dickinson wants to persuade readers that video games do not cause violent behavior in mentally healthy children.

Audience

His readers are his instructor, his classmates, and the students at Weber State University who read the journal *Weber Writes*.

Rhetorical appeals

Dickinson develops his **ethos** by stating that he is a gamer himself and that he's even worked in the industry.

By noting that the DC Sniper trained at a shooting range, Dickinson appeals to readers' sense of **logos** to question the connection between the DC Sniper and his video game experience.

Dickinson, *One-Way Path to Violence?* Continued

THE GENRE'S
CONVENTIONS

**Elements of the
genre**

**States a thesis or
makes a clear claim.**
Dickinson's is "I
believe that [violent
behavior in people
who play video
games] is not the
fault of the games
themselves, but
the lack of parental
supervision and
interaction with
today's youth."

**Presents an
argument based
on research.**
He presents
his argument
in paragraph 3
and develops it
in subsequent
paragraphs—
reasoning that
the DC Sniper,
Columbine shooters,
and Virginia Tech
shooter had histories
of mental illness,
and that is what
the crimes should
be attributed to.
He argues that
parents should
monitor children's
use of games and
take mental health
into account when
deciding what their
children can handle.
(Continued on p. 228.)

be that much more strict on what their kids play. As an avid gamer myself, and as someone who has workedin the industry, I understand the sense of accomplishment received from a well placed shot in *Modern Warfare* just as much as I understand that video games are not real. I was personally raised buying and playing games under the supervision of my parents, and am a strong supporter of such supervision. Even so, according to Jack Thompson and others with his mindset, I should be a ball of boiling hatred ready to explode at the slightest provocation.

Contrary to the claims of many naysayers, it is becoming easier to filter what a child does and does not play. A rating system implemented by the Entertainment Software Rating Board (ESRB) provides a fantastic way for parents to monitor what their kids are playing. This rating system issues an age range for each game, disclosing the full contents of the game. The most common ratings include E (Everyone, suitable for everyone age six and older), T (Teen, suitable for ages thirteen and older), and M (Mature, suitable for ages seventeen and older). The AO rating (Adult Only) is the only one higher than the M rating, and is actually considered to be a death sentence for games because brick-and-mortar stores will not sell them. AO- and M-rated games are the ones that come under the most fire from the media because they contain the most violent and bloody content. However, many people don't realize that in order to purchase an M-rated game from any major retailer, the customer must be at least seventeen years of age. Because of this age restriction, it is harder for young children to get their hands on violent content without parental approval.

There is no denying that video games have matured since their introduction in the '70s. Back then, games meant playing *Pong* or *Space Invaders* with friends and family. Today, games are becoming more and more complex, with violence playing a large role in almost all modern titles. Still, with parents staying involved in their kids' lives, it is possible to filter violent

Dickinson, *One-Way Path to Violence?* Continued

content and keep it to a minimum, which can prevent any type of aggressive behavior from developing. And with the ESRB and Web sites like *What They Play*, it is becoming easier and easier to keep children from playing games that are not age appropriate. Rather than focusing on trying to ban video games for their so-called influence on violent crime, an emphasis on parental supervision should be implemented in the fight against modern-day crime.

Works Cited

Adams, Duncan. "The Alienation and Anger of Seung-Hui Cho." *Roanoke.com*. The Roanoke Times, 31 Aug. 2007. Web. 27 Jan. 2010. <http://www.roanoke.com/vtinvestigation/wb/130177>.

Benedetti, Winda. "Were Video Games to Blame for Massacre?" *MSNBC.com*. MSNBC, 20 Apr. 2007. Web. 27 Jan. 2010. <http://www.roanoke.com/vtinvestigation/wb/130177>.

Biggs, John. "Why Video Games Don't Cause Violence." *CrunchGear.com*. CrunchGear, 18 Apr. 2007. Web. 27 Jan. 2010. <http://techcrunch.com/2007/04/18/why-video-games-dont-cause-violence/>.

Kutner, Lawrence, and Cheryl Olson. *Grand Theft Childhood: The Surprising Truth About Violent Video Games and What Parents Can Do*. New York: Simon & Schuster, 2008. Print.

Mikkelson, Barbara. "Columbine Doom Levels." *Snopes.com*. Snopes, 1 Jan. 2005. Web. 27 Jan. 2010. <http://www.snopes.com/horrors/madmen/doom.asp>.

Provan, Alexander. "The Education of Lee Boyd Malvo." Bidouan.org, 13 Jan. 2009. Web. 27 Jan. 2010. <http://www.bidoun.org/magazine/16-kids/the-education-of-lee-boyd-malvo-by-alexander-provan/>.

THE RHETORICAL SITUATION

Modes & media

Mode = written
Dickinson's assignment specified that he write an essay; however, sometimes assignments allow students the latitude to choose another mode, such as video or audio essay. Dickinson could have included visuals with his essay, perhaps screen shots of the video games mentioned in the essay or mug shots of the DC Sniper.

Medium = print
Again, Dickinson was required by his assignment to produce an essay in print form, but researched arguments often appear digitally, on blogs, for example.

Dickinson, *One-Way Path to Violence?* Continued

THE GENRE'S CONVENTIONS

Acknowledges counterarguments. For example, in paragraph 2, the author mentions that lawyers claimed there were connections between their clients' violence and use of video games.

Refutes or concedes counterarguments. For example, in paragraphs 4 and 5, the author discredits the links others have made between specific criminals and video game habits.

Cites specific examples, synthesizing them into his main argument. Rather than being general, the author specifies shooters (DC Sniper, Columbine, and Virginia Tech) and particular games (*Grand Theft Auto*, *Doom*, *Halo*, and *Counter-Strike*).

Style

Descriptive title. Dickinson's title makes it clear that his essay deals with kids and violence.

Gets readers' attention in the introduction. Dickinson accomplishes this by stating that players are "free to do just about anything they want" in the game *Grand Theft Auto*.

Closes with a simple, memorable statement. His final sentence reads: "Rather than focusing on trying to ban video games for their so-called influence on violent crime, an emphasis on parental supervision should be implemented in the fight against modern-day crime."

Strong authoritative voice and tone. The author chooses to avoid phrases such as "I think" and "in my opinion" but is still present in the essay.

Uses detail. For example, he names the names of violent criminals and identifies the games they're associated with.

Design

For this brief essay, the author decided that subheadings and explanatory notes would be inappropriate. When he submitted it for class, it was double-spaced. For use in *Weber Writes*, it was single-spaced to conform to that journal's design.

Sources

The author cites sources in the body of the text and at the end in a Works Cited list. His sources are varied and include Snopes.com, a respected Web site.

Questions: Analyzing Dickinson's researched argument

1. Purpose. Has Dickinson persuaded you that video games cannot be conclusively linked to violent behavior in players? Why or why not?

2. Audience. Besides Dickinson's professor and classmates, who else do you think might be an appropriate audience for this essay? Would Dickinson need to revise his essay to make it accessible for other audiences?

3. Rhetorical appeals. What are two techniques Dickinson uses to develop his ethos?

4. Rhetorical appeals. Dickinson's appeals to ethos and logos are discussed in the annotations. Can you find any appeals to pathos in the essay?

5. Modes & media. How would the inclusion of screen shots of the video games mentioned add to or detract from the essay?

6. Elements of the genre. How effective do you think Dickinson's refutation of the counterarguments is? Can you think of other refutations he could have used?

7. Style. Dickinson begins his essay by stating that players are "free to do just about anything they want" in *Grand Theft Auto*. What are some other ways Dickinson could have gotten readers' attention at the very beginning? For example, how could a reference to one of the criminals mentioned in the essay be used in the introduction?

8. Style. Dickinson writes in a strong, declarative voice rather than in a tentative "I'm just a student" voice. Find two or three sentences that are particularly strong and analyze the techniques Dickinson uses to come across as authoritative in these sentences.

9. Design. Because this is a short essay, Dickinson opted against using subheadings. If the essay were developed into a longer one, say fifteen pages, what are some subheadings he might use?

10. Sources. Look over Dickinson's Works Cited list. Are there some sources that appear to be more reliable than others?

Drafting a Researched Argument

CHECKLIST: Drafting a Researched Argument Thinking of writing a researched argument? Ask yourself the following questions.

<table>
<tr><td>WHAT'S MY RHETORICAL SITUATION?</td><td>WHAT GENRE CONVENTIONS MATTER?</td></tr>
</table>

☐ **Purpose.** What topic am I researching that might lend itself to an argument? What are some potential persuasive claims I could make about that topic? Have I discovered something about the topic that would contribute to other scholarly research?

☐ **Audience.** Assuming my readers are my classmates and professor—I need to think about how much they already know about my topic. How much background information will they need? What kind of terminology will they expect? How will they use the information I present?

☐ **Rhetorical appeals.** How will I establish my authority as a writer? How will I build a case for my conclusions using logic? What kinds of sources establish me as an expert and work to build my case?

☐ **Modes & media.** Can some of the information I present be shown visually with a chart or graphic? Do I want readers to access my article in print or digitally? Or do I want to make both options available?

☐ **Elements of the genre.** How will I make my thesis clear and declarative? How will I refer to my sources? How can I synthesize my sources to show readers that my sources are in conversation with each other?

☐ **Style.** How can I project an authoritative voice? How much detail will I need to provide so that readers understand the complexity and validity of my research?

☐ **Design.** How will I use design elements to my advantage? Will I use subheadings to organize and chunk information? Will I use images to illustrate points?

☐ **Sources.** Will my readers expect me to cite my sources in MLA, APA, or another format? Will my readers respect the types of sources I've referred to?

PRACTICE Want to experiment? Draft your own researched argument.

Think of a controversial topic you are curious about, perhaps even a bit uninformed about. Maybe campaign finance reform, the safety of bottled water, or the future of AIDS research. Ask your instructor or a librarian to help you find three reliable sources on the subject. Read the sources and then draft an argumentative thesis statement in which you take a position on the topic. Sketch out at least two counterarguments and your refutations of them.

AUTHOR'S/ARTIST'S STATEMENTS

Composers of all sorts often write a statement for their audience that explains their inspirations, intentions, and choices in their creative and critical processes. The liner notes that come with a CD, the program you receive at the theater or symphony, the Director's Commentary on a DVD, the Artist's Statement pinned to the wall at an art gallery—these are all forms of Authors' or Artists' Statements.

The magazine *Cook's Illustrated* is in the business of providing recipes, often with accompanying critical discussions. The point of the discussion—or what you could call a Cook's Statement—is to explain and discuss what went into the creation of the recipe, what went well, and what could have gone better, for example, and to discuss process. In the following discussion of the recipe for Thai Grilled-Beef Salad, recipe writer Andrew Janjigian explains what his goals were and the thought processes behind the decisions he made as he tinkered with the recipe. Janjigian is an associate editor for *Cook's Illustrated* and also works for America's Test Kitchen.

An Author's or Artist's—or Cook's—Statement assists the reader in understanding the process that led to the product. If you've watched a DVD recently, you may have found a Director's Commentary included along with the feature film or documentary. In Director's Commentaries (or Statements), the director—or an actor, choreographer, or other person associated with the film—talks about the considerations that went into making the film, such as casting, lighting, music, and blocking. The Director's Commentary, like an Author's Statement, makes visible, to some extent, the behind-the-scenes work that is invisible in the final product.

When our students create assignments—whatever genre or media they create in—we ask them to write an accompanying Author's or Artist's Statement that can give us insight into what they set out to do, how they did it, and what they might do to further improve the piece.

What are some examples of Authors' or Artists' Statements that you've seen lately? How does understanding a composer's perspective and intent contribute to how you relate to their work?

▲ AUTHOR PHOTO
Andrew Janjigian. *America's Test Kitchen.*

Thai Grilled-Beef Salad

Our goal was to look no further than the supermarket to replicate this salad's complex range of flavors and textures. Along the way, we learned a neat trick for grilling meat.

▷ BY ANDREW JANJIGIAN ◁

A scoop of rice turns this steak salad into a meal.

High-Steaks Decisions

Five Tastes of Thai Grilled-Beef Salad—and One More

One of the keys to this salad is balancing the signature flavor elements of Thai cuisine. In addition to achieving it, we added one more complementary flavor: the earthiness of toasted cayenne and sweet paprika.

HOT	SOUR	SALTY	SWEET	BITTER	EARTHY

Falling Water

Well Dressed

THAI GRILLED-BEEF SALAD
SERVES 4 TO 6

Unbeadable Thai Trick: Knowing When to Flip

TIME TO FLIP

3A. FOR A CHARCOAL GRILL

3B. FOR A GAS GRILL

Look: The Moisture Beads
Video available FREE for 4 months at www.CooksIllustrated.com/aug11

▲ RECIPE & COOK'S STATEMENT
Andrew Janjigian,
"Thai Grilled-Beef Salad" from *Cook's Illustrated*, July/August 2011. *America's Test Kitchen.*

Analyzing Author's/Artist's Statements: What to Look For

THE RHETORICAL SITUATION

Purpose The purpose of an Author's Statement is for an author (or artist or other composer) to discuss the decisions and choices he or she made in composing a specific text or other work. Let's say you've created an ad or a documentary film for your course. By writing an accompanying Author's or Artist's Statement, you can persuade your readers to see your finished piece in a particular way. A successful Author's Statement reflects your understanding of your chosen genre (and the elements, style, design, and use of sources that characterize it)—and of your specific rhetorical situation (your reasons for composing, your audience, how you use rhetorical appeals, and your choice of mode and medium).

Following is an example of a Director's Statement. It relates to the film *The Social Network*, directed by David Fincher. In the Director's Commentary for the film (included on the DVD), Fincher aims to persuade viewers that his choice in how to cast the main character was motivated by his desire to be realistic:

> I was looking for somebody who could just come out of the gates and be relentlessly who he is, and um, this QuickTime of an audition ended up on my computer and I turned it on and I watched Jesse Eisenberg. I think he did two takes of this scene, and I just thought, "Wow, like, that's pretty undeniable," and I remember dragging Aaron [Sorkin, the screenwriter on the film] into my office and saying, "Just watch this," and he looked at it and he said, "Well, our job's done."
> —**David Fincher**, from Director's Commentary for *The Social Network*

If you're writing an Author's Statement in an academic setting, your main purpose is to inform and persuade readers—your peers, your instructor, your audience—of the critical and creative thought you put into your composition.

Audience The audience for an Author's Statement is usually a particularly engaged and interested reader or viewer. Not everyone who saw the film *The Social Network* listened to David Fincher's Director's Commentary. Only the most interested viewers did; the ones who wanted to better understand the behind-the-scenes process. In an academic setting, your audience is made up of invested and critical readers and viewers, such as your professor and peers, who want to confirm that you've made deliberate choices throughout your composing process.

Rhetorical appeals In an Author's Statement, writers persuade readers by appealing mainly to logos and ethos. The author's credibility (ethos) is particularly important because, as with most persuasive pieces, the writer needs to come across as honest and thoughtful. Authors can establish ethos through the reasoning (logos) they present in their Authors' Statements. When writers logically present evidence to readers about the choices they made in organizing and presenting their work, readers are more likely to accept the claims the author makes.

To persuade, composers may sometimes appeal to their audience's emotions. For example, if a composer wrote a piece of music as a memorial and wanted it performed a certain way, that message would appear in the program.

Modes & media Authors choose modes and media for their Statements that are appropriate for those of the work they're discussing. An artist showing work online would probably create a digital Artist's Statement, whereas an artist showing work in a brick-and-mortar gallery would probably print out a text-based statement to hang next to his or her masterpieces.

Analyzing Author's/Artist's Statements: What to Look For   **233**

THE GENRE'S CONVENTIONS

Elements of the genre   In their Authors' and Artists' Statements, writers do
the following:

Discuss a specific composition—and make an argument. In an Author's or Artist's
Statement, writers discuss a particular composition—such as an essay, painting,
photo, documentary, ad, or other work. They refer directly to that work and provide specific details as they explain the "what, why, and how" of their creation.
For example, in the Cook's Statement example from *Cook's Illustrated*, Andrew
Janjigian explains that he set out to create a dressing that would successfully blend
"the four Thai flavor elements: hot, sour, salty, and sweet." He then explains how
he did that.

Writers also make a case for their compositions in order to persuade readers to
see their work in a particular way. For example, David Fincher (p. 233) wants us to
believe his casting was motivated by a desire for realism. Andrew Janjigian wants
us to see that his beef salad recipe succeeds in blending desired flavors.

Address readers directly. Writers use the *I* construction, which allows them to
speak plainly to readers about their choices. They also refer to the works they're
discussing in the Statement as "my essay" (or "my painting," "my photograph,"
etc.), indicating their ownership of the composition and the choices they made.

Explain their choice of genre—and how they worked with its conventions. The
Author's or Artist's Statement is a place for a composer to explain why he or she
chose to work in a particular genre. For example, let's say that for your composition
course, you chose to write an opinion piece on gun control. In a separate statement, submitted with your opinion piece, you might explain to your instructor and
classmates why you chose this genre. Pointing out your specific choices builds your
ethos and persuasiveness. You might note, for example, that the opinion piece was
the best choice of genre, because it allowed you to:

» Clearly present your opinion on the topic of gun control (and write in the first
person)

» Be brief (just a few paragraphs) and lively

» Deal with potential objections and offer potential solutions

» Invite readers to respond

**What are some
arguments a
musician might
make about a song
or album? What
are some claims a
fashion designer
might make about a
new line of clothing?**

Alternatively, maybe you created a photo essay, for your class or a wider audience. An accompanying statement—in which you explain why you found the photo essay to be the best way to communicate your ideas about gun control—would go a long way toward helping your viewers get the most out of your work.

Discuss their specific rhetorical situation—and related choices. The Author's or Artist's Statement gives you, as a composer, an opportunity to explain to audiences:

» Your purpose: why you composed the work—on that specific topic, in that specific way

» Your audience and use of rhetorical appeals: what you understand about your readers and how you connected with them through choices regarding ethos, pathos, and logos

» Your mode and medium: why you chose them and how they benefit your work overall

For example, if you created a collage—perhaps on the topic of body art and identity—in your Artist's Statement, you could explain to viewers:

» Your purpose or main point in creating a collage on the relationship between body art and identity—and what the relationship is

» Why you chose specific central images, how they contribute to your message, and how you hope your viewers will read them and relate to the collage overall

» How you wanted to connect with your viewers through pathos, logos, and ethos (for example, your arrangement of images might appeal to their logic or emotions)

» Why you decided to create the collage, say, in a digital format

Reflect on their compositions—and discuss successes and limitations. Writers use Authors' Statements as an opportunity to look back at a composition and to evaluate the extent of their achievement; they might also note what they would have done differently or better. For example, say you created an advertisement showing how marines achieve strength without steroids. You might note in an accompanying Author's Statement that you felt you'd succeeded in providing a captivating visual, an original slogan, and an emotional appeal. On the other hand, don't hesitate to mention in your Statement places where you could improve your work editorially or technically. The point here is to do your best and reflect on what you did well and talk about what you'd like to improve. This all adds to your ethos as a composer and to the persuasiveness of your work.

Provide context. In the Author's or Artist's Statement, it's useful for writers to give some background on their composition (their editorial or collage, etc.), such as how they became interested in the topic, what their inspirations were, or, if they've created a series of related works, how the piece fits in with other pieces. Andrew Janjigian explains in his Cook's Statement that he decided to create his own beef salad recipe because he hadn't found one that came close to achieving the quality of beef salads he'd eaten in Thai restaurants.

Style   Statement authors do the following:

Use detail. The persuasive and critical nature of the Statement depends on the use of specific detail. Janjigian, for example, names particular ingredients that he tried and describes the exact result he got, such as in his discussion of what happened when he used cayenne pepper instead of powdered Thai bird chiles: "Just ½ teaspoon of cayenne, in fact, overpowered the meat's smoky char."

Write in a tone that builds ethos. In their Statements, authors use critical, analytical language to make their points. They choose words related to their subject of inquiry to establish themselves as experts. When you write such a Statement, even though you're writing in the first person (*I*), use a serious, straightforward tone to emphasize that you have made deliberate, thoughtful choices.

Besides the essay format, what other forms might you use for an Author's or Artist's Statement? When might writing a song for this purpose be appropriate? Are there forms that would never work as a Statement? What forms? Why?

Design   Authors' Statements can often look very much like an academic essay, with indented paragraphs and little or no decoration except for subheadings that offer structure and organization. However, a writer might choose to design an Author's Statement to reflect the genre of the composition. For example, an Author's Statement might take the form of a letter written to a professor, a Director's Commentary, or a one-page Artist's Statement.

Sources   The most persuasive authors discuss the sources that informed their composing process. For example, in his Statement, student Michael Kipp mentions specific sources by title or author's name, including page numbers. Depending on the audience, sources may be cited according to MLA or APA or other academic formats, as in Michael Kipp's Statement on page 238. An artist who is inspired by another artist usually names his or her inspiration and cites specific works by that artist.

Michael Kipp (Student)

Artist's Statement: Why and How I Created My Collage: "Thank You"

Michael Kipp, a student at Red Rocks Community College, became interested in the concept of gratitude and happiness when he took a psychology course and studied positive psychology. As part of a second-semester research-based composition class, Kipp decided to focus his semester-long multigenre project on the idea of gratitude, looking at research in the field and reflecting on his own experience with feeling gratitude. One of the pieces Kipp created for the project was a collage illustrating gratitude, which includes a quote. Accompanying the collage is his Artist's Statement, analyzing the choices he made in creating the collage, such as design and organization, and illustrating how his collage achieves his purpose and uses rhetorical appeals to persuade his audience. *("Artist's Statement: Why and How I Created My Collage: 'Thank You.'" Reprinted Courtesy of Michael Kipp.)*

▲ STUDENT AUTHOR PHOTO & ◀ COLLAGE **Michael Kipp** and his composition, *Thank You*, the subject of his Artist's Statement on page 238. *Michael Kipp.*

What is the
composer,
Michael Kipp,
doing?

THE RHETORICAL
SITUATION

Purpose
Audience
Rhetorical appeals
Modes & media

see page 239

How do I
know this is
an **Artist's
Statement**?

THE GENRE'S
CONVENTIONS

Elements of the genre
Style
Design
Sources

see page 239

Michael Kipp
Artist's Statement: Why and How I Created My Collage: "Thank You"

"Psychologists have repeatedly shown that perceptions are more important than objective reality" ("Positive Thinking"). This quote embodies the message behind my collage. It ties in with messages from other research I've done on the science of happiness, including my reading of the article "Psychological Research: Gratitude," by Jerry Lopper. In that piece, Lopper quotes psychologist and researcher Dr. Alex Wood as saying: "Gratitude is a life orientation towards noticing and appreciating the positive in the world." These quotes suggest that feeling grateful requires mental work (Emmons, *Thanks!* 6). Gratitude is a part of our perception, a "life orientation," and without effort that perception will not arise or be maintained. Thus, to have an attitude of gratefulness, we must change our outlook on life. My purpose in creating this collage is to promote the idea that we make choices about how we perceive experience, and that practicing gratitude can make us happier.

My intended audience is made up of people who like art, psychology, and philosophy, who appreciate the abstract expression of concepts, and who may be persuaded to think about how a grateful attitude could be more important than one's objective reality—and how they may practice that in their own life to be happier.

In my collage I used *pathos* to convey these ideas—I wanted to sway my viewers emotionally, to cause them to feel curious and inspired when looking at the collage. I did this through my choices of composition, colors, and subjects, which are discussed in depth below. I used striking contrast and positioned the objects in ways the viewer would not expect, thus drawing attention to them. I also used *logos* by putting the piece together in a logical manner, and by grounding my concept in positive psychology research. Furthermore, by including

Kipp, *Artist's Statement*, Continued

the quote about perception and reality, I ask viewers to think about how the collage illustrates that concept. My goal is that my audience will ponder what each part of the collage represents and come to logical conclusions about the collage's representation of gratitude.

During my research, the following passage stood out for me: "A grateful outlook does not require a life full of material comforts but rather an interior attitude of thankfulness regardless of life circumstances" (Emmons and Shelton, "Gratitude" 465). I wanted to convey this idea visually by emphasizing contrasting experiences; a negative or challenging objective reality is represented by the black background, which is supposed to have a feel of encompassing and surrounding the sitting figure, which is asymmetrically placed within the piece. The figure herself is creating a positive perception of her reality, the potential of which is represented by the landscape and the rainbow, which arches upward and out—drawing the eye forward and to a higher point. A Spanish study confirmed that positive affect rises in persons who practice gratitude, which was found in a previous study (Martinez-Marti, Avia, and Hernandez-Lloreda 893).

Also, the landscape refers to the fact that grateful people experience a positive memory bias—they are more likely to recall positive memories, similar to the negative memory bias experienced in depression (Watkins 63). The idea of creation is also suggested by the plant, whose roots surround the woman's head. Her efforts to be thankful and practice gratitude are nourishing the plant, which grows upward, changing her reality, subjective and objective, for the better. The figure's pose is reminiscent of *The Thinker*, a nineteenth-century sculpture by Rodin, which suggests that changing one's attitude takes intentional, active thought. "People adapt quickly to positive changes in their lives and thus derive diminishing happiness returns" ("Positive Thinking"), so it may be that practicing gratitude helps counteract that adaptation.

Continues next page

THE RHETORICAL SITUATION

Purpose

Kipp's purpose is to persuade readers that "practicing gratitude can make us happier" and that his collage furthers that goal. He wants readers to know that he made thoughtful decisions when composing the collage.

THE GENRE'S CONVENTIONS

Elements of the genre

Kipp **discusses a specific composition** (his collage)—and makes an argument about it. He supports claims with evidence; for example, Kipp discusses how he used color and composition in the context of Emmons and Shelton's concept of an "interior attitude of thankfulness."

Kipp **addresses readers directly** (e.g., "I considered adding words") and uses *my* throughout (e.g., "my collage" and "my research").

(Continued on p. 240.)

Kipp, *Artist's Statement*, Continued

Audience

His readers are his
instructor and fellow
students. They want
to know why he
created a collage
and what research
informed it.

**THE GENRE'S
CONVENTIONS**

Kipp **explains why
he created a collage**
and how he worked
with established
conventions. For
example, he writes
that choosing this
genre meant he
could use a variety
of images—and
also use a black
background as part
of the composition.

He **talks about
his rhetorical
situation**—and
specific related
choices. For
example, he appeals
to his audience
through pathos,
hoping they "feel
curious and inspired"
when viewing the
collage.

The embracing arms in the collage represent several things: first, they represent the tendency for people who practice gratitude to be more prosocial, more likely to help others or return a favor, than less grateful people (Tsang 139). They also represent the positive social benefits we receive when we regularly practice gratitude (Watkins, Grimm, and Kolts 65). Finally, they represent that gratitude is an acknowledgment that one is dependent on others (Emmons and Shelton, "Gratitude" 463). The angle of the arms to the rainbow creates a triangle, which leads the eye to the point where they get close together and hit the frame. The frames represent precisely that—that gratefulness is a frame of mind. What is outside that frame is objective reality. The parallel lines created by the frames again pull the eye upward; their top ends create a diagonal line with the part of the plant where the last leaf connects to the stem, as well as the top of the mountain, which pulls the eye back to the left center of the piece, and finally back to the central figure. The shelf the books rest on and the bench the woman sits on repeat the parallel lines created in the frames, but are perpendicular to them. The red "Thank You" at the bottom of the piece pulls in the warm colors in the arms at the opposite side and serves as a sort of name tag—indicating that the collage is based on thankfulness, as is the woman's perception of her life.

All of these pieces contribute to the composition of my collage—even the use of a canvas was intentional, enhancing the idea of active creation. I used a collage because even though I am unfamiliar with the genre, I am familiar with painting and drawing, so I have some, although limited, background in composition and got to try something new. I also wanted to create in a medium other than text or a computer-based visual. Collages often have more cut out pieces pasted together, but the more I added, the less I felt like the collage conveyed the intended message. Covering too much of the black background defeated the purpose of that background—the

Kipp, *Artist's Statement,* Continued

negative space is as important as the positive space. I considered adding words, but found that I liked the collage better
when no words were used, that it was more powerful without
text—this is also why I moved "Thank You" off the canvas; it
complements the idea behind the picture, but is not included
within the composition itself. I added the perception and reality quote last—I think it gives the viewer more to think about,
particularly because it is the quote that inspired the entire
piece. It also extends the ideas I've presented, asking viewers
not only to feel and practice gratitude, but to affect their own
experiences of reality by doing so.

Works Cited

Emmons, Robert A. *Thanks! How the New Science of
Gratitude Can Make You Happier.* New York: Houghton
Mifflin Harcourt, 2007. Web. 10 Oct. 2012. <http://
books.google.com/books?id=tGCcH2l4jUUC>.

Emmons, Robert A., and Charles M. Shelton. "Gratitude and
the Science of Positive Psychology." *Handbook of Positive
Psychology.* Eds. C. R. Snyder and Shane J. Lopez. New
York: Oxford University Press, 2002. 459-471. Print.

Lopper, Jerry. "Psychological Research: Gratitude." *Suite101.*
Suite101, 19 May 2008. Web. 10 Oct. 2012. <http://
www.suite101.com/content/
psychological-research-gratitude-a54399>.

Martinez-Marti, Maria Luisa, Maria Dolores Avia, and Maria
Jose Hernandez-Lloreda. "The Effects of Counting Blessings
on Subjective Well-Being: A Gratitude Intervention in a
Spanish Sample." *Spanish Journal of Psychology* 13.2
(2010): 886-896. Web. 25 Nov. 2012. <http://
www.ucm.es/info/psi/docs/journal/v13_n2_2010/art886.pdf>.

Continues next page

THE RHETORICAL SITUATION

Rhetorical appeals
Kipp establishes
his credibility, or
ethos, in paragraph
1 by showing he's
done research on
positive psychology,
including quotes
from experts.

(Continued on p. 242.)

THE GENRE'S CONVENTIONS

Kipp **reflects on
his successes and
limitations.** For
example, he mentions
that though he has a
"limited" background
in design and visual
composition, he was
pleased by achieving a
"striking contrast" for
viewers through his
positioning of images.

Kipp **provides context**
by discussing his
interest in the concept
of gratitude and his
goal to show readers
"that practicing
gratitude can make us
happier."

Michael Kipp (Student), *Artist's Statement*   **241**

Kipp, *Artist's Statement,* Continued

Pursuit of Happiness.org / Teaching Happiness, Inc. "Positive
Thinking: Optimism and Gratitude." *The Pursuit of
Happiness.* Pursuit-of-Happiness.org (Teaching Happiness,
Inc.), n.d. Web. 26 Nov. 2012. <http://
www.pursuit-of-happiness.org/science-of-happiness/
positive-thinking/>.

Rodin, Auguste. *The Thinker.* 1880-81. Bronze sculpture.
Cleveland Museum of Art, Cleveland.

Tsang, Jo-Ann. "Gratitude and Prosocial Behaviour: An
Experimental Test of Gratitude." *Cognition & Emotion*
20.1 (2006): 138-148. *Academic Search Premier.* Web. 25
Nov. 2012.

Watkins, Philip C., Dean L. Grimm, and Russell Kolts.
"Counting Your Blessings: Positive Memories among
Grateful People." *Current Psychology* 23.1 (2004): 52-67.
Academic Search Premier. Web. 25 Nov. 2012.

THE RHETORICAL SITUATION

Kipp appeals to
logos by explaining
his choices logically
and using evidence
from his collage to
support his claims.
For example, when
he discusses his
use of **pathos**, he
shows how he used
contrast and layout
to make readers
curious.

Modes & media

Mode = written
Kipp uses only
words to make his
case for his collage.
He uses both his
own analysis and
outside research
to deliver his
reflections and
analysis.

Medium = print
Because Kipp
composed his
statement as a
researched academic
essay, he chose
to print it out and
submit it to his
instructor that way.
Of course, he could
also have submitted
the statement
digitally. In digital
format, readers could
easily click on the
sources in his Works
Cited page, for
example.

THE GENRE'S CONVENTIONS

Style

Kipp **uses specific
detail.** For example,
he talks about the
image of embracing
arms, and what they
represent in terms
of gratitude, how
their angle orients
the reader toward
a certain point, and
how the arms relate
to the frame.

His **word choice
reflects his critical
thought** (e.g.,
*intentional, sway,
ponder, grounding,
bias*).

Design

Kipp structures
and designs
his statement
as a traditional
researched essay
with an introduction,
body paragraphs,
conclusion,
parenthetical
citations, and Works
Cited list.

Sources

Kipp's sources for the
Artist's Statement
are the collage itself
and the research
he conducted on
gratitude. He refers
to source material,
such as a study by
Martinez-Marti, Avia,
and Hernandez-
Lloreda, and relates
that back to his
collage.

He cites his sources
per MLA style and
connects them to the
decisions he made
in composing his
collage.

Questions: Analyzing Kipp's Artist's Statement

1. Purpose. How does Kipp convince you that his collage illustrates that "practicing gratitude can make us happier"?

2. Audience. Although the primary audience for the piece is Kipp's instructor, are there other audiences that might be interested in reading the piece? If so, who? Why?

3. Rhetorical appeals. One of the ways Kipp establishes his ethos is by including research. How else does he establish his ethos?

4. Rhetorical appeals. Why would it be inappropriate for Kipp to use pathos in an Artist's Statement? Are there any circumstances where pathos might be appropriate for an Artist's Statement? What circumstances? Why?

5. Modes & media. How would including visuals enhance Kipp's Artist's Statement? Where might he incorporate visuals?

6. Elements of the genre. What types of evidence does Kipp use to support his claims? How effective is the evidence? Are there places where he might have included different evidence? If so, where and what?

7. Elements of the genre. Throughout the statement, Kipp shows how research influences his choices and motivations. Do you learn anything about Kipp's own personal motivation for exploring this subject? If so, how? If not, what would this add to the Artist's Statement?

8. Style. How does Kipp use language to establish his credibility?

9. Design. Kipp chose to submit his Artist's Statement in a traditional academic essay form. Would the piece be strengthened if he had used subheads and divided the Artist's Statement into sections? If so, what would be the different sections?

10. Sources. What are the different purposes the research serves in Kipp's Artist's Statement?

Drafting an Author's/Artist's Statement

CHECKLIST: Drafting a Statement Thinking of drafting an Author's/Artist's Statement? Ask yourself the following questions.

WHAT'S MY RHETORICAL SITUATION?

- ☐ **Purpose.** What is the central claim I want to make about my piece? What particular elements do I need to justify? What choices did I make as I created the piece? What motivated me to create the piece?

- ☐ **Audience.** Am I writing this Statement for my instructor? For fellow students? Will my Statement be read by people outside the academic setting? If so, how will this affect what I write?

- ☐ **Rhetorical appeals.** What makes me a credible writer on this subject? How will I show readers my credibility? How will I organize my information to support my claims?

- ☐ **Modes & media.** Will I present my Statement only in written form? Is it appropriate to incorporate visuals? If so, what types of visuals? How would the inclusion of audio enhance my Statement? Would it be appropriate to just use audio? Do I want to present my work in print or digital form?

WHAT GENRE CONVENTIONS MATTER?

- ☐ **Elements of the genre.** What persuasive point do I want to make about my piece? How can I support that point with specific examples and details from my composition and process? Are there aspects of the context that readers should know to fully understand and appreciate my work?

- ☐ **Style.** How can I use my tone to convey the seriousness with which I view my work? What details can I use to support the generalizations I make?

- ☐ **Design.** How will I organize my Statement? What visuals should I include? Should I use subheadings, or is my Statement short enough that subheadings aren't necessary?

- ☐ **Sources.** Is the piece I composed informed by source material? What inspired me? Where did I get the facts and information that I used? Will my audience expect formal citations?

PRACTICE Want to experiment? Draft your own Author's/Artist's Statement.

Look at a piece you wrote earlier in the semester or for another class. Reflect on the choices you made as you thought through and created the piece. Where did you put most of your energy and why? Where did you get your ideas? What did you tinker with? Then draft a brief statement in which you discuss your process and thoughts.

COLLAGES/VISUAL ARGUMENTS

Collage is an art form that involves gluing pieces of paper, ribbon, newspaper, photos, gems, buttons, and other small items to a paper, poster board, wood, or canvas background. Artists use a combination of everyday or "found" materials, assembling them to create a piece of art. Collage techniques have been used since tenth-century Japanese calligraphers glued colored pieces of paper to their poems; today, scrapbookers and other DIY artists use collage techniques.

Iconic artists, including Pablo Picasso (1881–1973), have used collage to express ideas—and to make arguments. One of Picasso's well-known collages is *Guitar, Sheet Music, and Glass*, completed in 1912, in which the artist glued pieces of sheet music and newspaper to a background.

Have you ever made a collage? If so, why? And for what audience? What was the overall message of your collage?

◀ COLLAGE
Pablo Picasso,
Guitar, Sheet Music, and Glass (1912).
© McNay Art Museum/ Art Resource, NY.

Let's look at Picasso's collage as a visual argument. What is Picasso arguing? And what choices make his argument(s) clear? Let's look at two of the choices he made.

1. Picasso chose to represent the objects in the collage in an abstract, rather than a realistic, way. Possible argument: Picasso is making a case for a break from traditional forms of art such as lifelike or still-life painting.

2. Picasso chose to use everyday materials drawn from everyday life (wallpaper, a cast-off piece of sheet music, etc.). Possible argument: Picasso is making the case for the value of the everyday in fine art. (This was a revolutionary idea back in 1912.)

What are some other examples of visual arguments? This book is filled with them— ads, comics, bumper stickers, photos, and other images. While the focus of this section is on the collage as a visual argument, much of the advice here also pertains to any type of visual argument.

POLITICAL CARTOON ▶
Rex F. May (a.k.a. Baloo), "My Point of View." *Reprinted by permission of Rex May.*

Analyzing Collages/Visual Arguments: What to Look For

THE RHETORICAL SITUATION

Purpose We (artists, nonartists, students) create visual artwork, including collages, in order to convey ideas or aesthetic concepts—and often to make a visual argument or commentary on a controversial issue, a moment in time, or a cultural theme. Some collage artists, for example, choose a particular shape for their composition to emphasize their point.

Audience Visual artists often appeal to a particular audience through their choice of subject. For example, the artist Kara Walker, who works with issues of race and gender, knows that her art appeals to people who are interested in slavery, racism, and feminism. In the piece on page 248, taken from an exhibit entitled "Kara Walker: Annotating History," Walker superimposes a figure over an original illustration from *Harper's Pictorial History of the Civil War* of 1866/1868.

◀ ARTIST PHOTO
Kara Walker with her work at her 2007–08 installation at the Whitney Museum of American Art. *Librado Romero/ NY Times.*

▲ COLLAGE
Kara Walker,
A Warm Summer Evening in 1863. Walker uses a silk-screening process to create layers in this mixed-media print. *Untitled collage on paper, Artwork G Kara Walker/Image courtesy of Sikkema Jenkins & Co., New York.*

Rhetorical appeals Visual composers use image, line, color, and other visual elements to express concepts and arguments. Depending on an artist's main point—and how he or she chooses to reach viewers—the artist will emphasize ethos, pathos, or logos. For example, the composer of the *Business Collage* on page 251 appeals to viewers' sense of logos by creating a chain of reasoning for the reader. The "$" and "Only" on the glasses in the collage tell the reader that the consumer organizes the world according to money and perceived bargains. Additionally, the composer appeals to viewers' sense of pathos by presenting a relationship between the pressure of consumerism (as symbolized by the coupons) and addictive behavior (as symbolized by the cigarette and the beckoning finger). The piece is persuasive because of the textual messages, the visual representation of a consumer, and the juxtaposition of all the elements.

The *Coffee Break* collage below was created in response to a contest called the NASA Remix Challenge. The composer combined real NASA photos and a picture of a café on Route 66. The artist establishes ethos by using real photos to remix ideas about the moon landing, and also appeals to viewers' pathos through humor. The original caption reads: "After 109 hours, 39 minutes in the lunar module, Neil Armstrong and Buzz Aldrin enjoy a double cafe mocha." The collagist persuades the viewer that Starbucks has no boundaries—they will even take their product to the moon.

Modes & media   Visual composers use a variety of visual elements to create their work. Collagists, specifically, cut images out of magazines, incorporate found objects and fabrics, and work with photos to create their assemblages. When text is a part of a collage, it is usually "found text" taken from something else rather than written specifically for the collage. Collages are delivered in a variety of media—in galleries, print magazines, and digital collections.

Visual composers arrange images in certain ways to create connections. Have you ever seen two images side by side and been struck by the combination? How does seeing an image on its own—or paired with another—alter how you experience it?

◀ COLLAGE
Jerry Taylor, *Coffee Break.* "Coffee Break" NASA remix, Jerry Taylor (jrtcel).

Elements of the genre   Visual composers do the following:

Convey a theme. If you think of a visual work as an argument, then the visual art-ist, like an editorial writer or film reviewer, for example, creates works that convey a central idea or commentary. In collages, artists juxtapose different images or use shape and form to convey a theme. For example, among the images the *Business Collage* artist chooses are a dollar sign and a price tag, which contribute to the overall commentary on greed, consumption, and "business."

Connect with culture and history. Visual artists—especially those making an argu-ment—often create or incorporate images that allude to a cultural or historical phenomenon. For example, in one of her collages, Kara Walker features an image of Ulysses S. Grant, the eighteenth U.S. president and commander of the Union army in the Civil War, and pastes onto it an image of an African American woman. Walker's collage makes clear the differences between her perspective and that of the nineteenth-century creators of the Grant image, and puts her work in the context of the Civil War.

Use layers and juxtapose images and materials. By definition, collages are com-posed of a variety of objects. Collagists use a variety of objects to bring texture and dimensionality to their work. All visual artists, especially those presenting an argument, consider how presentation and positioning of different items affect how viewers see the work.

Use color to direct the attention of the viewer. In Kara Walker's collage, the super-imposed silhouette stands out against the pale background image. Collage artists use the same principles as composers of advertisements, who might contrast the color of the text with the background of the page or screen so that the text is more prominent for the viewer.

Assemble parts. When artists assemble a collage, they use a variety of materials, such as scissors, glue, newspapers, magazines, books, and paint. Because you can make a collage out of anything, you can use materials you find in the kitchen or at a bus stop. For example, the Romanian-born Swiss artist Daniel Spoerri uses familiar objects in his pieces, such as kitchen plates and leftover food. Although collagists have the broadest range of materials, all visual artists use a variety of materials to assemble their pieces.

Style   Visual composers do the following:

Present varying degrees of detail. The amount of detail in a visual argument varies. In Picasso's collage (p. 245), he uses just a few elements to create his piece. In the *Coffee Break* collage (p. 249), the artist uses detail to emphasize the Starbucks brand.

Convey a tone. Artists convey their attitudes toward the subjects of their work. Some artists use parody to persuade viewers, for example, the creator of the *Coffee Break* collage.

Design   Visual composers do the following:

Vary the size and shape of their compositions. Collage artists, like other visual artists, are not limited by a particular size or form for their creations. Some pieces might be the size of a sheet of paper, while others might occupy an entire wall. In collage, in particular, by using shape in a deliberate way the artist conveys a point.

Embrace (or reject or remix) traditional artistic conventions. Collagists generally follow the con-

▲ COLLAGE **Stock Artist, Business Collage.** *CSA Images/ Printstock Collection/Getty Images.*

ventions of visual art, in terms of balance, contrast, and perspective. These conventions allow the artist to make sure that nothing in the piece gets more attention than he or she wants it to. Artists generally divide their canvases into sections. For example, the collagist who created *Coffee Break* divides his work into thirds, with each astronaut on the outer third of the piece. This keeps the artist from putting an image right smack in the middle, where it would dominate the piece. As with other art forms, when artists violate the rules of perspective and other conventions, they do it with a purpose, to call attention to the violation.

Present patterns/repeat certain elements. All visual artists must give their work a sense of order or coherence. This is true of collagists, whose works are made of seemingly random pieces, but which can be given order through the repetition of elements such as color or shape. The *Business Collage*, for instance, is held together visually by the predominant use of black and white, and by the curved shapes of the ears, chin, and glasses. Other artists use similar strategies, repeating shapes and colors to give a piece an overall sense of unity.

Use lines (or not). Collagists use the lines created by the edges of the images they've assembled to direct the audience's attention to particular elements, just as an arrow would. Notice, for example, how the flagpole in *Coffee Break* directs your attention to both the café flag and the astronaut's arm. Visual artists working in other media use lines similarly. Click through a museum Web site and find a painting and notice how the lines in the painting direct your attention.

Sources   To create collages, artists do the following:

Incorporate found objects. The cutouts and items that a collagist uses are considered "found objects" because they are not created for artistic purposes; rather, they are items that have been repurposed by an artist. Source material is often paper based, such as photos and cutouts from magazines and newspapers, but can be any item an artist chooses. Collage artists have used small objects like buttons and ribbons, parts of items like tree branches, and larger items, too. Visual artists working in other media get ideas and inspiration from many sources; for example, an artist might paint a portrait based on a photograph of a person or place.

Incorporate cultural materials. Artists may include cultural and historical materials such as documents and images.

Look around you and find three visual pieces in any medium—posters, ads, billboards, and so on. Which pieces are divided into thirds? What is the effect?

Guided Reading: Collage ▼

Richard Hamilton

Just What Is It That Makes Today's Homes So Different, So Appealing?

On page 254 is a collage created in 1956 by artist Richard Hamilton (1922–2011), entitled *Just What Is It That Makes Today's Homes So Different, So Appealing?* The dimensions of the original are 10¼ × 9¾ inches. When the collage was first displayed as part of an exhibit titled *This Is Tomorrow*, the image of the tape player in the collage had a sound source behind it, making the piece not just a collage but a multimodal composition. The *This Is Tomorrow* exhibit kick-started the pop art movement, and *Just What Is It That Makes Today's Homes So Different, So Appealing?* became one of the most recognized pieces of pop art ever produced. Pop art raised everyday materials and techniques to art status, featuring more ingenuity and cleverness than high art sensibility. The background of this collage is a flooring ad torn from a 1950s *Ladies' Home Journal*. *(Image on page 254: © R. Hamilton. All Rights Reserved, DACS 2013.)*

What do you think of pop art? Is everyday or "lowbrow" life worth looking at? How do the sensibilities of Hamilton, "the father of pop art," compare with your own? Learn more in his obituaries in digital editions of the *Guardian* and *The New York Times.*

◀ ARTIST PHOTO
Richard Hamilton.
Chris Morphet/Getty Images.

Hamilton, *Today's Homes*, Continued

**THE RHETORICAL
SITUATION**

Purpose
Audience
Rhetorical appeals
Modes & media

see page 255

What is the
composer,
**Richard
Hamilton**,
doing?

**THE GENRE'S
CONVENTIONS**

Elements of the genre
Style
Design
Sources

see page 255

How do I
know this is a
**collage/visual
argument**?

Hamilton, *Today's Homes,* *Continued*

Purpose

Hamilton makes an argument about 1950s domesticity, sexuality, and consumerism. He wants to persuade us that having all the new consumer culture wouldn't lead to a perfect life—it would merely lead to a perfect-*looking* life. He also comments on 1950s body ideals.

Audience

His viewers appreciate visual art, pop culture, and humor. When the piece was originally displayed in 1956, many audience members were probably curiosity seekers attracted by the hoopla around the exhibit.

Rhetorical appeals

The artist appeals to **pathos** by presenting erotic images—a bodybuilder and a nude woman on a couch—in a domestic situation. He establishes his **ethos** by including items that might be found in a home in the late 1950s.

Modes & media

Mode = visual and audio The visual aspect is most obvious. When the piece was exhibited in 1956 in *This Is Tomorrow*, it also had an audio element because of the sound source behind the radio.

Medium = paper In the original exhibition, the piece was viewed face-to-face. Reproductions can be conveyed in print, as in this book, or digitally, as in images of the piece on the Internet. Artwork typically makes a more profound impression when viewed face-to-face, in part because a small reproduction in a book simply can't make the same impact as a large piece can in person. Textures that are evident in a face-to-face viewing are usually lost in print or digital renderings.

Elements of the genre

Presents a theme. Hamilton's collage connects 1950s home life with romance (e.g., the framed comic book page), convenience (e.g., the canned ham), and tradition (e.g., the formal portrait on the wall).

Connects with history and culture. The images from 1950s pop culture invite viewers to make associations. For example, the canned ham connects with World War II, when fresh meat was scarce and convenience foods like Spam hit the market.

Layers images. The artist cut images from ads and magazines, then arranged them into a layered composition.

Works with color. Hamilton chooses mainly black and white, but uses color very deliberately. For example, the Tootsie Pop and the framed comic stand out.

Assembles the pieces. Hamilton used a transparent material to attach the pieces, so that it would not interfere with the visual impact.

Style

Brings in specific detail. For example, the artist makes sure the brands of the canned ham and the lollipop are visible.

Conveys a tone and attitude. Most living rooms don't feature a naked bodybuilder holding a giant lollipop, yet Hamilton uses images such as these to create an ironic and satirical tone.

Design

Consciously uses size and shape. Hamilton works with scale to create emphasis—note the different sizes of the women in the image.

Works with traditional art conventions. While this collage looks very modern, Hamilton conforms to established principles of balance, contrast, and perspective.

Repeats elements. For example, the rectangular shapes (the couches) highlight the idea that people are constrained by consumerism rather than liberated by it.

Uses lines. Hamilton creates strong horizontal and vertical lines with the edges of the cutouts, such as the couch, window, portrait, and framed comic.

Sources

The collage is made up of clippings from magazines (e.g., *Ladies' Home Journal*) and advertisements of the time.

Questions: Analyzing Hamilton's collage

1. Purpose. Hamilton is considered a creator of pop art. In an interview, he said that he considered pop art to be "popular (designed for a mass audience); transient (short-term solution); expendable (easily forgotten); low cost; mass produced; young (aimed at youth); witty; sexy; gimmicky; glamorous; and last but not least, Big Business." In what ways does Hamilton's collage seem consistent with his thoughts on pop culture? Explain.

2. Purpose. Hamilton's collage is titled *Just What Is It That Makes Today's Homes So Different, So Appealing?* How does the title direct your thinking about the artist's point in making the collage? How effective is the title? Why?

3. Audience. The collage uses images current for audiences in 1956. View some of the modern adaptations created by students at Joliet Junior College at www .redmagazine.com/web2012/feature_what_ the.html. How do you think the audiences for Hamilton's collage and the students' collages are similar and/or different?

4. Rhetorical appeals. How does Hamilton appeal to your emotions? What emotions is he appealing to and how?

5. Rhetorical appeals. What other rhetorical methods does Hamilton use to try to persuade us, his viewers, of his take on 1950s domestic culture?

6. Modes & media. You are viewing this piece at a smaller size than the original. Check out a bigger version of this collage from the Tate museum site, in London. What details do you notice in it that you didn't notice when you looked at the small printed reproduction in the book?

7. Elements of the genre. What ideas or themes do you notice in the collage?

8. Style. What difference would it make if the canned ham and lollipop weren't associated with particular brands?

9. Style. Do certain parts of the collage seem to attract more of your attention? For example, do your eyes more readily go to the romance comic book page on the wall or to the Tootsie Pop acting as a loincloth? Why?

10. Design. How many different materials can you identify in the collage? How does the use of different materials affect you as a viewer?

11. Design. How do the lines and use of color in the collage direct your attention toward particular elements?

12. Sources. The collage is made up of "found objects" rather than created from scratch. How does the fact that the collage is constructed of rather mundane scraps from magazines and advertisements, rather than painted or drawn, lend meaning to it? Keep in mind that the purposes and audiences for the scraps are probably different from the purposes and audiences of the collage. For example, the Tootsie Pop cutout in the collage was probably originally intended for an advertisement, not an artistic collage.

Drafting/Sketching a Collage/Visual Argument

CHECKLIST: Planning a Collage Thinking of sketching out a collage or other visual argument? Ask yourself the following questions.

WHAT'S MY RHETORICAL SITUATION?

☐ **Purpose.** What idea do I want to represent in a collage or other visual argument? Do I want to persuade others about a political issue? Do I want my viewers to take some type of action? What themes might I use to advance my ideas or arguments?

☐ **Audience.** Will my collage or other visual argument be viewed in a public space? Private space? What type of viewer is interested in my subject? Who do I want to influence?

☐ **Rhetorical appeals.** How will I establish my credibility? How will I persuade my viewer? Do I want to appeal to viewers' emotions through humor? Do I want to shock viewers? How will I organize my material to appeal to viewers' sense of logos?

☐ **Modes & media.** To create a visual argument, will I use only visuals, such as photographs? Will I incorporate text? Will the text be something I create or something I take from existing material? Do I want viewers to see the piece face-to-face, such as hanging on a wall? Or do I want to digitize the piece so that anyone can view it?

WHAT GENRE CONVENTIONS MATTER?

☐ **Elements of the genre.** What theme do I want to convey? How can I use shape, color, image, and other elements to convey this theme? What connotations and cultural associations do I want my audience to catch?

☐ **Style.** How can I layer and juxtapose materials to add dimensionality? What colors will convey my point? What materials will I use to put everything together? How much detail will I need to persuade my audience? Do I want to convey a satirical tone? A serious tone? Some other tone?

☐ **Design.** What size and shape will my visual argument be? Is there a particular shape I can use to convey my point? How will I use balance, contrast, perspective, and line to focus my audience's attention on particular elements? What elements can I repeat to give the piece a sense of order?

☐ **Sources.** What sources will I use? Should I consider cutting photos or pictures out of magazines, or printing images from the Internet (or embedding them if I'm creating a digital file)? What about objects, such as buttons, jewelry, or scraps? How about found objects such as a grocery list, a cocktail napkin, or a restaurant's bar coaster? Are there particular cultural or historical associations that I'd like my audience to make? If so, I need to consider working with (or from) these types of materials.

PRACTICE Want to experiment? Sketch your own collage.

Think of a point you'd like to argue about modern life, such as "social networking is making us lose our ability to communicate in person," and create a collage to make your argument. Begin by going through some magazines and cutting out images that you think will assist in making your point. Play with different ways of arranging the images together, overlapping them in different ways. Then think about other items you might want to add, such as buttons and pins, scraps of fabrics or other materials, printouts of images from the Internet, photos, or jewelry (for example, to make the argument mentioned about social networking, you might want to find and print out from the Internet an image of an old-fashioned calling card).

Alternatively, create a digital collage. Instead of cutting out images from magazines, find images online and incorporate them or take your own digital photos. Instead of buttons, pins, and fabric scraps, you can use a photo-editing application to create different effects, such as blurred photo edges or the addition of a particular pattern, similar to a pattern added with a rubber stamp in a traditional collage.

PART 2
COMPOSING IN GENRES
FROM START TO FINISH

5 EXPLORING TOPICS & CREATING A RESEARCH PROPOSAL

CONTENTS

▲ STUDENT AUTHOR
Jasmine Huerta.
iStockphoto.
RESEARCH PROPOSAL ▶
Jasmine Huerta,
Diabetes Project.

ENG 101, Professor Braziller

Research Proposal Assignment: What Is Your Focus?

Jasmine Huerta
Professor Amy Braziller
English 101
October 6, 20—

Research Proposal

1. Your research question

   How can diet—specifically, monitoring the intake of sugar, calories, and sodium—help someone with diabetes manage the disease and avoid taking insulin?

2. A working title for your project

   The working title for my project is "Living with Diabetes: Diet Is the Answer." I chose this topic because although some people are predisposed to diabetes because of genetics, they do have some control over the situation. For example, through their choices related to food and diet they can manage or perhaps even prevent the disease.

CHOOSING A TOPIC THROUGH BASIC RESEARCH

The Internet offers an unlimited source of topics, and beginning your reading can be exciting but overwhelming: You can easily locate millions of resources on any topic simply by doing a quick online search. That's why it's important to go about the process in an orderly fashion. This chapter will show you the steps you need to take.

Whenever you write—as a student in a composition classroom or a professional in a workplace—you focus on a specific topic. Sometimes you may be provided with a general theme or a specific topic or issue. For example, your instructor might ask you to respond to an essay you've read for class, or your manager at work might ask you to share your plans to improve business or increase sales in the next quarter. Other times, most often in the course of college work, you get to start from scratch and choose a topic purely out of your own interest and curiosity.

So how do you choose a topic? Where should you start? One place might be this book. The Index of Themes (p. T-1) organizes every reading in this text by topic, and the Index of Genres (p. G-1) will help you see the relationship between topic choice and genre choice.

> What issues do you care most about? What have you blogged or posted about lately? What topics from the news or your studies keep you up at night? What would you like to learn more about?

1. Brainstorm Topic Ideas: Read, Talk, Sketch, Enjoy.

The best way to get started on identifying a topic that is meaningful to you is to get your ideas flowing. Here are some ways to do that.

Begin by reading for ideas, and discuss those ideas with others.

Do some preliminary reading online, but be disciplined about it   Googling your topic is a way to explore your initial ideas, but at this stage, limit yourself to a few major sources in order to get a flavor for the topic. Some general sources might be *Salon, Slate, The New York Times,* or CNN. If you want to skim scholarly sources, try Google Scholar (scholar.google.com). If you go to *Wikipedia,* be sure to look at the source links for the entries you read. That's where you'll find the best leads. And don't be all day about it: Remember, you're generating ideas, not surfing mindlessly. For example, let's say you are interested in the topic of road rage: the problem of aggressive driving. While the *Wikipedia* "Road Rage" entry (see p. 262) may not be exceptionally informative (or particularly trustworthy), the "Sources," "Further reading," and "External links" sections can connect you to better sources, such as the National Highway Traffic Safety Administration's campaign to stop aggressive driving (see p. 263), and AAA's (the Automobile Association of America's) study on controlling road rage.

> For an Index of Sources & Contexts for material referenced in this chapter, see the e-Pages at **bedfordstmartins .com/bookofgenres.**

Talk to people   Discuss your topic ideas and questions with classmates, friends, family, and coworkers to find out what others have to say about the topic you're considering. Often, explaining why you're interested in a topic can help you focus. When others ask you to clarify your ideas, you will often discover what you really want to say.

Continue to generate ideas through brainstorming and sketching techniques.

Make a list   What do you care most about? Begin by making a list of things you are passionate about, your pet peeves, things you are curious about, things you don't understand, or things you'd like to change about the world. From your initial

◀ WEB SITE
National Highway Traffic Safety Administration, "Stop Aggressive Driving." The "Sources" and "External Links" sections of *Wikipedia's* "Road Rage" entry point readers to this authoritative government source (nhtsa.gov/ Aggressive). *Courtesy of the National Highway Traffic Administration.*

list, force yourself to double or triple the size of the list. Often the best topic ideas are the less obvious ones—ideas that will come to you when you push yourself to keep listing.

Freewrite   If you've identified a general topic area, or some of the ideas you've generated in your lists interest you, try freewriting. The goal here is to get your ideas written down, without judging what you're writing, or editing yourself, or trying to write beautifully. Experiment by making yourself write nonstop for ten to thirty minutes. As you keep your fingers moving, don't worry about making sense, or about readers being confused or impressed. No one is going to read this document but you. When you take away the pressure of producing smooth prose, you may be surprised to see the ideas you generate.

Mind map   Like list making and freewriting, mind mapping gives you a creative format for sketching out your early ideas about a topic. To begin, write the topic or idea you are exploring in the middle of a blank piece of paper (alternatively, you can use mind-mapping software such as MatchWare OpenMind or a free Web-based mind-mapping application such as Bubbl.us). As you think of details and related ideas, write them around the central topic, connecting them with lines that indicate their relationships.

Ideas come out of conversations. What comes up in your talks with friends? What was the topic of your last discussion or disagreement? What are some of your un-resolved questions about the topic?

Guided Process: How to Choose a Topic ▼

Sharon Freeman (Student)

From Coffee to Germs

▲ STUDENT AUTHOR
Sharon Freeman.
Here we look at
this student's early
brainstorming on a
possible research
topic (germs).
Shutterstock.

Below are three lists made by student Sharon Freeman. In the first list, she simply wrote down everything on her mind. For the second list, she wrote a question or two about each topic. By the third, she focused on germs and specific questions related to that topic.

TOPIC BRAINSTORM 1

Coffee

Chocolate

Democracy

Taxes

Germs

TOPIC BRAINSTORM 2

Coffee—is it worth it to pay more for organic or sustainably grown coffee?

Chocolate—is dark chocolate really good for you?

Democracy—how much say do citizens have compared with corporations these days? How much difference do huge campaign contributions make in how politicians vote and make laws?

Taxes—how much do I really pay in taxes (income taxes, sales taxes, property taxes, etc.), and how does it all get spent?

Germs—is antibacterial soap really necessary?

TOPIC BRAINSTORM 3

Germs

Do I need to use antibacterial soap, or does it make things worse?

Do you need both antibacterial soap and hand sanitizer, or just one?

How much money do people spend these days on antibacterial products and is it all just a hoax?

Aren't some germs actually good for you?

Has anyone actually gotten sick from someone at the gym not wiping down a machine? Seriously, what can you catch from someone else's sweat?

Why do some people get colds and other people don't?

How contagious are you when you have a cold? Should you really skip class and work?

How can you build your immunity against colds?

After brainstorming, Sharon did some freewriting about germs:

TOPIC FREEWRITE: "GERMS"

It seems like everyone I know is obsessed with germs. My roommate has little bottles of hand sanitizer stashed everywhere and she's constantly using the stuff and offering it to me. I feel weird when I say no, but honestly, I'm suspicious of the stuff. I wash my hands before cooking or eating and of course, after using the bathroom, and I almost never get sick, so it seems to me that I'm doing everything I need to do. What would spending money on hand sanitizer and obsessing over germs do for me? I think it's a moneymaking scheme. The companies that make soap now want to sell us soap AND hand sanitizer. And now we have to pay extra to get antibacterial soap, too. My parents don't use that and they're perfectly healthy. My dad hasn't had a cold in twenty years.

Sharon also sketched out a mind map in order to explore different views and aspects of her topic. In the map below, she broke out "Germs" into two aspects or subtopics:

TOPIC MIND MAP: "GERMS"

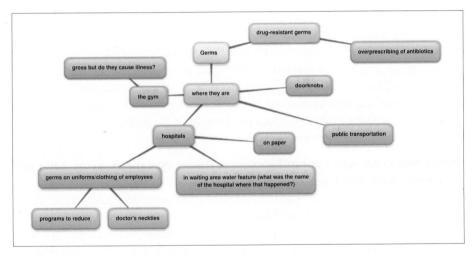

At this point, Sharon is ready to test some of her questions with some preliminary research, with a focus on:

1. Where germs are

2. How germs become drug resistant

From there, she focuses on the first subtopic—where germs are—and further breaks it down into aspects she could explore (in darker green):

» The gym

» Public transportation

» Hospitals

» Doorknobs

When you research a topic, how do you know what is fact and what is opinion (an argument supported with facts)? If you wanted just plain facts about how germs are spread—and not, say, an argument for or against hand sanitizers—what sources would you turn to? Medical reports? Editorials?

Sharon Freeman, *From Coffee to Germs*

Next, Sharon focuses on hospitals—and programs that hospitals could adopt for reducing the spread of germs among staff and patients. For example, "asking doctors not to wear germ-transporting neckties" could branch off the "programs to reduce" bubble.

There are still plenty of unexplored topic areas represented in this map. For example, Sharon could go back to her "Germs" bubble and add other aspects, such as the views of scientists, parents, and schools. Or she could focus on the relationship between drug-resistant germs and the use of hand sanitizer.

2. Explore Topic Ideas through Preliminary Research: Ask Yourself, Who's Saying What?

Once you've identified a topic area (road rage, germs, or something else), you're ready to dig a little deeper to better understand it. Keep a few possibilities in mind and conduct preliminary research on several related topics (or subtopics) so you can make an informed decision about which one to commit to; the viability of each topic will depend on what you find out at this point. As with the preliminary reading you did during brainstorming, you'll continue to draw on sources written for nonexperts. Later in your process, you'll move on to more specialized sources. As you conduct preliminary research, focus on the following:

Words and facts: Ask yourself some questions. Are there terms you need to define? And what are the facts? For example, if you are exploring road rage, you might ask yourself: How do law enforcement agencies define "road rage"? When is this term used, and why? Are there degrees of road rage that police recognize? And how does the court system define and prosecute road rage? For ex- ▶ ample, the Automobile Association of America (AAA), in a report it commissioned (see p. 267), makes a distinction between "road rage" and "aggressive driving."

As you gather facts, ask yourself: How many incidents of road rage have been recorded nationally? How many in your state, city, or neighborhood? What were the circumstances? What were the repercussions?

Opinions: Find out what others have to say on the subject, and notice what evidence they use to support their opinions In addition to facts, what opinions surround your topic? Who writes about the topic, and why are they concerned? On what sources do they base their statements or arguments? What sources do they draw on? And what sources might you want to use, too? In relation to the road rage topic, you might find out that some psychologists consider road rage a mental health issue, or that law enforcement in different places defines road rage as a crime, depending on whether someone is injured or killed. Source material for road rage might include legal statutes and news reports of incidents.

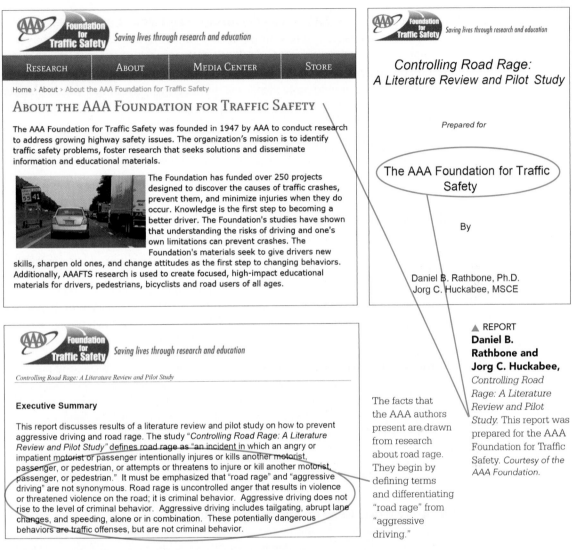

The facts that the AAA authors present are drawn from research about road rage. They begin by defining terms and differentiating "road rage" from "aggressive driving."

▲ REPORT
Daniel B. Rathbone and Jorg C. Huckabee, *Controlling Road Rage: A Literature Review and Pilot Study.* This report was prepared for the AAA Foundation for Traffic Safety. *Courtesy of the AAA Foundation.*

As you gather opinions on your topic, ask yourself: What are the advantages of—and motivations behind—each argument? For example, an organization that wants to stop road rage might define it as a mental health issue; this might make it easier for them to get funding for a safe driving program.

Your perspective: Form your own arguments in response to others   As you research, you will begin to form your own ideas and opinions about your topic. For example, learning how others define road rage might lead you to form your own definition. Or learning how psychologists understand and treat road rage could lead you to put forth an argument on how it should be handled by law enforcement. In other words, you will naturally begin responding to the ideas of others and kicking around possible arguments.

Conflicting views: Notice who disagrees about your topic   When you begin reading sources related to your topic, you might begin to notice that there are viewpoints that stand opposed to each other. Furthermore, as you dig into these disagreements, you might realize that the differing viewpoints are well researched and should not be immediately dismissed. In the case of road rage, you might find one article by a psychologist arguing that road rage is a result of a mental disorder and another article written by a sociologist claiming that road rage is not a mental condition, but rather a cultural condition based on societal behavior. Discovering well-researched, well-reasoned opposing stances related to your topic forces you to accept that there is not necessarily one "correct" viewpoint; reasonable people can disagree.

The irrational: Avoid arguments that are just too "out there"   In the course of your research, you may stumble upon the ideas of people who are unreasonable, ill informed, or both. For example, say you are researching *Apollo 11*, the first manned landing on the moon, in 1969, and the cultural impact of this event. You may encounter arguments by those who believe the landing was a hoax, despite factual evidence to the contrary. Moon landing deniers are considered by most people to be out of touch with reality; in this case, pursuing this strand of research is not worthwhile. Keep a critical eye as you read sources.

Comfort zone: Use sources that are right for you   While there is plenty of source material on the topics of road rage and *Apollo 11*, other topics, especially those that are very narrow or specialized, can be problematic. In certain cases, the information you need might be held in archives or scientific labs that you don't have access to; another problem is that the information you find might be so complex that you can't understand it. For example, a scholarly journal article on advanced economic theory is probably not an appropriate source for your purposes (unless you happen to be an expert in this area).

Detective work: Keep an eye out for subtopics   In your preliminary research you'll uncover subtopics you hadn't thought of before. For example, you may not have known that the phenomenon of road rage is discussed and researched by doctors and psychologists; a subtopic of road rage might be personality predictors for road rage.

The search: Pay attention to key terms   As you conduct preliminary research, you'll notice that certain terms pop up. For example, if you research road rage, you'll see that *defensive driving*, *aggressive driving*, *reckless driving*, and *intermittent explosive disorder* are terms that appear frequently in source materials. Follow up on these key terms by using them in your searches of the Internet and library databases.

What works: Test the viability of your topic by asking yourself a few questions Following is an assignment we give our students during their preliminary research phase. It includes the responses of a student, Jasmine Huerta, whose research topic is diabetes. (Note: We will see more of her work on this project later in the chapter.)

Through answering the assigned questions, Jasmine realizes that she has several interesting potential research questions to pursue. The list of key terms helped her continue and refine her research. She realized that the glycemic index is not 100 percent accepted, which surprised and intrigued her. By using the Internet to find key terms, exploring some of these potential subtopics, previewing and reading sources, and then reflecting on her process and discoveries, Jasmine narrows her topic from diabetes to the role of nutrition in the diabetic patient.

ENG 101, Professor Braziller

Topic Assignment: What Is Your Topic? How Viable Is It?

Jasmine Huerta
Professor Amy Braziller
English 101
September 26, 20—
Topic Idea: Diabetes

You've begun your preliminary research. Now, respond to the following questions to see how workable your topic may be.

1. What is the general topic area you are considering?

   I am interested in researching and writing about diabetes.

2. Why? Are you truly fascinated/curious/passionate about the topic? How did you become interested in this topic? (If your answer is no, explain why and then move on to the next topic without answering any more questions.)

   Diabetes runs in my family, so it's something I want to understand more about in case I am faced with it at some point. My six-year-old cousin has type 1 diabetes. My mother had gestational diabetes when she was pregnant with me. Most recently, my grandfather, who is a bit overweight (as is my cousin), was diagnosed with diabetes. I'm wondering if I am just destined to develop it at some point because of my family history. I also wonder if perhaps there are things I can do to prevent the disease, since I presently don't have diabetes. I worry about both my cousin and grandfather, so I'd like to see if there are some things they could do to keep their diabetes under control, rather than just relying on traditional medicine.

3. What surprising facts have you gathered so far about your topic? What further questions do you have that you need answered with data? And what sources are you thinking of using?

Continues next page

▲ STUDENT AUTHOR
Jasmine Huerta.
In this chapter, we follow this student as she chooses and investigates a topic (diabetes). Jasmine appears next on page 277.
iStockphoto.

◀ TOPIC ASSIGNMENT
Jasmine Huerta.
Shown here are Jasmine's very early ideas about her diabetes project and some information on what she's discovered during preliminary research.

Huerta, *Topic Assignment*, *Continued*

Surprising facts/data:

- According to *Wikipedia*'s entry "Diabetes" (accessed on 9/20/13): "Diabetic patients with neuropathic symptoms such as numbness or tingling in feet or hands are twice as likely to be unemployed as those without the symptoms."

- A link found on the American Diabetes Association to an article on SmartBrief .com stated that those who are exposed to secondhand smoke have a greater risk of contracting diabetes.

- According to an article about lifestyle and home remedies, found on the Mayo Clinic's page, diabetes can contribute to gum infections.

Potential sources:

- *Wikipedia*

- American Diabetes Association

- Mayo Clinic

4. Do reasonable people disagree about the topic? If so, what aspects of the topic do they disagree about? Who disagrees with whom? Name names. Articulate at least three positions you have found. (If your answer is no, explain why and then move on to the next topic without answering any more questions.)

There seems to be a bit of a debate about what makes the best approach for a diabetic diet. While surfing around on the Internet, one of the big debates I found discussed the glycemic index and how it relates to managing diabetes. It seems that people used to think you just had to avoid high-sugar foods, but after reading a few articles, I realized that many researchers want to look more closely at using the glycemic index (taking into account carbohydrates) in working with diabetic diets.

In an article titled "Low–Glycemic Index Diets in the Management of Diabetes," Miller et al. argue that this is a positive approach. I found an editorial written by Marion Franz in the publication *Diabetes Care* that argues with this approach: "The Glycemic Index: Not the most effective nutrition therapy intervention." In the Mayo Clinic's advice column, "Ask a Diabetes Specialist," someone wrote to Dr. Maria Collazo-Clavel, asking, "Is the glycemic-index diet useful for people with diabetes?" She responds that it's very complicated to use this as a measure, cautioning that it might not be the best approach for everybody.

5. Is the topic researchable in the time you have? Will you be able to conduct primary research? (If your answer is no, explain why and then move on to the next topic without answering any more questions.)

I don't see any issues with researching the topic this semester. In a short amount of time I was able to find many sources and potential ideas. Primary research also should be easy. As I mentioned in my answer above, I have a number of family members who deal with diabetes. I can easily interview them. I also would like to contact a doctor who treats people with diabetes and arrange an interview, perhaps by phone or e-mail. Another possibility for primary research is to find some blogs written by diabetics, so I could draw on some of their firsthand experiences.

Huerta, *Topic Assignment,* *Continued*

6. What are some subtopics that have emerged in your research?

- Nutrition to manage diabetes

- Medication to manage diabetes

- Alternative treatments for diabetes

- Prevention of diabetes

- Social issues connected to diabetes

7. What questions might you pursue in further research, based on what you've discovered during preliminary research?

- What types of diets are best for people with diabetes?

- How can diet prevent someone from getting diabetes if he or she has a family history of diabetes?

- How can following certain nutritional guidelines make diabetes go away?

- How can alternative treatments or natural medications be used instead of insulin?

- What countries have the highest rate of diabetes? What contributes to the high rate?

8. What are some key terms that keep coming up in relation to this topic?

- glycemic index

- metabolism

- blood sugar

- hypertension

- obesity

- glucose monitoring

- insulin

3. Commit to a Single Viable Topic: What Are You Most Curious About?

Once you've identified a general topic area, it's time to commit to one specific topic within it. The "What Is Your Topic? How Viable Is It?" assignment (p. 269) can assist you with this choice, as can the following questions:

Is your topic compatible with your assignment? And can you make a strong argument about it?   If your instructor has given you an assignment, read it carefully and consider the degree to which your topic will work. If you've

Attention, researchers! Looking for something to argue about?

Almost any topic offers argumentative angles: The key is to find the angles.

For example, while "reading" may not seem like the most provocative topic, a quick Google search reveals that it's the subject of much debate. Some questions around this debate include: Do college students read more or less than in the past? Is online reading cognitively different from reading books? What is the relationship between how much we read and our development of critical thinking skills?

The point is to keep an open mind to topics that seem vanilla. You may find some spice under the surface.

been asked to make an argument, you might find yourself gravitating toward controversial issues—such as gun control, abortion, and censorship. However, we urge you to consider other, less obvious topics. For example, if you are interested in the subject of gun control, rather than choosing the topic of concealed weapons and constitutional rights, you might take the topic of gun control and examine the power that gun control groups, such as the NRA, hold in the political arena.

Do you like your topic enough to stick with it?   If you are not truly curious about your topic, you probably won't remain interested in your research beyond the first week or so. Choose something you really want to learn about, that has some connection to you and your life.

What is your deadline, and how will it affect your plans for research? If your completed project is due in two weeks, choose a topic for which there is plenty of information that you can access easily. If you have more time, say an entire fifteen-week semester, you have the luxury of using a range of sources, and conducting interviews or surveys, for example, so you can select your topic accordingly. On the other hand, if your topic is so obscure that your only sources need to be ordered through interlibrary loan (which can take several weeks), it is not a good topic for either a two-week or fifteen-week deadline.

Will you find appropriate sources for your topic?   Some topics are so current that there is little or no published research available. For example, a friend who works in the field of bioengineering might tell you that scientists are developing crops with deeper roots to reduce the amount of carbon dioxide in the atmosphere, but because the research has just begun, there are no published articles about it. In this case, you might want to shift your topic toward an aspect of bioengineering that is more researchable in the present.

4. Form a Working Research Question—and Refine as You Go.

What's your general topic? What questions will move you from a basic, broad idea to more specific ideas?   Creating research questions focuses your attention from a general topic to a specific aspect of the topic, as follows:

GENERAL TOPIC	Race
WORKING RESEARCH QUESTIONS	Is the criminal justice system in the United States racist?
	Is racial profiling a form of racism?
	What is it like to be an immigrant in America?

While you'll ask (and answer) lots of questions in your research, your "research question" is the big question, the one that you are ultimately interested in answering. Once you've done some preliminary searching—and have a sense of what people are saying about your topic and what some of the subtopics are—you can formulate a working research question. As you continue your research, you will refine your question. For instance, you might decide to begin as follows:

WORKING RESEARCH QUESTION	Is racial profiling a form of racism?

But as you discover more about your topic, you might revise your question to reflect what you're learning, as follows:

REVISED RESEARCH QUESTION	Does racial profiling help or hinder law enforcement policies?

◀ WEB SITE
The American Civil Liberties Union. The ACLU is an excellent resource for racial profiling data and perspectives. *American Civil Liberties Union.*

The ACLU argues that the practice of racial profiling hinders law enforcement and alienates communities.

What questions—focused on finding facts and defining terms—can move you toward a final research question? As you begin your research, many of your questions will be focused on gathering facts and defining terms. If, as in the example above, you're researching the general topic of race, you will ask questions at the outset such as the following:

QUESTIONS TO HELP YOU UNCOVER FACTS & TERMS	What is the definition of *race*?
	What is the difference between *race* and *ethnicity*?
	Has the definition of *race* changed over time?
	What statistical data is there concerning race in the United States?

Your research question, however, should focus on more complex *analysis*. Following are some examples of revised, more final research questions:

RESEARCH QUESTIONS	How is race portrayed in the news media?
	What are the real-life effects of the news media's portrayal of race?
	What can news media outlets do to ensure that race is portrayed responsibly?
	What would happen if the portrayal of race in the news media were regulated by a governing body?

Notice how these questions require extensive research and even speculation, especially the last question. These would make solid research questions, while the first set of questions would not, although they would be useful questions to ask in the course of researching one of the questions in the second list.

Let's look at another example. Imagine you are researching graphic novel heroes. As you begin to familiarize yourself with your topic, you might ask:

QUESTIONS TO HELP YOU UNCOVER FACTS & TERMS	When did graphic novels become popular?
	What are some popular themes in graphic novels?
	What are the most commercially successful graphic novels?
	Who is the audience for the most commercially successful graphic novels?

With the answers to these questions, you can then focus on answering more critical, complex research questions, like these:

RESEARCH QUESTIONS   How do graphic novels subvert female stereotypes?

How does the portrayal of females in graphic novels differ from the portrayal of females in comic books?

How do graphic novels extend and build upon the archetypes of comic books?

How does the subversion of female stereotypes in graphic novels affect female readers?

◀ WEB SITE
Graphic Novel Reporter is a good source for facts and opinions on graphic works, and for investigating the themes, assumptions, and stereotypes built into graphic novels. *Copyright 2008–2010, GraphicNovelReporter .com. All rights reserved.*

As with the research questions about race, the final questions about graphic novels are much more focused on analysis than on simple fact-finding.

What is the general topic of your research? What are your questions about it so far? Which questions have to do with finding facts? Which ones are more about analysis? What, in your early research, has surprised you most?

The chart below shows some working research questions as they move from general concepts drawing on facts to more complex ideas involving speculation. As you read from left to right, you can see beginning/working research questions evolving into more final research questions. Notice also that as the questions get more speculative, they also become more debatable and argumentative.

QUESTIONS TO HELP YOU UNCOVER FACTS & TERMS

RESEARCH QUESTIONS

Broad/general →————————————————→ Specific, analytical, complex

TOPIC: **Race**	What is the definition of *race*? What is the difference between *race* and *ethnicity*?	▶ Has the definition of *race* changed over time?	▶ How is race portrayed in the news media? What are the effects of the news media's portrayal of race?	▶ What can news media outlets do to ensure that race is portrayed responsibly?	▶ What would happen if the portrayal of race in the news media were regulated by a governing body?

Broad/general →————————————————→ Specific, analytical, complex

TOPIC: **Graphic novels**	When did graphic novels become popular? What are the most commercially successful graphic novels? Who is the audience for the most commercially successful graphic novels?	▶ What are some popular themes in graphic novels?	▶ How do graphic novels subvert female stereotypes? How does the portrayal of females in graphic novels differ from the portrayal of females in comic books?	▶ How do graphic novels extend and build upon the archetypes of comic books?	▶ How does the subversion of female stereotypes in graphic novels affect female readers?

▲ CHARTS
Refining a research question. This chart shows the movement from broad topic questions to more specific research questions. Notice the movement from "What is race?" to "What if the government had a say in the portrayal of race in the media?"

CHECKLIST Refining Your Research Question

What are the qualities of a really good research question?

☐ **It is open-ended,** meaning it cannot be answered with a simple yes, no, or maybe, or a single number.

☐ **It uses specific, rather than general, terms.**

☐ **It can be answered in the time you have—and with the resources you have access to.** You might have a fascinating and specific research question, but if you can't feasibly research it in the time you have, it just won't work.

☐ **It is one you really want to find answers to.** The best research grows out of curiosity. No matter how good your research question is, if it isn't backed up by your genuine interest, it won't lead you to rich, interesting research.

MOVING FROM A RESEARCH QUESTION TO A PROPOSAL

Now that you've got an understanding of how to explore a topic and form working research questions, let's look at some next steps. In the following Guided Process, we circle back to Jasmine Huerta (remember her from the assignment on p. 269?) to see how she proceeds in her research on diabetes.

Guided Process: How to Research a Topic

Jasmine Huerta (Student)

Diabetes Project

While you may not follow every step that Jasmine takes as you work on your own research topic, tracing her process (through p. 296) may give you ideas for how to proceed.

Exploring a Topic: Diabetes

When Jasmine got started on her project, she knew she wanted to write about diabetes, but she wasn't sure how to focus. So she began with a few broad questions:

QUESTIONS TO HELP YOU UNCOVER FACTS & TERMS

What causes diabetes? Who is affected by it, and why?

What are the statistics of diabetes in the United States and around the world?

What is the latest medical research on diabetes?

What alternative treatments are there (as opposed to insulin)?

How can people avoid getting diabetes?

What is the relationship between nutrition and diabetes?

What is the relationship between metabolism and diabetes?

What is the role of glucose and the glycemic index?

▲ STUDENT AUTHOR
Jasmine Huerta moves from her working research question to a final proposal in this Guided Process section. *iStockphoto.*

From these fact-finding questions, which she investigated through research (we'll outline this process in a moment), Jasmine began to narrow the scope of her topic from the list of questions above to:

WORKING RESEARCH QUESTION

What is the relationship between nutrition and diabetes?

After still more research and analysis, she pursued this question:

REVISED RESEARCH QUESTION

How can diet—specifically, monitoring the intake of sugar, calories, and sodium—help someone with diabetes manage the disease and avoid taking insulin?

Ultimately, Jasmine moved from a research question to the argument she made in her final paper, which also became her title:

FINAL RESEARCHED ARGUMENT

Getting off insulin: A case for a nutritional approach for managing diabetes

▼ *WIKIPEDIA* ENTRY
"Diabetes mellitus."
Jasmine reads through this entry with special attention to the "References" and "External links" sections for further resources—as well as the "Management" and "Lifestyle" portions for information on diet, which are shown on page 279. *Courtesy of Wikimedia Foundation, Inc. All rights reserved.*

Finding Facts about Diabetes

What was Jasmine's process? First, through her early reading, and as a person with a family history of the disease, Jasmine realizes that what interests her most are the dietary concerns of diabetics. With this in mind, she begins to explore a few more sources.

Wikipedia is her starting point. Even though her instructor has cautioned the class against using *Wikipedia* as a source (see our advice about *Wikipedia* on p. 406), Jasmine sees it as a good starting point for general information, and perhaps some leads related to dietary concerns. She begins with the "Diabetes mellitus" page (when she typed in "Diabetes," she was redirected there). ▼

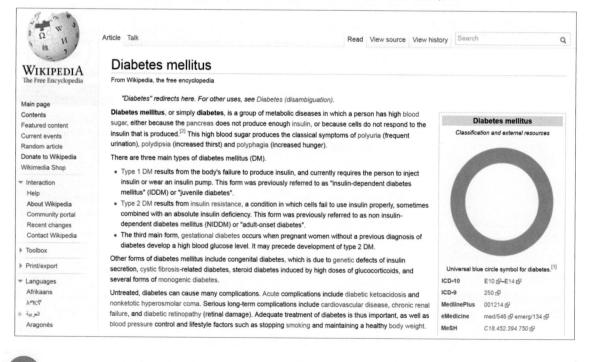

After reading through the overview, Jasmine realizes that she needs information about the differences between type 1 diabetes and type 2 diabetes (which the entry explains is the more common form, and the one that can be treated through diet). She discovers she'll also need to explore diabetes in terms of blood glucose levels, metabolism, body weight, and insulin.

Of particular interest are the "References" and "External links" sections of the "Diabetes mellitus" page, which offer Jasmine a head start on exploring other sources.

References

1. ^ "Diabetes Blue Circle Symbol" 🔗. International Diabetes Federation. 17 March 2006.
2. ^ *a b c d* Shoback, edited by David G. Gardner, Dolores (2011). *Greenspan's basic & clinical endocrinology* (9th ed.). New York: McGraw-Hill Medical. pp. Chapter 17. ISBN 0-07-162243-8.
3. ^ *a b* *Williams textbook of endocrinology* (12th ed.). Philadelphia: Elsevier/Saunders. pp. 1371–1435. ISBN 978-1-4377-0324-5.
4. ^ Lambert, P.; Bingley, P. J. (2002). "What is Type 1 Diabetes?". *Medicine* **30**: 1–5. doi:10.1383/medc.30.1.1.28264 🔗. Diabetes Symptoms 🔗 edit
5. ^ Rother KI (April 2007). "Diabetes treatment—bridging the divide". *The New England Journal of Medicine* **356** (15): 1499–501. doi:10.1056/NEJMp078030 🔗. PMID 17429082 🔗.
6. ^ *a b* "Diabetes Mellitus (DM): Diabetes Mellitus and Disorders of Carbohydrate Metabolism: Merck Manual Professional" 🔗. Merck Publishing. April 2010. Retrieved 2010-07-30.
7. ^ Dorner M, Pinget M, Brogard JM (May 1977). "Essential labile diabetes" (in German). *MMW Munch Med Wochenschr* **119** (19): 671–4. PMID 406527 🔗.
8. ^ Lawrence JM, Contreras R, Chen W, Sacks DA (May 2008). "Trends in the prevalence of preexisting diabetes and gestational diabetes mellitus among a racially/ethnically diverse population of pregnant women, 1999–2005". *Diabetes Care* **31** (5): 899–904. doi:10.2337/dc07-2345 🔗. PMID 18223030 🔗.

External links

- Diabetes 🔗 at the Open Directory Project
- American Diabetes Association 🔗
- IDF Diabetes Atlas 🔗
- National Diabetes Education Program 🔗

◄ WIKIPEDIA ENTRY DETAIL **"Diabetes mellitus."** The "References" and "External links" sections provide Jasmine with authoritative resources, including the American Diabetes Association, which she will investigate (see p. 281). *Courtesy of Wikimedia Foundation, Inc. All rights reserved.*

In addition, the "Lifestyle" section of the page links her to another entry titled "Diabetic diet."

Management

Main article: Diabetes management

Diabetes mellitus is a chronic disease which cannot be cured except in very specific situations. Management concentrates on keeping blood sugar levels as close to normal ("euglycemia") as possible, without causing hypoglycemia. This can usually be accomplished with diet, exercise, and use of appropriate medications (insulin in the case of type 1 diabetes, oral medications, as well as possibly insulin, in type 2 diabetes).

Patient education, understanding, and participation is vital, since the complications of diabetes are far less common and less severe in people who have well-managed blood sugar levels.[24][25] The goal of treatment is an HbA1C level of 6.5%, but should not be lower than that, and may be set higher.[26] Attention is also paid to other health problems that may accelerate the deleterious effects of diabetes. These include smoking, elevated cholesterol levels, obesity, high blood pressure, and lack of regular exercise.[26] Specialised footwear is widely used to reduce the risk of ulceration, re-ulceration, in at-risk diabetic feet. Evidence for the efficacy of this remains equivocal, however.[27]

Lifestyle

See also: Diabetic diet

There are roles for patient education, dietetic support, sensible exercise, with the goal of keeping both short-term and long-term blood glucose levels within acceptable bounds. In addition, given the associated higher risks of cardiovascular disease, lifestyle modifications are recommended to control blood pressure.[28]

Medications

Oral medications

Main article: Anti-diabetic medication

Metformin is generally recommended as a first line treatment for type 2 diabetes, as there is good evidence that it decreases mortality.[29] Routine use of aspirin, however, has not been found to improve outcomes in uncomplicated diabetes.[30]

Insulin

Main article: Insulin therapy

◄ WIKIPEDIA ENTRY DETAIL **"Diabetes mellitus."** The "Management," "Lifestyle," and "Medications" sections refer Jasmine to related entries. She notices that the "Lifestyle" section links to an entry for "Diabetic diet," which she decides to check out (see p. 280). *Courtesy of Wikimedia Foundation, Inc. All rights reserved.*

Create account 👤 Log in

Article Talk

Read Edit View history Search 🔍

Diabetic diet

From Wikipedia, the free encyclopedia

There is much controversy regarding what diet to recommend to sufferers of diabetes mellitus. The *'diet'* most often recommended is high in dietary fiber, especially soluble fiber, but low in fat (especially saturated fat). Recommendations of the fraction of total calories to be obtained from carbohydrate intake range from 1/6 to 75% – a 2006 review found recommendations varying from 40 to 65%.[1] Diabetics may be encouraged to reduce their intake of carbohydrates that have a high glycemic index (GI), although this is also controversial.[2] (In cases of hypoglycemia, they are advised to have food or drink that can raise blood glucose quickly, such as lucozade, followed by a long-acting carbohydrate (such as rye bread) to prevent risk of further hypoglycemia.) However, others question the usefulness of the glycemic index and recommend high-GI foods like potatoes and rice.

Display showing low fat and/or high fiber foods 🔗

Contents [hide]
1 History
2 Exchange scheme
3 Later developments
4 Carbohydrates
5 Low-carbohydrate alternatives
6 Vegan/vegetarian
7 Timing of meals
8 Special diabetes products
9 Alcohol and drugs
10 Specific diets
11 See also
12 Further reading
13 References
14 External links

Display showing refined, high fat/carbohydrate foods 🔗

History   [edit]

There has been long history of dietary treatment of diabetes mellitus – dietary treatment of diabetes mellitus was used in Egypt as long ago as 3,500 B.C., and was used in India by Sushruta and Charaka more than 2000 years ago. In the eighteenth century, these authors note, John Rollo argued that calorie restriction in the diabetic diet could reduce glycosuria in diabetes. However, more modern history of the diabetic diet may begin with Frederick Madison Allen, who, in the days before insulin was discovered, recommended that people with diabetes ate only a low-calorie diet to prevent ketoacidosis from killing them. This was an approach which did not actually cure diabetes, it merely extended life by a limited period. The first use of insulin by Frederick Banting in 1922 changed things, and at last allowed patients more flexibility in their eating.

Jasmine looks closely at the "External links" section of the *Wikipedia* page (p. 279) and decides to investigate the American Diabetes Association. She finds out that the ADA is a nonprofit group whose purpose is to control diabetes, especially through improving healthcare access and funding research and prevention.

The ADA site is organized into topics, including "Diabetes Basics," which in turn is broken down into related subtopics. In this section, Jasmine uncovers some interesting data, including:

» Prediabetes is a condition that develops prior to type 2 diabetes.

» Seven million people in the United States have undiagnosed diabetes.

» It is a myth that people get diabetes just because they eat too much sugar.

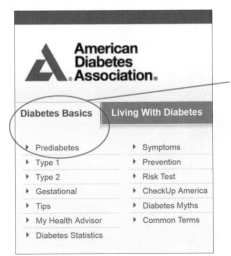

▲ WEB SITE
American Diabetes Association. Jasmine investigates the ADA site, where she focuses on the following content categories: "Diabetes Basics," "Prediabetes," "Living with Diabetes," "Recently Diagnosed," "Food & Fitness," and "MyFoodAdvisor," as shown below and through page 186. Copyright 2013 American Diabetes Association. From http://www.diabetes.org. Reprinted with permission from The American Diabetes Association.

◄ WEB SITE DETAIL
American Diabetes Association.
Jasmine is especially interested in the "Diabetes Basics" category and wonders what the ADA has to say about prediabetes, type 1, and type 2. Copyright 2013 American Diabetes Association. From http://www.diabetes.org. Reprinted with permission from The American Diabetes Association.

WEB SITE DETAIL ▶
American Diabetes Association.
Jasmine investigates the "Prediabetes" page and gets new information about the condition. *Copyright 2013 American Diabetes Association. From http://www.diabetes.org. Reprinted with permission from The American Diabetes Association.*

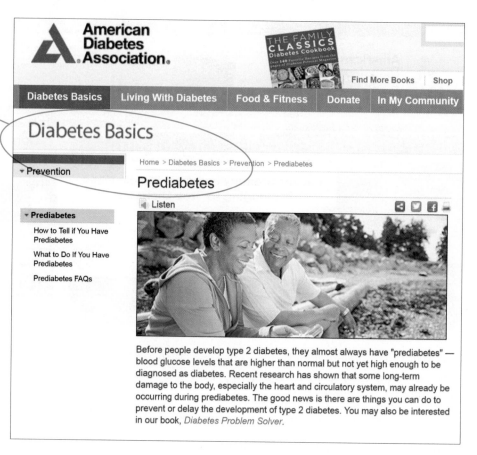

Jasmine is also interested in "Living With Diabetes," which is broken down into smaller topic areas.

WEB SITE DETAIL ▶
American Diabetes Association.
The "Living With Diabetes" content, Jasmine sees, addresses important topics she's interested in, including dealing with the diagnosis and daily care. *Copyright 2013 American Diabetes Association. From http://www.diabetes.org. Reprinted with permission from The American Diabetes Association.*

She's especially drawn to the "Food & Fitness" section, because of her interest in nutrition.

In the "Food & Fitness" section, Jasmine is surprised by the emphasis on recipes and meal planning as ways to control the disease. She finds the following information especially interesting:

» Beans, berries, and tomatoes are diabetes "superfoods."

» We shouldn't just look at the sugar content on food labels. It's more useful to examine the total carbohydrate number.

» Recipes for diabetics are not dull. The site includes recipes for Texas Tuna Burger, Asian Roast Pork Sliders, and Whole-Wheat Pancakes.

WEB SITE DETAIL ▶
**American Diabetes
Association.** On the
"MyFoodAdvisor"
page, Jasmine is
thrilled to find specific
recipes and nutritional
advice. *Copyright 2013
American Diabetes
Association. From http://
www.diabetes
.org. Reprinted with
permission from The
American Diabetes
Association.*

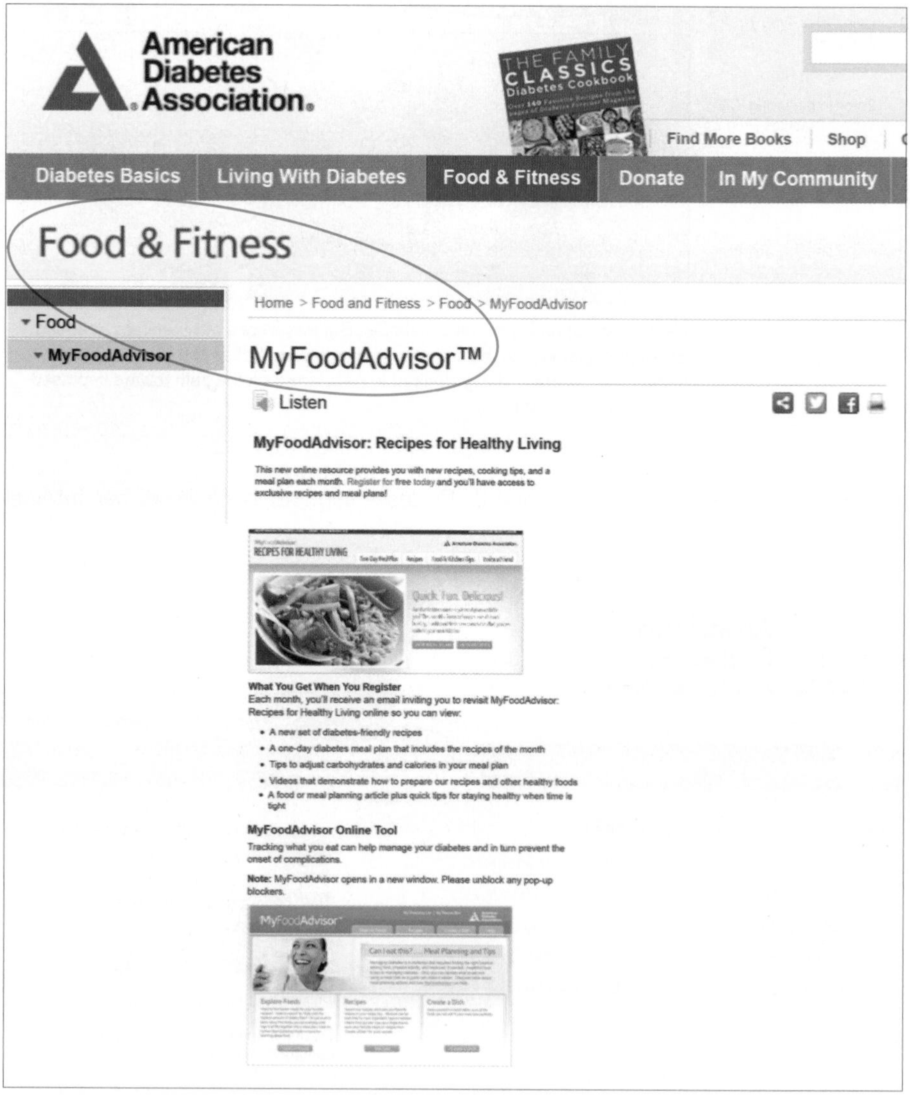

As Jasmine continues to read through the ADA site, she gets more absorbed in the idea that eating specific kinds of foods can assist in managing diabetes. She decides her next step is to find more information on nutrition, maybe even some more recipes designed for diabetics. A hospital or research facility might be another good source, she thinks, and she decides to check out the Mayo Clinic site.

◀ WEB SITE
Mayo Clinic. On their "Diabetes" page, the Mayo Clinic provides a definition of the disease. Jasmine is interested to see how this information compares to that of the ADA. *Mayo Foundation for Medical Education and Research.*

There she finds information on diabetes, along with meal plans and recipes. She gets even more interested in the relationship between diet and diabetes management.

◀ WEB SITE DETAIL
Mayo Clinic. On the "Diabetes meal plan recipes" page, Jasmine is pleasantly surprised by the range of foods that the Mayo Clinic recommends. *Mayo Foundation for Medical Education and Research.*

The following recipe, among many others, catches her eye.

WEB SITE DETAIL ▶
Mayo Clinic.
Jasmine finds that the
recipes are created
by Mayo Clinic
staff and include
specific pointers
from a dietitian. *Mayo
Foundation for Medical
Education and Research.*

| Patient Care | Health Information | MAYO CLINIC | For Medical Professionals | Research | Education |

Appointment   Find a Doctor   Find a Job   Log in to Patient Account   Give to Mayo Clinic

Recipe: Blackberry iced tea with cinnamon and ginger

Dietitian's tip:

Herbal tea isn't made from tea leaves. Instead, herbs, flowers or spices are steeped in water. Most herbal teas are caffeine-free.

By Mayo Clinic staff

Serves 6

Ingredients

6 cups water
12 blackberry herbal tea bags
8 3-inch-long cinnamon sticks
1 tablespoon minced fresh ginger
1 cup unsweetened cranberry juice
Sugar substitute, to taste
Ice cubes, crushed

Directions

In a large saucepan, heat water to just before boiling. Add tea bags, 2 of the cinnamon sticks and ginger. Remove from heat, cover and let steep for about 15 minutes.

Pass the mixture through a fine-mesh sieve, placed over a pitcher. Add the juice and sweetener to taste. Refrigerate until very cold.

To serve, fill 6 tall, chilled glasses with crushed ice. Pour the tea over the top of the ice and garnish with cinnamon sticks. Serve immediately.

Nutritional analysis per serving

Calories	30	Sodium	0 mg
Total fat	0 g	Total carbohydrate	7 g
Saturated fat	0 g	Dietary fiber	0 g
Monounsaturated fat	0 g	Protein	0 g
Cholesterol	0 mg		

The recipe itself, and the surrounding information, presents Jasmine with a few things to think about. First, the "Dietitian's tip" mentions that most herbal teas are caffeine-free, which makes her wonder about the connection between caffeine and the health of a diabetic. She also notices the use of cinnamon and ginger and wonders how these natural ingredients might benefit a diabetic. In the nutritional analysis of the recipe, Jasmine sees that the drink is low in calories and does not contain any sodium. She wonders if these are important concerns; before she started browsing recipes at the ADA and the Mayo Clinic, Jasmine knew that diabetics should avoid sugar, but she hadn't been taking sodium and calorie content into consideration.

At this point, Jasmine's working research question has evolved from:

| WORKING RESEARCH QUESTION | What is the relationship between nutrition and diabetes? |

to:

| REVISED, MORE SPECIFIC, WORKING RESEARCH QUESTION | How can diet—specifically, monitoring the intake of sugar, calories, and sodium—help someone with diabetes manage the disease? |

Now that Jasmine has done some exploratory, informational reading, she's ready to see what others have to say about managing diabetes through diet. She moves on to look for sources that will offer viewpoints and arguments about diabetes and nutrition.

Gathering Opinions about Diabetes

Jasmine looks for other sources—including a journal article, a Web site, and a You-Tube video—to provide current viewpoints on nutrition as prevention/treatment for diabetes.

1. American Diabetes Association.

At the ADA site, Jasmine finds an article (in their journal, *Diabetes Care*) that provides the organization's position on diabetes and nutrition. The ADA argues:

> There is not sufficient, consistent information to conclude that low–glycemic load diets reduce the risk for diabetes.
>
> —**ADA,** from "Nutrition Recommendations and Interventions for Diabetes"

JOURNAL ARTICLE/ ▶
POSITION STATEMENT
**American Diabetes
Association.** Jasmine
goes back to the
ADA to see if that
organization offers
any opinions or
recommendations
about diabetes
and nutrition. She
finds this position
statement. (Shown
here: the introductory
paragraph and
recommendations.)
*Copyright 2013
American Diabetes
Association. From http://
www//diabetes.org.
Reprinted with permission
from The American
Diabetes Association.*

American Diabetes Association Diabetes Care

Home | Current Issue | Archive | Contact Us | Subscribe | Help | Alerts |

Nutrition Recommendations and Interventions for Diabetes
A position statement of the American Diabetes Association

American Diabetes Association

Medical nutrition therapy (MNT) is important in preventing diabetes, managing existing diabetes, and preventing, or at least slowing, the rate of development of diabetes complications. It is, therefore, important at all levels of diabetes prevention (see Table 1). MNT is also an integral component of diabetes self-management education (or training). This position statement provides evidence-based recommendations and interventions for diabetes MNT. The previous position statement with accompanying technical review was published in 2002 (1) and modified slightly in 2004 (2). This statement updates previous position statements, focuses on key references published since the year 2000, and uses grading according to the level of evidence available based on the American Diabetes Association evidence-grading system. Since overweight and obesity are closely linked to diabetes, particular attention is paid to this area of MNT.

Recommendations

- Among individuals at high risk for developing type 2 diabetes, structured programs that emphasize lifestyle changes that include moderate weight loss (7% body weight) and regular physical activity (150 min/week), with dietary strategies including reduced calories and reduced intake of dietary fat, can reduce the risk for developing diabetes and are therefore recommended. (A)

- Individuals at high risk for type 2 diabetes should be encouraged to achieve the U.S. Department of Agriculture (USDA) recommendation for dietary fiber (14 g fiber/1,000 kcal) and foods containing whole grains (one-half of grain intake). (B)

- There is not sufficient, consistent information to conclude that low–glycemic load diets reduce the risk for diabetes. Nevertheless, low–glycemic index foods that are rich in fiber and other important nutrients are to be encouraged. (E)

- Observational studies report that moderate alcohol intake may reduce the risk for diabetes, but the data do not support recommending alcohol consumption to individuals at risk of diabetes. (B)

2. The Joslin Diabetes Center.

At this site, Jasmine read the views of Amy Campbell, a Joslin nutritionist and the coauthor of a book titled *16 Myths of a Diabetic Diet*. Campbell states that there is no such thing as a "diabetic diet." Jasmine finds the following quote from Campbell on a Joslin page titled "The Truth about the So-Called 'Diabetes Diet'":

> A person with diabetes can eat anything a person without diabetes eats.
>
> —**Amy Campbell,** from "The Truth about the So-Called 'Diabetes Diet'"

Joslin Diabetes Center

Affiliated with
Harvard Medical School

| Diabetes Information | Adult Clinic | Pediatrics | Healthcare Professionals | Research |

Diabetes Information | Diabetes Resource » Diabetes & Nutrition » The Truth About the So-Called "Diabetes Diet"

The Truth About the So-Called "Diabetes Diet"

Despite all the publicity surrounding new research and new nutrition guidelines, some people with diabetes still believe that there is something called a "diabetic diet." For some, this so-called diet consists of avoiding sugar, while others believe it to be a strict way of eating that controls glucose. Unfortunately, neither are quite right.

The "diabetes diet" is not something that people with type 1 or type 2 diabetes should be following. "That just simply isn't how meal planning works today for patients with diabetes," says Amy Campbell, MS, RD, LDN, CDE, a nutritionist at Joslin and co-author of *16 Myths of a Diabetic Diet*.

"The important message is that with proper education and within the context of healthy eating, a person with diabetes can eat anything a person without diabetes eats," Campbell states.

What's the truth about diabetes and diet?

We know now that it is okay for people with diabetes to substitute sugar-containing food for other carbohydrates as part of a balanced meal plan. Prevailing beliefs up to the mid-1990s were that people with diabetes should avoid foods that contain so-called "simple" sugars and replace them with "complex" carbohydrates, such as those found in potatoes and cereals. A review of the research at that time revealed that there was relatively little scientific evidence to support the theory that simple sugars are more rapidly digested and absorbed than starches, and therefore more apt to produce high blood glucose levels.

◀ RESEARCHED
ARGUMENT
Joslin Diabetes Center and Amy Campbell.
At the Joslin Diabetes Center page, Jasmine is surprised to see an argument against "the so-called 'diabetes diet.'" It seems to contrast with what she's read elsewhere at the American Diabetes Association Web site. *Copyright © 2012 by Joslin Diabetes Center (www.Joslin.org). All rights reserved. Reprinted with permission.*

3. Nature's Factory Products.

On YouTube, Jasmine finds a video produced by a business called Nature's Factory Products, which makes aloe vera–based products and markets them for various ailments. Jasmine was surprised by the company's claim that aloe helps treat diabetes. In their video, "How Aloe Vera can help Diabetics," the manufacturer claims that:

> Aloe vera can help regulate blood sugar levels and control inflammation caused by diabetes.
>
> —**Nature's Factory Products**

While she is skeptical about Nature's Factory Products' claims, Jasmine doesn't dismiss their argument altogether. She decides to keep this source in mind and to fact-check the claims made in the video by researching medical studies.

Now that she's gathered some facts and arguments about diabetes, Jasmine decides to meet with her instructor to talk about a final research question and plan her research proposal.

VIDEO AD ▶
Nature's Factory Products, From "How Aloe Vera Can Help Diabetics."
Jasmine discovered a video on YouTube by a company that makes nutritional supplements. In the video advertisement, Nature's Factory Products addresses the question: "What is Aloe Vera?" and argues that among its many benefits, the plant helps reduce blood sugar. Jasmine is intrigued by this and by the claims that aloe vera may improve the circulation, immune systems, and overall internal health of diabetics. She decides to keep this source in the mix—and to verify some of the claims made by Nature's Factory Products. She'll do this by reading medical studies on the relationship between aloe vera—and potential health benefits to diabetic patients.

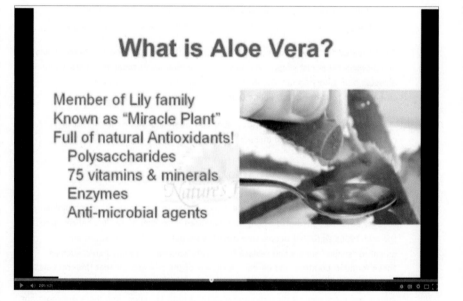

CHECKLIST Choosing a Topic

As you start your research, consider following these steps:

☐ **Brainstorm topic ideas.**

    ☐ Read what others have said.

    ☐ Google your topic (but stay focused).

    ☐ Discuss what you find with others.

☐ **Start writing informally.**

    ☐ Make a list of topics that interest you, then double it, then double it again.

    ☐ Freewrite about your topic.

    ☐ Sketch out a mind map.

☐ **Do preliminary research.**

    ☐ Ask questions of fact and definition so that you will understand the more complex research you do later.

    ☐ What arguments have others made about your topic? How do they support their views?

    ☐ Note key terms to aid in later research.

☐ **Commit to a topic. Consider these factors:**

    ☐ Is the topic compatible with the assignment?

    ☐ Have you found an argumentative angle?

    ☐ Will you stay interested in this topic?

    ☐ Are there enough appropriate sources available for you to research in the time you have?

    ☐ Overall, how viable is the topic? (See Jasmine Huerta's assignment, "What Is Your Topic? How Viable Is It?" on p. 269.)

☐ **Form a research question. Consider these factors:**

    ☐ Does your question focus more on stating facts and defining terms? Or are you making an argument? Providing an analysis?

    ☐ Is your question open-ended?

    ☐ Is your question specific enough? If not, how will you move from a general question to a more specific one?

    ☐ Are you truly interested in finding answers to this question?

    ☐ What are some challenges you may come up against as you research this question, and how can you deal with these challenges?

Creating a Research Proposal

A research proposal sets forth a writer's rationale for choosing a particular research question. For Jasmine, the proposal gives her an opportunity to fine-tune her research question and her focus. Your instructor may ask you to turn in a proposal or a working bibliography that outlines your sources (pp. 297–300). Or your instructor might simply ask you to think about your research before looking more carefully at sources.

Even if your instructor does not assign a formal research proposal, it can be a great tool for use in planning your project. Following is a research proposal assignment that we give our students.

ASSIGNMENT ▶
Research Proposal.

Creating a research
proposal is a great
way to help you
focus and plan.
See below for
Jasmine's completed
assignment.

ENG 101, Professor Braziller

Research Proposal Assignment: What Is Your Focus?

This proposal will help you solidify your ideas for your semester's research. Your proposal should
be approximately two double-spaced pages in MLA manuscript format. Your proposal should
include the following:

1. Your research question

2. A working title for your project

3. A summary of your project. Identify your topic and describe what you will be looking at
   in terms of the topic. Include some key terms and additional questions that will guide your
   research.

4. A description of your purpose for working on this project. Why did you choose this topic? What
   do you hope to learn from this project?

5. A discussion of the key challenges you will face or you imagine you will face. What concerns
   do you have regarding the research/project?

Following is Jasmine's research proposal, in response to the above assignment.

▲ STUDENT AUTHOR
Jasmine Huerta.

ASSIGNMENT ▶
Research Proposal.

Jasmine has explored
her topic and gathered
facts and opinions
from some solid
sources, and she is
now ready to share
her ideas for what she
plans to do next.

ENG 101, Professor Braziller

Research Proposal Assignment: What Is Your Focus?

Jasmine Huerta
Professor Amy Braziller
English 101
October 6, 20—

Research Proposal

1. Your research question

   How can diet—specifically, monitoring the intake of sugar, calories, and sodium—help
   someone with diabetes manage the disease and avoid taking insulin?

2. A working title for your project

   The working title for my project is "Living with Diabetes: Diet Is the Answer." I chose
   this topic because although some people are predisposed to diabetes because of
   genetics, they do have some control over the situation. For example, through their
   choices related to food and diet they can manage or perhaps even prevent the disease.

3. A summary of your project. Identify your topic and describe what you will be looking at
   in terms of the topic. Include some key terms and additional questions that will guide your
   research.

   I plan to research and write about different ways you can control diabetes through
   nutritional choices. While there are medications used to control the disease, such as

insulin, I'm more curious about natural approaches, such as diet. I want my readers to understand that diabetes doesn't have to be a death sentence and that even if you are predisposed to it, there are some simple things you can do to keep it from taking over your life or causing other health issues.

I also think, based on my research, that diet and nutrition might be just as powerful as insulin for some people. I wonder if doctors are too quick to prescribe insulin.

Much of the debate around diabetes has to do with the connection between diabetes and obesity. I wonder to what extent diabetes can be prevented by a healthy diet, one that helps people avoid obesity. Also, are there specific foods that children need to avoid? Are these different from what older people should avoid?

Besides researching different diabetes-related diets, I want to find out how people learn about these diets. Are there specific programs, initiatives, or educational tools used to get this information out to the public? How might schools and doctors share this information?

Following are some **key terms** I've discovered during my preliminary research: *glycemic index, metabolism, blood sugar, hypertension, obesity, glucose monitoring,* and *insulin.*

Following are some of the **questions that will guide my research:**

- What diets are best for diabetics?

- What foods do diabetics need to avoid?

- Can diet cure diabetes? If so, how?

- Can diet prevent someone from getting diabetes, even if he or she has a family history of the disease? If so, how?

- Can diet prevent someone's diabetes from getting worse? If so, how?

- Can dietary changes prevent or reduce a diabetic's dependence on insulin?

4. A description of your purpose for working on this project. Why did you choose this topic? What do you hope to learn from this project?

Diabetes runs in my family, so it's something that is very close to me. My cousin, who is only six years old, has type 1 diabetes. Just last month, my grandfather, who is somewhat overweight, but definitely not obese, was diagnosed with diabetes. When my mother was pregnant with me, she had gestational diabetes.

I believe I may be predisposed toward the disease, and I want to find out what I can do to avoid it. I also want to help my family by sharing what I learn—especially in terms of natural alternatives rather than traditional medicine.

5. A discussion of the key challenges you will face or you imagine you will face. What concerns do you have regarding the research/project?

My biggest challenge so far has been making sense of some terms I've encountered in my research. Some articles go into a lot of detail about the relationship of the glycemic index to insulin levels. Authors of these pieces also use technical terms such as *pancreatic islet cells, resistant starches,* and *macronutrients.*

Another challenge I might face is that my topic may be too narrow. Based on my research so far, it seems that many sources say yes, diet does contribute to diabetes prevention and management. But how might I expand on that? Will I end up just listing foods to eat and not to eat?

I think that trying to figure out if nutritional changes can actually replace insulin as treatment gives my project a good argumentative angle, but I am a little worried that I may end up arguing more strongly against insulin than I really want to.

I am also afraid of getting sidetracked and focusing too much on the obesity problem, especially in regard to children, and losing my focus on diabetes. While obesity is related, I really want to focus on preventing and managing the disease—and not so much on the causes of diabetes. While it's important to understand some of the causes, especially as they relate to nutrition, I'm more interested in prevention and treatment.

Now that Jasmine has written her proposal and submitted it to her instructor, she is ready to begin the next stage of her research.

CHECKLIST Creating a Research Proposal

What does a good research proposal do?

☐ **It assists you in organizing your project,** and includes five major components:
- Research question (the main thrust of your research)
- Working title
- Summary of the project (a sketch of the research you've done, the questions you've raised, and the possible direction you will take, including the potential argument you may make)
- Overall purpose (why you want to pursue this topic and project)
- Potential challenges

☐ **It shows that you have a clear focus for your research.** Your research question and working title are specific, showing your reader the angle you are researching. Throughout the proposal, you include details rather than vague generalities. For example, Jasmine doesn't just write, "I want to learn how people find out about these diets." She adds these details: "Are there specific programs, initiatives, or educational tools. . . ."

☐ **It illustrates that you have done some preliminary research.** Your summary includes key terms that you discovered while doing research. While Jasmine might have previously thought of the key terms *obesity* and *insulin,* she probably had not considered such terms as *glycemic index* and *glucose monitoring.*

☐ **It gives reasons why you have selected your area of research.** By communicating why you chose your topic, your reader understands your choice, and you see why this research matters to you. By articulating these reasons, you stay more engaged.

☐ **It shows that you have considered potential challenges.** Anticipating challenges prepares you for the bumps you might hit during research. Additionally, a good research proposal tells your reader about those challenges so that you might be given assistance. For example, when Jasmine writes that she has encountered technical terms such as *pancreatic islet cells,* her reader might point her to resources where she can get help deciphering these terms.

ORGANIZING YOUR SOURCES

Once you have a research question and a rough plan (as Jasmine does), you'll begin to gather and read more sources. In the next chapter, we're going to take you deeper into the research process. But before that, here's some advice on staying organized.

Be sure to keep track of every source you look at so that you can:

» Easily retrieve sources to verify facts

» Check that you aren't plagiarizing

» Make connections among sources

» Document your sources in your final paper

Use Simple Strategies: E-mail, Bookmark, Copy/Paste, Screen Capture

Following are some strategies for keeping track of your sources:

E-mail sources you find online to yourself.   Store the e-mails in a folder on your computer.

Bookmark sources on your computer.   Create folders for your bookmarks.

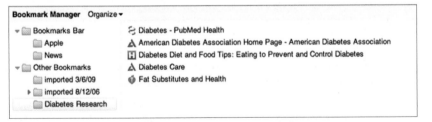

◀ BOOKMARK TOOLS
Featured on most PCs.

Use social bookmarking tools.   Sites such as Diigo have bookmarking/information storage functions.

◀ BOOKMARK TOOL
Diigo.

Copy and paste content from Web sites into a Word document. Below is a Word document into which we've pasted a section of the text of a commencement speech by the late novelist, David Foster Wallace, published by Kenyon College.

WORD DOCUMENT ▶
David Foster Wallace's
2005 commencement
speech at Kenyon
College, "This is
Water," copied/pasted
from *Kenyon College
Alumni Bulletin*.

SOURCE: Kenyon College Alumni Bulletin
(article)
http://bulletin.kenyon.edu/x4276.xml
David Foster Wallace, 2005 Commencement Speech, Kenyon College, "This is Water"
(speech text)
http://bulletin.kenyon.edu/x4280.xml

TEXT COPIED & PASTED FROM SOURCE:

This is Water

There are these two young fish swimming along, and they happen to meet an older fish swimming the other way, who nods at them and says, "Morning, boys, how's the water?" And the two young fish swim on for a bit, and then eventually one of them looks over at the other and goes, "What the hell is water?"

If at this moment you're worried that I plan to present myself here as the wise old fish explaining what water is to you younger fish, please don't be. I am not the wise old fish. The immediate point of the fish story is that the most obvious, ubiquitous, important realities are often the ones that are the hardest to see and talk about. Stated as an English sentence, of course, this is just a banal platitude-but the fact is that, in the day-to-day trenches of adult existence, banal platitudes can have life-or-death importance. That may sound like hyperbole, or abstract nonsense. So let's get concrete...

☞ **Attention, researchers! A note on cutting and pasting.**

If you copy and paste from a source, do so very carefully. Make sure you have a way of reminding yourself which words belong to others—and which ones belong to you. Review page 392 in Chapter 7 to see how cutting and pasting *can lead to inadvertent plagiarism*. If you decide you want to capture something exactly from a Web site, then copy and paste as above, highlighting the source information.

Create screen captures of online content. For this option, you would capture screens of your sources and paste them into a Word document (or save the screens as image files). We highly recommend this method of recording source material. Why? Because it prevents any potential confusion about what content came from where—and prevents you from inadvertently mixing up your own words with those from your source. A screen capture of the David Foster Wallace commencement speech as it appears online is on page 297.

◀ WEB PAGE
David Foster Wallace, "This is Water," his 2005 commencement speech at Kenyon College, from *Kenyon College Alumni Bulletin* (bulletin .kenyon.edu).

Create a List of Sources: Keep a Working Bibliography

We also highly recommend that you create a working bibliography—or, even better, an annotated working bibliography, which includes more detail. A working bibliography is simply a list of the sources you've gathered and plan to refer to. Keeping a list will provide you with the information required by all documentation styles, including MLA and APA (see p. 395 for Modern Language Association style and p. 415 for American Psychological Association style).

Your working bibliography, which you add to and revise as you research, will be the basis for your final Works Cited list and in-text citations. It will also help you evaluate your sources as a group, so you can make sure they represent a good range and so you can make any useful connections among your sources. (For information on evaluating and integrating sources, see Chapters 6 and 7.)

Better Yet, Keep an Annotated Working Bibliography

An annotated bibliography is a working bibliography (a list of your sources) that includes your own brief notes about each source. In your annotations, you summarize each source, capturing its essence in a few sentences. If the source is argumentative, you also note the main points of the writer's argument. In addition, note the potential reliability of the source: Is it from a reliable site, news organization, or publication? Was it created by a source you can trust? How well do the source and its author fit with your research? What might the source add? What might be its drawbacks? (For details on evaluating sources, see Chapter 6.)

Guided Process: How to Create a Bibliography ▼

Jasmine Huerta (Student)

Diabetes Project: Bibliography

▲ STUDENT AUTHOR
Jasmine Huerta.
iStockphoto.

Jasmine's Working Bibliography

Below is Jasmine's working bibliography for her project on nutrition and diabetes. In this case, Jasmine uses the MLA style of documentation.

Jasmine writes of her working bibliography:

> I pulled together a good range of dependable sources—including, for example, a peer-reviewed journal called *Diabetes Care*, the American Diabetes Association, and the Harvard School of Public Health. My sources are connected: Three focus on diabetes and the glycemic index and two focus specifically on low-glycemic foods. I made sure to include the detailed source information my instructor expects, and in MLA format.

Huerta 1

Working Bibliography
(for diabetes project-in-progress)

Brand-Miller, Jennie, et al. "Low–Glycemic Index Diets in the Management of Diabetes." *Diabetes Care* 26.8 (2003): 2261-2267. Web. 15 Sept. 2013. <http://
care.diabetesjournals.org/content/26/8/2261.long>.

"Diabetes Mellitus." *Wikipedia.* Wikimedia Foundation, 7 Sept. 2013. Web. 15
Sept. 2013. <http://en.wikipedia.org/wiki/Diabetes_mellitus>.

"Glycemic Index and Diabetes." *American Diabetes Association*. American Diabetes Association, n.d. Web. 15 Sept. 2013. <http://www.diabetes.org/
food-and-fitness/food/planning-meals/glycemic-index-and-diabetes.html>.

"Glycemic Index and Diabetes: Low-Glycemic-Index Foods." *WebMD Diabetes
Health Center*. WebMD, n.d. Web. 15 Sept. 2013. <http://
diabetes.webmd.com/glycemic-index-good-versus-bad-carbs>.

"Simple Steps to Preventing Diabetes." *The Nutrition Source*. Harvard School of
Public Health, n.d. Web. 15 Aug. 2013. <http://www.hsph.harvard.edu/
nutritionsource/diabetes-prevention/preventing-diabetes-full-story/
index.html>.

Jasmine's Annotated Bibliography

Here is how Jasmine describes her process:

> I began each entry with a basic summary. In my summaries, I note specific examples, such as unfamiliar terms or important evidence. I've also indicated my evaluation of how dependable each source is. When I quoted exact language from a source, I used quotation marks. I also made connections among my sources.

Huerta 1

Annotated Working Bibliography

Brand-Miller, Jennie, et al. "Low–Glycemic Index Diets in the Management of Diabetes." *Diabetes Care* 26.8 (2003): 2261-2267. Web. 15 Sept. 2013. <http://care.diabetesjournals.org/content/26/8/2261.long>.

The authors explore the controversy about whether a low-glycemic diet actually helps someone manage his or her diabetes. The article presents the research methods used, along with the results. Ultimately, the results of their study show that a low-glycemic diet did help patients manage their diabetes—in contrast to patients whose diets consisted of high-glycemic foods. The article is filled with unfamiliar terms such as "acarbose therapy." At the end is a list of footnotes and references that will be useful as I continue my research. This is a very reliable source because *Diabetes Care* is a peer-reviewed journal; also, the use of documentation reinforces the authors' ethos.

"Diabetes Mellitus." *Wikipedia*. Wikimedia Foundation, 7 Sept. 2013. Web. 15 Sept. 2013. <http://en.wikipedia.org/wiki/Diabetes_mellitus>.

This article gives a very comprehensive overview of diabetes. It begins by briefly explaining the different types of diabetes, such as types 1 and 2. It also includes a discussion of symptoms, causes, and ways to control the disease. Throughout the article, there are numerous hyperlinks to other Wikipedia pages that explain concepts further. Since I'm focusing on nutrition, I found the hyperlink to the "Diabetic Diet" page most useful, since this page included information on various diets and potential research sources. *Wikipedia* gears its information to someone beginning research, looking for possible angles to explore related to the topic. Additionally, it establishes its reliability by providing many source references at the end of the article. Many of the references were from medical journals.

"Glycemic Index and Diabetes." *American Diabetes Association*. American Diabetes Association, n.d. Web. 15 Sept. 2013. <http://www.diabetes.org/food-and-fitness/food/planning-meals/glycemic-index-and-diabetes.html>.

The ADA's page on the glycemic index and its relationship to diabetes is an informative summary on the topic. It has three subheads, so readers can immediately find information: "What is the glycemic index?" "What

Continues next page

Attention, bibliographers!

Although the latest MLA guidelines say it's okay to omit source URLs, we recommend that you include them in your papers, as shown in Jasmine's bibliographies (and in Chapter 7). Including URLs (or embedding hyperlinks in your paper) leaves no room for confusion about where you obtained information, and makes it easier and faster for your readers to check your sources.

Huerta, *Annotated Bibliography,* *Continued*

affects the GI of a food?" And, "Is the GI a better tool than carbohydrate counting?" The article discusses how the glycemic index is affected by many things and is not simply determined by a food's type. For example, factors such as length of ripening and cooking time affect a food's glycemic index. The article is written for a general reader, so I found that I could understand all its terms and get a beginning grasp of the glycemic index. This article, too, is very reliable since the American Diabetes Association is a respected and noted organization related to the field.

"Glycemic Index and Diabetes: Low-Glycemic-Index Foods." *WebMD Diabetes Health Center.* WebMD, n.d. Web. 15 Sept. 2013. <http:// diabetes.webmd.com/glycemic-index-good-versus-bad-carbs>.

WebMD's article provides a good overview of the glycemic index. The article briefly discusses how a diet of high-glycemic-index foods (pasta, rice) can contribute to weight gain and health issues. The article encourages readers to choose low-glycemic-index foods (vegetables, fruits) for a healthier diet. While the article tends to be fairly general, it does bring up some useful points; for example, it explains that several factors might alter the glycemic index, such as the combination of foods eaten. I trust the information presented here since WebMD is a trusted Web source for medical information, especially in terms of providing basic ideas to readers.

"Simple Steps to Preventing Diabetes." *The Nutrition Source.* Harvard School of Public Health, n.d. Web. 15 Aug. 2013. <http://www.hsph.harvard.edu/ nutritionsource/diabetes-prevention/preventing-diabetes-full-story/ index.html>.

This article focuses on ways to prevent type 2 diabetes. It gives statistics on the number of people affected by the disease and lists illnesses that the disease may cause, such as blindness. Prevention strategies are offered, such as diet and exercise. The writers sum up these strategies by saying, "Stay lean and stay active." This article, like the Brand-Miller piece, also includes a list of references, so I will add that to my potential project sources. Since this piece was published by a Harvard University site, I trust the information presented.

Drafting a Research Question, Proposal, & Bibliography

CHECKLIST: Beginning Your Research As you begin drawing on sources, forming your research questions, drafting your research proposal, and creating a bibliography, ask yourself the following questions.

WHAT'S MY RHETORICAL SITUATION?

☐ **Purpose.** What am I learning as I research? And how can I develop what I'm learning into a solid research question? Once I identify a research question, I'll need to refine it. Does it simply focus on facts (if so, it's not refined enough)? Or is it geared toward analysis and argument (if so, I'm heading in the right direction)? Once I come up with a research plan, I need to clearly articulate my approach, purpose, and potential challenges in my research proposal.

☐ **Audience.** What expectations will my readers (my instructor, classmates, and any audience beyond) have regarding the quality of my sources? (See Chapter 6 for more on evaluating source quality.) As I gather sources into an annotated bibliography, how can I make certain that my notes on each source show readers its potential usefulness?

☐ **Rhetorical appeals.** As I begin research, how will I know whether to trust an author and source? What about a given author and source gives me confidence, or doubts? What techniques and appeals do authors use that I can adopt for my own purposes? To what degree do they use logos (logic) and pathos (emotion) to reach readers? As I draft my research question, proposal, and bibliography, I need to make a solid case for my readers. Do I convey the reliability of my sources in my proposal and bibliography?

☐ **Modes & media.** How do modes and media come into play as I'm reading and choosing sources? My sources should represent a range of modes and media.

HOW DOES GENRE MATTER?

☐ **Elements of genres.** As I look at potential sources, I need to ask: Does the author of this source draw on other sources? Does the author document the work of others? For example, I'd expect a journalist to attribute quotations to specific people in a news article, but bloggers may not be meticulous about naming people quoted. How many different genres should I include among my sources—and in my bibliography?

☐ **Style.** When I look at a potential source, how much attention should I pay to the author's style? Are informal first-person pieces the right fit for my topic? Do I need to gather sources written in a variety of styles? To what extent do tone and level of detail contribute to a source's reliability? I should note each author's style and tone in my annotated bibliography.

☐ **Design.** When I look at a potential source, how important are design considerations? Some sources are very visual and graphically designed, but I should find a good mix.

☐ **Sources.** What makes a source particularly trustworthy? For example, if an author draws on documented sources, I may want to pay more attention to that text. If a source is drawn on by more than one author, I should check out that source and consider adding it to my working bibliography and commenting on it in my research proposal.

PRACTICE Want to experiment? Draft a research proposal. Create a working bibliography and annotate it.

Find a topic that interests you and work through the points in the above checklist until you develop a research question you are interested in. Then do the following:

1. Draft a research proposal for your professor that includes:

   • A working title for your project (you can always change the title later, when you have a better idea of what your finished project will actually cover).

   • A summary of the project, including which aspects of the topic you will research.

   • A list of the keywords you've identified in the research you've done so far.

   • A discussion of your purpose in working on the project. This is where you'll discuss why you are interested in answering the research question.

   • A discussion of the challenges you anticipate facing in your project and strategies you can use to deal with them.

2. Keep a working bibliography of all the sources you use, even ones you think you won't refer to in your final written report. You never know.

3. Annotate three sources you find particularly interesting or thought provoking. In your annotation, discuss:

   • What the summary is about

   • The argument the source makes

   • How reliable you judge this source to be and why

   • How this source might be used in your project

EVALUATING & CHOOSING SOURCES

◄WIKI ENCYCLOPEDIA
Wikipedia. *Courtesy of Wikimedia Foundation, Inc. All rights reserved.*

WIKIPEDIA
The Free Encyclopedia

In Chapter 5, we discussed how to begin your research to explore topics—and ultimately to come up with a research question and proposal. We assume in this chapter that you've done your preliminary research, you have a topic, and you are ready to focus in on an important aspect of that topic. In the following pages, we will discuss research in greater depth, covering how to identify a source that is appropriate, reliable, and useful to you.

GETTING STARTED WITH SOURCES

What Are Sources?

For an Index of Sources & Contexts for material referenced in this chapter, see the e-Pages at **bedfordstmartins.com /bookofgenres.**

The word *source* comes from the Anglo-French word *surse*, which means "to rise or to begin." Think of a source as a starting point. To cook something you've never made before, you might first refer to a cookbook, an online recipe database, or the Food Channel for inspiration. To plan a trip, you might begin with sources including maps, photos, and brochures. To begin a research paper, you might refer to Google and online databases such as *EBSCOhost* and *ProQuest*, and consult research librarians and professors to shape and define your ideas and narrow your topic.

LIBRARY HOMEPAGE ▶
Auraria Library Homepage. This library serves the Metropolitan State University of Denver and other institutions in the Denver area. Like most libraries, this one offers access to a range of databases, organized by title and subject area. *Auraria Library.*

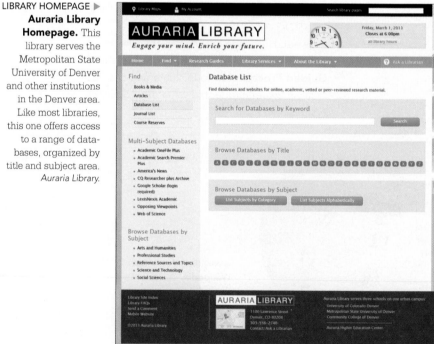

What research have you done for other courses? Where did you seek advice? What sources worked especially well? What do you wish you'd done differently or better?

In the context of this book, we see everything you read (or view, or listen to, or experience in any way), every text you encounter, every conversation you have, as a potential source for your writing. When you compose—whether in college or on the job—you draw on sources for information and opinions. These sources do more than get you started; they are also the texts that you'll converse with throughout your composing process, from your earliest topic ideas to your final project. (For more on early topic ideas, see Chapter 5. For information on later stages of research and writing, see Chapter 7.)

◀ ARTIFACT
The Crème Brûlée truck, also known as the Crème Brûlée Cart, is based in San Francisco. Researching food? A food truck or other eatery can be a valuable source of firsthand information. *The Crème Brûlée Cart.*

Can a food truck be a source? Sure. Especially if you're researching the trend of food trucks, or the growing number of people who identify themselves as "foodies." Maybe you're interested in comparing the old-time ice cream truck to the phenomenon of the food truck. Depending on your argument, you might use the truck as a starting point for your research, talking with its chef or operator to learn more about the business: its operation, clientele, and profitability. Or maybe about the food itself: the source of its ingredients and its nutritional value. (See Cremebruleecart .com: Better Living through Dessert.)

Where Do I Find Sources?

Sources are everywhere. Imagine that a friend tells you about an upcoming debate about the presence of the ROTC on campus; because she has provided you with information, your friend is a source. Let's say you become interested in the ROTC debate and decide to search your online campus newspaper for articles and editorials on the topic. Your campus paper and the materials it contains are sources.

STUDENT NEWSPAPER : ▶
EDITORIAL PAGE
*Accent: The Student
Voice of Austin
Community College.*
Here a student offers a
commentary on women's
healthcare in the state of
Texas, which has some
of the most restrictive
reproductive health
policies in the country.
Your own campus
publication may provide
an excellent source for
ideas, facts, and opinions
on your topic. *Courtesy of
The Accent (the accent.org).*

From there, you could learn more by talking to a member of the ROTC or a military recruiter, or a local activist organization opposed to military recruiting. The people you talk with and the discussions you have with them are sources.

What Can Sources Do for Me?

For one thing, they help you make decisions. You use sources all the time—not only to inform your school and work projects, but to aid you in making informed choices. For example, you want to choose a movie to see this weekend. You'd probably consult a variety of sources: Maybe you'd read film reviews, watch current movie trailers, or talk with a film-buff friend. Or imagine you're shopping for a car. You would probably do some research; you would probably visit some manufacturers' sites, talk to your mechanic and other car owners, or visit dealerships for test drives. You might check out the advice at Cars.com.

◀ WEB PAGE
Cars.com, "Quick Start Guide." We all draw on sources to conduct research in daily life, perhaps using consumer sites such as this one. Solid information helps us make better decisions. *Courtesy of Cars.com.*

Now that you have a sense of what sources are, the rest of this chapter will show you how to:

» Locate and preview sources

» Identify sources in terms of general versus specialized academic; and of primary versus secondary

» Read sources critically, with attention to author, purpose, audience, and other rhetorical concerns

» Evaluate what sources will be best for your own research and writing

What's a General Source?
What's a Specialized Academic Source?

When you look at a source, think about who created that text, and for what purpose and for what audience. That will guide you as to when and how to use that source.

General Sources

General sources are aimed at a general audience; that is, they're written by knowledgeable authors and are meant to be understood by nonexperts. For example, a

Did you ever start reading a source and realize that you were in over your head? What were the indicators? Have you ever had the opposite experience—you started reading a source and realized it was much too simple? What were the indicators?

journalist who regularly covers local politics for your newspaper might write a piece to inform readers about a scandal at city hall. To get the gist of the story, you don't have to know anything about local politics or politicians. General sources help you:

» Begin to understand the overall topic

» Begin to see what the subtopics are

» Discover keywords

» Find the different conversations that are related to the topic

» Begin to explore your research questions

ARTICLE: ▶
GENERAL SOURCE
Psychology Today.
Amy Alkon's article,
"The Truth about
Beauty," is aimed at
a general audience.
Courtesy of Psychol-
ogy Today. *Photo by Art
Steiber/August Images.*

An example of a general source is "The Truth about Beauty," an article written by Amy Alkon, a journalist and writer for the magazine *Psychology Today*. Alkon's purpose is to persuade her audience, primarily middle-aged women, about how men define beauty. Her ultimate goal in the article is to empower women so that they can understand their choices and the effects of their choices when it comes to beauty and landing a man. This is an example of a general source.

Specialized Academic Sources

These sources are aimed at (you guessed it!) specialized academic readers. They are usually written by scholars and other experts—professors, scientists, doctors, and researchers—who have studied the subject extensively. An example of a specialized academic source is an article from *JAMA* (*The Journal of the American Medical Association*) on a new clinical trial and its success. Readers of such an article would include doctors interested in new treatments that they can incorporate in their own practice. Although academic articles are aimed at people with expertise on a given subject, that doesn't mean you should avoid these sources. They may include information that you can use—and may become easier to understand as you deepen your research and gain an understanding of your topic (and associated terms and vocabulary). You might turn to these sources once you've built a foundation of understanding with your general sources. Specialized academic sources help you:

» Delve into a topic in depth

» See how experts view the subject

» Access the latest research in the field

» Access critiques of research in the field

» Find other academic sources through Works Cited lists and bibliographies

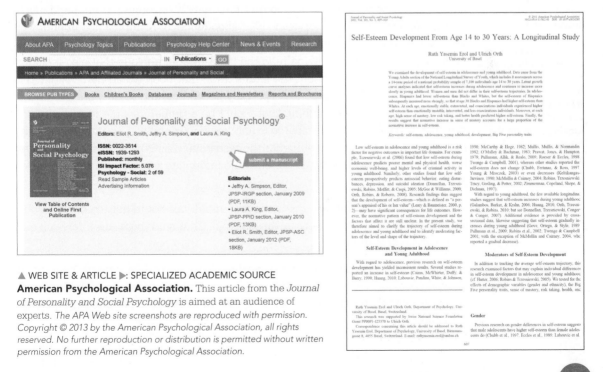

◢ WEB SITE & ARTICLE ▶: SPECIALIZED ACADEMIC SOURCE
American Psychological Association. This article from the *Journal of Personality and Social Psychology* is aimed at an audience of experts. *The APA Web site screenshots are reproduced with permission. Copyright © 2013 by the American Psychological Association, all rights reserved. No further reproduction or distribution is permitted without written permission from the American Psychological Association.*

An example of a specialized academic article is a piece on self-esteem development by Ruth Yasemin Erol and Ulrich Orth (see p. 309), which appeared in the American Psychological Association's publication, the *Journal of Personality and Social Psychology*. In the article, the authors examine the ways that early self-esteem affects health and happiness in later life. The primary audience for this piece consists of psychology and sociology scholars interested in social behavior.

☞ **Attention, researchers! A word about specialized sources.**

In addition to specialized academic sources, depending on your topic, you might also deal with specialized technical sources, such as technical manuals or drawings. For example, if you are researching ecotourism, you might use as a source a schematic drawing of a water treatment plant, one that an engineer might refer to on the job.

What Are Primary & Secondary Sources? Tertiary Sources?

What kinds of sources do you use every day that would be considered primary sources? What about secondary sources and tertiary sources? When you have a choice between different types of sources, say between asking your friend what time a concert starts and looking it up on the Internet, which do you usually choose and why?

Sources can be categorized as primary, secondary, or tertiary, based on the type of information an author uses—and the distance between the author and that information. A primary source is a record of information encountered firsthand, such as original photographs, interviews, correspondence, or historical documents. For example, if you read a letter written by a slave, that letter would be considered a primary source. However, if you read the letter in an anthology that also includes historical interpretations about the letters, then that book would be considered a secondary source. The categories of primary, secondary, and tertiary are not always clear-cut. Sometimes, something that would be a primary source in one circumstance would be a secondary source in another. For example, if Liz interviews Amy, the interview is a primary source for the researcher Liz; however, if Liz publishes this interview, and our editor Ellen reads the interview, it is a secondary source for Ellen.

We advise you to keep these distinctions in mind, but not to get too caught up in categorizing sources precisely in these terms. That said, here are a few rules of thumb to keep in mind:

1. A **primary source** is an original artifact, like a journal entry or photograph. If you were conducting research on the author Virginia Woolf, you might use one of her journal entries to get a sense of how her personal experiences shaped the novels she wrote.

2. A **secondary source** is written about an original artifact and often includes interpretation or analysis. If you were conducting research on Virginia Woolf, you might read a biography of her to get a sense of how her life intersected with historical events and to get a sense of the overall themes of her life.

3. A **tertiary source** is based on multiple secondary sources and presents un-contested information about a topic. In your hypothetical Virginia Woolf project, you might consult an encyclopedia of famous women to get a quick sense of the achievements Woolf is most famous for.

Primary Sources

In a primary text, a writer reports directly what he or she has witnessed, experienced, or created. For example, a piece of original music can be considered a primary source. Composers of primary sources rarely create their compositions to analyze, interpret, or evaluate data. If you are doing scientific research and encounter a rare plant specimen in the field, that plant specimen would be considered a primary source. If you are doing research on the Civil War and you find a map of a battlefield, that map would be considered a primary source. A place where you can find such a primary source is at the Library of Congress site, particularly in the American Memory collection, where the map of Gettysburg shown on page 312 and other Civil War maps are housed.

◀ WEB SITE FOR PRIMARY SOURCES **The Library of Congress** is an authoritative public archive of primary sources. The map on page 312 is from the LOC American Memory collection. *Library of Congress.*

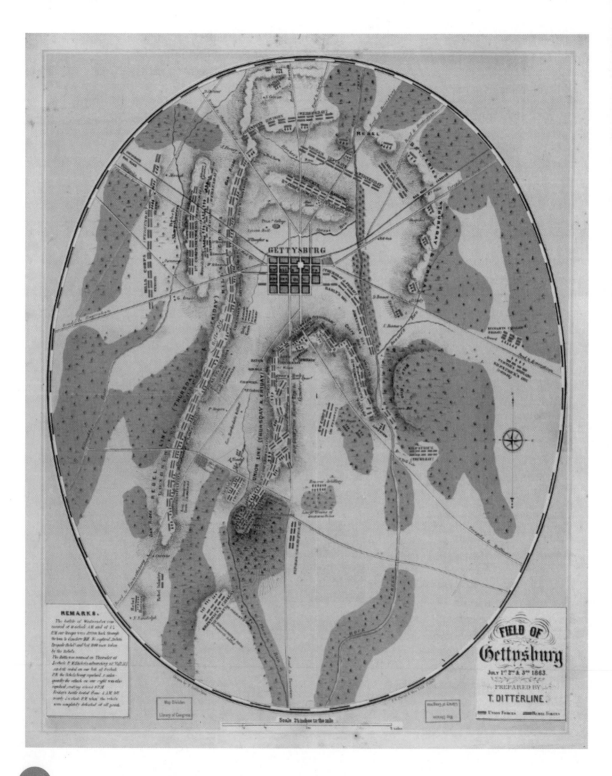

Secondary Sources

In a secondary source, a writer looks at a primary source—and offers an analysis, interpretation, or evaluation of that source. For example, a critique of a song (a primary source) is a secondary source. A critique of Lady Gaga's album *Born This Way* found in *Rolling Stone* magazine would be considered a secondary source; a YouTube video of Lady Gaga performing a song from *Born This Way* would be considered a primary source. If you were researching George Washington and found the biography *His Excellency: George Washington* by Joseph J. Ellis, that book would be considered a secondary source, while the George Washington Papers, original documents collected by the Library of Congress, are a primary source. (For more original documents, see the Manuscript Division at the Library of Congress.)

Tertiary Sources

Authors of tertiary texts synthesize, critique, and/or analyze secondary sources without adding new information. Essentially, authors of tertiary (or thirdhand) sources compile primary and/or secondary sources. They tend to present a generalized view of a given subject. For example, a music encyclopedia that mentions the critique (secondary source) of a piece of music (primary source) would be considered a tertiary source. *Wikipedia* is considered a tertiary source because it essentially summarizes information found in secondary sources.

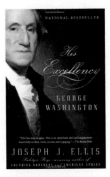

▲ SECONDARY SOURCE: BOOK
Joseph J. Ellis, *His Excellency: George Washington. Copyright © 2004 by Alfred A. Knopf, a division of Random House, Inc. from His Excellency: George Washington by Joseph J. Ellis. Used by permission of Alfred A. Knopf a division of Random House, Inc. Any third party use of this material, outside of this publication, is prohibited. Interested parties must apply directly to Random House, Inc. for permission.*

◀ PRIMARY SOURCE: DOCUMENTS
The Library of Congress. *The George Washington Papers. Library of Congress.*

The complete George Washington Papers collection from the Manuscript Division at the Library of Congress consists of approximately 65,000 documents. This is the largest collection of original Washington documents in the world. Document types in the collection as a whole include correspondence, letterbooks, commonplace books, diaries, journals, financial account books, military records, reports, and notes accumulated by Washington from 1741 through 1799. The collection is organized into nine Series or groupings. Commonplace books, correspondence, and travel journals, document his youth and early adulthood as a Virginia county surveyor and as colonel of the militia during the French and Indian War. Washington's election as delegate to the First and Second Continental Congresses and his command of the American army during the Revolutionary war are well documented as well as his two presidential administrations from 1789 through 1797. Because of the wide range of Washington's interests, activities, and correspondents, which include ordinary citizens as well as celebrated figures, his papers are a rich source for almost every aspect of colonial and early American history. In its online presentation, the George Washington Papers consists of approximately 152,000 images. This project is funded by Reuters America, Inc. and the Reuters Foundation.

▼ TERTIARY SOURCE: WIKI ENCYCLOPEDIA
Wikipedia. *Courtesy of Wikimedia Foundation, Inc. All rights reserved.*

◀ PRIMARY SOURCE:
MAP **The Library of Congress.**
"Field of Gettysburg." American Memory collection.
The Library of Congress.

When Should I Draw on a Primary Source? When Might a Secondary or Tertiary Source Be Best?

The kind of source you turn to depends on your purposes as a researcher and writer:

» When you want to get an overall sense of a topic or find uncontested factual information, look for a **tertiary source**.

» When you want original artifacts without the interpretation or analysis of others, look for a **primary source**.

» In most other cases, when you want to know how others have made sense of or interpreted primary sources, you should look for **secondary sources**.

Imagine you are conducting research about graphic novels and their presentation of female characters. Following are some sources you might turn to. They are organized into general and specialized academic categories. They are further divided by whether a given source is primary, secondary, or tertiary.

CHART ▶
Types of sources: primary, secondary, and tertiary, for a project on graphic novels and female characters. As you begin your research of any topic, keep in mind the variety of sources out there, aimed at different audiences, and composed for different purposes. Which are right for you?

	General sources	Specialized academic sources
PRIMARY SOURCES	• An interview with a graphic novelist that appears in the entertainment section of the newspaper • A graphic novel • A blog entry written by a graphic novelist about the creation of graphic novel characters • A movie poster for a film adaptation of a graphic novel	• An interview with a graphic novelist that appears in a peer-reviewed journal (an academic journal containing research by scholars in the field, reviewed by an editorial board of peers, such as other academic experts) • A professor's lecture about graphic novels in a literature course
SECONDARY SOURCES	• A book about the history of graphic novels geared toward a general audience • A blog entry by a fan of graphic novels that summarizes and comments on several different graphic novels	• A scholarly article about a graphic novel • A scholarly article that offers a feminist critique of graphic novels
TERTIARY SOURCES	• An encyclopedia entry about graphic novels • A review of a film adaptation of a graphic novel • A specialized encyclopedia of comic books and graphic novels	• A review of literature in a scholarly book on graphic novels • An annotated bibliography of articles about graphic novels

How Do I Preview a Source Critically?

Previewing your sources before committing to them is worth the effort. Ask yourself the following questions to identify what you might expect from a particular source, and whether you will want to use it in your research.

1. What Is the Overall Rhetorical Situation?

That is, what is the context of the source? Who wrote this piece, why, for whom, and how? And how does this impact the value of this text as a potential source?

Following is an example that we'll refer to throughout this section. It's an editorial published at Bloomberg.com.

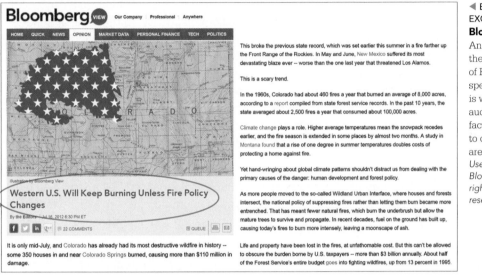

What's the Rhetorical Situation?

Bloomberg Editors, "Western U.S. Will Keep Burning Unless Fire Policy Changes"

To get a sense of the rhetorical situation of this Bloomberg editorial—or any potential source—ask and answer some basic questions:

▶ **Who wrote this piece?** The editorial board at Bloomberg, an influential news organization focused on business and finance and with clout in both of these areas.

▶ **Why?** The Bloomberg editors wanted to address the disastrous Colorado fires of the summer of 2012. Their purpose was to persuade readers that the government could adopt a course of action that could prevent future fires—and also save taxpayers money.

▶ **For whom?** Bloomberg's audience includes general readers with Internet access interested in business news and a "business take" on issues—both in Colorado and across the country—as well as business and government leaders who could do something about the problem.

▶ **How?** The editors collaborated to come up with their collective view on government policies regarding fires in the Rockies. They published their editorial in the opinion section of their Web site. The editorial includes hyperlinks to related materials, and there are options for commenting and linking out to social networking.

As you look at sources, think about the rhetorical context of each by paying attention to the authors and their purposes, their target audiences and how they appeal to them, and the modes and media that they use for delivering their messages.

Purpose   First, ask yourself: Who is the author of this piece? What are his or her reasons for writing? What assumptions does the author make? How does all of this fit in with what I'm looking for? Keep in mind:

» *What is the author's background?* This information will give you a sense of the author's credibility (ethos) and his or her perspective on the topic at hand. Begin by reading any biographical information provided and see if there are links to any other writing the author has done on this topic. For example, an article from a collection published by the surgeon general about the causes of heart disease is very likely to be more dependable than an article written by someone who is not a doctor. The authors of the editorial about fire policy (p. 315) are the members of Bloomberg's editorial board. Bloomberg is a well-respected news group focused on money and the marketplace, part of what makes this source a trustworthy one.

» *Is the author seeking to persuade?* Report information? Tell a story? All of the above? How does this fit with the type of information you're looking for? Begin by examining the title and then skim the piece with a critical eye.

» *What are the author's biases?* While you're skimming, keep an eye out for assumptions built into the text. For example, an article by Facebook founder Mark Zuckerberg on the value of social networking will be biased in favor of social networking, while an article written by a more neutral, objective author not employed in the social networking business may be less biased. While both sources may have value, you need to keep in mind the authors' viewpoints and how they fit with what you want to say. The Bloomberg editorial (p. 315) represents the viewpoints of editors whose priorities are business growth and other financial concerns rather than the environment and other aspects of fire policy.

Audience   Ask yourself: Where did I find this text? Was it published in a popular magazine? A specialized academic journal? At a particular Web site? If so, who is the main audience for that magazine, journal, or Web site?

» *Am I part of the author's primary audience?* Based on the text's origin and a quick read of its contents, is the author aiming at a general readership or a narrower, more specialized audience? Evaluate the piece in terms of whether you find it readable, challenging, or perhaps oversimplified or condescending. Ask yourself: How much subject knowledge does the author assume readers have? For example, an engineer writing for a technical journal will assume readers are also engineers or specialists in related fields. That engineer is not writing to a

Have you ever discovered something about a writer that made you question his or her reliability? Have you ever been unsure about a writer's trustworthiness and then made a discovery that changed your mind?

general reader. As for the editors at Bloomberg (p. 315), they write for business-people, not environmentalists, so their take on fire policy is likely going to mesh better with the concerns of the business community than those of tree huggers.

» *Am I* not *part of the author's primary audience?* Don't dismiss a source just because you're not part of the author's primary audience. There may be something to learn from the piece. Let's say you're researching mining safety violations and settlements, and you locate a brochure created by a mining company. The target audience for the brochure is the local community—including relatives of people killed in a recent disaster at the mine. Perhaps the brochure oversimplifies the situation and denies responsibility, or perhaps it offers an apology and reparations. In either case, understanding an author's rhetorical situation (in this case, a company trying to appeal to employees and families) is valuable to you as a researcher.

Rhetorical appeals   In general, what strategies does the author use to build his or her case and connect with readers?

» *Does the author use humor?* Again, examine the title and skim the composition. If the author uses humor, does it work to strengthen the piece? How well does a humorous piece fit in with your topic and research?

» *Does the author use ethos, logos, and pathos to connect with readers?* How much authority does the author convey in the writing? Is the writing logical? To what extent does it appeal to your emotions? For example, you might realize as you analyze an author's appeal to pathos that his or her argument is not logical. At that point (unless you want a piece that is not logical, perhaps so you can critique it), you might decide not to use the source. It's a good sign when authors of a source incorporate statistical data, as the Bloomberg editors do (see p. 315), for example, to build a logical case that current fire policy must change. In the case of the Bloomberg editorial, the numerical data particularly appeals to their business and government audience.

Modes & media

» *Modes* In what mode was the source produced—written, audio, video, or something else? How does the composer's choice of mode contribute to the composition? What assumptions do you have about the mode? For example, it's fair to assume that hearing an audio essay, which features the composer's voice, is a more intimate experience than reading an article online. By considering mode you're more aware of how the author appeals to his or her audience. For example, a documentary film can have more of a dramatic impact on viewers than a researched article on readers because viewers use multiple senses to experience a film.

Do you think that some modes are more reliable than others? For example, do you assume that printed sources are more authoritative than stories you hear on the radio? Why or why not?

» *Media* In what medium is the source delivered—print, digital, or something else? What does the composer's choice of medium tell you about his or her assumptions about the audience? For example, digital sources are used primarily by audiences with access to computers or smartphones. Think, too, about the relationship between medium and the currency of information. A composer who publishes online can make revisions to the piece, adding links to newer articles on the topic at hand. For example, the Bloomberg editorial (p. 315) is digital, with written and visual components. The digital nature allows for the composers to update hyperlinks throughout the editorial, connecting readers with the latest writing on the topic.

2. What Is the Genre of the Piece?

What are you looking at? What kind of composition is it? What qualities is this genre known for? What makes this text a potentially workable source, or not?

Following is an example that we'll refer to throughout this section. It's a photo essay published at *Time* magazine's Web site. The photos are by Danny Wilcox Frazier of Redux photography, and the text was written by editors at *Time*.

PHOTO ESSAY ▶
Time. This photo essay, "In Boise, Housing Struggles to Emerge From Its Malaise," includes photos by Danny Wilcox Frazier of Redux, and captions by *Time* editors. As you consider sources, think about the genre of those sources (see the box on p. 319). *Photo essay: Danny Wilcox Frazier / Redux. Time branding: © 2009. Time Inc. Reprinted/Translated from TIME. COM and published with permission of Time Inc. Reproduction in any manner in any language in whole or in part without written permission is prohibited. TIME and the TIME logo are trademarks of Time Inc. Used under license.*

TIME
Photos

In Boise, Housing Struggles to Emerge From Its Malaise

1 of 8 ◀ BACK | NEXT ▶

LightBox   LIFE   Pictures of the Week   TIME Covers

DANNY WILCOX FRAZIER / REDUX

◀ BACK | NEXT ▶

Nice House, But...
Vinny and Karla Trovato, along with their kids, Steven and Ashley enjoy their new home, in a subdivision north of Boise, but they are surrounded by empty lots and unsold homes.
• Why There's Hope About Housing

What's the Genre?

Time and Danny Wilcox Frazier/Redux, "In Boise, Housing Struggles to Emerge From Its Malaise"

When you look at a potential source, you want to understand its rhetorical situation (see the Bloomberg editorial on p. 315)—its authorship, purpose, audience, etc.

You also want a sense of the genre that the composer chose—will it work for you?—as well as the style, design, and other sources drawn on. Ask and answer the following questions:

▶ **What am I looking at?** The image on page 318 is from a photo essay published online, created by *Time* editors and a photographer.

▶ **What qualities is this genre known for?** Photo essayists combine images and words to tell a story and/or to make an argument. Here, the editors at *Time* show the impact of an economic crisis—and hoped-for recovery—on a community. The title, "In Boise, Housing Struggles to Emerge From Its Malaise," suggests the argument being made.

▶ **What makes this text a potentially workable source, or not?** The authorship of this photo essay and its publication in a respected magazine make it a promising source. Also promising is that the journalists who composed the piece also conducted interviews with residents. The genre makes it useful to a researcher looking for a persuasive visual/textual argument based in primary research.

Elements of the genre   Ask yourself: What do I know about the genre? What can I expect or assume about it? Keep in mind:

» *What is the scope of the information?* Different genres present different amounts and degrees of information: An encyclopedia entry provides an overview of information, while a peer-reviewed journal article provides in-depth treatment.

» *How reliable is the information?* Some genres are known for their reliability and objectivity, others less so. For example, in terms of factual accuracy, a peer-reviewed journal article is probably more reliable than a political ad. (See also Chapter 1, "Understanding Genres.")

» *What is the connection between genre and purpose?* There is a relationship between an author's purpose and his or her choice of genre. For example, an author writing a blog probably wants to inform and/or persuade others. On the other hand, the author of an encyclopedia entry seeks to provide uncontested knowledge, while the creator of a TV ad is definitely out to convince viewers to buy something. Previewing a source in terms of its genre gives you a set of expectations to consider before you decide whether to read the source more closely. (See also Chapter 1, "Understanding Genres.") For example, the authors of the photo essay (see p. 318) chose that genre for a reason. The *Time* editors and photographer Danny Wilcox Frazier, who collaborated on the photo essay, chose to focus on the human side of the housing crisis in Boise. Consider how differently the business-oriented Bloomberg editorial board might have dealt with the same issue, perhaps writing an opinion piece on the financial aspects of the crisis rather than on how people deal with losing their homes.

Style   When evaluating a source, pay attention to the style of the author. Ask yourself:

» *How does the author use language?* As you skim, pay attention to the writer's word choice and vocabulary level. To what extent do they contribute to (or undermine) the author's ethos? How formal or informal is the language? Does the writer use slang? If so, keep in mind that slang is not an indicator of unreliability, just as formal language is not an indicator of reliability.

» *What is the author's tone? How does he or she use voice?* Describe the author's presence in the text. How does he or she use stylistic techniques to create a memorable voice and tone? For example, if you want to learn about the day-to-day impact of Asperger's syndrome, you may be drawn to a first-person text (or video, etc.) created by someone who is being treated for Asperger's and who can explain it from an intimate point of view. For any source, pay attention to tone—some authors may be off-putting, while an author with an engaging voice and tone might get you to read a piece that you weren't initially sure about.

» *How well does the author's style work with the chosen genre?* Think of the author's style in the context of the genre the author composed in. For example, if the author has written an editorial, ask yourself: Is the style generally in keeping with other editorials? For example, is it direct and persuasive?

» *What special techniques does the author use? How much detail does he or she provide?* Does the author use literary techniques, such as dialogue, setting, and metaphor? How do these techniques work to get and keep your attention? And how specific does the author get in terms of detail? Paying attention to these factors will assist you in deciding whether to commit to the source; in the best cases, other authors provide examples of techniques that you can adapt in your own writing. Consider the *Time*/Frazier photo essay as a source (p. 318). The editors don't go into much detail in the textual part of the essay, but the photos they chose highlight the personal connections people have with their homes.

Design   All compositions—from the lowliest e-mail to the biggest-budget film—are designed. Ask yourself: Is the source I'm looking at presented in a way that draws me in?

» *How are text and images laid out?* How does the author use spatial arrangement to guide your reading? How does formatting, such as use of capital letters, bold, or special fonts, direct your attention or shape your understanding of the source's organization? Is color used to highlight information? As with style, you might notice how an author uses design elements to communicate with a reader and decide to try some of the same techniques yourself. Designs that you find annoying or gimmicky may turn you off to a source, and the opposite may happen too: Clever design that resonates with you can draw you in.

» *How are sound and other nontext/nonimage elements arranged?* How does the composer use sound to guide your listening? How does the composer use sound to evoke emotion? How do these elements direct your attention toward or away from aspects of the piece? Note, for example, how in the *Time*/Frazier photo essay (p. 318), the photos stand out against the black background.

Sources When you preview a text, learn what you can about its author's research methods, and therefore the text's validity. Ask yourself:

» *How did the author gather and analyze data?* For example, if you're looking at an article that draws its data from surveys of large groups, you expect to encounter a lot of statistics and charts that compile the data. You'd also hope that the data is dependable. For example, the *Time* editors who created the photo essay on the housing situation in Idaho visited the location and conducted interviews, gathering information firsthand.

» *What types of sources did the author draw on?* Pay attention to where the author obtained the information on which the piece is based. Also, keep in mind the type of information you're looking for. For example, if you want facts on a specific topic and the source you're looking at is anecdotal or only relies on the author's experiences rather than on scientific research, you might decide the source won't be of use to you after all.

» *Did the author document sources?* Are sources listed in a bibliography or Works Cited list? Within the text, are specific details about sources given, such as page numbers and dates of publication for written sources? For example, in the *Time*/Frazier photo essay (p. 318), the writers refer to the names of the homeowners in the text of the piece.

» *Did the author not conduct research?* Not all authors conduct outside research, especially when they compose in particular genres such as the memoir. In the case of the memoir, the source that informs the piece is the author himself or herself—it's based on his or her own experiences.

What is the price of drawing on unreliable sources? Have you ever lost faith in an author because of the sources he or she used? What were the sources? What made them seem unreliable?

PREVIEWING A SOURCE

Emily Kahn: Women in Comic Books Project

▲ STUDENT AUTHOR
Emily Kahn.
iStockphoto.

Let's follow a student, Emily Kahn, as she previews a possible source. Emily is interested in comics and graphic novels, and she plans to write an academic argument about the portrayal of women in these works. She locates a promising-looking article on the topic of women in graphic works in *Lightspeed: Science Fiction & Fantasy*, a weekly online magazine for fans of sci-fi and fantasy literature. The article, "The Objectification of Women in Comic Books," is by a writer named Jehanzeb Dar.

Before Emily reads the article in depth or adds it to her working bibliography, she will preview it. This means she'll dig around to better understand the context of the article. Keeping in mind the factors outlined above, Emily will set out to learn basic information about the publisher and author of the article—in addition to the author's purpose, audience, choice of genre, and more.

👉 **Attention, researchers! A word about previewing.**

When you find a source, do basic detective work before you commit to it. Start by getting to know its publisher and author. Ask yourself:

1. Where did the piece appear? Was it published by a scholarly journal? A well-known news outlet? An obscure but solid-looking blog? To what extent does the publisher have a specific point of view or agenda (e.g., *The Weekly Standard* states that it is a conservative publication)? How will this perspective fit in (or compare/contrast) with my project?

2. Who is the author? Someone I've heard of? Someone I don't know, but who seems to be a good writer?

---

1. What Is *Lightspeed* Magazine?

Emily first considers who publishes the magazine in which the article appears. She asks herself:

» What type of magazine is this?
» Who publishes it?
» What is the quality of the work presented there?
» Who is the main audience?
» Are the articles in the magazine peer-reviewed? Scholarly?

On the "About" page, she reads a note from the publisher:

◀ MAGAZINE *Lightspeed,* "About" page. Emily begins her initial research, locating an article, "The Objectification of Women in Comic Books," in an online magazine for sci-fi fans, titled *Lightspeed.* She goes to the "About" page to learn more about the publication and the people behind it. *John Joseph Adams.*

ABOUT

Lightspeed is an online science fiction and fantasy magazine. In its pages, you will find science fiction: from near-future, socio-logical soft SF, to far-future, star-spanning hard SF—and fantasy: from epic fantasy, sword-and-sorcery, and contemporary urban tales, to magical realism, science-fantasy, and folktales. No subject is off-limits, and we encourage our writers to take chances with their fiction and push the envelope.

Lightspeed was a finalist for the 2011 & 2012 Hugo Awards, and stories from Lightspeed have been nominated for the Hugo Award, the Nebula Award, and the Theodore Sturgeon Award.

Edited by bestselling anthologist John Joseph Adams, every month *Lightspeed* brings you a mix of originals and reprints, and featuring a variety of authors—from the bestsellers and award-winners you already know to the best new voices you haven't heard of yet. When you read *Lightspeed*, it is our hope that you'll see where science fiction and fantasy comes from, where it is now, and where it's going.

For Emily, the fact that *Lightspeed* has been nominated for a number of awards and that the editor seems to be knowledgeable are important selling points. While at first glance *Lightspeed* might look like a fanzine, she sees when she browses the contents that the nonfiction pieces published there seem sophisticated in terms of subject matter, cultural analysis, and the use of sources and Works Cited lists. *Light-speed* may be more scholarly than she'd originally thought, though it's very read-able for a general audience. She's not sure what to assume about it, so she reads on.

MAGAZINE ▶
Lightspeed. Emily
peruses the home-
page for the magazine
to get a sense of its
focus and audience.
John Joseph Adams.

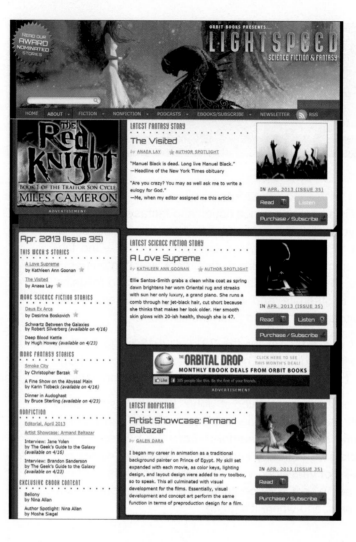

2. Who Are the Editors & Staff Members at *Lightspeed* Magazine?

Emily scrolls down to the masthead to find out more about the magazine's editorial staff.

She asks herself:

» What can I learn about who runs the magazine?

» Who is the publisher or main editor? What are his or her credentials? Is this an independent company, or is a parent company in charge?

» Who are the other editors and regular contributors to the magazine? What else have they written, and for what publications?

» Are the editors and contributors scholars? Critics? Fans of the genres of science and fantasy fiction? Authors themselves?

▲ STUDENT AUTHOR
Emily Kahn.
iStockphoto.

Emily is curious about the publisher and editor-in-chief, John Joseph Adams, and sees that he has won several awards as an anthologist and also is affiliated with Wired.com. She notices that *Lightspeed*'s monthly sponsor is Orbit Books, an imprint of Hachette, which publishes books by authors she has read, so that adds to the magazine's credibility. Reading down the masthead, she sees that many editors are published authors themselves who also write critical articles for other magazines devoted to fantasy, science fiction, horror, culture, and comics. Emily is pleasantly surprised that the editors of *Lightspeed* are more than enthusiastic consumers of science fiction and fantasy: They are experts as well. From the information Emily reads on the "About," "Our Staff," and "Our Sponsor" pages, she finds that *Lightspeed* magazine may be an appropriate source for her paper.

◀ MAGAZINE

Lightspeed, excerpt from the masthead on the "Our Staff" page. Emily browses *Lightspeed*'s staff page to learn about who puts the magazine together. *John Joseph Adams.*

Our Staff

John Joseph Adams
Publisher/Editor-in-Chief

John Joseph Adams, in addition to serving as publisher and editor of *Lightspeed* (and its sister magazine, *Nightmare*), is the bestselling editor of many anthologies, such as *The Mad Scientist's Guide to World Domination, Oz Reimagined, Epic: Legends of Fantasy, Other Worlds Than These, Armored, Under the Moons of Mars, Brave New Worlds, Wastelands, The Living Dead, The Living Dead 2, By Blood We Live, Federations, The Improbable Adventures of Sherlock Holmes,* and *The Way of the Wizard.* He has been nominated for six Hugo Awards and four World Fantasy Awards, and he has been called "the reigning king of the anthology world" by Barnes & Noble.com. John is also the co-host of Wired.com's *The Geek's Guide to the Galaxy* podcast. Find him on Twitter @johnjosephadams.

Robert Barton Bland
Assistant Publisher

Robert Barton Bland dabbles in writing, independent film, and, when struck by fancy, will even patronize the arts. He subsidized and helped found his sister's start-up dance company, Company Stefanie Batten Bland, currently a Baryshnikov Arts/Jerome Robbins New Fellow. Rob also produced the touring and creation of "Chapters an Evening of Repertory," which toured at Symphony Space in New York City, Saratoga Arts Festival, and in 2010 at Ris Orangis in France. In film, Rob is a two-time CINE Eagle Award winner for the independent shorts, "On Time" and "Writer's Block," and is currently executive producing a feature length independent film, '79 Parts, directed by Ari Taub. Rob is also an alum of Jeanne Cavelos's Odyssey Workshop (2001), and he is currently pecking away at an urban fantasy novel, *Divinity Bind.*

Rich Horton
Reprint Editor

Rich Horton is a Software Engineer living in the St. Louis area, working for a major Aerospace corporation. His job sometimes has a science fictional side, but he'd go to jail if he told you why. He also writes a monthly column for *Locus Magazine,* and columns and reviews for *Black Gate, SF Site,* and other publications. He edits *The Year's Best Science Fiction & Fantasy* series of anthologies for Prime Books, as well as such other anthologies as *War and Space: Recent Combat and Superheroes.*

Jack Kincaid
Podcast Host

Jack Kincaid is best known as the creator and producer of the cyberpunk audio drama series, Edict Zero – FIS. He is a speculative fiction writer with a handful of short stories published and many novels waiting in the wings. One novel, *Hoad's Grim,* he released as a podcast in 2008-2009. He is also a diverse voice actor whose work can be heard in audio dramas on the web and in podcasts such as *The Geek's Guide to the Galaxy,* among other places. His background includes theatre, A/V production, music, games, sound design, and early machinima. Find him on Twitter at @jackkincaid9.

Jim Freund
Podcast Editor

Jim Freund has been involved in producing radio programs of and about literary sf/f since 1967, when he began working at New York City's WBAI-FM at age 13. Jim has been sole host of the radio program, *Hour of the Wolf,* since 1974. Over the years, he has produced many radio dramas and lost track long ago of how many interviews and readings he has conducted. His work has been twice nominated for and was once a winner of the Major Armstrong Award for Excellence in Radio Production. Jim is currently Producer and Executive Curator of The New York Review of Science Fiction

Karen Jones
Art Director

Karen Jones is a freelance User Interface Designer based in Brooklyn, New York. Her creative pursuits include photography, vector-based art, and character design for video games. When she isn't working in Photoshop or Illustrator or looking for artists on Cool Vibe and Deviant Art, she's being chased by zombies on the Xbox 360, reading about the art and architecture of the ancient world, or traveling. Follow her on Twitter as @karenjUX.

Christie Yant
Assistant Editor

Christie Yant has published fiction in the magazines *Beneath Ceaseless Skies, Crossed Genres, Daily Science Fiction, Fireside, Shimmer,* has been featured on io9 and Wired.com, and has been included in the anthologies *The Way of the Wizard, Armored,* and *The Year's Best Science Fiction & Fantasy, 2011 Edition.* In the past, she has served as a book reviewer for Audible.com, and she occasionally narrates for StarShipSofa and blogs at Inkpunks.com, a website for aspiring and newly-pro writers. She lives in a former Temperance colony on the central coast of California, where she sometimes gets to watch rocket launches with her husband and her two amazing daughters. Learn more at inkhaven.net.

Our Sponsor

Lightspeed's sponsor this month is <u>Orbit Books</u>:

Orbit US is the Science Fiction and Fantasy imprint at Hachette Book Group USA. Our authors include Joe Abercrombie, Iain M. Banks, Gail Carriger, Lilith Saintcrow and Brent Weeks. They publish a wide range of fiction from both established and debut authors.

Orbit also publishes digital short stories from their authors. The stories are available at all major ebook retailers —currently in the US and Canada, and further afield in the very near future. You can find their short fiction program at www.orbitshortfiction.com.

3. Who Is Jehanzeb, the Author of the Article?

Emily sees that *Lightspeed* attributes the article to a writer named Jehanzeb, for whom no last name is given. She asks herself:

» How can I discover the last name of the author, so that I can learn more about this writer?

» Is there a biography somewhere? Maybe a link to a blog or personal Web site?

» What else has this author written—whether on this topic or others? And where has his work been published?

» How much credibility does the author convey?

Emily first needs to discover Jehanzeb's full name. She notices a brief biography at the end of the article, which links to Jehanzeb's blog, where the article was first published. She also sees that *Lightspeed* has published three other articles by Jehanzeb on the topic of women in comics. To learn more, Emily follows the link to Jehanzeb's *Broken Mystic* blog, where he posts poems, personal writing, and articles. There she links to

Jehanzeb is a film student who writes about Islam, Feminism, Politics, and Media. This piece was originally published on his <u>blog</u>.

Tagged as: comics

Related Posts

○ A Critique of Muslim Women in Comics -- AK Comics' Jalia and Aya

○ A Critique of Muslim Women in Comics -- The 99

○ Female, Muslim, and Mutant

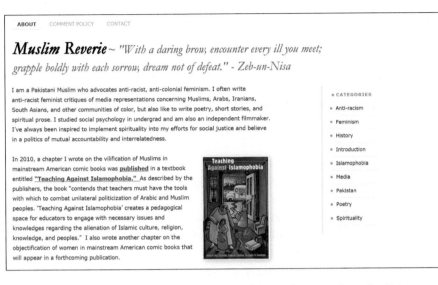

◀ PHOTO & BIO
Jehanzeb Dar, blog, *Muslim Reverie.* Emily discovers that Dar has an Internet presence; he's the author of a blog, and has been quoted in an Associated Press article (see below). *Jehanzeb Dar.*

a second blog, called *Muslim Reverie,* where Jehanzeb posts about "politics, current events, feminism, and media literacy." Here Emily discovers that his last name is Dar. She notices e-mail links at both blogs, so she can contact him directly. She thinks she might do that if she decides to use his article as a source in her research.

Now that Emily knows Jehanzeb's full name, she does a quick Google search to learn more about him. She wonders: Has Jehanzeb Dar published elsewhere—besides *Lightspeed* magazine and his blog? To what extent is he considered an expert on comics? A critic? She's interested to discover that Jehanzeb was interviewed by the Associated Press about the film *Prince of Persia.* In the AP article, which also appeared in media outlets including MSNBC's *Today, The Huffington Post, The Washington Times,* and *Bloomberg Businessweek,* among others, Jehanzeb argues that the role played by Jake Gyllenhaal (a white actor) should have gone to an actor of Middle Eastern descent. Dar also posted on his blog about the topic (see "This Prince Is Not Persian"). He is noted in different sources as a blogger, filmmaker, video gamer, and critic.

Critics: 'Airbender' & 'Prince' were 'whitewashed'
DEEPTI HAJELA, Associated Press
May 25th, 2010

NEW YORK (AP) — The hopes of many are resting on the shoulders of 12-year-old Aang.

Ever since he first came out of a block of ice in the Nickelodeon cartoon series "Avatar: The Last Airbender," the other tribes in his fictional, Asian-inspired world saw Aang and his power over the elements as their last chance for peace after a century of conflict.

Now Paramount Pictures and director M. Night Shyamalan also have high hopes for Aang: that he will attract audiences to see their big-screen — and big budget — version of "The Last Airbender," opening July 2.

"This part really needed to go to someone who's Persian," said Jehanzeb Dar, a blogger and independent filmmaker who is a fan of the video game but has no intention of supporting the movie.

"It's not only insulting to Persians, it's also insulting to white people. It's saying white people can't enjoy movies unless the protagonist is white," he said.

◀ ARTICLE EXCERPT
Associated Press / Deepti Hajela, excerpt from "Critics: 'Airbender' & 'Prince' Were 'Whitewashed,'" in which Jehanzeb Dar is quoted. *The YGS Group.*

By tracking down information through the bio that appeared with the article, through Jehanzeb's blogs, and through a Google search, Emily has turned up some rich information. As her mental picture of Jehanzeb gets clearer—as a writer, and as a thinker and critic who takes part in larger, public conversations about the presentation of race in popular culture—she becomes more interested in his article on women in comics as a source for her paper.

4. What Type of Article Is This? Will It Work for My Topic?

Now that Emily has a better sense of *Lightspeed* magazine and the writer Jehanzeb Dar, she's ready to do a closer reading of the article itself. Below is Dar's article, along with Emily's notes in the margins—you can see how she identifies her assumptions and also begins to read the piece closely and critically. At this point, she is still deciding on whether to use this source. Once she's done some annotating, she's ready to make her final call.

☞ **Attention, readers! A little history on this article.**

Jehanzeb Dar's article on women in graphic works was originally published at *Lightspeed* magazine (formerly *Fantasy* magazine). The piece included here is an updated version of the essay that Dar sent us for publication in this book. How did he revise his work? Why not read both versions of the article to find out? (Go to fantasy-magazine.com and search by author and title.)

Guided Process: How to Preview a Source ▼

Emily Kahn (Student)

Women in Comic Books Project: Previewing Jehanzeb Dar

As she reads, Emily asks herself the following questions:

▲ STUDENT AUTHOR
Emily Kahn.
iStockphoto.

» What is Dar's main purpose? And how does this fit in with my research questions?

» Who is his primary audience? Am I part of it? How does he connect with readers through rhetorical appeals?

» What genre is this piece? Based on what I know about the genre, what assumptions can I make?

» What is Dar's writing style? How do his techniques, voice, and tone affect me as a reader? How much detail does he use?

» Does the design of the article support what Dar seeks to achieve?

» What sources does he draw on? Does he document them? What type of sources are they—and how reliable are they?

(The following article appears by permission of Jehanzeb Dar. The Lightspeed *branding appears by permission of John Joseph Adams.)*

The Objectification of Women in Comic Books

by JEHANZEB

During World War II, a handsome American intelligence officer, Colonel Steve Trevor, crash-lands his plane on a mysterious island inhabited by the beautiful Amazons of Greek mythology. This new world is known as "Paradise Island" (what else would an island populated by Amazonian women be called, right?) and changes the course of human destiny. A princess by the name of Diana attends Trevor's wounds and subsequently falls in love with him. When she learns about the U.S. war against the Nazis, she dons a costume of America's red, white, and blue, and departs for the "Man's World." She becomes Wonder Woman— "beautiful as Aphrodite, wise as Athena, stronger than Hercules, and swifter than Mercury." She can fly like Superman and hurl heavy objects like the Hulk, and if you refuse to tell her the truth, she'll crack out her golden lasso and tie you up (especially if you're a heterosexual man).

At first glance, she may look like an empowered, kick-butt, feminist superheroine amidst a realm dominated by white heterosexual male superheroes. But is Wonder Woman really empowered? Is she really a symbol of feminism in comic books? Is her message really all about defending sisterhood, freedom, and democracy?

A historical overview is necessary to examine the role women have played in mainstream comic books as well as how intersecting dynamics of race and gender have impacted the way women are presented.

Continues next page

Emily's notes on Dar's essay

What genre is this?

Definitely an article/essay. The title indicates the author is making an argument about sexism in comics. I know it's a re-searched argument because there is a references/Works Cited page at the end.

What can I assume about this genre?

I assume Dar will make claims (and maybe counter-arguments) and support them with evidence from out-side sources.

What is the author's style?

His style is serious and scholarly, but the tone is kind of entertaining—he uses terms such as "kick-butt." He also uses lots of detail.

How does the au-thor use design?

I like the subhead-ings. They divide the article into sections on differ-ent portrayals of women in comics.

Emily's notes on Dar's essay

How does the author work with sources?

He cites sources in the text and in a References list. Looks like APA format.

Sources look to be from experts on comics and feminist and cultural critics. He also draws on comics themselves.

Who is the author?

Dar is a writer concerned with comics and critical of the portrayal of women in them. He also writes about issues related to race and popular culture.

What is the author's purpose?

The title says to me that Dar wants to persuade readers that women are objectified in comic books. As I read further, I see that he argues that even strong female characters are created to be alluring.

(Continued on p. 331.)

1. The Damsel in Distress

Originally, the only women that appeared in mainstream American comic books were white women, though they played very small roles. In the late 1930s, superpowered heroes like Superman and Captain Marvel dominated the stage while women scarcely had any presence. If women made appearances, they were depicted as dependent and "damsels in distress"—victims (typically of male violence) needing to be rescued by the male protagonist (who typically exerts more violence over the male villain). The "damsel in distress" is not only a prize that needs to be won by either the male villain or hero, but also an object that measures the masculinity of the male characters. For example, Superman's "masculinity is defined by what it is not, namely 'feminine,' and by all its associated traits—hard *not* soft, strong *not* weak, reserved *not* emotional, active *not* passive" (Brown, 2001, p. 168). The manner in which women service masculinity is apparent in the first issue of *Superman*, where news reporter and future love interest Lois Lane is kidnapped by criminals and eventually saved by Superman. A romantic relationship is not developed between the two characters and nothing is learned about who Lois is—she is only a weak "feminine" body reinforcing Superman's strong "masculinity" and "savior" role. Superman simply rescues her from villains, flies her to safety, and then flies away. Such one-dimensional portrayals were evident in other ways women were depicted: as the "girl-Friday . . . seductive vamp, or perhaps, the long-suffering girlfriend" (Lavin, 1998, p. 93). The stereotypical gender roles were quite obvious: men alone are capable of succeeding independently and being courageous, while women are dependent and weak beauties relegated to the background. These early attitudes toward women in comic books are quite suggestive of common sexist-defined role patterns where women are thought to be less intelligent than men and only have a place in the house as a caretaker and/or source of emotional support. As New York cartoonist Jules Feiffer states, "The ideal of masculine strength, whether Gary Cooper's, Lil Abner's, or Superman's, was for one to be

so virile and handsome, to be in such a position of strength, that he need never go near girls. Except to help them" (1965).

2. Women as Sex Objects

The role of women changed dramatically during World War II when patriotic characters emerged and surprisingly attracted the interest of new readers, who were both men and women. Arguably, the most noteworthy female character was Wonder Woman. As mentioned above, she possesses enormous superhuman strength, has the ability to fly, and can overcome any obstacle that comes her way. Even more interesting is how her love interest, Colonel Trevor, is constantly being rescued by her, as if he is the male version of the aforementioned Lois Lane. Rather than the male rescuing the female in every episode, it is reversed in the Wonder Woman comics. In the following years, other strong superheroine characters surfaced like Miss America—the female version of Captain America—Mary Marvel, Supergirl, She-Hulk, and many others. They carried the symbolic message that "girls could do anything boys could do, and often better, especially if they stuck together" (Robbins, 2002).

However, despite these new portrayals of strong and powerful female characters like Wonder Woman, something else was occurring: they were being depicted as sex objects. As stated by Michael Lavin: "Powerful super-heroines like DC's Wonder Woman or Marvel's She-Hulk may easily overcome the most overwhelming threats and obstacles, but they are invariably depicted as alluring objects of desire, wearing the scantiest of costumes." The images of women with large bust sizes, hourglass figures, bare legs, and half-naked appearances became enormously popular after the success of Wonder Woman. Believe it or not, comic books were filled with so many sexual images of women that they were known as "headlight comic books" (crudely referring to the female anatomy). Comic book historian Ron Goulart writes: "In the days before the advent of *Playboy* and *Penthouse*, comic books offered one way

Continues next page

Emily's notes on Dar's essay

Looks like this is a feminist critique of comics. He also includes a section on the future of comics, so he's looking forward too.

Who is the author writing for?

For the editors and readers of *Lightspeed* magazine; the audience is mainly people who are experts on comics and interested in critical commentary about comics.

How does the author use appeals?

Dar appears to make his points using logic; he establishes his ethos/intelligence/ expertise and uses sources. In this article he doesn't appeal to readers' emotions as a strategy.

to girl watch" (quoted in Lavin, p. 93). A prime example of "headlight comics" was in Bill Ward's *Torchy*, a series that ran from 1946 to 1950. The comic books contained dull and uninteresting storylines where the scriptwriters were merely making an excuse to draw Torchy as a tall, bare-legged blonde, who walked around in her underwear.

The escalating amount of sex and violence in comic books eventually led to complaints, particularly by psychologist Fredric Wertham who held a symposium in 1948 on the "Psychopathology of Comic Books." He also wrote a book, *Seduction of the Innocent*, which correlated a connection between "juvenile delinquency and comic book reading" (Lavin, 1998, p. 95). As a result, the Comics Code Authority established a written code that set the guidelines for comic book publishing. During this time, the comic book industry took a remarkable new turn where the constant objectification of women was seized. The brief period where comic books were geared more toward teenage girls wouldn't last long, as superheroes reemerged in the late 1960s, along with their scantily clad superheroines and damsels in distress. Women were drawn in the same stereotypical fashion, but this time, the artists took it one step further on the skimpy scale. Consider the White Queen, a female villain who appeared in the *X-Men* comics during the 1980s. She was "the stuff of male sexual fantasy: a push-up bustier, panties, and high-heel boots, all in white" (Lavin, 1998, p. 94).

Today, women are becoming more and more sexualized. As described by Jones and Jacobs (1995, p. 341):

> Females, perpetually bending over, arching their backs, and heaving their anti-gravity breasts into readers' faces, defied all laws of physics . . . the Victoria's Secret catalogue became the Bible of every super-hero artist, an endless source of stilted poses ripe for swiping by boys who wanted their fantasies of women far removed from any human reality.

One study conducted by Jessica H. Zellers shows an examination of how women are depicted in eighteen comic books. She finds that "of the sug-

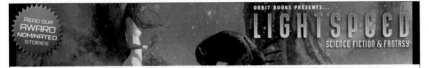

gestively clad, partially clad, or naked individuals . . . about three times as many were women (296) than men (107)." From the comic book sample where there were 1,768 male characters and 786 female characters, only 6 percent of all males were suggestively clad, partially clad, or naked; while of all the females, 38 percent were suggestively clad, partially clad, or naked. Additionally, of all males, 2 percent were naked, while of all females, 24 percent were naked. Zellers writes: "It is incredible that almost one out of every four females was, at some point, depicted in the nude" (2005, p. 34).

3. "Women of Color" as "Exotic Others"

Often in the analysis of women in comic books, nonwhite women, or women of color, are marginalized or given no mention at all. Without discussing the way women of color are depicted in mainstream American comic books, the analysis remains centered on white women and ignores the manner in which sexism and racism intersect. It would be a mistake to assume that "all women" suffer from the same mistreatment or objectification in comic books. As feminist bell hooks explains:

> A central tenet of modern feminist thought has been the assertion that "all women are oppressed." This assertion implies that women share a common lot, that factors like class, race, religion, sexual preference, etc. do not create a diversity of experience that determines the extent to which sexism will be an oppressive force in the lives of individual women. (1984, p. 5)

During the early history of comic books, which is often referred to as the Golden Age (late 1930s to early 1950s), people of color rarely appeared as superheroes. Lothar, Prince of the Seven Sons, was the first black character to appear in a comic strip titled *Mandrake the Magician*. Lothar was an "illiterate strongman dressed in animal skins" and catered to stereotypical images of "poverty and servitude" (Hogan, 2004, para. 3). A young black male superhero was featured in the 1940s war comic *Young Allies*, but was "nothing more than a minstrel stereotype in a zoot suit, who supplied comic relief"

Continues next page

Emily Kahn, *Women in Comic Books Project*

(Lendrum, 2005, p. 365). Such demeaning caricatures of black men in comic books paralleled the blackface performances in minstrel shows and American cartoons, which featured white actors and cartoon characters, including Mickey Mouse, wearing black makeup to create stereotypical depictions of African Americans. By the civil rights movement in the 1960s, significant changes had been made and new black characters emerged. However, the changes didn't guarantee a departure from stereotypes.

While black male superheroes, such as Black Panther, Luke Cage, Black Lightning, and Black Goliath, made their debuts in the 1960s and 1970s, they were presented as hypermasculine bodies (also note that three of the four black characters mentioned have their race emphasized in their names). That is, they were drawn with larger muscles than their white counterparts, were portrayed as more violent, and reinforced racial stereotypes of black men being "overly masculine" (Lendrum, 2005, p. 365). When black superheroines were introduced in the 1970s, particularly with the appearance of Storm, a mutant who has the ability to control the weather, their bodies were subjected to both sexist and racist stereotypes. In Storm's origin story, for example, she is recruited by X-Men leader Professor X, who finds her being worshipped as a rain goddess by a tribe in Africa. Storm is depicted as mythical and topless, although her long, flowing white hair conveniently covers her breasts. Not only is Storm depicted as a sex object, but she is also exoticized as a *racialized* sex object. As Jeffrey A. Brown, author of *Dangerous Curves: Action Heroines, Gender, Fetishism, and Popular Culture* (2011, p. 170), explains:

> In particular, women of color are consistently marketed and consumed as more bodily, more sexual, and more mysterious than their Caucasian counterparts. In short, ethnically identified women are routinely overwritten by cultural stereotypes and expectations of exotic Otherness, and all the sexual fantasies that implies.

While Storm adds diversity and challenges whiteness in the comic book genre, she also perpetuates the Otherness of women of color. In other words, due to her blackness, not only must she be a character from "over there," but she must also embody popular stereotypes and expectations white writers have about the continent of Africa. One can find a similar pattern when observing the Afghan Muslim super-heroine named Sooraya Qadir, or Dust, who made her 2002 debut in *X-Men*. Although she is intended to be a "positive" representation of Muslims in comic books, her character reinforces Orientalist stereo-types, that is, inaccurate presentations of "the East," particularly the Middle East, in order to reinforce "cultural superiority" of western civilization. Her face and body are fully veiled, though that didn't stop the artists from showing off her curvy figure.

She also needs to be rescued by a white man, namely Wolverine, from misogynist Afghan men who try to take off her clothes and molest her. When Wolverine brings Dust to the X-Men headquarters, she repeatedly says "*toorab*," the Arabic word for "dust." According to Wolverine, "It's all she says."

Dust is not only an "exoticized beauty" who speaks (one word) in a "foreign language" and hides her voluptuous figure behind a black veil, but also a vehicle for a disturbing imperialist narrative. For instance, if one considers how Wolverine slaughters a pile of Afghan militants and saves Dust from sexual molestation, one can see how Wolverine represents a western military intervention to "liberate" the "oppressed Muslim woman." In other words, Wolverine's violent presence in Afghanistan is justified because Dust needs rescuing from Afghan Muslim men (because Orientalism teaches us Islam is misogy-nistic). This narrative demonstrates how the woman of color, per-ceived as being "victimized" by her own people, becomes an object of imperial heteropatriarchal possession because her body, like her land, is violable and obtainable for Western masculinist power. Similarly, in Western politics and war propaganda, the struggle of Afghan women against sexist oppression is used to justify U.S. war and occupation

Continues next page

in Afghanistan, despite the fact that bombs and bullets kill Afghan women, men, and children (Smith, 2005, p. 7).

It is worth noting that more superheroines of color are appearing in contemporary comic books, specifically in those produced by the two major comic publishers, DC and Marvel. Brown (2011, p. 168) lists a significant number:

> Latina characters Arana, White Tiger, Fire, and Tarantula; the African American or African heroines Storm, Vixen, Onyx, Steel 2.0, Thunder, Lady Hawk, Misty Knight; the Asian Psylocke, Colleen Wing, Katana, and the most recent Batgirl, the Native North American Rainmaker, Dawnstar, and the most recent Shaman. . . .

These characters have undoubtedly enriched comic books with immense diversity, but only a quick glance at their names is needed to see how they're accompanied by racial stereotypes. Sexual objectification of women of color is accentuated as they are seen as "exotic" and "physically different, but in an exciting way." As Brown (2011, p. 176) states: "While white superheroines are clearly fetishized as sexual ideals as well, the inscription of hypersexuality coupled with ethnicity perpetuates specific cultural stereotypes of exotic Otherness."

4. Exploitation and Sexism

Although some comic book artists argue that drawing women voluptuously and provocatively is a symbol of their strength and power, there are other points that can be emphasized to argue that women are being exploited. Consider the creator of Wonder Woman: a psychologist named William Moulton Marston (pen name: Charles Moulton) who also invented the lie detector. Revealing Marston's intentions and goals on the character of Wonder Woman sheds light upon new attitudes toward women in the world of graphic novels. The fact that Wonder Woman comes from a woman-only "Paradise Island" is enough to suggest heterosexual male fantasy, but Marston also states, "Give [men] an alluring woman stronger than themselves to submit to, and they'll be proud to become her willing slaves." Though Wonder Woman is not subordinate to or weaker than her surrounding male characters in terms of strength and powers, she is being exoticized and idolized by her male creator. Her weapon is a golden lasso, which critics have called an erotic symbol of sexual control since she uses it to make her adversaries obey her commands. Marston has been criticized for his bondage fixations—a recurring theme of Wonder Women tying up both men and women. This theme was so prevalent that the editor of DC comics, Sheldon Mayer, was uncomfortable with it and tried to tone it down (but was unsuccessful). In one 1948 story of Wonder Woman, there are no fewer than seventy-five panels of Wonder Woman tying up men or women in ropes.

One may also find sexist undertones in how many other female characters have abilities and superpowers ranging from being skilled in mundane arts like gymnastics and mind control (Maher, 2005, para. 11). Women of color like the aforementioned Dust have powers that align with dull and unimaginative racial stereotypes. That is, since Dust is from Afghanistan, which is presented as a dusty landscape, she has the ability to manipulate, you guessed it, dust! Sarah Rainmaker, of Apache descent, has the ability to control the weather and, yep, make it rain! White female characters like Madame Mirage, White Queen, and Malice have the ability to use mind control to manipulate their opponents, mostly men! White Queen specifically uses her powers of mind control to manipulate and deceive men in order to gain wealth and power (Lavin, 1998, p. 94). The voluptuous Catwoman uses her beauty to manipulate Batman, Poison Ivy uses her seductive and deadly love potions to gain what she wants, and Malice is able to control the emotional centers of the brain. Hmm, what's next? A female character who marries a rich old man only to have him killed off just to inherit the wealth and property? Wait, they already have a character like that: White Rabbit from the Spider-Man comics!

Continues next page

Emily Kahn, *Women in Comic Books Project*

Sexist representations of women can be found in the work of Frank Miller, one of the most popular and successful comic book writers/artists, who is also notorious for his racist (see his *300* series) and sexist undertones. The misogyny in his comic books is too obvious to be missed. Elektra, for example, is a troubled female assassin and antiheroine. Miller named her after the Greek mythological character of the same name and, as in the myth, Elektra's character develops a sexual attraction to her father (which is the symptom of the Electra complex in neo-Freudian psychology). Early in her life, her Electra complex is strengthened when her father rapes her, but then she is told that it never really happened. "It was only a fantasy . . . and she wanted it to happen. Her belief in her desire for the father grows, but her father dies before she can resolve the Electra complex" (Baughman, 1990, p. 28). One can't help but ask, "What purpose does Elektra's Electra complex serve?"

Frank Miller has also subjected other female characters to subordinate positions, such as Ava Lord in his series *Sin City*. Ava Lord says to a male character: "You're right about me! I'm nothing but a selfish slut who threw away the only man she ever loved . . . I'm such a fool. Such a selfish stupid slut" (Maher, 2005, para. 13). Another character he sexualizes is Vicki Vale in his *All Star Batman and Robin the Boy Wonder* comics. She is drawn in her pink bras and panties while thinking about her upcoming date with Bruce Wayne (a.k.a. Batman). On one panel, she is sucking her finger suggestively, and on the bottom panel, there is a shameless close-up of her buttocks. Below is an excerpt from Frank Miller's script for artist Jim Lee. It speaks for itself:

> OK, Jim, I'm shameless. Let's go with an ASS SHOT. Panties detailed. Balloons from above. She's walking, restless as always. We can't take our eyes off her. Especially since she's got one fine ass.

As analyzed by a feminist comic book reader, Vicki Vale's character is there to "reassure the readership of their hetero-masculinity." She is quintessentially "watched by male watchers: the writer/director (Frank), his artist, and the presumed male audience that buys the book" (Rubinstein, para. 7).

5. The Heterosexual Male Gaze

One could argue that what is at work here is the concept of the "male gaze." This feminist theory was first introduced in the essay "Visual Pleasure and Narrative Cinema" by film theorist Laura Mulvey in 1975. Male gaze is described as "a symptom of power asymmetry" that "projects its fantasy onto the female figure." A defining characteristic of male gaze is how the heterosexual male lets the camera "linger on the curves of the female body." The male gaze "denies women agency, relegating them to the status of objects" (p. 7). When applied to comic books, what we see presented about women is through the gaze of the male. The women are presented as men would want to see them. Similarly, the same images are presented to women as something they should aspire to be if they want to be with a man. In other words, the power and control that characters like Wonder Woman have may be perceived as a woman's control or power over a man, but it is in fact fake control. The male writers can take it away at will. Consider the following "adjustments" made by male writers on the storylines of female characters: "Batwoman is killed, Batgirl is paralyzed, Mirage is raped, while Black Canary is tortured, made infertile, and de-powered!" (Maher, 2005, para. 14). In other words, femininity has no control at all, as long as male writers and artists persist with these depictions and attitudes.

However, the concept of the male gaze needs to be expanded upon in order to recognize the white heterosexual male gaze that is at work. When women of color are objectified, they are seen in the way white heterosexual men want to see them: as exotic, hypersexualized Others. A 2005 Marvel comics series titled *Daughters of the Dragon: Samurai Bullets* starred the black superheroine Misty Knight and her Asian partner Colleen Wing. Misty falls victim to "hypersexualized characterization," which begins early in the series when "her naked body is glimpsed in the shower over the course of two full pages"

Continues next page

Emily Kahn, *Women in Comic Books Project*   **339**

(Brown, 2011, p. 178). After losing a half-naked fight with a white female villain, Misty has rough sex with Iron Fist to "blow off some steam." Brown elaborates:

> Though the act is not depicted (thanks primarily to comics code restrictions), the aftermath is shown and it is clear the encounter was aggressive—headboards and lamps are broken—and as Misty dresses Danny [Iron Fist] lies spent in the broken bed, declaring "I think I need an I.V. drip and some pancakes." This scene has no bearing on the story except to mark Misty's assertive and animalistic hyper-sexuality. Rarely, if ever, do white superheroines hook up for random sexual encounters just to "blow off some steam."

Dust also serves as an example of how a Muslim woman is typically perceived in mainstream western media: veiled, oppressed, shy, and mysterious. Through the lens of the heterosexual male gaze, she is veiled and oppressed, but also "sexy," as is illustrated by her skin-tight *abaya*, or outer garment.

I found countless images of female characters in extremely provocative poses: bending over, arching their heads back, tossing their hair, fighting in the rain, and so on. Even the popular characters like Wonder Woman, Storm, Supergirl, and Jean Grey were not spared.

6. What Is the Future for Women in Comic Books?

According to the article "Why Don't 'Black Books' Sell?" by Alan Donald, the comic book industry and readership is dominated by young white men (2003, para. 6). Comics writer-artist Terry Brooks observes that most attendees at comic book conventions are white men. In addition to the racial homogeny, fans are "treated to the sight of several scantily clad professional models dressed in the costumes of popular comic book babes." The models are hired by comics companies to promote upcoming publications, and "for a small fee, any fan can immortalize the fantasy by having his picture taken with one of the role-playing women" (Lavin, 1998, p. 96).

This is not to say women and people of color don't read comic books. There certainly are some who do, but one may also argue that the sexism and racism contribute to the lower number of women readers, particularly women of color. According to comic book artist Trina Robbins:

> Women just don't go into comic-book stores. . . . A woman gets as far as the door, and after the cardboard life-size cut-out of a babe with giant breasts in a little thong bikini and spike-heel boots, the next thing that hits her is the smell. It smells like unwashed teenage boys, and it has this real porn-store atmosphere.

While one may argue that Robbins is generalizing about the nonpresence of women in comic books, she raises an important point about the atmosphere comic book stores create. The images on the covers of comic books featuring Wonder Woman, Catwoman, and other scantily clad superheroines (or random women dangling from the necks of their male saviors) are comparable to the sexualized images featured on the covers of "men's magazines" like *Maxim* and *Playboy*.

The increasing popularity of comic books has influenced other entertainment industries, especially Hollywood. Comic books are being adapted into movies more than ever before. Consider films like *The Dark Knight*, *X-Men*, *Iron Man*, and the Spider-Man films. These films are not only successful, but critically acclaimed as well. Now consider the protagonists of these films: predominantly white men. Has there been a Wonder Woman film in recent years? There have been two comic book films in the past decade with a female protagonist: *Catwoman* and *Elektra*. However, these films were critical and financial failures at the box office. Catwoman is portrayed as a shy black woman who transforms into a hypersexual, animalistic vigilante, while Elektra does battle in a midriff and has an onscreen kiss with another woman (I wonder how heterosexual male fans would react if Batman kissed another man?). Not only are the films taken less seri-

Continues next page

ously than the aforementioned comic book movies, but they also seem to be poor excuses to watch Halle Berry and Jennifer Garner fight crime in skintight and revealing costumes.

If there were a Wonder Woman movie, would she have the same fate as Catwoman and Elektra? Considering that Wolverine earned his own spin-off film, would we see a movie about Storm? If so, would the filmmakers depict these superheroines as complex and three-dimensional characters with dilemmas and inner struggles? The X-Men include powerful female characters who can move objects with their minds, control the weather, and run through walls, among other things, but the male characters take center stage. Also, if we look at characters like Supergirl, Batgirl, and Spider-Girl, we notice what they all have in common. That is, they would not have existed if it were not for the original male characters: Superman, Batman, and Spider-Man, respectively. Superman tells Supergirl that he will take care of her like a "big brother," but if Supergirl is the cousin of Superman, then why in the world would she need to be looked after? This is an example of how male dependency is prevalent in comic books, both implicitly and explicitly.

Sexist undertones and stereotypical images are getting worse and increasingly sleazier. Comic books have a unique blend of complex narratives and visual art, which makes them a very popular and appealing form of art, but they also reinforce stereotypes about women—stereotypes about the "ideal" feminine body image: large breasts, thin waists, toned buttocks, long legs, and so on. These "ideals" are misleading because they are setting a standard for beauty in women, and considering the growing popularity of the superhero genre in Hollywood films, more viewers are being attracted to comic books.

We need new interpretations of female comic book characters. Wardrobes have been reinterpreted in the *X-Men* films directed by Bryan Singer; instead of wearing tight leather or spandex, the characters are wearing less provocative clothing (see Anna Paquin's Rogue). However, if we focused only on clothing, we would be overlooking the way in which women are relegated to marginalized and/or stereotypical roles. In *X-Men: First Class*, the character Angel is a woman of color with superhuman powers, but she is depicted as a stripper. I mention this not to degrade real women who work in the profession, but rather to highlight the pattern in which women of color are consistently hypersexualized in media. Furthermore, Angel decides to betray Professor Xavier's human-friendly mutants by joining the more militant and antihuman mutants led by Magneto. Instead of seeing these stereotypes about gender and race reproduced in comic books and their film adaptations, we need to see more realistic, diverse, and complex female characters—characters that we can not only relate to, but also learn from.

Some admirable efforts have been produced by comic book writer Chris Claremont, who introduced "a string of independent, strong-willed, and generally admirable heroines" in the mid '70s (Lavin, 1998, p. 97). Fourteen-year-old Kitty Pryde (or Shadowcat) of the X-Men is an excellent example of a multilayered female character. She is a teenager who suffers from anxiety, peer pressure, and loneliness, and she has a longing to be treated as an adult. In addition to being a well-developed character, she is not drawn unrealistically with large breasts like Wonder Woman. Another positive female character, Jubilee, is also from the *X-Men* series.

As more female writers and artists make contributions to the industry, male writers and artists will need to be inspired to work against sexism, the objectification of women, and the sexualization of women of color. The more sexualized images and stereotypical roles of women in comic books persist and are left unchallenged, the more sexist ideals for beauty will be reinforced and the less we will see of inspiring superheroines—of all racial backgrounds—truly taking a stand for truth, justice, and liberty.

Continues next page

Emily Kahn, *Women in Comic Books Project*

References

Baughman, L. (1990). A psychoanalytic reading of a female comic book hero: *Elektra: Assassin. Women and Language, 13*, 27–30.

Brown, J. A. (2001). *Black superheroes, Milestone comics, and their fans*. Jackson: University Press of Mississippi. 168.

Brown, J. A. (2011). *Dangerous curves: Action heroines, gender, fetishism, and popular culture*. Jackson: University Press of Mississippi. 168, 170, 176, 178.

Donald, A., et al. (2003, September 9). The panel: Why don't 'black books' sell?" *Silver Bullet Comic Books*. Retrieved from http://www.silverbulletcomicbooks.com/panel/1063121223602.htm

Feiffer, J. (1965). *The great comic book heroes*. New York: Dial Press. 21.

Gorman, M. (2003). *Getting graphic! Using graphic novels to promote literacy with preteens and teens*. Worthington, Ohio: Linworth Publishing.

Hendrix, G. (2007, December 11). Out for justice. *The New York Sun*.

Hogan, E. (2004, February 5). Afros, icons, and spandex: A brief history of the African American superhero. *Open Your Mouth*. Retrieved from http://www.comicbookresources.com/?page=article&id=14623

hooks, b. (1984). *Feminist theory: From margin to center*. Cambridge, MA: South End Press. 5.

Jones, G., & Jacobs, W. (2005). *The comic book heroes* (rev. ed.). Rocklin, CA: Prima Publishing.

Lavin, M. (1998). Women in comic books. *Serials Review, 24*, 93–100.

Lendrum, R. (2005). The super black macho, one baaad mutha: Black superhero masculinity in 1970s mainstream comic books. *Extrapolation, 46*, 360–372.

Maher, K. (2005, June 2). Comic contempt. *The London Times*. Retrieved from http://www.thetimes.co.uk/tto/arts/film/article2429806.ece

Mulvey, L. (1975). Visual pleasure and narrative cinema. *Screen*, *16*(3), 6–18.

Robbins, T. (2002, September). Gender differences in comics. *Image & Narrative*. Retrieved from http://www.imageandnarrative.be /inarchive/gender/trinarobbins.htm

Robbins, T. Women in comics: An introductory guide. Retrieved from http://readingwithpictures.org/wp-content/uploads /2008/03/women.pdf

Rubinstein, A. [Tekanji]. (2006, August 26). FAQ: What is the male gaze? Retrieved from http://finallyfeminism101 .wordpress.com/2007/08/26/faq-what-is-the-"male-gaze"

Smith, A. (2005). *Conquest: Sexual violence and American Indian genocide*. Cambridge, MA: South End Press. 7.

Zellers, J. H. (2005). *Naked ladies and macho men: A feminist content analysis of a burgeoning graphic novels collection* (Unpublished master's thesis). University of North Carolina, Chapel Hill, NC. 34.

5. Should I Add This Source to My Working Bibliography?

Emily is now satisfied that the author of the article is knowledgeable and that the article itself is interesting, readable, and potentially quite useful for her research project. She decides to add it to her working bibliography. She will return to the piece again later. Emily's next step is to create a research plan. (See pp. 364–65 for information on research plans.)

EVALUATING A SOURCE

Evaluating a source is much like previewing a source (see pp. 322–28), only with more depth and attention to specifics. Once you've decided that a source is a potential "keeper," it's time to do a closer reading of it and decide whether it fits in with your research plan. Your main questions include:

» Is this a trustworthy source—do the author and publication convey an ethos of credibility?

» Will it work for my assignment—and further my purpose?

Calvin Sweet: Hurricane Katrina Project

▲ STUDENT AUTHOR
Calvin Sweet.
Shutterstock.

In the following pages, we will follow student Calvin Sweet as he looks at three different sources related to his topic, Hurricane Katrina. These sources, which appear on pages 354–63, are:

» **Madison Gray**, "The Press, Race and Katrina," an argument/editorial from *Time* magazine online.

» **Lincoln Shlensky**, "Hurricane Katrina, Race and Class: Part I," an argument/editorial from Shlensky's blog, titled *Aulula.*

» **Amardeep Singh**, "Race and Hurricane Katrina: two questions," an argument/editorial from Singh's self-titled blog, *Amardeep Singh.*

You'll read these sources along with Calvin in the next few pages. For now, here is information on each author, and the context in which his work appeared.

Madison Gray, "The Press, Race and Katrina"   Madison Gray, a journalist and the Home Page Producer for *Time*, makes choices about the content that appears daily at Time.com. On his LinkedIn page, he describes himself as a "writer, online editor, breaking news monitor, and critical thinker." Gray was educated at Central Michigan University and his experience includes work with AOL Black Voices and the Knight Digital Media Center. He writes in his biography for *Time*: "Looking at my years in this craft, you could call me jack-of-all trades, but I'm really a student. Beginning in my hometown of Detroit, first writing [for] business, then doing radio, transitioning to a major daily, and finally finding my way to the East Coast

◀AUTHOR PHOTO
Madison Gray. On his Twitter page, Madison Gray comments on his career to date: "Two decades, three continents, no apologies. I deliver news like Thelonius, baby: straight, no chaser." Gray's experience contributes to his ethos as a trustworthy source. *Kenneth Goldberg.*

to find a place in Internet news, the surprises keep on coming." Madison Gray wrote his editorial about Hurricane Katrina in 2006, almost one year after the storm. In it, Gray calls attention to his views on how journalists handled the reporting of Katrina, especially in terms of race. Gray's editorial appears on page 354.

Lincoln Shlensky, "Hurricane Katrina, Race and Class: Part I"   Dr. Lincoln Shlensky, author of the blog *Aulula*, is an assistant professor of English at the University of Victoria. During Hurricane Katrina, Shlensky was an assistant professor of English at the University of Alabama in Mobile. As a resident of Mobile, he was directly affected by Katrina. In his blog entry titled "Hurricane Katrina, Race and Class: Part I," he discusses his perspective on Katrina in relation to how the press covered the event. An excerpt from Shlensky's blog entry appears on page 358.

Home	Related Sites ▾	Student Resources ▾	University of Victoria ▾	Dr. Lincoln Z. Shlensky ▾

Lincoln Z. Shlensky, PhD
Assistant Professor
Department of English
University of Victoria

Lincoln Z. Shlensky is an assistant professor of English at the University of Victoria, where he specializes in cultural and media studies, with a focus on the postcolonial Caribbean, Jewish and diaspora studies, and film.

Employment

Assistant Professor. Department of English, University of Victoria, Victoria, British Columbia. July 2006–present.

Assistant Professor. Department of English, University of South Alabama, Mobile, Alabama. August 2003–July 2006.

Education

Ph.D., Comparative Literature (English, French, Hebrew)		
University of California, Berkeley	2003	
M.A., Comparative Literature (English, French)		
University of California, Berkeley	1991	
B.A., *magna cum laude*, Semiotics (Honors), Brown University	1987	

◀ AUTHOR CURRICULUM VITAE **Lincoln Shlensky.** This CV from Shlensky's Web site (shlensky.com) indicates that, like Gray, he may be an authoritative source. *By permission of Lincoln Z. Shlensky. Photo by Jason Francisco.*

Amardeep Singh, "Race and Hurricane Katrina: two questions"   Amardeep Singh is an associate professor of English at Lehigh University. His Lehigh blog includes postings on a variety of subjects: his vacation in Ireland, a book writ-

ten by a graduate school friend, Bollywood, and Hurricane Katrina, the topic of the posting below. In his blog posting titled "Race and Hurricane Katrina: two questions," Singh briefly explores how race played into the response to the hurricane. (Note: Singh now has a more current blog.) An excerpt from Singh's blog posting appears on page 361.

Before we read these sources on Hurricane Katrina in depth, we'll identify some guidelines for evaluating sources.

How Do I Evaluate a Source? How Is This Different from Previewing?

While some of this overlaps with advice on previewing sources, we are asking you to do a more in-depth analysis of texts than you did earlier in the chapter. To evaluate whether a source is strong enough to draw upon for your own writing, ask yourself the questions posed in the following section.

1. Is this source relevant to my project?   First, determine whether the source you're looking at is related to and useful for your project and research question(s). Ask yourself: Does the information in the source generate additional research questions related to my original question—does it get me deeper into my research? Does the source contribute to my knowledge on the topic—did I learn something new about the subject? In other words, does the author simply rehash what others have said, or does he or she say something new—or provide an alternative perspective? If the author simply duplicates knowledge, then the source is probably not a good choice for your project.

2. What is the author's level of credibility? When evaluating a source, you need to figure out how trustworthy the author is. Ask yourself:

» *What can I find out by Googling the author?* Learn about the author's education, degrees held, and any institutional, organizational, or professional affiliations. Find out whether the author is mentioned in other sources on the topic, and to what extent he or she is considered to be an "expert" on the subject by other experts in the field. Research other works by the author: One indicator of expertise is whether someone has published numerous times on the subject. However, don't discount the author's credibility just because this is the author's first piece on the subject—the author could be a rising scholar in the field.

» *What if I can't figure out who the individual author is?* If there is no obvious author, look at the reliability of the organization sponsoring the Web site. For example, if the site is the American Diabetes Association, you can assume that the information presented is researched and reliable because it is an organization that publishes researched articles on diabetes. Additionally, this organization funds research. On its Web site, the association states, "We provide objective and credible information."

No matter how much you might agree with the viewpoint conveyed in a source or how much you might like the way the author has presented information, establishing the author's credibility is absolutely necessary if you are to use this source in your research. If you cannot trust the author, then you should not use the source.

3. What is the author's purpose? To persuade? Inform? Tell a story? Some combination? Identify the author's purpose by reading the source critically and carefully. As you read, ask yourself the following questions to determine the author's objectives:

» What is the author's thesis? Does the thesis make an argument?

» Is the author trying to get me to agree with an opinion?

» Is the author presenting facts and information to teach me about the subject?

» Does the author use a narrative structure (include characters, conflict, setting)?

Once you have determined the purpose, ask yourself whether the author's purpose fits with your research question(s). A persuasive source can provide information that you can use to support or refute your argument. Informative and narrative sources may provide background for you or lend a personal perspective to your subject. For example, student Calvin Sweet's sources (see p. 346) are three

Have you ever Googled someone? If so, how did what you discovered affect your view of that person? If you've ever Googled yourself, how accurate was the information you found? What type of person did the information portray?

editorials in which authors seek to persuade readers about Hurricane Katrina. One of these texts, Madison Gray's "The Press, Race and Katrina" (p. 354), presents an argument critiquing the way the press handled the reporting of Katrina in relationship to race. Calvin knows this because as he reads the article, he notes that the author discusses and provides specific examples from the media. He also circles explicit related statements such as, "many journalists who monitored the coverage felt in hindsight that African Americans caught in Katrina's wake were misrepresented in the press."

When determining an author's purpose, remember that genre might be able to give you a clue. For example, if the source is an editorial, you can assume that the author's purpose is to persuade you; however, the author might also be telling a story to support that opinion. You need to read the source carefully to fully know the author's purpose.

Ultimately, by knowing the author's purpose you can determine whether the source is a good fit for your research topic. If your goal is to persuade your reader, then a source that provides useful evidence is a good fit. If the author's purpose is to tell a story and none of the information helps you advance your own claim, then you shouldn't use that source.

4. Who is the author's target audience? How does the author use rhetorical appeals to reach that audience? When you preview a source, you determine the author's audience (see "Previewing a Source," p. 322). In order to determine the audience, ask yourself the following questions:

» Does the place of publication offer clues about audience? (For example, an editorial in *Bloomberg Businessweek* is clearly aimed at a business audience.)

» Does the author use a formal or informal tone?

» What level of detail is presented in the piece?

» Does the author include information that assumes previous knowledge?

» Does the author use jargon or vocabulary used by experts?

When Calvin reads Shlensky's blog entry about Katrina (p. 358), he notices that the author uses informal language, such as "I'm doing okay." This tells Calvin that Shlensky's primary audience is people concerned about how Hurricane Katrina affected him.

Once you've determined the audience for the text, take a look at how the author appeals to that audience. Is the author establishing a sense of credibility that speaks to particular readers? Is the author using an emotional appeal to connect with the audience? Calvin notices that Shlensky begins his blog with an emotional appeal to those who know him, discussing the long lines for gas he experiences and his concern for those who live closer to where the hurricane hit.

Besides identifying the audience and analyzing rhetorical appeals, you also need to examine the evidence the author provides and determine whether it is appropriate for his or her intended audience. Pay attention, too, to how the author keeps readers' perspectives in mind, so that they will continue to read the piece. For example, when Calvin reads Singh's piece (p. 361), he notices that the author is mindful that his audience might be put off if he makes huge generalizations about racism, so he qualifies his statements by saying "I'm not trying to imply racism is afoot."

Knowing whether a source is written for a general audience or experts in the field helps you determine how appropriate the source is for research. For example, you may want to choose more specialized sources, written for a specific audience, if you're looking for detail and research so you can dig deeper into your topic inquiry. Or, if you want to make an argument—supported by research and data—about the impact of global warming on animals, you might turn to the journal *Nature* (written for a specialized audience), rather than *USA Today* (written for a general audience).

5. What is the source's genre? Does the author make the most of its conventions? Let's say you're considering using a news and opinion blog as a source. As you evaluate it, look at a few other examples to see how other bloggers typically convey information—and the types of conventions they tend to adhere to. How does your potential source compare with other blogs? Does your blogger take advantage of the conventions of the genre? For example, does he clearly identify himself as the author? Does he embed hyperlinks to additional details or sources? Does he invite feedback? If not, you might want to consider using a different source. When an author chooses to ignore the traditional conventions of a genre, he may also ignore other things, such as using reliable evidence to support opinions.

6. How does the author use evidence—and how reliable is that evidence? As you evaluate a source, pay close attention to how the author supports his claims and arguments. Look at:

» *Sufficient support: Does the author use enough evidence?* If not, that's a problem. A skilled persuasive writer will back up each claim with an appropriate example. Read the source and (1) make a note every time the author makes a claim, and (2) also note whether the claim is supported. Notice also whether the evidence is vague and general, or specific and detailed. For example, Madison Gray, the author of one of Calvin Sweet's sources on Hurricane Katrina, race, and the media, writes:

Do you read any blogs regularly? If so, think of two or three that you particularly enjoy. What do they have in common in terms of how the bloggers present information? Do they share design elements, such as headings and lists? Are there things that are done better on one blog than on the others?

CLAIM

"In fact, many journalists who monitored the coverage felt in hindsight that African Americans caught in Katrina's wake were misrepresented in the press."

Gray follows that claim with evidence—a quote from one person—that shows that at least one person believed there was misrepresentation. However, he doesn't sufficiently support his statement that "many journalists" felt that way. He could have made a stronger case by drawing on, say, a study of many journalists, or providing multiple quotes from journalists, for example.

INADEQUATE EVIDENCE

"I don't think African Americans were portrayed in the best light," said Camille Jackson, a staff writer for the Southern Poverty Law Center's Tolerance.org Web site. "It came out just how uncomfortable the media is when it comes to race, with the exception of a few."

👉 **Attention, researchers! A note about evidence.**

Wondering what we mean by "evidence"? Evidence is facts, examples, and source citations that authors use to illustrate and support each point they make in their compositions. Skilled authors use evidence to develop their arguments as well as their ethos. The type of evidence authors choose reflects upon them; for example, citing a celebrity gossip magazine as evidence suggests shallowness, while citing the *Wall Street Journal* suggests professionalism.

When you're evaluating a source, look at how the author uses evidence: Think of the evidence as the foundation upon which the argument is built. A shoddy foundation can cause even the most beautiful building to crumble.

» *Timeliness: Is the source and evidence current?* In most cases, you'll want to draw on sources that are as recent as possible. For example, if you are researching current trends in social media and how they affect elections, you would want the most up-to-date information. With this same topic, you might also choose to draw on perspectives from the past in order to compare how things might have changed. In either case, be sure to check the dates of your sources and when they were last updated, especially when you research online.

Timeliness mattered to Calvin Sweet when he conducted research on Hurricane Katrina. He knew he wanted a contemporary account of the hurricane, told by someone who had survived it. He wanted reporting based on actual events that occurred at the moment of the storm—so he looked for sources published on or around the storm date. He was excited to find Lincoln Z. Shlensky's blog entry, "Hurricane Katrina, Race and Class: Part I," dated September 2, 2005, just a few days after the August 29, 2005, landfall of the hurricane.

If Calvin had wanted a source focused on the longer-term aftermath of the storm—perhaps a yearlong study on the impact of the hurricane on people's lives—he'd probably have searched for sources written in 2006 or later. Such a source would likely draw on research conducted over time; the author could report the information provided in a study, or perhaps reflect on the situation, drawing on the study's data as supporting evidence for his claims. Depending on how you plan to use a source, its timeliness could make a difference. If you are looking for a contemporary account of an incident, then obviously a reflection written ten years later would not be appropriate.

7. Does the author cite sources?   As you evaluate a source, ask yourself: Does the author give credit to others? Does he mention the work of others in the text itself—perhaps with hyperlinks or a list of credits? How easily can I tell where the author obtained his or her information? If you can't tell what sources the author drew on, it's possible that the information isn't well researched or can't be supported.

Citation conventions—and by this we mean the format in which an author identifies his sources—can vary across genres. Before you can judge whether an author has cited sources properly, you need to be aware of the documentation conventions for the genre you are looking at. For example:

» Authors of newspaper articles usually cite sources in the body of the article itself, by using quotations and naming people and publications they've drawn on.

» Authors of blogs usually cite sources by providing hyperlinks to them, assuming the sources are online sources. You can see this in the two blog entries on Katrina featured in this chapter.

» Authors of peer-reviewed journal articles usually use strict source-citing conventions; for example, *The American Journal of Family Therapy*, a peer-reviewed journal on family behavioral health, requires authors to cite sources in accordance with the *Publication Manual of the American Psychological Association*. (See Chapter 7 for information on APA documentation style.) Considering that professional counselors rely on information in *The American Journal of Family Therapy* to inform their professional practice and research, it makes sense that source citation would be taken very seriously by the editors.

The Internet has made it possible to invent new genres quickly and easily. For example, just a short time ago, a "tweet" did not exist, but now the genre is incredibly popular. How do you think creators and users of these new genres decide how to cite their sources? What factors might contribute to their decisions?

Once you know something about the citation conventions of a genre, ask yourself: Does the author of the source I'm evaluating cite sources the way he should? For example, a journalist who doesn't mention any sources in an article or editorial should raise eyebrows—but a blogger who uses hyperlinks (rather than an academic style such as APA) should not. In a reliable text, an author makes it clear where he or she drew from the material of others. The author provides this information in the format that is common to that genre. If the source you're looking at falls short on this score, you may want to look for a different one.

Guided Process: How to Evaluate Sources ▼

Calvin Sweet (Student)

Hurricane Katrina Project: Evaluating 3 Sources

▲ STUDENT AUTHOR
PHOTO
Calvin Sweet.
Shutterstock.

Let's circle back to Calvin Sweet, who has identified a research question—and three sources that he's thinking of using.

RESEARCH QUESTION
How did the press treat race and class in their coverage of Hurricane Katrina and what are the consequences of that treatment?

Using the guidelines on pages 348–53, Calvin now evaluates his sources. His notes in the margins of each source show his thinking. He begins with Madison Gray's editorial for *Time*. (For biographical information on Madison Gray, see p. 346.) *(Article & Time branding: © 2009. Time Inc. Reprinted/Translated from TIME.COM and published with permission of Time Inc. Reproduction in any manner in any language in whole or in part without written permission is prohibited. TIME and the TIME logo are trademarks of Time Inc. Used under license.)*

Calvin's notes on Gray's argument

Relevant to my topic?

Yes. I want to look at media coverage of Katrina, as it relates to race and class. Madison Gray's critique of the storm coverage relates directly to my topic.

Credible author?

Yes. Gray writes for *Time*, so I trust he's a reliable journalist. He's also reported for the AP, *The New York Times*, and the *Detroit News*; he's a member of the New York Association of Black Journalists.

TIME

VIEWPOINT

The Press, Race and Katrina

Madison Gray

| Home | NewsFeed | U.S. | Politics | World | Business | Tech | Health | Science | Entertainment | Style | Opinion | Photos |

If you watched any television, listened to any radio, picked up a newspaper or visited a news Web site in the days that followed Hurricane Katrina last year, you probably were witness to the result of dozens of on-the-spot editorial decisions made by news managers around the country.

As much as we may have wanted to avoid the issue in those first confusing days, because New Orleans was 67% African American prior to the storm, race played a significant role in criticisms of government, both local and federal, humanitarian aid and not surprisingly, the media. Fortunately, the fourth estate has its own self-policing mechanisms and is much faster than government and other industries at evaluating and scrutinizing itself. But it is only in recent years that the media has taken a look at how it relates to the country's racial divisions, and Katrina provided an opportunity to do just that.

Keith Woods, faculty dean of the Poynter Institute, a St. Petersburg, Florida–based journalism training organization, said many

TIME

mistakes were made by the media, but in bringing attention to the crisis, the press got it right.

"The media brought a palpable sense of outrage with the coverage from the very beginning," said Woods. "If you looked at NPR, CNN, and scattered sightings of the networks and newspapers, where they did well was to recognize the size of the story and the need to stay with it."

But where race comes in is more difficult, he told me. Where journalism failed is not in any lack of emphasis on how disproportionately blacks were affected, but in how "too many people were making the surface observation that there were lots of blacks affected without spending the time parsing the facts that would make it meaningful or informative."

In fact, many journalists who monitored the coverage felt in hindsight that African Americans caught in Katrina's wake were misrepresented in the press.

"I don't think African Americans were portrayed in the best light," said Camille Jackson, a staff writer for the Southern Poverty Law Center's Tolerance.org Web site. "It came out just how uncomfortable the media is when it comes to race, with the exception of a few."

Jackson authored a series of articles for the Web site that spoke to media outlets referring to victims as "hoodlums," "animals" and "thugs." But she said it comes from cultural insensitivity in the media, which led to false news reports and eventually to a curtailing of emergency response.

She warned that the important lesson to be learned is "to be an honest journalist, to tell the whole story, and be aware of your

Continues next page

Calvin's notes on Gray's argument

I did a search for Gray on Google and found his 2008 article on Rodney King that won a journalism award. Race definitely factors into some of his articles.

Author's purpose?

Gray wants to persuade readers that "African Americans caught in Katrina's wake were misrepresented in the press." He also wants to inform about how journalists dealt with race in reporting the storm.

Audience?

Gray is writing for *Time* readers, especially African Americans who experienced Katrina and whose stories were not properly reflected in the press. His readers are also probably interested in journalism and concerned about media bias. Gray relies on ethos to appeal to readers' concerns.

Calvin's notes on Gray's argument

Identifiable genre/ mode/media?

This magazine article is an editorial: Gray's column is titled "Viewpoint." Its mode is written and it is published online.

Essentially, Gray's article is an argument. He presents his case in short paragraphs and works in sources and quotes: This technique is common to editorials and other journalistic writing.

Reliable evidence?

Gray's sources include a journalism dean, a journalist, and other media experts; he also refers to a congressional report. That all seems solid.

Gray writes: "many journalists who monitored the coverage felt in hindsight that African Americans caught in Katrina's wake were misrepresented in the press."

(Continued on p. 357.)

TIME

| Home | NewsFeed | U.S. | Politics | World | Business | Tech | Health | Science | Entertainment | Style | Opinion | Photos |

own personal biases. I know it's scary, but we're going to have to start talking about race so that we can get at the fear."

Buttressing criticisms of the press response to Katrina was a bipartisan Congressional report released in February that outright accuses the media of making a bad situation worse. It does not specify race in its pages, but its accusations implicate press reports that it says contributed to the confusion.

The report from the bipartisan House committee investigated preparations for and responses to Katrina and found that media reports of gunshots fired at rescue helicopters, rapes and murders in the Superdome, and mass rioting in the streets were unsubstantiated at best, and many were simply false. "It's clear accurate reporting was among Katrina's many victims," the report says. "If anyone rioted, it was the media."

But Margaret Engel, managing editor of the Newseum, an Arlington, Virginia–based interactive news museum, said there are more important things to consider, like images that seemingly cast a divide between black and white survivors. Two in particular were now-infamous captions placed with Agence France-Presse and Associated Press photos. The AFP photo caption described two whites as "finding" food, while the AP caption described a black youth as "looting" a store.

"That to me is much more troubling than reporters quoting cops who didn't really know," said Engel. "I think you'll find that some of the stories on that day of looting were wildly overstated. It's not good that the press reported that, but it is a footnote to the overall coverage which riveted the nation over the lack of response." She added: "I think for Congress to cast the media response as rumor-mongering is to miss the forest for the trees."

TIME

Despite the varied points of view, two things are clear. First, mistakes were made. As Woods pointed out, there has never been a how-to book on covering a disaster that nearly wipes out a whole city. Secondly, and most importantly, if African Americans in New Orleans are to be fairly served, the story must be told. "Now that the initial event has passed, the problem is maintaining people's attention," said Richard Prince, chairman of the National Association of Black Journalists' Media Monitoring Committee. "People are desperate for media attention because they fear the country will forget them. While a lot of reporters have covered the follow-up, it has not been compelling enough."

Prince said that the way to learn from what happened is for journalists to continually go to the Gulf Coast Region and find new stories, which are abundant. "They call it one of the worst natural disasters in the history of the country. So many people have a story to tell; somehow those stories have to be told."

Calvin's notes on Gray's argument

He supports this claim by mentioning one specific journalist. Are there others he could mention to back this statement more strongly?

Sources cited?

Gray attributes his information to sources when he quotes people and names them in the body of the editorial.

He also provides hyperlinks so readers can get more information. For example, I clicked on the Keith Woods link and it took me to the Poynter Institute, where Woods was faculty dean (until 2010 when he joined NPR).

After reading through the informative and persuasive piece in *Time*, Calvin decided he wanted a more personal lens into the issues of the press and its reporting of Katrina. He found Lincoln Shlensky's blog containing writing about his views related to press coverage of Katrina. Additionally, he found that Shlensky provided the argumentative take on the situation that he was looking for. (For more biographical information on Lincoln Shlensky, see p. 347). *(The following blog post is reprinted here by permission of Lincoln Z. Shlensky.)*

Calvin's notes on Shlensky's argument

Relevant to my topic?

Yes. Shlensky focuses on issues of race and how they affected the media's response to the disaster. This will be a valuable source for my research.

Credible author?

Yes. Shlensky is a college professor, and I trust that his research and sources are valid. His area of specialty is Caribbean literature (he holds a PhD), and according to his CV, he's presented numerous times on this subject, looking at issues of race in relationship to literature.

Because he's regularly subject to the peer review of fellow academics, I'd imagine Shlensky is careful with how he states things. Also, as an educator, he may look at his loss during Katrina through a more analytical than emotional lens.

AULULA

A LYTTELL POTTE

LINCOLN Z. SHLENSKY

Hurricane Katrina, Race and Class: Part I

I have been in Pensacola, Florida, since late Tuesday because my house in Mobile still is without electricity. I'm doing okay here, but I look forward to getting back home as soon as electricity is restored. The University is supposed to reopen on September 6th, but that may change, depending on conditions. Yesterday and today the gas stations here in Pensacola were mainly without gas, and I waited in a long line at the one station that (only briefly) had gas to offer. It's scary to see people begin to panic when basic commodities are in short supply; I can only imagine to what degree such a sense of panic must be magnified nearer to the epicenter, where essential necessities such as water, food, and sanitation are in severe shortage.

From my vantage—geographically and emotionally near the disaster, but safely buffered from its worst deprivations—much of the press coverage has not adequately dealt with the most difficult social issues that mark this still unfolding catastrophe. It is difficult to avoid concluding that one important cause of the slow response to the debacle has to do with the fact that most of the people who are caught up in it are poor and black. Here in Pensacola I keep hearing blame expressed towards the victims: "they should have heeded the call to evacuate." Even the FEMA chief said as much in a news conference today. So where, I must ask, were the buses he should have provided to take them away before Katrina hit? Where were the troops to supervise evacuation? Where were the emergency shelters and health services? People who ought to know better do not seem to understand or acknowledge the enormous differential in available resources— access to transportation, money, information, social services,

AULULA

etc.—that forms the background to this human catastrophe. Terms such as "looting" are tossed about in the press and on TV with no class or race analysis at all. In recent news reports, there is an emerging discussion of the *political* background to the calamity: the Bush administration's curtailment of federal funding for levee repair in order to pay for the war in Iraq, rampant commercial housing development on environmentally protected wetlands, financial evisceration of FEMA, and so on. But there's been little or no discussion of the economic background that makes New Orleans a kind of "Third World" nation unto itself, with fearsomely deteriorated housing projects, extraordinarily high crime and murder rates, and one of the worst public education systems in the country.

Major newspaper editors and TV producers have prepared very few reports about issues of race in this disaster, and those reports that have appeared so far seem to me deeply insufficient in their analysis of endemic class and race problems. I've been communicating with a national magazine reporter friend of mine since Tuesday night about the issues of race and class in this catastrophe; here's my email comment on this topic from earlier today:

CNN addressed the race question today on TV, but only to ask softball questions of Jesse Jackson, who to his discredit didn't exhibit even a modicum of the anger of one Louisiana black political leader, who said: "While the Administration has spoken of 'shock and awe' in the war on terror, the response to this disaster has been 'shockingly awful.'"

The *Washington Post* also ran a puff piece that doesn't ask any of the relevant questions, such as whether the Administration's response would have been faster if these were white people suffering the agonies of a slow motion disaster. Here's the <u>link</u> to the *Post*'s piece.

Michael Moore also had this to say in a letter to President Bush circulated today:

Continues next page

Calvin's notes on Shlensky's argument

Author's purpose?

Shlensky writes his post to persuade readers that "much of the press coverage has not adequately dealt with the most difficult social issues that mark this still unfolding catastrophe . . . [because] most of the people who are caught up in it are poor and black."

Audience?

Shlensky writes to those critical of the media. He appeals to his audience with ethos (using quotes and evidence from media coverage) and pathos, hoping his audience gets angry enough to demand attention to the issues of race.

AULULA

No, Mr. Bush, you just stay the course. It's not your fault that 30 percent of New Orleans lives in poverty or that tens of thousands had no transportation to get out of town. C'mon, they're black! I mean, it's not like this happened to Kennebunkport. Can you imagine leaving white people on their roofs for five days? Don't make me laugh! Race has nothing—NOTHING—to do with this!

(See Michael Moore's full letter <u>here</u>.)

A member of the Congressional Black Caucus had to remind reporters today to stop referring to those displaced by the flooding with the blanket term "refugees" (recalling, of course, the waves of Haitian or Central American or Southeast Asian refugees who sought shelter in the United States): these people are citizens, she said, deserving of the full protections guaranteed to all Americans.

The federal government promised on Wednesday that those receiving food stamps could get their full allotment at the beginning of September, rather than the usual piecemeal distribution throughout the month. How very generous. What these people need is relief money and access to services now—even the 50,000 or so exhausted and traumatized people whose images we've seen at the N.O. Superdome and at the Civic Center are just a few of the far larger number of those residents of the region displaced by the hurricane, many of whom live from monthly paycheck to paycheck. It will be months at the very least before these people can return home; their jobs may be gone for good. The mayor of New Orleans was actually caught off camera crying in frustration today at the slow pace of the federal response.

If there is a hopeful side to this tragedy, it is perhaps that Hurricane Katrina's damage and efforts to relieve those displaced by the storm may spark a wider national discussion about the ongoing and unaddressed issues of race and economic disparity in America. If that doesn't happen, I fear that there will be even further

AULULA

deterioration in the living conditions and economic predicament of those left destitute and homeless by Katrina—a situation in which our own government's years of neglect must be included as a crucial contributing factor. We must not let such a deterioration of conditions for those hardest hit by Katrina occur.

What happens next, when tens or hundreds of thousands of Americans require long-term recovery help, will be an important barometer of our society's ability to heal itself.

After realizing that Shlensky's blog contained a lot of evidence to support the writer's opinion, Calvin decided that another blog might give him additional anecdotes related to Katrina. Even though Amardeep Singh was not directly affected by the hurricane, his blog entry reflects his reaction to what occurred and raises questions to help Calvin dig deeper into his research. (For biographical information on Amardeep Singh, see p. 351.) *(The following blog post is reprinted here by permission of Amardeep Singh.)*

Amardeep Singh

Race and Hurricane Katrina: two questions

Though I haven't written about it this week, I've been watching and reading the coverage of Katrina in New Orleans with a mixture of awe and horror.

Two quick thoughts for discussion.

Continues next page

Calvin's notes on Singh's argument

Relevant to my topic?

While Singh touches on issues of race and raises an interesting point about how some media compared the devastation to

(Continued on p. 362.)

Calvin's notes on
Singh's argument

Amardeep Singh

**Calvin's notes on
Singh's argument**

that of third-world
countries, I'm not
sure that there's
enough informa-
tion here to be
useful. The source,
though, does make
me think about the
issues.

Credible author?

Like Shlensky,
Singh is a profes-
sor subject to peer
review. He has
published re-
searched articles,
so I expect this
same expertise in
his blog entries.

Like Shlensky,
Singh takes an
analytical,
academic-seeming,
approach, with no
direct experience
of Katrina.

Author's purpose?

Singh wants read-
ers to consider
why the media
is not examining
the issue of race
in relationship to
Katrina.

Audience?

Singh's audience is
most likely his fel-
low academics and
those who read his
blog.

**First, have you noticed that numerous articles refer to the affected
region as "third world" in its devastation?** (Example: CNN) I
always cringe when I read that.

But it's worth thinking about. Remember how after the Bombay
flood last month (37.1 inches in 24 hours), there were numerous
articles in the Indian media lamenting the city's inability to keep
things running smoothly? Well, it doesn't just happen in India.
Natural disasters happen to everyone; it isn't something to be
embarrassed about. (Still, I wish they wouldn't use poorer parts
of the world as a benchmark for the scale of the disaster.)

Here the authorities had access to good predictions for the storm,
and were able to execute a large-scale evacuation of *part of the
population* quickly. It would be great if monsoon rains could be
predicted with as much accuracy. Does anyone know the science
behind this? Why did no one have any idea that 37 inches of rain
were about to hit the city of Bombay last month?

[Update: The fact that they had good predictions makes it all the
more unbelievable that the post-hurricane evacuation of New
Orleans has been so inept.]

It is also worth considering that the area in question with Katrina
is much less densely populated than Bombay (1.5 million people
in the entire New Orleans metro area; compare to 20 million–
plus in greater Bombay).

The second issue circles around race within the United States.
If you watch the news footage of the post-Katrina rescue operations, you'll notice again and again that the people being rescued
seem to be overwhelmingly African American.

There could be any number of reasons for this. One is, it's quite
plausible to infer that more African Americans ignored or didn't
get the message about the mandatory evacuation before the
storm. Some folks may not have had the physical means to get

Amardeep Singh

out (i.e., a car & a credit card), or a place to go. Another factor might be topography: it's possible that many black neighborhoods are in low-lying areas (though I admit I don't know the New Orleans area very well). And finally, one shouldn't forget that in terms of sheer demographics, these areas as a whole have large African American populations.

I'm not trying to imply racism is afoot. Only this: the fact that blacks seem to have been disproportionately affected by this tragedy reminds us of the inequities that existed before the Hurricane happened. When we see folks being airlifted to safety, it should probably be on our minds that they were the ones who lived in the most vulnerable housing to begin with, and were also in many cases unable to think of leaving it behind.

I wish the mainstream media would take notice of this issue; thus far, though, I haven't seen anyone make reference to it. (Maybe after the shock of the storm dies down.)

The mayor of Biloxi, Mississippi, called Katrina "Our Tsunami", and judging from the pictures of Biloxi and Jackson, he may be right (though, as massive as the disaster is, it is still much smaller in scale than the Tsunami, which caused huge damage in *eight countries*, and left nearly 1000 times more people dead). But as with the tsunami, there is here a story behind the tragedy—a pattern of ongoing suffering that existed before the storm—that people aren't talking about.

This Boing Boing story doesn't help matters. Apparently, in some AFP photo captions, blacks who are carrying goods retrieved from closed or damaged stores are referred to as "looting," while white people doing the same thing are described "finding" the goods they're carrying.

Calvin's notes on Singh's argument

Identifiable genre/ mode/medium?

Like Shlensky, Singh blogs his argument. He uses hyperlinks, a comments section, links to previous posts, and lists contact information.

Reliable evidence?

Singh refers to CNN, *Boing Boing*, and the mayor of Biloxi's statement, but some generalizations either are not backed up or are backed with sparse evidence. For example, the statement "numerous articles refer to the affected region as 'third world' in its devastation" is followed up by only one example.

Sources cited?

Singh attributes his quotes, such as when he quotes the mayor of Biloxi, but doesn't cite common knowledge (such as the population of Bombay versus New Orleans).

Calvin Sweet, *Hurricane Katrina Project*   363

Calvin Sweet (Student)

Hurricane Katrina Project: Research Plan

Following his evaluation of the works of Gray, Shlensky, and Singh, Calvin maps his research out in a little more detail.

Research Assignment: Research Plan

Calvin Sweet
Professor Elizabeth Kleinfeld
English 102
February 1, 20—
Research Plan: Hurricane Katrina Project

1. Your research question.

   My research question is twofold: How did the press treat race and class in their coverage of Katrina, and what are the consequences of that treatment?

2. Your goals.

   My starting point was to find out how the press covered Katrina. I want to be a journalist, and I remember my cousin who interned at a newspaper in 2007 saying that the writers at that paper were still talking about how "slanted" the Katrina coverage was. One of my goals is to discover what the Katrina coverage was. In the research I've done so far, it looks like some people think the coverage treated both race and class unfairly. If my research continues to support this view, I'll argue that press coverage didn't adequately take race and class into account and that there were serious consequences because of that. I believe my research would be considered inductive, because I truly haven't made up my mind and even these thoughts I have now are completely based on the three sources I've read. The next source I read could make me see things differently.

3. Types of sources.

   I will continue reading blogs about Katrina. I think reading about people who experienced it gives me an understanding of what actually happened and how race and class mattered in what happened. I also need to read the press coverage, which I have just begun with the *Time* article. In fact, analyzing the press coverage itself will be a major part of my research. I can do *EBSCOhost* searches to find articles. To make my argument that there are consequences because of the coverage, I need to follow up on things like Shlensky's idea that this could all lead to more discussion of race and class. For example, I need to find out if there have been more discussions of race and class, maybe by

---

comparing how many articles a particular newspaper published on race and class issues in the two years before and the two years after Katrina. I will also watch Spike Lee's documentary *When the Levees Broke*. My assumption is that it will be like all of Lee's other films, in which race and class are examined.

For primary sources, I will look for YouTube videos by Katrina survivors to see how they portray race and class. I will also interview Professor Hughes in the African American studies department to see if she can share any insights with me.

4. Your timeline.

- Find and read more blogs: March 20-31

- Schedule interview with Professor Kleinfeld: April 1

- Write interview questions: April 5

- Conduct interview: April 7

- Watch Spike Lee film on Netflix: April 8-10

- Find and read press coverage: April 11-25

- Draft: April 25-May 6

- Revise: May 7-14

- Edit: May 14

- Submit: May 15

INTEGRATING & DOCUMENTING SOURCES

VIDEO STILL ▶
Stephen Colbert, during taping of *The Colbert Report.* Comedy and news programs can be interesting research sources. See MLA documentation for this source on page 402. *AP Photo/Joseph Kaczmarek.*

In this chapter, we focus on two things: (1) how to integrate sources, and (2) how to cite and document sources using two popular documentation styles. First, we'll show you how to incorporate sources into your own compositions, through quotations, paraphrases, and summaries (pp. 369–87). As you'll discover, there are reasons for choosing one method over the others, or combining methods, depending on your purposes. We'll follow the processes of student writers as they work with their sources (see Guided Processes in this chapter). We will also take a look at the issue of plagiarism. Composers who plagiarize use a source unethically, for example, by using an idea or language from a source without giving credit to that source with an attribution, parenthetical citation, and bibliographical entry. Plagiarism is not always a deliberate act; it can simply be the result of sloppiness. Whether it's intentional or not, plagiarism is a serious offense in any academic setting. However, if you follow the advice in this chapter (especially on pp. 387–92), you can be confident of your integrity and ethos as an author.

For an Index of Sources & Contexts for material referenced in this chapter, see the e-Pages at **bedfordstmartins.com /bookofgenres.**

In the second part of the chapter, we will show you how to cite sources within the text of your own compositions, and how to document them in lists at the end of your paper. Because the documentation styles of the Modern Language Association (MLA) and American Psychological Association (APA) are the ones most typically used in the humanities and social sciences, we've provided detailed coverage of both (MLA, pp. 395–414; APA, pp. 415–35). There are other popular styles—such as *Chicago* style, used by some of the humanities disciplines, and the American Medical Association (AMA) style, used by health and medical fields. If you are using those styles, we refer you to chicagomanualofstyle.org and amamanualofstyle.com.

INTEGRATING SOURCES INTO YOUR WRITING

When we talk about integrating sources, we mean a host of different and related activities. We mean using source material in our own compositions, perhaps to provide context for our ideas or evidence for our claims. We also mean showing how the source material we've used relates to other source material—does it agree with other sources? Does it contradict other sources? Does it provide a perspective missing in other sources? And finally, we mean citing our sources to give credit and documenting them in a Works Cited list so that interested readers can track the sources down for themselves.

Using a Parenthetical Citation or Signal Phrase

Here are examples of how Emily Kahn (the student introduced in Chapter 6) integrated an article into a paper she wrote. She found the article, "The Objectification of Women in Comic Books" by Jehanzeb Dar, online in the fantasy magazine, *Lightspeed*.

In this first example, Emily presents Dar's name in what's called a parenthetical citation. Parenthetical citations must include the author's last name and the page number from the source that the material is taken from. Because Dar's article is from an online magazine, there are no page numbers to list.

EMILY'S IN-TEXT CITATION (MLA style—names author in parentheses)
The writer argues that the comic book industry may begin to attract female readers and readers of color if comics authors reject sexism and racism. He concludes: "As more female writers and artists make contributions to the industry, male writers and artists will need to be inspired to work against sexism, the objectification of women, and the sexualization of women of color" (Dar 000).

author's last name — if there is a page number, it goes here

Alternatively, Emily could have cited Dar's article as follows, by naming him in a signal phrase.

EMILY'S IN-TEXT CITATION (MLA style—names author in a signal phrase)

author named in signal phrase

Jehanzeb Dar argues that if the comic book industry wants to attract female readers, then comic book authors need to reject sexism and racism. He concludes: "As more female writers and artists make contributions to the industry, male writers and artists will need to be inspired to work against sexism, the objectification of women, and the sexualization of women of color" (00-00).

were this a print article, with page numbers, the page referred to would go here

At the end of her paper, Emily provides a bibliographic entry for her references to Dar's article.

EMILY'S WORKS CITED ENTRY (MLA style)

author name: last, first   title of online article   title of online magazine

Dar, Jehanzeb. "The Objectification of Women in Comic Books." *Lightspeed*.

sponsor/publisher   publication date   medium   access date

John Joseph Adams, Aug. 2008. Web. 23 Aug. 2013.

article URL; not MLA-required, but we recommend

<http://www.fantasy-magazine.com/non-fiction/articles/the-objectification-of-women-in-graphic-novels/>.

Using the MLA style of documentation, Emily:

» Cites Dar's article in the text of her paper, using an in-text citation that includes his name (no page number available)

» Documents Dar's article with a corresponding entry in her Works Cited list

» Avoids plagiarism, by citing Dar's article in *both* her paper *and* her Works Cited list

Overview: Quoting, Paraphrasing, & Summarizing

Quoting   In the example on page 368, Emily quotes directly from Dar's article. To signify to her readers that she is using Dar's exact words, she surrounds his words with quotation marks:

> **EMILY'S DIRECT QUOTATION FROM THE SOURCE (Dar)**
> He concludes: "As more female writers and artists make contributions to the industry, male writers and artists will need to be inspired to work against sexism, the objectification of women, and the sexualization of women of color" (Dar).

Emily chooses to include a quotation in order to state the specifics of Dar's argument. The quotation also serves to back up her first sentence, in which she summarizes Dar's main argument.

Paraphrasing   Elsewhere in her paper, Emily paraphrases Dar's argument. To paraphrase, a writer takes the ideas of a source and puts them into his or her own words. A paraphrase rewords without significantly condensing a specific passage.

> **ORIGINAL PASSAGE FROM SOURCE (Dar)**
> The role of women changed dramatically during World War II when patriotic characters emerged and surprisingly attracted the interest of new readers, who were both men and women. Arguably, the most noteworthy female character was Wonder Woman.

> **EMILY'S PARAPHRASE**
> According to Dar, Wonder Woman was the most interesting character to come out of the comics of the World War II era.

Note that Emily rephrases Dar's sentences and condenses them into one. She also attributes the entire idea to Dar by naming him in a signal phrase: "According to Dar . . ." If the article were in print, she would also include a parenthetical note at the end with the page number on which the idea was mentioned.

As you can see in the examples above, Emily always gives credit to Dar when she refers to his ideas, even if she changes his words, as in a summary or paraphrase.

☞ **Attention, writers! A little summary goes a long way.**

Although summarizing an entire work is occasionally the way to go, we recommend that you do this sparingly.

Choose summary to step back and give a "big picture" view to your readers, or to provide context.

In general, focus on specific points and passages of your sources; draw on these through quotations, paraphrases, or a combination of these. Support your arguments with specifics from your sources and your paper will be richer, more detailed, and ultimately, more persuasive.

Integrating sources smoothly into your own writing allows you to maintain control over the authorial voice that your readers hear. For example, although the examples above show Emily referring to Dar's ideas, it is clear that she, not Dar, is the author of her paper. Dar's voice never overtakes Emily's. While she draws on the source through quotations, paraphrases, and summary, she does so smoothly. Like Emily, you'll need to decide how and when to use these methods of drawing on sources. You'll also need to decide whether you're going to cite them through signal phrases, such as "According to Dar," or through parenthetical citations, such as "(Dar 000)." And if your instructor has not requested that you use a particular documentation style, you'll need to decide which format to use: MLA, APA, or another method of documentation.

Summarizing   In the example on page 368, Emily summarizes the main point of Dar's entire article in her first sentence:

> **EMILY'S SUMMARY OF ENTIRE SOURCE**
> Jehanzeb Dar argues that if the comic book industry wants to attract female readers, then comic book authors need to reject sexism and racism.

Emily manages to summarize in one sentence a point Dar makes in nine paragraphs. A summary condenses material significantly and focuses only on the point made, not the details that support or illustrate the point. Emily wants to reference Dar's central argument, so summary makes sense.

Quoting

What Does It Mean to Quote from a Source?

When you quote from a source, you provide a passage from that text—in the author's exact language. The best time to quote from a text is when the language from a passage contributes in a crucial way to the argument you are making.

When you quote from a passage, you should:

Use the exact words from the original without alteration   If you do need to alter the words for the sake of agreement of verb tense, use brackets to indicate what you've altered. To shorten a passage, use ellipses.

> **ORIGINAL PASSAGE FROM SOURCE**
> "Sexist undertones and stereotypical images are getting worse and increasingly sleazier."

> **EMILY'S ALTERED QUOTE (changes shown in brackets)**
> Dar points out that "[s]exist undertones and stereotypical images [have gotten] worse and increasingly sleaz[y]."

Surround the quoted passage with quotation marks An exception is long quotes, which should be indented in a block. A long quote, per MLA, is more than four lines long; in APA style, it is more than forty words long.

Give credit to the author of the source being quoted An attribution phrase, such as "Dar points out that," gives credit and cues readers to hear someone else's voice for a moment or two. Conventions for crediting sources differ. As with summaries and paraphrases, you may need to provide a parenthetical citation and/or a bibliographic entry if that is appropriate for the genre you are composing in.

Quote from other authors to present their specific language for good reasons; for example, if a passage supports (or refutes) the point you're making.

Let's look at an example. Suppose a student named Omar Sadi is writing about the possible connection between extreme weather and global warming. One of his sources is *Yale Environment 360*, published by Yale University and its School of Forestry and Environmental Studies. In that journal, Omar finds an article that gathers the views of eight climate experts.

👉 **Attention, writers! A caution against quoting too much.**

Remember that every time you quote an author, you are, in effect, turning over the microphone to someone else. So when should you let someone else take the microphone? Perhaps if the author makes a point in language so vivid it deserves a moment in the spotlight. Or if the author's language or phrasing is particularly precise or interesting or humorous. Our point is this: Quote mindfully. Don't use quotations just because you think it will be too much work to paraphrase.

Forum: Is Extreme Weather Linked to Global Warming?

In the past year, the world has seen a large number of extreme weather events, from the Russian heat wave last summer, to the severe flooding in Pakistan, to the recent tornadoes in the U.S. In a Yale Environment 360 forum, a panel of experts weighs in on whether the wild weather may be tied to increasing global temperatures.

That global air and ocean temperatures are rising, and that human activity is largely to blame, is no longer a subject of debate among the vast majority of the world's climate scientists. But there is no such consensus when talk turns to another important question: Is climate change already causing more extreme weather events, including worsening downpours and flooding, intensifying heat waves, and more powerful hurricanes?

Yale Environment 360 asked eight leading climate experts whether they think there is growing evidence that human-caused global warming is contributing to an increased incidence of extreme weather — and to cite specific recent examples in their answers. Their responses varied, with some contending that rising temperatures already are creating more tempestuous weather and others saying that more extreme weather may be likely but that not enough data yet exists to discern a trend in that direction. Scientists in both camps said two physical phenomena — warmer air holds more moisture, and higher temperatures exacerbate naturally occurring heat waves — would almost by definition mean more extremes. But some argued that the growing human toll from hurricanes, tornadoes, floods, and heat waves is primarily related to burgeoning human population and the related degradation of the environment.

Gabriele C. Hegerl, professor of climate system science at the University of Edinburgh.
Not all extreme events are expected to increase or even change. For example, there is quite a bit of evidence that greenhouse gas increases have contributed to recent widespread changes in the frequency of extreme temperatures, but this encompasses both decreases in the number of cold days and nights and increases in the number of warm nights. The widespread recent warming, which for global and continental mean data has been found to be likely due largely to human influences, leads to a changing probability of extreme temperatures. However, there are also cases where the tail of the temperature distribution is changing differently from the mean. Warming can lead to more severe drought in regions and seasons where precipitation decreases or remains largely unchanged, while evaporation increases due to warmer temperatures. Furthermore, the warming atmosphere has been shown to become moister. This probably explains the statistically significant shift towards more extreme precipitation events worldwide, which cannot be explained by climate variability and is best explained by human influences.

Roger A. Pielke Jr., professor of environmental studies at the University of Colorado.
The IPCC [Intergovernmental Panel on Climate Change] defines "climate change" as a change in the statistics of weather occurring over 30 years or longer and persisting for decades. Thus, the detection of a change in climate requires long-term records. To suggest that particular extreme weather events are evidence of climate change is not just wrong, but wrongheaded — every bit as much as the claims made during a particularly cold and snowy winter (or even several in a row) that such events somehow disprove climate change. Weather is not climate and short-term climate variability is not climate change.

◀ ARTICLE
Yale Environment 360, Yale University's online magazine. The article "Forum: Is Extreme Weather Linked to Global Warming?" presents the views of climate scientists, including Gabriele C. Hegerl and Roger A. Pielke Jr. *Yale Environment 360*.

He decides that the experts' perspectives and voices will support his main argument, and he chooses to quote from the source as follows.

OMAR'S EFFECTIVE QUOTING

In a recent forum published by *Yale Environment 360*, a panel of experts addressed the question: Is extreme weather linked to global warming? Like many of the panelists, University of Colorado professor Roger A. Pielke Jr. said that because the Intergovernmental Panel on Climate Change defines climate change as a persistent change of weather that takes place over the course of thirty years or more, the question posed cannot be answered now. Instead, Pielke says, we need long-term studies and records to scientifically support a connection. He argues:

quotation from a source

> To suggest that particular extreme weather events are evidence of climate change is not just wrong, but wrongheaded. . . . Weather is not climate and short-term climate variability is not climate change.

So how do scientists explain the extreme weather of recent years? And what are the best ways of evaluating the impact of global warming on the weather? . . .

When Should I Quote from a Source?

A great time to quote from a source is when the ideas or language of the original is so striking that you can't truly capture them in a paraphrase or summary. For example, 9/11 hero Todd Beamer's words "let's roll" could be paraphrased as "we should act now," but such a paraphrase lacks the energy and emotion of the original. It would be best to quote Beamer. Here are some other instances when you might quote rather than paraphrase or summarize:

Quote from a source when the author or speaker is an expert in a given field   For example, the passage quoted from the *Yale Environment 360* article (p. 371) clearly provides the essence of one expert's views on a question that is central to student writer Omar's purpose. Quoting the exact words of an expert can carry weight, add credibility, and help support your argument.

Quote from a source when a paraphrase or summary would alter the author's meaning   For example, this might be the case when your source is a legal document, as in the following:

STUDENT'S QUOTATION FROM A LEGAL DOCUMENT

In the Supreme Court's historical ruling on school segregation, Chief Justice Earl Warren offered the court's final opinion in *Brown v. Board of Education*, ruling for the plaintiffs:

quotation from a source

> We conclude that in the field of public education the doctrine of "separate but equal" has no place. Separate educational facilities are inherently unequal. Therefore, we hold that the plaintiffs and others similarly situated for whom the actions have been brought are, by reason of the segregation complained of, deprived of the equal protection of the laws guaranteed by the Fourteenth Amendment.

It was this ruling that changed . . .

Note: Because the quoted passage is long, it is "blocked" rather than run in with the text; there are no quotation marks in this case.

Quote from a source when a paraphrase or summary would not capture the essence of the author's clear and memorable words and tone   For example, supermodel Linda Evangelista once famously said, "We don't wake up for less than $10,000 a day." If you were to paraphrase this, you would lose the tone and spirit of her comment.

Quote from a text if your purpose is to analyze that text   For example, if you were writing an analysis of a work of literature, you would include in your paper specific passages to discuss. Let's say you want to comment on mystery writer Agatha Christie's use of an omniscient narrator and want to give an example from her writing to illustrate your point. You might write something like this:

STUDENT'S QUOTATION OF A PASSAGE FOR ANALYSIS
In *Secret Adversary*, Christie uses her narrator to convey a quick analysis of a character's true nature:

> Although she was accustomed to take the lead, and to pride herself on her quick-wittedness, in reality she had relied upon Tommy more than she realized at the time. There was something so eminently sober and clear-headed about him, his common sense and soundness of vision were so unvarying, that without him Tuppence felt much like a rudderless ship (88).

quotation
from a source

The narrator's commentary on Tommy, conveyed through Tuppence's point of view, serves to . . .

How Do I Quote from a Source?

To quote a source, do the following:

» Integrate the quote into your prose by providing a context for the quotation. In other words, don't simply plop the quote into the prose, expecting your reader to understand how it fits within the material that precedes and follows it.

» Signal the reader that a quote is coming. This is usually best done by using the author's name (Kleinfeld discusses ". . .").

» If the quote is shorter than four lines, integrate it into your sentences. If the quote is longer than four lines, use a blocked quote format.

Guided Process: How to Quote from a Source ▼

Paul Pierre (Student)

Nonviolent Protest Project: Quoting Gandhi

▲ STUDENT AUTHOR
Paul Pierre.

Let's look at the process of student Paul Pierre. He's researching nonviolent protest and has come across some speeches by Mohandas K. Gandhi (commonly known as Mahatma Gandhi), the philosophical leader of the early twentieth-century independence movement in India. Gandhi became famous for using only nonviolent protest strategies.

Paul decides to read some of Gandhi's writings and speeches, and to summarize and paraphrase them within his own writing. However, when he reads "The Doctrine of the Sword," in which Gandhi defines nonviolence, Paul decides that Gandhi's original words are powerful and that he should quote them directly.

Paul located the text of this 1920 article by Gandhi at the Web site of a research foundation dedicated to the author. Gandhi's article was originally published in his weekly journal, *Young India*.

Comprehensive Site By Gandhian Institute Bombay Sarvodaya Mandal & Gandhi Research Foundation

Mahatma Gandhi's
writings, philosophy, audio, video & photographs

The Doctrine Of The Sword

By M. K. Gandhi

In this age of the rule of brute force, it is almost impossible for anyone to believe that anyone else could possibly reject the law of final supremacy of brute force. . . .

I do believe that where there is only a choice between cowardice and violence I would advise violence. Thus when my eldest son asked me what he should have done, had he been present when I was almost fatally assaulted in 1908, whether he should have run away and seen me killed or whether he should have used his physical force which he could and wanted to use, and defended me, I told him that it was his duty to defend me even by using violence. . . .

I am not a visionary. I claim to be a practical idealist. The religion of nonviolence is not meant merely for the Rishis and saints. It is meant for the common people as well. Nonviolence is the law of our species as

Paul's notes on Gandhi's article

1. *I read the whole article* and chose the passage I thought was most significant to my argument about nonviolence.

2. *I thought about how this source works with my other sources.* In my research, I've looked into how well-known political figures define *nonviolence*. Gandhi, probably the best known of these figures, offers a perspective that I think is crucial to present.

3. *I tried paraphrasing Gandhi's words.* Here's what I came up with:

MY PARAPHRASE
Gandhi named in signal phrase, so no parenthetical citation needed

For Gandhi, nonviolence was a type of active defiance.

I don't think it works. My paraphrase is a lot less powerful than Gandhi's original words.

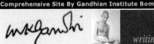

Comprehensive Site By Gandhian Institute Bombay Sarvodaya Mandal & Gandhi Research Foundation

Mahatma Gandhi's

writings, philosophy, audio, video & photographs

violence is the law of the brute. The spirit lies dormant in the brute and he knows no law but that of physical might. The dignity of man requires obedience to a higher law to the strength of the spirit.

I have therefore ventured to place before India the ancient law of self sacrifice. For Satyagrah and its offshoots, non-cooperation and civil resistance are nothing but new names for the law of suffering. The Rishis, who discovered the law of nonviolence in the midst of nonviolence, were greater geniuses than Newton. They were themselves greater warriors than Wellington. Having themselves known the use of arms, they realized their uselessness, and taught a weary world that its salvation lay not through violence, but through nonviolence.

Nonviolence in its dynamic condition means conscious suffering. It does not mean meek submission to the will of the evil-doer, but it means the putting of one's whole soul against the will of the tyrant. Working under this law of being, it is possible for a single individual to defy the whole might of an unjust empire to save his honor, his religion, his soul and lay the foundation for the empire's fall or its regeneration.

And so I am not pleading for India to practice nonviolence because it is weak. I want her to practice nonviolence being conscious of her strength and power. . . .

Paul's notes on Gandhi's article

4. *I decided to quote Gandhi directly.* Here's what I wrote and included in my final audio essay:

MY QUOTATION

Gandhi named in signal phrase, so no parenthetical citation needed

Gandhi was adamant that nonviolence is different from being passive, explaining, "Nonviolence in its dynamic condition means conscious suffering. It does not mean meek submission to the will of the evil-doer, but it means the putting of one's whole soul against the will of the tyrant."

5. *I cited the Gandhi article as a source in my Works Cited list.* Even though I created an audio essay about nonviolent protest, my instructor asked me to formally cite all my sources. I submitted (with my audio essay) an Artist's Statement in which I documented all my research according to MLA style. Here's the entry that corresponds with my in-text citation of the Gandhi article.

MY WORKS CITED ENTRY (MLA STYLE)

author name: title of short work
last, first   from a Web site

Gandhi, M. K. "The Doctrine of the Sword."
          title of site

Mahatma Gandhi Complete Informa-
               site sponsor

tion Web Site. Gandhian Institute
Bombay Sarvodaya Mandal.
   publication   date of
     date   medium   access

11 Aug. 1920. Web. 15 Sept.
      URL; not MLA-required,
       but recommended

2013. <http://www.mkgandhi.org/
nonviolence/D_sword.htm>.

Paul is satisfied that quoting is best in this case. Why? Because Gandhi's words are distinctive and indicate a tone and sensibility that would be lost in a summary or paraphrase.

Paraphrasing

What Does It Mean to Paraphrase a Source?

When you paraphrase a source, you basically restate what you've read from a text or a part of a text. Like when you summarize a source, you capture the author's main idea—usually the main idea behind an entire book or movie, for example—in your own words (for more on summary, see p. 384). However, when you *paraphrase* a source, you capture *all* of the author's ideas in your own words—including details and supporting evidence. Typically you won't paraphrase an entire source; instead you'll probably paraphrase a passage or a sentence or two.

Paraphrasing is handy when you want to share specifics but don't want to use the author's exact original wording. While quoting can be a good option (pp. 370–73), there are times when you want the voice to be all your own. There are still other times when an author's tone is not a good fit for your purpose and audience; in these cases, use paraphrase to present that author's perspective smoothly.

A paraphrase should:

> » Provide not only the big-picture message of a source, but also the details that the author uses to support his or her argument.

> » Be in your own words and voice, with the same level of formality and vocabulary as the rest of your piece.

> » Change both the words and the order of the ideas presented in the original.

> » Usually end up being close to the same length as the original.

> » Give credit to the author of the source being paraphrased. If you are using MLA or APA conventions, be sure to credit your source with an in-text citation and correlating entry for the Works Cited or References list.

Let's look at an example. Shelby Prince, a student writing about therapeutic uses of music (p. 377), found a blog called *The Contrapuntist*, where she read a post by Miguel Cano, titled "How Music Saved My Life, and Why Music Education Should Be Taken More Seriously." She wanted to integrate Cano's experience into her writing without shifting over to his voice. She decided to paraphrase.

ORIGINAL PASSAGE FROM *THE CONTRAPUNTIST*

That sad instrument became my life; it became my outlet to express my frustration with teenage life. I took it everywhere, practiced everywhere and played for everyone. Like every other 15-year-old, my dream was to become a rock star. I wanted to be like my guitar heroes Alex Skolnick (from Testament), and Marty Friedman (formerly from Megadeth). Eventually, I became introduced to classical guitar music.

☞ Attention, writers! How to paraphrase fairly.

When you paraphrase a passage from a source, make sure that the details you paraphrase are consistent with the "big picture" of your source; for example, if a source's author is positive overall about an experimental drug treatment, it would be unfair to paraphrase only the few negative details provided. However, it would be okay to mention the negative details, provided that you offer them in the context of the author's main (pro-treatment) argument.

The Contrapuntist
Culture Through | A Musical Lens

How Music Saved My Life, and Why Music Education Should Be Taken More Seriously

by CONTRAPUNTIST
In MUSIC EDUCATION

A few days ago I came across a story reported by Reuters that Venezuelan President Hugo Chavez public music programs have taken 300,000 kids out of slums in a country with some of the "highest murder rates in the world." I reminisced about how music saved my life. I grew up in a middle class home with a family that made decent income, but the city was plagued with gang activity and poverty when I lived there.

At the end of my freshman year of high school, my grandfather brought me my first nylon/classical guitar from Paracho, Mexico. It was a mediocre instrument, good for a beginner. In fact, if I tried to play it now, it's so warped that after hitting a few notes it would sound like Arnold Schoenberg meets Henry Cowell, while attempting to play J. S. Bach. Sad! That sad instrument became my life; it became my outlet to express my frustration with teenage life. I took it everywhere, practiced everywhere and played for everyone. Like every other 15-year-old, my dream was to become a rock star. I wanted to be like my guitar heroes Alex Skolnick (from Testament), and Marty Friedman (formerly from Megadeth). Eventually, I became introduced to classical guitar music.

SHELBY'S PARAPHRASE
Before classical guitar music entered his life, the blogger fantasized about becoming a rock star like Alex Skolnick or Marty Friedman, and became almost physically attached to the guitar. That guitar enabled him to cope with his teenage angst (*The Contrapuntist*).

parenthetical citation
names source

▲ BLOG POST
Miguel Cano, "How Music Saved My Life." This excerpt can be found at the *Contrapuntist* blog. *Miguel Cano.*

When Should I Paraphrase a Source?

Consider paraphrasing in the following situations:

When you don't want to quote an author directly You may decide not to quote because you don't want too many competing voices in your piece. In this case, you could paraphrase the sentences from your source, keeping your voice dominant. (See "When Should I Quote from a Source?" on p. 372.)

When *your* audience is very different from your source author's audience For example, the source you are using may have been written for a specialized or technical audience, and the language might not be suitable for your readers. That is the case in the first example on page 378. A student is writing for an audience of nonexperts about various approaches to treating people convicted of crimes. However, one of her sources is very technical; it was written for criminologists and who are familiar with legal terminology. This is an excellent opportunity to paraphrase. The following passage is from an article titled "A Comparative Recidivism Analysis of Releasees from Private and Public Prisons," by Lonn Lanza-Kaduce, Karen F. Parker, and Charles W. Thomas, from the journal *Crime & Delinquency*.

ORIGINAL PASSAGE

Recidivism was operationalized in alternative ways. FDOC records on arrest histories, sentencing, and the movement of inmates in and out of prison were the sources of the data, which were used to develop five different indicators of recidivism.

STUDENT'S PARAPHRASE

authors named in signal phrase; no parenthetical citation needed

Lanza-Kaduce, Parker, and Thomas examined the Florida Department of Correction's records, looking for signs that a prison releasee had returned to prison, such as a record of the releasee's being arrested again or sentenced to another prison term.

You want your writing to flow with your own ideas and words; you want your tone to dominate   Paraphrasing allows you to convey all of your source's information, but in your own consistent words and style. For example, imagine you are writing a blog entry in a very informal, snappy tone, and you want to paraphrase the very formal speech Queen Elizabeth II gave in Dublin in 2011.

ORIGINAL PASSAGE

Indeed, so much of this visit reminds us of the complexity of our history, its many layers and traditions, but also the importance of forbearance and conciliation. Of being able to bow to the past, but not be bound by it.

STUDENT'S PARAPHRASE (with humorous intent)

author named in signal phrase; no parenthetical citation needed

The Queen remarked that you gotta remember the past, baby, but you can't let it hold you back. Our relationship's had problems, she told the Irish, but that don't mean it's gotta end.

Note: This paraphrase style can work for nonacademic genres; however, for formal research papers, we do not recommend this technique.

For an entertaining look at the opposite situation—a writer paraphrasing extremely informal writing to make it more formal—check out the Twitter feed for Queen's English 50c, in which the writer (Andrew O'Neill, a British comedian) translates the rapper 50 Cent's tweets into "proper English."

How Do I Paraphrase a Source?

When you want to paraphrase a source, do the following:

Read (or view or listen to) the passage

Put the source away and write down the passage from memory   This ensures that you are articulating the ideas in your own words.

Restate the sentence or passage in your own words—while maintaining the sense of the author's original words   The following paraphrase retains the meaning of the original passage (from an article by Edison Elementary, "HG/HGT Education") while transforming it into a totally different voice and structure.

ORIGINAL PASSAGE
Giftedness is a collection of certain characteristics that have been displayed by remarkable adults and children past and present. Among the gifted there is great diversity; they are not a homogeneous group.

STUDENT'S PARAPHRASE author named in signal phrase; no parenthetical citation needed
According to educators at Edison Elementary, gifted adults or children are unique individuals who exhibit traits that make them stand out from their peers.

Think of paraphrasing as rephrasing. When you paraphrase, you do more than swap out key words with similar words. Below is an example of an unsuccessful paraphrase created through an inadvisable technique called "patch writing." When people patch write, they simply switch out key words and replace them with synonyms. The result is clunky at best.

The shaded words in the original (again, from the "HG/HGT Education" article by Edison Elementary) are the words the writer replaced with synonyms in the patch-written version.

ORIGINAL PASSAGE
Giftedness is a collection of certain characteristics that have been displayed by remarkable adults and children past and present.

STUDENT'S UNSUCCESSFUL PARAPHRASE (what NOT to do)
According to educators at Edison Elementary, specialness is a group of particular traits that have been shown by extraordinary people of all ages throughout time.

Notice how the patch-written version is not all that different from the original passage—only now it lacks style and voice. The writer chose to switch out words, for example, replacing *collection* with *group*. He also did not change the sentence structure or word order, and kept many of the smaller words (articles and prepositions) as they were in the original. The writer would have done better to use the original quote.

Compare your sentence(s) to the original, making sure that you have altered the language and style enough so that the words are your own

Compare your sentence(s) to the original, making sure that you haven't altered the meaning or intent of the author   Keep in mind that there are some words that you cannot change without changing the meaning of the author's content. Proper nouns and numbers, for example, should not be changed.

Always, always, always attribute your paraphrase to its source   Use the style that is appropriate to the genre you're composing in. For academic genres, see MLA and APA guidelines on pages 395–435.

▲ STUDENT AUTHOR
Paul Pierre.

Guided Process: How to Paraphrase a Source ▼

Paul Pierre (Student)

Nonviolent Protest Project: Paraphrasing Julia Bacha

Paul, who is writing about nonviolent protest, finds a presentation by documentary filmmaker Julia Bacha. In it, Bacha argues that nonviolent protest is ignored by the media and tells a story about nonviolent protest in a Palestinian town, a story she portrays in her documentary *Budrus*. Following is a step-by-step look at how Paul paraphrased from this source. Images presented on pages 381–83 are stills from Bacha's documentary film. *(Julia Bacha's presentation and images appear courtesy of Just Vision Media.)*

JUST VISION

HOME ABOUT US FILMS VISIONARIES RESOURCES GET INVOLVED EVENTS NEWS STORE **DONATE**

JULIA BACHA (Director, Producer, 2009)   العربية   עברית

Budrus

TRANSCRIPT: I'm a filmmaker. For the last 8 years, I have dedicated my life to documenting the work of Israelis and Palestinians who are trying to end the conflict using peaceful means. When I travel with my work across Europe and the United States, one question always comes up: Where is the Palestinian Gandhi? Why aren't Palestinians using nonviolent resistance?

The challenge I face when I hear this question is that often I have just returned from the Middle East where I spent my time filming dozens of Palestinians who are using nonviolence to defend their lands and water resources from Israeli soldiers and settlers. These leaders are trying to forge a massive national nonviolent movement to end the occupation and build peace in the region. Yet, most of you have probably never heard about them. This divide between what's happening on the ground and perceptions abroad is one of the key reasons why we don't have yet a Palestinian peaceful resistance movement that has been successful.

I'm [going to] talk about the power of attention, the power of your attention, and the emergence and de-

Paul's notes on Bacha's presentation

1. *I watched Bacha's entire presentation.* Then I watched it again. One section of what Bacha said really stood out for me—where she talks about a specific nonviolent protest in Budrus. I think I might want to use some of this in my audio essay. I watched that section of her talk a few times.

2. *Next, I read the transcript.* The entire text of Bacha's talk is available online. I focused especially on the passage that includes the Budrus story.

3. *I put the transcript aside, and paraphrased the passage from memory.* Here is what I came up with:

MY DRAFT PARAPHRASE (of Bacha)
Violent and nonviolent protesters are similar in that to be effective, they need an audience to respond to them. When the media fails to cover nonviolent protest, they deprive nonviolent protestors of an audience (Bacha).

parenthetical citation
names author of source

JUST VISION

HOME   ABOUT US   FILMS   VISIONARIES   RESOURCES   GET INVOLVED   EVENTS   NEWS   STORE   DONATE

JULIA BACHA   (Director, Producer, 2009)   العربية   עברית

velopment of nonviolent movements in the West Bank, Gaza and elsewhere—but . . . my case study is going to be Palestine. I believe that what's mostly missing for nonviolence to grow is not for Palestinians to start adopting nonviolence, but for us to start paying attention to those who already are. Allow me to illustrate this point by taking you to this village called Budrus.

About seven years ago, they faced extinction, because Israel announced it would build a separation barrier, and part of this barrier would be built on top of the village. They would lose 40 percent of their land and be surrounded, so they would lose free access to the rest of the West Bank. Through inspired local leadership, they launched a peaceful resistance campaign to stop that from happening.

Let me show you some brief clips, so you have a sense for what that actually looked like on the ground.

FROM THE DOCUMENTARY *BUDRUS*:

Palestinian Woman: We were told the wall would separate Palestine from Israel. Here in Budrus, we realized the wall would steal our land.

We were told the Wall would

Israeli Man: The fence has, in fact, created a solution to terror.

Man: Today you're invited to a peaceful march. You are joined by dozens of your Israeli brothers and sisters.

Continues next page

Paul's notes on Bacha's presentation

4. I reread the passage in the transcript and evaluated my draft paraphrase. I thought I could have done a better job in paraphrasing/restating what Bacha had to say.

5. I revised and finalized my paraphrase. I thought the wording of my draft paraphrase was not different enough from Bacha's original text, especially in voice and structure. Here's how I revised to correct those problems:

MY IN-TEXT CITATION (paraphrase of Bacha)

Bacha named in signal phrase, so no parenthetical citation needed

Julia Bacha points out that all protesters—including nonviolent ones—need an audience in order to matter. It's a problem that violent protests are the ones we read about, the ones that get attention. When the media fails to cover nonviolent protest, she argues, they deprive peaceful protesters of an audience and of the potential to make a difference.

6. I cited Bacha as a source in my Works Cited list. Although audio essays don't usually include a Works Cited list, my instructor asked me to submit one with my Artist's Statement. This caused me some strife because the MLA style for documenting digital sources is confusing to me. However, after consulting a handbook, I cited my source as follows:

MY WORKS CITED ENTRY (MLA style)

title of short work

author name   from Web site   site title

Bacha, Julia. "Budrus." *Just Vision.*

publication

site sponsor   date   medium

Just Vision, Inc. Aug. 2011. Web.

URL; not MLA-required, but recommended

access date

5 Sept. 2013. <www.justvision.org/budrus>.

JUST VISION

HOME   ABOUT US   FILMS   VISIONARIES   RESOURCES   GET INVOLVED   EVENTS   NEWS   STORE   DONATE

JULIA BACHA   (Director, Producer, 2009)   العربية   עברית

to a peaceful march.

Israeli Activist: Nothing scares the army more than non-violent opposition.

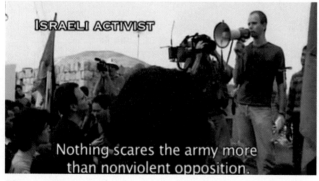

ISRAELI ACTIVIST

Nothing scares the army more
than nonviolent opposition.

Woman: We saw the men trying to push the soldiers, but none of them could do that. But I think the girls could do it.

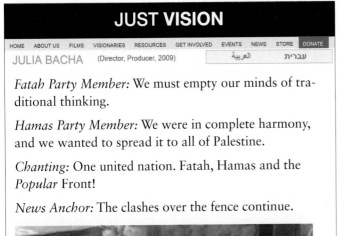

JUST **VISION**

HOME   ABOUT US   FILMS   VISIONARIES   RESOURCES   GET INVOLVED   EVENTS   NEWS   STORE   DONATE

JULIA BACHA   (Director, Producer, 2009)   العربية   עברית

Fatah Party Member: We must empty our minds of traditional thinking.

Hamas Party Member: We were in complete harmony, and we wanted to spread it to all of Palestine.

Chanting: One united nation. Fatah, Hamas and the *Popular* Front!

News Anchor: The clashes over the fence continue.

They were allowed to use any force necessary

Reporter: Israeli border police were sent to disperse the crowd. They were allowed to use any force necessary.

(Gunshots)

Man: These are live bullets. It's like Fallujah. Shooting everywhere.

Israeli Activist: I was sure we were all going to die. But there were others around me who weren't even cowering.

Israeli Soldier: A nonviolent protest is not going to stop the [unclear].

Protester: This is a peaceful march. There is no need to use violence.

Chanting: We can do it! We can do it! We can do it!

In the paraphrase above (and in his summary on p. 387), Paul strips out references to Palestinians and Israelis. He believes Bacha's idea is relevant to conflicts outside of the Middle East, so he captures Bacha's comparison of violent and nonviolent protest but omits the details of the parties involved.

Pierre, *Paraphrasing Julia Bacha*   383

Summarizing

What Does It Mean to Summarize a Source?

When you summarize a source, you pare the whole thing down to its essence. You eliminate all specific details and give your reader the main point of what the source's author is saying. For example, you might summarize a source in the text of a paper you are writing when you want to investigate or compare the main ideas behind several different sources.

When you summarize, you should:

» Capture the ideas of the source's author.

» Be considerably shorter than the original work. For example, if you are summarizing a two-page article, your summary might be only a paragraph or less. (In the example on p. 370, a student writer summarizes twenty-one paragraphs in just one sentence.)

» Write in your own words—not the words of the source's author.

» Give credit to the author of the source summarized. Depending on the genre you compose in, the conventions for crediting sources differ. (In the example below, the student uses a signal phrase to name her source author.)

☞ **Attention, researchers! Summarizing versus paraphrasing.**

When you summarize a passage from a source, you pick up on *the main points* the author is making and describe them in your own words. When you paraphrase, on the other hand, you do provide a type of summary—but one in which you restate/rephrase the author's words (not just the main points). Summarizing and paraphrasing are both subjective actions, and require you to retain the spirit of the author's meaning and ideas, even if you use them to contrast with your own.

Let's return to Shelby, the student who is writing about therapeutic uses of music. She finds an article in the blog section of *The Huffington Post* by opera singer Susanne Mentzer, titled "The Catharsis of Song."

Shelby decides she wants to include the opera singer's perspective in her paper, but she wants to do so broadly and briefly, in her Introduction, to draw in her readers. Following are the first few paragraphs from Mentzer's post—as well as Shelby's summary of the post (which she read in its entirety at the *Huffington Post* blog).

SHELBY'S SUMMARY OF AN ENTIRE ARTICLE
Opera singer Susanne Mentzer has used singing to alleviate both her own stress and tension and the stress and tension of others.

When Should I Summarize a Source?

As a researcher and writer, you might choose to summarize a source when you want to capture the main ideas of a source without going into details. As in the example of Shelby's summary above, the details of Mentzer's experiences, such as crying during rehearsal, are irrelevant to Shelby's point about the therapeutic nature of music; what matters to Shelby is that Mentzer, a professional singer, has experienced the therapeutic aspects of music in several different contexts.

THE **BLOG** | *Featuring fresh takes and real-time analysis from HuffPost's signature lineup of contributors*

Susanne Mentzer
Opera singer

The Catharsis of Song

Posted: 09/08/11 07:42 PM ET

The human singing voice has the power to release deep emotions. Many know of sounds that give us goosebumps. From the point of view of one who makes sounds, I refer to it as my primal scream therapy. The wonderfulness of singing can be the primal, super-human sound that pours out of one's body. It can also be humbling.

It is thought that hearing is the last sense to leave us when we die. Over the past year, I sang both my parents into the next world. In the ICU, for my mother, an amateur singer who was particularly proud of me, I think I sang my entire repertoire of hymns and arias, toned down to a low dynamic. At one point she awakened with a smile and said, in the slow, whispered voice of one who could barely breathe, "You were singing!" I am not sure if Dad heard me in his last hours, but I would like to think so. It was a privilege that I would not trade for the world.

Even in my career I have had my own cathartic release of emotion. I once sang a matinee opera performance in Bonn, Germany, after having just put my 10-month old son and his father into a taxi to the airport to fly to the States. It was excruciatingly painful to let my child go but I was contractually obligated to stay. I went to the theater, sang my guts out, and became a blubbering idiot during curtain calls. (Fortunately, it was a dramatic role, the Composer in Strauss's Ariadne auf Naxos.) My colleagues mentioned that I was really "on" that show and that I gave so much emotion. Only then did I share what I was really crying about.

Here's another example. Let's say your project is on skateboarding, and you want to draw on an NPR story by Sarah Reynolds titled "Fingerboarding: Skateboarding without 'Fear Factor.'" The audio article is four minutes long. Rather than detailing the whole recording, you decide you only care about fingerboarding and how popular it's become. This is a perfect situation for summarizing. Of course, you'd credit Sarah Reynolds in your text and Works Cited or References list.

How Do I Summarize a Source?

To summarize a source, do the following:

» Read (or view or listen to) the source.

» Put the source away and write down the main ideas from memory. This ensures that you are articulating the ideas in your own words.

» Look over the main ideas you wrote down and organize them. For example, begin with a general statement and then move on to the supporting ideas.

» Also, make sure you're simply capturing the main ideas and arguments of the source's author, and not adding any of your own opinions.

» Go back and reread or re-listen to or review the original source. Compare it to what you've written to make sure you haven't distorted any of the points. Make sure you also haven't left out any of the central points.

Attribute your summary to its source. Do this not only in your text but in your Works Cited or References list as well.

▲ ORIGINAL SOURCE
Susanne Mentzer, "The Catharsis of Song." This article was published at *The Blog,* which is hosted by *The Huffington Post.* Shown here are just the first few paragraphs. © 9/8/11 Huffington Post. All rights reserved. Used by permission and protected by the Copyright Laws of the United States. The printing, copying, redistribution, or retransmission of this Content without express written permission is prohibited.

▲ STUDENT AUTHOR
Paul Pierre.

Guided Process: How to Summarize a Source ▼

Paul Pierre (Student)

Nonviolent Protest Project: Summarizing Julia Bacha

Paul, who earlier in this chapter paraphrased a passage from a talk by Julia Bacha, decides that he wants to summarize a different passage. Following are the steps he took. *(Julia Bacha's presentation and images appear courtesy of Just Vision Media.)*

JUST VISION

| HOME | ABOUT US | FILMS | VISIONARIES | RESOURCES | GET INVOLVED | EVENTS | NEWS | STORE | DONATE |

JULIA BACHA (Director, Producer, 2009)   العربية   עברית

Budrus

TRANSCRIPT: When I first heard about the story of Budrus, I was surprised that the international media had failed to cover the extraordinary set of events that happened seven years ago, in 2003. What was even more surprising was the fact that Budrus was successful. The residents, after 10 months of peaceful resistance, convinced the Israeli government to move the route of the barrier off their lands and to the green line, which is the internationally recognized boundary between Israel and the Palestinian Territories. The resistance in Budrus has since spread to villages across the West Bank and to Palestinian neighborhoods in Jerusalem. Yet the media remains mostly silent on these stories. This silence carries profound consequences for the likelihood that nonviolence can grow, or even survive, in Palestine.

Violent resistance and nonviolent resistance share one very important thing in common; they are both a form of theater seeking an audience to their cause. If violent

Paul's notes on Bacha's presentation

1. *I revisited Bacha's talk,* and was struck by a passage in which she gives a viewpoint on Palestine and nonviolent resistance. I decided to include that material, in some way, in my audio essay.

2. *I reread the transcript,* focusing on the section on Palestine and non-violent resistance. I decided that it might be best to summarize Bacha's argument.

3. *I drafted a summary of the passage.* To do this, I put the transcript away, and tried to provide an overview of what Bacha said in this part of her talk. Here is what I wrote:

MY DRAFT SUMMARY (of Bacha's passage)

Bacha named in signal phrase, so no parenthetical citation needed

Bacha says that residents of the Palestinian town of Budrus were able to successfully protest against the Israeli building of a fence using nonviolent strategies; however, the news reports of the conflict all focused on a few incidents that involved violence.

4. *Next, I re-viewed Bacha's talk.* I wanted to make sure I had accurately captured her point. Satisfied that I had, I put the summary away for the night.

5. *I revised my summary of Bacha's point.* The next day, when I reread my

JUST VISION

HOME   ABOUT US   FILMS   VISIONARIES   RESOURCES   GET INVOLVED   EVENTS   NEWS   STORE   DONATE

JULIA BACHA   (Director, Producer, 200   العربية   עברית

actors are the only ones constantly getting front-page covers and attracting international attention to the Palestinian issue, it becomes very hard for nonviolent leaders to make the case to their communities that civil disobedience is a viable option in addressing their plight.

Paul's notes on Bacha's presentation

summary, I decided to cut back on some details of what Bacha had to say. Specifically, I opted not to mention that the Palestinians protested against Israel. For my audio essay, I wanted to stay focused on my main argument—that the media doesn't give enough attention to nonviolent protest—and didn't want to sidetrack my audience with the politics surrounding the protest itself. With this in mind, I revised as follows:

MY REVISED SUMMARY (of Bacha's passage)

Bacha describes and shows clips of protests in the Middle East that were completely nonviolent. This is in stark contrast to the media reports of the conflict, which failed to mention the nonviolent protests and focused on a handful of violent skirmishes.

6. *Next, I included my summary of Bacha's point in my audio essay. I drew on Bacha's words to support my argument that nonviolent protest is more powerful than violent protest.*

7. *I cited Bacha's talk as a source in my Works Cited list.*

MY WORKS CITED ENTRY (MLA style)

title of short work

author name   from Web site ┌— site title

Bacha, Julia. "Budrus." *Just Vision*.

publication

site sponsor   date   medium

Just Vision, Inc. Aug. 2011. Web.

URL; not MLA-required,

access date   but recommended

5 Sept. 2013. <www.justvision.org/budrus>.

Avoiding Plagiarism

Plagiarism is misrepresenting the ideas or words of others as your own. It includes submitting papers you didn't write, failing to adequately cite sources, and copying small bits and pieces from sources into your own work without properly documenting them. Plagiarism is unethical and committing an act of plagiarism can have serious consequences on your grade, your academic career, and your karma. Your school probably has a statement on academic integrity, defining penalties for acts of academic dishonesty. Be sure to familiarize yourself with the academic integrity policy at your school.

Comparing Passages from a Source

Some plagiarism is unintentional. Writers may read several sources that express similar ideas and only cite one of these sources. Or writers may forget which source they got an idea from and not cite any source at all. Another all-too-common type of unintentional plagiarism occurs when a writer tries to paraphrase a source but doesn't significantly change the original source's language. Here are a couple of examples:

Original passage   From a podcast by Adam Hinterthuer, found online at *Scientific American*:

> Want to live a happier life? Try surrounding yourself with happy friends or at least find friends with happy friends. A study published online December 4th in the *British Medical Journal* says happiness can quickly go viral within your social network.

Passage plagiarized   The writer misrepresents the source; the source's author, Hinterthuer, is cited, but the writer has gotten the content wrong. Hinterthuer mentions only one study—not "a lot":

> There is a lot of research indicating that happiness is contagious. Simply surrounding yourself with happy friends can make you a happier person (Hinterthuer).

Passage plagiarized   In this case, the writer needs to provide an in-text citation. He/she has not shown that this information was obtained from the source, Hinterthuer:

> Recent research indicates that happiness is contagious. Simply surrounding yourself with happy friends can make you a happier person.

Passage correctly presented with an in-text citation

SUMMARY WITH MLA IN-TEXT CITATION
Recent research indicates that happiness is contagious. Simply surrounding yourself with happy friends can make you a happier person (Hinterthuer).

WORKS CITED ENTRY
Hinterthuer, Adam. "Happiness Is Contagious." *Scientific American*. Scientific American, Inc. 5 Dec. 2008. Web. 20 Aug. 2011. <http://www.scientificamerican.com/podcast/episode.cfm?id=happiness-is-contagious-08-12-05>.

SUMMARY WITH APA IN-TEXT CITATION
Recent research indicated that happiness is contagious. Simply surrounding yourself with happy friends can make you a happier person (Hinterthuer, 2008).

REFERENCES LIST ENTRY
Hinterthuer, Adam. "Happiness is contagious." *Scientific American*. MP3 audio file.
    http://www.scientificamerican.com/podcast/episode.cfm?id=happiness-is
    -contagious-08-12-05.

It's important to realize that whether plagiarism is intentional or unintentional, it is a violation of academic ethics and most schools' codes of conduct. If in doubt about whether to cite a source, cite it. This will prevent you from unintentionally plagiarizing. (For more on avoiding plagiarism, see below.)

CHECKLIST Getting Help and Avoiding Plagiarism

☐ **Visit your writing center.** If you don't know how to properly summarize or paraphrase a source, consult your instructor or a writing-center tutor for help. It's never a good idea to plagiarize and then plan to apologize if caught. If you're not sure if you're using source material in a way that constitutes plagiarism, get help: Take your draft to your instructor or a tutor and explain what you're having trouble with. As long as you haven't yet turned in the paper, you haven't done anything wrong.

☐ **Use detection software.** If your school subscribes to a plagiarism-detection program like turnitin.com, you can submit a draft of your writing to the program and it will generate a report that indicates what percentage of the draft is from other sources. The report will alert you to places where you've used sources without properly citing them.

☐ **Manage your time.** Allow yourself enough time to complete your writing assignment. Sometimes students accidentally plagiarize because they don't give themselves time to properly double-check all their citations.

☐ **When in doubt, cite that source.** Remember, too, that using an image, audio clip, or video is just like quoting words from someone. These texts need to be cited just as any other source would be.

How to Avoid Plagiarism during Your Research & Composing Process

There are certain crucial moments when researchers and writers can make mistakes that can lead to plagiarism. Please be especially careful at these points:

When taking notes as you conduct research Get in the habit of recording the source's bibliographic information and using quotation marks anytime you use the exact words of a source, even if you use just a few words from the source. For example, you might write in your notes:

> **Source:** *Our Stressful Lives* site, http://www.ourstressfullives.com/pets-and-stress-relief.html
> *About the source:* This site is authored by a "Certified Stress Management Coach," Jill Rheaume, who has also published a stress management workbook. She offers a variety of tips for stress management. I found the following article from the "Pets and Stress Relief: Other Benefits" section of the site, mainly from paragraph 9.

Notes: Rheaume writes (in paragraph 3) that pets "make great listeners" and help reduce stress in many other ways. In paragraph 9 she writes: "Pets also increase the 'love chemical' oxytocin in our brains. In addition, they can also increase our serotonin, known as the 'happiness chemical.' Both of these things can help to reduce or even prevent stress and prove that our pets can increase our feelings of happiness and help to improve our moods."

▼ WEB SITE
Jill Rheaume,
Our Stressful Lives.
By permission of Jill
Rheaume, Owner/Editor
of OurStressfulLives.com.

Alternatively, you might want to create a screen capture of each source (or otherwise save the original content), so you can refer back to the original as you write.

Our Stressful Lives
Helping you live a less stressful life.^{SM}

HOME   WHAT'S NEW   SUBMISSIONS   PRODUCTS

About Me

Welcome to OurStressfulLives.com!

My name is Jill Rheaume and I live in Kansas, USA. Thank you for visiting my website and taking the time to get to know a bit about me and why I created this site.

For me, stress was always something that I struggled with. I enjoyed writing and journaling and that helped relieve some of my stress... but that by itself just wasn't good enough.

Then, in late 2007, I met a man who became my "life guru". He taught me that stress is not insurmountable and he gave me practical tools to manage my stress so that I could begin living a happier and healthier life.

I consider myself and my life a constant work in progress and one of the things I've learned along the way is that proper stress management is not only necessary, it is also my passion.

I have spent a lot of time researching and trying different techniques to better manage the day-to-day stress in my life and now that I've mastered my own stress, as a Stress Management Coach, my goal is to help you do the same.

Jill R.

Pets and Stress Relief

Pets and Stress Relief: How Your Pet Can Help You Relieve Your Stress

It's a proven fact that the pets that we love so much do actually help to relieve our stress... something that many pet owners probably already suspected.

I am personally a huge animal lover and so this is a particular topic that I am very excited to share with you.

Companionship

Our pets are great companions. They can help us avoid feelings of loneliness and are often our confidants... they make great listeners. And unless you've trained your pet to talk (as you can with some birds) they don't give back talk or argue.

Gaining the Health Benefits of Pets

Health Benefits of Pets

As an animal lover and pet owner, it seems quite obvious to me that my pets make me "feel better". They certainly cheer me up when I'm down, give me comfort when I'm sad or scared, and make me laugh when I least expect it. So I wondered... what are the health benefits of having a pet?

Stress Relief

Any pet owner can probably tell you a funny story about something their "little baby" did. Animals have a way of being quite humorous and laughter is a great way to relieve stress! But in addition to laughter, they can create feelings of calm and love through the natural increase of a chemical called <u>Oxytocin "the love hormone"</u>.

They can help to increase the amount of physical activity we receive and decrease our blood pressure. All of which can help relieve stress.

When quoting as you draft   Always put quotation marks around the words you're using from the source. (In this case, there are quotation marks within quotation marks.)

MLA QUOTATION (no in-text cite needed because author is named)
Rheaume writes: "Pets also increase the 'love chemical' oxytocin in our brains."

WORKS CITED ENTRY
Rheaume, Jill. "Pets and Stress Relief: Other Benefits." *Our Stressful Lives*. Rheaume
     Writing Co., n.d. Web. 20 Aug. 2013. <http://www.ourstressfullives.com/
     pets-and-stress-relief.html>.

APA IN-TEXT CITATION
Rheaume wrote: "Pets also increase the 'love chemical' oxytocin in our brains."

REFERENCES LIST ENTRY
Rheaume, Jill. "Pets and stress relief: Other benefits." OurStressfulLives.com. Re-
     trieved from http://www.ourstressfullives.com/pets-and-stress-relief.html.

When paraphrasing as you draft   Always credit the source you're paraphrasing. If you aren't sure if you've adequately rephrased the source's idea in your
own words, ask a friend, classmate, or writing-center tutor to compare the original
passage with your paraphrase. One trick to use when paraphrasing is to read the
passage you want to paraphrase and then put the source out of sight and rewrite
the idea in your own words. When you do this, you minimize the chance of accidentally using the words of the original. A paraphrase of the above content from Jill
Rheaume's site follows. Note that even though we're not using Rheaume's exact
words, we still provide the in-text citation.

PARAPHRASE WITH MLA IN-TEXT CITATION
Pets can make us healthier by raising the levels of oxytocin and serotonin in our brains
(Rheaume).

WORKS CITED ENTRY
Rheaume, Jill. "Pets and Stress Relief: Other Benefits." *Our Stressful Lives*. Rheaume
     Writing Co., n.d. Web. 20 Aug. 2013. <http://www.ourstressfullives.com/
     pets-and-stress-relief.html>.

PARAPHRASE WITH APA IN-TEXT CITATION
Pets can make us healthier by raising the levels of oxytocin and serotonin in our brains
(Rheaume).

REFERENCES LIST ENTRY
Rheaume, Jill. "Pets and stress relief: Other benefits." OurStressfulLives.com. Re-
     trieved from http://www.ourstressfullives.com/pets-and-stress-relief.html.

When summarizing as you draft   You can use the same strategies for summarizing that you use for paraphrasing.

SUMMARY IN MLA STYLE (no in-text citation needed because author is named)
Stress management coach Jill Rheaume writes that interactions with our pets can
make us happier and more loving by altering levels of certain chemicals in the brain.

WORKS CITED ENTRY
Rheaume, Jill. "Pets and Stress Relief: Other Benefits." *Our Stressful Lives*. Rheaume
     Writing Co., n.d. Web. 20 Aug. 2013. <http://www.ourstressfullives.com/
     pets-and-stress-relief.html>.

SUMMARY WITH APA IN-TEXT CITATION

Stress management coach Jill Rheaume wrote that interactions with our pets can make us happier and more loving by altering levels of certain chemicals in the brain (2008-2012, para. 9).

REFERENCES LIST ENTRY

Rheaume, Jill. "Pets and stress relief: Other benefits." OurStressfulLives.com. Retrieved from http://www.ourstressfullives.com/pets-and-stress-relief.html.

When drafting—without referring to notes   Don't trust your memory! Writers sometimes don't cite sources in their drafts, thinking they'll go back later and add citations. This is a dangerous practice because if you run out of time and end up not adding those citations, you've plagiarized. *Always cite your sources*, even in a rough draft.

When integrating sources   When in doubt as to whether or not you should cite a source, cite it. It's always better to give too much credit with source citations than to give insufficient credit. You may wonder, for example, if a piece of information counts as "general knowledge," and therefore doesn't need to be cited. If you're not sure if it counts as "general knowledge," go ahead and cite a source.

How to Avoid Plagiarism When Using Online Sources

As tempting as it is to copy and paste chunks of online sources into your notes or drafts, minimize this practice because it greatly increases your chances of accidentally plagiarizing. Get in the habit of putting quotation marks around every direct quote. If you paraphrase or summarize, copy the original text into a document and indicate clearly—with color coding, highlighting, labeling, or some other device—that it is the original content from your source, and then work on your composition in a separate document. Another strategy is to create screen captures of each online source, always accompanied by the URL that will lead you back to that content.

How to Avoid Plagiarism When Composing a Multigenre/Multimodal Project

All the above guidelines apply to multigenre/multimodal projects: Cite your sources in drafts, give credit generously, and be meticulous about using quotation marks around quoted material in your notes. Even if you are composing in a genre or mode that doesn't use the MLA or APA format for citations, you still need to credit your sources in ways that are appropriate to the genre or mode of your composition. Additionally, your instructor may want you to submit a Works Cited list or an Author's or Artist's Statement that includes MLA or APA citations. (See Chapter 1, p. 35, for example.)

DOCUMENTING SOURCES:
A GUIDE TO MLA & APA STYLES

Documenting (or citing) a source means giving credit to the authors of any texts—including images, video, sound, or any other composition—that inform your writing, whether you're writing a research paper or creating other types of research-based compositions.

When you document sources, you show your audience where you got your information. You also develop your ethos as an author by showing that you've used reliable source material. Failing to give credit to your sources is a form of dishonesty and is considered plagiarism (pp. 387–92); it leads readers to conclude that all of the ideas and facts that you state come from your own independent thinking or research.

Whether you quote, paraphrase, or summarize from a source, you need to cite it. (For more on quoting, see pp. 370–75; for paraphrasing, see pp. 376–83; for summarizing, see pp. 384–87.)

As composers, when we cite sources, we do so using specific documentation styles. The documentation style you will use depends on the audience you're writing for: Are you writing for an academic audience, your peers, or a general/popular audience? Another factor is the subject matter you're writing about—and the discipline associated with that subject. For example, are your target readers associated with the humanities, social sciences, or sciences? The style you choose also depends on the genre you're composing in (e.g., whether you're writing a straight-up research paper or something else). Following are some guidelines for choosing a documentation style.

☞ **Attention, researchers! Why don't musicians document their sources when they sample music?**

Many hip-hop musicians use sampling (taking a part of a song) when they create their songs. For example, Nas's song "Can't Forget About You" includes a sample from Nat King Cole's classic "Unforgettable." Not only does the sample figure in the song, but clearly Nas's title was inspired by Nat King Cole. He doesn't provide formal documentation because it is a convention within the music industry that some sampling is deemed appropriate. This, however, is subject to legal interpretation if the original composer wants to challenge the originality of the composition. To avoid potential legal issues, most musicians will obtain permission prior to including samples in their own compositions—and include some kind of credit in the liner notes. If there *are* liner notes.

Composers of other genres often draw upon other sources; however, because of the conventions of the genres they're working in, they might not use formal academic documentation. Such genres include obituaries, memoirs, sets of instructions, and poems.

How to Choose a Documentation Style

Are you writing a research paper for a specific academic discipline?

» For papers for an English course or other humanities course or peer-reviewed journal, you will almost always use the documentation style of the Modern Language Association (MLA; mla.org). However, in some English courses that focus on writing in or across disciplines, you might use the documentation style that is associated with your major area of study.

» For papers for a social science course or peer-reviewed journal, you will probably use the format of the American Psychological Association (APA; apastyle.org).

» For papers for a history course or peer-reviewed journal, you will likely use *Chicago* style, based on *The Chicago Manual of Style* (chicagomanualofstyle.org).

» For papers for a science course or peer-reviewed journal, you will probably use the style specified by the Council of Science Editors in *Scientific Style and Format: The CSE Manual for Authors, Editors, and Publishers* (councilscienceeditors.org).

Are you composing a photo essay, ad, or documentary, or in some other alternative genre? And are your subject and audience based in the humanities, social sciences, or sciences? While MLA tends to be the default documentation style of the English composition course, and is likely the format your instructor may require, you might have the option of deciding for yourself which documentation style would be best for your composition and chosen subject. For example, if your topic involves criminal justice or gender studies, you could make a case for using APA style. And if you are creating a lab report or doctor's notes, you might use the CSE documentation style.

Most of our students submit MLA-style Works Cited lists with their compositions, though some, depending on their chosen genres, subjects, and major areas of study, use APA, *Chicago*, or CSE. If you plan to use one of these styles, you might want to discuss it with your instructor first, and make a case for why that style would be best.

Are you composing an Author's Statement to accompany your genre composition? If you are creating an Author's Statement to accompany your composition (whether it's a research paper or alternative genre project), we recommend the MLA style of documentation, unless you've made a case for using APA, *Chicago*, or CSE. (For more on the Author's Statement—the reflective piece that can be submitted with any genre composition—see pp. 233–46.)

While there are several documentation styles for you to choose from, the following sections of this chapter provide basic guidance for using MLA and APA styles, as these are the styles you are most likely to use in conjunction with this textbook.

MLA Style

The MLA style of documentation is presented in the *MLA Handbook for Writers of Research Papers*, 7th ed. (New York: MLA, 2009). It is commonly used in English courses and other courses in the humanities. This style has been around a long time, but it has evolved to take into account the many types of sources we work with today.

The MLA style of documentation has two main components:

1. In-text citations

2. List of Works Cited (a.k.a. Works Cited list)

The in-text citation   Each time you cite a source in your paper—whether through a signal phrase or a parenthetical reference—you cue readers to a corresponding entry in your Works Cited list. When you include an in-text citation, you:

» Name the author of your source

» Provide a page number for that source (if there is one)

» Make sure you have a corresponding entry in your Works Cited list

The list of Works Cited   In your Works Cited list, at the end of your paper, you:

» Provide publication information about each source

» Alphabetize your sources by authors' last names (or by title if an author is not provided)

» And although MLA makes this optional, we recommend that you include a URL for each online source. (For more on this, see the box on p. 402.)

Following is an example of an in-text citation along with its corresponding entry in the Works Cited list.

IN-TEXT CITATION

"Parents with this philosophy know there may be things their daughter hides from them, but they don't take it as a personal insult or an indication that their relationship with their daughter is weak" (Wiseman 54).

author — exact page that quotation is from

WORKS CITED ENTRY

author:
last name, first name ⎴ title of book ⎴ place of publication ⎴ publisher ⎴ publication year

Wiseman, Rosalind. *Queen Bees and Wannabes.* New York: Three Rivers Press, 2002.

page number ⎴ format

54. Print.

In-text citations: General guidelines   There are two main ways to handle an in-text citation: by using a signal phrase or a parenthetical reference (or some combination).

SIGNAL PHRASE (author named in phrase)

author

Wiseman suggests that "parents with this philosophy know there may be things their daughter hides from them, but they don't take it as a personal insult or an indication that their relationship with their daughter is weak" (54).

exact page that quotation is from

PARENTHETICAL REFERENCE (author cited in parentheses)

"Parents with this philosophy know there may be things their daughter hides from them, but they don't take it as a personal insult or an indication that their relationship with their daughter is weak" (Wiseman 54).

author ⎴ exact page that quotation is from

Works Cited entries: General guidelines   For each in-text citation in your paper, you need to provide a corresponding entry in your Works Cited list. The following guidelines provide the basic format for the MLA Works Cited entry.

» Name the author by last name, followed by first name.

author ⎴ book title ⎴ place of publication ⎴ publisher ⎴ year ⎴ page range

King, Stephen. *Full Dark, No Stars.* New York: Scribner-Simon & Schuster, 2010. 1-12.

format

PDF e-book.*

» Provide additional authors' or editors' names in normal order. Note that for university presses you should use the abbreviation "UP."

coeditors: last name, first name, then first name and last name ⎴ "eds." for "editors"

Bearman, Peter, Kathryn M. Neckerman, and Leslie Wright, eds. *After Tobacco: What*

book title ⎴ place of publication ⎴ publisher ⎴ publication year

Would Happen If Americans Stopped Smoking? New York: Columbia UP, 2011.

page range ⎴ format

30-36. Print.

———

*Provide a page range if your source is an e-book with numbered pages.

» Present the titles of long works—books or entire Web sites—in italics.

author · book title · place of publication · publisher · publication year

Burroughs, Augusten. *Running with Scissors*. New York: Picador-St. Martin's, 2002.

page range · format

113-17. Print.

author · Web site title · Web site sponsor

Sullivan, Andrew. *The Dish: Biased & Balanced*. The Newsweek / Daily Beast Company,

copyright year · format · date of access · URL

2012. Web. 8 Sept. 2013. <http://andrewsullivan.thedailybeast.com/>.

» Present the titles of short works—articles or other short pieces from books or Web sites—in quotation marks.

author · article title · magazine title · magazine date · page range · format

Parker, James. "Notes from the Underworld." *The Atlantic* May 2011. 38-41. Print.

author · article title · news site title

Acosta, Judith. "Do Guns Make the Man?" *Huffingtonpost.com*.

Web site sponsor · publication date · format · access date

TheHuffingtonPost.com, Inc., 21 Jul. 2011. Web. 8 Sept. 2013. <http://

URL

www.huffingtonpost.com/judith-acosta/do-guns-make-the-man_b_901918.html>.

» Present titles with initial capital letters—except in the case of articles (*a*, *the*, etc.), prepositions (*to*, *from*, *with*, etc.), or coordinating conjunctions (*and*, *but*, *or*, *for*, etc.), unless these words come first or last.

author · book title · place of publication · publisher · publication year · page range · format

Hemingway, Ernest. *To Have and Have Not*. New York: Scribner's, 1937. 1-4. Print.

author · book title · place of publication · publisher · publication year

Grafton, Sue. *V Is for Vengeance*. New York: Marion Wood-Penguin Putnam, 2011.

page range · format

12-13. PDF e-book.

» For print works, present the city of publication, but not the state.

author · book title · place of publication · publisher · publication year · page range

Atwood, Margaret. *The Blind Assassin*. New York: Anchor-Random House, 2001. 22-24.

format

Print.

» For print works, abbreviate publisher's names. For works published by an imprint, list the imprint, a hyphen, and the name of the publisher. The following book was published by Knopf, a division of Random House.

Lahiri, Jhumpa. *Unaccustomed Earth.* New York: Knopf-Random House, 2008. 52-56. [author] [book title] [place of publication] [publisher] [publication year] [page range]

PDF e-book. [format]

» For both print and online works, provide the date that the piece was published. For online sources, also include the date you accessed the source. For online sources, provide the URL in angle brackets at the end of the entry.

Sumners, Christina. "Animal Acumen: Elephantine Intelligence." *Inside NOVA.* [author] [article title] [site title]

PBS Online by WGBH Educational Foundation, 26 Aug. 2011. Web. 9 Sept. 2013. [site sponsor] [publication date] [format] [access date]

<http://www.pbs.org/wgbh/nova/insidenova/2011/08/elephants.html>. [URL]

» Provide the format or platform in which the work was delivered, such as "Print," "Web," "CD," "DVD," or "Lecture."

Gates, Henry Louis, Jr. *Life upon These Shores: Looking at African American History:* [author] [book title]

1513–2008. New York: Knopf-Random House, 2011. 112-14. Print. [place of publication] [publisher] [publication year] [page range] [format]

» Note that although MLA does not require it, we suggest that—for the sake of your audience—you identify the format of your source; in the first example below the format is: "video game." In other cases, as shown here, the identifier may be "video."

Microsoft. *Halo Reach.* Redmond: Microsoft Corp., 14 Sept. 2010. Xbox 360. Video game. [author] [title] [place of publication] [publisher] [publication year] [platform] [format]

Creative Commons. "Wanna Work Together?" Video. *Creative Commons.* [author] [title] [format] [site title]

Creative Commons, 2006. Web. 8 Sept. 2013. <http://creativecommons.org/videos/wanna-work-together>. [site sponsor] [publication date] [format] [access date] [URL]

Organize your Works Cited list alphabetically. For entries of more than one line, indent additional lines five spaces (this is called hanging indentation).

Works Cited

Acosta, Judith. "Do Guns Make the Man?" *Huffingtonpost.com.* TheHuffingtonPost.com, Inc., 21 Jul. 2011. Web. 8 Sept. 2013. <http://www.huffingtonpost.com/judith-acosta/do-guns-make-the-man_b_901918.html>.

Atwood, Margaret. *The Blind Assassin.* New York: Anchor-Random House, 2001. 22-24. Print.

Bearman, Peter, Kathryn M. Neckerman, and Leslie Wright, eds. *After Tobacco: What Would Happen If Americans Stopped Smoking?* New York: Columbia UP, 2011. 30-36. Print.

Burroughs, Augusten. *Running with Scissors.* New York: Picador-St. Martin's, 2002. 113-17. Print.

Creative Commons. "Wanna Work Together?" Video. *Creative Commons.* Creative Commons, 2006. Web. 8 Sept. 2013. <http://creativecommons.org/videos/ wanna-work-together>.

Gates, Henry Louis, Jr. *Life upon These Shores: Looking at African American History: 1513–2008.* New York: Knopf-Random House, 2011. 112-14. Print.

Grafton, Sue. *V Is for Vengeance.* New York: Marion Wood-Penguin Putnam, 2011. 12-13. PDF e-book.

Hemingway, Ernest. *To Have and Have Not.* New York: Scribner's, 1937. 1-4. Print.

King, Stephen. *Full Dark, No Stars.* New York: Scribner-Simon & Schuster, 2010. 1-12. PDF e-book.

Lahiri, Jhumpa. *Unaccustomed Earth.* New York: Knopf-Random House, 2008. 52-56. PDF e-book.

Microsoft. *Halo Reach.* Redmond: Microsoft Corp., 14 Sept. 2010. Xbox 360. Video game.

Parker, James. "Notes from the Underworld." *The Atlantic* May 2011: 38-41. Print.

Sullivan, Andrew. *The Dish: Biased & Balanced.* The Newsweek / Daily Beast Company, 2012. Web. 8 Sept. 2013. <http://andrewsullivan.thedailybeast.com/>.

Sumners, Christina. "Animal Acumen: Elephantine Intelligence." *Inside NOVA.* PBS Online by WGBH Educational Foundation, 26 Aug. 2011. Web. 9 Sept. 2013. <http://www.pbs.org/wgbh/nova/insidenova/2011/08/elephants.html>.

MLA Models

Models for Basic Situations

1. Author is named in a signal phrase   When citing a source in the text of your paper, you need to name your author. You can do this in a signal phrase or in a parenthetical reference (along with the source's page number) following your citation. It's simplest to name the author in a signal phrase and keep the parenthetical reference brief. The following citation refers to material from Jonathan Safran Foer's book *Eating Animals* (New York: Little, Brown and Company, 2009).

IN-TEXT CITATION

Jonathan Safran Foer argues that we can't trust language. "When it comes to eating animals," he writes, "words are as often used to misdirect and camouflage as they are to communicate" (45).

WORKS CITED ENTRY

Foer, Jonathan Safran. *Eating Animals*. New York: Little, Brown and Company, 2009. 1-86. Print.

2. Author is named in parentheses   If you decide not to name your author in a signal phrase, then name the author in your parenthetical reference along with the page number; don't use any punctuation between the name and page number.

IN-TEXT CITATION

Others argue that in addition to distrusting factory farming, we should also distrust the words associated with it, such as "natural" and "free range" (Foer 45).

WORKS CITED ENTRY

Foer, Jonathan Safran. *Eating Animals*. New York: Little, Brown and Company, 2009. 1-86. Print.

3. Individual author name is not provided   If you cannot locate an author name for your source, use the title. Provide the complete title of the text (or video, etc.) in a signal phrase—or give a shortened version of the title in the parenthetical reference. (Note: If the author is an organization, see example 6 on p. 403.) Following are sample citations for an article titled "Best Places to Live: 2012" that appears on CNN's *Money Magazine* site.

IN-TEXT CITATION (title in signal phrase; no page number available)

According to a recent *Money Magazine* article, "Best Places to Live: 2012," Carmel, Indiana, is the winner of all American small towns in terms of housing, finances, and overall quality of life.

OR (shortened title in parentheses; no page number available)

Carmel, Indiana, was recently determined to be the best American small town to live in ("Best Places to Live").

WORKS CITED ENTRY

"Best Places to Live: 2012." *Money Magazine*. CNN, Sept. 2012. Web. 31 Aug. 2013.
  <http://money.cnn.com/magazines/moneymag/best-places/2012/snapshots/
  PL1810342.html?iid=spl100>.

4. Author identified by screen name only   Some online sources identify an
author, but not by a traditional first and last name. For example, the author of an
eHow article is simply identified as an "eHow Contributor."

IN-TEXT CITATION (no page number available)

Another piece of career-building advice is to ask for extra training and to research and
learn more about your industry (eHow Contributor).

WORKS CITED ENTRY

eHow Contributor. "How to Get Along with the Boss." *eHow Money*. Demand Media, 4
  Nov. 2010. Web. 29 Aug. 2013. <ehow.com/how_2057947_get-along-boss.html>.

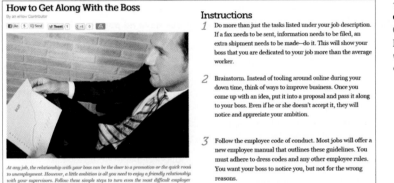

5. More than one author   Some sources have multiple authors. If your source
has *two or three authors*, include all of their names. Following is a reference to *The
Worst-Case Scenario Survival Handbook: Life*, a book by Joshua Piven and David
Borgenicht (San Francisco: Chronicle Books, 2006).

IN-TEXT CITATION (two authors)

To escape a stampede of giraffes, the best plan of action is to dive or wade into the
nearest body of water. Giraffes tend to avoid water unless they are thirsty (Piven and
Borgenicht 185).

WORKS CITED ENTRY

Piven, Joshua, and David Borgenicht. *The Worst-Case Scenario Survival Handbook:
  Life*. San Francisco: Chronicle Books, 2006. Print.

For four or more authors, use the phrase "et al." (short for the Latin phrase *et alia*,
which means "and others"). Following is a reference to an article published in

Nutrition Journal titled "A Survey of Energy Drink Consumption Patterns among College Students." It was written by Brenda M. Malinauskas, Victor G. Aeby, Reginald F. Overton, Tracy Carpenter-Aeby, and Kimberly Barber-Heidal.

IN-TEXT CITATION (four or more authors; no page number available)
According to a 2007 study, college students consume Red Bull and other energy drinks when they feel sleep-deprived (67%), need an energy boost (65%), drink alcohol (54%), study or complete a major project (50%), drive long distances (45%), and have hangovers (17%) (Malinauskas et al.).

WORKS CITED ENTRY
Malinauskas, Brenda M., et al. "A Survey of Energy Drink Consumption Patterns among College Students." *Nutrition Journal* 6:35 (2007): n. pag. Web. 31 Aug. 2013. <http://www.nutritionj.com/content/6/1/35>. "n. pag." means "not paginated"

☞ **Attention, researchers using MLA! Does your source have no page numbers?**

Most digital sources do not have page numbers. When using these sources, do your best to meet MLA's requirements:

1. Provide the author, title, publisher/publication title, date of publication, and access date. Also:

   » Identify the source's format: "Print" or "Web" (for most of your sources).
   » Note whether the source is a "Photograph," "Chart," "Map," "Cartoon," "Episode," etc. We also urge you to provide URLs for your online sources.

The Works Cited entry for a clip from *The Colbert Report* you found online would look like this:

▲ VIDEO STILL
Stephen Colbert, during taping of *The Colbert Report* at the University of Pennsylvania, April 4, 2008. *AP Photo/Joseph Kaczmarek.*

WORKS CITED ENTRY (for online chip)
episode title   name of show/series   label
"The Word: Let Them Buy Cake." *The Colbert Report.* Episode.
writer/producer   network   episode date   Web site   format
By Stephen Colbert. Comedy Central, 13 Dec. 2011. *Colbert Nation.* Web.
access date   URL
16 Aug. 2013. <http://www.colbertnation.com/the-colbert-report-videos/404252/december-13-2011/the-word---let-them-buy-cake>.

2. For an electronic source not found online, include a label of its type. The most common: "Film," "JPEG file," "MP3 file," "DVD," "CD-ROM," "Xbox 360," "Radio," and "Television."

If you saw the film *The Dark Knight Rises* in a theater, you would cite it like this:

WORKS CITED ENTRY (for movie)
movie title   director   major performers
The Dark Knight Rises. Dir. Christopher Nolan. Perf. Christian Bale, Tom Hardy, and
release
distributor   date   medium
Anne Hathaway. Warner Brothers, 2012. Film.

6. Author is an organization   Follow the same basic format as for sources with any other type of author.

IN-TEXT CITATION (no page number available)
Mental health is a human and civil rights issue (Mental Health America).

WORKS CITED ENTRY
Mental Health America. "Position Statement 21: Rights of Persons with Mental Health and Substance Use Conditions." *Mental Health America*. Mental Health America, 2012. Web. 30 Sept. 2013. <http://www.nmha.org/go/position-statements/21>.

7. No page numbers   Most online sources (unless the source is a PDF) have no page numbers. The box on page 402 and examples 3 and 4 (pp. 400–01) show how to handle entries for sources without page numbers.

Another example: a video by *South Park* creators Trey Parker and Matt Stone, which animates a lecture by the philosopher Alan Watts, was found on YouTube.

IN-TEXT CITATION
The animated version of Watts's main arguments about life, music, and how success is measured creates a layered experience for viewers (Parker and Stone).

WORKS CITED ENTRY
Parker, Trey, and Matt Stone. "Life and Music." *YouTube*. YouTube, 18 June 2007. Web. 30 Sept. 2013. <http://www.youtube.com/watch?v=ERbvKrH-GC4>.

8. Source used more than once in a paragraph   If you refer to a source multiple times in one paragraph, you can provide the author's name(s) just once, as long as it's clear it's still the same source. For example, see the citation for the article titled "Panic Disorder" from *The Journal of the American Medical Association*. The authors are Janet M. Torpy, Alison E. Burke, and Robert M. Golub.

IN-TEXT CITATION
According to research published in *The Journal of the American Medical Association*, not everyone who has a panic attack gets diagnosed with panic disorder (Torpy, Burke, and Golub). Still, as the article makes clear, many Americans suffer from mental health issues.

WORKS CITED ENTRY
Torpy, Janet M., Alison E. Burke, and Robert M. Golub. "Panic Disorder." *Journal of the American Medical Association* 305:12 (2011): 20-30. Web. 30 Sept. 2013. <http://jama.jamanetwork.com/article.aspx?articleid=646264>.

☞ **Attention, researchers using MLA! Why provide URLs in your Works Cited list?**

Even though the latest MLA guidelines make this optional, we believe it makes sense to provide URLs. They make it easy for your readers (especially your instructor) to check out your sources. Providing URLs benefits your audience, makes you more persuasive, and builds your ethos.

Models for Specific Types of Sources

9. Book   For more in-text citation models for books, see examples 1, 2, and 5 (pp. 400 and 401). The following is from *Unbearable Lightness: A Story of Loss and Gain* by Portia de Rossi.

IN-TEXT CITATION
In Hollywood, where thinness is demanded at any cost but is extolled as the product of health and fitness, those who strive for perfection have to lie. As one actress puts it: "How could I possibly explain my weight maintenance when it was attributed to starving and bingeing?" (de Rossi 90).

WORKS CITED ENTRY
de Rossi, Portia. *Unbearable Lightness: A Story of Loss and Gain*. New York: Atria
    Books-Simon and Schuster, 2010. Print.

10. Article or essay   The following models show how to cite online and print articles. In February 2012, *National Geographic* published an article by Tom O'Neill—"Lady with a Secret"—in two forms: online and in print.

IN-TEXT CITATION (article from online magazine)
A chalk-and-ink drawing, titled *La Bella Principessa*, may be the work of Leonardo da Vinci (O'Neill).

WORKS CITED ENTRY
O'Neill, Tom. "Lady with a Secret." *National Geographic*. National Geographic Society,
    Feb. 2012. Web. 31 Oct. 2013. <http://ngm.nationalgeographic.com/2012/
    02/lost-da-vinci/o-neill-text>.

IN-TEXT CITATION (article from print magazine)
A chalk-and-ink drawing, titled *La Bella Principessa*, may be the work of Leonardo da Vinci (O'Neill 102).

WORKS CITED ENTRY
O'Neill, Tom. "Lady with a Secret." *National Geographic* Feb. 2012: 102-09. Print.

11. Source quoted in another source   The following models show how to cite a source that is quoted in another source, whether online or print. "Is Anybody Out There?" by Phil Plait was published by *Discover* magazine in two different forms—in a print edition (in its November 2010 issue) and online at discovermagazine.com (on January 27, 2011). Plait's article features several quotations from four major astronomers. To cite one of those quotations, use the phrase "qtd. in" to indicate that you did not read the quoted source itself, but rather found the quoted material in another source.

IN-TEXT CITATION (article from an online magazine)

According to Gibor Basri, professor of astronomy at Berkeley, proof of whether "anybody's out there" may come down to a radio signal. "There are about 60 radio telescopes scanning the skies for these signals right now," he says. "That would be the definitive answer to the search for life: If you get an intelligent signal, then you know for sure" (qtd. in Plait).

WORKS CITED ENTRY

Plait, Phil. "Is Anybody Out There?" *Discover*. Kalmbach Publishing Company, 27 Jan. 2011. Web. 1 Apr. 2013. <http://discovermagazine.com/2010/nov/ 25-is-anybody-out-there/article_view?b_start:int=0&-C=>.

IN-TEXT CITATION (article from a print magazine)

According to Gibor Basri, professor of astronomy at Berkeley, proof of whether "anybody's out there" may come down to a radio signal. "There are about 60 radio telescopes scanning the skies for these signals right now," he says. "That would be the definitive answer to the search for life: If you get an intelligent signal, then you know for sure" (qtd. in Plait 49).

WORKS CITED ENTRY

Plait, Phil. "Is Anybody Out There?" *Discover* Nov. 2010: 49-51. Print.

12. Encyclopedia or dictionary entry—or wiki entry   In your signal phrase or parenthetical reference, provide the word or phrase that you looked up in the dictionary or encyclopedia. If the work or entry has an author, provide that also.

IN-TEXT CITATION (for online encyclopedia)

The phrase "carpe diem," which traces back to an ancient Roman poet, means to seize or "pluck the day" ("Carpe diem").

ENCYCLOPÆDIA BRITANNICA
ADVOCACY FOR ANIMALS | BLOG | HELP | SCHOOL & LIBRARY PRODUCTS | SHOP

carpe diem

Introduction   Related   Contributors & Bibliography

carpe diem, (Latin: "pluck the day") phrase used by the Roman poet Horace to express the idea that one should enjoy life while one can. The sentiment has been expressed in many literatures, especially in 16th- and 17th-century English poetry. Two of the best-known examples are Robert Herrick's "To the Virgins, to Make Much of Time" and Andrew Marvell's "To His Coy Mistress."

◀ **ENCYCLOPEDIA ENTRY**
"Carpe diem" from *Encyclopaedia Britannica Online*. See MLA documentation for this source on page 406. *Reprinted with permission from Encyclopaedia Britannica, © 2012 by Encyclopaedia Britannica, Inc.*

"Carpe diem." *Encyclopaedia Britannica. Encyclopaedia Britannica Online.* Encyclopaedia Britannica, Inc., 2012. Web. 30 Sept. 2013. <http://www.britannica.com/EBchecked/topic/96702/carpe-diem>.

WIKI ENTRY ▶

Wikipedia, "Wombat" entry. *Courtesy of Wikimedia Foundation, Inc. All rights reserved. Photo by JJ Harrison.*

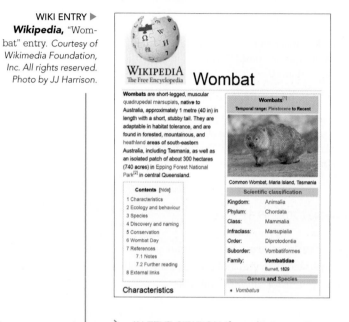

IN-TEXT CITATION (for online source)

The wombat is in danger because of destruction to its habitat; meanwhile, a project by a Swiss mining company is experimenting with relocating some of these animals from their native region in Australia to a new colony elsewhere in the country ("Wombat").

WORKS CITED ENTRY

"Wombat." *Wikipedia.* Wikimedia Foundation, Inc., 27 Feb. 2013. Web. 1 Sept. 2013. <http://en.wikipedia.org/wiki/Wombat>.

☞ **Attention, *Wikipedia* lovers!**

Check with your instructor about using *Wikipedia* as a source. It is a public wiki that can be edited by anyone. Tip: *Wikipedia* can be a great place to start your research, especially because the "Reference," "Further reading," and "External links" sections can often lead you to excellent and reliable sources to use in your research project. For example, the "Wombat" entry provides links to Australian governmental information, BBC articles, and books authored by wombat experts. See also *Wikipedia*'s entry "Researching with Wikipedia" (or go to wikipedia.org and type in "Researching with Wikipedia").

---

13. Entire Web site In the extremely rare instance that you will want to cite an entire Web site—rather than a specific portion of it, such as an article—use the following model. (For information on citing a short work from a Web site, see example 14 below.) MLA requires that for Web sources, you provide a sponsor or a publisher name. In cases where a Web site has an individual author, you should provide that person's name as the sponsor/publisher.

Web site with no author

IN-TEXT CITATION

It is possible for an Internet radio station, drawing from a database and using your preferences for artists, songs, and genres, to personalize your experience, playing only the music you want to hear (Pandora).

Web site sponsor/publisher (shortened)

WORKS CITED ENTRY

Pandora Internet Radio. Pandora Media, Inc., 2011. Web. 2 Sept. 2013. <http://www.pandora.com/>.

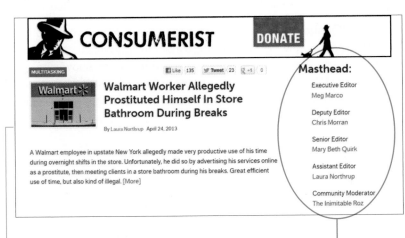

◀ WEB SITE
The Consumerist.
Copyright 2012 Consumer Media LLC, an affiliate of Consumers Union of U.S., Inc., Yonkers, NY 10703-1057, a nonprofit organization. Reprinted with permission from the Consumerist.com for educational purposes only. www.consumerist.com.

Web site with author or editor

IN-TEXT CITATION

One consumer-focused site gives an unflinching critique of big business, addressing the question: What is the worst company in America? (Marco et al.)

Web site editors

WORKS CITED ENTRY

Marco, Meg, et al., eds. *The Consumerist.* Consumer Media, LLC, 2010. Web. 30 Sept. 2013. <http://consumerist.com/>.

14. Short work from a Web site Most of what you cite from the Internet can be categorized as a "short work from a Web site." A short work is any text (of any type and medium) that is not book length or that appears as an internal page or section of a Web site. A short work can be an article, report, poem, song, video, and so on.

Short work with no author

IN-TEXT CITATION

To avoid deep vein thrombosis during air travel, it can help to wear loose clothing and to stroll through the cabin once every hour ("Healthy Travel").

title of short work from a Web site

WORKS CITED ENTRY

"Healthy Travel Tips." *Delta*. Delta Air Lines, Inc., 2012. Web. 30 Sept. 2013. <http://www.delta.com/traveling_checkin/travel_tips/health/index.jsp>.

Short work with an author

IN-TEXT CITATION

A new genetically engineered salmon produced by a biotech firm will not be labeled as such, according to standards set by the Food and Drug Administration (Bittman).

author

WORKS CITED ENTRY

Bittman, Mark. "Why Aren't GMO Foods Labeled?" *Opinionator. Newyorktimes.com*. New York Times Company, 15 Feb. 2011. Web. 30 Sept. 2013. <http://opinionator.blogs.nytimes.com/2011/02/15/why-arent-g-m-o-foods-labeled/>.

15. Video, movie, or TV show   In general, cite these sources as you would a short work from a Web site (see example 14). When citing a movie or any work that includes a director, begin with the title and then identify the director, as shown below. IMPORTANT: Although MLA style does not require it, we recommend that you note in your Works Cited entry the type of composition your source is—by including the words *video*, *movie*, and so on.

IN-TEXT CITATION

The opening scene of one episode of *Family Guy* is all about consumption: Peter can't resist the cookie dough batter, while Stewie is tempted by the Abercrombie catalog ("Big Bang Theory").

episode title

WORKS CITED ENTRY (for online episode)

"The Big Bang Theory." *Family Guy*. Dir. Seth MacFarlane. Fox, 8 May 2011. Video. *Hulu*. Web. 30 Sept. 2012. <http://www.hulu.com/watch/237564/family-guy-the-big-bang-theory>.

16. Video game, online game, or software   To cite an entire video game, follow the format for an entire Web site (see example 13). For a clip from a video game, follow the format for a short work from a Web site. As we recommend for videos, movies, and TV shows (see example 15), we also recommend that you include identifier words such as *game*, *software*, and so on.

Entire video game

IN-TEXT CITATION

The goal of one popular game is to plow, plant, and harvest on "your own" virtual land (Zynga).

video game publisher

WORKS CITED ENTRY

Zynga. *FarmVille 2*. Game. Facebook, 2012. Web. <FarmVille.com>.

Clip from video game

IN-TEXT CITATION

Players can build their enterprises by acquiring such animals as the arctic fox and the armadillo (Zynga).

    video game publisher

WORKS CITED ENTRY

Zynga. "My Mastery." *FarmVille 2*. Game. Facebook, 2012. Web. <FarmVille.com>.

    clip title

17. Visuals (photos, maps, charts, posters) Cite these as you would a short work from a Web site (see example 14) or other, longer work. Include the following, if available: author's or artist's name, title of the work, name of publication, and date of publication. Also note the type of the composition, for example, "Photograph," "Map," "Chart," or "Poster."

IN-TEXT CITATION

The image is a reminder that among those evicted by the Chicago Housing Authority are families with small children (Reblando).

    photographer

WORKS CITED ENTRY

Reblando, Jason. "Jessica Moore's Son Maurice Booker (left), 5, with a Friend." Photograph. *Newyorktimes.com*. New York Times Company, 3 Sept. 2011. Web. 30 Sept. 2013. <http://www.nytimes.com/2011/09/04/us/04cncfirststrike.html?_r=1>.

18. Comic strip/graphic work Think of comic strips as short works—from longer works such as Web sites, magazines, and so on—and cite them as you would a short work or article from a Web site (see example 14), online journal, book,

◀ COMIC STRIP
Tak Toyoshima,
"Why Oppose Openly Gay Soldiers in the Military?" From *Secret Asian Man*.
Tak Toyoshima creator/ illustrator Secret Asian Man.

or other source. Include the label "Cartoon" or "Comic strip" right after the title. For graphic novels (fiction) or memoirs (nonfiction), follow the format that you would for a book. In some cases, the author is also the illustrator; when that is not the case, be sure to include the name of the illustrator along with the abbreviation "illus."

Comic strip

IN-TEXT CITATION

The comic offers social commentary on issues such as racism, immigration, gay rights, the military, and consumption (Toyoshima).

author/artist

WORKS CITED ENTRY

Toyoshima, Tak. "Why Oppose Openly Gay Soldiers in the Military?" Comic strip.
Secretasianman.com. Secret Asian Man, 22 Aug. 2010. Web. 30 Sept. 2013.
<http://www.secretasianman.com/home.htm>.

Excerpt from a graphic memoir *(author is also illustrator)*

IN-TEXT CITATION

In 1980, a year after Iran's Islamic Revolution, she and her female classmates were obliged to wear a veil to school (Satrapi 3).

author/artist

WORKS CITED ENTRY

Satrapi, Marjane. *Persepolis.* New York: Pantheon-Random House, 2004. 1-8. Print.

Excerpt from a graphic novel *(with an author and an illustrator)*

IN-TEXT CITATION

The story opens with a journal entry that makes clear the character's obsessions with gore, filth, and death, not to mention Communists and intellectuals (Moore 1).

artist   *author*

WORKS CITED ENTRY

Moore, Alan. *Watchmen.* Illus. Dave Gibbons. New York: DC Comics, 2008. 1-32. Print.

19. Advertisement   To cite an ad, name the product being advertised, along with the word "Advertisement." Following are the in-text citation and Works Cited entry for an ad for Dove Visible Care Body Wash, found at the company Web site. For the in-text citation, provide a shortened version of the product name.

IN-TEXT CITATION

A recent ad campaign for body wash claims to renew and soften skin, promising "visible results in just one week" (Dove Visible Care).

ad title (shortened)

WORKS CITED ENTRY

Dove Visible Care Body Wash. Advertisement. *Dove.* Unilever, 2011. Web. 30 Sept. 2013.
<http://www.dovecloseup.com/default.aspx#home>.

20. Personal e-mail, letter, or interview   To cite an e-mail message (that you've written or received), provide the author's name, the subject line, the words "Message to" followed by the name of the recipient of the message, and the medium "E-mail" at the end. For a letter you've received, provide the author's name and the phrase "Letter to the author," along with the medium ("MS" for handwritten or "TS" for typed). To cite an interview that you've conducted, provide the interviewee's name and "Personal interview."

E-mail *(received)*

IN-TEXT CITATION

Once customers search for a flight, hotel, or car, the organization e-mails periodic pricing updates, which can lead to a better deal for the consumer (Hotwire).

author of e-mail

WORKS CITED ENTRY

Hotwire. "Another Way to Save on Portsmouth Hotels." Message to the author. 15 Sept. 2013. E-mail.

Letter *(received)*

IN-TEXT CITATION

I received an unsettling report of suspicious activity involving my personal credit information (Experian).

author of letter

WORKS CITED ENTRY

Experian National Consumer Assistance Center. Letter to the author. 15 Jan. 2013. TS.

Interview *(conducted)*

IN-TEXT CITATION

The world-traveling journalist admitted that while she might have wanted to stay home on her couch eating Ben and Jerry's Chunky Monkey, she did not have the time: Moscow, Afghanistan, and Cairo awaited (Amanpour).

person interviewed

WORKS CITED ENTRY

Amanpour, Christiane. Personal interview. 21 Feb. 2013.

21. Blog post or social media posting   Cite as you would a short work from a Web site (see example 14); if the entry has no title, use the phrase "Weblog entry" or "Weblog comment."

IN-TEXT CITATION

One journalist who covered the James "Whitey" Bulger story was surprised by the shabbiness of the mob fugitive's Santa Monica apartment (Brady-Myerov).

author

WORKS CITED ENTRY

Brady-Myerov, Monica. Weblog entry. *Facebook.* Facebook.com, 24 June 2011. Web. 30 Sept. 2013. <facebook.com>.

Monica Brady-Myerov

The sun is up on Whitey Bulger's former hideout. I'm surprised at how modest and almost shabby it is, compared to what he could have afforded!

◀ BLOG POST
Monica Brady-Myerov, reporter, social media post. *Monica Brady-Myerov.*

22. Audio recording or podcast Cite audio recordings or podcasts that you've accessed online in the same way you would a short work from a Web site (see example 14). If you've downloaded such sources as digital files, identify the medium as such (for example, "MP3 file").

Podcast from Web

IN-TEXT CITATION
It's holiday time, and an unemployed writer takes a job as a Macy's Christmas elf ("Sedaris Returns").
    podcast title

WORKS CITED ENTRY
"Sedaris Returns as Crumpet the Elf on NPR." *Morning Edition*. National Public Radio, 24 Dec. 2004. Web. 30 Sept. 2013. <http://www.npr.org/templates/story/story.php?storyId=4243755>.

Podcast downloaded as digital file (MP3)

WORKS CITED ENTRY
"Sedaris Returns as Crumpet the Elf on NPR." *Morning Edition*. National Public Radio, 24 Dec. 2004. MP3 file.

Song from the Web (via iTunes)

IN-TEXT CITATION
The artist performs her iconic song in "Single Ladies (Put a Ring on It)" as her alter ego, Sasha Fierce (Knowles).

WORKS CITED ENTRY
Knowles, Beyoncé. "Single Ladies (Put a Ring on It)." *I Am . . . Sasha Fierce*. Columbia, 2008. iTunes. Web. 30 Sept. 2013. <http://itunes.apple.com/us/album/i-am...-sasha-fierce/id296016891>.

Song downloaded as digital file (MP3)

WORKS CITED ENTRY
Knowles, Beyoncé. "Single Ladies (Put a Ring on It)." *I Am . . . Sasha Fierce*. Columbia, 2008. MP3 file.

23. Phone app Cite a phone app as you would a Web site; or if you're referring to part of the app, cite it as you would a short work from a Web site (see example 14). Identify the medium as a "Phone app."

IN-TEXT CITATION
The creators of the app pitch it as a "one-stop GPS outdoor recreation app," with maps created for the screen—maps that are not simply shrunken versions of outdated USGS maps ("Intermap").
    app title

"Intermap." AccuTerra. Phone app. *iTunes,* 13 Jul. 2011. Web. 9 Sept. 2013. <http://
   itunes.apple.com/us/app/accuterra-unlimited-maps-gps/id355787609?mt=8>.

24. Government or business document   For a government document, provide the author, title, and date. If there is no author, provide the name of the government agency (and department, if any). Note the medium—whether it's print or
from the Web—and follow the rules for a short work from a longer work (e.g., a book
or Web site). For a historical document, such as the one included below, provide the
title in regular roman letters (no italics and no quotation marks).

Government document

IN-TEXT CITATION
He wrote: "[A]ll persons held as slaves within any State or designated part of a State, the
people whereof shall then be in rebellion against the United States, shall be then,
thenceforward, and forever free" (Lincoln).
                                        author

WORKS CITED ENTRY   title of document
Lincoln, Abraham. Emancipation Proclamation. 1 Jan. 1863. *Library of Congress*, 30 Jul.
   2010. Web. 30 Sept. 2013. <http://www.loc.gov/pictures/item/97507511/resource/
   cph.3b53030/?sid=40c1ec586dad774d8a08ebfbf8cdff07>.

Business document *(annual report)*

IN-TEXT CITATION
Even a major corporation such as Microsoft has felt the sting of the global recession
(Ballmer).
   author
WORKS CITED ENTRY   title of document
Ballmer, Steven A. "Microsoft Corporation: Annual Report 2012." *Microsoft.com.*
   Microsoft Corp., 10 Oct. 2012. Web. 12 Sept. 2013. <http://www.microsoft.com/
   investor/reports/ar12/index.html>.

25. Literary work (novel, poem, fairy tale, etc.)   Provide the author, title,
publisher's city, publisher, and date. Also include the medium, for example, "Print"
or "E-book." MLA recommends that you identify the brand platform for e-books—
such as "Kindle file" or "Nook file"—but we consider this optional, especially with
companies and brands so often in flux. Include platform information, at the end of
the Works Cited entry, as shown.

Novel *(print)*

WORKS CITED ENTRY
McCarthy, Cormac. *All the Pretty Horses.* New York: Borzoi-Knopf, 1992. Print.

Novel *(e-book)*

WORKS CITED ENTRY

McCarthy, Cormac. *All the Pretty Horses*. New York: Vintage-Random House, 11 Aug. 2010. E-book. <amazon.com>. Kindle file.

Poem *(online)*

WORKS CITED ENTRY

Crane, Hart. "At Melville's Tomb." *Poetry Out Loud*. National Endowment for the Arts. n.d. Web. 11 Apr. 2013. <www.poetryoutloud.org/poem/172021>.

26. Selection from an anthology or textbook   Begin with the selection author and title, followed by the anthology or textbook title, editors, publisher's city, publisher, year, page range, and medium (e.g., "Print").

IN-TEXT CITATION

The cost of fruits and vegetables versus the cost of meat and dairy has a lot to do with government subsidies (The Physicians Committee).

author of selection (shortened)

WORKS CITED ENTRY   ⎡author of selection

information on textbook where selection appears — The Physicians Committee for Responsible Medicine. "Why Does a Salad Cost More Than a Big Mac?" *Bedford Book of Genres: A Guide*. Ed. Amy Braziller and Elizabeth Kleinfeld. Boston: Bedford/St. Martin's, 2013. 121. Print.

27. Object/artifact (cereal box, etc.)   If you find an object or artifact online, cite it as a short work from a Web site, (see example 14), but include a description of the item in your Works Cited entry. If you find such a source in the physical world, cite it as a work with an author and include a descriptor as shown below.

IN-TEXT CITATION

Children might be drawn to the sunny yellow box, but parents likely focus on the red heart and the soft claim about lowering cholesterol (Cheerios).

name of object

Object *(found online)*

WORKS CITED ENTRY

Cheerios. Cereal box. *Cheerios.com*. General Mills, n.d. Web. 30 Sept. 2013. <http://www.cheerios.com/Products/Cheerios>.

Object *(found in physical world)*

WORKS CITED ENTRY

Cheerios. Cereal box. General Mills, n.d.

▲ OBJECT
Cheerios box.
iStockphoto.

APA Style

The APA style of documentation is the style presented in the *Publication Manual of the American Psychological Association*, 6th ed. (Washington: APA, 2010). It is commonly used in the behavioral and social science disciplines, which include courses in psychology and in sociology, and some English and cultural studies courses.

The APA style of documentation has two main components:

1. In-text citations

2. List of References

The in-text citation Your in-text citations refer your readers to your list. Each time you cite a source in your paper—whether through a signal phrase or a parenthetical reference—you cue readers to a corresponding entry in your References list. When you include an in-text citation, you:

» Name the author of your source

» Provide the source's year of publication—and (if it's a print source) a corresponding page number

» Make sure you have a corresponding entry (for each in-text citation) in your References list

The References list In your References list, at the end of your paper, you:

» Provide publication information about each source

» Alphabetize your sources by authors' last names (or by title if an author is not provided)

The following example shows an in-text citation along with its corresponding entry in the References list.

IN-TEXT CITATION

As students who visit our writing centers are working with

author ⌐ publication year

multimodal compositions (Sheridan, 2010), it makes sense to open up our idea of what it means to help with the entire composing processes (p. 3).

└ exact page where information is from

publication

author | year | title of chapter | editors

Sheridan, D. M. (2010). Writing centers and the multimodal turn. In D. M. Sheridan &

title of book

J. A. Inman (Eds.), *Multiliteracy centers: Writing center work, new media, and multimodal rhetoric* (pp. 1-22). Cresskill, NJ: Hampton Press.

page range of chapter | place of publication | publisher

In-text citations: General guidelines

There are two main ways to handle an in-text citation: by using a signal phrase or a parenthetical reference (or some combination).

SIGNAL PHRASE (author named in phrase)

publication

authors | year

Kingsolver, Kingsolver, and Hopp (2007) explained to readers that they "had come to the farmland to eat deliberately" (p. 23).

exact page that quotation is from

PARENTHETICAL REFERENCE (author named in parentheses)

In discussing psychiatric illnesses, the author argued, "Psychiatry has found a way to medicalize all human behavior and offer a pharmaceutical intervention for everything" (Plante, 2012, para. 3).

author publication year | for this online source, no page number is available, but source has paragraph numbers

References entries: General guidelines

Provide a corresponding entry in your References list for each in-text citation in your paper. The following guidelines provide the basic format for the APA References list entry.

» Give the author's last name, followed by initials for all first and middle names. Provide additional authors' names with each last name followed by initials for first and middle names.

author: last name + initial(s) | publication year | title of book

Ben-Shahar, T. (2007). *Happier: Learn the secrets to daily joy and lasting fulfillment.*

place of publication | publisher | page range | publication year | title of article

New York, NY: McGraw-Hill, 20-32.

authors: last name + initial(s) | publication year | title of article

Watkins, P. C., Woodward, K., Stone, T., & Kolts, R. L. (2003). Gratitude and happiness:

title of article

Development of a measure of gratitude, and relationships with subjective well-being.

title of journal | volume | page range

Social Behavior and Personality, 31, 131-151.

☞ **Attention, researchers! A note about APA & tense.**

When you use a signal phrase to discuss a source, you must introduce the source by using the past or present perfect tenses. For example: "Lady Gaga (2013) said," or "Lady Gaga (2013) has argued." For more examples, see the APA in-text citation models provided in this chapter (pp. 419–35).

Note that MLA dictates a different approach, and requires you to use the present tense: for example: "Lady Gaga (2013) says," or "Lady Gaga (2013) argues." See pages 400–414 for MLA models.

» Present the titles of long works—books or entire Web sites—in italics. Capitalize the first word of the title; other words in the title (except proper nouns) are lowercased. If there is a subtitle, capitalize the first word of the subtitle.

author: last
name + initial(s)   publication
              year   title of book
Deutsch, D. (2011). *The beginning of infinity: Explanations that transform the world.*
       place of publication   publisher   page range
       New York, NY: Viking Penguin, 112-133.

» Present the titles of short works from books or Web sites without quotation marks or italics. Capitalize the first word of the title; other words are lowercased (though be sure to retain the capitalization of proper nouns). If there is a subtitle, capitalize the first word of the subtitle. IMPORTANT: For all online sources, include the URL. Although APA suggests you provide the URL for the source's homepage, we recommend that you provide the exact URL for the specific article or other work you're referring to. For example, the article cited below is from Salon.com. The URL takes readers to the page for the article itself, not Salon's homepage.

author: last   publication year,
name + initial(s)   month, day   title of article   title of magazine
Mustich, E. (2011, June 15). Can students be disciplined for online speech? *Salon*
       paragraph range   article URL
       (paras. 1-6). Retrieved from http://news.salon.com/2011/06/15/students
       _online_speech/singleton

» For print works, present the city and state of publication, and spell out the entire name of the publisher.

author: last   publication
name + initial(s)   year   title of book
Lieber, L. (2008). *The Einstein theory of relativity: A trip to the fourth dimension.*
       place of publication   publisher   page range
       Philadelphia, PA: Paul Dry Books, 17-24.

» For both print and online works, provide the date that the piece was published. For online sources, provide the URL, but not the access date—unless there is a chance the content of the source may change.

author: last   publication
name + initial(s)   year   title of book
Clark, D. P. (2010). *Germs, genes, and civilization: How epidemics shaped who we are*
                place of publication   publisher   page range
       today. Upper Saddle River, NJ: Pearson Education, Inc., 19-23.

author: last name + initial(s) | publication year, month, day | title of photo essay

Lewis, T. (2012, August 13). Slimy but cute: 10 newly discovered amphibians

descriptive label | title of magazine | photo essay URL

[Photo essay]. *Wired*. Retrieved from http://www.wired.com/wiredscience/2012/08/new-amphibian-species/

» If your source is a work that would benefit from clarification, provide that term in brackets. (See models for these on pp. 430–33.)

author | publication year, month, day | title of newspaper editorial

The Denver Post Editorial Board. (2012, January 20). School trans fat ban not needed

descriptive label | title of newspaper | editorial URL

[Editorial]. *The Denver Post*. Retrieved from http://www.denverpost.com/opinion/ci_19778812

Organize your References list alphabetically. For entries of more than one line, indent additional lines five spaces (this is called hanging indentation).

References

Ben-Shahar, T. (2007). *Happier: Learn the secrets to daily joy and lasting fulfillment*. New York, NY: McGraw-Hill, 1-12.

Clark, D. P. (2010). *Germs, genes, and civilization: How epidemics shaped who we are today*. Upper Saddle River, NJ: Pearson Educational, Inc., 19-23.

The Denver Post Editorial Board. (2012, January 20). School trans fat ban not needed [Editorial]. *The Denver Post*. Retrieved from http://www.denverpost.com/opinion/ci_19778812

Deutsch, D. (2011). *The beginning of infinity: Explanations that transform the world*. New York, NY: Viking Penguin, 112-133.

Kingsolver, B., Kingsolver, C., & Hopp, S. L. (2007). *Animal, vegetable, miracle: A year of food life*. New York, NY: HarperCollins, 23.

Lewis, T. (2012, August 13). Slimy but cute: 10 newly discovered amphibians [Photo essay]. Wired. Retrieved from http://www.wired.com/wiredscience/2012/08/new-amphibian-species/

Lieber, L. (2008). *The Einstein theory of relativity: A trip to the fourth dimension*. Philadelphia, PA: Paul Dry Books, 17-24.

Mustich, E. (2011, June 15). Can students be disciplined for online speech? *Salon* (paras.1-6). Retrieved from http://news.salon.com/2011/06/15/students_online_speech/singleton

Plante, T. (2012, February 1). The psychopathology of everything [Editorial Weblog post]. *Do the right thing: Spirit, science, and health. Psychology Today*, para. 3. Retrieved from http://www.psychologytoday.com/blog/do-the-right-thing/201202/the-psychopathology-everything

Sheridan, D. M. (2010). Writing centers and the multimodal turn. In D. M. Sheridan & J. A. Inman (Eds.), *Multiliteracy centers: Writing center work, new media, and multimodal rhetoric* (pp. 1-22). Cresskill, NJ: Hampton Press.

Watkins, P. C., Woodward, K., Stone, T., & Kolts, R. L. (2003). Gratitude and happiness: Development of a measure of gratitude, and relationships with subjective well-being. *Social Behavior and Personality, 31*, 131-151.

APA Models

Models for Basic Situations

1. Author is named in a signal phrase   When citing a source, name your author in a signal phrase—that is, name the author in the body of your text, and provide the source publication year and page number in parentheses. Or use a parenthetical reference—as shown in the example below—and provide everything in parentheses: the author's last name, the source publication year, and page number.

The simplest, cleanest method is to name the author in a signal phrase and keep the parenthetical reference brief:

IN-TEXT CITATION
David Myers (2011) identified shifts in the study of human behavior. He wrote: "I find myself fascinated by today's psychology, with its studies of the neuroscience of our moods and memories, the reach of our adaptive unconscious, and the shaping power of the social and cultural context" (p. 4).

REFERENCES LIST ENTRY
Myers, D. (2011). *Psychology* (10th ed.). New York, NY: Worth Publishers, 1-4.

2. Author is named in parentheses   If you don't name your author in a signal phrase, then do so in your parenthetical reference along with the publication year and page number; use commas between the name, year, and page number.

IN-TEXT CITATION
Part of what has made the study of psychology so interesting is the current focus on neuroscience, the adaptive unconscious, and social and cultural factors (Myers, 2011, p. 4).

REFERENCES LIST ENTRY
Myers, D. (2011). *Psychology* (10th ed.). New York, NY: Worth. 1-4.

3. Individual author name is not provided   In the rare case that you cannot locate an author name for your source, use the title (or the first word or two of the title) in parentheses. (Note: If the author is an organization, see example 6.)

Following are sample citations for a brief article titled "Psych Basics: Charisma" that appears on *Psychology Today's* site.

IN-TEXT CITATION (title in signal phrase; no page number available)
According to a current *Psychology Today* article, "Psych Basics: Charisma" (2012), charming and influencing others requires "confidence, exuberance, and optimism" (para. 1).

OR (shortened title in parentheses; no page number available)
Charisma is said to be a quality that you either have or you don't ("Charisma," 2012, para. 1).

REFERENCES LIST ENTRY
Psych basics: Charisma. (2012). *Psychology Today*, para. 1. Retrieved from http://
www.psychologytoday.com/basics/charisma

ALTERNATIVE APPROACH: If you consider the publisher, *Psychology Today*, as the author, here is how the in-text citation and References list entry would work:

IN-TEXT CITATION (organization treated as author)
There are physical aspects to charisma, as well: smiling, using body language, and speaking with a friendly voice (*Psychology Today*, 2012, para. 1).

REFERENCES LIST ENTRY
Psychology Today. (2012). Psych basics: Charisma. *Psychology Today*, para. 1.
Retrieved from http://www.psychologytoday.com/basics/charisma

4. Author identified by screen name only Some online sources identify an author, but not by a traditional first and last name. For example, the author of an eHow article is simply identified as an "eHow Contributor."

IN-TEXT CITATION (no page number available)
Among the suggestions for improving memory were doing crossword puzzles, reading, and playing word games (eHow Contributor, 2011).

REFERENCES LIST ENTRY
eHow Contributor. (2011, September 6). How to sharpen your memory. *eHow.*
Retrieved from http://www.ehow.com/how_5594193_sharpen-memory.html

5. More than one author   Some sources have multiple authors. In general, you will list only up to five names in your in-text citations; for your References list, you can list up to seven authors, using an "&" just before the final name. Below is a reference to *The Worst-Case Scenario Survival Handbook: Work*, a book by Joshua Piven and David Borgenicht (San Francisco: Chronicle Books, 2003).

IN-TEXT CITATION (two authors)
To avoid taking a nightmare job, the authors recommended that applicants should schedule a morning interview and observe the mood of workers as they arrive: slouching, pouting, or looking dejected are all signs of low morale (Piven & Borgenicht, 2003, p. 16).

REFERENCES LIST ENTRY
Piven, J., & Borgenicht, D. (2003). *The worst-case scenario survival handbook: Work.*
San Francisco, CA: Chronicle Books, 1-32.

For three to five authors, identify all authors the first time you use the source in text; afterward, use only the first author's name and the phrase "et al." (short for the Latin phrase *et alia*, which means "and others"). Note: The article cited in the example below is from a database; many databases provide a DOI number for use in your References list entry. If there is no DOI, then use the phrase "Retrieved from" followed by the URL.

IN-TEXT CITATION (three to five authors)
A recent study found a boost in girl power in India, thanks to affirmative action laws that gave women leadership roles in their village councils. In terms of career goals, the gender gap for teen girls in the villages with women leaders closed by 32% (Beaman, Duflo, Pande, & Topalova, 2012, pp. 582-586).

LATER CITATIONS
(Beaman et al., 2012, pp. 582-586)

REFERENCES LIST ENTRY (article retrieved from database with DOI)
Beaman, L., Duflo, E., Pande, R., & Topalova, P. (2012, January 12). Female leadership raises aspirations and educational attainment for girls: A policy experiment in India. *Science, 335,* 582-586. doi:10.1126/science.1212382

REFERENCES LIST ENTRY (article from publisher site, abstract or summary only)
Beaman, L., Duflo, E., Pande, R., & Topalova, P. (2012, January 12). Female leadership raises aspirations and educational attainment for girls: A policy experiment in India [Abstract]. *Science, 335,* 582-586. Retrieved from http://www.sciencemag.org/content/335/6068/582.abstract

For six or more authors, for your in-text citations, name the first author listed, followed by "et al." In your References list entry, list up to seven authors. If there are more than seven authors, list the first six followed by three ellipsis dots and the last author's name. Following is a reference to an article published in the British journal *Animal Behaviour* titled "Firefly Flashing and Jumping Spider Predation." It was written by Skye M. Long, Sara Lewis, Leo Jean-Louis, George Ramos, Jamie Richmond, and Elizabeth M. Jako.

IN-TEXT CITATION (six or more authors)
Sadly for fireflies, flashing does more than entice mates; it can attract predators, including two species of attacking spiders (Long et al., 2012, pp. 81-86).

REFERENCES LIST ENTRY (up to seven authors)
Long, S. M., Lewis, S., Jean-Louis, L., Ramos, G., Richmond, J., & Jako, E. M. (2012). Firefly flashing and jumping spider predation. *Animal Behaviour, 83*, 81-86. doi:10.1016/j.anbehav.2011.10.008

6. Author is an organization   Follow the same basic format as for sources with any other type of author.

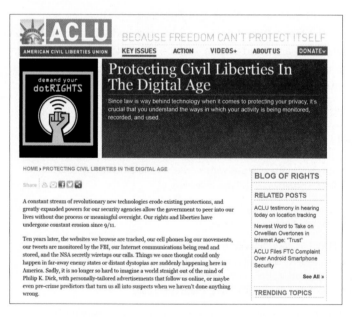

IN-TEXT CITATION
The American Civil Liberties Union argued that since 9/11, our civil liberties have "undergone constant erosion" thanks to expanded powers of government security agencies (ACLU, 2012, para. 1).

OR

Since 9/11, Americans' civil liberties, especially in the digital realm, have been under attack by security agencies such as the NSA and FBI (American Civil Liberties Union [ACLU], 2012, para. 1).

LATER CITATIONS
(ACLU, 2012)

REFERENCES LIST ENTRY
American Civil Liberties Union. (2012). Protecting civil liberties in the digital age, paras. 1-3. Retrieved from http://www.aclu.org/protecting-civil-liberties-digital-age

7. No page numbers   Most print sources have numbered pages, but unless your online source is provided as a PDF file, it probably will not include page numbers. Examples 3 and 6 show in-text citations for sources that have no page numbers; in those cases we provided paragraph numbers. Here is another example of an online source that lacks page numbers: a video by Erik Qualman, which presents statistics on social media, was found on YouTube.

◀ VIDEO
Erik Qualman,
"Social Media is about People," from YouTube. *Erik Qualman.*

IN-TEXT CITATION

Erik Qualman's (2011) video provided a fast-paced barrage of statistics showing the rapid growth of social media.

REFERENCES LIST ENTRY

Qualman, E. [Screen name: Socialnomics09] (2011, June 8). Social media revolution 2011 [Video file]. Retrieved from http://www.youtube.com/watch?v=3SuNx0UrnEo

8. Source used more than once in a paragraph   Let's say that you give the author's name in a signal phrase in the text of your paper (and the publication date and page number in parentheses). To refer to that same source later in the same paragraph, simply provide the page number (or paragraph number).

For a print source

The example below refers to an article by Rob Sheffield about *Mad Men*; it appeared in the print edition of *Rolling Stone* on March 29, 2012.

IN-TEXT CITATION

Sheffield (2012) wrote that Draper built his career by "hustling in the dirty world of American dreams" (p. 36). I've always assumed that, unlike the rest of us, Don Draper, the cool ad man, is immune to the beautiful lies he sells. But as the writers further developed the character, he has become more impulsive, a man looking for Disney happiness and fresh starts. What's clear is this: "[T]his guy believes in Hollywood happy endings" (p. 36).

REFERENCES LIST ENTRY

Sheffield, R. (2012, March 29). More desperate than mad. *Rolling Stone* (1153), p. 36.

For an online source

The example below refers to an article by Miriam Coleman about Madonna's 2012 Super Bowl performance; it was published at *Rolling Stone*'s Web site on February 5, 2012. Note that while there are no page numbers for this source, we have provided paragraph numbers.

IN-TEXT CITATION

Miriam Coleman (2012) detailed how Madonna was "ushered in on a golden chariot pulled by a phalanx of centurions" for the first part of her Super Bowl performance (para. 1). As a high priestess of popular culture, Madonna understands fanfare and branding, not to mention big entrances and exits: "In the final moment of the show, gold beams projected up into the sky as Madonna disappeared from the stage in a massive plume of smoke" (para. 3).

REFERENCES LIST ENTRY

Coleman, M. (2012, February 5). Madonna's glittering Super Bowl spectacle. *Rolling Stone*, paras. 1-3. Retrieved from http://www.rollingstone.com/music/news/madonnas-glittering-super-bowl-spectacle-20120205

☞ **Attention, researchers using APA! Does your source have no page numbers?**

For most online sources (anything that's not a PDF), you will not be able to provide page numbers. However, for online articles and other text-based digital sources, you can provide paragraph numbers. Paragraph numbers help your readers see exactly where you drew from a source.

For sources you cannot provide paragraph numbers for—videos, audio recordings, and many other types of digital media—we recommend that you do your best to provide whatever information will guide your audience to a particular moment in that video or audio recording. You can provide a time range, for example.

Let's look again at the Qualman video presented as part of example 7 (p. 423). Here is how you might cite a particular moment from that source.

◀ VIDEO
Erik Qualman,
"Social Media is about People" from YouTube. *Erik Qualman.*

IN-TEXT CITATION
According to Erik Qualman's (2011) video on the role of social media, "If Facebook were a country it'd be the world's 3rd largest" (0:42-0:44).

Let's say that elsewhere in your paper you refer to other moments of the video, which is two minutes and thirty-five seconds long. This is what a very precise References list entry would look like.

REFERENCES LIST ENTRY
Qualman, E. (2011, June 8). Social media revolution 2011 [Video file]. Retrieved from http://www.youtube.com/watch?v=3SuNx0UrnEo (0:01-2:35)

Models for Specific Types of Sources

9. Book   For more in-text citation models for books, see examples 1, 2, and 5. The following is from *Just Kids* by Patti Smith.

☞ **Attention, researchers! Citing entire works is a rarity.**

When working with sources, 99.9 percent of the time you refer to specific passages and pages from a source—and include them in both your in-text citation and the corresponding References list entry. In the *extremely* rare instance that you need to summarize an entire work (as shown in the example below), you do not need to provide specific page numbers. Unless you are creating an annotated bibliography (p. 299), we do not recommend that you make a practice of summarizing entire sources.

→ IN-TEXT CITATION (that summarizes entire work)
In her memoir, Patti Smith (2010) described numerous adventures with the artist Robert Mapplethorpe, highlighting stories from when they lived in the Chelsea Hotel.

REFERENCES LIST ENTRY
Smith, P. (2010). *Just kids*. New York, NY: HarperCollins.

IN-TEXT CITATION (that quotes from a specific passage)
Smith (2010) writes: "My mother gave me *The Fabulous Life of Diego Rivera* for my sixteenth birthday. I was transported by the scope of his murals, descriptions of his travels and tribulations, his loves and labor" (p. 12).

REFERENCES LIST ENTRY
Smith, P. (2010). *Just kids*. New York, NY: HarperCollins, 1-12.

IN-TEXT CITATION (that paraphrases a specific passage)
She was quite taken by a sixteenth birthday gift from her mother: *The Fabulous Life of Diego Rivera* (Smith, 2010, p. 12).

REFERENCES LIST ENTRY
Smith, P. (2010). *Just kids*. New York, NY: HarperCollins, 1-12.

10. Article or essay   The following models show how to cite online and print articles. In February 2012, a magazine called *5280: The Denver Magazine* published an article by Josh Dean—"The Australian Shepherd Is From"—in two forms: online and in print.

IN-TEXT CITATION (article from an online magazine)
According to Dean (2012), "[D]ogs that appeared to be Aussies were doing their jobs all over the West, but no one seemed interested in documenting their provenance" (para. 1).

REFERENCES LIST ENTRY
Dean, J. (2012, February). The Australian shepherd is from [Electronic version]. *5280: The Denver Magazine*, paras. 1-38. Retrieved from http://www.5280.com /magazine/2012/02/australian-shepherd

IN-TEXT CITATION (article from a print magazine)
In his article, Dean (2012) argued that although the Australian shepherd "isn't Colorado's official state dog . . . it really should be" (p. 75).

REFERENCES LIST ENTRY

Dean, J. (2012, February). The Australian shepherd is from. *5280: The Denver Magazine*, 70-75, 110-118.

11. Source quoted in another source   The following models show how to cite a source that is quoted in another source, whether online or print. "Is Anybody Out There?" by Phil Plait was published by *Discover* magazine in two different forms—in a print edition (in its November 2010 issue) and online at discovermagazine.com (on January 27, 2011). Plait's article features several quotations from four major astronomers. To cite one of those quotations, you need to use the phrase "as cited in" to indicate that you did not read the quoted source itself, but rather found the quoted material in another source.

IN-TEXT CITATION (article from an online magazine)

According to Gibor Basri, professor of astronomy at Berkeley, proof of whether "anybody's out there" may come down to a radio signal. "There are about 60 radio telescopes scanning the skies for these signals right now," he said. "That would be the definitive answer to the search for life: If you get an intelligent signal, then you know for sure" (as cited in Plait).

REFERENCES LIST ENTRY

Plait, P. (2011, January). "Is anybody out there?" *Discover* (paras. 1-3). Retrieved from http://discovermagazine.com/2010/nov/25-is-anybody-out-there/article_view?b _start:int=0&-C=.

IN-TEXT CITATION (article from a print magazine)

According to Gibor Basri, professor of astronomy at Berkeley, proof of whether "anybody's out there" may come down to a radio signal. "There are about 60 radio telescopes scanning the skies for these signals right now," he says. "That would be the definitive answer to the search for life: If you get an intelligent signal, then you know for sure" (as cited in Plait, 2010).

REFERENCES LIST ENTRY

Plait, P. (2010, November). Is anybody out there? *Discover*, 49-51.

12. Encyclopedia or dictionary entry—or wiki entry   When the author or authors of an entry are named, follow the format that you would for an article (see example 10). When no author is named, use the name of the publisher or publication—or begin the citation with the title of the entry. If there is a publication date, provide it. If not, then indicate that there is no date by using "n.d." in parentheses following the author's name.

IN-TEXT CITATION (for online dictionary)   *publisher name*

According to Merriam-Webster (2012), psychoanalysis is used to "treat emotional disorders."

REFERENCES LIST ENTRY

Merriam-Webster. (2012). Psychoanalysis. Retrieved from http://www.merriam-webster .com/dictionary/psychoanalysis

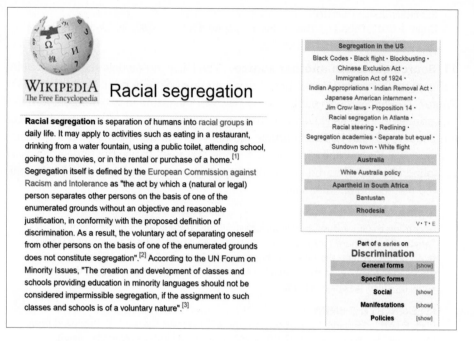

Unlike *Merriam-Webster*, *Wikipedia* is a multiple-authored wiki: This means that the authors and the content itself change all the time. Following is a model for citing a *Wikipedia* entry. We've included a "Retrieved from" date, because any *Wikipedia* entry cited today may be quite different by tomorrow.

IN-TEXT CITATION (for a wiki)
Racial segregation (2012), according to *Wikipedia*, is defined as "the separation of humans into racial groups in daily life" (para. 1).

REFERENCES LIST ENTRY
Wikipedia. (2012, February 6). Racial Segregation. Retrieved February 8, 2012, from http://en.wikipedia.org/wiki/Racial_segregation (para.1)

☞ **Attention, *Wikipedia* lovers!**

Check with your instructor about using *Wikipedia* as a source. It is a public wiki that can be edited by anyone. Tip: *Wikipedia* can be a great place to start your research, especially because the "Reference," "Further Reading," and "External Links" sections can often lead you to excellent and reliable sources to use in your research project. For example, the "Racial segregation" entry provides links to *The Washington Post*, *The American Historical Review*, and books authored by experts on apartheid. You can also go to wikipedia.org and type in "Researching with Wikipedia."

13. Entire Web site   In the extremely rare instance that you will want to cite an entire Web site—rather than a specific portion of it, such as an article—use the following model. (For information on citing a short work from a Web site, see example 14 below.) APA requires that for Web sources, you provide the name of the organization that authored the page, the publication date (use "n.d." if there is none), the name of the site, and the URL.

Note: All Web sites have an author—or at least a hosting organization. If an individual person or persons are not named as authors, then consider the organization that hosts or publishes the site to be the author. Similarly, if you find an article at MSNBC.com that does not list an individual author, then you should consider MSNBC.com as the author of that article.

Web site with an organization as author

IN-TEXT CITATION   Web site sponsor/publisher
Fastweb (2012) divided its scholarship links into categories including "Art Scholarships," "Hispanic Scholarships," and "Scholarships for College Freshmen."

REFERENCES LIST ENTRY
Fastweb. (2012). Retrieved from http://www.fastweb.com

14. Short work from a Web site   Most of what you cite from the Internet can be categorized as a "short work from a Web site." A short work is any text (of any type and medium) that is not book length or that appears as an internal page or section of a Web site. A short work can be an article, report, poem, song, video, and so on. In some cases, you will include a descriptive label (see example 15 on p. 430).

Short work with an organization as author

IN-TEXT CITATION   Web site sponsor/publisher
The WebMD entry "Anxiety Disorders" (2009) defined various types of disorders, such as panic disorder and social anxiety disorder.

REFERENCES LIST ENTRY
WebMD (2009). Anxiety disorders. Retrieved from http://www.webmd.com/anxiety
    -panic/guide/mental-health-anxiety-disorders

Short work with an individual author

IN-TEXT CITATION
All is not necessarily lost in a relationship if someone cheats. Sometimes, according to Clark-Flory (2012), infidelity might bring couples closer and "[open] new lines of communication" (para. 1).

REFERENCES LIST ENTRY
Clark-Flory, T. (2012, January 23). When infidelity heals. *Salon*. Retrieved from http://
    life.salon.com/2012/01/23/when_infidelity_heals/singleton/

15. Video, movie, or TV show   In general, if you find these sources online, cite them as you would a short work from a Web site (see also example 14). Include an identifying label in brackets: "Television series episode," "Film," and so on.

> IN-TEXT CITATION
>
> During the *Big Bang Theory* episode "The Friendship Connection," the character Wolowitz spent time trying to choose an astronaut nickname (Lorre, Kaplan, & Reynolds, 2012).

> REFERENCES LIST ENTRY (for a TV episode)
>
> Lorre, C., Kaplan, E., & Reynolds, J. (Writers), & Cendrowski, M. (Director). (2012, February 2). The friendship connection [Television series episode]. In Lorre, C., Prady, B., & Molaro, S. (Producers), *Big bang theory*. New York, NY: CBS.

> REFERENCES LIST ENTRY (for a different episode, online)
>
> Lorre, C., Kaplan, E., & Reynolds, J. (Writers), & Cendrowski, M. (Director). (2012, January 19). The recombination hypothesis [Television series episode]. In Lorre, C., Prady, B., & Molaro, S. (Producers), *Big bang theory*. Retrieved from http://www.cbs.com/shows/big_bang_theory/video/2188321432/the-big-bang-theory-the-recombination-hypothesis

16. Video game, online game, or software   To cite an entire video game, follow the format for an entire Web site and include a description—"Video game," "Online game," or "Computer software"—in brackets. For a clip from a video game, follow the format for a short work from a Web site (see example 14).

Entire video game

> IN-TEXT CITATION
>
> The goal of one popular game was to plow, plant, and harvest on "your own" virtual land (Zynga, 2009).
>
> video game publisher

> REFERENCES LIST ENTRY
>
> Zynga. (2009). *FarmVille* 2 [Online game]. Zynga. Retrieved October 13, 2012 from http://www.farmville.com/

Clip from video game

> IN-TEXT CITATION
>
> Players can build their enterprises by acquiring such animals as the arctic fox and the armadillo (Zynga, 2009).
>
> video game publisher

> REFERENCES LIST ENTRY
>
> Zynga. (2009). My mastery. [Online game clip]. *FarmVille 2*. Zynga. Retrieved February 13, 2012 from http://www.farmville.com/

17. Visuals (photos, maps, charts, posters)   Cite these works as you would a short work from a Web site (see example 14), or other longer work. Include the following, if available: author's or artist's name, date of composition, title of the work, and publication's name. Also note the medium of the composition—"Photograph," "Map," "Chart," "Poster," and so on—in brackets.

IN-TEXT CITATION
Most visitors spend time in the capital city of Kuala Lumpur, located in the southwestern part of the country (Lonely Planet, 2012).
<u>author of map</u>

REFERENCES LIST ENTRY
Lonely Planet. (2012). Malaysia [Map]. Retrieved from http://www.lonelyplanet.com/maps /asia/malaysia/

18. Comic strip/graphic work   Think of comic strips as short works—from longer works such as Web sites, magazines, and so on—and cite them as you would a short work or article from a Web site, online journal, book, or other source. Include the description—"Cartoon" or "Comic strip"—in brackets. For graphic novels (fiction) or memoirs (nonfiction), follow the format that you would for a book. In some cases, the author is also the illustrator; when that is not the case, in parentheses after the title, indicate the illustrator's name followed by the word "illustrator."

Comic strip

IN-TEXT CITATION   author/artist
Thomas's (2012) comic strip offered a commentary on the mentality of social media users.

REFERENCES LIST ENTRY
Thomas, C. (2012, February 5). Watch your head [Comic strip]. *The Washington Post Writer's Group.* Retrieved from http://www.cartoonistgroup.com/properties /wpwg.php?id=106&today=2012-02-05

Excerpt from a graphic memoir (author is also illustrator)

IN-TEXT CITATION   author/artist
In her graphic memoir, Crumb (2007, pp. 1-7) chronicled her life journey from New York to the south of France.

REFERENCES LIST ENTRY
Crumb, A. K. (2007). *Need more love: A graphic memoir.* London, United Kingdom: MQ Publications, 1-7.

Excerpt from a graphic novel (with an author and an illustrator)

IN-TEXT CITATION   author
Powell (2008) retold the classic story of Little Red Riding Hood in graphic novel form.

REFERENCES LIST ENTRY   artist
Powell, M. (2008). *Red Riding Hood: The graphic novel.* (Victor Rivas, illustrator.) North Mankato, MN: Stone Arch Books, 1-4.

19. Advertisement   To cite an ad, name the product being advertised, along with the word "Advertisement" in brackets. Following are the in-text citation and

References list entry for an ad created by the BBDO advertising firm for FedEx Kinko's. We found it at the Ads of the World Web site (which is not a publication).

IN-TEXT CITATION

One ad for FedEx Kinko's featured a larger-than-life highlighter (BBDO, 2007).

author of ad

REFERENCES LIST ENTRY

BBDO advertising firm. (2007, March). FedEx Kinko's Giant Highlighter [Advertisement]. Retrieved from http://adsoftheworld.com/media/ambient /fedex_kinko_giant_highlighter?size=_original

20. Personal e-mail, letter, or interview   Even though APA does not require you to list e-mails, personal interviews, letters, memos, or other personal communications in your References list, we recommend you do so for the sake of clarity. To cite an item in the text of your paper, include the author's first and middle initials (if known) and last name and the term "personal communication" (regardless of whether it was an interview, letter, or e-mail), and then the full date of the communication. In your References list, you can indicate in brackets the medium of the item, such as "E-mail."

E-mail *(received)*

IN-TEXT CITATION

Metro State's first Undergraduate Research Conference was scheduled to take place in April (P. Ansburg, personal communication, February 9, 2012).

author of e-mail

REFERENCES LIST ENTRY

Ansburg, P. (2012, February 9). First annual metro state undergraduate research conference [E-mail].

Interview *(conducted)*

IN-TEXT CITATION

person interviewed

I spoke to one tutor who described a method known as "glossing" (P. Calzia, personal communication, May 2, 2011).

REFERENCES LIST ENTRY

Calzia, P. (2011, May 2). Writing center discussion [Interview by E. Kleinfeld].

21. Blog post or social media posting   Cite postings as you would any short work from a Web site (see example 14). In your References list entry, add in brackets a brief description of the item: "Web log," "Facebook post," "Twitter post," and so on. Note: APA requires that you use the term "Web log." As with example 4, use the author's screen name if that is all that is provided.

IN-TEXT CITATION

author

Marino (2012) used social media to convey some of the items on his bucket list.

Marino, B. (2012). Bucket list [Facebook post]. Retrieved from http://www.facebook.com
    /billy.marino1

22. Audio recording or podcast

22. Audio recording or podcast Cite podcasts that you've accessed online in the same way you would cite a short work from a Web site (see example 14). Audio recordings should be cited similarly to works of art, regardless of whether they are downloaded from the Web or not.

Podcast from Web

IN-TEXT CITATION
Conan (2012) introduced listeners to historian Noah Andre Trudeau and described Trudeau's mission to collect artifacts from President Lincoln's presidency.

REFERENCES LIST ENTRY
Conan, N. (2012, February 9). Historian seeks artifacts from Lincoln's last days [Audio
    podcast]. Retrieved from National Public Radio Web site: http://www.npr.org
    /programs/talk-of-the-nation/

Song from the Web (via iTunes)

IN-TEXT CITATION
Ritter's (2010) song "The Curse" played with the ideas of love at first sight and coming back from the dead.

REFERENCES LIST ENTRY
Ritter, J. (2010). The curse [Song]. On *So Runs the World Away*. Brea, CA: Pytheas
    Recordings. Retrieved from http://itunes.apple.com/us/album/change-of-time
    /id362130747?i=362130766&ign-mpt=uo%3D4

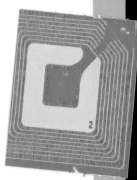

23. Phone app Cite a phone app as you would an advertisement, but include "Phone app" in brackets. Use the date of the most recent iteration of the phone app as the publication date. Put the developer's or publisher's name where you would put an author for a print source.

IN-TEXT CITATION
The social media app called MassUp was created to help bicyclists gather in large groups (Bedno, 2010).
    app publisher

REFERENCES LIST ENTRY
Bedno, A. (2010, November 17). MassUp [Phone app.]. Retrieved from http://www
    .apple.com/webapps/sports/massup.html

24. Government or business document For a government document, provide the author, government organization and department, title, and date, as well as publication information. If there is no author, provide the name of the government agency (and department, if any).

Government document

IN-TEXT CITATION

One of the top concerns of organizers of farmers' markets was the availability of parking for customers (Ragland & Tropp, 2006, pp. 6-10).

authors

REFERENCES LIST ENTRY

Ragland, E., & Tropp, D. U.S. Department of Agriculture, Agricultural Marketing

title of document

Service. (2006). *USDA national farmers market managers survey.* Washington, DC: U.S. Department of Agriculture, 6-10.

Business document *(annual report)*

IN-TEXT CITATION (for document found online; no page numbers)

The company that makes Clif Bars had in place a plan that allowed employees to purchase stock in the company (Pham & Hammond, 2010).

authors

REFERENCES LIST ENTRY

title of document

Pham, T., & Hammond, E. (Eds.). Clif Bar & Company (2010). All aspirations: Clif Bar & Company annual report [PDF file]. Retrieved from http://www.clifbar.com /uploads/default/ClifBar_AA2010.pdf

25. Literary work (novel, poem, fairy tale, etc.)   Provide the author, date, title, publisher's city, and publisher. For a selection (such as an essay) within a longer work (such as a collection of essays), provide the selection title before the full title.

IN-TEXT CITATION

One technique the author used was simile. For example, she described "bundled dough mounds" as being "as white and round as babies" (McCoy, 2012, p. 1).

Novel *(print)*

REFERENCES LIST ENTRY

McCoy, S. (2012). *The baker's daughter: A novel.* New York, NY: The Crown Publishing Group, 1-232.

Novel *(e-book)*

REFERENCES LIST ENTRY

McCoy, S. (2012). *The baker's daughter: A novel* [Kindle version]. Retrieved from http://www.amazon.com/The-Bakers-Daughter-Novel-ebook/dp/B004W3IEI6

26. Selection from an anthology or textbook   Include the selection author, publication date, and selection title, followed by the anthology editors, anthology title, page range of selection, publisher's city, and publisher.

IN-TEXT CITATION

The cost of fruits and vegetables versus the cost of meat and dairy has had a lot to do with government subsidies (The Physicians Committee, 2012).

author of selection (shortened)

author of selection

The Physicians Committee for Responsible Medicine. (2012). Why does a salad cost
more than a Big Mac? [Chart]. In A. Braziller & E. Kleinfeld (Eds.), *Bedford book
of genres: A guide* (p. 121). Boston, MA: Bedford/St. Martin's.

information on
textbook where
selection appears

27. Object/artifact (cereal box, etc.)   If you find an object or artifact online, cite
it as a short work from a Web site, but include a description of the item in brackets.
If you find such a source in the physical world, cite it as a work with an author and
include a descriptor in brackets.

IN-TEXT CITATION
The box is a cheerful sunny yellow meant to attract children, but parents likely focus
on the red heart and the soft claim about lowering cholesterol (General Mills, 2012).

author is an organization

▲ OBJECT
Cheerios box.
iStockphoto.

Object *(found online)*

REFERENCES LIST ENTRY
General Mills. (n.d.). Cheerios [Cereal box]. Retrieved from http://www.cheerios.com
/Products/Cheerios

Object *(found in physical world)*

REFERENCES LIST ENTRY
General Mills. (n.d.). Cheerios [Cereal box].

COMPOSING IN GENRES

CONTENTS

FILM STILL ▶
Hugh Jackman as
Wolverine, from
X-Men: a source
for student Gwen
Ganow's superhero
project. *Everett
Collection.*

By now you are familiar with a variety of genres (introduced in Chapters 1–4) and the choices writers and artists make. You've experienced a range of rhetorical situations and seen how composers work with genres. You've learned how to identify sources and draw on them to develop your ideas—from basic topic to research question to research plan (Chapters 5–7).

You've built your foundation. Now it's time to choose your genre—and create your own composition. To help you with this process, we've provided a model. In this chapter, we'll follow Gwen Ganow, one of Amy's former students, as she drafts, chooses her genre, revises, finishes, and polishes a film review and an accompanying Author's Statement.

As you'll see, choosing a genre and drafting are related activities that sometimes overlap. Sometimes you need to start drafting before you can decide on a genre, or vice versa.

In this chapter, we'll guide you through the following processes, along with Gwen, as she moves from exploratory draft to finished genre composition and accompanying Author's Statement. *(Gwen Ganow's superhero project presented in Chapters 8 through 10 appears by permission of Gwen Dalynn Ganow.)*

▲ STUDENT AUTHOR PHOTO **Gwen Ganow,** Amy's student at Red Rocks Community College. *This image appears throughout chapter by permission of Gwen Dalynn Ganow.*

ROUGH DRAFTING

At this stage, you know your topic. You've formed a research question and gathered sources, and have a general idea of what you want to say. (For help with topics and research questions, see Chapter 5.) You may have decided on your genre, but don't worry if you haven't. Perhaps you know you want to persuade your audience about the importance of spaying and neutering pets, but aren't sure whether you'll create an editorial, a collage, or an ad, for example. Regardless, you'll want to get your ideas out of your head and down on paper (or up on your computer screen).

Advice for Rough Drafting

As you begin your rough/exploratory draft, remember that it is just for you. No one else ever needs to see it. Think of your first draft not as an organized, perfect piece of writing with a clear purpose, but as a messy opportunity for creativity and experimentation.

Don't worry about a thesis, or about being logical or eloquent. Instead, focus on quantity rather than quality. That's right: quantity not quality. Think of words in the first draft as raw materials. You want as much raw material to work with as possible. Imagine an artist beginning a painting. Would she have only the exact amount of paint she needs to create her piece? What if she changes her mind

☞ **Attention, composers! Wondering how to begin?**

As you think about what form your composition will take, ask yourself the following:

• What do I want to accomplish? Who is my primary audience, and how will I connect with my audience?

• What genre will work best for my rhetorical situation and be most persuasive?

• What genre(s) am I already an expert in? Which are the most challenging? Which work best with my schedule?

For an Index of Sources & Contexts for material referenced in this chapter; see the e-Pages at **bedfordstmartins.com /bookofgenres.**

midway through the painting and wants to use more yellow than red? Wouldn't it make sense for her to begin with extra paint in each color to allow her the flexibility to modify her ideas? Writing and other kinds of composing are similar. Beginning with more words than you need gives you more options. Here are some pointers for getting your first draft written:

1. Set a timer for thirty minutes and force yourself to write for the entire time, not stopping for anything. That means no stopping to reread and correct or to refer to sources or models, and definitely no stopping to check Facebook.

2. Don't stop to correct or edit what is on the page.

3. Write until you have five thousand words or you run out of time.

Don't worry about grammar, punctuation, spelling, transitions, topic sentences, organization, titles, and so on. Don't even worry about genre or what the finished piece will look or sound like. Once you have your thoughts down, you can think logically about your purpose, audience, and the points you want to convey.

At this stage, if you're putting pressure on yourself to write flawless, beautiful prose, remind yourself of the term *rough draft*—with *rough* being defined as coarse, rugged, crude, unrefined, graceless, unfinished, tentative, imperfect, or approximate. Take a little more pressure off by thinking of Anne Lamott's phrase "shitty first draft." Everybody, including published authors, writes them.

Let's take a look at one student's drafting process. When Gwen Ganow took a composition class with Amy at Red Rocks Community College, she composed an argument about superheroes and social attitudes, starting with this question:

> **RESEARCH QUESTION**
> **To what extent do superheroes reflect real-world values and attitudes?**

She then moved from that question to an exploratory rough draft.

▲ STUDENT AUTHOR PHOTO **Gwen Ganow.**

Guided Reading: A Rough Draft

Gwen Ganow (Student)

Superhero Project: Rough Draft

Gwen began with some exploratory drafting to solidify what she wanted to say about superhero comics and social attitudes.

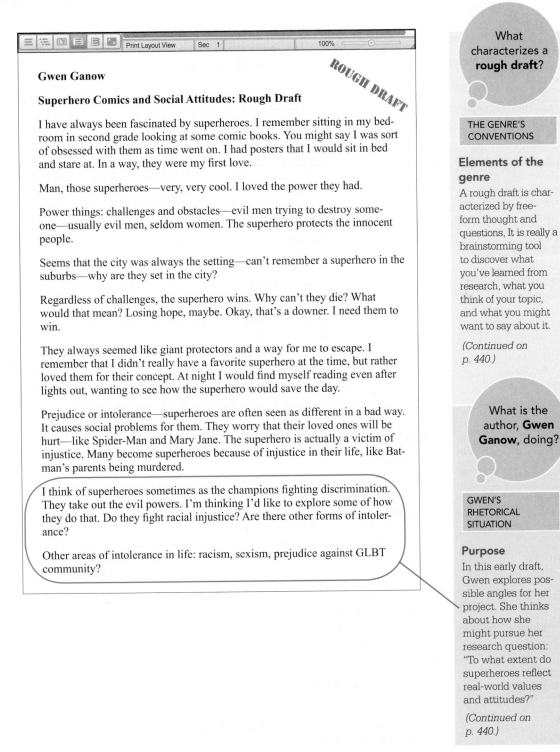

Gwen Ganow

Superhero Comics and Social Attitudes: Rough Draft

I have always been fascinated by superheroes. I remember sitting in my bedroom in second grade looking at some comic books. You might say I was sort of obsessed with them as time went on. I had posters that I would sit in bed and stare at. In a way, they were my first love.

Man, those superheroes—very, very cool. I loved the power they had.

Power things: challenges and obstacles—evil men trying to destroy someone—usually evil men, seldom women. The superhero protects the innocent people.

Seems that the city was always the setting—can't remember a superhero in the suburbs—why are they set in the city?

Regardless of challenges, the superhero wins. Why can't they die? What would that mean? Losing hope, maybe. Okay, that's a downer. I need them to win.

They always seemed like giant protectors and a way for me to escape. I remember that I didn't really have a favorite superhero at the time, but rather loved them for their concept. At night I would find myself reading even after lights out, wanting to see how the superhero would save the day.

Prejudice or intolerance—superheroes are often seen as different in a bad way. It causes social problems for them. They worry that their loved ones will be hurt—like Spider-Man and Mary Jane. The superhero is actually a victim of injustice. Many become superheroes because of injustice in their life, like Batman's parents being murdered.

I think of superheroes sometimes as the champions fighting discrimination. They take out the evil powers. I'm thinking I'd like to explore some of how they do that. Do they fight racial injustice? Are there other forms of intolerance?

Other areas of intolerance in life: racism, sexism, prejudice against GLBT community?

ROUGH DRAFT

Print Layout View   Sec 1   100%

What characterizes a **rough draft**?

THE GENRE'S CONVENTIONS

Elements of the genre

A rough draft is characterized by free-form thought and questions, It is really a brainstorming tool to discover what you've learned from research, what you think of your topic, and what you might want to say about it.

(Continued on p. 440.)

What is the author, **Gwen Ganow**, doing?

GWEN'S RHETORICAL SITUATION

Purpose

In this early draft, Gwen explores possible angles for her project. She thinks about how she might pursue her research question: "To what extent do superheroes reflect real-world values and attitudes?"

(Continued on p. 440.)

THE GENRE'S CONVENTIONS

GWEN'S RHETORICAL SITUATION

Style

Gwen is not worried about style, grammar, or how the draft reads. It's not meant to be perfect. Her writing is very casual, as if she's writing in a journal to herself.

Design

A rough draft is not designed. It's typically a Microsoft Word document.

Sources

Gwen does not discuss sources in this draft, but she could have, depending on how far along she was in her research process.

She allows herself to be unfocused as she starts with her fascination with superheroes. After doing this low-stakes drafting she realizes that she wants to cover how superheroes fight intolerance.

Audience

At this point, Gwen is writing for herself and her instructor, Amy. They'll go over this draft together to try to pin down a

direction. Gwen will later identify a specific outside-of-the-classroom audience.

Rhetorical appeals

Gwen is not concerned right now about ethos, logos, and pathos. She's in exploration mode.

Modes & media

Gwen e-mailed this Word document to her instructor.

After writing her first draft, Gwen talked with Amy about directions she might take with her topic. Together they decided that Gwen should look back at her initial research, specifically the sources dealing with the history of comics.

CHECKLIST Getting Started on a Rough Draft? Keep the following questions in mind.

Exploration

☐ **What do I already know about my topic?** What intrigues me about this topic? What questions do I still have about it?

☐ **Based on my research so far, what arguments am I familiar with about this topic?** Are there some that resonate for me more than others? Do I have an opinion on this topic?

☐ **Is there a way to narrow my topic** by time, place, demographics, or something else? For example, if I write about gun control, do I focus on guns on college campuses (narrow by place) or the growth of shooting ranges geared toward women (narrow by demographics)?

Rhetorical Situation

☐ **What is my purpose?** What do I want to say—and how do I want to say it? Do I want to tell a story? Inform? Persuade? Some combination?

☐ **Who am I composing for?** Is my primary audience mainly the other students in this course? My instructor? Anyone with access to the course space or blog? Or to the campus newspaper or Web site? Who makes up my secondary audience? Am I writing for a broader, more public audience too? For others on campus? For anyone with an Internet connection?

☐ **How will I connect with my audience?** How will I establish my authority as a composer (ethos) so that my readers will trust me? What is the most logical way for me to present what I have to say? To what extent will I want to appeal to my audience's emotions? For example, if I want to persuade people to take a certain action, how will I cultivate their enthusiasm?

REREADING & ANNOTATING SOURCES

We believe that critical reading is a crucial part of the composing process. By critical reading, we mean more than simply moving your eyes across a page of text. When you read critically, you read with an eye for detail, noticing not just *what* another author or artist says but *how* she says it. For example, imagine you are reading an article in *The Onion* that you think is hilarious. As you read, you relate to the content and subject, but you might also zoom in on what the author does to make the piece so funny: maybe using a lot of exaggeration and sarcasm, as well as clever details. You might then try using exaggeration and sarcasm in a piece you are writing, to heighten the humor.

Earlier in this book, we focused on reading a variety of genres (Chapters 1–4), on reading to explore topics and creating a research plan (Chapter 5), and on previewing, evaluating, and choosing sources (Chapter 6). When you read as part of your composing process, we recommend the following steps.

Steps for Rereading & Annotating Sources

Step 1. Preview each source.   If you've already done this earlier in your process, do it again to refresh your memory. (For a more thorough explanation, see "How Do I Preview a Source Critically?" on pp. 314–21.) Ask yourself the following:

» Who is the author of this text (remember, a text can be written words, video, an audio podcast, or something else)? What, if anything, do I know about him or her? Are any details or credentials provided?

» What can I figure out from the title? A title will usually hint at an author's topic and purpose. Consider two titles: "How to Conserve Water at Home" and "Political Factors Affecting Nationwide Water Conservation Efforts." Both pieces are obviously about saving water, but the titles make clear that the authors wrote for different purposes and audiences. The first piece is most likely aimed at homeowners and is probably very straightforward; the second piece sounds more technical and may have been written for scientists, a government agency, or some other specialized audience.

» What can I determine about this piece based on where it was published or appeared?

Step 2. Mark up each source.   This means writing notes on the piece you are reading (or if the piece is not text-based—say you're working with video—using the annotating tools at your disposal). Annotating is different from highlighting. Highlighting allows you to remind yourself of what you found interesting or important as you read, but it doesn't allow you to record why you found things interesting or important. Annotating is more active; it gives you the chance to record your critical thoughts as you read more closely. It also keeps you engaged with the text, as it allows you to "talk back" to it.

We advise that you follow steps 3–7 as you annotate, incorporating these points into your notes.

Step 3. Identify each author's purpose & main points.   What is the author's purpose? How clear is it? Can you put it in your own words? This is a good way to check your own understanding of what you're reading. If you can summarize what you've read in your own words—that is, without quoting the piece you've read—then you probably understand it. By the same token, if you can't summarize it in your own words, chances are you don't fully grasp what you've read and you should reread more carefully.

Step 4. Identify each author's audience.   Who do you think is the composer's primary audience? What makes you think so? Can you tell who the author's secondary audiences might be? How does the author address his or her audience? What kind of relationship does the author try to create with the audience? For example, if the author writes in the first person and addresses the audience as "you," that creates a sense of intimacy. How do you feel toward the author and why?

Step 5. Analyze each author's use of sources, evidence, & rhetorical appeals.   Notice whether the piece presents statistics, anecdotes, personal experiences, or other types of evidence to support its points. Also note whether the piece is using ethos, pathos, or logos. As you notice these things, keep in mind that if you are positively affected by the use of evidence and rhetorical appeals in the piece, you might want to try the same techniques in your own writing.

Step 6. Pay some attention to the genre and the conventions that are evident.   Keep your eyes open for how genre conventions help you identify the genre. Begin thinking about how you could incorporate the conventions into your own genre piece. Which features and conventions get your attention and guide you through the piece? For example, do images give you a clearer picture of statistics that would otherwise confuse you?

Step 7. Notice each author's style & techniques.   Be aware of how the writing affects you, and notice techniques you might want to try yourself. Whenever you see an author doing something particularly effective or interesting—say, integrating dialogue or introducing an image or presenting an argument—note how the author does it so that you can try it yourself.

CHECKLIST Analyzing Sources & Genres as You Draft? Keep the following questions in mind.

The Rhetorical Situation

☐ **Purpose.** What seems to be the author's purpose? How is that purpose made clear? How is that purpose achieved? How could I use similar techniques to establish my purpose in the piece I'm drafting?

☐ **Audience.** Who seems to be the targeted audience for the piece? How is that made clear? How are vocabulary, examples and details, organization, and other elements geared toward the targeted reader? How could I use similar techniques to engage my audience?

☐ **Rhetorical appeals.** How does the author use rhetorical appeals to connect with the audience? How could I use similar appeals in my own piece?

☐ **Modes & media.** How does the author's choice of mode and medium affect my level of engagement with the piece? For example, if the piece is a video, does the background music keep me interested or distract me? Can I use the author's choices about mode and medium as models for my own choices? Or as cautionary tales?

The Genre's Conventions

☐ **Elements of the genre.** How does the author use the elements of the genre to guide me through the piece? If I am composing in the same genre, how can I use the elements of the genre to guide readers through the piece?

☐ **Style.** How do the word choices, sentence structures, use of literary devices (like metaphor), and other stylistic techniques used by the author get me engaged in the piece? How can I use similar stylistic techniques to keep my readers engaged?

☐ **Design.** How has the author used design elements, such as color, images, and font, to emphasize the purpose and main point? How could I use similar design elements to convey my purpose and main point?

☐ **Sources.** What kinds of sources does the author refer to? How are these sources cited? How does the author make it clear when source material has been consulted? How can I use the author's strategies with sources as a model (or anti-model) for what I want to do?

▲ STUDENT AUTHOR
PHOTO **Gwen
Ganow.**

Guided Process: How to Reread & Annotate a Source ▼

Gwen Ganow (Student)

Superhero Project: An Annotated Source

Gwen decided to return to her sources, which included Dwight Decker's essay "Fredric Wertham: Anti-Comics Crusader Who Turned Advocate" (see p. 445), Brandford Wright's book *Comic Book Nation*, and various comic books by Alex Ross. She focused on the Dwight Decker essay, which she had found through a simple Google search on the history of comics. She especially liked how the author of the piece approached comics as a subject worthy of serious study. She also liked the author's tone and thought she might want to use a similar tone in her own writing. In this way, Gwen read this piece as both a source of information and a source of inspiration for *how* to write about her topic.

Gwen found Dwight Decker's article at *The Art Bin*, a magazine published by Karl-Erik Tallmo of Slowfox Press and archived at the press's blog. Decker notes at the end of his article: "This is a re-written version of an article that appeared in the magazine *Amazing Heroes* in 1987. Also available in Swedish. © Dwight Decker, 1987, 1997." *Amazing Heroes* (1981–1992, published by Fantagraphics Books) was a magazine about comics for comic book fans.

Also included with Decker's article is the following biography:

"Born 1952, Dwight R. Decker has been an active comics fan since 1967. By day he is a technical writer in the electronics industry, and by night he works as a freelance comics translator for publishers in the United States and Europe. [Decker] publishes his own fanzine, *Torch*, [and is] presently living in Phoenix, Arizona."

(*"Fredric Wertham—Anti-Comics Crusader Who Turned Advocate" by Dwight Decker is reprinted here by permission of the author, © Dwight Decker.*)

Fredric Wertham — Anti-Comics Crusader Who Turned Advocate

by Dwight Decker

Illustration:
Asa Harvard

In the late 1940s and early 1950s, a distinguished psychiatrist named Dr. Fredric Wertham made a name for himself in the United States by leading a crusade against violent comic books. His 1954 book exposing the comic-book industry, *Seduction of the Innocent*, is still remembered in American comics fandom as a wildly exaggerated and overwrought polemic and has gone on to become a collector's item in its own right. Even the comic books mentioned in the text or used as source illustrations have also become collector's items because of their association with him and the book. Facing a public relations nightmare and hearings by the U.S. Senate subcommittee on juvenile delinquency, fearful publishers either went out of business or banded together to form a Comics Code Authority that would censor comic books before some outside body did it for them.

American comics fans have no cause to love Dr. Wertham. They remember him as the man who attacked comics with his hysterical book, helped kill EC Comics (the one publisher doing anything like adult-level material), and brought on the Comics Code that reduced American comics to a childish mentality. Many fans have associated Dr. Wertham with Senator Joseph McCarthy, well-known for his anti-Communist crusade at about the same time, and legends circulate of Dr. Wertham accusing comic books of being a Communist plot or some such.

"*Seduction of the Innocent*—the influence of comic books on today's youth." On the book's inner flap you could read: "90,000,000 comic books are read each month. You think they are mostly about floppy-eared bunnies, attractive little mice and chipmunks? Go take a look."

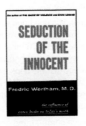

The actual story is somewhat different, and much more complicated. As an indicator of the general trend of Dr. Wertham's thinking, consider these three quotes from his various books:

> I have known many adults who have treasured throughout their lives some of the books they read as children. I have never come across any adult or adolescent who had outgrown comic-book reading who would ever dream of keeping any of these "books" for any sentimental or other reason. —*Seduction of the Innocent* (1954)

> When *Seduction of the Innocent* appeared in the middle fifties, it started a grass-roots social reaction. . . . A change occurred. Murder in comic books decreased, and so did the number of crime-comic-book publishers. Within a few years after the publication of *Seduction of the Innocent*, twenty-four out of twenty-nine crime-comic-book publishers went out of business. But it was only a partial victory. We now meet some of the child

Continues next page

Gwen's notes on Decker's article

Decker draws on a bunch of sources, including passages from Wertham's books, articles, and, later, his fanzine, as well as a *New York Times* obituary.

Decker builds ethos through his authoritative tone, and logos by backing up his points with specific evidence, organized chronologically.

Decker informs and draws on sources—but presents his opinions about Wertham's crusade against comics and the contradictions when Wertham reinvents himself. So I'd characterize the piece as a researched argument.

Researched arguments are characterized by, well, research and are typically documented according to a scholarly style, unless they are created for a popular, nonacademic audience (as is the case here).

comic-book readers as parents of the "battered child" or in similar roles. Moreover, very many of the old comic books are still around at reduced prices. —*A Sign for Cain* (1966)

Comic-book collecting which started as a nice nostalgic hobby is in some danger of becoming an overpriced, overcommercialized transaction. —*The World of Fanzines* (1974)

A man probably has a right to change his mind over the course of twenty years, but did Dr. Wertham really change his? How did a prominent psychiatrist and author get mixed up with comic books in the first place?

Fredric Wertham, 1895–1981.

According to his obituary in the *New York Times* (December 1, 1981), Fredric Wertham was born in Munich, Germany, in 1895. He studied at Kings College in London and at the Universities of Munich and Erlangen, and received his MD from the University of Würzburg in 1921. He did post-graduate study in London, Vienna, and Paris, and correspondence with Sigmund Freud led him to take up psychiatry as his life's work. He settled in the United States in 1922, becoming a citizen in 1927.

Wertham's subsequent career was impressive. He held the posts of senior psychiatrist for the New York City Department of Hospitals and director of the mental hygiene clinics at Bellevue Hospital and later Queens General Hospital. He was also director of the Lafargue Clinic in Harlem, a mental hygiene clinic for the poor in a mostly black section of New York City. His article for the *American Journal of Psychotherapy*, "Psychological Effects of School Segregation," was submitted to the United States Supreme Court as an important piece of evidence in the legal case that led to the 1954 ruling that declared racial segregation in schools to be unconstitutional.

Where Dr. Wertham made his name was as a consulting psychiatrist for the court system. The psychiatric clinic he directed for the New York City court was probably the first clinic in the United States in which all convicted felons received a psychiatric examination. His recommendations led to the modernization of facilities and methodology at many mental and criminal holding institutions.

Dr. Wertham was also an author. His first book was *The Brain as an Organ* (1934), a straightforward scientific work. *Dark Legend,* however, was a psychological case history of a seventeen-year-old boy who murdered his mother, written for a more general audience and with literary allusions. The reviews were mostly favorable, though an MD referred to "slips and inconsistencies which definitely mar the book as a scientific study." Criticisms of sloppy writing would dog every book Wertham wrote. His 1949 book, *Show of Violence,* is a general study of murder in which he discusses some of the major murder cases he was involved with as either a court witness or a consultant.

Parents and educators had been complaining about comic books for years. As early as December, 1940, when comic books were still in their infancy, the *National Education Association Journal* ran an article discussing "An Antidote to the Comic Magazine Poison." Dr. Wertham ran into comic books in the course of his work with juvenile offenders, and noting that many of the delinquents read them avidly, concluded that they were important environmental factors leading the kids to crime and violence. He presented his case in an article published in the May 29, 1947, issue of the *Saturday Review of Literature,* and after that he was off and running in his crusade against violent comic books. Over the next seven years, he would give lectures, write articles, and testify as an expert witness before legislative committees investigating the comic-book menace, culminating in the publication of his book *Seduction of the Innocent* in 1954.

Latterday American comics fans, who look back at the anti-comics crusade with fear and loathing, and fret nervously over whether it might happen again, tend to ignore the point that comics publishers of the early '50s virtually cut their own throats. While Dr. Wertham overstated his case to a sometimes ludicrous degree, he didn't have to: comics really were as crude, violent, and tasteless as he claimed, as any parent or legislator could easily confirm. With the postwar eclipse of costume heroes, comic books moved into increasingly violent and graphic crime and horror. Parents and legislators were worried enough about children seeing pictures of endless murders and mutilations and severed body parts in comics that were anything but fuzzy bunny books; then a distinguished psychiatrist came along and told them exactly what they had suspected all along—yes, children who read crime comic books became hardened to violence, and even accepted it as a useful problem-solving device. Comic books taught children to be cruel, sexually warped, dishonest, and contemptuous of soft virtues like pity or love. Comic books were still relatively mild in 1947 when Dr. Wertham began his crusade, but some publishers lost all restraint into the 1950s, running increasingly violent and gory stories that only confirmed everything he said.

Outside the forbidden pages of de Sade, you find draining a girl's blood only in children's comics.

One of Dr. Wertham's samples from the book, with his own caption.

Seduction of the Innocent is a remarkable book. Like most of Dr. Wertham's publications, it is short on proof of its assertions and long on polemics, anecdotes related without any sources cited, and literary quotations or allusions crowbarred into the text. Several generations of comics fans have had a chance to discover the book and react to it now, and everything you've heard about it is probably true. Dr. Wertham does accuse Superman of being a fascist, Batman and Robin of being a homosexual fantasy of a man and a boy living together, and Wonder Woman of being just plain kinky (judging from the early years of that strip, with all the downright astonishing emphasis on bondage and submission, I'd have to say he called that one pretty well). He does make the claim that comic-book drawings contain "pictures within pictures" for "those who know how to look," his Exhibit A being the shading of a man's shoulder muscles that supposedly evoke a woman's naked torso when squinted at right. Dr. Wertham does badly misinterpret a few stories, notably an EC one in which some overly patriotic citizens beat a man to death for not saluting the flag, only to discover at the end that he was blind and couldn't see it; Wertham claimed that the story *favored* rough treatment of insufficiently patriotic individuals, somehow missing the point of a fairly heavyhanded story.

Mr. Decker's own fanzine *Torch*.
By permission of Douglas Jones.

NOTE: Several paragraphs are intentionally omitted. Decker's final paragraphs appear below. —Eds.

Continues next page

Gwen's notes on Decker's article

This researched argument originally appeared in *The Art Bin*, an early online magazine, now archived by its publisher, Karl-Erik Tallmo.

This researched argument, in effect, is posted on a blog, but does not reflect the typical conventions such as hyperlinks and comments, for example. This may be because it was published in the early days of the Internet, before blog conventions were what they are now.

I like the use of text and images—and also Decker's personable but authoritative style. He isn't simply an excited comics fan; he seems like a scholar and takes comics seriously. He persuades me that comics are a worthy topic of study and that I could write about them seriously myself.

Dr. Wertham's account in the introductory chapter [of his book *The World of Fanzines*] of how he got involved with fanzines is interesting, as he doesn't mention *Seduction of the Innocent* or his anti-comic book work in the '50s. The unknowing reader is left with the impression that Wertham is simply a public figure known for his "writings or talks on such subjects as mass media, youth problems, or violence," and fanzine editors sent him their publications just to communicate pleasantly with the nice gentleman in response. Wertham gives no hint of his personal position in the world of fanzines as a near-legendary bogeyman, regarded by many of their editors and contributors as incarnate evil walking the earth.

He seemed to only reluctantly acknowledge comic books and science fiction as the source of fanzines and fandom, and gave a couple of the most skewed capsule histories of the genres I've ever seen, concentrating on their anti-war and non-violent aspects. In discussing the comics fanzines' emphasis on superheroes, he offered the remark that "the creative imagination of fanzine writers and artists, especially the younger ones, tends in the direction of heroes, maybe in that lies a message for our unheroic age." This is more than a little remarkable coming from the man who in *Seduction* classified superheroes as a bizarre variant of "crime comics" and thought Superman in particular was a fascist avatar. Mostly, he glosses over the comic-book connection of comics fandom, treating it puzzledly or condescendingly when he can't avoid it, and seems to proceed on the premise that fandom just spontaneously organized itself as a communications vehicle for teenagers, with comic books only an incidental, even accidental aspect of it all. As usual, Dr. Wertham concentrates on violence and is delighted to report that there isn't any in the world of fanzines.

The World of Fanzines is a masterpiece of scholarship gone off the track. It's the only book you'll find about its subject in most libraries even though the author never quite understood what he was writing about. He never said as much—he couldn't admit it for the sake of professional pride, perhaps—but *The World of Fanzines* contradicts everything Dr. Wertham wrote about comic books and their readers in his previous books.

In the end, he decided, we'd turned out pretty much all right.

CHOOSING A GENRE TO COMPOSE IN

After reviewing your sources and creating a rough, exploratory draft, you should have a better sense of what you want to say about your topic. Your next decision is to choose a genre. You may find the checklist on page 450 helpful.

Steps for Choosing a Genre to Compose In

Step 1. Revisit your topic & research question. Remember that rough draft? Since you've done more reading and analyzed a variety of genres, what's changed for you? How might that affect your focus?

Step 2. Focus on your purpose. Look over your initial draft and highlight some of the main ideas you want to explore. Make a list of four or five of them. Next, choose the idea that energizes you the most, the one that you will be most excited to write about. Then, decide on the primary purpose of the piece you are composing.

Step 3. Really think about your audience. Consider your audience. Keep in mind that aspects of your topic that are obvious to you may not be obvious to your audience.

Step 4. Strategize on how you'll use rhetorical appeals. Start thinking about how to appeal to your audience's senses of ethos, logos, and pathos. Many composers begin with only a general sense of how they will use rhetorical appeals, but while drafting realize which appeals will be most effective.

Step 5. Consider your mode & medium. Once you have narrowed the scope of your purpose and audience, think about whether you want to work with text, visuals, video, audio, or some combination. Consider the advantages of each, as well as your skills and the tools available to you. If you have access to a multimodal composing lab on campus, you may be more interested in experimenting with sound and images than if you have to teach yourself how to use sound- and image-editing software.

Step 6. Narrow your choices down to three possible genres. Now that you have your purpose and audience, and are developing a sense of how you'll work with text and other media, put together a short list of potential genres you want to consider composing in. At this point, it can be helpful to look at the particular conventions of the genres you are considering.

Step 7. Look at examples of the three genres you're interested in. There are many features to consider when looking at genre:

» **Is point of view important for your purpose and audience?** Determining the point of view for your genre piece helps you narrow your genre selection. If you need your piece to be first person so that it includes your perspective, then make sure you choose a genre that accommodates this point of view.

» **What type of connection do you want to establish with your audience?** If you want to remain at a critical distance from your audience in order to establish a more authoritative voice, you might choose a genre that emphasizes ethos in its rhetorical appeal. If you want to make a closer connection with your audience, perhaps appealing to their emotions regarding the topic, then you might choose a genre that emphasizes pathos.

» **What tone do you want to use in order to achieve your purpose?** Some writers, especially those composing a scientific report, for example, adopt a formal tone, one that perhaps incorporates jargon from the field that will be familiar to his or her readers. If you want your piece to have that level of formality, make sure to choose a genre that utilizes formality. On the other hand, if you desire to convey your message using a more informal tone, look for genres whose style is marked by a less formal tone.

Step 8. Zero in on how you'll use your sources. Finally, you'll need to think about how you will use sources in your piece—and how the genre you're considering typically deals with sources. You may realize that you need to do more research or simply reread the sources you've gathered more carefully. You'll also want to look at samples of the genre you're thinking of working in. Keep this in mind: Genre decisions at this point are still tentative; as you draft, you may stumble upon a completely different genre idea that fits your purpose, audience, and other aspects of your rhetorical situation. Keep an open mind as you draft. Remember that the drafting process is a process of discovery.

CHECKLIST Choosing a Genre? Keep the following questions in mind.

The Rhetorical Situation

☐ **Purpose.** What is my purpose? Which genres are best for what I want to do? If I want to persuade, should I consider creating an advertisement? An editorial? Something else?

☐ **Audience.** How familiar is my audience with my topic? What assumptions might my audience make about my topic? What expectations will my audience have about my piece?

☐ **Rhetorical appeals.** How will I connect with my audience? For example, if I create an ad or an editorial, how will I work within that genre to be as compelling and convincing as possible?

☐ **Modes & media.** What is the best mode for saying what I want to say? If I rely on text only, will anything be lost? And what medium would be best?

The Genre's Conventions

☐ **Elements of the genres.** What are my favorite genres? Which ones do I know the most about? Which ones do I want to try out? Which ones can I get help with? Among the sources I've drawn on in my research, which ones stood out? What are their genres? What features make a particular genre what it is? How would I use (or not use) those features?

☐ **Style.** What are my strengths as a writer/composer? What tone will be most appropriate for my composition, considering the genre I choose to use? For example, if I create an ad, can I be funny? What kind of vocabulary would I use? How much detail would be appropriate?

☐ **Design.** Once I choose the genre for my composition, how will it look (or sound)? Will I use a conventional design, or perhaps tailor a standard layout or structure to my own purposes?

☐ **Sources.** What do I already know about my topic? What sources have I gathered? Which ones will work best as sources for my composition, and why? To what extent will I need to draw on my sources? Will I need to quote from them? Document them?

Guided Process: How to Choose a Genre to Compose In ▼

Gwen Ganow (Student)

Superhero Project: Brainstorm to Refine Topic & Purpose

In the following pages, Gwen Ganow decides which genre she'd like to compose in. She does so by:

▲ STUDENT AUTHOR
PHOTO **Gwen
Ganow.**

1. Brainstorming about her topic and rhetorical situation
2. Looking at three examples of persuasive genres: an ad, a researched argument, and a film review
3. Deciding how she wants to use sources—and which genre will work best overall. In this section, Gwen moves from brainstorming about a possible genre to compose in—to making a final choice about which genre will be best for her project. (Spoiler alert: It's a film review.)

☰ ☷ ◻ ▤ ▤ ▤	Print Layout View	Sec 1	100% ⊙

Gwen Ganow

~~BRAINSTORM~~

Superhero Project: Brainstorm

WHERE AM I WITH MY TOPIC AND RESEARCH QUESTION?

Okay, I've sketched out a rough draft and looked at an argument about superheroes. But I need to think through my topic a little more. Here are some ideas and questions I'm tossing around:

- Now that I've read some more, I may focus totally on superheroes, rather than comics as a whole. Good idea?
- Most comics have superheroes. Why? Also, they are kind of underdogs with power. What does that have to do with the real world?
- Superheroes are sort of in the real world—but also in a kind of magical world where they always persevere. Why this duality?
- Superheroes use their power to protect others. Why do they care so much? And why do fans seem to need superheroes to win?
- Superheroes mainly fight injustice. Superheroes are themselves almost always victims of injustice.
    - I like the injustice angle, which gets back to my idea of writing about a social issue. Not sure what I'll say, but I may present an argument about superheroes, power, and social inequality.

WHAT IS MY PURPOSE?

I need to decide what I want to say. Also, how and why. What do I want to present to my audience about superheroes? Do I want to:

Continues next page

Gwen's notes on her project

My early research question about comics and social attitude—"To what extent do superheroes reflect real-world values and attitudes?"—is too broad.

Will revise to something like: How/why are superheroes victims of injustice? What does that have to do with their fight against injustice?

Ganow, *Superhero Project: Brainstorm,* *Continued*

Gwen's notes on her project

What I really want to do is present some type of persuasive argument about superheroes.

Print Layout View   Sec   1   100%

Tell a story?

I could tell a story about a superhero fighting some evil. The story would show some societal intolerance, maybe racism, and it would show how the superhero struggles but ultimately wins. But that's not really a fresh concept. Also, what would be the advantage of telling a story? Would I create a work of fiction with a moral or lesson—or a narrative essay? I'm not sure that's right for my topic.

Report information?

I might present information about how a superhero fights injustice. Instead of telling a story, I would give concrete information so that my reader sees how the superhero ultimately promotes tolerance. How do superheroes promote tolerance? If I took on that question, I'd need to provide information. I'd also offer analysis through my perspective. More like arguing a case. Hmm.

Persuade?

I could try to convince people that we need superheroes in the world to fight intolerance. I might use my idea of how we need hope and how superheroes give us that hope. Also, what are superheroes—and why do we need them? So I'd be defining superheroes, but also creating a persuasive argument. The question now is, how? Would an advertisement be a good idea, or some other persuasive genre?

WHO IS MY AUDIENCE?
Okay, who do I want my target readers/viewers to be?

Mainly, people who enjoy comics. Probably they read them as children and teens because they loved the stories and heroes. Also, my classmates and instructor. Beyond the people in my course, I'd like to aim at a primary audience of people who are really into comics—who know something about them and their history. A kind of expert audience.

I know I want to make a case about superheroes. I see my primary audience as comic and superhero fans like me. I see my secondary audience as people who may have less interest in superheroes.

So I have a mix of potential readers—my primary, expert audience of comics fans—and people in my classroom who may have varying levels of knowledge and interest in the topic.

What do they know about superheroes?

My primary audience already knows something about superheroes. They aren't necessarily as obsessed as I am, but they have a certain passion about the topic. They do have some level of specialized knowledge, which means I'll have to craft my argument in ways to hook in uninterested people—but also speak to my core readers (appreciative fans).

What expectations will they have?

As comic book lovers/experts, my target audience will expect me to be well-informed about superheroes. If I'm going to persuade them of something, I'll need to draw on evidence and details from comics to support my points. Whatever genre I choose for my composition, something visual and narrative will appeal to this audience.

Ganow, *Superhero Project: Brainstorm,* *Continued*

| ≣ | ⬚ | ◱ | ▤ | ▤ | ▦ | Print Layout View | Sec 1 | | 100% | ◉ |

What assumptions might they already hold about superheroes?

For most comic readers, superheroes save the day. They represent good battling evil (or vice versa) and usually do a lot of rescuing (or sabotage). At least
these are my own assumptions as a comics expert.

HOW WILL I USE RHETORICAL APPEALS?

Ethos

I think of ethos as having to do with authority. As an author, if I want to
persuade my audience, it's going to be crucial to convince them that my information and argument are credible—and that I am qualified (or authorized)
to make the argument. I've grown up with comics and have a good base of
knowledge; I'll establish that in my composition. That will help me with my
ethos.

Logos

I associate logos with logic. I'll need to build a logical case for my audience.
How to do this will become clearer once I choose a genre, I think. But I'll
need to be methodical and organized. Depending on the form my composition takes, I'll have to find ways to present and support my argument clearly.
Thinking back to some of my sources, I like how Dwight Decker does that in
his researched essay. Maybe reread?

Pathos

Emotions. Hmm. I'm not totally sure how I'll work with pathos. But part of
what makes me care about superheroes is my emotional connection to them as
people who care—who put themselves "in harm's way," as they say, to help
and rescue others. I hadn't thought of tapping into emotions in my piece, but
it might come in handy, especially if I emphasize superheroes as righters of
wrongs and fighters of injustice. I also may want to use humor as a persuasive
strategy.

WHAT MODES AND MEDIA WILL I WORK WITH?

Even though I don't know what genre I'll compose in, I should probably think
of the media I'm most comfortable with. That might impact my choice of
genre. Okay, so will my composition be:

Visual? Textual?

My composition will probably have more text than visuals. My comics-fan
audience may expect visuals, but I'm more comfortable working in text—and
presenting arguments that way. Also, I'll be drawing on sources. How would
I do that in a nontextual medium? Though it might be fun to branch out into
working with images.

I'm a good writer, but I feel less comfortable as an artist. Maybe I can use
existing images from comics in my work to support my points. (Many of my
sources are visual.) Or maybe it doesn't matter that creating visuals isn't my
strong suit. Should I experiment?

Continues next page

Gwen's notes on her project

I'll be making an argument, so it makes sense to emphasize ethos (my own authority as a comics fan) and logos (logic) to reach my audience. Also pathos—my primary audience has an emotional relationship with comics.

I think I'll use both words and im-ages—but mainly words. I'd like my sources to be ap-parent, especially to online readers. I'd also like to be able to integrate/ embed media such as video.

Gwen Ganow, *Brainstorm to Refine Topic & Purpose* 453

*Ganow, **Superhero Project: Brainstorm,** Continued*

Gwen's notes on her project

I want to be persuasive—what genres will help me convince my audience of comics lovers of my views on superheroes? Given my skills and timeframe, I'd consider three possibilities: an ad, a researched argument (which I could morph into a presentation), or a film review.

Sound? Motion (video or animation)? Other digital delivery?

I probably won't use sound, but I would consider using video clips from superhero films or animated works. I'd need to use existing content because I don't have expertise in creating this stuff myself. Also, I have a limited time frame. In a future iteration of this project, I might use other media. I might even collaborate with someone who knows how to work with video.

If I create a written text for a digital environment, I can embed links. That might be an easy way to bring in my sources. I'd like to build into my work some existing clips from films and animations.

WHAT ARE SOME PERSUASIVE GENRES? WHICH ONE SHOULD I CHOOSE?
Here are the genres I'm familiar with that are associated with persuading. Which option do I like best?

Ad?

I like that I could mix visuals with text if I made an ad. Where would I publish this ad? It would need to be somewhere that comic book fans would see it. Not sure where that would be. I also like the idea of making a commercial. Sounds fun. An ad is very obviously persuasive. This could work for me, though it wouldn't showcase my sources. But I could include them in an Artist's Statement. If my ad is image centered, then I will be creating a type of visual argument. That may be a good way to reach comic book lovers.

Editorial?

I could easily write an editorial, and maybe include some images. But I've done a lot of research, and I'd really like to show off my sources. How might this work? Most editorials are pretty short, and I'm not sure how much space I'll need to make my case. Yeah, I don't think a traditional newspaper-type editorial will work, given that I want to use images. But maybe a researched argument?

Researched argument?

This may be a better option than an editorial. I've done research and want to draw on that. If I choose this genre, I won't have to worry about length problems and could easily include visuals to make my case. I'm now thinking I could present this online in a magazine, journal, or blog. I see researched arguments and presentations as related genres. Could work. This genre would give me a framework for arguing about superheroes, and I could include related/supporting images and clips.

Collage or other visual argument—such as a comic?

It would be cool to create a persuasive comic, but I'd want help with the images and don't have a lot of time. While I love the idea of creating some kind of visual argument—I think my best bet is to work existing visuals into my composition in a meaningful way.

Presentation?

I can see myself translating a researched argument into a presentation at some point.

Ganow, *Superhero Project: Brainstorm*, *Continued*

☰ ☷ ◫ ☰ ☷ ▦	Print Layout View	Sec 1		100%	⊙

Personal statement? Resume & cover letter?
These genres don't apply to my topic, purpose, or audience. Onward!

Film review?
Hmm, this is a possibility. I love superhero / comics movies, and there are a
lot of them out there. And as an avid film-viewer I do read a lot of film reviews. I could review a film that focuses on a superhero. Interesting thought. A
film review is kind of like an editorial or researched argument in that I'd make
a case mainly through writing.

For more on **rhetorical
appeals,** see Chapter 1,
page 11.

For more on **argument
and persuasion,** see
Chapter 4, "Persuasive
Genres."

Gwen Ganow (Student)

Superhero Project: 3 Annotated Persuasive Genres

Now that Gwen has narrowed her choice of genre down to three types—an ad, a
researched argument, and a film review—she looks at an example of each:

» AD: **Douglas & Gordon,** "He Was No Ordinary Estate Agent," from the Douglas &
Gordon Web site

» RESEARCHED ARGUMENT: **Shannon Cochran,** "The Cold Shoulder: Saving Superheroines from Comic-book Violence," from *Bitch* magazine online

» FILM REVIEW: **A. O. Scott,** "*Iron Man*: Heavy Suit, Light Touches," from *The New York
Times* online

She annotates these sources, reading them not only for information about her topic,
but also to find out more about the genres and their conventions. For example, how
did the composers of these works incorporate sources?

As she reads these sources closely, she asks herself: Which of these persuasive
genres—an ad, researched argument, or film review—should I ultimately choose for
my composition?

Gwen analyzes and annotates each piece according to the author's/artist's
rhetorical situation and use of genre conventions.

How do I know this is an ad? And do I want to create one?

Gwen's notes on Douglas & Gordon ad

Elements of the genre

I like this ad's simplicity. The real estate agent superhero is vivid and colorful. The name of the agency is easy to find; the brand is reinforced by the logo on the hero's chest and beside the company name.

Style

Not much text—mainly the headline—and what's there is conversational. Effective.

Design

The image plays on pop culture. The ad creators mimic comic books with the speech bubble and text boxes.

Sources

The ad makers draw on the image of Superman. But they don't have to cite this source. That's handy.

Text of ad:
He was no ordinary estate agent.
With over 45 years experience in property and a team of more than 150 well trained, enthusiastic everyday superheroes, D&G is dedicated to providing you with an extraordinary service. We're here to fight for truth, justice and the best deal on your property.
Ad reprinted here by courtesy of Douglas & Gordon.

What are the ad's composers, Douglas & Gordon, doing?

Gwen's notes on Douglas & Gordon ad

Purpose
Douglas & Gordon want to persuade viewers that their agents can save the day. If I created an ad, what would my argument be?

Audience
This ad is aimed at people buying or selling real estate. I've identified my main audience as comic book lovers. But where would I place an ad so it reaches my audience?

Rhetorical appeals
The ad creators appeal to pathos/emotion through the message that their agents can rescue you. They appeal to ethos through the company branding.

Modes & media
This ad is online, but could easily translate to a print magazine, for example. I like that.

Next, Gwen looks at an example of a researched argument, asking herself: Would I want to compose in this genre? *(Shannon Cochran's article is reprinted here courtesy of* Bitch Magazine.*)*

How do I know this is a researched argument? Do I want to write one?

THE GENRE'S CONVENTIONS

Gwen's notes on Cochran's article

Elements of the genre
In a researched argument, the writer makes a case by presenting claims and backing them up with evidence and sources. Here, Shannon Cochran, who wrote this piece for the feminist magazine *Bitch*, refers to her sources clearly and in keeping with how sources are treated in magazine articles (e.g., not MLA or APA). She makes it easy to tell what's from a source—e.g., in the first paragraph, she clearly attributes a quotation from DC director Dan DiDio. She also synthesizes different sources together.

The Cold Shoulder   Shannon Cochran

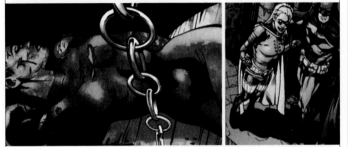

Saving Superheroines from Comic-book Violence

There's a new Bat in Gotham City. Like Bruce Wayne, she's a rich socialite by day and a black-clad vigilante at night. And, also like Bruce Wayne, in both incarnations she's apt to sweep the ladies off their feet. Kate Kane, the new, revamped Batwoman, isn't the first lesbian character to debut in the DC Comics universe, but she might have the highest profile. Last June, DC Executive Director Dan DiDio issued a press release saying the move was intended "to get a better cross-section of our readership and the world."

But the new Caped Crusader may find Gotham City a hostile work environment. Many of the series' previous female characters met with unfortunate fates. An earlier Batwoman was murdered, a female Robin was tortured to death with a power drill, one Batgirl was shot by the Joker, and another one was turned to villainy. In fact, it's so common for female superheroes to be killed in gruesome ways, comic-book fans have a term for it: "women in refrigerators." The phrase was coined in 1999 by comic-book writer Gail Simone, whose many credits include a stint on the Superman title *Action Comics* as well as current authorship of the *Birds of Prey* series.

The women-in-refrigerators syndrome got its name from a 1994 *Green Lantern* story arc, in which the titular hero's girlfriend is strangled and later discovered in a fridge. In an e-mail interview, Simone explains: "I and some male friends started making a list of the characters that had been killed, mutilated, or depowered (also a telling trend, as the more powerful a female character was, the more likely it was that she would lose those powers). It was shockingly long, and almost no one in the already small pool of valid superheroines escaped the wave of gynocentric violence."

Continues next page

What is the composer, Shannon Cochran, doing?

THE RHETORICAL SITUATION

Gwen's notes on Cochran's article

Purpose
Cochran argues that female superheroes should not be victimized in comic books. I like how she clearly states her argument. That's something I would do if I were to write a researched argument.

Audience
Cochran is writing for feminists who are into comics. Her audience is kind of like mine—readers with a perspective on comics and social issues.

Gwen's notes on
Cochran's article

Style

She writes in the third person, and sometimes in the first person, here and there. Her tone is a little formal, especially in places where she draws on sources. I like that she treats the subject seriously, but in a lively way.

Design

Cochran designed this piece for easy reading—it's organized into blocked paragraphs—with visuals placed in the foreground. I like that, but I think the author could have used more visuals and made more of what digital media offers.

bitchmedia

But so what? Don't superheroes die all the time in comic books, regardless of their biology? Sure, but as Simone says: "First, there's [always been] a larger selection of male characters, so a handful killed made barely a ripple. Second, they didn't seem to be killed in the same way—they tended to die heroically, to go down fighting. Whereas in many cases, the superLADIES were simply found on the kitchen table already carved up." Furthermore, she points out, most of the men recovered with lightning speed. Take Batman and Batgirl: "Both had their backs broken [Batman broke his in a dramatic Batcave confrontation with the villain Bane; Batgirl broke hers when she was ambushed in her home and shot in the spine by the Joker, never given a chance to fight]. Less than a year later, Batman was fine. Batgirl—now named Oracle—was in a wheelchair and remained so for many years."

Alan Moore, the writer responsible for the story arc that led to Batgirl's shattered spine, provides some insight into the editorial perspective behind the decision. As he told the industry magazine *Wizard*: "I asked DC if they had any problem with me crippling Barbara Gordon—who was Batgirl at the time—and if I remember, I spoke to Len Wein, who was our editor on the project, and he said, 'Hold on to the phone, I'm just going to walk down the hall and I'm going to ask [former DC Executive Editorial Director] Dick Giordano if it's alright,' and there was a brief period where I was put on hold and then, as I remember it, Len got back onto the phone and said, 'Yeah, okay, cripple the bitch.'"

Moore later regretted the story arc that retired Batgirl, stating in several interviews that he felt the decision was shallow and ill-conceived. However, Barbara Gordon was far from the only victim of the women-in-refrigerators syndrome. The list Simone created in 1999 included more than 90 female characters, among them Aquagirl, Hawkwoman, Elasti-Girl, Nova, Lady Flash, and at least two different Supergirls. In the eight years since, few of the list's characters have returned to life or regained their powers.

Simone also contacted other comic creators, both male and female, asking for their reactions to the list. Her letters were circulated on message boards and fan sites, provoking widespread debate and discussion in the comic-book world. Simone and her compatriots decided to create a Web site detailing the women-in-refrigerators phenomenon (now archived at http://unheardtaunts .com/wir/). The site includes Simone's original list, along with a number of the responses it sparked.

For female fans like myself, Simone had pinpointed a problem we felt keenly but had not been able to articulate. "WiR syndrome" was the terminology we needed to make our discontent with the industry's sexism coherent, and Simone's list was the ammunition behind

Gwen's notes on
Cochran's article

Rhetorical appeals

Cochran builds her ethos with her research sources. She also appeals to readers' pathos, e.g., through her choice of visuals, which convey both sex and violence; her images are meant to tap into readers' emotions and get a reaction. Like her, I'd use my research to convey my authority; I'm now more convinced of the value of visuals and pathos in persuading readers.

our arguments. And it seemed that her observations impacted the industry. "For whatever reason," Simone notes, "the next generation of writers paid a great deal more attention to making fun, entertaining, kick-ass superheroines." Notable examples include characters like Mark Andreyko's Manhunter at DC, or over at Marvel, Brian Michael Bendis's Jessica Jones, Tamora Pierce's White Tiger, and Dan Slott and Juan Bobillo's She-Hulk (thankfully reinvented as much more than a green slice of cheesecake). According to Simone, these characters have generated more female fans.

But many female fans are still angry over treatment of past characters. Although Stephanie Brown might not be well known to casual fans of the Batman mythos, readers of DC's Batman titles knew her for 12 years as Spoiler, a young and impulsive vigilante with a sunny optimism that made her an endearing foil to Batman's endlessly brooding ways. Robin's girlfriend for many years, Stephanie eventually filled out Robin's tights herself when the former Boy Wonder resigned his post. Shortly after, in 2004, Stephanie met her grisly end by the aforementioned power-drill torture by the supervillain Black Mask. The sequence spanned multiple issues and featured graphic artwork that blatantly sexualized the teenage heroine during her bondage and torture. An action figure of Black Mask, complete with power drill, was subsequently issued. No action figure of the Girl Wonder was ever made.

It felt like comics were backsliding badly. Before Stephanie Brown took over for Robin, I'd gone years without reading a *Batman* comic. It was a cover picture of Stephanie in action under the brassy logo "Robin: Girl Wonder" that had reinvigorated my interest. Soon I was buying four *Batman*-related titles every month and splurging for the occasional *Teen Titans* crossover. Stephanie's brutal death felt like a kick in the gut. I'd been a rube to fall for a promise that DC never intended to keep.

And I wasn't the only one angry about it. Mary Borsellino, a graduate student in cultural studies at Melbourne University, posted a rant on her blog that articulated her "rage and disgust" at Stephanie's treatment. Within two hours, her post had gathered about a hundred comments from like-minded fans.

"I felt like this was a sign," Borsellino wrote in an e-mail exchange, "that this was something that needed to be sustained. So I registered Girl-Wonder.org that evening."

Project Girl Wonder was initially dedicated to protesting the treatment of Stephanie Brown, but quickly took on a life of its own. While Stephanie remains the site's official symbol, Girl-Wonder.org's mission has expanded into a campaign demanding better treatment for *all* women in comics. As the site proclaims: "Batman and other

Continues next page

superhero stories are the modern age's fables, and if we don't stop the spread of this rot now they will be irrevocably corrupted by it. Stephanie Brown is a symbol of the need for change. And we're going to see that the change begins." The site attracted more than 100,000 visitors in its first couple months, with hundreds of registered users filling the message boards. In the years since, Girl-Wonder.org has organized a letter-writing campaign, distributed literature about the WiR problem to conventions and local comic stores, and sparked a new wave of debate within the industry.

For Borsellino, the Girl Wonder campaign is fueled not only by depictions in the comics, but also by the apparent disdain shown by industry editors toward their female audience. In an e-mail interview, Borsellino wrote: "Less than a week [after Stephanie's death], [DiDio] started shooting his mouth off in an interview, and described Stephanie's death-by-torture as having a 'major impact' on the lives of heroes." This statement bothered Borsellino because it was untrue (Stephanie's death didn't seem to impact male superheroes) and because of what it implied. "It completely failed to acknowledge that anybody could possibly have the girl as their hero. No, the girls are the ones who die and thereby make the boys, the real heroes, sad. It's pathetic." DiDio provoked another wave of outrage when, in response to a question from a fan at a comics convention, he allegedly intimated that Stephanie Brown deserved her torture and death because she had failed to obey Batman's orders to stay out of the fight with Black Mask.

Simone believes the anger against DiDio may be misdirected: "I'm not against shock and repulsion as story elements at all, in fact. I think comics that are slightly lurid are wonderfully compelling, and my own work regularly contains things that are simply inappropriate for anyone, thank God. And thankfully, Dan is dead serious about more diversity in both the characters and creators. It's not just more good female characters we need—it's more good gay characters, more good Asian characters, more good African-American characters, and on and on."

But the reality isn't so rosy. A former industry employee who maintains a blog at occasionalsuperheroine.blogspot.com recently removed all of her previous posts and replaced them with a twelve-part "Goodbye to Comics," in which she referenced the sexual harassment that had been a daily part of her job until she was driven to resign.

DiDio and other industry honchos might make the right noises about increasing diversity and female audiences, but even in death, Stephanie Brown has been treated unfairly. While another fallen Robin (Jason Todd, now resurrected as Red Hood) was honored with a permanent memorial in the Batcave, no sign of Stephanie's service has been installed. According to Coordinating Editor Jann

Jones, no plans for a memorial are in the works. For the boys: glorious deaths and dramatic returns. For the girls: punishment, torture, and forgotten fates.

Meanwhile, Girl-Wonder.org has expanded to include three regular columnists who keep tabs on the ongoing portrayals of female superheroes in the mainstream and alternative comics; they also recommend comics featuring strong female characters. Academic papers with titles like "The Secret Origins of Jessica Jones: Multiplicity, Irony and a Feminist Perspective on Brian Michael Bendis's *Alias*" or "Wonder Woman: Lesbian or Dyke? Paradise Island as a Woman's Community" are archived on the site. Two independent Web comics are hosted by Girl-Wonder.org, and Borsellino says she'd like to see the support for creators expand: "Someday I'd love to generate the funds to get more female creators to conventions, so their work can be seen by editors, and to perhaps have a Girl-Wonder.org publishing imprint to get titles into stores, even if only in small numbers."

The future will belong to those creators. "We are making strides at DC," Simone affirms. "I write a book with an Asian lead [*The All-New Atom*], another with a nearly all-female cast [*Birds of Prey*], another with a cast of senior citizens [*(Welcome to) Tranquility*], and another with an openly lesbian couple, among others. That would have been almost unimaginable a few years back. We've got a lot to do, but I'm very optimistic and excited to be part of it."

Borsellino is also looking forward to a brighter future for female characters and fans, but she thinks that groups like hers will be necessary to keep the industry in line. "I want Girl-Wonder.org to stand like a watchdog. We're working on forging contacts with media groups, so that the next time DC or Marvel try to do something as sickening as [the arc in which Stephanie Brown was murdered], they'll have to consider that there's this group of very noisy, very angry feminists watching their every move and hitting their speed-dial as they do it."

Both Simone and Borsellino are optimistic about DC's new Batwoman. "I think it could be an amazing book," Simone says. But Borsellino notes that her presence has come with a price. "To get Kate Kane, we lost Cass Cain, Stephanie Brown, and Leslie Thompkins entirely [the latter, though not killed, was exiled to Africa]. Barbara Gordon and Helena Bertinelli were permanently relocated to Metropolis. Onyx has vanished without any follow-up. So that's six female characters—one Asian, one poor, one elderly, one disabled, one Italian, and one black—traded off the team in order to get one rich, white, young, pretty, gay woman."

Hopefully, Batwoman will be strong and capable enough to navigate the streets of Gotham City on her own. But it can't hurt that there's a legion of real-life Girl Wonders to watch her back. We've lost enough of our heroines already.

Gwen then looks at an example of a film review. *(A. O. Scott's review reprinted here from* The New York Times, *May 2, 2008. © 2008 The New York Times. All rights reserved.)*

How do I know this is a **film review**? Do I want to write one?

THE GENRE'S CONVENTIONS

Gwen's notes on Scott's review

Elements of the genre

In a film review, a writer presents an argument about a movie and backs that up by drawing on moments from the film, and even from film history. Here, Scott's lead paragraph gets readers' attention and identifies the genre of the film. In his review Scott makes clear what he thinks of the film.

Style

Scott writes in the third person. His tone is mostly formal but is sometimes informal, e.g., his use of exclamation points and phrases including: "Yeah, that guy." He even addresses the reader as "you." I like that informality a lot.

The New York Times

Movies
Heavy Suit, Light Touches

By A. O. SCOTT

MOVIE REVIEW | 'IRON MAN'
Iron Man (2008)

Zade Rosenthal/Paramount Pictures

Iron Man, based on the Marvel comic and with Robert Downey Jr. as the title character, opens on Friday nationwide. Jon Favreau directed.

The world at the moment does not suffer from a shortage of super-heroes. And yet in some ways the glut of anti-evil crusaders with cool costumes and troubled souls takes the pressure off of *Iron Man*, which clanks into theaters today ahead of Hellboy, Batman, and the Incredible Hulk. This summer those guys are all in sequels or redos, so *Iron Man* (a Marvel property not to be confused with the Man of Steel, who belongs to DC and who's taking a break this year) has the advantage of novelty in addition to a seasonal head start.

And *Iron Man*, directed by Jon Favreau (*Elf*, *Zathura*), has the advantage of being an unusually good superhero picture. Or at least—since it certainly has its problems—a superhero movie that's good in unusual ways. The film benefits from a script (credited to Mark Fergus, Hawk Ostby, Art Marcum, and Matt Holloway) that generally chooses clever dialogue over manufactured catchphrases and lumbering exposition, and also from a crackerjack cast that accepts the filmmakers' invitation to do some real acting rather than just flex and glower and shriek for a paycheck.

There's some of that too, of course. The hero must flex and furrow his brow; the bad guy must glower and scheme; the girl must

What is the composer, **A. O. Scott**, doing?

THE RHETORICAL SITUATION

Gwen's notes on Scott's review

Purpose

Scott wants to persuade readers that *Iron Man* is a film to see. He shows readers that it's a "superhero movie that's good in unusual ways." I like that his purpose is extremely clear and that he draws on moments in the film to support his claims.

Audience

As a film critic for *The New York Times*, Scott writes for anyone generally interested in movies. In this case, his audience also consists of people familiar with the Marvel comic, people who like Robert Downey Jr., and people who like imagined worlds. My audience is similar: They are fans of comics and people who like superheroes.

Gwen's notes on
Scott's review

Design

Scott's review
appears online; he
and *The New York
Times* designers
include hyperlinks
to enhance the
content.

Sources

Scott's primary
source is the movie
Iron Man.

Note: The entire
text of this review
is available online.

The New York Times

shriek and fret. There should also be a skeptical but supportive
friend. Those are the rules of the genre, as unbreakable as the
pseudoscientific principles that explain everything (An arc reactor!
Of course!) and the Law of the Bald Villain. In *Iron Man* it all plays
out more or less as expected, from the trial-and-error building of
the costume to the climactic showdown, with lots of flying, chasing
and noisemaking in between. (I note that there is one sharp, subversive surprise right at the very end.)

What is less expected is that Mr. Favreau, somewhat in the manner of those sly studio-era craftsmen who kept their artistry close
to the vest so the bosses wouldn't confiscate it, wears the genre
paradigm as a light cloak rather than a suit of iron. Instead of the
tedious, moralizing, pop-Freudian origin story we often get in the
first installments of comic-book-franchise movies — childhood
trauma; identity crisis; longing for justice versus thirst for revenge;
wake me up when the explosions start — *Iron Man* plunges us immediately into a world that crackles with character and incident.

It is not quite the real world, but it's a bit closer than Gotham or Metropolis. We catch up with Tony Stark in dusty Afghanistan, where
he is enjoying a Scotch on the rocks in the back of an armored
American military vehicle. Tony is a media celebrity, a former M.I.T.
whiz kid and the scion of a family whose company makes and sells
high-tech weaponry. He's also a bon vivant and an incorrigible
playboy. On paper the character is completely preposterous, but
since Tony is played by Robert Downey Jr., he's almost immediately as authentic and familiar — as much fun, as much trouble — as
your ex-boyfriend or your old college roommate. Yeah, that guy.

Tony's skeptical friend (see above) is Rhodey, an Air Force officer
played with good-humored sidekick weariness by Terrence Howard. The girl is one Pepper Potts (Gwyneth Paltrow, also in evident
good humor), Tony's smitten, ultracompetent assistant. His
partner and sort-of mentor in Stark Enterprises is Obadiah Stane,
played by Jeff Bridges with wit and exuberance and — spoiler
alert! — a shaved head.

These are all first-rate actors, and Mr. Downey's antic energy and
emotional unpredictability bring out their agility and resourceful-
ness. Within the big, crowded movements of this pop symphony
is a series of brilliant duets that sometimes seem to have the
swing and spontaneity of jazz improvisation: Mr. Downey and
Ms. Paltrow on the dance floor; Mr. Downey and Mr. Howard
drinking sake on an airplane; Mr. Downey and Shaun Toub working on blueprints in a cave; Mr. Downey and Mr. Bridges sparring
over a box of pizza.

Those moments are what you are likely to remember. The plot is
serviceable, which is to say that it's placed at the service of the

Continues next page

Gwen's notes on
Scott's review

Rhetorical appeals

Scott uses logos
by retelling some
of the plot to
make his case. He
chooses language
that conveys
pathos ("bon
vivant" and "incor-
rigible playboy"),
playfulness, and
sophistication.
I like this combina-
tion. I wonder if I
could manage that.

Modes & media

This piece is
primarily a text
document avail-
able in print and
online. The digital
version includes
embedded links
to sources and
related materials.
I also want to
write for the digital
environment and
use these tech-
niques.

The New York Times

actors (and the special-effects artists), who deftly toss it around and sometimes forget it's there. One important twist seems glaringly arbitrary and unmotivated, but this lapse may represent an act of carefree sabotage rather than carelessness. You know this ostensibly shocking revelation is coming, and the writers know you know it's coming, so why worry too much about whether it makes sense? Similarly, the patina of geopolitical relevance is worn thin and eventually discarded, and Tony's crisis of conscience when he discovers what his weapons are being used for is more of a narrative convenience than a real moral theme.

All of which is to say that *Iron Man*, in spite of the heavy encumbrances Tony must wear when he turns into the title character, is distinguished by light touches and grace notes. The hardware is impressive, don't get me wrong, but at these prices it had better be. If you're throwing around a hundred million dollars and you have Batman and the Hulk on your tail, you had better be sure that the arc reactors are in good working order and that the gold-titanium alloy suit gleams like new and flies like a bird.

And everything works pretty well. But even dazzling, computer-aided visual effects, these days, are not so special. And who doesn't have superpowers? Actually, Iron Man doesn't; his heroism is all handicraft, elbow grease and applied intelligence. Those things account for the best parts of *Iron Man* as well.

Iron Man is rated PG-13 (Parents strongly cautioned). It has a lot of action violence, none of it especially graphic or gruesome. Also, Iron Man has sex, and not with the suit on. But not completely naked either.

Opens on Friday nationwide.

Directed by Jon Favreau; written by Mark Fergus, Hawk Ostby, Art Marcum and Matt Holloway based on the character created by Stan Lee, Larry Lieber, Don Heck and Jack Kirby; director of photography, Matthew Libatique; edited by Dan Lebental; music by Ramin Djawadi; production designer, J. Michael Riva; visual effects by John Nelson; produced by Avi Arad and Kevin Feige; released by Paramount Pictures and Marvel Entertainment. Running time: 2 hours 6 minutes.

With: Robert Downey Jr. (Tony Stark), Terrence Howard (Rhodey), Jeff Bridges (Obadiah Stane), Shaun Toub (Yinsen) and Gwyneth Paltrow (Pepper Potts).

Gwen Ganow (Student)

Notes on Final Genre Choice

Now that Gwen has decided she wants to write a film review, she needs to think about that genre in terms of how she'll pull in sources and work with evidence. She does some more brainstorming to think this through.

She wants to figure out how she might work in the research she's done, and what kind of evidence she'll need to draw on to convince readers to agree with her evaluation of whatever film she will review.

| ☰ ☷ ▢ ☰ ☰ ▣ | Print Layout View | Sec 1 | 100% ⊙ |

NOTES

Gwen Ganow

Genre Choice: Film Review

I like the idea of composing an ad or a researched argument, but I think that a film review is a genre that my target audience can connect with. Why? Because superheroes are a big part of pop culture and tons of films feature them. I assume that, like me, my comic- and superhero-loving audience sees these films and reads reviews of them.

How will I draw on sources in my genre composition?

Okay, I'm going to write a film review. Now what?

- **What film will I review?** It has to be one about superheroes. Should I choose something contemporary? Or a classic? And once I choose, should I read others' reviews of that film or will those sources just distract me?
- **How will I work with research I've done? What more do I need to find out about?** Once I know what film I'll review, I will need to learn about other works the director, writer, and producer have been involved in. Maybe the actors too. Also, how can I draw on research I've already done? I'm thinking that one of my sources in particular—a book I've read titled *Who Needs a Superhero?* by H. Michael Brewer—could come in handy, in addition to the film itself, which is my main source.
- **What do I know about film reviews?** I may need to do more reading on the film review as a genre. What makes a film review successful? Maybe I should look at more examples. I'll reread the section in Chapter 4 on film reviews and take a closer look at the Roger Ebert example. He's a known and respected reviewer.
- **Do I need to know more about how comics fans think of superhero movies?** Especially when a story is moved from the page to the screen? I might need to do some primary research on this. Maybe I should interview some comics fans.

Gwen's notes on her genre choice

The film review is a genre I know, and a great venue for presenting an argument about superheroes.

I need to choose a superhero film to review. But which one?

I need to read more film reviews—especially those by Roger Ebert.

I need to look back at my other sources—and maybe interview people from my potential audience.

COMPOSING YOUR GENRE PIECE

Remember that "shitty first draft" we mentioned at the beginning of this chapter? Let's circle back to that. It might not look much like an editorial or an investigative journalism piece or whatever genre you've chosen. That's okay. But now that you've followed Gwen to this point, you may have more ideas about what you want to do—and why and how. Hopefully you have a more solid sense of your own rhetorical situation and have focused in on a genre that you want to compose in.

When you do return to your draft, try this: Review the conventions of the genre you've chosen, and start nudging your rough draft into the shape of your chosen genre. For example, if you're writing an editorial, you'll want a pithy first paragraph that makes the issue you're discussing and your position on it clear. If you're composing an ad, step back and think about how visuals could work with your text.

Steps for Composing

You have your topic, your basic ideas, and the genre figured out. Now it's time to start composing in the genre.

Step 1. Write a solid draft.   Review the exploratory rough draft you created earlier in this process and begin fleshing it out so it has a beginning, middle, and end, or whatever elements are appropriate for your chosen genre. It should include, at least in rough form, the main points you want to make, and include some examples or evidence you'll use to support your points.

Working from this draft, follow the steps below to evaluate and revise it.

 Attention, composers! Wondering about media?

What medium will best suit your genre and rhetorical situation? Will you reach your audiences best through a print or physical medium—or in a digital environment? If you're composing online, will you use audio? How about video or animation? What medium will your primary audience respond to best?

Step 2. Evaluate your use of sources & evidence.   Look at a really good example of the genre you're working in—and compare it to yours. How does that author support claims with evidence? Draw on sources? What kind of evidence will your audience expect and respond to? Will anecdotes and personal stories be convincing to your audience, or will they be more convinced by statistics and references to peer-reviewed studies?

Note: Refer to the sample of your genre as you complete steps 3–7.

Step 3. Confirm the scope of information to provide.   How much coverage of the topic is appropriate for the genre you've selected? Examine the sample of the genre you're comparing your draft to. Does it present an overview of the subject? What is the level of detail?

Step 4. Consider your use of style.   Think about voice, tone, language, and point of view. Is the genre you're composing in characterized by the use of first or third person? How explicit and present will your voice and experience be in the piece? Look at the example you're comparing your piece to. Does that composer use an objective, authoritative tone, or a personal, subjective tone, or something else?

Step 5. Look at how you use rhetorical appeals. Look at your draft and the sample genre piece you're consulting. To what extent does the other author use ethos, pathos, and/or logos? How effective is his/her approach, and what might you want to adapt for your own work?

Step 6. Look at your organization. How have you organized your content? Is this the best way, considering who your audience is and what you're trying to achieve? Is it logical? Persuasive? Does the sample you're consulting have anything to offer you in terms of a model for improving your work?

Step 7. Consider your mix of words & images. This is also a moment to think about design and medium. Are you being as effective as you could be? Again, consult your example.

Step 8. Make a list of what you want to work on when you revise. Base your list on what you've determined in steps 2–7.

Step 9. Revise your draft based on your revision list. After you've revised, reread your work and make notes to address things you want to improve for the next draft.

Step 10. Revise a little more. Get your work in the best shape you can in the time you have.

👉 **Attention, composers! A word on design.**

What are the design features of the genre you're composing in? How will you use design? Consider:

Layout. In your genre, how are elements typically arranged spatially? How are visuals presented? How will your layout help readers/viewers quickly orient themselves?

Color. How can you use color to guide your audience's attention? What colors are often associated with your genre? For example, many ads are designed with bright colors.

Chunking & fonts (if you're working with text). Will it be best to present information in short paragraphs organized under headings? Or are you going to do something else? How can a font help you achieve your purpose and reach your audience? What fonts are associated with your genre? For example, Times New Roman works in newspapers; sans serif fonts work well in a digital environment.

Context. Is the design you have in mind appropriate, considering when and where and how your audience will encounter the piece?

Guided Process:
How to Compose a Genre Piece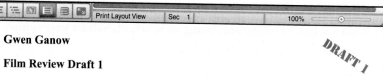

Gwen Ganow (Student)

Superhero Project: Film Review Draft 1

▲ STUDENT AUTHOR
PHOTO **Gwen
Ganow.**

Gwen has a clear sense of her genre—as well as her rhetorical situation. She now gets down to writing. In the following section, she writes a first draft of her film review. She then spends time evaluating it—reading it against a published film review—to see how she might improve her own. In this process, she reviews her work for how well she deals with purpose, audience, and other rhetorical concerns, as well as how well she works in the genre of the film review itself. After this process, she revises her work, creating a second and third draft.

**Gwen's notes on
her film review**

I decided to review the film *X-Men*— it's a significant film in the superhero genre that my audience will be familiar with. This is my first attempt at a draft.

☰ ☷ ◫ ☰ ☷ ◙	Print Layout View	Sec 1		100% ⊙

Gwen Ganow

Film Review Draft 1

DRAFT 1

X-Men

The punctuated equilibrium concept of Niles Eldredge and Stephen Jay Gould states that evolution and speciation occur at a rapid rate followed by long periods of stasis. The film *X-Men* explores how a modern American society would react to its own punctuated equilibrium in which a new, superhuman species rises and suddenly integrates with "normal" humans. Through the events and emotions of the movie *X-Men*, our past and current social issues of prejudice and intolerance as an American society become exposed.

X-Men opens with a powerful image of prejudice and intolerance, a Nazi concentration camp. While unloading a new trainload of Jews, Nazi soldiers rip a young boy from the arms of his parents. He sits in the rain crying and watches helplessly as his parents are herded off to other buildings. His yellow Star of David, his label of difference, is the only color against the dismal backdrop of rain, mud, and hate. The young boy survives his Nazi captors and grows up to be a mutant with the power to move and control metal.

The movie leaves the scene of war and enters the chambers of Congress where a Senate committee hearing is taking place. Magneto attends this committee hearing of the Senate because he is curious about what the American government is doing about the so-called "mutant problem" in the United States. Senator Kelly, a staunch supporter of the Mutant Registration Act, is debated by Dr. Jean Grey (a mutant herself). Jean Grey argues against the Mutant Registration Act and says, "Mutants who have revealed themselves publicly have been met with fear, hostility, and violence." To this, Senator Kelly responds with the questions, "Are they dangerous? Do you want your children in school with mutants? Do you want your children to be taught by mutant teachers?"

Ganow, *Film Review Draft 1,* Continued

| ≡ ⋮≡ ▦ ▤ ▥ ▦ | Print Layout View | Sec 1 | 100% ⊙ |

To shield the younger generation from the violence created by the words of intolerance spoken by Senator Kelly, Charles Xavier (a mutant with powerful psychic abilities) creates Xavier's School for Gifted Youngsters and makes it a place for young mutants who have recently discovered that they are very different from their peers and have run away from home. Here he offers these young men and women a place of refuge and sense of inclusiveness. This is a safe environment where they can be taught how to control their developing minds and powers by some of Xavier's finest past students like Storm, Cyclops, and Jean Grey, who become mentors to a new generation of young mutants, afraid of the world around them. Charles Xavier never gives up hope that humanity will come to realize the error of their judgment. He teaches his students that intolerance should not be returned with even more intolerance.

Magneto's view of humanity is radically different from the views of Charles Xavier. Magneto sees nothing wrong with trying to solve the plight of mutants by using violence and fear against humans. He devises a plan using his own powers combined with a radiation-generating machine to change non-mutants into mutants. By doing this, he feels that vengeance will be carried out by putting would-be persecutors into the lives of the people they sought to persecute and chooses Senator Kelly as his first test subject. Magneto tells the senator, "Humankind has always feared what it doesn't understand. You have nothing to fear from God and nothing to fear from me. Not anymore."

The fear, intolerance, and violence toward mutants that is conveyed in *X-Men* closely ties in with the fear, intolerance, and violence endured by the GLBT community today. Sometimes, the reality of the comic book universe resembles our own reality more than we would like to admit. The movie *X-Men* questions whether we as Americans really believe in freedom for all or whether we really mean freedom for some.

Gwen Ganow

Superhero Project: Evaluation of Film Review Draft 1

Next, Gwen evaluates her film review by comparing it to an excellent example of the genre: A. O. Scott's review "*Iron Man*: Heavy Suit, Light Touches," which she looked at earlier. She evaluates Scott's use of evidence and sources, his scope and use of rhetorical appeals, and his organization and use of visuals. Then she applies this lens to her own review. *(A. O. Scott's review reprinted here from* The New York Times, *May 2, 2008.)*

Gwen's notes on Scott's review

Scott's use of evidence & sources

Scott contextualizes *Iron Man* with other movies of the same genre. He also refers to the director, his other films, and the scriptwriters.

He gives lots of plot details but never gives the story away. He supports each claim with brief snippets from the plot. E.g., when he talks about the "brilliant duets" (paragraph 7), he backs that up with evidence from specific scenes.

Scott's scope

Scott's scope is in line with his purpose: to evaluate the film overall—to make an argument in favor of it. He chooses key details about characters and from specific scenes to support his claims and overall case.

He summarizes quite a bit: He offers just a snapshot of the plot by providing setting, character descriptions, and parts of the story.

The New York Times
Movies
Heavy Suit, Light Touches
By A. O. SCOTT

MOVIE REVIEW | 'IRON MAN'
Iron Man (2008)

Iron Man, based on the Marvel comic and with Robert Downey Jr as the title character, opens on Friday nationwide. Jon Favreau directed.

The world at the moment does not suffer from a shortage of superheroes. And yet in some ways the glut of anti-evil crusaders with cool costumes and troubled souls takes the pressure off of *Iron Man*, which clanks into theaters today ahead of Hellboy, Batman, and the Incredible Hulk. This summer those guys are all in sequels or redos, so *Iron Man* (a Marvel property not to be confused with the Man of Steel, who belongs to DC and who's taking a break this year) has the advantage of novelty in addition to a seasonal head start.

Gwen's notes on her own review

My use of evidence & sources

In my own review, I contextualize *X-Men* in terms of the theory of "punctuated equilibrium" (and cite Eldredge and Gould as my source).

I support my claims about the "powerful image of prejudice and intolerance" (paragraph 2) with plot details and specifics from a scene.

Like Scott, the evidence I use to support my argument includes details from the plot and other aspects of the film and its creators.

My scope

I go into way more detail than Scott does, maybe because I am retelling the plot chronologically. Is this a problem? Do I need to pull back from some of my details to give more summary? Should I choose my details more carefully?

Print Layout View | Sec 1 | 100%

Gwen Ganow

Film Review Draft 1

DRAFT 1

X-Men

The punctuated equilibrium concept of Niles Eldredge and Stephen Jay Gould states that evolution and speciation occur at a rapid rate followed by long periods of stasis. The film *X-Men* explores how a modern American society would react to its own punctuated equilibrium in which a new, superhuman species rises and suddenly integrates with "normal" humans. Through the events and emotions of the movie *X-Men*, our past and current social issues of prejudice and intolerance as an American society become exposed.

Ganow, *Film Review Draft 1*, *Continued*

Gwen's notes on Scott's review

Scott makes broad statements when he delivers snappy and fun one-liners. E.g., in his line "The hero must flex and furrow his brow," Scott makes a generalization about action movies.

Scott's style

I like Scott's writing style. It's almost as if I can hear him speaking, especially in lines such as: "The hero must flex and furrow his brow; the bad guy must glower and scheme; the girl must shriek and fret."

He chooses each word carefully and keeps his language varied and interesting. E.g., he uses a variety of terms (*film*, *picture*) to refer to the movie.

Scott writes in the third person, but I like how he sometimes invites the reader in by using the word *we*.

X-Men opens with a powerful image of prejudice and intolerance, a Nazi concentration camp. While unloading a new trainload of Jews, Nazi soldiers rip a young boy from the arms of his parents. He sits in the rain crying and watches helplessly as his parents are herded off to other buildings. His yellow Star of David, his label of difference, is the only color against the dismal backdrop of rain, mud, and hate. The young boy survives his Nazi captors and grows up to be a mutant with the power to move and control metal.

The movie leaves the scene of war and enters the chambers of Congress where a Senate committee hearing is taking place. Magneto attends this committee hearing of the Senate because he is curious about what the American government is doing about the so-called "mutant problem" in the United States. Senator Kelly, a staunch supporter of the Mutant Registration Act, is debated by Dr. Jean Grey (a mutant herself). Jean Grey argues against the Mutant Registration Act and says, "Mutants who have revealed themselves publicly have been met with fear, hostility, and violence." To this, Senator Kelly responds with the questions, "Are they dangerous? Do you want your children in school with mutants? Do you want your children to be taught by mutant teachers?"

To shield the younger generation from the violence created by the words of intolerance spoken by Senator Kelly, Charles Xavier (a mutant with powerful psychic abilities) creates Xavier's School for Gifted Youngsters and makes it a place for young mutants who have recently discovered that they are very different from their peers and have run away from home. Here he offers these young men and women a place of refuge and sense of inclusiveness. This is a safe environment where they can be taught how to control their developing minds and powers by some of Xavier's finest past students like Storm, Cyclops, and Jean Grey, who become mentors to a new generation of young mutants, afraid of the world around them. Charles Xavier never gives up hope that humanity will come to realize the error of their judgment. He teaches his students that intolerance should not be returned with even more intolerance.

Gwen's notes on her own review

My style

I'm not sure my voice comes through enough in my review. I think I sound knowledgeable, but I'm not so sure how present I am in the writing in terms of voice, personality, or humor.

My review does not seem as personal or subjective as Scott's. I think my perspective is more objective. Is that a strong point? Or a problem?

My use of rhetorical appeals

I want to establish myself as a kind of expert on superheroes and film. I like how Dwight Decker established his ethos in his researched essay. I'm modeling my language on his. Is it right for a film review? I'm not sure how well I've conveyed my ethos. I also need to persuade my audience, so I need to appeal to pathos.

Gwen's notes on Scott's review

Scott's use of rhetorical appeals

Scott builds his ethos by drawing on evidence and by crediting the film's creators. He also makes it clear that he is very qualified to write about superhero action flicks.

He also appeals to readers through pathos. He entices readers to go see *Iron Man* through his language and tone.

Scott's organization

Scott begins with general comments about superheroes and the popularity of superhero movies before he moves onto *Iron Man*.

Next, he situates the film within its genre, hinting at his opinion of the movie. He outlines some of his expectations.

He makes claims that he supports with details of the plot and characters; he closes with a final evaluation of the film.

Scott's use of visuals

He includes a few visuals. The large still featuring Robert Downey Jr., who plays the lead, is pretty striking. There is also a small picture further into the review.

Gwen's notes on her own review

My organization

I move through the plot, giving readers a general sense of the story.

I don't discuss the film in terms of a broader context. Should I? I'm also not sure I present my argument clearly enough. I think I need to be more direct.

My use of visuals

I haven't yet incorporated any images/film stills into my review, but I need to. Which characters/key scenes do I want to show? Why?

What to focus on when I revise

Revise/reorganize the review so it isn't just a chronological plot summary. Will be challenging. Maybe I should think about the main points I want to make, and then choose supporting details from the plot as needed, much as Scott does.

Establish a clearer sense of voice. Also, should I worry about the shift from third to first person? How much personality can I inject into my review?

Make sure I'm giving a clear evaluation of the film. I need my argument about the film to be stronger. Is it worth seeing? Why or why not? Also, I want readers to see the dilemma of the hero as related to that of the GLBT community.

Do more to establish ethos and appeal to readers' emotions.

Pay more attention to language. For example, don't just use the word *movie* throughout.

Incorporate visuals—also maybe embed video.

Gwen Ganow (Student)

Superhero Project: Film Review Draft 2

Gwen returns now to her draft and begins to rework it, based on her evaluation of it, her comparison of it to the A. O. Scott review, and her list of what to focus on when she revises.

☰ ☷ ▣ ▤ ▦ ▥	Print Layout View	Sec 1		100% ◔ ─── ○

Gwen Ganow

Film Review Draft 2

DRAFT 2

X-Men: Mutants R Us

As a "hard-core" comic book fan, I always considered the 2000 *X-Men* film the epitome of a true comic book movie. What sets the *X-Men* apart from other comic book films is that the story behind the X-Men is not overshadowed by special effects. In *X-Men*, equilibrium is punctured; humans face a sudden and dramatic evolutionary change, one that results in the existence of "mutants." The mutants are humans with superhuman powers, who look human enough to integrate invisibly into society. The movie explores how American society might react to the existence of these mutants, exposing our past and current social issues of prejudice and intolerance. Bryan Singer, best known for 1995's *The Usual Suspects*, directs from the screenplay written by David Hayter.

Created by Stan Lee and Jack Kirby in 1963, X-Men are children of parents who were exposed to atmospheric radiation and became genetically altered. The mutant kids are outsiders in the world, and are envied and feared by "normal" humans. The alienation of the X-Men is similar to that of other groups of people who have experienced prejudice, like African Americans, Jews, Japanese, and homosexuals. Singer makes this parallel explicit with the opening scene.

X-Men opens with a powerful image of prejudice and intolerance, a Nazi concentration camp. While unloading a new trainload of Jews, Nazi soldiers rip a young boy from the arms of his parents. He sits in the rain crying and watches helplessly as his parents are herded off to other buildings. His yellow Star of David is the only color against the dismal backdrop of rain, mud, and hate. The young boy survives his Nazi captors and grows up to be a mutant known as Magneto with the power to move and control metal.

The movie leaves the scene of war and enters the chambers of Congress where a Senate committee hearing is taking place on the Mutant Registration Act, which would require mutants to register with the government and list their special abilities, making it impossible for them to blend in unnoticed with the rest of society. Magneto, played by Ian McKellen, attends this committee hearing because he is curious about what the American government is doing about the so-called "mutant problem." Senator Kelly, played by Bruce Davison, a staunch supporter of the Mutant Registration Act, is debated by Dr. Jean Grey, a mutant herself, played by Famke Janssen. Kelly supports the Mutant

Continues next page

Gwen's comments on her film review

Overall, I've done a better job evaluating the film and making an argument about it. It's clear what I think of the movie and why.

This draft is more interesting and readable. I've done more to appeal to my audience of superhero/comic lovers. For example, my first sentence and paragraph are aimed at drawing them in.

My writing still seems stiff in places. I want to make the style and tone a little more casual; also, I want to tighten up the wording and do more to make this flow.

Ganow, *Film Review Draft 2*, *Continued*

**Gwen's comments
on her film review**

This doesn't look
like a film review
yet. I'll need to
apply design prin-
ciples and add at
least one image.
Maybe some links,
too. If this is going
to be delivered
digitally, I should
take advantage of
hyperlinking.

Print Layout View   Sec 1   100%

Registration Act, believing that mutants are a danger to "normal" humans and should be locked away, while Grey argues that forcing mutants to register would create the potential for them to be treated as freaks.

The performers share good chemistry, with Hugh Jackman's Wolverine's and James Marsden's Cyclops's one-upmanship bringing humor to their scenes. Patrick Stewart's Charles Xavier seems both fatherly and professorial, and Anna Paquin as Rogue does a fine job conveying fear about her future as a mutant and lovesickness over Wolverine. Rebecca Romijn makes an impression in a role that relies more on physical presence than lines.

In *X-Men*, responses to prejudice by the victims of prejudice are explored through the actions of two important mutants, both leaders of mutant groups. Charles Xavier, a mutant with powerful psychic abilities, creates a school for the gifted for young runaway mutants. Here he offers these young men and women a place of refuge and a sense of inclusiveness. This is a safe environment where they can be taught how to control their developing minds and powers by some of Xavier's finest past students like Storm, Cyclops, and Jean Grey, who become mentors to a new generation of young mutants, afraid of the world around them. Xavier's "turn the other cheek" philosophy links him to the Jesus Christ of the Christian culture. The fact that Charles Xavier provides a safe house for people rejected by humanity also links him to our real-life organizations like NAACP, GLBT (gay, lesbian, bisexual, and transgender) resource centers, and some of our churches.

The other leader is Magneto, who fronts the Brotherhood of Mutants. Magneto's perspective on humanity stems from his experiences as a young boy at a WWII concentration camp, which was captured in the film's opening scene. This experience left Magneto distrustful of humanity and convinced that mutants are bound to suffer the same fate met by the inmates of the Nazi death camps. To preserve the survival of his mutant species, Magneto declares war on humankind. Magneto's view of humanity is radically different from the views of Charles Xavier. Magneto sees nothing wrong with trying to solve the plight of mutants by using violence and fear against humans.

Although the film is worth seeing for the performances and direction alone, the special effects, while relatively low-key for a superhero movie, are stunning. Magneto's spinning contraption, the fight scenes, and Storm's weather conjuring add to the fun. Finally, while there is seldom a clear right and wrong in real life, Singer's film makes it easy for us to take the right side. The heroes of the film are clearly Professor Xavier's X-Men. In this way, Singer allows us to imagine the consequences of violence and anger, as shown by Magneto's band of mutants, and ultimately root for Xavier's more tolerant gang.

Gwen Ganow (Student)

Superhero Project: Film Review Final

Gwen revises some more: this time with plenty of attention to design, images, and embedded links. She also polishes her writing, and continues to evaluate her choice of mode and medium, with thoughts of future iterations of her project. Below is an excerpt from her final review.

Print Layout View Sec 1 100%

Gwen Ganow

Film Review Final

FINAL

X-Men: Mutants R Us

As a "hard-core" comic book fan, I always considered the 2000 *X-Men* film the epitome of a true comic book movie. What sets the *X-Men* apart from other comic book films is that the story behind the X-Men is not overshadowed by special effects. In *X-Men*, it's the story that matters. In the world of this film, the equilibrium of existence has been punctured; humans face a sudden and dramatic evolutionary change, one that results in the existence of "mutants." The mutants are humans with superhuman powers, who look human enough to integrate invisibly into society. The movie explores how American society might react to the existence of these mutants, exposing our past and current social issues of prejudice and intolerance.

Bryan Singer, best known for 1995's *The Usual Suspects*, directs from the screenplay written by David Hayter. . . .

The performers share good chemistry, with Hugh Jackman's Wolverine's and James Marsden's Cyclops's one-upmanship bringing humor to their scenes. Patrick Stewart's Charles Xavier seems both fatherly and professorial, and Anna Paquin as Rogue does a fine job.

Hugh ▶ Jackman as Wolverine, from *X-Men* (2000). *Everett Collection.*

Gwen's notes on her film review

My writing is a little smoother now and flows better.

I've decided that I want to deliver my film review digitally. I'm taking advantage of digital tools, including embedded links. E.g., I've added a link to the film trailer at Amazon, which illustrates the points I make in paragraph 1, and included another link to the director's bio at IMDb. I like the digital format, too, because I can give readers the option to comment on my work and to share it on social media.

As for future versions of this material, I'd consider an audio podcast. Podcasts give a clear sense of the writer's voice, views, and personality, something I'm striving for.

COMPOSING AN ACCOMPANYING AUTHOR'S OR ARTIST'S STATEMENT

What is an Author's or Artist's Statement? It's a piece of reflective and persuasive writing in which you explain the choices you made in a separate composition. Artists, filmmakers, novelists, and other composers commonly write statements of the intentions, processes, and inspirations behind a particular work or body of work. In this case, we're talking specifically about the Statement that you can write to accompany the genre piece you've created.

Advice for Composing Your Statement

Your Statement is a critical analysis of what you did and why, how successful you think you were, what you might have done differently, and any plans you may have for further revision—or even of repurposing the project for something else. If your genre piece is not ultimately as successful as you'd hoped, consider the Statement a chance to explore what didn't work and what you might do differently next time. The Statement is an opportunity to explain to your audience (particularly your peer and instructor audience) such specifics as why you chose your genre, what your rhetorical purposes were, how you wanted to affect your audience, and how your research informed your composition.

If your instructor asks you to write such an accompanying Statement, approach the drafting of it just as you would for any persuasive writing that brings in sources. Refer to the pieces you worked with along the way when composing your genre piece: Draw on any brainstorm lists, notes, and revisions of drafts. This will help you reconstruct your process and remember the choices you've made. Just as with any other composition, you'll want to get reader feedback and revise. (For more on Author's and Artist's Statements, see pp. 237–46. For more on revision, see Chapter 9.)

Following are instructions that we give our students for creating their Statements. Note: This is the assignment that Gwen will respond to on pages 478–79.

ENG 101, Professor Braziller

Assignment: Compose an Author's or Artist's Statement

For this course, every genre piece you create must be accompanied by an Artist's or Author's Statement. In that document, please explain:

- **The rhetorical choices you made as you composed your genre piece.**
  Define your purpose, audience, and how you wished to affect your audience.

Please also cover your use of rhetorical appeals, and the mode and medium you chose to work in.

- **How you worked within (or broke out of) genre conventions.**
Discuss the elements that define the genre most typically, and how you responded to those in your composition. Discuss your style (written and other), your use of design, and how you drew on sources. In fact, as you write, please draw on sources and cite them in the text of your paper and in a list at the end.

Note: Your Statement should be documented in MLA or APA style. Within the text of your Statement, please draw on specific sources that informed your composition. Include *both* in-text citations and a list of Works Cited or References at the end of your Statement. Remember, you're reflecting on your process—and persuading your readers that you made thoughtful choices. Maybe your choices weren't all perfect, but that's okay. This is your chance to explain your intentions.

Use these questions to guide your Statement.

Rhetorical choices

- What was your purpose? For example, did you set out to tell a story, report information, or present a persuasive argument? Or some combination? How well do you think you achieved your purpose? What, if anything, might you have done differently?

- Who was your intended primary audience? Secondary audience? Why? Characterize the people in each group. What are their assumptions and expectations about your topic? How did you speak to these audiences? What message did you want them to take away from your composition? For example, did you want them to take a specific action?

- Did you use one or more of the rhetorical appeals (ethos, logos, pathos), and how effective were you in reaching your audience through the appeals?

- How and why did you choose the mode and medium you decided on? What are the advantages to these choices? How might you alter your choices in future iterations of the project?

Genre conventions

- Why did you choose the genre you did? What elements of the genre interested you most? How did you use or subvert the conventions of the genre?

- What choices did you make in terms of style (including organization, language, voice, and tone)? What did you consider in making these choices?

- Evaluate your design. Why did you choose to work with text, images, video, and audio (and any other elements) as you did? How effective do you think you were? What might you have done differently if you had had more time?

- What sources did you draw on for this piece? How did you decide which sources were right for you? How did you integrate them into your composition? Did you cite them according to the conventions of your genre?

Guided Process: How to Compose an Author's Statement ▼

Gwen Ganow (Student)

Superhero Project: Author's Statement Draft 1

Following is Gwen's first draft of her Statement to accompany her film review.

▲ STUDENT AUTHOR
PHOTO **Gwen
Ganow.**

**Gwen's notes
on her Author's
Statement**

My purpose
Do I convey clearly
and persuasively
enough why I
chose to write a
film review? Not
sure. Also, should I
comment more on
process? And what
might I have done
differently or better?

My audience
Have I succeeded
in explaining my
choices to readers?

**My use of rhetorical
appeals**
I focused on using
pathos and logos.
Have I emphasized
one over the other?
Is that a good idea?

**My choice of and
use of modes &
media**
I should talk more
directly about
modes and media.
I'll ask my instruc-
tor about this.

≡ ≣ ◫ ☰ ≣ ▥ | Print Layout View | Sec 1 | | 100% ⊙

Gwen Ganow

Author's Statement Draft 1

DRAFT 1

Why I Wrote a Film Review of *X-Men*

There are two reasons I chose to write a film review. As a "hard-core" comic book fan, I always considered *X-Men* as a good example of what a true comic book movie should be. What sets the movie apart from other comic book movies is that the story behind *X-Men* is not overshadowed by special effects. The second reason I chose to do a film review was to show another perspective on how comic books are interrelated with our modern culture. Superheroes, heroes, antiheroes, and villains don't just come to us through the pop culture pages of a comic book. They have also expanded their influence to include the American silver screen. The stories of these comic book characters are now told by our Hollywood actors and actresses.

Created by Stan Lee and Jack Kirby in 1963, the X-Men are the children of humans who were exposed to atmospheric radiation and became genetically altered. These children are born with "differences" and become outsiders in a world that considers them mutants. Even though they do not show any outward signs of difference, their extrahuman powers evoke the envy and fear of ordinary people (Brewer 134). We can link the alienation of the X-Men to groups of people who have gone through their own form of prejudice in real life. African Americans, Jews, Japanese, and homosexuals have all endured the pain of living in an American society that is quick to respond in fear to someone who may be different from the norm.

In *X-Men*, solutions to the problems of prejudice are explored through the actions of two important mutants. Both of these men are leaders, one being the leader of the X-Men, the other the leader of the Brotherhood of Mutants. Charles Xavier creates a school for the gifted for young ostracized mutants. He teaches his mutant students to use their powers to benefit humanity, even if that same humanity hated and distrusted them (Brewer 142). Xavier's "turn the other cheek" philosophy links him to the Jesus Christ of Christian culture. The fact that Xavier provides a safe house for people rejected by humanity also links him to our real life organizations like NAACP, GLBT resource centers, and some of our churches.

Magneto's perspective on humanity stems from his experiences as a young boy at a WWII concentration camp. This experience left Magneto distrustful of humanity, and he is convinced that mutants are bound to suffer the same

Ganow, *Author's Statement Draft 1*, *Continued*

fate met by the inmates of the Nazi death camps (Brewer 143). To preserve the survival of his mutant species, Magneto declares war on humankind. We can link the thoughts and actions of Magneto to our own real-world thoughts and actions. We, as humans, have always wanted to put our persecutors into the shoes and lives of the persecuted. If we were given the technology to right the wrongs against us, would we create a machine similar to Magneto's? As humans, why are we quick to return violence with more violence?

Overall, I wanted my readers to see my passion for the subject. I wanted to persuade them, using pathos, to understand that you could read the film as a larger statement on the intolerance GLBT people often face. One of the ways I achieved this was by relying on logos, helping my readers follow the film logically, using strategies employed in other film reviews, such as giving snippets of the plot and using some of the plot summary to highlight the film's strength.

I studied several film reviews to help me figure out how to best create my review. One of the things that was missing from my initial draft was placing the film in a broader context. Thus, in my revision I began the review by discussing my relationship to comics (even if briefly) and then moved on to the film itself. I also incorporated the theory of punctuated equilibrium to help establish my ethos; I know about the theory because of my zoology/biology major. Another thing I wanted to make sure to achieve in the film review was a clear evaluation of the film. My earlier draft did not really make this clear; it primarily consisted of a retelling of some of the plot. In the revision I made sure to include this, not only in the close of the review but with some word choices in the review, such as "powerful image," "good chemistry," and "fine job."

When comic book fans or superhero film fans finish reading my review, I hope that they will see that *X-Men* is definitely an appealing film. More importantly, though, I want my audience to realize that lessons about ourselves can be learned through the story of the X-Men. By witnessing and learning from the actions of a misguided mutant like Magneto, humankind can learn how to be more understanding and tolerant—like Charles Xavier.

Works Cited

Brewer, H. Michael. *Who Needs a Superhero? Finding Virtue, Vice, and What's Holy in the Comics*. Grand Rapids: Baker Books, 2004. Print.

X-Men. Dir. Bryan Singer. Perf. Hugh Jackman, Ian McKellen, and Patrick Stewart. Marvel Studios, 2000. Film.

Gwen's notes on her Author's Statement

My use of sources

My instructor has asked me to use MLA-style citation in this Statement. I've supported my claims with evidence, but need to double-check my in-text citations in the next draft.

Should I include images in my Statement, too? Would that help me make my case?

After reading Gwen's Statement and considering her purposes, do you think she made a good choice of genre? Why or why not? Has she observed all the conventions of film reviews? Has she ignored any? What are the effects of her choices?

If you were Gwen, what would be your main goals in revising this draft Statement?

From this point, Gwen will discuss the draft with her classmates and instructor, and get ready to revise her Statement. For more on the next steps (and to see where Gwen goes from here), see Chapter 9, "Revising & Remixing Your Work."

9 REVISING & REMIXING YOUR WORK

CONTENTS

POWERPOINT SLIDE ▶
Gwen Ganow, Remix of film review project. *Slide: Gwen Dalynn Ganow. X-Men poster: Everett Collection.*

While feedback can help during any stage of your composing process, once you have a solid draft of your work, it's an ideal time to get some advice on how to make it even better. In this chapter, we pick up where we left off with Gwen Ganow (remember her from Chapter 8?). She's finished her genre piece—a film review of the movie *X-Men*—and has a first draft of her accompanying Author's Statement, which still needs work. In the first part of this chapter, she revises two drafts and polishes her final Statement, working with her own ideas and those she gets from peer review.

For an Index of Sources & Contexts for material referenced in this chapter, see the e-Pages at **bedfordstmartins.com/bookofgenres**.

Later, Gwen decides she wants to remix her genre project: to repurpose her film review and create something entirely new. Later in this chapter, we provide guidelines for remixing any genre project—that is, advice for how to work with your topic, research, and any composing you've already done, to make something totally different.

REVISING YOUR WORK

Why revise, you ask? Because your first draft is geared toward getting your ideas out of your head and onto the page. Some people call this a writer-based draft. A writer-based draft usually has gaps in development and logic. The purpose and sense of audience are usually unclear. They become clear through revision, and as you move toward a more audience-focused composition.

Revising Based on Your Own Observations

Gwen has a solid first draft of her Author's Statement to accompany her film review. Now she wants some input from others—from her instructor and classmates—on how to revise her Statement so it's more analytical and persuasive. As noted in

▲ STUDENT AUTHOR PHOTO
Gwen Ganow. *Gwen Dalynn Ganow.*

◀ DRAFT AUTHOR'S STATEMENT & FILM REVIEW **Gwen Ganow.** (Gwen's film review appears in Chapter 8.) *Gwen Dalynn Ganow.*

Chapter 8, her Statement is, arguably, more important than the film review she wrote. Gwen's Author's Statement gives her an opportunity to explain the choices she made in addressing her rhetorical situation and working with her genre. But it's also a document in which she can reflect on and learn from her own process.

When you create an Author's or Artist's Statement, you develop skills that will transfer into other settings. You learn to reflect critically on your own work—so that you can improve on it. This is a skill, a habit, even, that you (and all of us) can use in other coursework and outside of school—in future professions or when creating for any audience.

Need another reason why reflecting on your genre project (and revising your Author's or Artist's Statement) is a good idea? Here's an example. In art school, students hardly ever create the "perfect" painting or sculpture or installation in one course or semester. Often, they'll sketch, paint drafts, or create models that they'll use later, as maps or inspiration when they can flesh out their vision for the composition in a different or fuller way. Drafting, thinking critically, and revising go a long way in making great authors and artists truly great. Why not be great?

Revising Based on Peer Review

Let's say that, like Gwen, you've created your genre piece and/or your Author's or Artist's Statement. You've done some revising, and you feel that you've done the best you can. Maybe you can no longer review the content objectively, because you've been working on it for a while. Asking others for feedback on your draft is an excellent way to find out how well you've met your purposes or reached your audience. Readers/viewers/listeners will experience your composition with fresh eyes and ears. They can help you figure out where you need to make connections more explicit, where you need to develop examples, and where the draft could be restructured, among other things.

Respondents to your work can be classmates, a teacher, a tutor, friends, parents, or coworkers. Ideally your respondents are from your intended primary audience. These individuals are most likely to give you solid advice on how well you're doing in terms of your rhetorical situation and chosen genre. The respondents you choose, even if they're not part of your primary audience, should be those whose opinions you value, people whom you can trust to respond constructively. They should be able to articulate clearly their reactions to your draft.

Ask for responses at any point in your composing process. For example, at the beginning, when you're brainstorming, you can ask others to talk with you about your ideas and approach to your topic. Once you have a rough draft or a first solid draft, you can ask others to respond to your focus, development, voice, and organization.

☞ Attention, authors & artists! Who should respond to your drafts?

Friends, family, and roommates may not be familiar with your topic, but they can tell you whether your argument is logical, for example, or whether your introductory paragraph is clear. They can point out spots in the draft where they got confused, or found inconsistencies, or wanted more explanation or evidence.

That said, responses from your classmates, writing center tutor, or instructor, or from others in your target audience, are probably going to be most helpful. We recommend that you ask at least one person from your intended primary audience to respond to your draft.

Once you have completed your first or second draft, ask respondents to give you feedback on how clearly you convey your purpose, how well you're reaching your audience, and what you might do better or differently. Respondents can also help you see counterarguments and other perspectives at this stage. Near the end of your composing process, ask respondents to take a finer focus: Ask whether your transitions between ideas are consistent, and whether you need to do any fine-tuning in regard to working in your genre, for example.

To get feedback that will be helpful, ask yourself: What do I want to know from my respondents? What would be most helpful to know at this stage? Here are some questions you might ask respondents:

» Would you take a look at my paper (or watch my video, or listen to my podcast, etc.) and tell me what you think? As someone who isn't (or is) familiar with my topic, how well do you think I am conveying my ideas? How persuasive do you find the writing? I'm looking for "big picture" comments right now.

» I'm really struggling with adding specific details (or some other issue). Can you read my draft and point out some places where I could add more detail?

» Other respondents have found some parts of my composition confusing (or identified some other specific problem). Could you take a look at this and let me know if you're sometimes confused, and at what point you start to feel that way?

Gathering responses doesn't mean you'll implement every change that your respondents suggest. You may ultimately decide not to make a particular recommended change, perhaps because you disagree with the suggestion or think the reader misunderstood your purpose. But even if you disagree with a reader comment, consider why the reader made it. And if more than one person makes the same recommendation, you might want to consider it more seriously.

CHECKLIST Questions to Ask People Responding to Your Draft.

Wherever you are in your composing process, it can be helpful to get feedback. Here are some more questions you might want to ask your respondents.

☐ **What kind of genre does this piece appear to be? How can you tell?**
Possible follow-up questions:

    ☐ Can you suggest some ways to make it read more like an encyclopedia entry/photo essay/blog/other genre piece?

    ☐ Can you suggest any areas that are not consistent with the genre?

☐ **What would you say is the purpose of this document? How can you tell?**
Possible follow-up questions:

    ☐ Can you suggest some ways to make the purpose of the piece clearer?

    ☐ Can you point to some places where the purpose is not consistent?

☐ **How would you characterize the rhetorical appeals the genre piece uses?**
Possible follow-up questions:

  ☐ Can you suggest ways to make the appeal to my audience more defined?

  ☐ Can you suggest some ways to emphasize ethos so that my reader accepts the piece's credibility?

  ☐ Can you suggest some ways to emphasize pathos so that my reader understands the emotion behind the piece?

☐ **How would you characterize the writing style of this document?**
Possible follow-up questions:

  ☐ Can you point to some places where that style is particularly apparent?

  ☐ Can you point to some places where that style is not apparent?

  ☐ Can you point to some places where the style is inconsistent?

  ☐ Can you suggest some ways to make the style more consistent with that of an encyclopedia entry/photo essay/blog/other genre piece?

☐ **How would you characterize the tone of this document?**
Possible follow-up questions:

  ☐ Can you point to some places where that tone is particularly apparent?

  ☐ Can you point to some places where that tone is not apparent?

  ☐ Can you point to some places where the tone is inconsistent?

  ☐ Can you suggest some ways to make the tone more consistent with that of an encyclopedia entry/photo essay/blog/other genre piece?

☐ **How would you characterize the voice in this document?**
Possible follow-up questions:

  ☐ Can you point to some places where that voice is particularly strong?

  ☐ Can you point to some places where that voice is not as strong?

  ☐ Can you point to some places where the voice is inconsistent?

  ☐ Can you suggest some ways to make the voice more consistent with that of an encyclopedia entry/photo essay/blog/other genre piece?

☐ **How do the design elements direct your attention?**
Possible follow-up questions:

  ☐ Can you suggest some ways I might better use design to help me get into my topic?

  ☐ Can you suggest some ways to emphasize the visual elements?

  ☐ Can you suggest some ways to help the text have more impact on the reader?

  ☐ Can you suggest some ways design elements might clarify for readers that this is an encyclopedia entry/photo essay/blog/other genre piece?

☐ **How can you tell that research has informed the piece?**
Possible follow-up questions:

  ☐ Can you suggest some ways I might make the piece appear more credible?

  ☐ Can you suggest some areas where I might make the research connection more explicit?

  ☐ Can you suggest some topics I might research to help me achieve my purpose?

Guided Process: Integrating Peer Feedback: Draft to Finished Composition ▼

Gwen Ganow (Student)

Superhero Project: Author's Statement
Draft 1—with Peer Review

Let's circle back to Gwen Ganow and her draft of the Author's Statement that will accompany her film review.

Draft 1   Gwen asks her respondents—a few of her classmates—the following questions about her Author's Statement:

» Have I made my purpose in writing a film review clear?

» Have I clearly communicated the ways I used rhetorical appeals to reach my audience?

» Is my tone reflective and persuasive enough for an Author's Statement?

Her readers report back that they want more information about how Gwen thinks she demonstrated her passion for the subject. They also suggest that she clearly connect her research and what she incorporated into her review, to make her Statement more reflective and persuasive. Finally, one respondent recommends that Gwen rethink the organization of the second half of her Statement.

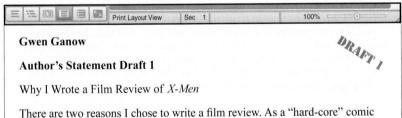

```
▤ ▤ ▣ ▤ ▤ ▣  Print Layout View    Sec  1              100%  ◁────◉────▷
```

Gwen Ganow

Author's Statement Draft 1

DRAFT 1

Why I Wrote a Film Review of *X-Men*

There are two reasons I chose to write a film review. As a "hard-core" comic book fan, I always considered *X-Men* as a good example of what a true comic book movie should be. What sets the movie apart from other comic book movies is that the story behind *X-Men* is not overshadowed by special effects. The second reason I chose to do a film review was to show another perspective on how comic books are interrelated with our modern culture. Superheroes, heroes, antiheroes, and villains don't just come to us through the pop culture pages of a comic book. They have also expanded their influence to include the American silver screen. The stories of these comic book characters are now told by our Hollywood actors and actresses.

Created by Stan Lee and Jack Kirby in 1963, the X-Men are the children of humans who were exposed to atmospheric radiation and became genetically

Continues next page

Ganow, *Author's Statement Draft 1*, *Continued*

altered. These children are born with "differences" and become outsiders in a world that considers them mutants. Even though they do not show any outward signs of difference, their extrahuman powers evoke the envy and fear of ordinary people (Brewer 134). We can link the alienation of the X-Men to groups of people who have gone through their own form of prejudice in real life. African Americans, Jews, Japanese, and homosexuals have all endured the pain of living in an American society that is quick to respond in fear to someone who may be different from the norm.

In *X-Men*, solutions to the problems of prejudice are explored through the actions of two important mutants. Both of these men are leaders, one being the leader of the X-Men, the other the leader of the Brotherhood of Mutants. Charles Xavier creates a school for the gifted for young ostracized mutants. He teaches his mutant students to use their powers to benefit humanity, even if that same humanity hated and distrusted them (Brewer 142). Xavier's "turn the other cheek" philosophy links him to the Jesus Christ of Christian culture. The fact that Xavier provides a safe house for people rejected by humanity also links him to our real life organizations like NAACP, GLBT resource centers, and some of our churches.

Magneto's perspective on humanity stems from his experiences as a young boy at a WWII concentration camp. This experience left Magneto distrustful of humanity, and he is convinced that mutants are bound to suffer the same fate met by the inmates of the Nazi death camps (Brewer 143). To preserve the survival of his mutant species, Magneto declares war on humankind. We can link the thoughts and actions of Magneto to our own real-world thoughts and actions. We, as humans, have always wanted to put our persecutors into the shoes and lives of the persecuted. If we were given the technology to right the wrongs against us, would we create a machine similar to Magneto's? As humans, why are we quick to return violence with more violence?

Overall, I wanted my readers to see my passion for the subject. I wanted to persuade them, using pathos, to understand that you could read the film as a larger statement on the intolerance GLBT people often face. One of the ways I achieved this was by relying on logos, helping my readers follow the film logically, using strategies employed in other film reviews, such as giving snippets of the plot and using some of the plot summary to highlight the film's strength.

I studied several film reviews to help me figure out how to best create my review. One of the things that was missing from my initial draft was placing the film in a broader context. Thus, in my revision I began the review by discussing my relationship to comics (even if briefly) and then moved on to the film itself. I also incorporated the theory of punctuated equilibrium to help establish my ethos; I know about the theory because of my zoology/biology major. Another thing I wanted to make sure to achieve in the film review was a clear evaluation of the film. My earlier draft did not really make this clear; it primarily consisted of a retelling of some of the plot. In the revision I made sure to include this, not only in the close of the review but with some word choices in the review, such as "powerful image," "good chemistry," and "fine job."

Ganow, *Author's Statement Draft 1*, *Continued*

≡ ≔ ◫ ▤ ▤ ▦	Print Layout View	Sec 1		100% ——○——

When comic book fans or superhero film fans finish reading my review, I hope
that they will see that *X-Men* is definitely an appealing film. More importantly,
though, I want my audience to realize that lessons about ourselves can be
learned through the story of the X-Men. By witnessing and learning from the
actions of a misguided mutant like Magneto, humankind can learn how to be
more understanding and tolerant—like Charles Xavier.

Works Cited

Brewer, H. Michael. *Who Needs a Superhero? Finding Virtue, Vice, and
    What's Holy in the Comics*. Grand Rapids: Baker Books, 2004. Print.
X-Men. Dir. Bryan Singer. Perf. Hugh Jackman, Ian McKellen, and Patrick
    Stewart. Marvel Studios, 2000. Film.

With these factors in mind, Gwen created a list of what to focus on in her next draft.

Gwen Ganow (Student)

Superhero Project: Author's Statement Revision List

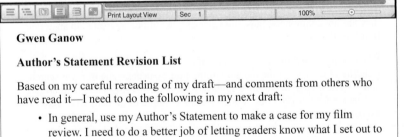

≡ ≔ ◫ ▤ ▤ ▦	Print Layout View	Sec 1		100% ——○——

Gwen Ganow

Author's Statement Revision List

Based on my careful rereading of my draft—and comments from others who
have read it—I need to do the following in my next draft:

- In general, use my Author's Statement to make a case for my film
  review. I need to do a better job of letting readers know what I set out to
  do, and why, and how.
- Explain how I use rhetorical appeals (or at least intended to use them).
  In my draft I've listed the appeals I worked with, but have not organized my ideas well enough for readers. Just stating my passion is not
  enough. I need to include an example or two to back up that claim.
- Connect my research to the choices and claims that I make in my
  review.
- Add signal phrases to clearly separate my research from my own ideas.

Gwen then implemented these revisions in the following draft. The blue text in the body of the Statement indicates places where Gwen reworked her Statement.

Gwen Ganow (Student)

Superhero Project: Author's Statement Draft 2

Gwen's notes on draft 2 of her Author's Statement

I'm giving readers more context for why I chose to write my film review.

Here I connect with my research—through citing a specific source.

≡ ≡ ◫ ≡ ≣ ▣   Print Layout View   Sec 1   100% ◁━━━━○

DRAFT 2

Gwen Ganow

Author's Statement Draft 2

Why I Wrote a Film Review of *X-Men*

There are several reasons I chose to write a film review. As a "hard-core" comic book fan, I always considered *X-Men* as a good example of what a true comic book movie should be. What sets the movie apart from other comic book movies is that the story behind *X-Men* is not overshadowed by special effects. The second reason I chose to do a film review was to show another perspective on how comic books are interrelated with our modern culture. Superheroes, heroes, antiheroes, and villains don't just come to us through the pop culture pages of a comic book. They have also expanded their influence to include the American silver screen. The stories of these comic book characters are now told by our Hollywood actors and actresses. My final reason for writing a film review is that I wanted to choose a genre that I felt my peers would be interested in reading. Many of my classmates are moviegoers, and even if they are not comic book fans, they probably would be interested in an action film like *X-Men*.

When writing the film review, I wanted to demonstrate I had a clear understanding of the role of the outsider in the film by using some of my research and my knowledge about the original comic book story. Created by Stan Lee and Jack Kirby in 1963, the X-Men are the children of humans who were exposed to atmospheric radiation and became genetically altered. H. Michael Brewer, in his book *Who Needs a Superhero?*, discusses how these children are born with "differences" and become outsiders in a world that considers them mutants. Even though they do not show any outward signs of difference, their extrahuman powers evoke the envy and fear of ordinary people (134). If we think about the movie in terms of a larger context, we can link the alienation of the X-Men to groups of people who have gone through their own form of prejudice in real life. African Americans, Jews, Japanese, and homosexuals have all endured the pain of living in an American society that is quick to respond in fear to someone who may be different from the norm.

Brewer also discusses how in *X-Men* solutions to the problems of prejudice are explored through the actions of two important mutants. Both of these men are leaders, one being the leader of the X-Men, the other the leader of the

Ganow, *Author's Statement Draft 2*, *Continued*

☰ ☷ ▦ ▤ ▤ ▦	Print Layout View	Sec 1		100% ─○─

Brotherhood of Mutants. Charles Xavier creates a school for the gifted for young ostracized mutants. He teaches his mutant students to use their powers to benefit humanity, even if that same humanity hated and distrusted them (142). Xavier's "turn the other cheek" philosophy links him to the Jesus Christ of Christian culture. The fact that Xavier provides a safe house for people rejected by humanity also links him to our real life organizations like NAACP, GLBT resource centers, and some of our churches.

In his book, Brewer also focuses on how Magneto's perspective on humanity stems from his experiences as a young boy at a WWII concentration camp. This experience left Magneto distrustful of humanity, and he is convinced that mutants are bound to suffer the same fate met by the inmates of the Nazi death camps (143). To preserve the survival of his mutant species, Magneto declares war on humankind. We can link the thoughts and actions of Magneto to our own real-world thoughts and actions. We, as humans, have always wanted to put our persecutors into the shoes and lives of the persecuted. If we were given the technology to right the wrongs against us, would we create a machine similar to Magneto's? As humans, why are we quick to return violence with more violence?

I've worked in signal phrases to make my research more apparent and to make my Statement more readable.

Overall, I wanted my readers to see my passion for the subject. One of the ways I did this was by opening with the fact that I am a "hard-core" comic book fan. Besides demonstrating my passion, I wanted to persuade my readers, by using pathos, to understand that you could read the film as a larger statement on the intolerance GLBT people often face. One of the ways I achieved this was by relying on logos, helping my readers follow the film logically, using strategies employed in other film reviews, such as giving snippets of the plot and using some of the plot summary to highlight the film's strength. While both pathos and logos are important for reaching my audience, I realized that if I did not establish my ethos, people would not care about what I had to say. By incorporating the theory of punctuated equilibrium, which I know about because of my zoology/biology major, and connecting it to the film, I help readers view me as a knowledgeable and informed writer.

I've made it clearer how I set out to use ethos, pathos, and logos, and backed that up with details.

I studied several film reviews to help me figure out how to best create my review. One of the things that was missing from my initial draft was placing the film in a broader context. Thus, in my revision I began the review by discussing my relationship to comics (even if briefly) and then moved on to the film itself. Another thing I wanted to make sure to achieve in the film review was a clear evaluation of the film. My earlier draft did not really make this clear; it primarily consisted of a retelling of some of the plot. In the revision I made sure to include this, not only in the close of the review but with some word choices in the review, such as "powerful image," "good chemistry," and "fine job."

When comic book fans or superhero film fans finish reading my review, I hope that they will see that *X-Men* is definitely an appealing film. More importantly, though, I want my audience to realize that lessons about ourselves can be learned through the story of the X-Men. By witnessing and learning from the actions of a misguided mutant like Magneto, humankind can learn how to be more understanding and tolerant—like Charles Xavier.

Continues next page

Ganow, *Author's Statement Draft 2,* Continued

≡	≔	▣	▤	▦	▧	Print Layout View	Sec 1	100%	─○─

Works Cited

Brewer, H. Michael. *Who Needs a Superhero? Finding Virtue, Vice, and What's Holy in the Comics*. Grand Rapids: Baker Books, 2004. Print.

X-Men. Dir. Bryan Singer. Perf. Hugh Jackman, Ian McKellen, and Patrick Stewart. Marvel Studios, 2000. Film.

At this point, Gwen asks her respondents to read the above draft with the following questions in mind:

» Is my tone persuasive enough?

» Have I said enough about the film reviews I studied as models?

» What is the single most important revision I can make to strengthen my Author's Statement?

Respondents suggest that Gwen:

» Improve her persuasiveness by looking carefully at the word choices in her Author's Statement

» Make more-specific comments about the film reviews she used as models for her own review

» Refer to more than one outside source

Gwen agrees with the first two suggestions, but feels that adding more sources is not necessary to achieve her purpose. With this feedback and her own ideas in mind, Gwen creates a quick revision list before moving on to her final draft.

Gwen Ganow (Student)

Superhero Project: Author's Statement Revision List

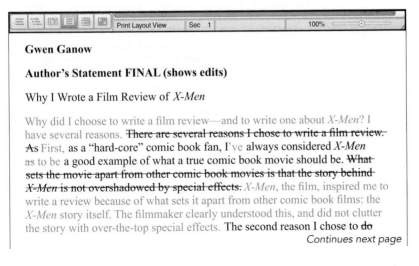

☰ ⇎ ⧉ ☰ ☷ ▣ Print Layout View   Sec 1   100% ⊙

Gwen Ganow

Author's Statement Revision List

I think I'm making a pretty good case for my review—and am specifically explaining my intentions to my readers. I've incorporated research successfully. Now I just have a little more to do:

- Back up my choices by referring specifically to the film reviews I used as models for my own composition.
- Fine-tune my writing to make it more persuasive overall; also, make sure I'm choosing the most persuasive words and phrasing.
- Check my Statement for mechanics, grammar, tense, spelling, and so on. Proofread.

With these points in mind, Gwen revises her Statement a final time. The document below (created in Microsoft Word) shows Gwen's edits as tracked changes.

Gwen Ganow (Student)

Superhero Project: Author's Statement Final (shows edits)

☰ ⇎ ⧉ ☰ ☷ ▣ Print Layout View   Sec 1   100% ⊙

Gwen Ganow

Author's Statement FINAL (shows edits)

Why I Wrote a Film Review of *X-Men*

Why did I choose to write a film review—and to write one about *X-Men*? I have several reasons. ~~There are several reasons I chose to write a film review.~~ ~~As~~ First, as a "hard-core" comic book fan, I've always considered *X-Men* ~~as to be~~ a good example of what a true comic book movie should be. ~~What sets the movie apart from other comic book movies is that the story behind *X-Men* is not overshadowed by special effects.~~ *X-Men*, the film, inspired me to write a review because of what sets it apart from other comic book films: the *X-Men* story itself. The filmmaker clearly understood this, and did not clutter the story with over-the-top special effects. The second reason I chose to ~~do~~

Continues next page

Ganow, *Author's Statement: Final (shows edits)*, *Continued*

| ≡ | ⋮≡ | ▣ | ▤ | ▤ | ▣ | Print Layout View | Sec 1 | 100% | ⊙ |

write a film review is a little broader: I wanted to comment on ~~was to show another perspective on~~ how comic books are ~~interrelated~~ intertwined with ~~our~~ modern popular culture. Superheroes, heroes, antiheroes, and villains don't just come to us through ~~the pop culture pages of a~~ comic books anymore. They ~~have also~~ come to us through Hollywood, brought to life ~~expanded their influence to include the American silver screen. A~~ by the actors and actresses who portray the characters and stories of America's favorite superheroes. ~~The stories of these comic book characters are now told by our Hollywood actors and actresses.~~ My final reason for choosing to write a film review, rather than a researched journal article, for example, is that I wanted to choose a genre that I ~~felt~~ knew my peers would relate to. ~~be interested in reading.~~ Many of my classmates are moviegoers and readers of reviews: ~~, and e~~Even if they are not comic book fans, they are likely to ~~probably would~~ be interested in an action film like *X-Men*, and therefore in a review of the film.

~~When writing the~~ In my ~~film~~ review, I wanted to demonstrate ~~I had~~ a clear understanding of the role of the outsider in *X-Men*. ~~the film.~~ To do this, I drew on ~~by using some of my~~ research and my own knowledge ~~about~~ of the original *X-Men* comic book story. Created by Stan Lee and Jack Kirby in 1963, the X-Men are the children of humans who were exposed to atmospheric radiation and became genetically altered. H. Michael Brewer, in his book *Who Needs a Superhero?*, discusses how these children are born with "differences" and become outsiders in a world that considers them mutants. Even though they do not show any outward signs of difference, their extrahuman powers evoke the envy and fear of ordinary people (134). If we think about the movie in terms of a larger context, we can link the alienation of the X-Men to groups of people who have gone through their own form of prejudice in real life. African Americans, Jews, Japanese, and ~~homosexuals~~ gay men and lesbians have ~~all~~ endured the pain of living in an American society that is quick to respond in fear to someone who may be different from the norm.

Brewer also discusses how in *X-Men* authors Lee and Kirby explore solutions to the problems of prejudice ~~are explored~~ through ~~the actions of~~ two important mutants: Charles Xavier and Magneto. Both of these characters ~~men~~ are leaders; Xavier ~~, one being the leader of~~ leads the X-Men, while Magneto ~~the other the leader of~~ leads the Brotherhood of Mutants. ~~Charles~~ Xavier creates a school for the gifted for young ~~ostracized~~ outcast mutants~~,~~ where he ~~He~~ teaches ~~his mutant students~~ them to use their powers to benefit humanity, even if that same humanity hate~~d~~ and distrust~~ed~~s them (142). Xavier's "turn the other cheek" philosophy links him to the Jesus Christ of Christian culture. The fact that Xavier provides a safe house for people rejected by humanity also links him to our real-life organizations ~~like~~ such as the NAACP, GLBT resource centers, and some of our churches.

In his book, Brewer also focuses on how Magneto's perspective on humanity stems from his experiences as a young boy at a WWII concentration camp. ~~This experience~~ Life in the camp left Magneto distrustful and despairing of humanity, and ~~he is~~ convinced that mutants are bound to suffer the same fate as Jews imprisoned and murdered in ~~met by the inmates of the~~ Nazi death camps (143). To preserve the survival of his mutant species, Magneto declares war on humankind. ~~We can link~~ I see Magneto's ~~the thoughts and actions~~ distrust and violence as related to contemporary life and the collective urge to "right wrongs," gain

Ganow, Author's Statement: Final (shows edits), Continued

power, or find revenge through warfare. ~~of Magneto to our own real-world thoughts and actions. We, as humans, have always wanted to put our persecutors into the shoes and lives of the persecuted.~~ If we had the technology available to Magneto in *X-Men*, would we use it the same way? ~~were given the technology to right the wrongs against us, would we create a machine similar to Magneto's? As humans, why are we quick to~~ Would we return violence with more violence?

In my review, I consciously worked with rhetorical appeals. Overall, I wanted my readers to see my passion for my topic—toward superheroes, society, and the film *X-Men*. ~~the subject.~~ I worked to establish ethos ~~One of the ways I did this was opening with the fact that I am~~ by letting readers know I am a "hard-core" serious comic book fan and think of myself as somewhat of an expert on the genre. Besides demonstrating my passion, I wanted to persuade my readers ~~;~~ by using pathos, by appealing to emotion to persuade them to ~~understand that you could~~ read the film as a larger statement—a statement on the intolerance that "outsiders," specifically GLBT people, often face. I supported my argument logically, with ~~One of the ways I achieved this was by relying on logos, helping my readers follow the film logically,~~ key points from the plot, ~~using~~ and used strategies I learned from other film reviewers, such as using summary and highlighting particular moments in a film. ~~employed in other film reviews, such as giving snippets of the plot and using some of the plot summary to highlight the film's strength.~~ While both pathos and logos ~~are~~ were important for reaching my audience, I realized that if I did not establish my ethos, people would not care about what I had to say. For example, I ~~By~~ incorporat~~ing~~ed the theory of punctuated equilibrium that I learned about in my studies as a ~~; which I know about because of my~~ zoology/biology major, and used that as a lens for reading ~~and connecting it to~~ the film ~~;~~. I believe this perspective, and the fact that I am a longtime and avid comics reader, helped my audience see ~~I help readers view~~ me as a knowledgeable and informed writer.

I studied several film reviews to help me figure out how to best create my own review. ~~One of the things~~ Something that I did not do in ~~was missing from~~ my initial draft was to place ~~placing~~ the film in a broader context. ~~Thus, in my revision~~ In my next draft, I began with a brief discussion of ~~the review by discussing~~ my relationship to comics ~~(even if briefly)~~ and then moved on to the film itself. Another thing I focused on in revisions was ~~wanted~~ to make sure ~~to achieve in the film review was~~ I gave a clear opinion ~~a clear evaluation~~ of the film. I did not do this in ~~My~~ my earlier draft, ~~did not really make this clear; it primarily consisted of a~~ which was also too focused on retelling ~~of some of~~ the plot ~~.~~—and not focused enough on evaluating it. In my revised review, ~~the revision~~ I made sure to be more straightforward in my opinion, and to choose words that supported my observations clearly. I sharpened up my language to make it more persuasive and precise, using phrases ~~include this; not only in the close of the review but with some word choices in the review;~~ such as "powerful image ~~;~~" and "good chemistry ~~;~~." ~~and "fine job."~~

When comic book fans or superhero film fans ~~finish reading~~ read my review, I want them to ~~hope that they will~~ see that *X-Men* is ~~definitely an appealing~~ a film worth seeing—and one that offers insight into human experience. ~~More importantly, though,~~ I want my audience to realize that—through the story of the

Continues next page

Attention, authors & artists! Are you using the e-Portfolio tool that came with this book?

If so, take advantage of how it can support your composing process and showcase your creations.

Ganow, *Author's Statement: Final (shows edits),* Continued

| | Print Layout View | Sec 1 | 100% |

X-Men—we can learn ~~lessons~~ about ourselves. ~~can be learned through the story of the X-Men.~~ Maybe we can learn something from ~~By witnessing and learning from the actions of a~~ the misguided mutant ~~like~~ Magneto, ~~humankind can learn how to be more understanding~~ and his tolerant, loving counterpart, ~~—like~~ Charles Xavier.

Works Cited

Brewer, H. Michael. *Who Needs a Superhero? Finding Virtue, Vice, and What's Holy in the Comics.* Grand Rapids: Baker Books, 2004. Print.

X-Men. Dir. Bryan Singer. Perf. Hugh Jackman, Ian McKellen, and Patrick Stewart. Marvel Studios, 2000. Film.

The following document shows Gwen's work with her edits accepted.

Gwen Ganow (Student)

Superhero Project: Author's Statement Final (edits incorporated)

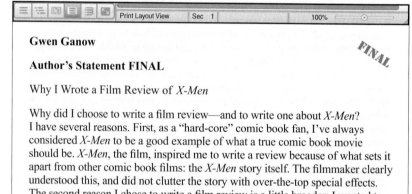

Gwen Ganow

Author's Statement FINAL

FINAL

Why I Wrote a Film Review of *X-Men*

Why did I choose to write a film review—and to write one about *X-Men*? I have several reasons. First, as a "hard-core" comic book fan, I've always considered *X-Men* to be a good example of what a true comic book movie should be. *X-Men*, the film, inspired me to write a review because of what sets it apart from other comic book films: the *X-Men* story itself. The filmmaker clearly understood this, and did not clutter the story with over-the-top special effects. The second reason I chose to write a film review is a little broader: I wanted to comment on how comic books are intertwined with modern popular culture. Superheroes, heroes, antiheroes, and villains don't just come to us through comic books anymore. They come to us through Hollywood, brought to life by the actors and actresses who portray the characters and stories of America's favorite superheroes. My final reason for choosing to write a film review, rather than a researched journal article, for example, is that I wanted to choose a genre that I knew my peers would relate to. Many of my classmates are moviegoers and

| | | | | Print Layout View | Sec 1 | | 100% | |

readers of reviews: Even if they are not comic book fans, they are likely to be interested in an action film like *X-Men*, and therefore in a review of the film.

In my review, I wanted to demonstrate a clear understanding of the role of the outsider in *X-Men*. To do this, I drew on research and my own knowledge of the original *X-Men* comic book story. Created by Stan Lee and Jack Kirby in 1963, the *X-Men* are the children of humans who were exposed to atmospheric radiation and became genetically altered. H. Michael Brewer, in his book *Who Needs a Super-hero?*, discusses how these children are born with "differences" and become outsiders in a world that considers them mutants. Even though they do not show any outward signs of difference, their extrahuman powers evoke the envy and fear of ordinary people (134). If we think about the movie in terms of a larger context, we can link the alienation of the X-Men to groups of people who have gone through their own form of prejudice in real life. African Americans, Jews, Japanese, and gay men and lesbians have endured the pain of living in an American society that is quick to respond in fear to someone who may be different from the norm.

Brewer also discusses how in *X-Men* authors Lee and Kirby explore solutions to the problem of prejudice through two important mutants: Charles Xavier and Magneto. Both of these characters are leaders; Xavier leads the X-Men, while Magneto leads the Brotherhood of Mutants. Xavier creates a school for the gifted for young outcast mutants, where he teaches them to use their powers to benefit humanity, even if that same humanity hates and distrusts them (142). Xavier's "turn the other cheek" philosophy links him to the Jesus Christ of Christian culture. The fact that Xavier provides a safe house for people rejected by humanity also links him to our real-life organizations such as the NAACP, GLBT resource centers, and some of our churches.

In his book, Brewer also focuses on how Magneto's perspective on humanity stems from his experiences as a young boy at a WWII concentration camp. Life in the camp left Magneto distrustful and despairing of humanity, and convinced that mutants are bound to suffer the same fate as Jews imprisoned and murdered in Nazi death camps (143). To preserve the survival of his mutant species, Magneto declares war on humankind. I see Magneto's distrust and violence as related to contemporary life and the collective urge to "right wrongs," gain power, or find revenge through warfare. If we had the technology available to Magneto in *X-Men*, would we use it the same way? Would we return violence with more violence?

In my review, I consciously worked with rhetorical appeals. Overall, I wanted my readers to see my passion for my topic—toward superheroes, society, and the film *X-Men*. I worked to establish ethos by letting readers know I am a serious comic book fan and think of myself as somewhat of an expert on the genre. Besides demonstrating my passion, I wanted to persuade my readers by using pathos, by appealing to emotion to persuade them to read the film as a larger statement—a statement on the intolerance that "outsiders," specifically GLBT people, often face. I supported my argument logically, with key points from the plot, and used strategies I learned from other film reviewers, such as using summary and highlighting particular moments in a film. While both pathos and

Continues next page

☞ **Attention, authors & artists! A word on using technology for peer review.**

If you are drafting your composition in a Microsoft Word or Apache OpenOffice document, there are features that allow you to track your changes so others can edit and add comments on your draft electronically. This might be handy if you can't arrange to meet with a reader in person. E-mail your draft to a reader, or share it in a space such as Google Drive (drive.google.com) or DropBox (dropbox .com).

Ganow, *Author's Statement: Final,* *Continued*

≡ ≒ ◫ ▤ ▤ ◫ | Print Layout View | Sec 1 | 100% ⊂━━━○━

logos were important for reaching my audience, I realized that if I did not establish my ethos, people would not care about what I had to say. For example, I incorporated the theory of punctuated equilibrium that I learned about in my studies as a zoology/biology major, and used that as a lens for reading the film. I believe this perspective, and the fact that I am a longtime and avid comics reader, helped my audience see me as a knowledgeable and informed writer.

I studied several film reviews to help me figure out how to best create my own review. Something that I did not do in my initial draft was to place the film in a broader context. In my next draft, I began with a brief discussion of my relationship to comics and then moved on to the film itself. Another thing I focused on in revisions was to make sure I gave a clear opinion of the film. I did not do this in my earlier draft, which was also too focused on retelling the plot—and not focused enough on evaluating it. In my revised review, I made sure to be more straightforward in my opinion, and to choose words that supported my observations clearly. I sharpened up my language to make it more persuasive and precise, using phrases such as "powerful image" and "good chemistry."

When comic book fans or superhero film fans read my review, I want them to see that *X-Men* is a film worth seeing—and one that offers insight into human experience. I want my audience to realize that—through the story of the X-Men—we can learn about ourselves. Maybe we can learn something from the misguided mutant Magneto and his tolerant, loving counterpart, Charles Xavier.

Works Cited

Brewer, H. Michael. *Who Needs a Superhero? Finding Virtue, Vice, and What's Holy in the Comics*. Grand Rapids: Baker Books, 2004. Print.

X-Men. Dir. Bryan Singer. Perf. Hugh Jackman, Ian McKellen, and Patrick Stewart. Marvel Studios, 2000. Film.

REMIXING YOUR WORK INTO DIFFERENT GENRES

Sometimes we ask our students to remix their finished genre piece into a different genre. For example, Gwen, who composed a film review on superheroes and justice, thought at one point that she'd create a presentation, animation, or advertisement. Remixing her film review would be an opportunity to work in a different genre on a topic she had already researched and written about—and to think about the different ways of reaching an audience that other genres allow.

Guided Process: Remixing a Genre Project ▼

Gwen Ganow (Student)

Remix of Film Review
PowerPoint: "We Are All Mutants"

Gwen wants to shape her film review into something new. When our students create remixes, we ask them to think their projects through as shown in the following assignment.

ENG 101, Professor Braziller

Assignment: Remix Your Genre Project

What is a remix? When you remix an object or composition, you repurpose it. For example, Martha Stewart might repurpose flowerpots to be utensil holders in her kitchen. Originally intended for outdoor use to hold soil and plants, the pots will need to be overhauled for indoor kitchen use. Stewart would probably wash them, apply a nontoxic sealant, and paint them or decorate them in some way. The finished product—the utensil holder that was formerly a flowerpot—is a remix.

How will you create a remix? Your assignment is to remix one of the genre pieces you've already composed. You will repurpose your creation for a different context. This may involve changing the purpose, audience, and/or message of your original piece. You should not have to do significant new research for your remix. Your energy should go toward revising your original material to fit into a new mode and/or genre appropriate to your new context.

For example, you might remix an editorial you wrote about school funding into a short YouTube video. The editorial was originally geared toward politicians or taxpayers, but you now imagine an audience of college students. Thus, you need to make the editorial interesting and palatable to college students. You also need to take into account the conventions of the new genre.

You might also consider taking parts from several of your genre pieces and weaving them together into a new work. Quilters do this when they take scraps of fabric from outgrown clothing and sew them together into a new item: a quilt.

Gwen repurposes her film review to create a PowerPoint presentation that begins with a top 10 list (inspired by the "Top Ten" lists feature of the *Late Show with David Letterman*). In this case, her purpose is to persuade an audience of fans who watched the film when it came out in the year 2000, to watch it again. She chooses the genre of the top 10 list because it gives her the opportunity to use humor to persuade. Her plan is to share her list with friends and fans on social media sites, and to ask them to contribute their own lists of reasons for watching the *X-Men* movie again.

Following are her first three slides.

POWERPOINT SLIDE ▶
Gwen Ganow, Remix
of film review.
*Slides: Gwen Dalynn
Ganow. X-Men poster:
Everett Collection.*

◀ POWERPOINT SLIDES
Gwen Ganow, "We
Are All Mutants."
Gwen Dalynn Ganow.

Top **10** reasons to watch
the original *X-Men* movie again

10. The year 2000 was a wicked long time ago.

9. Hugh Jackman cage-fight scenes.

8. Pre-*True Blood* Anna Paquin. Halle Berry. Lycra.

7. Need refresher on details of Mutant Registration Act.

6. Xavier School for Gifted Youngsters is way cooler than Hogwarts.

Top **10** reasons to watch
the original *X-Men* movie again

5. That scene where Jackman flips the fork-fingered bird.

4. Far too long since a Holocaust survivor with magnetic-field-control superpowers tried for world domination.

3. "Trust a few and fear the rest" starting to sound like a good idea.

2. Humans (except for Patrick Stewart) still totally overrated.

1. You are *such* a geek.

CHECKLIST **Remixing a genre piece?** Keep the following questions in mind.

WHAT'S MY RHETORICAL SITUATION?	WHAT GENRE CONVENTIONS MATTER?

☐ **Purpose.** What is the purpose of my new, remixed composition? How can I make that purpose clear?

☐ **Audience.** Who is the targeted audience for my remix? How can I take my new audience's expectations, values, and concerns into account? What kind of vocabulary, examples and details, organization, and other elements should I use to appeal to my new audience?

☐ **Rhetorical appeals.** How can I use rhetorical appeals to connect with my new audience?

☐ **Modes & media.** What mode and medium will be most likely to engage my new audience?

☐ **Elements of the genre.** How can I use the elements of my new genre to guide my new audience's experience?

☐ **Style.** How can I use word choice, sentence structure, literary devices (like metaphor), and other stylistic techniques to keep my new audience engaged?

☐ **Design.** How can I use design elements, such as color, images, and font, to emphasize my purpose and main point?

☐ **Sources.** What kinds of sources should I use to convince my new audience of my point? How should I cite these sources appropriately in my new genre?

10 ASSEMBLING A MULTIGENRE PROJECT

CONTENTS

MULTIGENRE PROJECT ▶
Neil Carr,
"Video Games and
Violence."
Neil Carr.

What is a multigenre project? It's a collection of three or more genre compositions, built around a single topic. A multigenre project is an opportunity to experiment. It also gives you the chance to practice in a variety of rhetorical situations, forms of composition, and types of media.

Let's look at an example. You've conducted research on the topic of, say, the significance of the bond between people and dogs. Through the course of your research, brainstorming, and drafting, you decide that you want to make the case that dogs were essential to the rise of civilization (persuasive). You also want to present a history of the relationship between humans and canines (informative), and perhaps even tell a story of a particular relationship (narrative). You are strong in a variety of genres and media (better at some than others). Your audience is one of general readers; that is, it's an unspecialized audience, but one with some interest in dogs and humanity. A multigenre project for your topic could include a few of these genres and media options:

» INFORMATIVE. An **annotated timeline** tracing human-canine interactions from ancient times to the present.

» PERSUASIVE. A brief TED talk–style video **presentation** on how and why dogs were critical to human civilization.

» NARRATIVE. A **story** of how dogs and humans relate now.

» PERSUASIVE. A **photo essay** or **slide show** that demonstrates how dogs benefit humans by reducing stress.

» INFORMATIVE. An **annotated map** locating where humans first settled and domesticated dogs.

» NARRATIVE. An **interview** with a dog behaviorist, a therapy dog trainer, or a psychologist who uses dogs to treat humans.

» PERSUASIVE. An **Author's or Artist's Statement** that brings everything together.

Alternatively, maybe you want to put together a collection of genre pieces that are entirely persuasive. Why not? There are a lot of interesting options. In this chapter, we want to introduce you to possibilities. Elsewhere in this book, we provide advice on how to compose in specific genres; here we're going to show you how, once you've composed your individual genre pieces, you can put them together into a coherent whole. We also provide you with sample projects by student authors and artists Neil Carr, Gwen Ganow, and Dawson Swan.

For another example of a **multigenre project,** see Kristen LaCroix's work in Chapter 1.

THE POSSIBILITIES OF THE MULTIGENRE PROJECT

Just like any research endeavor, a genre project allows you to join a conversation about a particular subject or issue. Whether you research and compose a single genre piece or multiple related pieces, you address a research question, make clear arguments, and draw on sources, all while keeping a strong sense of purpose and audience. Unlike more traditional academic projects, genre projects let you break away from (or embrace, if you prefer) the usual forms such as the research paper. Multigenre projects go a step beyond: They open up unlimited channels and formats for you to convey your points. Nothing is out of bounds. Think handmade objects, videos, blogs, animations, photo essays, collages, and other visual arguments. Further, genre projects, and multigenre projects in particular, offer you the chance to connect with audiences beyond the classroom.

Your Rhetorical Situation

When you begin thinking about creating a multigenre project, consider the following:

Furthering your purpose   You can do this by assembling a coherent collection. Think of each genre piece as a chapter that contributes to a whole. You will unify the pieces by building in relationships among them by choosing a sequence and package (more on this on pp. 504–506)—and by composing an Introduction that pulls everything together. For multigenre projects, we recommend that you compose a separate Author's or Artist's Statement for each of your individual genre pieces, and use the Introduction to discuss how the pieces work together. However, it also works to create one Author's or Artist's Statement for the entire project. Check with your instructor about specific preferences. (For more on Author's and Artist's Statements, see Chapter 4, pp. 231–44.)

Reaching your audience   You might do this by providing different *perspectives*. As you decide on the genres to compose in, think about whether you want to convey multiple perspectives on your topic through each piece. For example, if you are presenting an argument, you could address a different point of view in each composition.

Using rhetorical appeals to your advantage   Imagine how you might use each genre piece to make your case through different rhetorical appeals. Maybe in one genre you emphasize ethos; in another, logos; and in another, pathos. Or maybe you want to organize your project around a single rhetorical appeal.

Choosing modes and media   Think about using a mix of modes and media throughout your pieces so that your audience has different ways to connect with your message. Some of the best projects we've seen are a combination of textual, visual, and audio compositions.

The Conventions of the Multigenre Project

For advice, examples, and guidelines for composing in individual genres, see Chapters 1–4.

Every multigenre project will be different—a culmination of one author's choices about which genres to mix together, which perspectives to represent, which voices or tones to incorporate. There are no "conventions" for a multigenre work beyond the use of multiple genres to convey ideas to an audience. Typically, we ask student composers of multigenre projects to provide an Introduction, a separate Author's or Artist's Statement for each individual piece, or a single statement in which they reflect on each of their genre pieces. The Statement(s) should include Works Cited lists.

THE STEPS TO ASSEMBLING A MULTIGENRE PROJECT

For help with **Author's and Artist's Statements,** see Chapter 4, pages 237–46, and Chapter 8, pages 476–79.

1. Introduce your project and provide context   Write a one- to two-page Introduction that gives your audience an overview of your topic, your scope, and what sparked your interest in your topic. Provide a brief explanation for your rationale for the sequence of your genre pieces (more on that below). You can provide more details—and cite and document your research—in your Author's or Artist's Statement(s), which is typically longer than the Introduction and includes a list of References or Works Cited. Alternatively, you can combine your Introduction and Statement into one document, as some of our students have done.

Your Introduction should also provide any context that your audience will need to fully understand your project and individual genre pieces. This means you may need to provide a brief history of your topic, the people who are key to its larger discussion, and the main controversies surrounding it.

2. Sequence your genre pieces   Do this in a way that will make sense to your audience. Each piece should prepare your audience for the one that follows it. Sequencing helps orient your audience, and it also helps you methodically achieve your purpose. Here are some scenarios:

» If your goal is to convince your audience to take action on a specific problem, begin with a composition that highlights that problem, and end with a piece that offers a possible solution and/or makes a direct call to action. An alternative approach could be to begin with a visual piece that shows what could happen if no one took action to solve the problem.

» If your purpose is to compare or contrast specific views on your topic, you might arrange your pieces to highlight differences and similarities.

» If one of your goals is to tell a story, sequence your pieces into a narrative structure (consider a beginning, middle, and end), and bring out narrative elements such as character and conflict.

» If you want to emphasize a particular rhetorical appeal, think about how the order of your genre pieces could do that. For example, to emphasize pathos, you could begin and end with the pieces that will evoke the most emotion in your audience. Alternatively, if establishing your ethos is more important, you might begin with a piece that establishes your expertise and credibility, such as a researched journal article.

3. Title your project   Your title should reflect your topic and your "take" on your topic. Create a title that will spark the interest of your target audience, a title that is memorable and provocative. The title should reflect your project's message but can go beyond simply stating it. Consider how the tone and word choice of the title will build expectations in readers' minds about what the project will or will not do.

Here are some titles our students have come up with:

» Dawson Swan's project on nature and mental health: "The Threat of Nature Deficit Disorder" (p. 514)

» Gwen Ganow's project on how the concept of superheroes intersects with "real life": "When Worlds Collide: Why Superheroes Matter" (p. 511)

» Scarlet Moody's project on Rwanda radio: "The Rwandan Genocide and Radio-Television's Libre des Milles Collines"

» Emma Jones's project on Alzheimer's disease: "The Road of Life"

4. Create an Author's or Artist's Statement   Use your Statement to discuss your research, explain your rhetorical choices, and evaluate your project overall. (See Chapter 4, pp. 231–44, and Chapter 8, pp. 476–79, for advice and examples.) We encourage our students to write a Statement for each genre piece, and provide an Introduction or project-wide Statement to unify their work.

5. Package your project creatively   While a standard research paper is generally packaged quite simply, with a cover page or perhaps in a folder, a multigenre project can be packaged more imaginatively. As with every other aspect of your project, your package and delivery will impact your audience and indicate your tone and angle on your subject. For example, a multigenre project packaged in a

---

☞ **Attention, authors & artists! Need some ideas for genres?**

Working on a multigenre project? Great. There are lots of genres to choose from. Here are just a few (they can be delivered in digital, print, and/or 3-D physical media): researched arguments, editorials, articles, user manuals, brochures, encyclopedia articles, obituaries, exposés, editorials, letters to the editor, interviews, book reviews, essays, surveys, business letters, poems, personal letters, short stories, scripts, journal entries, memoirs, advice columns, political speeches, eulogies, tabloid articles, restaurant menus, top 10 lists, resumes, directions, syllabi, Web pages, photographs, collages, photo essays, charts, graphs, advertisements, comics, cartoons, posters, movie posters, skit performances, paintings, sketches, musical scores, musical performances, sculptures, audio essays, film clips, and scrapbook pages.

miniature black coffin indicates somberness, while a project presented in a minia-ture pink-polka-dotted coffin suggests a humorous and ironic approach.

Here are some ways students have packaged their projects in the past:

» A project on globalization: All the components were rolled up inside a mailing tube covered with stamps and postal marks from around the world.

» A project on the drinking age: All the genre pieces were presented in a wire wine bottle carrier.

» A project on education: The title page was designed to look like the cover of a teacher's grade book, and all the pieces inside had pale blue columns on the borders (like grade books have).

Which of the project titles on page 505 most pique your interest? Why? What does each title suggest about the scope and focus of the project?

CHECKLIST **Assembling a Multigenre Project?** Keep the following questions in mind.

Wherever you are in your composing process, it can be helpful to get feedback. Here are some more questions you might want to ask your respondents.

THE RHETORICAL SITUATION

☐ **Purpose.** What is the overall purpose of my project? What are the purposes of my individual genre pieces? What is the ef-fect of reading/viewing each piece in iso-lation versus reading/viewing each piece as a group? When all are experienced together, how is the effect different from reading/viewing each piece in isolation? How can I sequence or package my pieces to best achieve my overarching purpose? What title will signal my overall purpose to my readers?

☐ **Audience.** How does my Introduction and Author's/Artist's Statement work to draw my audience in? If I aim to persuade my audience, how does the sequencing encourage readers/viewers to accept my point of view? What kind of packaging will capture the attention of my audience?

☐ **Rhetorical appeals.** How do my indi-vidual genre compositions, Author's/Artist's Statements, and Introduction, taken together, establish my credibility (ethos)? Is there a clear logical aspect to

the project (logos)? Is there something that will resonate emotionally (pathos) with readers? Given my audience, should I emphasize one appeal over another, perhaps highlighting it in my Intro-duction? Given my purpose, can I use sequencing to begin and end my project with a particular appeal?

☐ **Modes & media.** Have I used a mix of modes and media throughout my pieces so that my audience has different ways to connect with my message? Have I bal-anced one mode/medium with others so that the project overall isn't text-heavy or too visual?

THE GENRE'S CONVENTIONS

There are no conventions for multigenre projects. However, there are conventions for individual genres. See Chapters 1–4 for advice and examples.

EXAMPLES OF MULTIGENRE PROJECTS

Let's take a look at some student projects. We've annotated these to highlight the components of each project and how the student assembled them into a whole. We've also indicated how our students handled their rhetorical choices (regarding purpose, audience, rhetorical appeals, and modes and media) and the possibilities of the multigenre project (elements, style, design, and use of sources).

Guided Reading: A Multigenre Project

Neil Carr (Student)

Video Games and Violence: Who Should We Blame When Kids Are Violent?

One multigenre project will look very different from another. Here is student author Neil Carr's multigenre project on video games and violence.

(Project reprinted by permission of Neil Carr.)

◄ STUDENT AUTHOR PHOTO
Neil Carr.
Courtesy Neil Carr.

What is the author/artist, Neil Carr, doing?

NEIL'S RHETORICAL SITUATION

Purpose
Neil wants to persuade his audience that video games and their makers should not be blamed for the violent real-life behavior of some players.

Audience
Neil identifies his primary audience as general readers who do not have specialized knowledge of video games. He's

aiming at regular citizens/taxpayers. He sequences his compositions so that his audience will get a sense of the humanity of gamers themselves, as well as the escape aspects of gaming, before he moves on to more detailed research findings.

Rhetorical appeals
Neil's choice to compose both a film script and an audio diary—both narrative and persuasive genres—indicates that appealing to pathos and ethos is important to him.

What are the parts? How do they work together?

MULTIGENRE PIECES

Neil's project consists of:
An informative and persuasive **researched essay** on studies of video games and violence (p. 508).

A narrative and persuasive **audio diary** of a truancy officer (see recorder).

(Continued on p. 508.)

**MULTIGENRE
PIECES**

A narrative and persuasive **film script** of the story of two boys, one who plays video games and one who doesn't, comparing their tendencies toward violence.

The **film** (on DVD).

To unify his project, Neil provides:

An **Introduction** with contextual information.

An **Author's Statement** in which he discusses his research, explains his rhetorical choices, and evaluates his project as a whole.

Packaging for his print pieces—a binder with an illustrated cover—and a recorder that contains his audio piece.

**NEIL'S RHETORICAL
SITUATION**

Modes & media

Neil chooses film and audio to engage his audience in a narrative, persuasive, and entertaining way. However, he opts to present his own views and research findings on the topic in a traditional research paper.

**Multigenre
conventions**

There are no conventions for multigenre projects. However, there are conventions for individual genres. See Chapters 1–4 for examples.

Let's look at the audio diary from Neil's multigenre project.

What makes this an **audio diary**?

What is the author/artist, **Neil Carr**, doing?

THE GENRE'S CONVENTIONS

Elements of the genre

A diary entry is a first-person narrative in which the writer records thoughts and observations.

Style

A diary entry is very casual; it often reads/sounds like a person's speaking voice. In this case, Neil has adapted some literary narrative elements, and has written this piece almost like dialogue or even a short scene from a play.

Design

In this case, Neil has provided a transcript of the audio diary. He has formatted it as a Word document; it looks like an essay.

Print Layout View   Sec 1   100%

Neil Carr

Audio Diary of a Truancy Officer (transcript)

March 31, 2013. This is truancy officer Mike Rendar, and this is the first entry of my audio diary. I've never done one of these before, but I decided to start because I've been put on a new duty—a pretty strange one. See, as a truancy officer, I usually patrol looking for kids trying to ditch their classes. When I find them, I ticket them—or rather, their parents—and get them to where they need to be. Well, I got called in by Sergeant Purser yesterday, on my day off, so he could tell me about my new assignment.

It seems that some kid named Thomas Miller was expelled from school yesterday for fighting. I guess with everything that's been going on lately . . . the school shootings and violence and all . . . Higher-ups must think the kid is gonna hurt someone.

I looked into the kid's profile, and I can see what they mean, but I just don't think it's gonna happen. Call it a hunch. [sigh] Oh, well. I'll begin my observation today . . . Here we go.

I spent all day yesterday watching this kid . . . nothing. He lives in a crappy little apartment with his dad. They live on the bottom floor, so I can go peek in the window sometime. At first, I waited in my car because the shades were all closed. Finally, the kid's dad opened the shades and left about 7:30 AM. Probably for work.

Once Dad left, I looked in to see what was going on. Nothing. Kid was probably sleeping. A couple hours later, I checked again. Kid was playing some video game. I checked again an hour later—same story. An hour later—no change.

That was when I realized this whole damn thing is political. The chief just doesn't want to get caught with his pants down . . . who can blame him. Anyway, the most exciting thing the kid did all day was switch from playing the video game to surfing the Net. I couldn't see what Web sites he was going to. Coulda been buying knitting needles . . . or looking up a recipe for a bomb.

April 1, 2013. It's morning again and I'm sitting in my car outside the kid's apartment . . . again. I've had way too much time to think just sitting here. I'm starting to wonder if what I'm doing is even legal. Course, even if it isn't, I wouldn't bring it up with Sergeant Purser. Up until now, I've enjoyed my job and I'd like to keep it. Besides, there's probably some new amendment to the Patriot Act.

Continues next page

NEIL'S RHETORICAL SITUATION

Purpose

Neil channels the voice of a truancy officer to make a point about video gamers. This piece fits in with the broader purpose of his multigenre project: to persuade others that video games and their producers should not be blamed for the violent behavior of some gamers.

Audience

Neil's audience includes his classmates, his instructor, and a general audience.

If this had been a "real" audio diary by Officer Rendar, the audience could have been the court, if he'd been asked to submit his observations.

Carr, *Audio Diary (transcript)*, *Continued*

Sources

Typically the source for a diary entry is the writer's own experience. In this case, however, Neil is channeling a truancy officer's voice and experience. He has also based this on his research on how gamers respond to video games, and what video games may or may not have to do with violence.

Print Layout View   Sec   1   100%

But this kid never leaves the damn house. I wanna go invite him out to Denny's . . . McDonald's, 7-Eleven, anything! Who doesn't leave their house?

It's the end of the day. Another day this kid hasn't moved. Seems to be having fun with his games, though. At least one of us is having a good time. He went online again today. I hope the kid is getting a girlfriend or something. [chuckle]

I wonder if his dad even knows he's been expelled. Wouldn't surprise me if he didn't . . . They never talk to each other.

April 2, 2013. I think I got too many of my personal thoughts in this thing yesterday. I guess I forgot I may have to turn this over to a court someday. Hopefully not. Problem is, it might be the only thing keeping me sane on this job. Hmm, either way I gotta try and keep it more professional today.

I just checked on the Miller kid . . . like I do every hour. He's back at it, playing his game. His father left approximately forty-five minutes ago. I'm going to go approach the window and see what I can see.

Ah geez . . . I went up to the window, and I was being as sneaky as a person can be in daylight, but I think the kid might've seen me . . . [pause] Hmmm, you know, I didn't think about this before, but if he sees me . . . [chuckle] I won't have to do this crappy duty anymore. I'll lie low out here for a while, maybe he didn't notice me after all.

[laughing] Wow, now that was surprising. The kid walks out his door, looks me straight in the eye, and hocks a loogie from his patio to the hood of my car. Man, that kid has got range! Since he didn't pull a gun and blow me away, I doubt the kid's actually gonna hurt anyone. Still, he's got some nerve to go spitting on a cop car.

Anyway, my cover is blown so I'm heading back to Purser's office now . . . He'll probably rip me a new one, but that's better than working this job. What a waste. Rendar out.

Rhetorical appeals

Neil clearly appeals to ethos by choosing a truancy officer to be the speaker in this creative audio diary. The officer has authority and knowledge of teen behavior. Neil also appeals to pathos by presenting the officer as a sympathetic character; he also uses humor.

Modes & media

Neil created an audio diary, which could just as easily have been a video diary. Either can be delivered in a digital environment. When he submitted his project, he included this paper transcript of the recording.

Guided Reading: A Multigenre Project ▼

Gwen Ganow (Student)

When Worlds Collide: Why Superheroes Matter

In her multigenre project, "When Worlds Collide: Why Superheroes Matter," Gwen Ganow represents a variety of genres and media, as her table of contents shows (see p. 512). (To learn more about Gwen's project, see Chapters 8 and 9.) *(Project reprinted by permission of Gwen Dalynn Ganow.)*

▲ STUDENT AUTHOR
PHOTO
Gwen Ganow.

When Worlds Collide:
Why Superheroes Matter

Gwen Ganow
Project Contents

What are the parts? How do they work together?

MULTIGENRE PIECES

Gwen's project consists of:

A persuasive **researched argument** essay that examines the power of superheroes (item 2).

(Continued on p. 512.)

What is the author/artist, Gwen Ganow, doing?

GWEN'S RHETORICAL SITUATION

Purpose
Gwen's overall purpose is to persuade her audience that superheroes can help convey hope and strength to marginalized people who experience intolerance.

MULTIGENRE PIECES

An informative and narrative **collage** that combines a number of paintings of comic book superheroes, original comic book artwork, and quotations from the comic books (item 3).

A narrative and persuasive **journal entry** written from the perspective of a young boy who reads comic books during the 1950s (item 4).

An informative **brochure** about a support group for gay superheroes and their allies (item 5).

A persuasive **film review** of the movie *X-Men* (item 6).

A persuasive **Power-Point presentation** on the movie *X-Men*, featuring a **top 10 list** (item 7).

A narrative **memoir** in which Gwen explores her experience with comic books with her mother, who is also a comic book fan (item 8).

To unify her project, Gwen provides:

An **Introduction** that offers context. In it, she explains her research and rhetorical choices, and evaluates her project (item 1).

Packaging. Gwen puts her project together in a Word document that she can e-mail to her instructor. This format suits her project because some of her genre pieces—such as her film review and PowerPoint—include embedded links to film clips and other media.

GWEN'S RHETORICAL SITUATION

Audience

Gwen's primary audience is made up of comic book readers; her choice for sequencing the genre pieces reflects her desire for readers to be immersed in the world of the superhero right away.

Rhetorical appeals

Gwen's choice to compose a film review, researched argument, and brochure indicates that appeals based on ethos and logos are most important to her. However, she also conveys pathos, especially in her journal entry, memoir, and film review.

Modes & media

Gwen decides on a mix of text and visuals in her project to help readers visualize, relate to, and interpret the world of the superhero.

Multigenre conventions

There are no conventions for multigenre projects. However, there are conventions for individual genres. See Chapters 1–4 for examples.

What makes this a **persuasive brochure**?

THE GENRE'S CONVENTIONS

Elements of the genre

Brochures are usually used to inform and/or persuade an audience, which is the case here. They are usually brief, to the point, and visual.

Style

Gwen uses a casual but persuasive tone, and plays with the concept of the superhero to move readers/viewers to action.

Design

She works in two columns to present her content. In column 1 she chooses gay pride flags instead of bullets to telegraph the message behind the brochure. In column 2 she presents her eye-catching images and centers the invitation to the meeting.

Sources

Gwen draws on the sources she has used in her research. See her Works Cited list in Chapter 9 (p. 487).

Let's examine the brochure from Gwen's multigenre project.

Superhero GSA Brochure

Gay/Straight Alliance: Be a Superhero

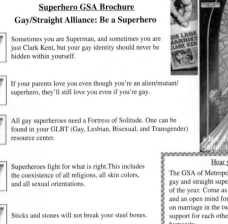

Sometimes you are Superman, and sometimes you are just Clark Kent, but your gay identity should never be hidden within yourself.

If your parents love you even though you're an alien/mutant/superhero, they'll still love you even if you're gay.

All gay superheroes need a Fortress of Solitude. One can be found in your GLBT (Gay, Lesbian, Bisexual, and Transgender) resource center.

Superheroes fight for what is right. This includes the coexistence of all religions, all skin colors, and all sexual orientations.

Sticks and stones will not break your steel bones.

Secrets hurt everyone, even superheroes.

Bigotry and hatred can be just as deadly as kryptonite. Always stand up for yourself, and let strength and hope guide your path.

You're not alone. Superheroes have to struggle and fight for what they believe in.

Captain America fights for freedom, democracy, and the American way. He desires these things for ALL Americans.

Hear ye! Hear ye!

The GSA of Metropolis would like to invite all gay and straight superheroes to its first meeting of the year. Come as you are with an open heart and an open mind for a "brown bag" discussion on marriage in the twenty-first century. Through support for each other, we can lead the way for humanity.

The GSA meeting will be held at the time and place stated below:

GSA Headquarters
5655 W. Kent Ave.
Metropolis
Special Guest Speaker, Captain America
5-7 p.m.
Capes and refreshments will be provided.

What is the author/artist, **Gwen Ganow**, doing?

GWEN'S RHETORICAL SITUATION

Purpose

In this brochure, Gwen makes a case for gay marriage, arguing for tolerance and presenting an invitation to a GSA (Gay/Straight Alliance) meeting. The brochure relates to her project on superheroes, "otherness," and acceptance.

Audience

The audience for this piece is specifically gay teens, but Gwen also makes it relevant for her wider audience of comics/superhero fans as well as her classmates and instructor.

Rhetorical appeals

Gwen uses mainly pathos in this piece, both in her list (e.g., "Secrets hurt" and "You're not alone") and by choosing festive images of kissing couples.

Modes & media

This piece can be used as a physical flyer or shared on digital media (in which case it can include links to the GSA, for example).

Guided Reading:
A Multigenre Project ▼

Dawson Swan (Student)

The Threat of Nature Deficit Disorder

In his multigenre project, Dawson Swan represents a variety of genres and media, as the image below shows. *(Project reprinted by permission of Dawson Swan.)*

▲ STUDENT AUTHOR PHOTO **Dawson Swan.**

MULTIGENRE PIECES

A **compilation CD**, leaning against a rock, of songs about nature, accompanied by liner notes that identify each song and the message it sends about nature.

A research-based **magazine article**, rolled up and "planted" in a green flowerpot.

To unify his project, Dawson provides:

An **Introduction** that prepares his audience to experience his project and serves as his Author's/Artist's Statement. In it, he explains his research and rhetorical choices and evaluates his project (item 1).

Packaging consisting of a Roadmaster wagon, which represents childhood play and nature.

DAWSON'S RHETORICAL SITUATION

Audience

Dawson's primary audience is educated adults; his choice for packaging the components reflects his view that exposure to nature is important for all children.

Rhetorical appeals

Dawson's choice of the poster with a small child, the music CD, and the wagon used as packaging indicate that appeals to pathos are most important to him.

Modes & media

Dawson's project includes print (the magazine article), audio (the CD), and visual pieces (the poster, the artwork with the CD, and the packaging).

Multigenre conventions

There are no conventions for multigenre projects. However, there are conventions for individual genres. See Chapters 1–4 for examples.

Let's take a closer look at Dawson's Introduction to his multigenre project.

What makes this an Introduction to a multigenre project?

THE GENRE'S CONVENTIONS

Elements of the genre

Dawson begins by acknowledging that many people will initially view his topic as a joke; this helps him build rapport with his readers. He gives an overview of the different pieces in the project and prepares readers for what to expect.

Style

Dawson writes in a formal tone, which develops his ethos as someone who takes this issue seriously.

Design

The design of Dawson's Introduction is minimal; he formats his Introduction into paragraphs for easy reading.

Print Layout View | Sec 1 | 100%

Dawson Swan

Introduction

The Threat of Nature Deficit Disorder

"Things are not like they used to be." I've heard this said many times in reference to technology, nature, parenting, music, and the world in general. That phrase will always be true because change is inevitable, but there is one change that is occurring unnoticed today that I believe requires our urgent attention. This change has resulted in a condition that has recently been identified as nature deficit disorder (NDD). Richard Louv introduced this condition in his book *Last Child in the Woods: Saving Our Children from Nature-Deficit Disorder*. Most people have never heard of this "disease," and when they do hear about it, their initial reaction is that it is a joke, just a clever play on words. Unfortunately NDD and the misery it causes are very real.

In today's society, it seems we no longer have time to relax, to take a walk outside and smell the roses. Instead, we are bombarded by tight schedules, economic pressures, and chronic stress. The former secretary of education Richard Riley was quoted as saying, "The top ten jobs that will be in demand in 2010 didn't exist in 2004. Students are being prepared for jobs that don't exist, using technologies that haven't been invented, to solve problems that we don't know about yet" (qtd. in Fisch). This shows how incredibly overwhelming it can be to simply live in our culture and to plan for the future, let alone find time to be outside.

Due to continually advancing technology, globalization is becoming a reality. The quantity of data created every day is increasing exponentially. Toddlers are learning to use technology scientists wouldn't have dreamed of thirty years ago. As a result, it is becoming vitally important to train our children about technology. Fortunately the young generations are easily able to learn to use technology, but there is always much more to be learned as technology continues to advance. The increasing need for technological "geeks" is drawing more and more of us into cyberspace and shoving nature off into a corner.

Ironically, going "green" is becoming increasingly popular. Our culture is reveling in new ways to better the environment and preserve nature, but it is seriously missing the point because the culture, particularly pop culture, has little firsthand knowledge of nature. We would rather stay inside and watch the hit TV show *Planet Earth* on our massive high-definition TVs than take a walk outside. Instead of climbing a mountain or sitting on our porch watching the sunset, we would rather sit in front of a computer monitor and look at beautiful photographs of exotic places. This misguided relationship with nature has created a synthetic

---

What is the author/artist, Dawson Swan, doing?

DAWSON'S RHETORICAL SITUATION

Purpose

Dawson introduces his topic and argues for its importance.

Audience

The audience for this piece is people who don't understand the gravity of nature deficit disorder, so Dawson takes a serious tone.

Rhetorical appeals

Dawson appeals to logos when he explains his genre choices and the order in which he wants them viewed/read and why.

Swan, *Nature Deficit Disorder,* Continued

THE GENRE'S
CONVENTIONS

Sources

Dawson incorporates three outside sources: two books and a video that went viral in 2007 about how the world is changing.

☰ ☷ ▣ ▤ ▥ ▦ Print Layout View   Sec 1   100% ▭▭○▭

environment and a secondhand relationship with the earth—an environment that is convenient and controlled. While those who have generated this environment are supposedly pursuing the natural, they have only created a vague reflection of the real thing. Our culture is sadly lacking in an understanding of the true meaning of "natural."

Now you may ask, "Why should I care? I get enough nature from the Discovery Channel and an occasional ski trip." Well, look at it this way. The generation that is currently approaching, or is already in, the child-rearing stage is the largest generation ever (Tapscott 20). The men and women of this generation are going to begin having children, and the decisions they make about how they raise their children will have a monumental impact on the future.

The logical next question you may ask is, "Is NDD a real threat?" Yes it is, and its effects can be devastating: obesity, ADD, emotional disorders, high blood pressure, and chronic pain that kids develop decades before they should. These conditions have always been there, but now they are disturbingly prevalent.

This project serves a couple of purposes: First, I want to inform people of NDD, and if they already know about it, I want to increase their knowledge and alert them to how urgent it is to take action. Second, I hope that this project gives inspiration to fight NDD. It can be as easy as walking outside, looking up at the stars, or smelling the fragrance of a wildflower in the night air.

I planned each part of the project to fit into a different category of media so I could communicate to more people. My first piece is a poster that can be displayed nearly anywhere, and it quickly draws people in—far more than an essay or a brochure can. A poster evokes emotion and thoughts of childhoods spent playing outside. This sets them up for my second piece.

The second and third pieces actually merge into a CD album, which can reach people on multiple levels. The artwork for the album is made up of photographs I have taken of nature during the last couple of years. These pictures grab the attention of the viewer and create a relaxing and thought-provoking environment for them to take part in as they experience the second half of the album—the music and lyrics (I searched through hundreds of songs to find specific songs about nature). I wrote an Introduction to the album that describes the purpose of each piece and its message.

My fourth piece is a magazine article. It could appear in parenting magazines because my primary audience is people

Continues next page

DAWSON'S
RHETORICAL
SITUATION

Modes & media

The mode and medium were dictated by the assignment, which specified that the Introduction be a print-based essay. Dawson felt that visuals did not need to be part of the Introduction because the project itself was so eye-catching. So he used text exclusively to explain his decisions.

Swan, *Nature Deficit Disorder,* Continued

---

who are moving into, or are in, the childbearing years, and because children are most susceptible to NDD.

I have concluded that these pieces fit together best in a conference setting where the poster in a booth would initially draw people. Then they would see the CD. It could be considered a fund-raiser for my topic or maybe just a sampler. After leafing through the pages of artwork and listening to the music, people would want to know what it's all about, and they could read the magazine article. The article brings everything home and explains NDD in depth. Between these four pieces, a variety of media are used to grab people's attention, engaging both their minds and hearts. NDD is a compelling subject that affects everyone. Although a presentation of the simple facts of NDD would be enough to win people over, the potential of engaging them emotionally just as nature herself does, is fulfilled through photographs, poetry, and music.

Works Cited

Fisch, Karl. "Did You Know 2.0." *YouTube*. 22 July 2007. Web. 13 Oct. 2012. <http://www.youtube.com/watch?v=pMcfrLYDm2U&feature=related>.

Louv, Richard. *Last Child in the Woods: Saving Our Children from Nature-Deficit Disorder.* North Carolina: Algonquin, 2005. Print.

Tapscott, Don. *Growing Up Digital: The Rise of the Net Generation.* New York: McGraw-Hill, 1998. Print.

Who does Dawson seem to be writing his Introduction to? How can you tell? How would you describe the voice he uses? How well does he prepare you for experiencing his project?

Reader

PART 3
READER

11 IDENTITY

CONTENTS

POSTER/AD ▶
Homeless Coalition
of Hillsborough
County. *Reprinted*
by permission of the
Homeless Coalition of
Hillsborough County.
Photo by Brian Adams
Photographics Inc.

What do our online profiles, tattoos, or bumper stickers say about who we are? How about the magazines and blogs we read? The things we carry and the things we wear? And how do we define and represent ourselves in other genres and media—such as music, poems, movies, advertisements, or national slogans?

As individuals and as members of a larger community, we may define ourselves based on where we live, our religion, heritage, race, class, gender, and sexual orientation. We may also identify ourselves through favorite activities or sports teams, educational major, or profession, for example.

When we express something about identity, we create. What we create depends on what we want to say and the people we want to say it to—and also on how we say it. In other words, our creative expression depends not only on our choices about our purpose, message, and audience, but also on the genres and media that we choose as vehicles for that expression.

For example, if you wanted to share something about your own identity with your friends, you might create a musical mixtape or playlist. As you compile that music, would you choose songs that reflect where you're from? Would the lyrics say something about your likes and dislikes, or some other aspect of you?

Now, imagine that instead you've decided to say something about who you are in the form of a narrative essay, or through a poem, blog, or YouTube video. What might change? What different choices would you need to make in order to represent your ideas about identity through these genres?

In this chapter, you will encounter a range of voices commenting on personal and cultural identity. You'll read the works of well-known writers such as Garrison Keillor, as well as a group of homeless people and their advocates, a professor of psychology, and a car manufacturer. Their work represents a variety of genres: a humor essay, a researched argument, a nursery rhyme, an ad, and an interview, to name a few. As you read, pay attention to how these authors use different types of compositions and media to present ideas and arguments about identity.

What do your tastes say about who you are? What about the things you dislike?

The first set of readings explores how our material possessions reflect who we are, with an excerpt from Sam Gosling's book *Snoop: What Your Stuff Says About You* and an ad for a luxury car. Consider how many quick judgments you make about others based on their possessions. For example, if you notice your mom has traded in her old phone for a smartphone, you might identify her as a tiny bit cooler today than she was yesterday.

The second set of readings explores some of how we think of and shape ourselves—through our words (as in Garrison Keillor's "Last Words"), our behaviors (as in Paul Bloom's "First Person Plural"), and our bodies (as in Hanna Rosin's "A Boy's Life" and a nursery rhyme that asks: "What are little boys [and girls] made of?").

The chapter then moves toward more social aspects of identity. How does where we're from, or where we live now, affect who we are? Beginning with an editorial by Matthew Yglesias on race and identity in the United States, a group of readings on American identity includes a brief social history of the Jewish American deli (Ted Merwin) and a collection of ads that invites us to revise assumptions we might have about who the homeless are ("Not What You Expected?" from the Homeless Coalition of Hillsborough County).

Closing the chapter is an exploration of the subcultures we identify with, such as being a geek (eHow's wiki entry "How to Become a Geek") or a punk rocker (Deborah Solomon's interview with Patti Smith).

STARTER PROJECTS: Identity

1. **Identity & heritage: Make a list.** Make a quick list of the nationalities you identify with as being part of your family heritage. For example, if your great-grandparents on your mother's side emigrated from Ireland and your father's mother emigrated from El Salvador and his father from Mexico, list Irish, Salvadoran, and Mexican. Then jot down your traits or characteristics that you associate with each of those lines of heritage. What assumptions about national identity does your list reveal?

2. **Identity & stuff: Make a list.** Make another quick list, this time of your most prized possessions. These could be items with market value, such as a car, or things with sentimental value, such as scrapbooks. What does this list reveal about you? How might this list be misconstrued by others? For example, one prized possession might be a very expensive stereo system that you made significant sacrifices to pay for. Could someone assume you're from a higher income bracket than you are, based on the fact that you own such expensive stereo equipment?

3. **Identity & advertising: Create a collage.** Search through a variety of magazines with plenty of advertisements and photographs and cut out pictures that define someone's identity as an American. Then create a collage with these pictures showing what you think an American identity looks like. Create a title for your collage. What assumptions might someone make about being an American based on the collage?

IDENTITY & STUFF

When we're in someone else's home, we sometimes draw conclusions about that person based upon the pictures (or lack of pictures) on the wall, the books (or lack of books) in the bookcase, the type of furniture, or the neatness (or lack of neatness). The clothes we wear, the cars we drive, and our belongings often mark aspects of our identity. Even the type of computer we use (Mac or PC) conveys an aspect of our identity. Is it fair to draw conclusions about a person based on his or her "stuff"? The two pieces that follow explore how our "stuff" conveys aspects of who we are.

Researched Argument

Sam Gosling

From Snoop: What Your Stuff Says About You

In his book *Snoop: What Your Stuff Says about You*, Sam Gosling examines how our possessions reflect our personalities and shape how other people perceive us. Gosling, a professor of psychology at the University of Texas at Austin, focuses his research on ways individuals create environments that mirror their personalities. In short, he is interested in developing a "science of snooping." *(Snoop: What Your Stuff Says About You: Copyright © May 12, 2009, Sam Gosling. Reprinted by permission of Basic Books, a member of the Perseus Book Group.)*

◀ **AUTHOR PHOTO** *By permission of Sam Gosling.*

The Arrival of the Mystery Box

A FedEx package awaited me in the mailroom. Nothing much distinguished the box from other boxes. It was your standard box, brown and about the size of a shoebox, but squarer. What made this delivery different was the unusual set of instructions that came with it. I was not to open it until given permission to do so. Just in case I was in doubt, the words *DO NOT OPEN* were boldly inscribed in black ink across the top flap. According to instructions left on my voice mail, at a prearranged time I was to videotape myself opening the package. So at 3:00 PM the next day I took the box to a small room equipped with a video camera. Once inside, I pointed the camera to the spot where I would be standing and switched it on. I moved into view of the camera lens and pulled a small scrap of paper from my pocket. There was a number scribbled on the paper. I punched it into my cell phone.

"This is Dr. Gosling. I'd like to speak to Gary."

"I'll put you through."

A click. Then a pause.

"Gary speaking."

"It's Sam here. I'm ready."

"Go ahead and open it up."

Free at last to exercise my Pandoran urges, I slit the box open. "Inside you will see some things belonging to one person," said Gary. "They're all taken from that person's bathroom." (I noticed he was careful not to say *his* or *her*.) "Take the objects out one by one," he continued, "and tell me what they say about the owner."

As I removed the objects, I turned each one over in my hands. A small tube of skin cream, a CD, slightly scratched, of dance music, a brown plastic hair brush, and a Polaroid photo of the owner's sink area. As I inspected each item for clues I narrated my reasoning to the camera. "Well, the brush is quite large, probably belonging to a man." My theory was supported by the Polaroid photo, which showed a sink area with the surrounding surfaces generally devoid of sweet-smelling stuff and with levels of grime and (dis)organization more likely to be associated with males than females. I noted that the hairs trapped on the brush were short, straight, and dark. Perhaps the person was Asian or Hispanic. The

> Think about the objects on your bathroom counter. What clues do they give about you?

Sam Gosling, From Snoop: What Your Stuff Says About You   527

photo showed that the door on the bathroom vanity wasn't closed properly and the hairdryer cord was hanging out; the tube of skin cream had been squeezed in the middle, not from the end, and some crusty residue was stuck to the cap. The CD was a compilation of house music, a genre stereotypically associated with gay clubs. Combine that with the evidence that the person is concerned with his (I'm now pretty sure the owner is a male) appearance and a coherent picture begins to emerge.

After a few minutes, Gary asked: "So, what can you tell me about the owner of these items?" On the basis of what I'd inspected, I said I believed the owner was an Asian male in his mid to late twenties and that he was quite possibly gay. I had underestimated his age by a few years—he was in his early thirties—but I was right about the rest. Gary seemed pleased.

What was going on here? What was I doing talking to this faceless voice under such strange circumstances?

The mysterious caller was a television producer planning a new reality series that would deal with the familiar, almost irresistible, human urge to snoop. If you're anything like me, you do more than passively observe the surroundings when you enter someone's living space for the first time. I find it hard not to look around and collect, filter, and process information about the occupant. Would I be so kind as to excuse the host while she goes to the bathroom? Absolutely! She's gone. Right. Hightail it over to the bookcase. Scan the books. A guidebook to budget travel in Madagascar. A tiny gift edition of Virginia Woolf's *A Room of One's Own*. Interesting. Now the photos. Hmm, all but one show my host with a big group of friends, and each picture projects an image of drunken hilarity. No time to dwell, I just heard the toilet flush and there are still the CDs, the trash basket, and that pile of junk on the windowsill. And all this is before I've had a chance to snoop through her medicine cabinet. . . . I mean, kindly be excused to powder my nose. (Medicine cabinets are such quintessential snooping sites that I've often thought it would be fun to surprise snoopers with a "visitors' book" inside.)

> " What can a physical space tell you about someone you have never met or even seen? "

The television producers were taking this common impulse to its logical endpoint: What can a physical space tell you about someone you have never met or even seen? The vision for the program—unlike MTV's popular show *Room Raiders*—included a role for an expert who would provide insight into the snooping process.

Why were the producers talking to me? I am a professor of psychology at the University of Texas, and I specialize in the study of personality differences and how people form impressions of others in daily life. My research focuses on the same question driving the television program: how people's possessions can tell us even more about their personalities than face-to-face meetings or, sometimes, what their best friends say about them. Indeed, my first study on this topic, which I conducted when I was still a graduate student at UC Berkeley, was the scientific equivalent of what the producers had in mind for their show. The study examined what observers could learn about men and women they had never met purely on the basis of snooping around their bedrooms.

The "bedroom study," as it came to be called, yielded fascinating findings in its own right, and, to my surprise, the research and the ideas underlying it sparked significant interest beyond the halls of academe. Although other psychologists have looked at personality impressions based on small snippets of information, like video clips or short interactions, no one had examined rooms before. And no one had come up with such a rich bounty of information. The media reported our results with obvious glee. They gave their stories headlines such as "Object Lessons," "Behind Enemy Lines," and "Room with a Cue."

I continued my research in graduate school and have developed it further since taking up my post at the University of Texas in 1999. My graduate students and I have conducted many studies on personality in everyday life: We've peeked under beds and peered into closets; we've riffled through music collections; we've scrutinized Facebook profiles. We've visited eighty-three dorm rooms and nearly a hundred offices in banks, real estate firms, business schools, advertising agencies, and architecture studios. And we've examined how people reveal their personalities in such ordinary contexts as their Web pages, their books, the words they use in casual conversation, and where they live.

In the years we've been doing this research my teammates and I have learned how people form impressions of others based on their stuff, and we have trained our eyes to exploit clues that will tell us what a person is really like. Did the Virginia Woolf volume mean that my friend was an ardent feminist? Or perhaps the book was merely one of many she was assigned for a course on British literature? Did the photos of drunken hilarity mean she was using alcohol as an escape? Or was she just a party girl? Some ten years into the research, we'd assembled an enormous amount of information showing how people portray and betray their personalities.

So perhaps the television people were on the mark. Maybe I could say something useful about this topic.

• • •

Two weeks after the arrival of the box, I found myself in Los Angeles. We were to shoot a pilot episode the next day. As I stood on Hollywood Boulevard in front of Mann's Chinese Theater and stared down at the famous footprints on the sidewalk, I thought about how I could contribute to the program. I hoped I would be able to explain the different ways people leave behavioral footprints in the places they occupy. I hoped I would be able to guide the contestants away from common errors of judgment such as jumping to conclusions on the basis of only one clue or being misled by the things that tend to grab your attention. And I hoped to do this without oversimplifying the science underlying my research.

As I mulled these questions over in my mind I began to realize that there was no single source that brought together all the strands of snooping research. So, soon after my Los Angeles adventure, as I returned to Texas to continue my work, I began formulating my plans for this book.

The task facing me in my research is not much different from the task we all face as we attempt to make sense of the social worlds in which we live; that is, we draw meaning from artifacts. Of course, we usually don't realize that we're doing this because we do it unconsciously and with great ease. When you first meet someone, you don't notice that you're forming an impression by integrating information—from his shaved head or the maps on his living room wall, from the first words that pop out of his mouth or the firmness of his handshake.

> **❝ We draw meaning from artifacts. ❞**

But underlying the apparent ease with which we paint these portraits is a set of complex mental processes that have only recently been systematically investigated.

And sometimes these processes go awry. For example, our dorm-room snoopers were pretty good at judging students' political values just by glancing around their living spaces. But they were far from perfect judges. They correctly used obvious cues such as explicit political décor—bumper stickers, posters of political icons such as Malcolm X, Che Guevara, or Ronald Reagan. But there were clues that they shouldn't have used but did, and clues that they should have used but didn't. In our studies, judges used the presence of art and books on art to infer that occupants leaned to the Left. But despite what you might think, these things bore no relation to political affiliation. What *did* give clues to (conservative) political leanings, though, was sports-related décor, a clue our judges completely overlooked.

This tells us that although common sense often gets it right, it can also lead us in the wrong direction. And without learning about the studies we can never know whether we're using the kind of common sense that's useful or misleading.

What's more, our common sense can fool us into thinking that the results of studies merely confirm what we already know. I was struck by this 20/20 hindsight bias during a recent presentation. Before I begin a talk I usually ask my audience to guess what the bedroom studies showed. This turns out to be difficult to do. Few people are able to predict that attractiveness is easy to pick up in bedrooms but that nervousness is tougher to crack. On this particular occasion I made the mistake of unveiling my findings without asking the audience to guess in advance. And this time, something different happened: the attendees did not seem at all surprised by the results. Thus, I learned once again that just because something makes sense after the fact doesn't mean it was obvious all along. . . .

Space Invaders

Each of us faces similar challenges every day. You piece together bits of evidence, wherever you can find them, to form coherent portraits of the characters who populate your social spheres. You draw on information from your long history with dear old friends, you make snap judgments from thin slices of behavior in brief social interactions—the so-called zero-acquaintance contexts—and, if you're a snooper, you use clues left by people you've never met. You integrate new information, toss out current beliefs, and fill the gaps with new working hypotheses. But what are the mechanisms by which personality reaches out and connects to the physical world? How exactly does the self send its signals?

> " *How exactly does the self send its signals?* "

These were the questions driving my research when, in 1997, I assembled my first team of environmental assessors to help me develop a science of snooping. One of our goals was to explore the ways in which people have an impact on their personal spaces. What evidence of their characters do they leave behind? What elements of personality are most likely to leave traces? I also wanted to examine the judgments my assessors made on the basis of these spaces. I was not trying to improve the judging process, but to examine ordinary, everyday evaluations—the kind you and I might make, not the sort that would interest the FBI.

After much discussion with my graduate adviser, I formulated a plan. I would recruit a bunch of volunteers who, at a specified time, would vacate their rooms.

While they were gone, I would send in a team of judges to form an impression of the recently departed purely from evidence in their rooms. Next, I would send in another team of coders to assess the physical features of the space. We would also give the rooms' occupants personality tests and collect information about them from their friends.

As an impoverished graduate student, all I could offer the volunteers as an incentive was feedback on how others viewed them on the basis of their rooms. To my surprise, almost a hundred people signed up; then, as word of the study got out, others came around, virtually begging to be included.

As soon as I set foot in the first room, I knew we were on to something. The rooms varied much more than I had expected, not only in the quantity of objects but also in the nature of the objects themselves. Some rooms contained little more than a modest bed in the corner. Others were so full of objects and so adorned with decorations that our assessors had to be careful not to crush the evidence they were there to examine. And even in the overflowing rooms there was much variation in the objects that fought for territory on the shelves, chairs, beds, floors, and windowsills.

One such room exhibited a magnificent collection of *Star Wars* figurines and toys, a theme echoed in the posters adorning the walls and ceiling. Winnie the Pooh and friends were featured in a surprising number of rooms. Some spaces were meticulously arranged; others suggested that the occupant was aiming for a level of organization best described as "somewhere in the room." Some spaces were dark and stale, others light and breezy. Some were cozy, others cold.

As we examined the rooms, we began to notice their occupants' psychological footprints and to glimpse the different ways personality is expressed. Three broad mechanisms—identity claims, feeling regulators, and behavioral residue— seemed to connect people to the spaces that surrounded them. [The first mechanism] stood out especially clearly in the room of an occupant I'll call Cindy. . . .

Identity Claims: Cindy's Signals

We spend many hours in our personal environments, but there is no obvious functional reason why we should decorate them. The strawberry motif on the quilt hardly guarantees sweet dreams, and the stuffed piranha on top of the computer monitor won't help an ad writer produce snappy copy. Nonetheless, we continue to decorate our spaces, and the decorating is far from random; these changes to a space, which on a superficial level seem "nonfunctional," may

How do you "craft" your environment?

have a big impact on what is done there. Indeed, the results of one survey on worker comfort and engagement in the *Gallup Management Journal* reported that "employees working in a comfortable environment are much more likely to be engaged and to make a positive contribution to the organization's financial success." The survey was careful to point out that "comfort" extends well beyond physical conditions. The psychological environment that people craft is also crucial. This is certainly consistent with observations we have gathered—the extensive and persistent efforts by many of our subjects to decorate and modify their spaces strongly suggest a need to affect their psychological surroundings.

One way we make spaces our own is to adorn them with "identity claims"— posters, awards, photos, trinkets, and other mementos—that make deliberate symbolic statements. Cindy's room was laden with such symbols. My research teammates and I noticed them even before we stepped into the room. A sorority sticker stuck to the door announced an allegiance to one group. A bumper sticker, "Be Your Own Goddess," broadcast public self-affirmation with a feminist twist. Once across the threshold, we found more. On the dry-erase board was a quote from Nietzsche, "Where the will to power is lacking, there is decline," and written in caps along the bottom of the board was "Think Positive!" Hanging from the wall were cheerleading pompoms.

Identity claims are either directed toward others or directed at the self, and both kinds have their own psychological functions. People use other-directed identity claims—like Cindy's pompoms and the goddess bumper sticker—to signal how they want to be regarded. Since it is crucial that a person's audience understand the intended message, other-directed identity claims rely on objects that have shared meanings. The bumper sticker conveys pride in Cindy's gender and the pompoms affirm her loyalty to the university.

> ❝ People use other-directed identity claims to signal how they want to be regarded. ❞

In workplaces, office doors (or, these days, the outside of cubicle walls) are great repositories of other-directed identity claims. Next time you're visiting someone at work, I encourage you to cruise the corridors and trawl for the messages people are sending about themselves. Should your hallway wanderings lead you to my door, you will find a large poster produced by despair.com, a company that parodies inspirational posters promoting teamwork, trust, and other wholesome values. My poster shows a stunning photo of the Leaning Tower of Pisa set against a spectacular sunset. The message below reads: "Mediocrity. It takes a lot less time and most people won't notice the difference until it's too late." I didn't think deeply about the symbolic value of the poster when I first hung it up, but I now realize I was trying to convey an image of someone who not only has an ironic sense of humor but also has a broader distrust of facile feel-good moments.

Posters on the outside of office doors (as opposed, of course, to those hung on the inside where they face the occupant) are particularly interesting because the owners rarely see them. They are thus paragons of other-directed identity claims. These statements are typically intended to convey honest messages about their owners. But they can also be strategic, even deceptive. The student who adorned his dorm room with images of such hip icons as Bruce Lee and Tupac and cult movies such as *Reservoir Dogs* clearly wanted his visitors to see him as "cool." But we'd need to look further to see how cool he really is.

Your other-directed identity claims may vary, depending on whom you're trying to influence—the things you do to impress your boss might overlap only partially with the things you would do to wow a potential mate. However, it is increasingly difficult to keep our audiences separate, as the freelance television producer Colleen Kluttz discovered. According to a story in the *New York Daily News*, a friend posted a picture of Kluttz on her [social media] profile showing Kluttz with half-closed eyes; the caption indicated that she had smoked an illegal substance. Although the photo and caption were a joke between two friends, there was nothing to stop prospective employers from Googling her. After losing a couple of jobs at the eleventh hour, Kluttz suspected that her professional and personal worlds had collided so she had the photo removed.

As we begin to live out more and more relationships online, it's harder and harder to keep our various identities distinct. And it's harder to project the approved identities only to the audience we want to target. I'm not wild about the nerdy, decidedly uncool high-school picture of me easily discoverable online by all those people who I am hoping will view me as a sophisticated, devastatingly cool international man of mystery.

> **"** It's harder and harder to keep our various identities distinct. **"**

In addition to making statements to others about how we would like to be regarded, we can make symbolic statements for our own benefit. These self-directed identity claims reinforce how we see ourselves. In Cindy's room, objects on her desk included an inscribed gavel and a button expressing support for a local mayoral candidate. Their placement, right where Cindy would get to see them, suggests they were primarily there for her own

What are your "identity claims"? Which ones are meant for others? Which are just for you?

benefit—reminders, perhaps, of her accomplishments on the debate team and her involvement as a volunteer during the previous local elections. Both symbols raised hypotheses about some core features of Cindy's identity to be supported or rejected by further evidence.

Mass-produced posters are a good source of cultural symbols. A former colleague of mine displayed a small poster of Martin Luther King Jr. on her office wall. Like Cindy's gavel and political buttons, MLK's placement above my colleague's desk was deliberate and significant. It would be easy to miss the poster because, from the visitor's perspective, it was partially obscured by the computer monitor; but if you sat at her desk you would notice that the image was hung in a spot that didn't even require my colleague to move her head to see her idol—a quick rightward flick of the eyes, away from the document she was reading on the computer screen, is all that was needed. The arrangement suggested to me that she used this icon of progressive thought and values to inspire and reinforce the way she viewed herself. The poster appeared to be there more for her benefit than for that of visitors.

> **ff** *She used this icon to inspire and reinforce the way she viewed herself.* **ff**

As with many cultural icons, the meaning of MLK is reasonably clear, but identity claims directed at the self can also make use of artifacts whose meaning may be obscure to outsiders. As long as the items have personal meaning, they work. A pebble collected from a beach during a vacation in Morocco could provide someone with a connection to her Moroccan heritage. A fountain pen awarded to the occupant at her high school science fair could bolster her current identity as a chemist. Private artifacts can convey a broad message to the snooper even if the exact significance is unclear. In combination with other objects, the pebble or fountain pen could suggest that the collector is sentimental about a certain era in her life.

One simple experimental method for measuring identity—a person's view of who he or she is—is the Twenty Statements Test, which consists of twenty lines, each beginning, "I am . . ." followed by a blank space. Participants fill in as many of the blanks as they can in twelve minutes. (Think for a moment of the kinds of things you might come up with.) Typically, people generate about seventeen responses in the allotted time. The "Twenty Answers" can vary widely and include such responses as a girl, an athlete, a blonde, married, and from Chicago. Some respondents refer to themselves simply as *religious* or *a student*; others describe themselves more specifically as *Christian, Baptist*, or *a poor Christian*, or *pre-med, studying engineering*, or *a pretty good student*. Even this small set of responses gives us a sense of the potential range of identities that can be expressed by this method.

Sam Gosling, From *Snoop: What Your Stuff Says About You*   535

Photographs on display are the pictorial analogs of the "I am . . ." test because they capture a moment the person wanted to record ("Here I am being me"): "I am a freewheeling world traveler" (a picture of a grungy young man on the roof of a train as it climbs through the mountains of Rajasthan). "I am a loving daughter" (a teenager hugging her parents as she arrives home from a trip). "I am a successful student" (a young man collecting an award during a graduation ceremony).

In fact, the Twenty Statements Test has been adapted for pictorial use. Instead of filling in the blanks, people are given a camera and a twelve-exposure roll of film (this test was developed long before the advent of digital cameras) and given the following instructions: "We want you to describe to yourself how you see yourself. To do this we would like you to take (or have someone else take) twelve photographs that tell who you are. These photographs can be of anything just as long as they tell something about who you are." This exercise mirrors closely what people do informally when they select and display photographs in their homes, offices, cars, and wallets.

Tattoos are usually regarded as classic other-directed identity claims. Not only do they proclaim a particular value or attitude or allegiance, the permanence of tattoos signals that the wearer anticipates a continued commitment to that value—you don't tattoo yourself with a message you believe is going to be transitory; "Perot for President" is better expressed on a T-shirt or bumper sticker than inked across your forehead. But not all tattoos are for the benefit of others. Before heading to California to attend graduate school, my friend Amanda had her arm tattooed with an outline of the state of Texas. Not surprising—she had a strong allegiance to her home state. But the placement of the tattoo is what made this a striking self-directed identity claim: It was on her inner forearm and, from my perspective, it was upside down. This might seem odd until we realize that it was there to remind Amanda herself of her home state, not to signal to others where she was from. The placement meant that she could look down and think of Texas; it couldn't have served this purpose had she put it on her biceps or shoulder blade. This example underscores the importance of paying attention to location when considering identity claims. Placement determines the psychological function that the clue serves.

Identity claims can be made on T-shirts, buttons, necklaces, nose rings, tattoos, e-mail signatures, posters, flags, bumper stickers, and just about any other space big enough to accommodate a symbol of some sort. In his book about iPods, *The*

> What images hang on your walls? Why did you choose each one?

Perfect Thing, Steven Levy describes "wars" in which iPod wearers thrust their digital music players into one another's faces to demonstrate how hip they are. In the 1980s, when "ghetto blasters" or "boom boxes" were de rigueur, it was easy (unavoidable, actually) to broadcast your musical tastes to others. But as headphones took these acoustic emblems off the streets and directly into our skulls, we were denied this form of expression. Although less intrusive than filling a subway car with the latest number from the Fat Boys, the screen of the iPod has rescued, at least partially, the opportunity to let others know what's currently rocking your world.

And now we have music players that let you broadcast your musical tastes to anyone within wireless range. Although "squirting," as it has been called, was designed to allow you to share your songs with those who have compatible players, it can also be used to check out other people's music libraries and playlists. . . . [A] glimpse of a person's music collection can put you on the fast track to learning about his or her personality, political views, artistic tendencies, and even preferences in alcohol.

In practice, it can be hard to tell whether an identity claim is self-directed or other-directed. Displaying a poster of Martin Luther King Jr. may simultaneously reinforce your view of yourself and communicate your values to others, but it is useful to treat the two kinds of claims as separate because they reflect separate and distinct motivations. For example, this distinction may help us understand the difference between public and private spaces. In a home, what distinguishes the hallway, dining room, living room, and guest bathroom, which are, sure to be seen by others, from spaces that require a higher security clearance, such as the bedroom, study, or private

> **❝** *It can be hard to tell whether an identity claim is self-directed or other-directed.* **❞**

bathroom? Perhaps there is religious iconography, such as a cross or menorah, in the public places but reminders of family in the private places. Or, if the occupant is less concerned with privacy for the family and instead experiences his spiritual identity at a more private level, it could be the other way around, with the iconographic symbols hidden away and the family photos displayed for all to see.

For the snooper, it is invaluable to detect such distinctions because they hint at a potential fractionating of the self.

What do you find most interesting about other people's stuff?

Ad

Acura

The Acura TSX

The advertisement for the Acura TSX (see p. 539) is available online, and was originally obtained from a print issue of *Food & Wine* magazine. Like most ads for luxury goods, this one is selling not only the product itself, but a lifestyle. Notice how the people in the ad do not actually appear in or even with the car.

COMPANY HOMEPAGE ▶
Acura's Web site sells the brand as visionary and of high quality. *Courtesy of American Honda Motor Company, Inc.*

Old luxury has a glass of
warm milk and turns in early.
Modern luxury goes out all night and
still makes it into the office by eight.
A new generation has arrived.

TSX

>> commercial-archive.com

Introducing the all-new Acura TSX. This is modern luxury. Loaded with innovations like dynamic Traffic Rerouting™ and Zagat® reviews, it can find you an uncrowded road or a crowded club. Its ELS Surround® Sound could turn punk rock into a symphonic experience. And its re-tuned i-VTEC® engine achieves both more power, and an ultra-low emissions rating. The TSX with Technology Package. It's luxury for a whole new generation. See it at acura.com.

ACURA
ADVANCE

The text of the ad (left to right):

"Old luxury has a glass of warm milk and turns in early. Modern luxury goes out all night and still makes it into the office by eight. **A new generation has arrived.**

Introducing the all-new Acura TSX. This is modern luxury. Loaded with innovations like dynamic Traffic Routing and Zagat reviews, it can find you an uncrowded road or a crowded club. Its ELS Surround Sound could turn punk rock into a symphonic experience. And its re-tuned i-VTEC engine achieves both more power, and an ultra-low emissions rating. The TSX with Technology Package. It's luxury for a whole new generation. See it at acura.com."

Fine print (upper right corner):

"Traffic Rerouting requires XM NavTraffic subscription. XM NavTraffic available in select markets. First 90 days of service included. © 2008 Acura. Acura, TSX, i-VTEC and Traffic Rerouting are trademarks of Honda Motor Co., Ltd. Zagat Survey. ELS Surround is a registered trademark of Panasonic Corporation of North America. All rights reserved."

▲ **AD** Acura's TSX.
Courtesy of American Honda Motor Company, Inc.

To what extent can you relate to this ad? Who do you think it's meant for?

Acura, *The Acura TSX*   **539**

Identity & Stuff

ANALYZING RHETORICAL SITUATIONS

1. Researched essay. What is the central point in Sam Gosling's researched essay? What evidence does he use to support his claim?

2. Researched essay. How would you characterize the tone of Gosling's piece? How does his tone help him appeal to his audience?

3. Ad. What are some of the ways the Acura ad conveys that this car is "modern luxury"?

4. Ad. How does the ad use lighting, contrast, and framing to convey its message?

5. Researched essay & ad. Using Gosling's argument about "what your stuff says about you," what does the Acura TSX ad say about someone who buys this car? Based on the ad, what "stuff" would you expect to find in the Acura TSX owner's house?

6. Researched essay & ad. Both Gosling and the creators of the Acura ad attempt to persuade their audiences. What are the strategies used in each piece? How effective are they?

COMPOSING IN GENRES

7. Create an inventory list. Create an inventory of items found in your bedroom or dorm room. Exchange your list of objects (anonymously) with another classmate. Then present the inventory you received to the class, discussing the personality traits you'd expect based on the items listed. After you present the inventory, have the person who created it identify himself and discuss the correctness of the personality traits presented.

8. Research personality traits. Sam Gosling's Web site contains a variety of links related to research on personality traits. For example, one link he provides is to the work of Anthony Little and David Perrett, who research how personality information is perceived from facial expressions. Go to their site (alittlelab.com) and take one of the tests. Write a report about the test methods and results.

9. Take the "Twenty Statements Test." Refer back to Gosling's description of the Twenty Statements Test. Create your own list by writing twenty lines that begin with "I am . . ." followed by a trait that identifies you. Alternatively, do a Twelve Photos Test by taking a dozen photos of yourself that "describe to yourself how you see yourself." Include captions to yourself with your twelve photos. Write a reflective essay in which you consider these questions: What do these exercises tell you about how you measure and express your own identity? What do they tell you about your idea of self or selves?

10. Analyze an ad. Write a visual analysis of the Acura TSX ad showing how its visual aspects help achieve its rhetorical purpose. Take into account such design features as text placement, choice of photographs, font size, lighting, and framing.

11. Design an ad. Redesign the Acura ad for a different audience than the one intended in the ad shown here. You might consider redesigning the ad for an older audience, such as people who typify "old luxury."

12. Create an ad. Using the Acura ad as your template, create an advertisement for your car or your mode of public transportation. The ad should reveal aspects of your personality and appeal to an audience of your peers.

13. Analyze ads. View some television ads for the Acura TSX on YouTube. What are some differences and similarities between the television ads and the print ad shown here? How do you account for these?

SHAPING IDENTITY

Most of us identify ourselves in multiple ways—shaping and reshaping who we are in relation to the world as we grow and change. In the course of a normal day, you may function as a son or daughter, a spouse or partner, a parent, a friend, a student, an employee, a sports fan, an athlete, a pet owner. You convey your identity through your words, through your actions and choices, and also through your body. For example, maybe you have a tattoo that lets the world know you're really into dragons or butterflies, or that you've been in prison (hopefully not!), or that you love your mom. This group of readings begins with a piece on the presentation of identity in obituaries (Garrison Keillor), then takes a psychological turn, looking at the idea that we all have "multiple selves" (Paul Bloom). The final two readings in this group delve into issues surrounding the transgendered and present a nineteenth-century nursery rhyme that makes plenty of assumptions about what it means to be male or female.

When you read the final two pieces in this group, keep in mind that though we often use the terms *gender* and *sex* interchangeably, there is an important difference between the two. *Sex* is a biological identity having to do with whether we are born with male or female genitals; *gender*, on the other hand, refers to our culturally constructed roles and behaviors. From the time we are born, we are identified by our sex. Until fairly recently, it was standard practice for hospitals to identify the sex of newborns with pink caps for girls and blue caps for boys. Many birthday cards for young children reinforce typical gender roles by showing pictures of pretty ballerinas for girls and firemen and trucks for boys. Gender, however, is not a simple binary of masculine and feminine. Sometimes people identify themselves as gender variant, deviating from the expectations of their biological sex.

Humor Essay

Garrison Keillor

Last Words

Garrison Keillor is an author and radio-show host best known for
his Lake Wobegon novels and his live radio variety show, *A Prairie
Home Companion*. Born in 1942, he was inducted into the Radio
Hall of Fame in 1994. Keillor's hosting *Prairie Home Companion*
is characterized by droll humor and gentle satire. He plays up his
identity as a midwestern American of Lutheran background. Keillor
says, "A bit of advice: Stay off the obituary page as long as possible. There's no telling what they'll write about you." The following
essay was originally published by *Salon* (Salon.com). *(Salon artwork
is reprinted by permission of the Salon Media Group. The essay "Last Words" was
originally published as a syndicated column published by Tribune Media Services.
Copyright 2009, Garrison Keillor. Reprinted by permission. All rights reserved.)*

Last words

BY GARRISON KEILLOR

A bit of advice: Stay off the obituary page as long as possible. There's no telling what
they'll write about you.

**What is the "inven-
tory" of your life so
far? What would you
want your obituary
to include—and
what would you
want left out?**

I enjoy a well-crafted obituary as much as the next man, and now that people of
my own generation (what????) are appearing there, the obituary page becomes
closer and closer to my heart.

Yesterday I thought I might have to write one for my older brother after he
slipped while skating and cracked his head open and was rushed to intensive
care, and so I was reviewing a few salient facts of his life—his long off-and-on
romance with Natalie Wood, his invention of sunscreen, his real estate empire in
the Caribbean—but now he is conscious and showing signs of intelligence so it
looks as if I'm off the hook.

I like to read English obituaries, which are more frank than American obits.
Americans go to great lengths not to speak ill of the dead and lean toward the

comforting eulogy, but the obituary is not meant to comfort. It is meant to take inventory of a life. And thereby remind us that we too are mortal and someday the world will look at us with a cool clear eye and measure our contribution to the common good. ("His weekly column was always neatly typed and contained very few serious grammatical errors.") To make the dead guy into a demigod does not serve the common good.

> **"** *The obituary is not meant to comfort. It is meant to take inventory of a life.* **"**

This morning I read the obituary of an English writer I'd never heard of named Edward Upward, who died last Friday at the age of 105. (In fact, he outlived his obituarist, Alan Walker, who died in 2004.)

Ed went to Cambridge and was a friend of W. H. Auden and Christopher Isherwood and his career seems to have wilted in the heat of their brilliance. They became famous and he got a job teaching school. And then he joined the Communist Party, which is a heavy load of bricks to carry, and he married a hard-line Communist named Hilda, and he wrote an essay announcing that good writing could only be produced by Marxists, whereupon he suffered writer's block for twenty years. (Talk about poetic justice.)

"The middle decades were bleak for Upward," wrote Mr. Walker. "During a sabbatical year designed to give Upward the chance to write, he suffered a nervous breakdown." And then when he did publish again, he had become an antique. His autobiographical trilogy, "The Spiral Ascent," was received by critics like you'd receive a door-to-door vacuum-cleaner salesman.

And then there was the problem of walking around with the name Edward Upward.

It is a sobering tale for a fellow writer to read, and the main lessons of Upward's life, as I see it, are these.

1. Don't hang out with brilliant people who are likely to outshine you—unless you are a satirist. In which case, do. And stand quietly in back and take notes.

2. Writers shouldn't join parties and especially not the Communist Party.

3. Avoid making big pronouncements such as "The only good art is Marxist art." You say it, feeling you're on the cutting edge of history, but it's only going to come back and bite you in the butt.

4. If you must write an autobiography, give it a better title than "The Spiral Ascent."

I am a satirist. I am not now, nor have I ever been, a member of the Communist Party. I might have joined if Natalie Wood had tried to recruit me, but she did

Garrison Keillor, *Last Words*   543

not. I am a Democrat but mainly for the atmosphere and so I can meet normal people who do real work. I don't write essays or autobiographies.

And thanks to Edward Upward, I have decided not to take a sabbatical after all. You go off to the woods for a year and it puts you under terrible pressure to write *Moby-Dick* or something worthy of having had an entire year in which to write, and the longer you work at this masterpiece, the shabbier it looks, the whale turns into a guppy, and at the end of the year you have torn up almost everything you wrote and you are filled with self-loathing and bitter regret. No thanks. I am sticking to my post and recommend that you do, too. And stay off the obituary page as long as possible. One hopes for an opulent send-off but it's not going to happen, dear heart, and so you may as well go ahead and live your life because your obituary is bound to be a big disappointment.

Essay ▼

Paul Bloom

First Person Plural

Paul Bloom is a professor of psychology at Yale University. He has
written several books on language, including *How Children Learn the
Meanings of Words*. His research interests include moral reasoning
and the relationships between art and fiction. In "First Person Plural,"
Bloom discusses different ways scientists and social scientists understand the multiple selves of an individual. This essay first appeared in
The Atlantic and on *The Atlantic Online*. (*The Atlantic artwork is reprinted
by permission of* The Atlantic. *The essay "First Person Plural" is reprinted with permission. Copyright © 2008, The Atlantic Media Co., as first published in* The Atlantic
Magazine. *All rights reserved. Distributed by Tribune Media Services.*)

▲ AUTHOR PHOTO
Paul Bloom. © *Sigrid
Estrada.*

| Politics | Business | Tech | Entertainment | Health | Sexes | National | Global | China | Magazine |

First Person Plural

PAUL BLOOM

An evolving approach to the science of pleasure suggests that each of us contains multiple
selves—all with different desires, and all fighting for control. If this is right, the pursuit of
happiness becomes even trickier. Can one self "bind" another self if the two want different
things? Are you always better off when a Good Self wins? And should outsiders, such as
employers and policy makers, get into the fray?

Imagine a long, terrible dental procedure. You are rigid in the chair, hands
clenched, soaked with sweat—and then the dentist leans over and says, "We're
done now. You can go home. But if you want, I'd be happy to top you off with a
few minutes of mild pain."

There is a good argument for saying "Yes. Please do."

The psychologist and recent Nobel laureate Daniel Kahneman conducted a series
of studies on the memory of painful events, such as colonoscopies. He discovered

*Which of your
"selves" is in charge
right now?*

that when we think back on these events, we are influenced by the intensity of the endings, and so we have a more positive memory of an experience that ends with mild pain than of one that ends with extreme pain, even if the mild pain is added to the same amount of extreme pain. At the moment the dentist makes his offer, you would, of course, want to say no—but later on, you would be better off if you had said yes, because your overall memory of the event wouldn't be as unpleasant.

Such contradictions arise all the time. If you ask people which makes them happier, work or vacation, they will remind you that they work for money and spend the money on vacations. But if you give them a beeper that goes off at random times, and ask them to record their activity and mood each time they hear a beep, you'll likely find that they are happier at work. Work is often engaging and social; vacations are often boring and stressful. Similarly, if you ask people about their greatest happiness in life, more than a third mention their children or grandchildren, but when they use a diary to record their happiness, it turns out that taking care of the kids is a downer—parenting ranks just a bit higher than housework, and falls below sex, socializing with friends, watching TV, praying, eating, and cooking.

The question "What makes people happy?" has been around forever, but there is a new approach to the science of pleasure, one that draws on recent work in psychology, philosophy, economics, neuroscience, and emerging fields such as neuroeconomics. This work has led to new ways—everything from beepers and diaries to brain scans—to explore the emotional value of different experiences, and has given us some surprising insights about the conditions that result in satisfaction.

But what's more exciting, I think, is the emergence of a different perspective on happiness itself. We used to think that the hard part of the question "How can I be happy?" had to do with nailing down the definition of *happy*. But it may have more to do with the definition of *I*. Many researchers now believe, to varying degrees, that each of us is a community of competing selves, with the happiness of one often causing the misery of another. This theory might explain certain puzzles of everyday life, such as why addictions and compulsions are so hard to shake off, and why we insist on spending so much of our lives in worlds—like TV shows and novels and virtual-reality experiences—that don't actually exist. And it provides a useful framework

> ❝ *Each of us is a community of competing selves.* ❞

for thinking about the increasingly popular position that people would be better off if governments and businesses helped them inhibit certain gut feelings and emotional reactions.

Like any organ, the brain consists of large parts (such as the hippocampus and the cortex) that are made up of small parts (such as "maps" in the visual cortex), which themselves are made up of smaller parts, until you get to neurons, billions of them, whose orchestrated firing is the stuff of thought. The neurons are made up of parts like axons and dendrites, which are made up of smaller parts like terminal buttons and receptor sites, which are made up of molecules, and so on.

This hierarchical structure makes possible the research programs of psychology and neuroscience. The idea is that interesting properties of the whole (intelligence, decision making, emotions, moral sensibility) can be understood in terms of the interaction of components that themselves lack these properties. This is how computers work; there is every reason to believe that this is how we work, too.

But there is no consensus about the broader implications of this scientific approach. Some scholars argue that although the brain might contain neural subsystems, or modules, specialized for tasks like recognizing faces and understanding language, it also contains a part that constitutes a person, a self: the chief executive of all the subsystems. As the philosopher Jerry Fodor once put it, "If, in short, there is a community of computers living in my head, there had also better be somebody who is in charge; and, *by God, it had better be me*."

More-radical scholars insist that an inherent clash exists between science and our long-held conceptions about consciousness and moral agency: If you accept that our brains are a myriad of smaller components, you must reject such notions as character, praise, blame, and free will. Perhaps the very notion that there are such things as *selves*—individuals who persist over time—needs to be rejected as well.

The view I'm interested in falls between these extremes. It is conservative in that it accepts that brains give rise to selves that last over time, plan for the future, and so on. But it is radical in that it gives up the idea that there is just one self per head. The idea is that instead, within each brain, different selves are continually popping in and out of existence. They have different desires, and they fight for control—bargaining with, deceiving, and plotting against one another.

> " *Within each brain, different selves are continually popping in and out of existence.* "

The notion of different selves within a single person is not new. It can be found in Plato, and it was nicely articulated by the eighteenth-century Scottish philosopher David Hume, who wrote, "I cannot compare the soul more properly to any thing than to a republic or commonwealth, in which the several members are united by the reciprocal ties of government and subordination." Walt Whitman gave us a pithier version: "I am large, I contain multitudes."

The economist Thomas Schelling, another Nobel laureate, illustrates the concept with a simple story:

> As a boy I saw a movie about Admiral Byrd's Antarctic expedition and was impressed that as a boy he had gone outdoors in shirtsleeves to toughen himself against the cold. I resolved to go to bed at night with one blanket too few. That decision to go to bed minus one blanket was made by a warm boy; another boy awoke cold in the night, too cold to retrieve the blanket . . . and resolving to restore it tomorrow. The next bedtime it was the warm boy again, dreaming of Antarctica, who got to make the decision, and he always did it again.

Examples abound in our own lives. Late at night, when deciding not to bother setting up the coffee machine for the next morning, I sometimes think of the man who will wake up as a different person, and wonder, *What did he ever do for me?* When I get up and there's no coffee ready, I curse the lazy bastard who shirked his duties the night before.

To what extent does who you are depend on the situation you're in?

But anyone tempted by this theory has to admit just how wrong it feels, how poorly it fits with most of our experience. In the main, we do think of ourselves as singular individuals who persist over time. If I were to learn that I was going to be tortured tomorrow morning, my reaction would be terror, not sympathy for the poor guy who will be living in my body then. If I do something terrible now, I will later feel guilt and shame, not anger at some other person.

It could hardly be otherwise. Our brains have evolved to protect our bodies and guide them to reproduce, hence our minds must be sensitive to maintaining the needs of the continuing body—my children today will be my children tomorrow; if you wronged me yesterday, I should be wary of you today. Society and human relationships would be impossible without this form of continuity. Anyone who could convince himself that the person who will wake up in his bed tomorrow is *really* someone different would lack the capacity for sustained self-interest; he would feel no long-term guilt, love, shame, or pride.

The multiplicity of selves becomes more intuitive as the time span increases. Social psychologists have found certain differences in how we think of ourselves versus how we think of other people—for instance, we tend to attribute our own bad behavior to unfortunate circumstances, and the bad behavior of others to their nature. But these biases diminish when we think of *distant* past selves or *distant* future selves; we see such selves the way we see other people. Although it might be hard to think about the person who will occupy your body tomorrow morning as someone other than you, it is not hard at all to think that way about the person who will occupy your body twenty years from now. This may be one reason why many young people are indifferent about saving for retirement; they feel as if they would be giving up their money to an elderly stranger.

> ❝ *The multiplicity of selves becomes more intuitive as the time span increases.* ❞

One can see a version of clashing multiple selves in the mental illness known as dissociative-identity disorder, which used to be called multiple-personality disorder. This is familiar to everyone from the dramatic scenes in movies in which an actor is one person, and then he or she contorts or coughs or shakes the head, and—boom!—another person comes into existence. (My own favorite is Edward Norton in *Primal Fear*, although—spoiler alert—he turns out in the end to be faking.)

Dissociative-identity disorder is controversial. It used to be rarely diagnosed, then the number of reported cases spiked dramatically in the 1980s, particularly in North America. The spike has many possible explanations: the disorder was first included as a specific category in the 1980 version of the *Diagnostic and Statistical Manual of Mental Disorders*, just as an influential set of case studies of multiple personalities was published. And increased popular interest was fueled by the 1973 novel *Sybil* and its 1976 movie adaptation, which starred Sally Field as a woman with sixteen different personalities.

As a child, did you like to pretend that you were an animal, or a cartoon character? What did you enjoy most about these "alternative" or play selves?

Some psychologists believe that this spike was not the result of better diagnosis. Rather, they say it stemmed in part from therapists who inadvertently persuaded their patients to *create* these distinct selves, often through role-playing and hypnosis. Recent years have seen a backlash, and some people diagnosed with the disorder have sued their therapists. One woman got a settlement of more than $2 million after alleging that her psychotherapist had used suggestive memory "recovery" techniques to convince her that she had more than 120 personalities, including children, angels, and a duck.

Paul Bloom, *First Person Plural*   549

Regardless of the cause of the spike, considerable evidence, including recent brain-imaging studies, suggests that some people really do shift from one self to another, and that the selves have different memories and personalities. In one study, women who had been diagnosed with dissociative-identity disorder and claimed to be capable of shifting at will from one self to another listened to recordings while in a PET scanner. When the recordings told of a woman's own traumatic experience, the parts of the brain corresponding to auto-biographic memory became active—but only when she had shifted to the self who had endured that traumatic experience. If she was in another self, different parts of the brain became active and showed a pattern of neural activity corresponding to hearing about the experience of a stranger.

> **"** Memory is notoriously situation-dependent even for normal people. **"**

Many psychologists and philosophers have argued that the disorder should be understood as an extreme version of normal multiplicity. Take memory. One characteristic of dissociative-identity disorder is interpersonality amnesia—one self doesn't have access to the memories of the other selves. But memory is notoriously situation-dependent even for normal people—remembering something is easiest while you are in the same state in which you originally experienced it. Students do better when they are tested in the room in which they learned the material; someone who learned something while he was angry is better at remembering that information when he is angry again; the experience of one's drunken self is more accessible to the drunk self than to the sober self. What happens in Vegas stays in Vegas.

> **"** Personality also changes according to situation. **"**

Personality also changes according to situation; even the most thuggish teenager is not the same around his buddies as he is when having tea with Grandma. Our normal situation dependence is most evident when it comes to bad behavior. In the 1920s, Yale psychologists tested more than ten thousand children, giving them a battery of aptitude tests and putting them in morally dicey situations, such as having an opportunity to cheat on a test. They found a striking lack of consistency. A child's propensity to cheat at sports, for instance, had little to do with whether he or she would lie to a teacher.

More-recent experiments with adults find that subtle cues can have a surprising effect on our actions. Good smells, such as fresh bread, make people kinder and more likely to help a stranger; bad smells, like farts (the experimenters used fart spray from a novelty store), make people more judgmental. If you ask people to unscramble sentences, they tend to be more polite, minutes later, if the sentences contain positive words like *honor* rather than negative words like *bluntly*. These findings are in line with a set of classic experiments conducted by Stanley Milgram in the 1960s—too unethical to do now—showing that normal people could be induced to give electric shocks to a stranger if they were told to do so by someone they believed was an authoritative scientist. All of these studies support the view that each of us contains many selves—some violent, some submissive, some thoughtful—and that different selves can be brought to the fore by different situations.

The population of a single head is not fixed; we can add more selves. In fact, the capacity to spawn multiple selves is central to pleasure. After all, the most common leisure activity is not sex, eating, drinking, drug use, socializing, sports, or being with the ones we love. It is, by a long shot, participating in experiences we know are not real—reading novels, watching movies and TV, daydreaming, and so forth.

Enjoying fiction requires a shift in selfhood. You give up your own identity and try on the identities of other people, adopting their perspectives so as to share their experiences. This allows us to enjoy fictional events that would shock and sadden us in real life. When Tony Soprano kills someone, you respond differently than you would to a real murder; you accept and adopt some of the moral premises of the Soprano universe. You become, if just for a moment, Tony Soprano.

Some imaginative pleasures involve the creation of alternative selves. Sometimes we interact with these selves as if they were other people. This might sound terrible, and it can be, as when schizophrenics hear voices that seem to come from outside themselves. But the usual version is harmless. In children, we describe these alternative selves as imaginary friends. The psychologist Marjorie Taylor, who has studied this phenomenon more than anyone, points out three things. First, contrary to some stereotypes, children who have imaginary friends are not losers, loners, or borderline psychotics. If anything, they are slightly more socially adept than other children. Second, the children are in no way deluded: Taylor has rarely met a child who wasn't fully aware that the character lived only in his or her own imagination. And third, the imaginary friends are genuinely different selves. They often have different desires, interests, and needs from the child's; they can be unruly, and can frustrate the child. The writer Adam Gopnik wrote

> **"** *Some imaginative pleasures involve the creation of alternative selves.* **"**

about his young daughter's imaginary companion, Charlie Ravioli, a hip New Yorker whose defining quality was that he was always too busy to play with her.

Long-term imaginary companions are unusual in adults, but they do exist— Taylor finds that many authors who write books with recurring characters claim, fairly convincingly, that these characters have wills of their own and have some say in their fate. But it is not unusual to purposefully create another person in your head to interact with on a short-term basis. Much of daydreaming involves conjuring up people, sometimes as mere physical props (as when daydreaming about sports or sex), but usually as social beings. All of us from time to time hold conversations with people who are not actually there.

Sometimes we get pleasure from sampling alternative selves. Again, you can see the phenomenon in young children, who get a kick out of temporarily adopting the identity of a soldier or a lion. Adults get the same sort of kick; exploring alternative identities seems to be what the Internet was invented for. The sociologist Sherry Turkle has found that people commonly create avatars so as to explore their options in a relatively safe environment. She describes how one sixteen-year-old girl with an abusive father tried out multiple characters online—a sixteen-year-old boy, a stronger, more assertive girl—to try to work out what to do in the real world. But often the shift in identity is purely for pleasure. A man can have an alternate identity as a woman; a heterosexual can explore homosexuality; a shy person can try being the life of the party.

How do you "fight your Bad Self"?

Online alternative worlds such as *World of Warcraft** are growing in popularity, and some people now spend more time online than in the real world. One psychologist I know asked a research assistant to try out one of these worlds and report on what it is like and how people behave there. The young woman never came back—she preferred the virtual life to the real one.

Life would be swell if all the selves inhabiting a single mind worked as a team, pulling together for a common goal. But they clash, and sometimes this gives rise to what we call addictions and compulsions.

---

*As this book goes to press, alternative worlds and adventure games continue to be popular; however, users are moving away from subscriber-based (payment-required) games and toward those available for free. (See for example, "World of Warcraft Subscribers Are Leaving, Activision Warns," by Dave Lee, technology reporter for the BBC, May 9, 2013.)

This is not the traditional view of human frailty. The human condition has long been seen as a battle of good versus evil, reason versus emotion, will versus appetite, superego versus id. The iconic image, from a million movies and cartoons, is of a person with an angel over one shoulder and the devil over the other.

The alternative view keeps the angel and the devil, but casts aside the person in between. The competing selves are not over your shoulder, but inside your head: The angel and the devil, the self who wants to be slim and the one who wants to eat the cake, all exist within one person. Drawing on the research of the psychiatrist George Ainslie, we can make sense of the interaction of these selves by plotting their relative strengths over time, starting with one (the cake eater) being weaker than the other (the dieter). For most of the day, the dieter hums along at his regular power (a 5 on a scale of 1–10, say), motivated by the long-term goal of weight loss, and is stronger than the cake eater (a 2). Your consciousness

> **❝** *The self who wants to be slim and the one who wants to eat cake exist within one person.* **❞**

tracks whichever self is winning, so *you* are deciding not to eat the cake. But as you get closer and closer to the cake, the power of the cake eater rises (3 . . . 4 . . .), the lines cross, the cake eater takes over (6), and that becomes the conscious *you*; at this point, you decide to eat the cake. It's as if a baton is passed from one self to another.

Sometimes one self can predict that it will later be dominated by another self, and it can act to block the crossing—an act known as self-binding, which Thomas Schelling and the philosopher Jon Elster have explored in detail. Self-binding means that the dominant self schemes against the person it might potentially become—the 5 acts to keep the 2 from becoming a 6. Ulysses wanted to hear the song of the sirens, but he knew it would compel him to walk off the boat and into the sea. So he had his sailors tie him to the mast. Dieters buy food in small portions so they won't overeat later on; smokers trying to quit tell their friends never to give them cigarettes, no matter how much they may later beg. In her book on gluttony, Francine Prose tells of women who phone hotels where they are going to stay to demand a room with an empty minibar. An alarm clock now for sale rolls away as it sounds the alarm; to shut it off, you have to get up out of bed and find the damn thing.

You might also triumph over your future self by feeding it incomplete or incorrect information. If you're afraid of panicking in a certain situation, you might deny yourself relevant knowledge—you don't look down when you're on the tightrope; you don't check your stocks if you're afraid you'll sell at the first sign of a downturn. Chronically late? Set your watch ahead. Prone to jealousy? Avoid conversations with your spouse about which of your friends is the sexiest.

Working with the psychologists Frank Keil, of Yale University, and Katherine Choe, now at Goucher College, I recently studied young children's understanding of self-binding, by showing them short movies of people engaged in self-binding and other behaviors and asking them to explain what was going on. The children, aged four to seven, easily grasped that someone might put a video game on a high shelf so that another person couldn't get it. But self-binding confused them: They were mystified when people put away the game so that they themselves couldn't get hold of it.

But even though young children don't understand self-binding, they are capable of doing it. In a classic study from the 1970s, psychologists offered children a marshmallow and told them they could either have it right away, or get more if they waited for a few minutes. As you would expect, waiting proved difficult (and performance on this task is a good predictor, much later on, of such things as SAT scores and drug problems), but some children managed it by self-binding—averting their eyes or covering the marshmallow so as to subvert their temptation-prone self for the greater pleasure of the long-term self.

How would you describe your "long-term," adult self?

Even pigeons can self-bind. Ainslie conducted an experiment in which he placed pigeons in front of a glowing red key. If they pecked it immediately, they got a small reward right away, but if they waited until the key went dark, they got a larger one. They almost always went for the quick reward—really, it's hard for a pigeon to restrain itself. But there was a wrinkle: the key glowed green for several seconds before turning red. Pecking the key while it was green would prevent it from turning red and providing the option of the small, quick reward. Some of the pigeons learned to use the green key to help themselves hold out for the big reward, just as a person might put temptation out of reach.

For adult humans, though, the problem is that the self you are trying to bind has resources of its own. Fighting your Bad Self is serious business; whole sections of bookstores are devoted to it. We bribe and threaten and cajole, just as if we were dealing with an addicted friend. Vague commitments like "I promise to drink only on special occasions" often fail, because the Bad Self can weasel out of them, rationalizing that it's *always* a special occasion. Bright-line rules like "I

“ *Fighting your Bad Self is serious business.* ”

will never play video games again" are also vulnerable, because the Bad Self can argue that these are unreasonable—and, worse, once you slip, it can argue that the plan is unworkable. For every argument made by the dieting self—"This diet is really working" or "I really need to lose weight"—the cake eater can respond with another—"This will never work" or "I'm too vain" or "You only live once." Your long-term self reads voraciously about the benefits of regular exercise and healthy eating; the cake eater prefers articles showing that obesity isn't really such a problem. It's not that the flesh is weak; sometimes the flesh is pretty damn smart.

It used to be simpler. According to the traditional view, a single, long-term-planning self—a *you*—battles against passions, compulsions, impulses, and addictions. We have no problem choosing, as individuals or as a society, who should win, because only one interest is at stake—one person is at war with his or her desires. And while knowing the right thing to do can be terribly difficult, the decision is still based on the rational thoughts of a rational being.

Seeing things this way means we are often mistaken about what makes us happy. Consider again what happens when we have children. Pretty much no matter how you test it, children make us less happy. The evidence isn't just from diary studies; surveys of marital satisfaction show that couples tend to start off happy, get less happy when they have kids, and become happy again only once the kids leave the house. As the psychologist Daniel Gilbert puts it, "Despite what we read in the popular press, the only known symptom of 'empty-nest syndrome' is increased smiling." So why do people believe that children give them so much pleasure? Gilbert sees it as an illusion, a failure of affective forecasting. Society's needs are served when people believe that having children is a good thing, so we are deluged with images and stories about how wonderful kids are. We think they make us happy, though they actually don't.

The theory of multiple selves offers a different perspective. If struggles over happiness involve clashes between distinct internal selves, we can no longer be so sure that our conflicting judgments over time reflect irrationality or error. There is no inconsistency between someone's anxiously hiking through the Amazon wishing she were home in a warm bath and, weeks later, feeling good about being the sort of adventurous soul who goes into the rain forest. In an important sense, the person in the Amazon is not the same person as the one back home safely recalling the experience, just as the person who honestly believes that his children are the great joy in his life might not be the same person who finds them terribly annoying when he's actually with them.

Even if each of us is a community, all the members shouldn't get equal say. Some members are best thought of as small-minded children—and we don't give six-year-olds the right to vote. Just as in society, the adults within us have the right—indeed, the obligation—to rein in the children. In fact, talk of "children" versus "adults" within an individual isn't only a metaphor; one reason to favor the longer-term self is that it really is older and more experienced. We typically spend more of our lives not wanting to snort coke, smoke, or overeat than we spend wanting to do these things; this means that the long-term self has more time to reflect. It is less selfish; it talks to other people, reads books, and so on. And it tries to control the short-term selves. It joins Alcoholics Anonymous, buys the runaway clock, and sees the therapist. As Jon Elster observes, the long-term, sober self is a truer self, because it tries to bind the short-term, drunk self. The long-term, sober self is the adult.

> **❝** *The longer-term self really is older and more experienced.* **❞**

Governments and businesses, recognizing these tendencies, have started offering self-binding schemes. Thousands of compulsive gamblers in Missouri have chosen to sign contracts stating that if they ever enter a casino, anything they win will be confiscated by the state, and they could be arrested. Some of my colleagues at Yale have developed an online service whereby you set a goal and agree to put up a certain amount of money to try to ensure that you meet it. If you succeed, you pay nothing; if you fail, the money is given to charity—or, in a clever twist, to an organization you oppose. A liberal trying to lose a pound a week, for instance, can punish herself for missing her goal by having $100 donated to the George W. Bush Presidential Library.

The natural extension of this type of self-binding is what the economist Richard Thaler and the legal scholar Cass Sunstein describe as "libertarian paternalism"—a movement to engineer situations so that people retain their choices (the libertarian part), but in such a way that these choices are biased to favor people's better selves (the paternalism part). For instance, many people fail to save enough money for the future; they find it too confusing or onerous to choose a retirement plan. Thaler and Sunstein suggest that the default be switched so that employees would automatically be enrolled in a savings plan, and would have to take action to opt out. A second example concerns the process of organ donation. When asked, most Americans say that they would wish to donate their organs if they were to become brain-dead from an accident—but only about half actually have their driver's license marked for donation, or carry an organ-donor card. Thaler and Sunstein have discussed a different idea: People could easily opt out of being a donor, but if they do nothing, they are assumed to consent. Such proposals are not merely academic musings; they are starting to influence law and policy, and might do so increasingly in the future. Both Thaler and Sunstein act as advisers to politicians and policy makers, most notably Barack Obama.

So what's not to like? There is a real appeal to anything that makes self-binding easier. As I write this article, I'm using a program that disables my network connections for a selected amount of time and does not allow me to switch them back on, thereby forcing me to actually write instead of checking my e-mail or reading blogs. A harsher (and more expensive) method, advised by the author of a self-help book, is to remove your Internet cable and FedEx it to yourself—guaranteeing a day without online distractions. One can also chemically boost the long-term self through drugs such as Adderall, which improves concentration and focus. The journalist Joshua Foer describes how it enabled him to write for hour-long chunks, far longer than he was usually capable of: "The part of my brain that makes me curious about whether I have new e-mails in my inbox apparently shut down."

> **There is a real appeal to anything that makes self-binding easier.**

It's more controversial, of course, when someone else does the binding. I wouldn't be very happy if my department chair forced me to take Adderall, or if the government fined me for being overweight and not trying to slim down (as Alabama is planning to do to some state employees). But some "other-binding" already exists—think of the mandatory waiting periods for getting a divorce or buying a gun. You are not prevented from eventually taking these actions, but you are forced to think them over, giving the contemplative self the chance to override the impulsive self. And since governments and businesses are constantly asking people to make choices (about precisely such things as whether to be an organ donor), they inevitably have to provide a default option. If decisions have to be made, why not structure them to be in individuals' and society's best interests?

The main problem with all of this is that the long-term self is not always right. Sometimes the short-term self should not be bound. Of course, most addictions are well worth getting rid of. When a mother becomes addicted to cocaine, the pleasure from the drug seems to hijack the neural system that would otherwise be devoted to bonding with her baby. It obviously makes sense here to bind the drug user, the short-term self. On the

> **Sometimes the short-term self should not be bound.**

other hand, from a neural and psychological standpoint, a mother's love for her baby can also be seen as an addiction. But here binding would be strange and immoral; this addiction is a good one. Someone who becomes morbidly obese needs to do more self-binding, but an obsessive dieter might need to do less. We think one way about someone who gives up Internet porn to spend time building houses for the poor, and another way entirely about someone who successfully thwarts his short-term desire to play with his children so that he can devote more energy to making his second million. The long-term, contemplative self should not always win.

This is particularly true when it comes to morality. Many cruel acts are perpetrated by people who can't or don't control their short-term impulses or who act in certain ways—such as getting drunk—that lead to a dampening of the contemplative self. But evil acts are also committed by smart people who adopt carefully thought-out belief systems that allow them to ignore their more morally astute gut feelings. Many slave owners were rational men who used their intelligence to defend slavery, arguing that the institution was in the best interests of those who were enslaved, and that it was grounded in scripture: Africans were the descendants of Ham, condemned by God to be "servants unto servants." Terrorist acts such as suicide bombings are not typically carried out in an emotional frenzy; they are the consequences of deeply held belief systems and long-term deliberative planning. One of the grimmest examples of rationality gone bad can be found in the psychiatrist Robert Jay Lifton's discussion of Nazi doctors. These men acted purposefully for years to distance themselves from their emotions, creating what Lifton describes as an "Auschwitz self" that enabled them to prevent any normal, unschooled human kindness from interfering with their jobs.

> **❝** *We benefit, intellectually and personally, from the interplay between different selves.* **❞**

I wouldn't want to live next door to someone whose behavior was dominated by his short-term selves, and I wouldn't want to be such a person, either. But there is also something wrong with people who go too far in the other direction. We benefit, intellectually and personally, from the interplay between different selves, from the balance between long-term contemplation and short-term impulse. We should be wary about tipping the scales too far. The community of selves shouldn't be a democracy, but it shouldn't be a dictatorship, either.

Researched Essay

Hanna Rosin

A Boy's Life

Hanna Rosin is an editor at *The Atlantic* and *Slate*, regularly contributes to *The Atlantic*, and has written for *The Washington Post* and *The New Yorker*. In her essay "A Boy's Life," which appeared in *The Atlantic* and on *The Atlantic Online*, she examines the life of a child who was biologically a boy but identified as a girl. She examines the various struggles parents face with young transgender children and the different debates surrounding transgender children coming out as transgendered socially. *(The Atlantic artwork is reprinted by permission of* The Atlantic. *The essay "A Boy's Life" is reprinted with permission. Copyright © 2008, The Atlantic Media Co., as first published in* The Atlantic Magazine. *All rights reserved. Distributed by Tribune Media Services.)*

▲ AUTHOR PHOTO
Hanna Rosin. *By permission of Nina Subin.*

| Politics | Business | Tech | Entertainment | Health | Sexes | National | Global | China | **Magazine** |

A Boy's Life

HANNA ROSIN

Since he could speak, Brandon, now 8, has insisted that he was meant to be a girl. This summer, his parents decided to let him grow up as one. His case, and a rising number of others like it, illuminates a heated scientific debate about the nature of gender—and raises troubling questions about whether the limits of child indulgence have stretched too far.

The local newspaper recorded that Brandon Simms was the first millennium baby born in his tiny southern town, at 12:50 AM. He weighed eight pounds, two ounces and, as his mother, Tina, later wrote to him in his baby book, "had a darlin' little face that told me right away you were innocent." Tina saved the white knit hat with the powder-blue ribbon that hospitals routinely give to new baby boys. But after that, the milestones took an unusual turn. As a toddler, Brandon would scour the house for something to drape over his head—a towel, a doily, a moons-and-stars bandanna he'd snatch from his mother's drawer. "I figure he wanted something that felt like hair," his mother later guessed. He spoke his first full sentence at a local Italian restaurant: "I like your high heels," he told a woman in a fancy red dress. At home, he would rip off his clothes as soon as Tina put them on him, and instead try on something from her closet—a purple undershirt, lingerie, shoes. "He ruined all my heels in the sandbox," she recalls.

As a child, when you were allowed to dress yourself, what look did you opt for? Why?

At the toy store, Brandon would head straight for the aisles with the Barbies or the pink and purple dollhouses. Tina wouldn't buy them, instead steering him to neutral toys: puzzles or building blocks or cool neon markers. One weekend, when Brandon was two and a half, she took him to visit her ten-year-old cousin. When Brandon took to one of the many dolls in her huge collection—a blonde Barbie in a pink sparkly dress—Tina let him bring it home. He carried it everywhere, "even slept with it, like a teddy bear."

For his third Christmas, Tina bought Brandon a first-rate army set—complete with a Kevlar hat, walkie-talkies, and a hand grenade. Both Tina and Brandon's father had served in the army, and she thought their son might identify with the toys. A photo from that day shows him wearing a towel around his head, a bandanna around his waist, and a glum expression. The army set sits unopened at his feet. Tina recalls his joy, by contrast, on a day later that year. One afternoon, while Tina was on the phone, Brandon climbed out of the bathtub. When she found him, he was dancing in front of the mirror with his penis tucked between his legs. "Look, Mom, I'm a girl," he told her. "Happy as can be," she recalls.

❝ *'Look, Mom, I'm a girl.'* **❞**

"Brandon, God made you a boy for a special reason," she told him before they said prayers one night when he was five, the first part of a speech she'd prepared. But he cut her off: "God made a mistake," he said.

Tina had no easy explanation for where Brandon's behavior came from. Gender roles are not very fluid in their no-stoplight town, where Confederate flags line the main street. Boys ride dirt bikes through the woods starting at age five; local county fairs feature muscle cars for boys and beauty pageants for girls of all ages. In the army, Tina operated heavy machinery, but she is no tomboy. When she was younger, she wore long flowing dresses to match her long, wavy blond hair; now she wears it in a cute, Renée Zellweger–style bob. Her husband, Bill (Brandon's stepfather), lays wood floors and builds houses for a living. At a recent meeting with Brandon's school principal about how to handle

❝ *'The way I was brought up, a boy's a boy and a girl's a girl.'* **❞**

the boy, Bill aptly summed up the town philosophy: "The way I was brought up, a boy's a boy and a girl's a girl."

School had always complicated Brandon's life. When teachers divided the class into boys' and girls' teams, Brandon would stand with the girls. In all of his kindergarten and first-grade self-portraits—"I have a pet," "I love my cat," "I love to play outside"—the "I" was a girl, often with big red lips, high heels, and a princess dress. Just as often, he drew himself as a mermaid with a sparkly purple tail, or a tail cut out from black velvet. Late in second grade, his older stepbrother, Travis, told his fourth-grade friends about Brandon's "secret"—that he dressed up at home and wanted to be a girl. After school, the boys cornered and bullied him. Brandon went home crying and begged Tina to let him skip the last week.

In what style was your hair cut when you were a child? Did you like it? Why or why not?

Since he was four, Tina had been taking Brandon to a succession of therapists. The first told her he was just going through a phase; but the phase never passed. Another suggested that Brandon's chaotic early childhood might have contributed to his behavior. Tina had never married Brandon's father, whom she'd met when they were both stationed in Germany. Twice, she had briefly stayed with him, when Brandon was five months old and then when he was three. Both times, she'd suspected his father of being too rough with the boy and had broken off the relationship. The therapist suggested that perhaps Brandon overidentified with his mother as the protector in the family, and for a while, this theory seemed plausible to Tina. In play therapy, the therapist tried to get Brandon to discuss his feelings about his father. She advised Tina to try a reward system at home. Brandon could earn up to twenty-one dollars a week for doing three things: looking in the mirror and saying "I'm a boy"; not dressing up; and not wearing anything on his head. It worked for a couple of weeks, but then Brandon lost interest.

" The therapist suggested that perhaps Brandon overidentified with his mother. "

Tina recounted much of this history to me in June at her kitchen table, where Brandon, now eight, had just laid out some lemon pound cake he'd baked from a mix. She, Bill, Brandon, his half sister, Madison, and Travis live in a comfortable double-wide trailer that Bill set up himself on their half acre of woods. I'd met Tina a month earlier, and she'd agreed to let me follow Brandon's development over what turned out to be a critical few months of his life, on the condition that I change their names and disguise where they live. While we were at the table talking, Brandon was conducting a kind of nervous fashion show; over the course of several hours, he came in and out of his room wearing eight or nine different outfits, constructed from his costume collection, his mom's shoes and scarves, and his little sister's bodysuits and tights. Brandon is a gymnast and likes to show off splits and back bends. On the whole, he is quiet and a little somber, but every once in a while—after a great split, say—he shares a shy, crooked smile.

About a year and a half ago, Tina's mom showed her a Barbara Walters *20/20* special she'd taped. The show featured a six-year-old boy named "Jazz" who, since he was a toddler, had liked to dress as a girl. Everything about Jazz was familiar to Tina: the obsession with girls' clothes, the Barbies, wishing his penis away, even the fixation on mermaids. At the age of three, Jazz had been diagnosed with "gender-identity disorder" and was considered "transgender," Walters explained. The show mentioned a "hormone imbalance," but his parents had concluded that there was basically nothing wrong with him. He "didn't ask to be born this way," his mother explained. By kindergarten, his parents were letting him go to school with shoulder-length hair and a pink skirt on.

Tina had never heard the word *transgender*; she'd figured no other little boy on earth was like Brandon. The show prompted her to buy a computer and Google "transgender children." Eventually, she made her way to a subculture of parents who live all across the country; they write in to listservs with grammar ranging from sixth-grade-level to professorial, but all have family stories much like hers. In May, she and Bill finally met some of them at the Trans-Health Conference in Philadelphia, the larger of two annual gatherings in the United States that many parents attend.

> ❝ *Tina had never heard the word* transgender; *she'd figured no other little boy on earth was like Brandon.* ❞

Four years ago, only a handful of kids had come to the conference. This year, about fifty showed up, along with their siblings—enough to require a staff dedicated to full-time children's entertainment, including Jack the Balloon Man, Sue's Sand Art, a pool-and-pizza party, and a treasure hunt.

Diagnoses of gender-identity disorder among adults have tripled in Western countries since the 1960s; for men, the estimates now range from one in 7,400 to one in 42,000 (for women, the frequency of diagnosis is lower). Since 1952, when army veteran George Jorgensen's sex-change operation hit the front page of the *New York Daily News*, national resistance has softened a bit, too. Former NASCAR driver J. T. Hayes recently talked to *Newsweek* about having had a sex-change operation. Women's colleges have had to adjust to the presence of "trans-men," and the president-elect of the Gay and Lesbian Medical Association is a trans-woman and a successful cardiologist. But nothing can do more to normalize the face of transgender America than the sight of a seven-year-old (boy or girl?) with pink cheeks and a red balloon puppy in hand saying to Brandon, as one did at the conference:

"Are you transgender?"

"What's that?" Brandon asked.

"A boy who wants to be a girl."

"Yeah. Can I see your balloon?"

Around the world, clinics that specialize in gender-identity disorder in children report an explosion in referrals over the past few years. Dr. Kenneth Zucker, who runs the most comprehensive gender-identity clinic for youth in Toronto, has seen his waiting list quadruple in the past four years, to about eighty kids—an increase he attributes to media coverage and the proliferation of new sites on the Internet. Dr. Peggy Cohen-Kettenis, who runs the main clinic in the Netherlands, has seen the average age of her patients plummet since 2002. "We used to get calls mostly from parents who were concerned about their children being gay," says Catherine Tuerk, who since 1998 has run a support network for parents of children with gender-variant behavior, out of Children's National Medical Center in Washington, D.C. "Now about 90 percent of our calls are from parents with some concern that their child may be transgender."

In breakout sessions at the conference, transgender men and women in their fifties and sixties described lives of heartache and rejection: years of hiding makeup under the mattress, estranged parents, suicide attempts. Those in their twenties and thirties conveyed a dedicated militancy: they wore nose rings and Mohawks, ate strictly vegan, and conducted heated debates about the definitions of *queer* and *he-she* and *drag queen*. But the kids treated the conference like a family trip to Disneyland. They ran around with parents chasing after them, fussing over twisted bathing-suit straps or wiping crumbs from their lips. They looked effortlessly androgynous, and years away from sex, politics, or any form of rebellion. For Tina, the sight of them suggested a future she'd never considered for Brandon: a normal life as a girl. "She could end up being a *mommy* if she wants, just like me," one adoring mother leaned over and whispered about her five-year-old (natal) son.

It took the gay-rights movement thirty years to shift from the Stonewall riots to gay marriage; now its transgender wing, long considered the most subversive, is striving for suburban

In elementary school, what expectations about looking like a girl or a boy were placed upon you? How did you respond?

> ❝ Now [the] transgender wing . . . is striving for suburban normalcy too. ❞

normalcy too. The change is fueled mostly by a community of parents who, like many parents of this generation, are open to letting even preschool children define their own needs. Faced with skeptical neighbors and school officials, parents at the conference discussed how to use the kind of quasi-therapeutic language that, these days, inspires deference: Tell the school the child has a "medical condition" or a "hormonal imbalance" that can be treated later, suggested a conference speaker, Kim Pearson; using terms like *gender-identity disorder* or *birth defect* would be going too far, she advised. The point was to take the situation out of the realm of deep pathology or mental illness, while at the same time separating it from voluntary behavior, and to put it into the idiom of garden-variety "challenge." As one father told me, "Between all the kids with language problems and learning disabilities and peanut allergies, the school doesn't know who to worry about first."

A recent medical innovation holds out the promise that this might be the first generation of transsexuals who can live inconspicuously. About three years ago, physicians in the United States started treating transgender children with puberty blockers, drugs originally intended to halt precocious puberty. The blockers put teens in a state of suspended development. They prevent boys from growing facial and body hair and an Adam's apple, or developing a deep voice or any of the other physical characteristics that a male-to-female transsexual would later spend tens of thousands of dollars to reverse. They allow girls to grow taller, and prevent them from getting breasts or a period.

> ❝ Physicians in the United States started treating transgender children with puberty blockers. ❞

At the conference, blockers were the hot topic. One mother who'd found out about them too late cried, "The guilt I feel is overwhelming." The preteens sized each other up for signs of the magic drug, the way other teens might look for hip, expensive jeans: a sixteen-year-old (natal) girl, shirtless, with no sign of breasts; a seventeen-year-old (natal) boy with a face as smooth as Brandon's. "Is there anybody out there," asked Dr. Nick Gorton, a physician and trans-man from California, addressing a room full of older transsexuals, "who would not have taken the shot if it had been offered?" No one raised a hand.

After a day of sessions, Tina's mind was moving fast. "These kids look happier," she told me. "This is nothing we can fix. In his brain, in his *mind*, Brandon's a girl." With Bill, she started to test out the new language. "What's it they say? It's nothing wrong. It's just a medical condition, like diabetes or something. Just a variation on human behavior." She made an unlikely friend, a lesbian mom from

Seattle named Jill who took Tina under her wing. Jill had a five-year-old girl living as a boy and a future already mapped out. "He'll just basically be living life," Jill explained about her (natal) daughter. "I already legally changed his name and called all the parents at the school. Then, when he's in eighth grade, we'll take him to the [endocrinologist] and get the blockers, and no one will ever know. He'll just sail right through."

"I live in a small town," Tina pleaded with Jill. "This is all just really *new*. I never even heard the word *transgender* until recently, and the shrinks just kept telling me this is fixable."

> **❝** *'The shrinks just kept telling me this is fixable.'* **❞**

In my few months of meeting transgender children, I talked to parents from many different backgrounds, who had made very different decisions about how to handle their children. Many accepted the "new normalcy" line, and some did not. But they all had one thing in common: In such a loaded situation, with their children's future at stake, doubt about their choices did not serve them well. In Brandon's case, for example, doubt would force Tina to consider that if she began letting him dress as a girl, she would be defying the conventions of her small town, and the majority of psychiatric experts, who advise strongly against the practice. It would force her to consider that she would have to begin making serious medical decisions for Brandon in only a couple of years, and that even with the blockers, he would face a lifetime of hormone injections and possibly major surgery. At the conference, Tina struggled with these doubts. But her new friends had already moved past them.

"Yeah, it is fixable," piped up another mom, who'd been on the *20/20* special. "We call it the disorder we cured with a skirt."

> **❝** *'We call it the disorder we cured with a skirt.'* **❞**

In 1967, Dr. John Money launched an experiment that he thought might confirm some of the more radical ideas emerging in feminist thought. Throughout the '60s, writers such as Betty Friedan were challenging the notion that women should be limited to their prescribed roles as wives, housekeepers, and mothers. But other feminists pushed further, arguing that the whole notion of gender was a social construction, and easy to manipulate. In a 1955 paper, Money had written: "Sexual behavior and orientation as male or female does not have an innate, instinctive basis." We learn whether we are male or female "in the course of the various experiences of growing up." By the '60s, he was well-known for having established the first American clinic to perform voluntary sex-change operations, at the Johns Hopkins Hospital, in Baltimore. One day, he got a letter from the parents of infant twin boys, one of whom had suffered a botched circumcision that had burned off most of his penis.

Money saw the case as a perfect test for his theory. He encouraged the parents to have the boy, David Reimer, fully castrated and then to raise him as a girl. When the child reached puberty, Money told them, doctors could construct a vagina and give him feminizing hormones. Above all, he told them, they must not waver in their decision and must not tell the boy about the accident.

In paper after paper, Money reported on Reimer's fabulous progress, writing that "she" showed an avid interest in dolls and dollhouses, that she preferred dresses, hair ribbons, and frilly blouses. Money's description of the child in his book *Sexual Signatures* prompted one reviewer to describe her as "sailing contentedly through childhood as a genuine girl." *Time* magazine concluded that the Reimer case cast doubt on the belief that sex differences are "immutably set by the genes at conception."

The reality was quite different, as *Rolling Stone* reporter John Colapinto brilliantly documented in the 2000 best seller *As Nature Made Him*. Reimer had never adjusted to being a girl at all. He wanted only to build forts and play with his brother's dump trucks, and insisted that he should pee standing up. He was a social disaster at school, beating up other kids and misbehaving in class. At fourteen, Reimer became so alienated and depressed that his parents finally told him the truth about his birth, at which point he felt mostly relief, he reported. He eventually underwent phalloplasty, and he married a woman. Then four years ago, at age thirty-eight, Reimer shot himself dead in a grocery-store parking lot.

> **"** *In the new conventional wisdom, we are all pre-wired for many things previously thought to be in the realm of upbringing, choice, or subjective experience.* **"**

Today, the notion that gender is purely a social construction seems nearly as outmoded as bra-burning or free love. Feminist theory is pivoting with the rest of the culture, and is locating the key to identity in genetics and the workings of the brain. In the new conventional wisdom, we are all pre-wired for many things previously thought to be in the realm of upbringing, choice, or subjective experience: happiness, religious awakening, cheating, a love of chocolate. Behaviors are fundamental unless we are chemically altered. Louann Brizendine, in her 2006 bestselling book, *The Female Brain*, claims that everything from empathy to chattiness to poor spatial reasoning is "hardwired into the brains of women." Dr. Milton Diamond, an expert on human sexuality at the University of Hawaii and long the intellectual nemesis of Money, encapsulated this view in an interview on the BBC in 1980, when it was becoming clear that Money's experiment was failing: "Maybe we really have to think . . . that we don't come to this world neutral; that we come to this world with some degree of maleness and femaleness which will transcend whatever the society wants to put into [us]."

Diamond now spends his time collecting case studies of transsexuals who have a twin, to see how often both twins have transitioned to the opposite sex. To him, these cases are a "confirmation" that "the biggest sex organ is not between the legs but between the ears." For many gender biologists like Diamond, transgender children now serve the same allegorical purpose that David Reimer once did, but they support the opposite conclusion: They are seen as living proof that "gender identity is influenced by some innate or immutable factors," writes Melissa Hines, the author of *Brain Gender*.

This is the strange place in which transsexuals have found themselves. For years, they've been at the extreme edges of transgressive sexual politics. But now children like Brandon are being used to paint a more conventional picture: Before they have much time to be shaped by experience, before they know their sexual orientation, even in defiance of their bodies, children can know their gender, from the firings of neurons deep within their brains. What better rebuke to the *Our Bodies, Ourselves* era of feminism than the notion that even the body is dispensable, that the hard nugget of difference lies even deeper?

In most major institutes for gender-identity disorder in children worldwide, a psychologist is the central figure. In the United States, the person intending to found "the first major academic research center," as he calls it, is Dr. Norman Spack, an endocrinologist who teaches at Harvard Medical School and is committed to a hormonal fix. Spack works out of a cramped office at Children's Hospital in Boston, where the walls are covered with diplomas and notes of gratitude scrawled in crayons or bright markers ("Thanks, Dr. Spack!!!"). Spack is bald, with a trim beard, and often wears his Harvard tie under his lab coat. He is not confrontational by nature, but he can hold his own with his critics: "To those who say I am interrupting God's work, I point to Leviticus, which says, 'Thou shalt not stand idly by the blood of your neighbor'"—an injunction, as he sees it, to prevent needless suffering.

Spack has treated young-adult transsexuals since the 1980s, and until recently he could never get past one problem: "They are never going to fail to draw attention to themselves." Over the years, he'd seen patients rejected by families, friends, and employers after a sex-change operation. Four years ago, he heard about the innovative use of hormone blockers on transgender youths in the Netherlands; to him, the drugs seemed like the missing piece of the puzzle.

The problem with blockers is that parents have to begin making medical decisions for their children when the children are quite young. From the earliest signs of puberty, doctors have about eighteen months to start the blockers for ideal results. For girls, that's usually between ages ten and twelve; for boys, between twelve and fourteen. If the patients follow through with cross-sex hormones and sex-change surgery, they will be permanently sterile, something Spack always discusses with them. "When you're talking to a twelve-year-old, that's a heavy-duty conversation," he said in a recent interview. "Does a kid that age really think about fertility? But if you don't start treatment, they will always have trouble fitting in."

When Beth was eleven, she told her mother, Susanna, that she'd "rather be dead" than go to school anymore as a girl. (The names of all the children and parents used as case studies in this story are pseudonyms.) For a long time, she had refused to shower except in a bathing suit, and had skipped out of health class every Thursday, when the standard puberty videos were shown. In March 2006, when Beth, now Matt, was twelve, they went to see Spack. He told Matt that if he went down this road, he would never biologically have children.

"I'll adopt!" Matt said.

"What is most important to him is that he's comfortable in who he is," says Susanna. They left with a prescription—a "godsend," she calls it.

Now, at fifteen and on testosterone, Matt is tall, with a broad chest and hairy legs. Susanna figures he's the first trans-man in America to go shirtless without having had any chest surgery. His mother describes him as "happy" and "totally at home in his masculine body." Matt has a girlfriend; he met her at the amusement park where Susanna works. Susanna is pretty sure he's said something to the girl about his situation, but knows he hasn't talked to her parents.

Susanna imagines few limitations in Matt's future. Only a minority of trans-men get what they call "bottom" surgery, because phalloplasty is still more cosmetic than functional, and the procedure is risky. But otherwise? Married? "Oh, yeah. And his career prospects will be good because he gets very good grades. We envision a kind of family life, maybe in the suburbs, with a good job." They have "no fears" about the future, and "zero doubts" about the path they've chosen.

Blockers are entirely reversible; should a child change his or her mind about becoming the other gender, a doctor can stop the drugs and normal puberty will begin. The Dutch clinic has given them to about seventy children since it started the treatment, in 2000; clinics in the United States and Canada have given them to dozens more.

According to Dr. Peggy Cohen-Kettenis, the psychologist who heads the Dutch clinic, no case of a child stopping the blockers and changing course has yet been reported.

This suggests one of two things: Either the screening is excellent, or once a child begins, he or she is set firmly on the path to medical intervention. "Adolescents may consider this step a guarantee of sex reassignment," wrote Cohen-Kettenis, "and it could make them therefore less rather than more inclined to engage in introspection." In the Netherlands, clinicians try to guard against this with an extensive diagnostic protocol, including testing and many sessions "to confirm that the desire for treatment is very persistent," before starting the blockers.

Spack's clinic isn't so comprehensive. A part-time psychologist, Dr. Laura Edwards-Leeper, conducts four-hour family screenings by appointment. (When I visited during the summer, she was doing only one or two a month.) But often she has to field emergency cases directly with Spack, which sometimes means skipping the screening altogether. "We get these calls from parents who are just frantic," she says. "They need to get in immediately, because their child is about to hit puberty and is having serious mental-health issues, and we really want to accommodate that. It's like they've been waiting their whole lives for this and they are just desperate, and when they finally get in to see us . . . it's like a rebirth."

Spack's own conception of the psychology involved is uncomplicated: "If a girl starts to experience breast budding and feels like cutting herself, then she's probably transgendered. If she feels immediate relief on the [puberty-blocking] drugs, that confirms the diagnosis," he told *The Boston Globe*. He thinks of the blockers not as an addendum to years of therapy but as "preventative" because they forestall the trauma that comes from social rejection. Clinically, men who become women are usually described as "male-to-female," but Spack, using the parlance of activist parents, refers to them as "affirmed females"—"because how can you be a male-to-female if really you were always a female in your brain?" . . .

Out on the sidewalk in Philadelphia, Tina was going through Marlboro after Marlboro, stubbing them out half-smoked against city buildings. The conference's first day had just ended, with Tina asking another mom, "So how do you know if one of these kids stays that way or if he changes?" and the mom suggesting she could wait awhile and see.

"Wait? Wait for what?" Tina suddenly said to Bill. "He's already waited six years, and now I don't care about any of that no more." Bill looked worried, but she threw an army phrase at him: "Suck it up and drive on, soldier."

The organizers had planned a pool party for that night, and Tina had come to a decision: Brandon would wear exactly the kind of bathing suit he'd always wanted. She had spotted a Macy's a couple of blocks away. I walked with her and Bill and Brandon into the hush and glow, the headless mannequins sporting golf shorts with eighty-dollar price tags. They quietly took the escalator one floor up, to the girls' bathing-suit department. Brandon leaped off at the top and ran to the first suit that caught his eye: a teal Hannah Montana bikini studded with jewels and glitter. "Oh, I love this one," he said.

"So that's the one you want?" asked Tina.

Brandon hesitated. He was used to doing his cross-dressing somewhat furtively. Normally he would just grab the shiniest thing he saw, for fear his chance would evaporate. But as he came to understand that both Tina and Bill were on board, he slowed down a bit. He carefully looked through all the racks. Bill, calm now, was helping him. "You want a one-piece or two-piece?" Bill asked. Tina, meanwhile, was having a harder time. "I'll get used to it," she said. She had tried twice to call Brandon "she," Tina suddenly confessed, but "it just don't sound right," she said, her eyes tearing.

Brandon decided to try on an orange one-piece with polka dots, a sky-blue-and-pink two-piece, and a Hawaiian-print tankini with a brown background and pink hibiscus flowers. He went into a dressing room and stayed there a long, long time. Finally, he called in the adults. Brandon had settled on the least showy of the three: the Hawaiian print with the brown background. He had it on and was shyly looking in the mirror. He wasn't doing backflips or grinning from ear to ear; he was still and at peace, gently fingering the price tag. He mentioned that he didn't want to wear the suit again until he'd had a chance to wash his feet.

At the pool party, Brandon immediately ran into a friend he'd made earlier, the transgender boy who'd shared his balloon puppy. The pool was in a small room in the corner of a hotel basement, with low ceilings and no windows. The echoes of seventy giddy children filled the space. Siblings were there, too, so it was impossible to know who had been born a boy and who a girl. They were all just smooth limbs and wet hair and an occasional slip that sent one crying to his or her mother.

Bill sat next to me on a bench and spilled his concerns. He was worried about Tina's stepfather, who would never accept this. He was worried that Brandon's father might find out and demand custody. He was worried about Brandon's best friend, whose parents were strict evangelical Christians. He was worried about their own pastor, who had sternly advised them to take away all of Brandon's girl-toys and girl-clothes. "Maybe if we just pray hard enough," Bill had told Tina.

Are you "comfortable in your own skin"? Why or why not?

Brandon raced by, arm in arm with his new friend, giggling. Tina and Bill didn't know this yet, but Brandon had already started telling the other kids that his name was Bridget, after the pet mouse he'd recently buried ("My beloved Bridget. Rest With the Lord," the memorial in his room read). The comment of an older transsexual from Brooklyn who'd sat behind Tina in a session earlier that day echoed in my head. He'd had his sex-change operation when he was in his fifties, and in his wild, wispy wig, he looked like a biblical prophet, with breasts. "You think you have troubles now," he'd yelled out to Tina. "Wait until next week. Once you let the genie out of the bottle, she's not going back in!"

> **❝** *Brandon had already started telling the other kids that his name was Bridget.* **❞**

Dr. Kenneth Zucker has been seeing children with gender-identity disorder in Toronto since the mid-'70s, and has published more on the subject than any other researcher. But lately he has become a pariah to the most-vocal activists in the American transgender community. In 2012, the *Diagnostic and Statistical Manual of Mental Disorders*— the bible for psychiatric professionals—will be updated. Many in the transgender community see this as their opportunity to remove gender-identity disorder from the book, much the same way homosexuality was delisted in

> **❝** *[Zucker] seems unlikely to bless the condition as psychologically healthy, especially in young children.* **❞**

1973. Zucker is in charge of the committee that will make the recommendation. He seems unlikely to bless the condition as psychologically healthy, especially in young children.

I met Zucker in his office at the Centre for Addiction and Mental Health, where piles of books alternate with the Barbies and superheroes that he uses for play therapy. Zucker has a white mustache and beard, and his manner is somewhat Talmudic. He responds to every question with a methodical three-part answer, often ending by climbing a chair to pull down a research paper he's written. On one of his file cabinets, he's tacked up a flyer from a British parents' advocacy group that reads: "Gender dysphoria is increasingly understood . . . as having biological origins," and describes "small parts of the brain" as "progressing along different pathways." During the interview, he took it down to make a point: "In terms of empirical data, this is not true. It's just dogma, and I've never liked dogma. Biology is not destiny."

Hanna Rosin, *A Boy's Life*   571

In his case studies and descriptions of patients, Zucker usually explains gender dysphoria in terms of what he calls "family noise": neglectful parents who caused a boy to overidentify with his domineering older sisters; a mother who expected a daughter and delayed naming her newborn son for eight weeks. Zucker's belief is that with enough therapy, such children can be made to feel comfortable in their birth sex. Zucker has compared young children who believe they are meant to live as the other sex to people who want to amputate healthy limbs, or who believe they are cats, or those with something called ethnic-identity disorder. "If a five-year-old black kid came into the clinic and said he wanted to be white, would we endorse that?" he told me. "I don't think so. What we would want to do is say, 'What's going on with this kid that's making him feel that it would be better to be white?'"

When you were growing up, what were the gender roles like in your family? How did this affect you?

Young children, he explains, have very concrete reasoning; they may believe that if they want to wear dresses, they are girls. But he sees it as his job—and the parents'—to help them think in more-flexible ways. "If a kid has massive separation anxiety and does not want to go to school, one solution would be to let them stay home. That would solve the problem at one level, but not at another. So it is with gender identity." Allowing a child to switch genders, in other words, would probably not get to the root of the psychological problem, but only offer a superficial fix.

Zucker calls his approach "developmental," which means that the most important factor is the age of the child. Younger children are more malleable, he believes, and can learn to "be comfortable in their own skin." Zucker says that in twenty-five years, not one of the patients who started seeing him by age six has switched gender. Adolescents are more fixed in their identity. If a parent brings in, say, a thirteen-year-old who has never been treated and who has severe gender dysphoria, Zucker will generally recommend hormonal treatment. But he considers that a fraught choice. "One has to think about the long-term developmental path. This kid will go through lifelong hormonal treatment to approximate the phenotype of a male and may require some kind of surgery and then will have to deal with the fact that he doesn't have a phallus; it's a tough road, with a lot of pain involved."

> ❝ *Younger children are more malleable, he believes, and can learn to 'be comfortable in their own skin.'* ❞

Zucker put me in touch with two of his success stories, a boy and a girl, now both living in the suburbs of Toronto. Meeting them was like moving into a parallel world where every story began the same way as those of the American families I'd met, but then ran in the opposite direction.

When he was four, the boy, John, had tested at the top of the gender-dysphoria scale. Zucker recalls him as "one of the most anxious kids I ever saw." He had bins full of Barbies and Disney princess movies, and he dressed in homemade costumes. Once, at a hardware store, he stared up at the glittery chandeliers and wept, "I don't want to be a daddy! I want to be a mommy!"

His parents, well-educated urbanites, let John grow his hair long and play with whatever toys he preferred. But then a close friend led them to Zucker, and soon they began to see themselves as "in denial," recalls his mother, Caroline. "Once we came to see his behavior for what it was, it became painfully sad." Zucker believed John's behavior resulted from early-childhood medical trauma—he was born with tumors on his kidneys and had invasive treatments every three months—and from his dependence during that time on his mother, who has a dominant personality.

When they reversed course, they dedicated themselves to the project with a thoroughness most parents would find exhausting and off-putting. They boxed up all of John's girl-toys and videos and replaced them with neutral ones. Whenever John cried for his girl-toys, they would ask him, "Do you think playing with those would make you feel better about being a boy?" and then would distract him with an offer to ride bikes or take a walk. They turned their house into a 1950s kitchen-sink drama, intended to inculcate respect for patriarchy, in the crudest and simplest terms: "Boys don't wear pink, they wear blue," they would tell him, or "Daddy is smarter than Mommy—ask him." If John called for Mommy in the middle of the night, Daddy went, every time.

When I visited the family, John was lazing around with his older brother, idly watching TV and playing video games, dressed in a polo shirt and Abercrombie & Fitch shorts. He said he was glad he'd been through the therapy, "because it made me feel happy," but that's about all he would say; for the most part, his mother spoke for him. Recently, John was in the basement watching the Grammys. When Caroline walked downstairs to say good night, she found him draped in a blanket, vamping. He looked up at her, mortified. She held his face and said, "You never have to be embarrassed of the things you say or do around me." Her position now is that the treatment is "not a cure; this will always be with him"—but also that he has nothing to be ashamed of. About a year ago, John carefully broke the news to his parents that he is gay. "You'd have to carefully break the news to me that you were straight," his dad told him. "He'll be a man who loves men," says his mother. "But I want him to be a happy man who loves men."

The girl's case was even more extreme in some ways. She insisted on peeing standing up and playing only with boys. When her mother bought her Barbies, she'd pop their heads off. Once, when she was six, her father, Mike, said out of the blue: "Chris, you're a girl." In response, he recalls, she "started screaming and freaking out," closing her hand into a fist and punching herself between the legs, over and over. After that, her parents took her to see Zucker. He connected Chris's behavior to the early years of her parents' marriage; her mother had gotten pregnant and Mike had been resentful of having to marry her, and verbally abusive. Chris, Zucker told them, saw her mother as weak and couldn't identify with her. For four years, they saw no progress. When Chris turned eleven and other girls in school started getting their periods, her mother found her on the bed one night, weeping. She "said she wanted to kill herself," her mother told me. "She said, 'In my head, I've always been a boy.'"

> **Chris, Zucker told them, saw her mother as weak and couldn't identify with her.**

But about a month after that, everything began to change. Chris had joined a softball team and made some female friends; her mother figured she had cottoned to the idea that girls could be tough and competitive. Then one day, Chris went to her mother and said, "Mom, I need to talk to you. We need to go shopping." She bought clothes that were tighter and had her ears pierced. She let her hair grow out. Eventually she gave her boys' clothes away.

Now Chris wears her hair in a ponytail, walks like a girl, and spends hours on the phone, talking to girlfriends about boys. Her mother recently watched her through a bedroom window as she was jumping on their trampoline, looking slyly at her own reflection and tossing her hair around. At her parents' insistence, Chris has never been to a support group or a conference, never talked to another girl who wanted to be a boy. For all she knew, she was the only person in the world who felt as she once had felt.

> **At her parents' insistence, Chris has never been to a support group. . . . For all she knew, she was the only person in the world who felt as she once had felt.**

The week before I arrived in Toronto, the Barbara Walters special about Jazz had been re-aired, and both sets of parents had seen it. "I was aghast," said John's mother. "It really affected us to see this poor little peanut, and her parents just going to the teacher and saying 'He is a "she" now.' Why would you assume a four-year-old would understand the ramifications of that?"

"We were shocked," Chris's father said. "They gave up on their kid too early. Regardless of our beliefs and our values, you look at Chris, and you look at these kids, and they have to go through a sex-change operation and they'll never look right and they'll never have a normal life. Look at Chris's chance for a happy, decent life, and look at theirs. Seeing those kids, it just broke our hearts." . . .

It's not impossible to imagine Brandon's life going in another direction. His early life fits neatly into a Zucker case study about family noise. Tina describes Brandon as "never leaving my side" during his early years. The diagnosis writes itself: father, distant and threatening; mother, protector; child overidentifies with strong maternal figure. If Tina had lived in Toronto, if she'd had the patience for six years of Dr. Zucker's therapy, if the therapy had been free, then who knows?

> " Brandon's . . . early life fits neatly into a Zucker case study about family noise. "

Yet Zucker's approach has its own disturbing elements. It's easy to imagine that his methods—steering parents toward removing pink crayons from the box, extolling a patriarchy no one believes in—could instill in some children a sense of shame and a double life. A 2008 study of twenty-five girls who had been seen in Zucker's clinic showed positive results; twenty-two were no longer gender-dysphoric, meaning they were comfortable living as girls. But that doesn't mean they were happy. I spoke to the mother of one Zucker patient in her late twenties, who said her daughter was repulsed by the thought of a sex change but was still suffering—she'd become an alcoholic, and was cutting herself. "I'd be surprised if she outlived me," her mother said.

> " Twenty-two [girls] were no longer gender-dysphoric. . . . But that doesn't mean they were happy. "

When I was reporting this story, I was visibly pregnant with my third child. My pregnancy brought up a certain nostalgia for the parents I met, because it reminded them of a time when life was simpler, when a stranger could ask them whether their baby was a boy or a girl and they could answer straightforwardly. Many parents shared journals with me that were filled with anguish. If they had decided to let their child live as the other gender, that meant cutting off ties with family and friends who weren't supportive, putting away baby pictures, mourning the loss of the child they thought they had. It meant sending their child out alone into a possibly hostile world. If they chose the other route, it meant denying their child the things he or she most wanted, day after day, in the uncertain hope that one day, it would all pay off. In either case, it meant choosing a course on the basis of hazy evidence, and resolving to believe in it.

About two months after the conference, I visited Brandon again. On Father's Day, Tina had made up her mind to just let it happen. She'd started calling him "Bridget" and, except for a few slipups, "she." She'd packed up all the boy-clothes and given them to a neighbor, and had taken Bridget to JC Penney for a new wardrobe. When I saw her, her ears were pierced and her hair was just beginning to tickle her earlobes. "If it doesn't move any faster, I'll have to get extensions!" Tina said.

That morning, Tina was meeting with Bridget's principal, and the principal of a nearby school, to see if she could transfer. "I want her to be known as Bridget, not Bridget-who-used-to-be-Brandon." Tina had memorized lots of lines she'd heard at the conference, and she delivered them well, if a little too fast. She told the principals that she had "pictures and medical documentation." She showed them a book called *The Transgender Child*. "I thought we could fix it," she said, "but gender's in your brain." Brandon's old principal looked a little shell-shocked. But the one from the nearby school, a young woman with a sweet face and cropped curly hair, seemed more open. "This is all new to me," she said. "It's a lot to learn."

> **'I thought we could fix it, but gender's in your brain.'**

The week before, Tina had gone to her mother's house, taking Bridget along. Bridget often helps care for her grandmother, who has lupus; the two are close. After lunch, Bridget went outside in a pair of high heels she'd found in the closet. Tina's stepfather saw the child and lost it: "Get them damned shoes off!" he yelled.

"Make me," Bridget answered.

Then the stepfather turned to Tina and said, "You're ruining his fucking life," loud enough for Bridget to hear.

Tina's talk with Karen, the mother of Bridget's best friend, Abby, hadn't gone too smoothly, either. Karen is an evangelical Christian, with an anti-gay-marriage bumper sticker on her white van. For two years, she'd picked up Brandon nearly every day after school, and brought him over to play with Abby. But that wasn't going to happen anymore. Karen told Tina she didn't want her children "exposed to that kind of thing." "God doesn't make mistakes," she added.

> **Karen told Tina she didn't want her children 'exposed to that kind of thing.' 'God doesn't make mistakes,' she added.**

Bridget, meanwhile, was trying to figure it all out—what she could and couldn't do, where the limits were. She'd always been a compliant child, but now she was misbehaving. Her cross-dressing had amped up; she was trying on makeup, and demanding higher heels and sexier clothes. When I was over, she came out of the house dressed in a cellophane getup, four-inch heels, and lip gloss. "It's like I have to teach her what's appropriate for a girl her age," says Tina.

Thursdays, the family spends the afternoon at a local community center, where both Bridget and her little sister, Madison, take gymnastics. She'd normally see Abby there; the two of them are in the same class and usually do their warm-up together, giggling and going over their day. On the car ride over, Bridget was trying to navigate that new relationship, too.

"Abby's not my best friend anymore. She hits me. But she's really good at drawing."

"Well, don't you go hitting nobody," Tina said. "Remember, sticks and stones."

When they arrived at the center and opened the door, Abby was standing right there. She looked at Bridget/Brandon. And froze. She turned and ran away. Madison, oblivious, followed her, yelling, "Wait for us!"

Bridget sat down on a bench next to Tina. Although they were miles from home, she'd just seen a fourth-grade friend of her stepbrother's at the pool table, and she was nervous.

"Hey, we need to work on this," said Tina. "If anybody says anything, you say, 'I'm not Brandon. I'm Bridget, his cousin from California. You want to try it?'"

"No. I don't want to."

"Well, if someone keeps it up, you just say, 'You're crazy.'"

Tina had told me over the phone that Brandon was easily passing as a girl, but that wasn't really true, not yet. With his hair still short, he looked like a boy wearing tight pink pants and earrings. This meant that for the moment, everywhere in this small town was a potential land mine. At the McDonald's, the cashier eyed him suspiciously: "Is that Happy Meal for a boy or a girl?" At the playground, a group of teenage boys with tattoos and their pants pulled low down did a double take. By the evening, Tina was a nervous wreck. "Gosh darn it! I left the keys in the car," she said. But she hadn't. She was holding them in her hand.

After gymnastics, the kids wanted to stop at the Dairy Queen, but Tina couldn't take being stared at in one more place. "Drive-thru!" she yelled. "And I don't want to hear any more whining from you."

On the quiet, wooded road leading home, she could finally relax. It was cool enough to roll down the windows and get some mountain air. After high school, Tina had studied to be a travel agent; she had always wanted to just "work on a cruise ship or something, just go, go, go." Now she wanted things to be easy for Brandon, for him to disappear and pop back as Bridget, a new kid from California, new to this town, knowing nobody. But in a small town, it's hard to erase yourself and come back as your opposite.

> " In a small town, it's hard to erase yourself and come back as your opposite. "

Maybe one day they would move, she said. But thinking about that made her head hurt. Instead of the future, she drifted to the past, when things were easier.

"Remember that camping trip we took once, Brandon?" she asked, and he did. And together, they started singing one of the old camp songs she'd taught him.

Smokey the Bear, Smokey the Bear,

Howlin' and a-prowlin' and a-sniffin' the air.

He can find a fire before it starts to flame

That's why they call him Smokey,

That's how he got his name.

"You remember that, Brandon?" she asked again. And for the first time all day, they seemed happy.

Nursery Rhyme ▼

Unknown

What Folks Are Made Of

How do the ideas in this eighteenth-century rhyme compare to today's attitudes about female and male identities?

The ballad "What Folks Are Made Of" developed over time in the oral folk tradition before being written down. The second and third stanzas, popularly known as "What Are Little Boys Made Of?," are attributed to the English poet Robert Southey (1774–1843); however, it's not certain that he is, in fact, the author of these lines. "What Are Little Boys Made Of?" was eventually gathered into a Mother Goose collection, while the rest of the ballad remains less well-known.

MOTHER GOOSE'S MELODY

A FACSIMILE REPRODUCTION

OF

THE EARLIEST KNOWN EDITION

WITH AN INTRODUCTION AND NOTES

BY

COLONEL W. F. PRIDEAUX, C.S.I.

LONDON
A. H. BULLEN
47 GREAT RUSSELL STREET
MCMIV

MOTHER GOOSE's
MELODY:

OR,

Sonnets for the Cradle.

IN TWO PARTS.

PART I. Contains the moſt celebrated Songs and Lullabies of the old Britiſh Nurſes, calculated to amuſe Children and to excite them to Sleep.

PART II. Thoſe of that ſweet Songſter and Nurſe of Wit and Humour, Maſter William Shakeſpeare.

EMBELLISHED WITH CUTS.

And Illuſtrated with NOTES and MAXIMS, Hiſtorical, Philoſophical and Critical.

LONDON:
Printed for FRANCIS POWER, (Grandſon to the late Mr. J. NEWBERY,) and Co. No. 65. St. Paul's Church Yard, 1791.
] Price Three Pence.]

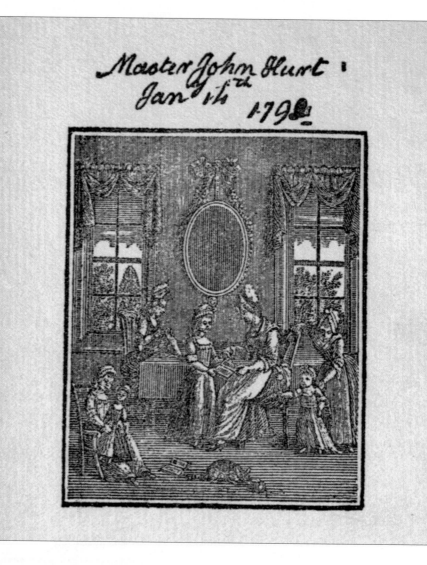

What are little babies made of, made of?
What are little babies made of?
    Diapers and crumbs and
    sucking their thumbs;
That's what little babies are made of.

What are little boys made of, made of?
What are little boys made of?
    Snips and snails and puppy-dog tails;
That's what little boys are made of.

What are little girls made of, made of?
What are little girls made of?
    Sugar and spice and everything
    nice;
That's what little girls are made of.

What are young men made of, made of?
What are young men made of?
    Sighs and leers and crocodile tears;
That's what young men are made of.

What are young women made of,
   made of?
What are young women made of?
    Rings and jings and other fine
    things;
That's what young women are made of.

What are our sailors made of, made of?
What are our sailors made of?
    Pitch and tar, pig-tail and scar;
That's what our sailors are made of.

What are our soldiers made of, made of?
What are our soldiers made of?
    Pipeclay and drill, the foeman to
    kill;
That's what our soldiers are made of.

What are our nurses made of, made of?
What are our nurses made of?
    Bushes and thorns and old cow's
    horns;
That's what our nurses are made of.

What are our fathers made of, made of?
What are our fathers made of?
    Pipes and smoke and collars
    choke;
That's what our fathers are made of.

What are our mothers made of,
   made of?
What are our mothers made of?
    Ribbons and laces and sweet
    pretty faces;
That's what our mothers are made of.

What are old men made of, made of?
What are old men made of?
    Slippers that flop and a bald-
    headed top;
That's what old men are made of.

What are old women made of, made of?
What are old women made of?
    Reels, and jeels, and old spinning
    wheels;
That's what old women are made of.

What are all folks made of, made of?
What are all folks made of?
    Fighting a spot and loving a lot,
That's what all folks are made of.

Shaping Identity

ANALYZING RHETORICAL SITUATIONS

1. Humor Essay. Garrison Keillor argues that an obituary "is not meant to comfort. It is meant to take inventory of a life." Do you agree with him? Why or why not?

2. Essay. Do you trust Paul Bloom as an authority on the subject of our multiple identities? Why or why not? How does Bloom establish and develop his ethos?

3. Essay. Bloom refers to governmental structures several times in his essay as a metaphor for the competing selves in an individual. How effective do you think this metaphor is? Can you think of a more effective metaphor?

4. Researched article. Hanna Rosin discusses a variety of issues surrounding transgender children transitioning at a young age. What is her central claim? What evidence does she use to support that claim?

5. Researched article. Rosin frames her discussion of the issues using the story of Brandon Simms. She also mixes in other narratives and provides a report on research on the issue. Why do you think she has chosen this particular strategy for this article?

6. Researched article. Who do you think is the audience for Rosin's piece? Consider her tone, evidence, and references as you formulate your answer.

7. Nursery rhyme. In "What Folks Are Made Of," what does the line "Snips and snails and puppy-dog tails" tell you about little boys? Does the nursery rhyme privilege one gender over another? Why or why not?

8. Researched article & nursery rhyme. How do some of the stories in Rosin's piece illustrate the gender dichotomy evident in the nursery rhyme?

Shaping Identity

9. Write life lessons. Keillor lists four "lessons of Upward's life," gleaned from Upward's obituary. Locate a detailed obituary from a major city newspaper or a funeral home Web site—or the obituary of a famous or historical person—and list some of the life lessons that can be learned. You may choose to be satirical, as Keillor is, or serious.

10. Create a photo essay. Create a photo essay of portraits that reflect identity. You might choose to have the series focus on yourself, on someone else, or on a group of individuals. Think about how you want to define identity and how the photos will convey that. Review the photo essay you created. How might you revise it to take into account the multiple selves within each individual that Bloom writes about?

11. Conduct primary research. Bloom notes that "[d]issociative-identity disorder is controversial." Survey or interview several psychology professors on your campus to find out where they stand on the issue and why.

12. Research medical approaches. Rosin's article discusses the use of hormone blockers in transgender children. She also discusses the developmental approach used by Dr. Zucker. Research both approaches and then write an argument essay that advocates for one of the approaches.

13. Write a nursery rhyme. Write a new version of the nursery rhyme from the perspective of someone like Brandon Simms, the child discussed in Rosin's article.

14. Create a collage. Create a collage that illustrates the concepts in the nursery rhyme. Review Chapter 10 and the guided reading of a collage in Chapter 4 (p. 253) before you start.

15. Write a film review. Transgender issues have been explored in several contemporary films (e.g., *Boys Don't Cry*, *Hedwig and the Angry Inch*, *Normal*, and *Transamerica*). Watch one of the films and then write a review. Before you write, review the guided reading of a film review in the e-Pages for Chapter 4.

RESEARCH EXPERIMENTS: Identity

1. **Investigate & analyze a subculture as an outsider.** Identify a subculture group that you are not a member of, perhaps computer nerds, hunters, skateboarders, parents, chess players, organic food eaters, or bluegrass music fans. Then, observe the group. Depending on the group you choose, you might attend an event, such as a bluegrass concert or chess club meeting; visit a retail outlet such as a skateboarding shop, Babies "R" Us, or computer or video game store; or visit a computer lab.

   a. **Conduct three observations of at least 30 minutes each. Take detailed observation notes** that include information about what you see, hear, smell, etc. Consider:

   - What are people wearing? Describe their clothing, hairstyles, jewelry, piercings, tattoos, and so on.

   - How do people position themselves in the space? How close do they stand or sit to each other? Do people move within the space or do they take a position, such as sitting at a table, and maintain it?

   - How does the space look? Describe the furniture and décor.

   - How do people speak to each other? What role does body language play? How loudly or softly do they speak?

   - What kinds of props do people have? Do they bring equipment with them? How do they use their props or equipment?

   b. Once you've completed your three observations, **review all your notes and look for commonalities** that tie the people together as members of the same subculture. What inferences can you make or what conclusions can you draw based on what you've seen? Answer the following questions:

   - Why do people come to this space? What needs or desires draw them there?

   - What sort of people come to this space? How do they behave within this space?

   - What types of behaviors seem to be encouraged or discouraged, based on what you've observed?

   - What roles do socializing and consumption seem to play in the gatherings you've observed?

   c. **Write an analytical essay** that makes a point about your subculture that might surprise readers, providing photos and quotations and references to details from your observations throughout to support your point. Your finished essay should **include a variety of media, such as a mixture of text, photographs, drawings, sketches**, and so on.

For example, observations of bluegrass fans might indicate that they are much more fashion savvy than stereotypes about them imply. An essay on this might include photos of bluegrass fans wearing designer sunglasses, chic blouses, and trendy heels to support the point. Quotations from overheard conversations about taste, shopping, or fashion might be woven throughout.

2. **Brand your family: create a motto, logo, & illustrated history.** Your family reunion is coming up and you've been nominated to put together a family history. The history will ultimately take the form of a paper scrapbook, Web page, or blog. You've also been asked to design a T-shirt that family members will wear for a group portrait. The T-shirt needs to feature a slogan that makes a statement about your family.

- **Brainstorm a motto** that says something about your family's identity. For example, Amy might design a T-shirt that says "The Brazillers: Even the Adults Are Children," to reflect the playful nature of her extended family.

- **Interview at least three family members** and ask them to consider your motto. Does it ring true for them? Would they identify your family with some other phrase or slogan? Ask interviewees to recall at least three memorable family episodes that support or refute your motto, and have them share photos with you (and video, if you have multimedia access).

- **Write up the best anecdotes** and/or include transcripts of your family interviews. Illustrate the stories (and/or transcripts) with family photos. If you have multimedia access, include audio and video recordings of your interviews, as well as any multimedia materials you gather from family members.

- **Revise your motto as needed**, based on feedback from interviewees.

- **Design a logo** that complements your family motto. Perhaps you'll use one of the photos you've collected or another image that works for your slogan and family history. For example, Amy could create a logo that portrays stick-figure people playing on a seesaw to illustrate the playful nature of her family, or work with a photo of family members at play.

- **Assemble your motto, logo, & illustrated family history** in a paper scrapbook or on a Web page or blog.

- **Write a reflective essay** that explains the choices you made along the way in your project. How did your audience (family) and purpose (to tell family stories and reflect family identity) affect your decisions and revisions? To what extent does what you've created offer a true picture of your family?

- **Alternative project:** Adapt the above assignment so that it's about you and a group of your friends.

12 THE BODY

CONTENTS

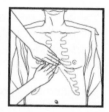

INSTRUCTIONS ▶
University of Washington School of Medicine.
Courtesy of Health Sciences, University of Washington.

e For e-Pages content, visit **bedfordstmartins .com/bookofgenres.**

How do we define ourselves in relation to our bodies? Are we what we eat—the healthy green salad *and* the late-night extra-cheesy mac and cheese? Are we our muscles? Our belly fat? Our illnesses and addictions? Our physical disabilities? Evidence of our attitudes toward our bodies can be found in various genres of everyday life. Consider these questions: What do our food labels say about how we fortify our bodies? How are our bodies described in routine documents such as medical forms and histories? How do we represent our bodies in advertising, and in art and literature?

Opening this chapter is a cluster titled "Bodies 101," presented in the e-Pages. The famous American poet Walt Whitman celebrates the body, reveling in its parts and "soul," while a medical history of President Ronald Reagan presents the body as a list of ailments and surgeries, and the American Medical Association provides instructions on performing cardiopulmonary resuscitation.

A cluster titled "Food, Obesity, & Fat Advocacy" presents multiple views about what we eat and what we weigh, with a news flash that lard may be good for us. Michael Pollan's "Six Food Rules" suggests that how we eat is just as important as what we eat. Regina Schrambling discusses the taboo on lard, and why it seems to be lifting. Essayist Laura Fraser traces the history of ideal body types; Juliet Samuel and bloggers Paul McAleer and Carrie Padian explain the growing fat acceptance movement in America, and Daniel Engber draws connections among health, social class, and obesity in his provocatively titled essay "Give Me Your Tired, Your Poor, Your Big Fat Asses."

A group of readings on "The Brain & Mental Health" brings you inside the zinging mind of a bipolar memoirist named Andy Behrman and takes a scholarly look with author Joan Arehart-Treichel at how women are portrayed in drug ads. A letter and painting reveal the final days of the famous and troubled Dutch painter Vincent van Gogh, followed by Lyn Garrity's article describing the artist's final days.

Finally, "Cigarettes, Drugs, & Alcohol," a cluster presented in the e-Pages, looks at the consequences of bad habits and untreated disease. Doctors happily peddle smokes in a portfolio of vintage cigarette ads, while a dark spoof on Joe Camel shows a sobering outcome. A chart and a map by the producers of the HBO series *Addicted* provide quick facts on the long-term effects of ten popular drugs and reveal America's dependence on a range of mind- and body-altering substances.

STARTER PROJECTS: The Body

1. **The body & mind: Annotate your picture.** What is the connection between your mind and body? How do the abilities and limitations of your mind affect your body, and vice versa? To what extent do you identify yourself in the world in terms of your intelligence? In terms of your physical appearance? Draw a picture or print out a photo of yourself and annotate your image. Describe your mind and the way you think. Characterize your body and what it can and can't do. Make connections. Examine these relationships. How does this relate back to your identity?

2. **The body & health: Make a list.** What does it mean to live a "healthy" life? What actions have you taken to keep yourself healthy or improve your health? How regularly do health concerns figure into your decision making? How does your financial situation affect your health? Make a list of your habits and lifestyle choices that you consider healthy; make a separate list of habits and choices you'd like to improve.

3. **The body & poetry: Write a haiku.** In anticipation of the Walt Whitman poem on the body that you will read in the e-Pages, come up with a few lines that characterize your attitude toward the physical self, or the "wonders" of the body. For example, you might write a verse in praise of circulation, or the ability to dance or breathe, or something else. Wax rhapsodic. Alternatively, write a complaint piece about some aspect of your body that's not working as well as you'd like.

4. **The body & medicine: Draft your medical history.** Have you ever been in the hospital? Had surgery? Seen a chiropractor or acupuncturist? Draft a history of your life in purely medical terms, beginning with your birth. What is it like to look at your life in these terms?

5. **The body & chapter concept: Keep your eyes peeled.** In early drafts of this book, we titled this chapter "Health." Our editor later suggested changing the title to "The Body." As you read through this chapter, consider how you might understand the readings differently if the chapter were still titled "Health."

Perhaps the fact that we say "as American as apple pie" is an indicator that Americans love dessert. An onslaught of studies shows that Americans consume too much sugar, too much fat, and not nearly enough plants and fiber. Despite the growing interest in vegetarianism, organic foods, and other supposedly healthy foods, our nation's obesity rate continues to climb. This cluster examines some of the connections among obesity, food, and health, focusing on what we should be eating (Pollan), what we thought we had to avoid but perhaps shouldn't (Schrambling), and explores changing social views of obesity (Fraser) and the growing fat acceptance movement (Samuel, McAleer, and Padian). The cluster ends with an examination of the connection between obesity and poverty (Engber).

List/Argument

Michael Pollan

Six Food Rules

▲ BOOK COVER
Food Rules: An Eater's Manual, by Michael Pollan (Penguin Books 2009).

Food journalist Michael Pollan, who has been described as a "neo-foodie rock star," is the author of several best-selling books on food, including *The Omnivore's Dilemma* and *In Defense of Food*. In his book *Food Rules: An Eater's Manual*, Pollan gives a few of the rules he's come up with for healthy eating. *(The text that follows originally appeared in* Food Rules: An Eater's Manual *and was presented there as rules 11, 19, 36, 39, 47, and 58. Copyright © 2010 by Michael Pollan. Used by Permission. All rights reserved.)*

Avoid foods you see advertised on television.

Food marketers are ingenious at turning criticisms of their products—and rules like these—into new ways to sell slightly different versions of the same processed foods: They simply reformulate (to be low-fat, have no HFCS or transfats, or to contain fewer ingredients) and then boast about their implied healthfulness, whether the boast is meaningful or not. The best way to escape these marketing ploys is to tune out the marketing itself, by refusing to buy heavily promoted foods. Only the biggest food manufacturers can afford to advertise their products on television: More than two thirds of food advertising is spent promoting processed foods (and alcohol), so if you avoid products with big ad budgets, you'll automatically be avoiding edible foodlike substances. As for the 5 percent of food ads that promote whole foods (the prune or walnut growers or the beef ranchers), common sense will, one hopes, keep you from tarring them with the same brush—these are the exceptions that prove the rule.

> **❝** *More than two-thirds of food advertising is spent promoting processed foods.* **❞**

If it came from a plant, eat it; if it was made in a plant, don't.

Don't eat breakfast cereals that change the color of the milk.

This should go without saying. Such cereals are highly processed and full of refined carbohydrates as well as chemical additives.

How do you decide what to eat? To what extent are you persuaded by advertising?

Eat all the junk food you want as long as you cook it yourself.

There is nothing wrong with eating sweets, fried foods, pastries, even drinking soda every now and then, but food manufacturers have made eating these formerly expensive and hard-to-make treats so cheap and easy that we're eating them every day. The french fry did not become America's most popular vegetable until industry took over the jobs of washing, peeling, cutting, and frying the potatoes—and cleaning up the mess. If you made all the french fries you ate, you would eat them much less often, if only because they're so much work. The same holds true for fried chicken, chips, cakes, pies, and ice cream. Enjoy these treats as often as you're willing to prepare them—chances are good it won't be every day.

Eat when you are hungry, not when you are bored.

> **❝** We eat out of boredom, for entertainment, to comfort or reward ourselves. **❞**

For many of us, eating has surprisingly little to do with hunger. We eat out of boredom, for entertainment, to comfort or reward ourselves. Try to be aware of why you're eating, and ask yourself if you're really hungry—before you eat and then again along the way. (One old wives' test: If you're not hungry enough to eat an apple, then you're not hungry.) Food is a costly antidepressant.

Do all your eating at a table.

No, a desk is not a table. If we eat while we're working, or while watching TV or driving, we eat mindlessly—and as a result eat a lot more than we would if we were eating at a table, paying attention to what we're doing. This phenomenon can be tested (and put to good use): Place a child in front of a television set and place a bowl of fresh vegetables in front of him or her. The child will eat everything in the bowl, often even vegetables that he or she doesn't ordinarily touch, without noticing what's going on. Which suggests an exception to the rule: When eating somewhere other than at a table, stick to fruits and vegetables.

Essay ▼

Regina Schrambling

Lard: After Decades of Trying, Its Moment Is Finally Here

In the following essay, food writer Regina Schrambling posits that pig-based lard may actually be better for us than vegetable-based shortening. Schrambling notes that lard "has always been a ridiculously hard sell," but that shortening is now coming under fire for containing trans fats. With many nutritionists arguing that trans fat is a killer, lard, with its saturated fats, seems much more attractive. Schrambling writes for *Slate*, where this essay first appeared; her writing can also be found on the *Gastropoda, Gastriques*, and *Epicurious* blogs.

HOME / FOOD : WHAT TO EAT. WHAT NOT TO EAT.

Lard

After decades of trying, its moment is finally here.

By Regina Schrambling

Wait long enough and everything bad for you is good again. Sugar? Naturally better than high-fructose corn syrup. Chocolate? A bar a day keeps the doctor away. Caffeine? Bring it on.

Lard, however, has always been a ridiculously hard sell. Over at least the last fifteen years, it's repeatedly been given a clean bill of health, and good cooks regularly point out how superior this totally natural fat is for frying and pastries. But that hasn't been enough to keep Americans from recoiling—lard's negative connotations of flowing flesh and vats of grease and epithets like *lardass* and *tub of lard* have been absurd hurdles. But no longer. I'm convinced that the redemption of lard is finally at hand because we live in a world where trendiness is next to godliness. And lard hits all the right notes, especially if you euphemize it as rendered pork fat—bacon butter.

> **"** *The redemption of lard is finally at hand.* **"**

Lard has clearly won the health debate. Shortening, the synthetic substitute foisted on this country over the last century, has proven to be a much bigger health hazard because it contains trans fats, the bugaboo du jour. Corporate food scientists figured out long ago that you can fool most of the people most of the time, and shortening (and its butter-aping cousin, margarine) had a pretty good ride after Crisco was introduced in 1911 as a substitute for the poor man's fat. But shortening really vanquished lard in the 1950s when researchers first connected animal fat in the diet to coronary heart disease. By the '90s, Americans had been indoctrinated to mainline olive oil, but shortening was still the go-to solid fat over lard or even butter in far too many cookbooks.

I have to admit even I was suckered by the nutrition nuttiness, despite having been all but weaned on lard in a Mexican neighborhood in Arizona. The great Mexican cooks in kitchens on either side of our house used it to make wondrously supple flour tortillas and almost airy tamales, while my Oklahoma-born dad worked it into biscuits and melted it for frying anything in his cast-iron skillet before we could afford, as he always put it, to "eat like white folks." (Peasant food has cachet only if you are not forced to live on it.) As a food writer, I learned early on that it was considered a four-letter word in recipes, even when it was essential for authenticity. (You can substitute butter in Mexican aniseed cookies called *bizcochos*, but they won't be as crisp, crunchy, and delicate.)

> ❝ *Now you could even argue that lard is good for you.* ❞

Do you or your friends or family cook with lard? Why or why not?

That's all changed. Now you could even argue that lard is good for you. As Jennifer McLagan points out in her celebrated book, *Fat: An Appreciation of a Misunderstood Ingredient, with Recipes*, lard's fat is also mostly monounsaturated, which is healthier than saturated fat. And even the saturated fat in lard has a neutral effect on blood cholesterol. Not to mention that lard has a higher smoking point than other fats, allowing foods like chicken to absorb less grease when fried in it. And, of course, fat in general has its upsides. The body converts it to fuel, and it helps absorb nutrients, particularly calcium and vitamins.

What matters more, though, is that lard has become the right ingredient at the right time. It fits perfectly into the Michael Pollan crusade to promote foods that have been processed as minimally as possible: Your great-grandmother surely cooked with it, so you should, too.

Add to that the new awareness that what you eat matters environmentally—if you are going to eat an animal on a planet at risk from too many humans raising too many animals to eat, you have to eat the whole thing. Lard is just about the last stop before the squeal when pork producers are extracting every savory bit from a pig.

That environmental consciousness coupled with competitive cooking has resulted in the nose-to-tail trend set off by British chef Fergus Henderson. Walk into any high-end restaurant these days and pork chops are less prevalent than pig's ears, trotters, and jowls. The salumi/charcuterie craze has also been great for enhancing lard's profile, particularly thanks to lardo—pork belly cured Tuscan-style with wine and herbs and served in thin slices over warm bread or on pizza. If Mario Batali says it's good, diners everywhere listen.

The best lard is leaf lard, from the fat around the kidneys of a hog, preferably a heritage hog. Flying Pigs Farm sells this at the Greenmarket in Union Square in New York City for six dollars per eight-ounce container, and it sells out fast. Lard from the supermarket can still be pretty scary; most of it has been hydrogenated to make it last longer.

To what extent do you pay attention to the *kinds* of fats contained in the food you eat?

(As I learned from lard crusader Zarela Martinez in New York, you can make your own if you can get your hands on top-quality fat from a small producer— back, belly, or kidney fat will all work. Cut it into chunks and cook them very slowly over low heat until the fat seeps out and only crispy bits are left. Strain it and save the fat in the refrigerator almost indefinitely. Salt the cracklings and eat them as what Mexicans call *chicharrones*.)

Only one thing may put lard back on the slippery slope: Google the word as news, and it might as well be lard-fearing 1969 all over again. Newspaper food pages still routinely advise using olive or canola oils rather than "fattening" or "artery-clogging" lard. Or they print idiotic utterances like "you get all the lard you need at McDonald's" (a chain that actually abandoned beef tallow for frying its fries only to be saddled with a trans-fatty substitute). Occasionally an article will make a valid point—lard is still anathema to vegetarians and halal observers—but more often there will be surprise that lard does not taste anything like pig.

> " [Lard] fits perfectly into the Michael Pollan crusade. "

Which is one more reason it is taking off at last. It's stealth fat.

Researched Essay ▼

Laura Fraser

The Inner Corset: A Brief History of Fat in the U.S.

▲ AUTHOR PHOTO
Laura Fraser. *By permission of Christina Taccone.*

Laura Fraser is a freelance journalist and author of the memoirs *An Italian Affair* and *All Over the Map,* as well as an exposé of the weight loss industry, *Losing It: America's Obsession with Weight and the Industry That Feeds on It*, in which she traces how American opinions about female weight have shifted from the nineteenth century to the present. Before 1880, she writes, "a beautiful woman had plump cheeks and arms, [and] full, substantial hips. Women were sexy if they were heavy." Fraser explores how this image of female attractiveness shifted, due in part to economics, immigration, and food availability, between 1880 and 1930, when "American women could never be too thin." The following essay is an excerpt from *Losing It.*[*] *(Copyright © 1997 by Laura Fraser. Reprinted with the permission of the Author, all rights reserved.)*

Once upon a time, a man with a thick gold watch swaying from a big, round paunch was the very picture of American prosperity and vigor. Accordingly, a hundred years ago, a beautiful woman had plump cheeks and arms, and she wore a corset and even a bustle to emphasize her full, substantial hips. Women were *sexy* if they were heavy. In those days, Americans knew that a layer of fat was a sign that you could afford to eat well and that you stood a better chance of fighting off infectious diseases than most people. If you were a woman, having that extra adipose blanket also meant that you were probably fertile, and warm to cuddle up next to on chilly nights.

> ❝ Women were sexy *if they were heavy.* ❞

---

[*]For the purposes of this book, we have edited Fraser's use of sources so that the in-text citations and references list conform to the APA style of documentation. —Eds.

Between the 1880s and 1920s, that pleasant image of fat thoroughly changed in the United States. Some began early on to hint that fat was a health risk. In 1894, Woods Hutchinson, a medical professor who wrote for women's magazines, defended fat against this new point of view. "Adipose," he wrote, "while often pictured as a veritable Frankenstein, born of and breeding disease, sure to ride its possessor to death sooner or later, is really a most harmless, healthful, innocent tissue" (Hutchinson, 1894, p. 395). Hutchinson reassured his *Cosmopolitan* readers that fat was not only benign, but also attractive, and that if a poll of beautiful women were taken in any city, there would be at least three times as many plump ones as slender ones. He advised them that no amount of starving or exercise—which were just becoming popular as a means of weight control—would change more than 10 percent of a person's body size anyway. "The fat man tends to remain fat, the thin woman to stay thin—and both in perfect health—in spite of everything they can do," he said in that article.

> ❝ *Hutchinson reassured his* Cosmopolitan *readers that fat was attractive.* ❞

But by 1926, Hutchinson, who was by then a past president of the American Academy of Medicine, had to defend fat against fashion, too, and he was showing signs of strain. "In this present onslaught upon one of the most peaceful, useful and law-abiding of all our tissues," he told readers of the *Saturday Evening Post*, "fashion has apparently the backing of grave physicians, of food reformers and physical trainers, and even of great insurance companies, all chanting in unison the new commandment of fashion: 'Thou shalt be thin!' " (Hutchinson, 1926, p. 60).

Hutchinson mourned this trend, and was dismayed that young girls were ridding themselves of their roundness and plumpness of figure. He tried to understand the new view that people took toward fat: "It is an outward and visible sign of an inward and spiritual disgrace, of laziness, of self-regard," he explained in that article, but he remained unconvinced. Instead, he longed for a more cheerful period in the not-so-distant past when a little fat never hurt anyone, and he darkly warned that some physicians were deliberately underfeeding girls and young women solely for the purpose of giving them a more svelte figure. "The longed-for slender and boyish figure is becoming a menace," Hutchinson (1926, p. 60) wrote, "not only to the present, but also the future generation."

And so it would. But why did the fashion for plumpness change so dramatically during those years? What happened that caused Americans to alter their tastes,

Laura Fraser, *The Inner Corset: A Brief History of Fat in the U.S.* 597

not only to admire thinner figures for a time, but for the next
century, culminating in fin de siècle extremes of thinness, where women's magazines in the 1990s would print ads featuring gaunt models side-by-side with
photo essays on anorexia?

**❝ Why did the fashion for plumpness
change so dramatically? ❞**

Many things were happening at once, and with dizzying
speed. Foremost was a changing economy: In the late
1800s, for the first time, ample amounts of food were
available to more and more people who had to do less and
less work to eat. The agricultural economy, based on family farms and home
workshops, shifted to an industrial one. A huge influx of immigrants—many of
them genetically shorter and rounder than the earlier American settlers—fueled
the industrial machine. People moved to cities to do factory work and service
jobs, stopped growing their own food, and relied more on store-bought goods.
Large companies began to process food products, distribute them via railroads,
and use refrigeration to keep perishables fresh. Food became more accessible and
convenient to all but the poorest families. People who once had too little to eat
now had plenty, and those who had a tendency to put on weight began to do so.

**❝ Europeans had long considered
slenderness a sign of class distinction. ❞**

When it became possible for people of modest means to
become plump, being fat no longer was a sign of prestige.
Well-to-do Americans of northern European extraction
wanted to be able to distinguish themselves, physically and
racially, from stockier immigrants. As anthropologist
Margaret Mackenzie notes, the status symbols flipped: It became chic to be thin
and all too ordinary to be overweight (personal communication, June 12, 1996).

In this new environment, older cultural undercurrents suspicious of fat began to
surface. Europeans had long considered slenderness a sign of class distinction
and finer sensibilities, and Americans began to follow suit. In Europe, during
the late eighteenth and early nineteenth centuries, many artists and writers—the
poets John Keats and Percy Bysshe Shelley, and authors Emily Brontë, Edgar
Allan Poe, and Anton Chekhov—had tuberculosis, which made them sickly
thin. Members of the upper classes believed that having tuberculosis, and being
slender itself, were signs that one possessed a delicate, intellectual, and superior
nature. "For snobs and parvenus and social climbers, TB was the one index of
being genteel, delicate, [and] sensitive," writes essayist Susan Sontag in *Illness as
Metaphor* (1977, p. 28). "It was glamorous to look sickly." So interested was the
poet Lord Byron in looking as fashionably ill as the other Romantic poets that
he embarked on a series of obsessive diets, consuming only biscuits and water, or

What do you see
as the relationship
between body im-
age and social class
in the U.S.?

vinegar and potatoes, and succeeded in becoming quite thin. Byron—who, at five feet six inches tall, with a clubfoot that prevented him from walking much, weighed over two hundred pounds in his youth—disdained fat in others. "A woman," he wrote, "should never be seen eating or drinking, unless it be *lobster salad* and *champagne*, the only truly feminine and becoming viands" (quoted in Schwartz, 1986, p. 38). Aristocratic European women, thrilled with the romantic figure that Byron cut, took his diet advice and despaired of appearing fat. Aristocratic Americans, trying to imitate Europeans, adopted their enthusiasm for champagne and slenderness.

Laura Fraser, *The Inner Corset: A Brief History of Fat in the U.S.*

Americans believed that it was not only a sign of class to be thin, but also a sign of morality. There was a long tradition in American culture that suggested that indulging the body and its appetites was immoral, and that denying the flesh was a sure way to become closer to God. Puritans such as the minister Cotton Mather frequently fasted to prove their worthiness and to cleanse themselves of their sins. Benjamin Franklin, in his *Poor Richard's Almanack*, chided his readers to eat lightly not only to please God, but also a new divinity, Reason: "Wouldst thou enjoy a long life, a healthy Body, and a Vigorous Mind, and be acquainted also with the wonderful works of God? Labour in the first place to bring thy Appetite into Subjection to Reason" (Franklin, 1970, p. 238). Franklin's attitude toward food not only reveals a puritanical distrust of appetite as overly sensual, but also presaged diets that would attempt to bring eating in line with rational, scientific calculations. "The Difficulty lies, in finding out an exact Measure;" he wrote, "but eat for Necessity, not Pleasure, for Lust knows not where Necessity ends" (p. 238).

At the end of the nineteenth century, as Hutchinson observed, science was also helping to shape the new slender ideal. Physicians came to believe that they were able to arrive at an exact measure of human beings; they could count calories, weigh people on scales, calculate their "ideal" weights, and advise those who deviated from that ideal that they could change themselves. Physicians were both following and encouraging the trend for thinness. In the 1870s, after all, when plumpness was in vogue, physicians had encouraged people to *gain* weight. Two of the most distinguished doctors of the day, George Beard and S. Weir Mitchell, believed that excessive thinness caused American women to succumb to a wide variety of nervous disorders, and that a large number of fat cells was absolutely necessary to achieve a balanced personality (Banner, 1983, p. 113). But when the plump figure fell from favor, physicians found new theories to support the fashion. They hastily developed treatments—such as thyroid, arsenic, and strychnine—to prescribe to their increasing numbers of weight loss patients, many of whom were not exactly corpulent, but who were more than willing to part with their pennies along with their pounds.

As the twentieth century got underway, other cultural changes made slenderness seem desirable. When many women ventured out of their homes and away from their strict roles as mothers, they left behind the plump and reproductive physique, which began to seem old-fashioned next to a thinner, freer, more modern body. The new consumer culture encouraged the trend toward thinness with fashion illustrations and ads featuring slim models; advertisers learned early to offer women an unattainable dream of thinness and beauty to sell more products. In short, a cultural obsession with weight became firmly established in the United States when several disparate factors that favored a desire for thinness—economic status symbols, morality, medicine, modernity, changing women's roles, and consumerism—all collided at once.

Thinness is, at its heart, a peculiarly American preoccupation. Europeans admire slenderness, but without our Puritanism they have more relaxed and moderate attitudes about food, eating, and body size (the British are most like us in being heavy and fixated with weight loss schemes). In countries where people do not have quite enough to eat, and where women remain in traditional roles, plumpness is still widely admired. Other westernized countries have developed a slender ideal, but for the most part they have imported it from the United States. No other culture suffers from the same wild anxieties about weight, dieting, and exercise as we do because they do not share our history.

> **❝** *Thinness is, at its heart, a peculiarly American preoccupation.* **❞**

The thin ideal that developed in the United States from the 1880s to the 1920s was not just a momentary shift in fashion; it was a monumental turning point in the way that women's bodies were appraised by men and experienced by women. The change can be traced through the evolution of three ideal types: the plump Victorian woman, the athletic but curvaceous Gibson Girl, and the boyishly straight-bodied flapper. By 1930, American women knew how very important it was for them to be thin. From then on, despite moments when voluptuousness was admired again (e.g., Marilyn Monroe), more American women could never be too thin.

References

Banner, L. (1983). *American beauty*. Chicago, IL: University of Chicago Press. 113.

Franklin, B. (1970). *The complete Poor Richard almanacks*, Vol. 1, 1733–1747. Barre, MA: Imprint Society. 238.

Hutchinson, W. (1894, June). Fat and its follies. *Cosmopolitan*. 395.

Hutchinson, W. (1926, August 21). Fat and fashion. *The Saturday Evening Post*. 60.

Schwartz, H. (1986). *Never satisfied: A cultural history of diets, fantasies, and fat*. New York, NY: The Free Press. 38.

Sontag, S. (1977). *Illness as metaphor*. New York, NY: Farrar, Straus and Giroux. 28.

What is the relationship between body ideals and the selling of products in America?

Essay ▼

Juliet Samuel

Fat Pride World Wide: The Growing Movement for Avoirdupois Acceptance

Juliet Samuel, now a journalist for *The Times* (in the United Kingdom), wrote this essay for *Reason* magazine when she worked there as an intern. In "Fat Pride World Wide," Samuel points out that people who are overweight suffer discrimination that can have serious consequences; for example, medical professionals' prejudices against overweight people can cause them to attribute health problems to weight rather than digging deeper to find another cause. Potential adoptive parents can be told by a judge that they are "too fat" to be good parents. *(Reason artwork appears by permission of Reason.com. "Fat Pride World Wide" appears by permission of Reason magazine and Reason.com, 10/23/07.)*

HOME   REASON24/7   REASONTV   HIT & RUN   MAGAZINE   POLL   SUBSCRIBE   DONATE

Politics | Policy | Economics | Civil Liberties | Culture | Science/Tech |

Fat Pride World Wide
The growing movement for avoirdupois acceptance

Juliet Samuel

According to fat pride activist Marilyn Waan, the American medical establishment has lost its head over the nationwide "obesity epidemic," and its prejudice is claiming victims. In one case, Waan says, a doctor told a fat woman complaining of shooting lights in her vision that the problem must be her weight. Her next doctor discovered a brain tumor.

Meanwhile, the U.S. Centers for Disease Control and Prevention, along with healthcare consortium Kaiser Permanente, have found a great new way to fight childhood obesity: the Amazing Food Detective. The computer game, released last week, features ten "case files" of unhealthy children—click on each prisoner-style mug shot and you proceed to help a fat child make a healthy choice. The solution to chubby twelve-year-old Emily's dilemma is to install a security camera to catch and stop her eating at home. (After all, "Those large portions were quite suspicious!") Little Cole has to learn that he can only eat raw carrots and bananas because "Healthy snacks are the way to go!" And the game comes complete with a time-out after twenty minutes: "You should take a break and do something active, like 100 pushups!" Gee whiz—that sounds fun!

Have you ever felt judged because of your weight? If so, how did you respond?

And medical professionals are on the same bandwagon. "Our doctors have the same superstitions that everyone else has," Waan says. "They act on them in ways that are not scientific." It's not difficult to find serious grievances from fat patients. On one recently started blog, *First, Do No Harm*, a woman with Cushing's syndrome, a muscle-wasting disease that turns muscle to fat, says she was told that she just needed to go on a diet.

❝ A woman with a disease that turns muscle to fat says she was told to go on a diet. ❞

In response, fat people are mobilizing. The "fat pride" or "fat acceptance" movement might provoke the scorn of skinnies, but it is growing in number and makes a compelling case. Much of the organizing takes place online, where fat people share stories of abuse, gripe about prejudicial scientific studies, and debate the finer points of weight discrimination. Some groups, like one started by Waan, often delve directly into activism, with members urging one another to write complaints about discriminatory food advertisements or boycott insensitive organizations. Other groups are simply about offering mutual support. SeaFATtle, a group started by activist Mary McGhee, began simply as a way for fat women to swim together without fear of catcalls.

Admittedly, agitating through a fat women's swimming club might not be the best way to attract serious attention. But the claims fat pride puts forward aren't so unreasonable: The movement holds that the nation's "public health crisis" isn't really about health at all. It's about bad science and intolerance.

❝ The nation's 'public health crisis' isn't really about health at all. ❞

Listen to any public health official and you'd think obesity was a scientific slam dunk, but studies on the exact causes and effects of weight gain are highly ambiguous. One study of twenty-five thousand men by the Cooper Institute for

Aerobics Research, for example, found that a fit fatso is actually healthier than a sedentary skinny: Over an eight-year period even those technically classified as "obese" (a BMI of over 30) were less likely to die from heart attacks, strokes, and cancer than inactive people of normal weight. And many of the studies released as "proof" of America's impending death by gristle fail to take into account confounding variables, like yo-yo dieting, a sedentary lifestyle, and fat distribution on the body.

Are critics of obesity concerned only about the health of others, or is there something else going on?

But even if the science were sound, public officials and antifat crusaders still confuse bad health with moral depravity. Paul Campos, a law professor at Colorado University and author of *The Obesity Myth*, claims that this "moral panic" sticks because it finds an "ideological resonance." On the right it appeals to an ascetic attitude; on the left it taps into anxieties about capitalist overconsumption and manipulative force-feeding by corporations.

Unfortunately, the "obesity crisis" has real victims. At five hundred pounds, Gary Sticklaufer was judged too fat to make a good adoptive father to his own cousin—despite having adopted and raised several other children without problems. His cousin was forcibly taken from his care. Meanwhile, fat women are regularly told by their doctors that to become pregnant would be irresponsible, despite a lack of medical evidence demonstrating a higher risk for overweight women. And in the United Kingdom it's now commonplace to raise concerns over fat children with a view to placing them in foster care. In short, cutting a slim figure is now a moral imperative for responsible parenting, and those who refuse the "cure" to this aesthetic "disease" are summarily punished.

" In the U.K. it's commonplace to raise concerns over fat children with a view to placing them in foster care. "

The anti-obesity campaign is waging war against the very people it purports to help and, in doing so, undermines the very medical authorities it relies on to perpetuate the crisis. Fat people are tired of being patronized by politicians, mistreated by doctors, and barraged by crises and "cures." Many, like *Big Fat Blog* writer Paul McAleer, have simply concluded, "A lot of people don't like fat people." And hard as it may be to accept, many fat people don't want to be "helped" by quack dieticians, misguided doctors, and opportunist politicians. Most, in fact, just want to be left alone.

Blog Pages ▼

Paul McAleer & Carrie Padian/*Big Fat Blog*

About Big Fat Blog *& About Fat Acceptance*

▲ AUTHOR PHOTO **Paul McAleer.**
By permission of Paul McAleer.

▲ AUTHOR PHOTO **Carrie Padian.**
Courtesy of Carrie Padian.

Founded by Paul McAleer and now hosted by Carrie Padian and the Fat Rights Coalition, *Big Fat Blog* is a forum for members and guest contributors to write about size discrimination. Contributors to the blog comment on social attitudes toward obesity and argue for fat acceptance. Following are the "About *Big Fat Blog*" and "About Fat Acceptance" pages from the site. *(Big Fat Blog artwork and text appear courtesy of Carrie Padian.)*

About

Welcome to *Big Fat Blog*!

Big Fat Blog—BFB for short—was founded in August 2000 by Paul McAleer and has its roots in size discrimination research he did in college. After giving a lecture on sizism, he put his materials on the Web, but they soon grew stale. Thankfully there was this new site called Blogger, which would allow him to keep the site updated easily, and the rest is history.

Since its inception, *BFB* has had guest bloggers, coauthors, and contributors, but the majority of the content was written by Paul. In April 2009, Carrie Padian of the Fat Rights Coalition took over content creation and daily management of the site. *BFB* still focuses on the media as it did in 2000 but has expanded to support the fatosphere with an events calendar, forums, activism, and lots more.

BFB has been recognized as one of the grandparents of the fatosphere, helping in a small way to encourage others to blog about fat acceptance and fat rights. As of August 2008, the site has 2,700 registered members (though many are lurkers or inactive), and averages 65,000 unique visitors each month.

Do you think "fat rights" are civil rights? Why or why not?

BFB has been featured in many publications and corners of the media, including, but not limited to, the *San Francisco Chronicle*, *USA Today*, the *Chicago Tribune*, *The New York Times*, the Associated Press, the *Orlando Weekly*, Australia's *The Age*, the BBC, MSNBC, CNN, *Time*, *Marie Claire*, *Figure*, and Elastic Waist's *The Daily Special*.

What *BFB* Is

Big Fat Blog (BFB) is a site devoted to fat acceptance. We publicize and comment on issues that affect social justice for fat people:

- Media trends and reporting

- Medical research

- Societal issues

- Stereotypes

- Body size in history and anthropology

- Fat people's experiences in the world, both positive and negative

- Social justice and fat activism

BFB also has forums that are only accessible to members.

Whether you're just getting into fat acceptance or are a seasoned activist, a HAES-friendly professional, or an ally, we welcome your participation. We welcome people of all backgrounds, orientations, abilities, political persuasions, and so on.

What Fat Acceptance Is

Fat acceptance has two parts: the political and the personal. Politically, we seek to expose and oppose prejudice and discrimination against fat people. Personally, we accept our bodies and reject the idea that weight loss is a positive goal. We address health and fitness directly, not by using weight as a proxy for health.

> " *We seek to expose and oppose prejudice and discrimination against fat people.* "

Some of us exercise regularly and pay attention to nutrition. That's called Health at Every Size, or HAES, and it often has a bit of weight loss as a *side effect*. We do not think that deliberate weight change is safe or effective for most people.

What *BFB* Isn't

BFB isn't a dating site. We don't care if you're attracted to fat people or not. If you need medical, legal, or psychological advice, *BFB* can't provide it. *BFB* isn't an open forum; it's for people of a specific ideological persuasion. We enjoy a good debate, but we are not interested in debating whether the basic tenets of fat acceptance are valid or whether fat people who are self-accepting have a right to exist.

> " *We accept our bodies and reject the idea that weight loss is a positive goal.* "

Most *BFB* members are former weight loss dieters, weight loss pill-takers, and/or weight loss surgery survivors. *BFB* is not a place for the discussion of weight loss dieting ("diet talk"). When we do discuss deliberate weight loss, it's generally to provide a counterpoint to the common assumption that weight loss and weight loss methods are always beneficial or harmless.

Gray Areas

If you are in favor of fat acceptance but don't practice it in your own life, then we ask you not to discuss your weight loss attempts on *BFB*. As always, weight loss evangelists will be unceremoniously booted.

If you're not a fat acceptance person but want to write a guest post espousing a point of view or introducing an idea that might be interesting for us to discuss, then by all means, send it to the administrators via the contact form and we'll consider publishing it. No guarantees.

About Fat Acceptance

Ask a person what "fat acceptance" means and you're bound to get different answers. There are a few basic tenets everyone in the movement agrees upon and things vary from there. I asked *BFB* readers to define fat acceptance, and here are their answers.

Carolyn

The essence of fat acceptance, for me, is that normal, healthy people come in a variety of sizes. As a large-size person, I should be able to pursue my educational dreams, have romances, fly in airplanes, visit theme parks, go to school, change careers, be promoted . . . in other words—live! I have the same rights to life, liberty, and the pursuit of happiness as thin people. It is bigotry and prejudice to try to interfere in civil rights because someone is "too big."

Fat acceptance also involves recognizing the deceitful practices of the weight loss industry and countering them.

Fat acceptance involves accepting our friends, coworkers, and family at the size they are now. It involves recognizing the way advertising and media reports have skewed our ideas about size and health, and size and beauty—and recognizing that many of us have internalized those attitudes and ideas.

Fat acceptance is a dedication to the idea that worth is based on character, decency, dependability, and integrity. We accept ourselves, fat or not; we accept our fellow human beings, fat or not. We recognize that beauty has to do both with outer appearance and inner joy and peace. Size is a simple description of our appearance, not who we are!

What are your ideas about "health, size, and beauty"? Do you accept your own body as it is?

❝ *Normal, healthy people come in a variety of sizes.* **❞**

Yammer

Fat acceptance [is] a political, cultural, and personal advocacy movement in North America that seeks to identify, redress, and prevent discrimination against people defined as fat.

Examples of discrimination include physical inaccessibility (e.g., airplane seats unusable to the "bigger than average"), social malice (e.g., fat jokes, aesthetic barriers to employment), and medical misinformation (e.g., assumptions that all fat is pathological, or that slimming diets are effective and reasonable preconditions of treatment).

Also called size acceptance.

2DayIs4Me

I want fat people to be able to claim our full-fledged (and in no way "second class") personhood in the world. I want more than the absence of discrimination. I want fat to be a nonissue in the social and political realms, and a *neutral*—but not *ignored*—issue in the medical realm.

To me, that is more than "fat acceptance"—I don't want nonfat people to offer me mere "acceptance" (as though it were a handout of some kind). I want to be valued according to my ideas, my work, my contributions to society, my spirit, my ethics, and how I live within the human community, but *not* according to the size of my body or people's erroneous assumptions about "how it got that way."

> ❝ I don't want nonfat people to offer 'acceptance' (as though it were a handout of some kind). ❞

Micki

It's telling the truth to yourself and others: Diets don't work, you can be healthy and beautiful at any size, and you deserve love and respect.

Hojoki

Fat acceptance is the total surrender to the truth of your body.

In addition, there's a bit of debate on the term "fat acceptance" itself. Other terms you might see to describe this include "size acceptance," "fat liberation," and "fat revolution." I personally like all of these terms—the latter two go well beyond "just" acceptance and encourage a stronger, more positive image.

If you have any thoughts on what fat acceptance means to you, send them in!

Paul McAleer & Carrie Padian/*Big Fat Blog, About Big Fat Blog & About Fat Acceptance*

609

Essay

Daniel Engber

Give Me Your Tired, Your Poor, Your Big Fat Asses

▲ AUTHOR PHOTO
Daniel Engber.
Courtesy of Daniel Engber.

In "Give Me Your Tired, Your Poor, Your Big Fat Asses," first published at *Slate*, Daniel Engber discusses the complex relationship between obesity, poverty, and health. Engber notes that "poverty and obesity tend to overlap in some complicated ways." For example, because poor neighborhoods have fewer grocery stores, people in low-income areas have less access to fresh, healthy foods; they are also less likely to be able to afford a health club membership. Engber is a columnist for *Slate* and has written for other publications, including *The Washington Post* and *Discover* magazine. *(Slate artwork reprinted by permission: from* Slate, *September 28 © 2009, The Slate Group. The essay "Give Me Your Tired, Your Poor, Your Big Fat Asses" by Daniel Engber: © 2009 The Slate Group. All rights reserved. Used by permission and protected by the Copyright Laws of the United States. The printing, copying, redistribution, or retransmission of the Material without express written permission is prohibited.)*

Slate

Give Me Your Tired, Your Poor, Your Big Fat Asses ...

Does poverty make people obese, or is it the other way around?

By Daniel Engber

In my last column ("Let Them Drink Water!"), I suggested that a tax on sweetened soft drinks would move the nation toward an apartheid of pleasure in which the poor must drink from the faucet while the rich enjoy superpremium fruit juice. I also argued that the soda tax discriminates on economic grounds, since rates of soft drink consumption tend to be highest in poor, nonwhite communities. But supporters of the measure counter that these very communities would benefit most from drinking less soda and that revenue from a regressive fat tax could be spent on laudable progressive goals—like universal healthcare.

The relationship between poverty and obesity keeps turning up in the debate over healthcare reform. Among the 46 million people in America who lack medical insurance, about two-thirds earn less than twice the poverty level. Advocates for universal coverage say that we can pay for all these new patients by cutting back on obesity rates, since excess fat accounts for 9 percent of the country's spending on medical care. (During the campaign, then-Senator Obama claimed this might save the Medicare system $1 trillion.) Some even suggest that a reform package should include special taxes or higher premiums for fat people. That idea starts to seem misguided, though, when you consider that poverty and obesity tend to overlap in some complicated ways.

> ❝ *It might be more important to help poor people than fat people.* ❞

As a matter of public health, it might be more important to help poor people than fat people. According to epidemiologist Peter Muennig, the relative risk of mortality for being obese is between 1 and 2. That means that, controlling for other factors, someone who's really fat is up to twice as likely to die early as someone whose body mass index is in the normal range. But if you compare people from the top and bottom of the wage scale (with everything else held constant), the risk ratio goes up to about 3.5. In other words, it's much better for your health to be rich and fat than poor and thin.

Those in greatest need, furthermore, tend to be both poor and fat. We know, for instance, that the lower your income, the more likely you are to inhabit an "obesogenic" environment. Food options in poor neighborhoods are severely limited: It's a lot easier to find quarter waters and pork rinds on the corner than fresh fruit and vegetables. Low-income workers may also have less time to cook their own meals, less money to join sports clubs, and less opportunity to exercise outdoors.

If poverty can be fattening, so, too, can fat be impoverishing. Paul Ernsberger, a professor of nutrition at Case Western Reserve University, lays out this argument in an essay from *The Fat Studies Reader*. Women who are two standard deviations overweight (that's sixty-four pounds above normal) make 9 percent less money, which equates to having 1.5 fewer years of education or three fewer years of work experience. Obese women are also half as likely to attend college as their peers and 20 percent less likely to get married. (Marriage seems to help alleviate poverty.)

> ❝ *Obese women are half as likely to attend college as their peers.* ❞

When it comes to public health, the relationship between poverty and obesity gets more convoluted. Being fat can make you poor, and being poor can make you sick, which means that being fat can make you sick irrespective of any weight-related diseases. Fatness (or the lifestyle associated with obesity) also creates its own health problems, regardless of how much money you have—and health problems tend to make people poor, through hospital bills and missed days of work. So fat can be impoverishing irrespective of any weight-related discrimination.

The point here is that sickness, poverty, and obesity are spun together in a dense web of reciprocal causality. Anyone who's fat is more likely to be poor and sick. Anyone who's poor is more likely to be fat and sick. And anyone who's sick is more likely to be poor and fat.

Sociologists describe these patterns in terms of social gradients. The "health-wealth gradient" refers to the fact that, as a general rule, the richer you are, the healthier you are. This applies across different countries and across the full range of social classes within the same country. (It's not just that the very poorest people are sick.) No one knows exactly what causes the health-wealth gradient or why it's so resilient. It may be that rich people have access to better healthcare. Or, as we've seen, it could be that being sick costs you money. Then there's the possibility that poor people have a greater incentive to behave in unhealthy ways: Since they don't have as much money to spend on happiness, they "spend" their health instead. (The pleasures of smoking and eating, for example, are easy on the wallet and hard on the body.)

> " The richer you are, the healthier you are. "

Related to the health-wealth gradient is what we might call the "girth-wealth" gradient. In 1989, a pair of researchers named Albert Stunkard and Jeffery Sobal pored over several decades' worth of data on obesity rates and concluded that socioeconomic status and body size were inversely related among women in developed countries. A recent review by Lindsay McLaren found that the pattern of poor women being fatter than rich ones has begun to spread into the developing world. (For men, the girth-wealth gradient tends to go in the opposite direction, and the health effects of obesity are somewhat diminished.)

Both gradients appear to be deeply entrenched in modern life, and we shouldn't count on universal health coverage to erase either one. International surveys suggest that the development of free medical care—through the National Health Service in the United Kingdom, for example—doesn't much alter the fundamental relationship between health and wealth. It's also not clear that expanded health coverage is likely to make the poor any less fat. A [recent] study even suggests that the opposite might be true—a public option could end up increasing obesity rates among the newly insured.

The mere existence of these gradients does suggest that if we spread around the wealth a little better, poor people would end up healthier—and thinner—than they were before. According to British economists Richard Wilkinson and Kate Pickett, this benefit wouldn't necessarily come at the expense of the rich. Their new book, *The Spirit Level: Why Greater Equality Makes Societies Stronger*, uses data from the World Bank, the World Health Organization, and the U.S. Census to argue that disparities in income produce a wide range of social ills—like obesity, teen pregnancy, mental illness, murder, and infant mortality—that could be addressed by shrinking the gap between the haves and the have-nots. Indeed, the United Kingdom's Labor government has taken up this charge in recent years, with a series of measures to reduce inequality in the name of public health.

What do you think of "spread[ing] around the wealth," to help make the poor healthier?

The United States could try to do the same, by raising the minimum wage or increasing earned-income tax credits. In 2001, Princeton economist Angus Deaton considered the implications of a Robin Hood health policy. (His thoughtful and accessible paper on the topic is well worth reading.) Deaton concluded that a direct redistribution of wealth might be an efficient way to improve the health of the poorest Americans. But he warned that equality shouldn't be treated as an end in itself. A fancy new treatment, for example, might steepen the health-wealth gradient when it's first introduced, since only the rich can afford it. But that doesn't mean we should avoid medical breakthroughs for the sake of public health. According to Deaton, a saner approach would be to invest in education, since better schooling seems to improve your health and raise your income, too.

Do you agree with punishing measures such as the "soda tax"? Why or why not?

You don't hear anyone suggesting that better schools could pay for healthcare reform, though. Instead, we've pegged our hopes on a national weight loss regime—a redistribution of girth instead of wealth. If being poor can make you fat and vice versa, then we can't solve one health problem while ignoring the other. Yet we act as though the war on obesity can be separated out from the war on poverty: Consider the soda tax—an anti-obesity measure that shifts money away from the poor.

Why are we so fixated on body size? Another social gradient might be playing out in this policy debate: It turns out that the richer you are, the more likely you are to be on a diet. (Among fat people, more wealth correlates with lower self-esteem.) So it's only natural that we'd be hung up on the issue of obesity—we're projecting.

Food, Obesity, & Fat Advocacy

ANALYZING RHETORICAL SITUATIONS

1. List/argument. Who do you think Michael Pollan sees as his main audience for this piece? What does he want readers to think or do after reading it? Which of his food rules seem most commonsensical to you? Which seem less so? Why?

2. List/argument. How does Pollan establish his ethos in this piece? How about pathos and his use of humor? How do these strategies work in terms of his overall persuasiveness? Point to specific sentences to support your answer.

3. Essay. What connotations does the word *lard* have for you? How surprising do you find Regina Schrambling's claim that lard is actually good for you? Why?

4. Essay. According to Laura Fraser, what factors have contributed to the shift in how fat is viewed in the United States?

5. Essay. How does Juliet Samuel support the movement's claim that "the nation's 'public health crisis' isn't really about health at all. It's about bad science and intolerance"?

6. Blog pages. What mission and goals do the creators and contributors of *Big Fat Blog* lay out in their "About" page? What audience(s) is the blog aimed at? How do the readers of *Big Fat Blog* define the term "fat acceptance"?

7. Essay. Does Daniel Engber convince you that "sickness, poverty, and obesity are spun together in a dense web of reciprocal causality"? Why or why not? Explain.

8. List/argument & essay. Review Pollan's food rules. Thinking about what Engber says about the connection between poverty and obesity, how feasible do you think it would be for someone living in poverty to follow Pollan's rules?

COMPOSING IN GENRES

9. Compose a food diary. For one week, keep track of the food you eat. Record everything you consume, the nutritional value of each item (you may prefer to rate each food's nutritional value on a scale of 1–10), and the cost of each item. After a week, consider the following:

- Which of Pollan's rules did you follow? Which did you not follow? Based on your food diary, would you add other rules to Pollan's list?

- What do you spend most of your food budget on? Fruits and vegetables, whole grains, dairy products, snack foods, or other items?

- What kinds of changes could you make to increase the nutritional value of your diet?

- How much would it cost to make your diet more nutritious?

10. Compose your own (good or bad) food rules. Using Pollan's list as a model, compose your own guidelines for healthy (or unhealthy) eating. Consider creating a satire of his list and using humor. *Alternative assignment:* Apply Pollan's rules to food served at a popular chain restaurant. Some chains, such as Au Bon Pain and Starbucks, provide nutritional information for each item they serve, in their stores or on their Web sites. Research and record the ingredients of a few items served at the establishment of your choice. How well do these items correlate with Pollan's rules?

11. Research lard & compose a cost-benefit analysis. Schrambling claims that lard is better for you than shortening, but she admits that "[l]ard from the supermarket can still be pretty scary; most of it has

Food, Obesity, & Fat Advocacy

been hydrogenated to make it last longer." The alternative to supermarket lard is either paying six dollars for eight ounces or making it yourself. Research how supermarket lard is made and how much it costs. Present a comparison of the costs and benefits of supermarket lard and gourmet lard to the class.

12. Research obesity & poverty in your state. Is there a connection? Interview an economics professor (or more than one) on campus about the links between obesity and poverty. Also, visit the Centers for Disease Control's Web site (www.cdc.gov/obesity) to investigate obesity in your state. How does it compare to other states? Does the obesity rate in your state correlate to income levels? What plans, if any, are in the works for making your state healthier? Ask the professor to respond to your findings. Present this information to your class, along with maps and other data.

13. Research the fat acceptance movement & create a documentary. What is "sizeism"? Investigate how, when, where, and why people are discriminated against because of their size. What are fat acceptance activists and scholars special-izing in fat studies doing to fight discrimination? To what extent is there a movement, and what might its future direction be? What needs to change in order for there to be fat acceptance in a society obsessed with thinness? Conduct research on size discrimination and gather primary research through video interviews with activists and scholars. Create a ten-minute video aimed at a general, nonexpert audience in which you address the preceding questions and/or make an argument.

14. Analyze the usability of public spaces & write an annotated list of recommendations. Observe several different spaces on your campus, such as a student lounge, a classroom, and a professor's office. Are these spaces created to accommodate bodies of all sizes? What conclusions can you draw about your campus's fat acceptance based on these spaces? What would you do to increase the level of fat acceptance on campus? If there is a fat acceptance group on your campus, interview members for opinions on campus life from a fat acceptance point of view. Write up your findings and recommendations in a report for your school's administration.

THE BRAIN & MENTAL HEALTH

Mental health as a personal and social issue is reflected in many aspects of our culture. For example, TV ads for drugs for depression ("Depression hurts . . .") run as frequently as do car ads. In the arts and literature, we associate certain public figures with mental health issues; examples include Vincent van Gogh and Virginia Woolf, as well as Kurt Cobain, Russell Brand, and Pete Wentz. This group of readings focuses on personal experiences of manic depression (Behrman and van Gogh) and the ways in which mental health drugs are marketed (Arehart-Treichel).

Memoir ▼

Andy Behrman

From Electroboy: A Memoir of Mania

In his memoir, *Electroboy: A Memoir of Mania*, Andy Behrman tells the story of his bipolar life, traces the ways his condition affected his behavior, and details the therapies—including electroshock treatments—that he's used to keep his manic depression controlled. In the following excerpt, from an *Electroboy* chapter titled "Oz," Behrman describes what mania feels like: "blips and burps of madness," "full of excitement, color, noise, and speed," "cluttered," "psychotic," and "removed from reality." (*The following excerpt appears by permission of Electroboy.com.*)

▲ AUTHOR PHOTO
Andy Behrman.
Photo by permission of Stephen Dummit, © 2013 DummitPhotography.com.

Manic depression is about buying a dozen bottles of Heinz ketchup and all eight bottles of Windex in stock at the Food Emporium on Broadway at 4:00 AM, flying from Zurich to the Bahamas and back to Zurich in three days to balance the hot and cold weather (my "sweet and sour" theory of bipolar disorder), carrying $20,000 in $100 bills in your shoes into the country on your way back from Tokyo, and picking out the person sitting six seats away at the bar to have sex with only because he or she happens to be sitting there. It's about blips and burps of madness, moments of absolute delusion, bliss, and irrational and dangerous choices made in order to heighten pleasure and excitement and to ensure a sense of control. The symptoms of manic depression come in different strengths and sizes. Most days I need to be as manic as possible to come as close as I can to destruction, to get a real good high—a $25,000 shopping spree, a four-day drug binge, or a trip around the world. Other days a simple high from a shoplifting excursion at Duane Reade for a toothbrush or a bottle of Tylenol is enough. I'll admit it: There's a great deal of pleasure to mental illness, especially to the mania associated with manic depression. It's an emotional state similar to Oz, full of excitement, color, noise, and speed—an overload of sensory stimulation—whereas the sane state of Kansas is plain and simple, black and white, boring and flat. Mania has such a dreamlike quality that often I confuse my manic episodes with dreams I've had. . . .

It's an emotional state similar to Oz, full of excitement, color, noise, and speed.

Mania is about desperately seeking to live life at a more passionate level, taking second and sometimes third helpings on food, alcohol, drugs, sex, and money, trying to live a whole life in one day. Pure mania is as close to death as I think I have ever come. The euphoria is both pleasurable and frightening. My manic mind teems with rapidly changing ideas and needs; my head is cluttered with vibrant colors, wild images, bizarre thoughts, sharp details, secret codes, symbols, and foreign languages. I want to devour everything—parties, people, magazines, books, music, art, movies, and television. In my most psychotic stages, I imagine myself chewing on sidewalks and buildings, swallowing sunlight and clouds. . . .

To what extent do you relate to what Behrman describes?

Pure mania is as close to death as I think I have ever come.

Manic depression, or bipolar disorder, is a disease that crippled me and finally brought me to a halt, a relatively invisible disease that nobody even noticed. Its symptoms are so elusive and easy to misread that seven psychotherapists and psychiatrists misdiagnosed me. Often the manic phase is mild or pleasant and the doctor sees the patient during a down cycle, misdiagnosing the illness and prescribing the wrong medication. . . .

Manic depression for me is like having the most perfect prescription eyeglasses with which to see the world. Everything is precisely outlined. Colors are cartoonlike, and, for that matter, people are cartoon characters. Sounds are crystal clear, and life appears in front of you on an oversized movie screen. I suppose that would make me the director of my own insanity, but I can only wish for that kind of control. In truth, I am removed from reality and have no direct way to connect to it. My actions are random—based on delusional thinking, warped intuition, and animal instinct. When I'm manic, my senses are so heightened, I'm so awake and alert, that my eyelashes fluttering on the pillow sound like thunder.

Andy Behrman, From *Electroboy: A Memoir of Mania*

Journal News Article ▼

Joan Arehart-Treichel

Women's Depiction in Drug Ads: Holdover from a Bygone Era?

According to *The New York Times* "Health Guide" page on depression: "Women, regardless of nationality, race, ethnicity, or socioeconomic level, have twice the rate of depression than men. . . . While men are more likely than women to die by suicide, women are twice as likely to attempt suicide." In the following article, mental health writer Joan Arehart-Treichel reports on a study published in *The Journal of Nervous and Mental Disease* that looked at the portrayal of women and men in ads for antidepressant medications. She writes: "In spite of the expansion of women's roles over the last twenty years, ads for psychotropic drugs in scientific journals often persist in portraying women in traditional settings and roles." What might explain this portrayal? Arehart-Treichel is a senior staff writer for *Psychiatric News*, a publication of the American Psychiatric Association, where this piece first appeared. *(The Psychiatric News artwork and "Women's Depiction in Drug Ads: Holdover from a Bygone Era," by Joan Arehart-Treichel: Reprinted with permission from Psychiatric News (Copyright © 2004). American Psychiatric Association.)*

PSYCHIATRIC NEWS

From The American
Psychiatric Association

psychiatryonline   DSM Library   Books   Journals   Topics   APA Guidelines   CME & Self-Assessment   News   For Patients

Women's Depiction in Drug Ads: Holdover From a Bygone Era?

Joan Arehart-Treichel

Women in the last two decades have taken advantage of countless new options in their work and personal lives—except, it seems, in drug ads.

In spite of the expansion of women's roles over the last twenty years, ads for psychotropic drugs in scientific journals often persist in portraying women in traditional settings and roles.

A study that led to this finding was conducted by Donna Stewart, MD, chair of women's health at University Health Network and the University of Toronto in Canada, and colleagues. Results appeared in the April *Journal of Nervous and Mental Disease*.

In their study, Stewart and her colleagues examined how often women and men were portrayed in psychotropic drug ads placed in three psychiatric journals during three different time periods. The journals were *The American Journal of Psychiatry*, *The Canadian Journal of Psychiatry*, and *The British Journal of Psychiatry*. The study periods were 1981, 1991, and 2001.

> ❝ Ads for psychotropic drugs often portray women in traditional settings and roles. ❞

The proportion of women and men displayed in ads in all three journals in 1981 was about equal, the researchers found. However, the proportion of women had increased to 80 percent in *The Canadian Journal of Psychiatry* in 2001 and to 88 percent in *The American Journal of Psychiatry* in 2001. In contrast, the proportion of women portrayed in *The British Journal of Psychiatry* in 2001 had declined to 40 percent.

What ads for psychotropic drugs have you seen lately? What images are used?

Trying to impart meaning to the findings, the researchers noted that given that women are known to be more at risk of depression than men, one possibility is that more antidepressant ads are run in these two journals today than in the earlier years and that women are depicted in the ads more often because they are more likely to seek treatment for depression. In fact, the researchers learned, only women were displayed in antidepressant ads in *The American Journal of Psychiatry* in 2001. But another reason why women appear in more psychotropic drug ads in *The Canadian Journal of Psychiatry* and *The American Journal of Psychiatry* today, the researchers suspected, may be a form of gender discrimination against women.

> ❝ Another reason why women appear in more ads may be a form of gender discrimination against women. ❞

CHART This ▶
infographic appeared
with Joan Arehart-
Treichel's article.
*Graphic from: "Who
Is Portrayed in
Psychotropic Drug
Advertisements?"
Munce, Sarah E. P. BSc;
Robertson, Emma K.
PhD; Sanson, Stephanie
N. MA; Stewart, Donna
E. MD, FRCPC Journal
of Nervous and Mental
Disease: April 2004,
Volume 192, Issue 4,
pp. 284–288.*

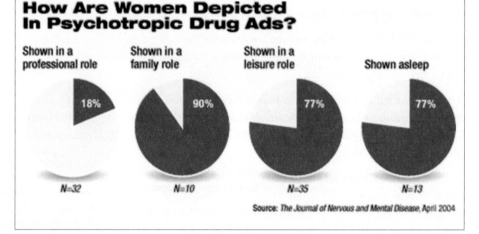

How Are Women Depicted In Psychotropic Drug Ads?

Shown in a professional role — 18% — N=32

Shown in a family role — 90% — N=10

Shown in a leisure role — 77% — N=35

Shown asleep — 77% — N=13

Source: *The Journal of Nervous and Mental Disease*, April 2004

In fact, when the researchers examined the types of roles in which women and men were cast in the ads in the three journals across the three time spans studied, they found that most of the men were portrayed at work or in professional roles, implying productivity, independence, and a higher socio-economic status, while most of the women were shown at home, in the garden, in a social situation, or asleep, implying traditional and dependent work roles.

> ❝ *Most of the men were portrayed at work or in professional roles.* ❞

"These findings," the investigators suggested, "seem to indicate that, despite the great diversification and expansion of women's roles over the last twenty years, there is a consistent tendency in pharmaceutical advertising to represent women submissively (i.e., sleeping) or even in a sexualized manner (i.e., well-dressed, slim, younger, attractive) in traditional settings and roles. . . ."

What are some potential hazards of portraying mainly women in drug ads aimed at the doctors who prescribe these drugs?

Stewart told *Psychiatric News* that she hoped clinical psychiatrists will "look beyond the images in pharmaceutical advertisements, which may not accurately reflect the images of many patients suffering from depression or psychosis—multicultural patients, men, the poor, the elderly, the disabled, and the physically unglamorous."

Letter & Painting ▼

Vincent van Gogh

"Dear Theo" & Portrait of Dr. Gachet, Seated at a Table

In May 1890, the Dutch painter Vincent van Gogh (1853–1890) went to the countryside of Auvers-sur-Oise (in France), hoping to be inspired by the landscape. Additionally, he hoped that his visit would help him with his mental illness struggles. Dr. Paul-Ferdinand Gachet, a physician and an amateur artist, treated van Gogh and recommended painting as a therapy. Following is a small sketch and the *Portrait of Dr. Gachet, Seated at a Table*, created by van Gogh in June 1890. A month later, he committed suicide (and died on July 29). Also included here are excerpts from a letter that van Gogh sent to his brother Theo on Tuesday, June 3, 1890. The letter, translated from French to English, is from the Van Gogh Museum's collection of the artist's writings. What, if anything, can art—and personal correspondence—suggest about a person's state of mind? *(The Vincent Van Gogh Museum artwork and "Dear Theo" letter written by Vincent van Gogh reprinted by permission of the Van Gogh Museum, Amsterdam.)*

▲ AUTHOR PHOTO
Vincent van Gogh (c. 1871), at around age eighteen. *J.M.W. de Louw, Vincent van Gogh op 19-jarige leeftijd, 1873 Den Haag, foto, 9.1 x 5.7 cm. Van Gogh Museum, Amsterdam (Vincent van Gogh Stichting) b4784V/1962.*

Van Gogh Museum huygens ing				Help | Quick Guide | Updates | Credits | Contact | Home	
Vincent van Gogh *The Letters*	by period	Search		Van Gogh as a letter-writer	About this edition
	by correspondent	keyword or number(s) ››		Correspondents	Chronology
	by place	Advanced search		Biographical & historical context	Concordance, lists, bibliography
	with sketches	Search results		Publication history	Book edition
877					« 876 | 878 »
To Theo van Gogh. Auvers-sur-Oise, Tuesday, 3 June 1890.					SEARCH THIS LETTER PRINT

My dear Theo,

For several days now I'd have liked to write to you with a rested mind, but have been absorbed in work. This morning your letter arrives, for which I thank you and for the 50-franc note it contained. Yes, I think that it would be good for many reasons that we were all together again here for a week of your holidays, if longer isn't possible. I often think of you, Jo, and the little one, and I see that

LETTER FACSIMILE ▼
An image of Vincent
van Gogh's June
3, 1890, letter to
his brother Theo,
featuring a sketch
of the portrait of
Dr. Gachet that he
was working on at
the time. *Reprinted
by permission of the
Van Gogh Museum
Foundation.*

the children here look well in the healthy fresh air. . . . [Y]ou'll certainly enjoy furthering your acquaintance with [Dr. Gachet], and he's already counting on it, speaks of it every time I see him, that you'll all come. He certainly appears to me as ill and confused as you or I, and he's older and a few years ago he lost his wife,[1] but he's very much a doctor, and his profession and his faith keep him going, however. We're already firm friends. . . . I'm working on his portrait, the head with a white cap, very fair, very light, the hands also in light carnation, a blue frock coat and a cobalt blue background, leaning on a red table on which are a yellow book and a foxglove plant with purple flowers.[2] It's in the same sentiment as the portrait of myself that I took when I left for here.

Mr. Gachet is absolutely *fanatical* about this portrait, and wants me to do one of him if I can, absolutely like that, which I also wish to do. He has now also come to understand the last portrait of the Arlésienne, one of which you have in pink—he comes back all the time, when he comes to see the studies, to these two

portraits and he accepts them fully, but fully as they are. I hope to send you a
portrait of him soon. . . .

I'll very probably also do the portrait of his daughter, who is 19,[3] and with
whom I can easily imagine Jo will quickly make friends.

So I'm looking forward to doing the portraits of all of you in the open air, yours,
Jo's, and the little one's.

I still haven't found anything interesting in the way of a possible studio, and yet
I'll have to take a room to put in the canvases which are surplus at your apartment and which are at Tanguy's. For they still need a great deal of retouching.
But anyway, I live from day to day—the weather is so fine. And my health is
good, I go to bed at 9 o'clock but I get up at 5 o'clock most of the time.

I have hopes that it won't be disagreeable to be together again after a long
absence. And I also hope that I'll continue to feel much surer of my brush than
before I went to Arles. And Mr. Gachet says that he would consider it highly
improbable that it should recur, and that it's going completely well. But he, too,
complains bitterly of the state of things everywhere in the villages where the least
foreigner has come, that life there becomes so horribly expensive. He says that
he's astonished that the people where I am lodge and feed me for that, and that
I'm still fortunate, compared to others who have come and whom he's known.
That if you come, and Jo and the little one, you can't do better than stay at this
same inn. Now nothing, absolutely nothing, keeps us here but Gachet—but the
latter will remain a friend, I'd assume. I feel that at his place I can do not too bad
a painting every time I go there, and he'll certainly continue to invite me to dinner each Sunday or Monday.

But up to now, however agreeable it is to do a painting there, it's a chore for me
to dine and lunch there for the excellent man goes to the trouble of making dinners in which there are 4 or 5 courses, which is as abominable for him as it is for
me, for he certainly doesn't have a strong stomach. What has held me back a little
from saying something about it is that I see that, for him, it reminds him of the
days of yore when people had family dinners, which anyway we too well know.

But the modern idea of eating one, at most two, courses is, however, certainly
progress, and a healthy return to true antiquity.

Anyway *père* Gachet is a lot, yes, a lot like you and I. I was pleased to read in
your letter that Mr. Peyron asked for news of me when he wrote to you.

How would you
characterize van
Gogh's tone and
outlook in this
letter?

Vincent van Gogh, *"Dear Theo"* & Portrait of Dr. Gachet, Seated at a Table   623

What does van
Gogh's attitude
toward his brother
seem to be? And
toward Dr. Gachet?

I'm going to write to him this very evening that things are going well, for he was very kind to me and I'll certainly not forget him. . . .

[H]is house, you will see, is full, full like an antique dealer's, of things that aren't always interesting, it's terrible, even. But in all of this there's this good aspect, that there would always be what I need there for arranging flowers or still lifes. I've done studies for him, to show him that should he not be paid in money we'll nevertheless still compensate him for what he does for us. . . .

[I] need as soon as possible 12 tubes zinc white from Tasset and 2 medium tubes geranium lake.

❝ Better still, perhaps, to seek a little
friendship and live from day to day. ❞

Then as soon as you could send them I'd be absolutely set upon copying all of Bargue's *Études au fusain* again, you know the nude figures. I can draw them quite quickly, let's say the 60 that there are in a month, so you might send a copy on loan, I'd make sure not to stain or dirty it. If I neglected to keep on studying proportions and the nude I'd find myself in a bad position later on. Don't think this absurd or futile.

Gachet also told me that if I wanted to give him great pleasure he would like me to redo for him the copy of Delacroix's *Pietà*, which he gazed at for a long time. Later he'll probably give me a hand with the models, I feel that he'll understand us completely, and that he'll work with you and me without reservation, with all his intelligence, for the love of art for art's sake. And he'll perhaps have me do some portraits. Now to have clients for portraits one must be able to show different ones that one has done. That's the only possibility I can see of placing something. But however, certain canvases will one day find collectors. Only I think that all the fuss created by the large prices paid lately for Millets & etc. has further worsened the state of things as regards the chance one has of merely recouping one's painting expenses. It's enough to make one dizzy. So why are we thinking about it, it would stupefy us. Better still, perhaps, to seek a little friendship and live from day to day. I hope that the little one will continue to be well, and you two also until we see each other again, more soon, I shake your hand firmly.

Vincent

Notes

1. Gachet was sixty-two years old. In 1868 he had married Blanche Elisa Castets, who had died on May 25, 1875, in Paris.
2. The letter sketch *Doctor Gachet* was made after the painting of the same name.
3. Marguerite Gachet was twenty years old. Van Gogh painted her portrait at the end of June (according to letter 893 in the museum's online collection).

◀ PAINTING
**Vincent van Gogh,
*Portrait of
Dr. Gachet, Seated
at a Table.*** In June
1890, van Gogh
painted this portrait,
which he described in
a letter to his brother
(pp. 621–624). Van
Gogh later wrote
of this work: "I've
done the portrait
of M. Gachet with
a melancholy
expression, which
might well seem like
a grimace to those
who see it. . . . Sad
but gentle, yet clear
and intelligent, that
is how many portraits
ought to be done." He
created two versions
of the portrait: the
one shown here, and
another that uses
more yellow and paler
tones. These were
among the last works
van Gogh painted
before his suicide.
*Reprinted by permission
of Erich Lessing/Art
Resource, NY.*

Article

Lyn Garrity

Van Gogh in Auvers

ARTS & CULTURE

Van Gogh in Auvers

The artist's tumultuous last days

By Lyn Garrity

On the evening of July 27, 1890, Vincent van Gogh stumbled back to his tiny room at the Auberge Ravoux in Auvers-sur-Oise, just north of Paris. When the innkeeper looked in on the artist, alarmed by his groans, he found van Gogh doubled over in pain from a self-inflicted gunshot wound to the chest. The innkeeper, Ravoux, summoned the village doctor and van Gogh requested that his personal doctor, Paul-Ferdinand Gachet, come as well.

> **"** The doctors concurred that it was not possible to remove the bullet. **"**

After examining the patient, the doctors concurred that it was not possible to remove the bullet. So at van Gogh's request, Gachet filled a pipe, lit it, and placed it in the artist's mouth. Van Gogh puffed quietly, while the doctor sat attentively at his side. The two had developed a warm friendship during the ten weeks van Gogh had been in Auvers.

Van Gogh's brother Theo had arranged for Gachet, who specialized in homeopathy and nervous disorders, to care for him during his recovery after van Gogh moved to Auvers on May 20, 1890, from the asylum in Saint-Rémy. The painter Camille Pissarro had recommended Gachet to Theo because of the doctor's affinity for artists. Gachet's circle of friends included Cézanne, Pissarro, and other Impressionist painters, and he avidly collected art. Gachet also enjoyed painting and engraving, signing his works with the name Paul van Ryssel.

With his red hair, Gachet also possessed an uncanny resemblance to van Gogh, which only fostered a stronger bond between the two men. Van Gogh noted to his youngest sister, Wilhelmina, "I have found a true friend in Dr. Gachet, something like another brother, so much do we resemble each other physically and also mentally."

Tempering the rapport, though, was van Gogh's observation that the "eccentric" doctor suffered from "nervous trouble" just as serious as the artist's. But despite these initial reservations, van Gogh soon began visiting Gachet's home regularly, sharing multicourse meals and painting portraits of the doctor and his daughter. One of these portraits, titled the *Portrait of Dr. Gachet*, is among van Gogh's most famous paintings and emphasizes the physician's melancholic nature more than his medical expertise. Describing the portrait to Gauguin, van Gogh wrote the doctor possessed "the heartbroken expression of our time."

> ❝ *Van Gogh wrote [that Gachet] possessed 'the heartbroken expression of our time.'* ❞

The artist's productivity soared in his new surroundings. Indeed, some catalogs have attributed some seventy works to van Gogh during his time in Auvers. As he wrote to Theo and his sister-in-law, Jo, he found Auvers to be "profoundly beautiful, it is the real country, characteristic and picturesque."

But by July, intimations of trouble crept into his correspondence and canvases. Describing in a letter to Theo several scenes of wheat fields "under troubled skies" that he had recently painted, van Gogh commented that it didn't take much effort "to express sadness and extreme loneliness." Some of his anxiety might have been fed by recent news that Theo, who financially supported him, was experiencing problems with his employers and thinking about leaving to start his own business. The situation must have exacerbated van Gogh's growing feelings of distress.

What are some differences between how van Gogh presented himself in his letter to Theo and how he is presented in this article?

Although it is not exactly clear why van Gogh chose to end his life, his intention to do so in that Auvers wheat field was unmistakable. While Gachet attended to his wounded friend, the doctor expressed his wish to save him.

> ❝ *It is not exactly clear why van Gogh chose to end his life.* ❞

Lyn Garrity, *Van Gogh in Auvers*   627

> **"** *His intention to do so in that Auvers wheat field was unmistakable.* **"**

"Then it has to be done all over again," replied van Gogh. At some point during the two days that van Gogh lay dying, Gachet sketched his prostrate friend.

Theo heard the news the next day and rushed to Auvers to be by his brother's side. Comforted by Theo's presence, van Gogh told his brother, "I wish I could pass away like this." They were among his last words. He died on July 29 at 1:30 AM.

A small group of friends and family attended his funeral, abundant with sunflowers. Among the mourners was Gachet, who spoke a few words. "He was an honest man . . . and a great artist," Gachet eulogized. "He had only two goals, humanity and art."

The Brain & Mental Health

ANALYZING RHETORICAL SITUATIONS

1. Memoir. What is Andy Behrman's main message? What is most striking to you about his description of his manic depression?

2. Memoir. Does Behrman come across as a reliable narrator to the reader? Why or why not? Explain.

3. Journal news article. According to Joan Arehart-Treichel, what are some of the possible reasons that so many drug advertisements are aimed at women? What is the impact of leaving other groups out of such advertising?

4. Letter & painting. Describe the tone of Vincent van Gogh's letter to his brother. What is your impression of his state of mind? How does knowing that van Gogh suffered from mental illness affect your interpretation of the portrait of Dr. Gachet? Explain.

5. Memoir & journal news article. How would Behrman's message be changed if he had presented his experience as a journal news article for a medical audience, as Arehart-Treichel did, rather than as a personal memoir? Consider especially how medical information is conveyed in the two pieces.

6. Memoir & painting. Compare Behrman's memoir and van Gogh's painting. What ideas and feelings do they each evoke? How are they similar and dissimilar? To what extent do these pieces make emotional appeals to the reader/viewer? How do the different artistic mediums function to convey mood?

The Brain & Mental Health

7. Research bipolar disorder. Locate two or three first-person accounts of bipolar disorder. Write an essay that compares and contrasts the accounts. Alternatively, interview friends or peers with manic depression. How do their experiences compare with each other? With Behrman's experience?

8. Write a film review. Watch a fictional movie or a documentary that depicts someone diagnosed as bipolar. Some films you might consider are *Michael Clayton*, *Mad Love*, *Mr. Jones*, *Pollock*, and *Sylvia*. Characterize the filmmaker's portrayal of mental illness. What strikes you most about the protagonist's experience?

9. Create a timeline of treatments for bipolar disorder. Research the various treatments for bipolar disorder over the past twenty-five years and create a timeline that illustrates the treatments. How has treatment evolved? What still needs work? What is planned for the future?

10. Investigate the portrayal of women in drug ads. The study mentioned in Arehart-Treichel's article finds that women are portrayed in stereotypical ways in ads for psychotropic drugs. Research and gather several ads for drugs in which women are depicted. Write an essay in which you take a position regarding how women are portrayed in these ads. Alternatively, research ads for drugs that show men and/or people of color. What is your take on how the drug company views the audience for the ads?

11. Create a parody drug ad. Find several advertisements for prescription drugs in magazines, and then create a parody of a prescription drug ad (perhaps an *Onion*-style ad; see theonion.com).

12. Research artists with mental illness. What other artists (past and present) have been diagnosed with symptoms of mental illness similar to van Gogh's? Create a list of those artists and then create a bibliography of sources used in your research. What characterizes the experiences of these artists? How did their illnesses affect their art and lives? What medical treatment, if any, did they receive, and how successful were the treatments? Use the bibliography as the basis for a longer project or a researched essay that focuses on a few of these artists.

RESEARCH EXPERIMENTS: The Body

1. **Create a marketing campaign for a grocery store.** Imagine you work for a marketing firm or ad agency hired by a local grocery store or chain to attract a new group of shoppers. Perhaps the store is Whole Foods and you've been asked to draw in shoppers who do not fall into a high-income bracket (e.g., "Whole Foods: You Don't Need to Drop Your Whole Paycheck"). Or maybe the store is a local Asian market with a mostly local Asian clientele, and the owners want to expand their customer base by attracting students and senior citizens from other neighborhoods.

   a. To begin your project, **choose a real grocery store**. Then, **visit that grocery** store at least three times.

   b. **Observe and take detailed notes** about the following:

   - Who are the shoppers? Who aren't the shoppers? Who could/should be shopping here but isn't?

   - What products and services does the store offer?

   - How much of an emphasis is there on organic foods? On locally grown foods? On other specific qualities?

   - How big is the store? How much space is allocated to different types of products? Are there lots of choices? Or are there limited but selective choices?

   - From a shopper's point of view, what are the main strengths of the store? What makes it special? What could it do better?

   - How are products and sales advertised in the store, and whom does the advertising seem to be aimed at?

   - How do customers get to the store? (What transportation is nearby?) What are the parking options?

   c. Next, review the notes you've compiled. **Decide what group of potential shoppers you will target** with your marketing. **Consider these questions:** How will you entice them to shop at the store? What are the needs and values of this group? How can you (and the store itself) appeal to their needs and values?

   d. Then take this information and create the pieces of your marketing campaign. Your ultimate goal is to sell your campaign in a presentation to your class (who will pose as your peers at the marketing firm or ad agency and/or as owners of the grocery store who hired your firm). **Create at least three different pieces for your campaign**, perhaps a series of print ads, storyboards for television ads, scripts for radio ads, slogans for bumper stickers or billboards, or YouTube videos. Your final presentation to your class should include the following:

- A description of your target group

- Your specific goal and message

- A rationale for the marketing campaign (including the needs and wants of the target group)

- A presentation of the pieces of the marketing campaign that you created

2. **Create an illustrated timeline for a controlled substance.** Begin by researching advertisements past and present for a particular controlled substance, such as a prescription drug, cigarettes, or alcohol. How has the substance/product been advertised over time?

a. Research and create the timeline:

- **Identify and print out** as many images of ads as you can find online, keeping careful track of the original dates of each. Make sure your ads represent a wide time span, from the nineteenth century to the present if possible.

- **Choose four or five** of the most interesting ads, again keeping in mind the desired time range.

- **Research the historical, political, and cultural events** that were taking place as your substance/product was advertised.

- **Create a timeline** that incorporates the ads with corresponding historical, political, and cultural events you have identified.

b. Analyze:

- **Look for ways that history, politics, and culture affected your product's ad campaign.** For example, do ads from the Great Depression reflect the nation's economic desperation in any way? Are women depicted differently in ads after the Pill (that is, birth control pills) became available? Are certain social or ethnic groups represented in new or different ways?

- **Write an essay** to accompany your timeline. Be sure to write about each ad and each point in your timeline. **Analyze** how history, politics, and culture impacted the way your product was advertised over time. Alternatively, you can write analytical annotations to accompany your timeline.

13   THE ENVIRONMENT

CONTENTS

For e-Pages content, visit **bedfordstmartins.com/bookofgenres**.

OBJECT/AD **Surfrider Foundation,** ▶ "Catch of the Day: Plastic Surprise." *By permission of Saatchi & Saatchi LA.*

What are your top ten concerns about the environment? Climate change, energy, water, biodiversity, chemicals, oil spills, air pollution, waste management, ozone layer depletion, damage to oceans and fisheries, and deforestation are listed as the top ten environmental concerns in Daniel C. Esty and Andrew S. Winston's book *Green to Gold: How Smart Companies Use Environmental Strategy to Innovate, Create Value, and Build Competitive Advantage.*

Our planet is changing because of our environmental practices. The earth's temperature is going up, sea levels are rising, and atmospheric CO_2 is expanding. A visit to the Environmental Protection Agency (EPA) Web site shows how deforestation and rising greenhouse gases (the result of burning coal and oil) are contributing to our planet's woes. Ice caps are melting, glaciers are retreating, and the migratory patterns of animals and insects are being disrupted. Further, the World Health Organization warns that global climate change causes highly infectious diseases such as malaria and dengue fever to spread more quickly. Consider also that climate change creates droughts, floods, and extreme weather that kill people, crops, and animals.

But perhaps we can fix this by "Going Green"? This chapter begins with a set of readings focused on ethics and the climate crisis. Al Gore lays out a number of inconvenient truths, while Alex Williams ("Buying into the Green Movement") looks at the ethics of buying eco-products, that is, consuming more in the name of the environment. Three journalists at *Wired* magazine offer "10 Green Heresies," a set of controversial fixes that takes on "ten sacred cows" of environmentalism.

In a cluster titled "Corporate Greening," Anna Lenzer exposes the business practices of Fiji Water, a company that offers a less-than-shining example of environmental (and local) friendliness ("Spin the Bottle"), and Jen Quraishi, a blogger for *Mother Jones*, examines the corporate misdeeds of several popular brands of bottled water ("H2Uh-Oh"). Eric Hagerman refutes corporate claims in his *Wired* article Little Green Lies."

In "Pollution & Activism," a cluster presented in the e-Pages, President Obama lays out a plan for dealing with the 2010 BP oil spill, and Leyla Kokmen of *Utne Reader* reports on the disproportionate impact of pollution on people of color and citizens living in poverty, and on a growing movement to change that ("Environmental Justice for All"). A billboard created by the Environmental Defense Fund and placed in New York City highlights the pollution caused by traffic congestion. Finally, a Credo Action letter advocates a ban on fracking.

Readings in the e-Pages cluster "Plastics, Recycling, & Wildlife" explore the impact of pollution on animals. Even though things look grim for Flipper and his ocean pals (see the Surfrider Foundation's "Catch of the Day: Plastic Surprise" and Oceana's "Love Flipper and His Friends?"), there is hope. A waste management company explains an efficient recycling program ("Zero-Sort" brochure) and the Environmental Protection Agency, through a comic and infographic, shows how to keep plastics out of the ocean and paper out of our landfills.

Closing this chapter is a group of readings that look at the relationship between food and the environment. How does what we eat—and how we produce and distribute what we eat—impact our bodies and our planet? Writer Jonathan Safran Foer argues strongly against eating meat, *Food & Wine* reporter Christine Lennon examines why some vegetarians are choosing to eat meat, and James E. McWilliams of *Forbes* magazine debunks what he calls "the locavore myth."

STARTER PROJECTS: The Environment

1. **The environment & your concerns: Make a list.** List your top ten environmental worries. Which items appear at the top of your list? Which items might you be able to do something about individually? Which items on your list need government involvement?

2. **The environment & food: Brainstorm local options.** Think about the food you regularly buy at the supermarket. Which foods that you purchase are grown or produced locally? Which ones travel here from other continents? Are there ways you might be able to eat more local foods?

3. **The environment & personal choices: Take an inventory.** What changes, if any, have you made in your daily life to take the environment into account? For example, some people wrap gifts in newspaper comics instead of in wrapping paper; others ride their bikes to work instead of driving. How hard was it to make these changes? Which ones became habits that you don't even have to think about anymore? Are there some changes you've made that never became habits?

GOING GREEN: ETHICS & CRISIS

It is commonplace to think about the environmental impact of our actions, at least in a cursory sense. We regularly use terms such as *carbon footprint, environmentally responsible,* and *low emissions.* However, scientists and world leaders don't always agree on the best course of action to take. This cluster examines some of the ethical questions raised by our responses to the climate crisis: Is "green" shopping really good for the environment (Williams)? What are the moral issues surrounding global climate change (Gore)? And what are some possible—even unconventional—solutions to the climate crisis (Power, Reiss, and Pearlstein)?

Editorial ▼

Alex Williams

Buying into the Green Movement

In the following editorial, *New York Times* reporter and feature writer Alex Williams questions the "easy fix" of a green economy. But is the "greening" of consumerism 100 percent positive? And what about the global impact of consuming, let alone consuming more? We talk about "greening" our homes, our workplaces, and our shopping habits, but what is green? And what is, as Alex Williams would ask, merely "light green"?

AUTHOR PHOTO ▶
Alex Williams.
Courtesy of Alex Williams.

Here's one popular vision for saving the planet: Roll out from under the sumptuous hemp-fiber sheets on your bed in the morning and pull on a pair of $245 organic cotton Levi's and an Armani biodegradable knit shirt.

Stroll from the bedroom in your eco-McMansion, with its photovoltaic solar panels, into the kitchen remodeled with reclaimed lumber. Enter the three-car garage lighted by energy-sipping fluorescent bulbs and slip behind the wheel of your $104,000 Lexus hybrid.

> **❝** *That vision of an eco-sensitive life as a series of choices about what to buy appeals to millions . . . and arguably defines the current environmental movement as equal parts concern for the earth and for making a stylish statement.* **❞**

Drive to the airport, where you settle in for an 8,000-mile flight—careful to buy carbon offsets beforehand—and spend a week driving golf balls made from compacted fish food at an eco-resort in the Maldives.

That vision of an eco-sensitive life as a series of choices about what to buy appeals to millions of consumers and arguably defines the current environmental movement as equal parts concern for the earth and for making a stylish statement.

Some thirty-five million Americans regularly buy products that claim to be earth friendly, according to one report, everything from organic beeswax lipstick from the west Zambian rain forest to Toyota Priuses. With baby steps, more and more shoppers browse among the 60,000 products available under Home Depot's new Eco Options program.

> **❝** *Some thirty-five million Americans regularly buy products that claim to be earth friendly.* **❞**

Such choices are rendered fashionable as celebrities worried about global warming appear on the cover of *Vanity Fair*'s "green issue," and pop stars like Kelly Clarkson and Lenny Kravitz headline Live Earth concerts at sites around the world.

Consumers have embraced living green, and for the most part the mainstream green movement has embraced green consumerism. But even at this moment of high visibility and impact for environmental activists, a splinter wing of the movement has begun to critique what it sometimes calls "light greens."

Critics question the notion that we can avert global warming by buying so-called earth-friendly products, from clothing and cars to homes and vacations, when the cumulative effect of our consumption remains enormous and hazardous.

"There is a very common mind-set right now which holds that all that we're going to need to do to avert the large-scale planetary catastrophes upon us is make slightly different shopping decisions," said Alex Steffen, the executive editor of Worldchanging.com, a Web site devoted to sustainability issues.

> **❝** *The genuine solution is to significantly reduce one's consumption of goods and resources.* **❞**

The genuine solution, he and other critics say, is to significantly reduce one's consumption of goods and resources. It's not enough to build a vacation home of recycled lumber; the real way to reduce one's carbon footprint is to only own one home.

Buying a hybrid car won't help if it's the aforementioned Lexus, the luxury LS 600h L model, which gets 22 miles to the gallon on the highway; the Toyota Yaris ($11,000) gets 40 highway miles a gallon with a standard gasoline engine.

It's as though the millions of people whom environmentalists have successfully prodded to be concerned about climate change are experiencing a SnackWell's moment: Confronted with a box of fat-free devil's food chocolate cookies, which seem deliciously guilt-free, they consume the entire box, avoiding any fats but loading up on calories.

The issue of green shopping is highlighting a division in the environmental movement: "the old-school environmentalism of self-abnegation versus this camp of buying your way into heaven," said Chip Giller, the founder of *Grist.org*, an online environmental blog that claims a monthly readership of eight hundred thousand. "Over even the last couple of months, there is more concern growing within the traditional camp about the *Cosmo*-izing of the green movement—'55 great ways to look eco-sexy,'" he said. "Among traditional greens, there is concern that too much of the population thinks there's an easy way out."

The criticisms have appeared quietly in some environmental publications and on the Web.

George Black, an editor and a columnist at *OnEarth*, a quarterly journal of the Natural Resources Defense Council, recently summed up the explosion of high-style green consumer items and articles of the sort that proclaim "green is the new black," that is, a fashion trend, as "eco-narcissism."

> **❝** *'Green consumerism is an oxymoronic phrase.'* **❞**

Paul Hawken, an author and longtime environmental activist, said the current boom in earth-friendly products offers a false promise. "Green consumerism is an oxymoronic phrase," he said. He blamed the news media and marketers for turning environmentalism into fashion and distracting from serious issues.

"We turn toward the consumption part because that's where the money is," Mr. Hawken said. "We tend not to look at the 'less' part. So you get these anomalies like 10,000-foot 'green' homes being built by a hedge fund manager in Aspen. Or 'green' fashion shows. Fashion is the deliberate inculcation of obsolescence."

He added: "The fruit at Whole Foods in winter, flown in from Chile on a 747—it's a complete joke. The idea that we should have raspberries in January, it doesn't matter if they're organic. It's diabolically stupid."

Environmentalists say some products marketed as green may pump more carbon into the atmosphere than choosing something more modest, or simply nothing at all. Along those lines, a company called PlayEngine sells a nineteen-inch wide-screen LCD set whose "sustainable bamboo" case is represented as an earth-friendly alternative to plastic.

But it may be better to keep your old cathode-tube set instead, according to *The Live Earth Global Warming Survival Handbook*, because older sets use less power than plasma or LCD screens. (Televisions account for about 4 percent of energy consumption in the United States, the handbook says.)

"The assumption that by buying anything, whether green or not, we're solving the problem is a misperception," said Michael Ableman, an environmental author and longtime organic farmer. "Consuming is a significant part of the problem to begin with. Maybe the solution is instead of buying five pairs of organic cotton jeans, buy one pair of regular jeans."

For the most part, the critiques of green consumption have come from individual activists, not from mainstream environmental groups like the Sierra Club, Greenpeace, and the Rainforest Action Network. *Sierra*, the magazine of the Sierra Club, has [published] articles hailing an "eco-friendly mall" featuring sustainable clothing (under development in Chicago) and credit cards that rack up carbon offsets for every purchase, as well as sustainably harvested caviar and the celebrity-friendly Tango electric sports car (a top-of-the-line model is $108,000).

One reason mainstream groups may be wary of criticizing Americans' consumption is that before the latest era of green chic, these large organizations endured years in which their warnings about climate change were scarcely heard.

Much of the public had turned away from the Carter-era environmental message of sacrifice, which included turning down the thermostat, driving smaller cars, and carrying a cloth "Save-a-Tree" tote to the supermarket.

How does Alex Williams support his argument about consumption and the environment? Which voices and evidence stand out most to you? Why?

Now that environmentalism is high profile, thanks in part to the success of *An Inconvenient Truth*, the 2006 documentary featuring Al Gore, mainstream greens, for the most part, say that buying products promoted as eco-friendly is a good first step.

"After you buy the compact fluorescent bulbs," said Michael Brune, the executive director of the Rainforest Action Network, "you can move on to greater goals like banding together politically to shut down coal-fired power plants."

John Passacantando, the executive director of Greenpeace USA, argued that green consumerism has been a way for Wal-Mart shoppers to get over the old stereotypes of environmentalists as "tree-hugging hippies" and contribute in their own way.

This is crucial, he said, given the widespread nature of the global warming challenge. "You need Wal-Mart and Joe Six-Pack and mayors and taxi drivers," he said. "You need participation on a wide front."

It is not just ecology activists with one foot in the 1970s, though, who have taken issue with the consumerist personality of the "light green" movement. Anticonsumerist fervor burns hotly among some activists who came of age under the influence of noisy, disruptive antiglobalization protests.

In 2006, a San Francisco group called the Compact made headlines with a vow to live the entire year without buying anything but bare essentials like medicine and food. A year in, the original ten "mostly" made it, said Rachel Kesel, twenty-six, a founder. The movement claims some 8,300 adherents throughout the country and in places as distant as Singapore and Iceland.

"The more that I'm engaged in this, the more annoyed I get with things like 'shop against climate change' and these kind of attitudes," said Ms. Kesel, who continues her shopping strike and counts a new pair of running shoes—she's a dog walker by trade—as among her limited purchases in eighteen months.

"It's hysterical," she said. "You're telling people to consume more in order to reduce impact."

For some, the very debate over how much difference they should try to make in their own lives is a distraction. They despair of individual consumers being responsible for saving the earth from climate change and want to see action from political leaders around the world.

Individual consumers may choose more fuel-efficient cars, but a far greater effect may be felt when fuel-efficiency standards are raised for all of the industry, as the

Senate voted to do on June 21, 2007, the first significant rise in mileage standards in more than two decades.

"A legitimate beef that people have with green consumerism is, at the end of the day, the things causing climate change are more caused by politics and the economy than individual behavior," said Michel Gelobter, a former professor of environmental policy at Rutgers who is now president of Redefining Progress, a nonprofit policy group that promotes sustainable living.

"A lot of what we need to do doesn't have to do with what you put in your shopping basket," he said. "It has to do with mass transit, housing density. It has to do with the war and subsidies for the coal and fossil fuel industry."

In fact, those light-green environmentalists who chose not to lecture about sacrifice and promote the trendiness of eco-sensitive products may be on to something.

Michael Shellenberger, a partner at American Environics, a market research firm in Oakland, California, said that his company ran a series of focus groups in April for the environmental group Earthjustice, and was surprised by the results.

People considered their trip down the Eco Options aisles at Home Depot a beginning, not an end point.

"We didn't find that people felt that their consumption gave them a pass, so to speak," Mr. Shellenberger said. "They knew what they were doing wasn't going to deal with the problems, and these little consumer things won't add up. But they do it as a practice of mindfulness. They didn't see it as antithetical to political action. Folks who were engaged in these green practices were actually becoming more committed to more transformative political action on global warming."

Correction: July 8, 2007. An article last Sunday about eco-friendly consumerism misstated the number of products sold through the Home Depot Eco Options program. It is 2,500—not 60,000, which was the number originally submitted by the store's suppliers for inclusion in the program.

Argument ▼

Al Gore

From An Inconvenient Truth

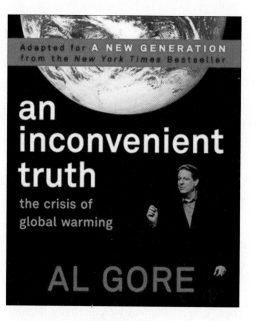

Following is an excerpt from *An Inconvenient Truth*, a book by
former vice president and Nobel Prize recipient Al Gore. The book
was the basis for Gore's Academy Award–winning documentary
of the same title. Both the book and the documentary have helped
raise awareness about environmental concerns, especially those related to global warming. Gore has studied global climate change for
several decades and is author of several books on the environment
and globalization, including *Earth in the Balance* and *The Future:
Six Drivers of Global Change. (The following excerpt from* An Inconvenient
Truth: *Copyright © 2006 by Al Gore. Permission granted by Rodale, Inc., Emmaus,
PA 18098.)*

After more than thirty years as a student of the climate crisis, I have a lot to share. I have tried to tell this story in a way that will interest all kinds of readers. My hope is that those who read the book and see the film will begin to feel, as I have for a long time, that global warming is not just about science and that it is not just a political issue. It is really a moral issue.

> **"** *Global warming is really a moral issue.* **"**

Although it is true that politics at times must play a crucial role in solving this problem, this is the kind of challenge that ought to completely transcend partisanship. So whether you are a Democrat or a Republican, whether you voted for me or not, I very much hope that you will sense that my goal is to share with you both my passion for the Earth and my deep sense of concern for its fate. It is impossible to feel one without the other when you know all the facts.

I also want to convey my strong feeling that what we are facing is not just a cause for alarm, it is paradoxically also a cause for hope. The Chinese expression for "crisis" consists of two characters side by side: 危机. The first is the symbol for "danger," the second the symbol for "opportunity."

The climate crisis is, indeed, extremely dangerous. In fact it is a true planetary emergency. Two thousand scientists, in a hundred countries, working for more than twenty years in the most elaborate and well-organized scientific collaboration in the history of humankind, have forged an exceptionally strong consensus that all the nations on Earth must work together to solve the crisis of global warming.

The voluminous evidence now strongly suggests that unless we act boldly and quickly to deal with the underlying causes of global warming, our world will undergo a string of terrible catastrophes, including more and stronger storms like Hurricane Katrina, in both the Atlantic and the Pacific.

We are melting the North Polar ice cap and virtually all of the mountain glaciers in the world. We are destabilizing the massive mound of ice on Greenland and the equally enormous mass of ice propped up on top of islands in west Antarctica, threatening a worldwide increase in sea levels of as much as twenty feet.

The list of what is now endangered due to global warming also includes the stable configuration of ocean and wind currents that has been in place since before the first cities were built almost ten thousand years ago.

Al Gore, *From* An Inconvenient Truth

We are dumping so much CO_2 into the environment that we have literally changed the relationship between the Earth and the sun. So much of that CO_2 is being absorbed into the oceans that if we continue at the current rate we will increase the saturation of calcium carbonate to levels that will prevent formation of corals and interfere with the making of shells by any sea creature.

> ❝ *It is not an asteroid colliding with the Earth and wreaking havoc; it is us.* ❞

Global warming, along with the cutting and burning of forests and other critical habitats, is causing the loss of living species at a level comparable to the extinction event that wiped out the dinosaurs sixty-five million years ago. That event was believed to have been caused by a giant asteroid. This time it is not an asteroid colliding with the Earth and wreaking havoc; it is us.

Last year, the national academies of science in the eleven most influential nations came together to jointly call on every nation to "acknowledge that the threat of climate change is clear and increasing" and declare that the "scientific understanding of climate change is now sufficiently clear to justify nations taking prompt action."

So the message is unmistakably clear. This crisis means "danger!"

Why do our leaders seem not to hear such a clear warning? Is it simply that it is inconvenient for them to hear the truth?

If the truth is unwelcome, it may seem easier just to ignore it. But we know from bitter experience that the consequences of doing so can be dire.

For example, when we were first warned that the levees were about to break in New Orleans because of Hurricane Katrina, those warnings were ignored. Later, a bipartisan group of members of Congress chaired by Rep. Tom Davis (R-VA) said in an official report, "The White House failed to act on the massive amounts of information at its disposal," and that a "blinding lack of situational awareness and disjointed decision making needlessly compounded and prolonged Katrina's horror."

Today, we are hearing and seeing dire warnings of the worst potential catastrophe in the history of human civilization: a global climate crisis that is deepening and rapidly becoming more dangerous than anything we have ever faced.

And yet these clear warnings are also being met with a "blinding lack of situational awareness"—in this case, by the Congress, as well as the president.

As Martin Luther King Jr. said in a speech not long before his assassination: "We are now faced with the fact, my friends, that tomorrow is today. We are confronted with the fierce urgency of now. In this unfolding conundrum of life and history, there is such a thing as being too late."

But along with the danger we face from global warming, this crisis also brings unprecedented opportunities.

What are the opportunities such a crisis offers? They include not just new jobs and new profits, though there will be plenty of both. We can build clean engines; we can harness the sun and the wind; we can stop wasting energy; we can use our planet's plentiful coal resources without heating the planet.

The procrastinators and deniers would have us believe this will be expensive. But in recent years, dozens of companies have cut emissions of heat-trapping gases while saving money. Some of the world's largest companies are moving aggressively to capture the enormous economic opportunities offered by a clean energy future.

But there's something even more precious to be gained if we do the right thing.

The climate crisis also offers us the chance to experience what very few generations in history have had the privilege of knowing: *a generational mission*; the exhilaration of a compelling *moral purpose*; a shared and unifying *cause*; the thrill of being forced by circumstances to put aside the pettiness and conflict that so often stifle the restless human need for transcendence; *the opportunity to rise*.

When we do rise, it will fill our spirits and bind us together. Those who are now suffocating in cynicism and despair will be able to breathe freely. Those who are now suffering from a loss of meaning in their lives will find hope.

When we rise, we will experience an epiphany as we discover that this crisis is not really about politics at all. It is a moral and spiritual challenge. At stake are the survival of our civilization and the habitability of the Earth.

The understanding we will gain—about who we really are—will give us the moral capacity to take on other related challenges that are also desperately in need of being redefined as moral imperatives with practical solutions: HIV/AIDS and other pandemics that are ravaging so many; global poverty; the ongoing redistribution of wealth globally from the poor to the wealthy; the ongoing genocide

How does Al Gore use rhetorical appeals (ethos, logos, and pathos) to make his case about climate change? How does this impact your experience as a reader?

in Darfur; the ongoing famine in Niger and elsewhere; chronic civil wars; the destruction of ocean fisheries; families that don't function; communities that don't commune; the erosion of democracy in America; and the refeudalization of the public forum.

Consider what happened during the crisis of global fascism. At first, even the truth about Hitler was inconvenient. Many in the West hoped the danger would simply go away. They ignored clear warnings and compromised with evil, and waited, hoping for the best.

After the appeasement at Munich, Churchill said: "This is only the first sip, the first foretaste of a bitter cup which will be proffered to us year by year—unless by supreme recovery of moral health and martial vigor, we rise again and take our stand for freedom."

But when England and then America and our allies ultimately rose to meet the threat, together we won two wars simultaneously in Europe and the Pacific.

By the end of that terrible war, we had gained the moral authority and vision to create the Marshall Plan—and convinced taxpayers to pay for it! We had gained the spiritual capacity and wisdom to rebuild Japan and Europe and launch the renewal of the very nations we had just defeated in war, in the process laying the foundation for fifty years of peace and prosperity.

This too is a moral moment, a crossroads. This is not ultimately about any scientific discussion or political dialogue. It is about who we are as human beings. It is about our capacity to transcend our own limitations, to rise to this new occasion. To see with our hearts, as well as our heads, the response that is now called for. This is a moral, ethical, and spiritual challenge.

We should not fear this challenge. We should welcome it. We must not wait. In the words of Dr. King, "Tomorrow is today."

I [had] an experience seventeen years ago that, for me, stopped time.* During that painful period I gained an ability I hadn't had before to feel the preciousness of our connection to our children and the solemnity of our obligation to safeguard their future and protect the Earth we are bequeathing to them.

---

*In 1989, the Gores' six-year-old son, Albert, was hit by a car. Gore has said of the experience: "Our lives were consumed with the struggle to restore [Albert's] body and spirit." —Eds.

Imagine with me now that once again, time has stopped—for all of us—and before it starts again, we have the chance to use our moral imaginations and to project ourselves across the expanse of time, seventeen years into the future, and share a brief conversation with our children and grandchildren as they are living in the year 2023.

Will they feel bitterness toward us because we failed in our obligation to care for the Earth that is their home and ours? Will the Earth have been irreversibly scarred by us?

Imagine now that they are asking us: "What were you thinking? Didn't you care about our future? Were you really so self-absorbed that you couldn't—or wouldn't—stop the destruction of Earth's environment?"

What would our answer be?

We can answer their questions now by our actions, not merely with our promises. In the process, we can choose a future for which our children will thank us.

Brief Arguments ▼

Matt Power, Spencer Reiss, & Joanna Pearlstein

Inconvenient Truths: 10 Green Heresies

The following readings are from *Wired*, a magazine that reports on technology's effects on culture, the economy, and the environment. Three writers collaborated on the article: Matt Power, an environmental reporter; Spencer Reiss, a contributing editor at *Wired* and former foreign correspondent for *Newsweek*; and Joanna Pearlstein, *Wired*'s research editor. These ten brief arguments present some surprising suggestions for dealing with the problem of global warming. *(Wired artwork and "Inconvenient Truths: 10 Green Heresies": Copyright © 2013 Condé Nast. Matt Power, Spencer Reiss, Joanna Pearlstein. All rights reserved. Originally published in Wired Magazine. Reprinted by permission.)*

GEAR SCIENCE ENTERTAINMENT BUSINESS SECURITY DESIGN OPINION VIDEO

SCIENCE : PLANET EARTH

Inconvenient Truths: Get Ready to Rethink What It Means to Be Green

By Matt Power Spencer Reiss Joanna Pearlstein

The environmental movement has never been short on noble goals. Preserving wild spaces, cleaning up the oceans, protecting watersheds, neutralizing acid rain, saving endangered species—all laudable. But today, one ecological problem outweighs all others: global warming. Restoring the Everglades, protecting the Headwaters redwoods, or saving the Illinois mud turtle won't matter if climate change plunges the planet into chaos. It's high time for greens to unite around the urgent need to reduce emissions of greenhouse gases.

Just one problem. Winning the war on global warming requires slaughtering some of environmentalism's sacred cows. We can afford to ignore neither the carbon-free electricity supplied by nuclear energy nor the transformational potential of genetic engineering. We need to take advantage of the energy efficiencies offered by urban density. We must accept that the world's fastest-growing economies won't forgo a higher standard of living in the name of climate science—and that, on the way up, countries like India and China might actually help devise the solutions the planet so desperately needs.

Some will reject this approach as dangerously single-minded: The environment is threatened on many fronts, and all of them need attention. So argues Alex Steffen.[*] That may be true, but global warming threatens to overwhelm any progress made on other issues. The planet is already heating up, and the point of no return may be only decades away. So combating greenhouse gases must be our top priority, even if that means embracing the unthinkable. Here, then, are ten tenets of the new environmental apostasy.

10 Green Heresies

1. **Live in cities.** Urban living is kinder to the planet than the suburban lifestyle.

2. **A/C is okay.** Air conditioning actually emits less CO_2 than heating.

3. **Organics are not the answer.** Surprise! Conventional agriculture can be easier on the planet.

4. **Farm the forests.** Old-growth forests can actually contribute to global warming.

5. **China is the solution.** The People's Republic leads the way in alternative-energy hardware.

6. **Accept genetic engineering.** Superefficient Frankencrops could put a real dent in greenhouse gas emissions.

7. **Carbon trading doesn't work.** Carbon credits were a great idea, but the benefits are illusory.

8. **Embrace nuclear power.** Face it. Nukes are the most climate-friendly industrial-scale form of energy.

9. **Buy used cars—not hybrids.** Don't buy that new Prius! Test-drive a used car instead.

10. **Prepare for the worst.** Climate change is inevitable. Get used to it.

---

[*]Alex Steffen is an environmental journalist and author. He is cofounder of the media organization Worldchanging.com. —Eds.

Matt Power, Spencer Reiss, & Joanna Pearlstein, *Inconvenient Truths: 10 Green Heresies*

10 GREEN HERESIES

1. Live in cities. Urban living is kinder to the planet than the suburban lifestyle.

To many Americans, ecological nirvana is a bucolic existence surrounded by wilderness. But the Thoreauvian desire for more elbow room has led to sprawl, malls, and cougar attacks. The edge-city upshot is a national cadre of 3.5 million "extreme commuters," who spend more than three hours a day in transit, many of them spewing CO_2 between exurb home and city office. Automobile exhaust in the United States contributes roughly 1.9 billion tons a year to the global carbon cloud, more than the emissions of India, Japan, or Russia. Even worse are the 40 million lawn mowers used to tame the suburban backcountry: Each spews eleven cars' worth of pollutants per hour.

> " *Manhattan is perhaps the greenest place in the United States.* "

The fact is, urban living is kinder to the planet, and Manhattan is perhaps the greenest place in the United States. A Manhattanite's carbon footprint is 30 percent smaller than the average American's. The rate of car ownership is among the lowest in the country; 65 percent of the population walks, bikes, or rides mass transit to work. Large apartment buildings are the most efficient dwellings to heat and cool.

And guess what high-speed means of transportation emits less atmospheric carbon than trains, planes, and automobiles? The humble counterweight elevator put into service in 1857, which has made vertical density possible from Dubai to Taipei.

2. A/C is okay. Air conditioning actually emits less CO_2 than heating.

As a symbol of American profligacy, the air conditioner may rank second only to the automobile. Energy-sucking A/C props up an unsustainable lifestyle in scorching desert cities like Phoenix, while the cheerful New Englander splitting wood and tending his potbelly stove is the epitome of ecological harmony—so goes the green cant. But this stereotype gets it wrong. When it's 0 degrees outside, you've got to raise the indoor thermometer to 70 degrees. In 110-degree weather, you need to change the temperature by only 40 degrees to achieve the same comfort level. Since air conditioning is inherently more efficient than heating (that is, it takes less energy to cool a given space by 1 degree than to heat it by the same amount), the difference has big implications for greenhouse gases.

In the Northeast, a typical house heated by fuel oil emits 13,000 pounds of CO_2 annually. Cooling a similar dwelling in Phoenix produces only 900 pounds of CO_2 a year. Air conditioning wins on a national scale as well. Salving the summer swelter in the United States produces 110 million metric tons of CO_2 annually. Heating the country releases nearly eight times more carbon over the same period. Meanwhile, chilly northeasterners can at least take heart in one thing: With global warming you can turn the heat down.

3. Organics are not the answer. Surprise! Conventional agriculture can be easier on the planet.

The path to virtue, we all know, begins with organics. Meat, milk, fruit, veggies—organic products are good for our bodies and good for the planet. Except when they're not good for the planet. Because while there may be sound health reasons to avoid eating pesticide-laden food, and perhaps personal arguments for favoring the organic-farmers' collective, the truth is that when it comes to greenhouse gases, organics can be part of the problem.

Take milk. Dairy cows raised on organic feed aren't pumped full of hormones. That means they produce less milk per Holstein—about 8 percent less than conventionally raised cattle. So it takes twenty-five organic cows to make as much milk as twenty-three industrial ones. More cows, more cow emissions. But that's just the beginning. A single organically raised cow puts out 16 percent more greenhouse gases than its counterpart. That double whammy—more cows and more emissions per cow—makes organic dairies a cog in the global warming machine.

How about that burger? Organic beef steers take longer to achieve slaughter weight, which gives them more time to emit polluting methane. And if you're eating hamburgers made from grass-fed cattle, don't award yourself any prizes just yet. While pastured beef offers some environmental benefit—these cows don't require carbon-intensive corn for feed, and the land they graze stores carbon more efficiently than land used for crops or left alone—they're burping up nearly twice as much methane as cattle fed grain diets, according to the UN's Food and Agriculture Organization. If you really want to adopt a climate-friendly diet, cut out meat entirely. Researchers at the University of Chicago showed that the meat-intensive diet of the average American generates 1.5 more tons of greenhouse gases per year than the diet of a vegetarian.

> **❝** *If you really want to adopt a climate-friendly diet, cut out meat entirely.* **❞**

But even organic fruits and veggies are a mixed bushel: Organic fertilizers deliver lower-than-average yields, so those crops require more land per unit of food. And then there's the misplaced romanticism. Organic isn't just Farmer John; it's Big Ag. Plenty of pesticide-free foods are produced by industrial-scale farms and then shipped thousands of miles to their final destination. The result: refrigerator trucks belching CO_2. Organic produce can be good for the climate, but not if it's grown in energy-dependent hothouses and travels long distances to get to your fridge. What matters is eating food that's locally grown and in season. So skip the prewashed bag of organic greens trucked from two time zones away—the real virtue may come from that conventionally farmed head of lettuce grown in the next county.

4. Farm the forest. Old-growth forests can actually contribute to global warming.

Ronald Reagan's infamous claim that "trees cause more pollution than automobiles" contained a grain of truth. In warm weather, trees release volatile chemicals that act as catalysts for smog. But the Gipper didn't mention another point that's even more likely to make nature lovers blanch. When it comes to fighting climate change, it's more effective to treat forests like crops than like majestic monuments to nature.

Over its lifetime, a tree shifts from being a vacuum cleaner for atmospheric carbon to an emitter. A tree absorbs roughly 1,500 pounds of CO_2 in its first fifty-five years. After that, its growth slows, and it takes in less carbon. Left untouched, it ultimately rots or burns and all that CO_2 gets released.

Last year, the Canadian government commissioned a study to determine the quantity of carbon sequestered by the country's woodlands, which account for a tenth of global forests. It hoped to use the CO_2-gathering power of 583 million acres of woods to offset its Kyoto Protocol–mandated responsibility to cut greenhouse gas emissions. No such luck. The report found that during many years, Canadian forests actually give up more carbon from decomposing wood than they lock down in new growth.

A well-managed tree farm acts like a factory for sucking CO_2 out of the atmosphere, so the most climate-friendly policy is to continually cut down trees and plant new ones. Lots of them. A few simple steps: Clear the oldest trees and then take out dead trunks and branches to prevent fires; landfill the scrap. Plant seedlings and harvest them as soon as their powers of carbon sequestration begin to flag, and use the wood to produce only high-quality durable goods like furniture and houses. It won't make a glossy photo for the Sierra Club's annual report, but it will take huge amounts of carbon out of the atmosphere.

5. China is the solution. The People's Republic leads the way in alternative-energy hardware.

Pop quiz: Who's the volume dealer in alternative-energy hardware? If you said choking, smoking, coal-toking China, give yourself a carbon credit.

Consider solar cells, the least carbon-intensive option after nuclear, wind, and biomass, according to an analysis by the International Atomic Energy Agency. In 2007, photovoltaic factories in the People's Republic tripled production, grabbing 35 percent of the global market and making China the world's number one producer. How about rechargeable lithium-ion batteries, critical for superefficient electric vehicles? Chinese manufacturers will soon rule that world, too. Windmills? "Prepare for the onslaught of relatively inexpensive Chinese turbines," says Steve Sawyer, head of the Global Wind Energy Council. His forecast: China will produce enough gear to generate 10 gigawatts of power annually.

China has three big reasons for jumping feet first into the carbon fight. Obviously, there's the threat of climate change—flooding in China's coastal cities, drought in the country's interior. Second, there's political instability: Air and water pollution is already a flash point for public protests. And then there's the burgeoning export market for green products stamped "made in China."

Will renovating the planet spur the first wave of homegrown Chinese tech innovation? Jeff Immelt, CEO of General Electric, thinks so. "China has as much or more at stake than anyone," he said at a recent corporate summit. "Solar energy, carbon sequestration—we're going to be blown away by China's progress over the next couple of decades."

6. Accept genetic engineering. Superefficient Frankencrops could put a real dent in greenhouse gas emissions.

Keeping six billion people fed boosts global warming more than all the world's cars, trucks, trains, ships, and planes put together. Agriculture accounts for almost 14 percent of greenhouse gas emissions worldwide, according to the

> **❝** *Agriculture accounts for almost 14 percent of greenhouse gas emissions worldwide.* **❞**

latest report from the Intergovernmental Panel on Climate Change. One response is to eat fewer of the two- and four-legged greenhouse gas factories known as animals. Before you send back that T-bone, though, call in the bioengineers.

Genomics experts have been optimizing food crops for decades, punching in traits for lower herbicide use, less tilling, and higher yields—carbon cutters, all. But the fountainhead of agricultural emissions is nitrogen-based fertilizer, whose manufacture (mainly from natural gas) and poor take-up rates add up to nearly one-third of agriculture's contribution to global warming. Monsanto, DuPont, and Syngenta, along with a flotilla of venture-backed start-ups, are trying to change that. California-based Arcadia Biosciences is already peddling genes for nitrogen-efficient rice that the company reckons could save the equivalent of 50 million tons of CO_2 a year. Arcadia's CEO, a lifelong Sierra Club member, is working to get carbon credits for Chinese farmers who make the switch.

What some greens deride as Frankencrops are also the only serious hope for biofuels. Right now, their net carbon benefit is negligible. Corn engineered for high yields and low fertilizer will help, but even better will be plants under development whose stalks and leaves can easily be turned into fuel.

The plunging cost of gene synthesis should help bio geeks deliver on another big promise: a new economy in which biochemical reactions replace industrial processes. J. Craig Venter's Synthetic Genomics is working with BP on microorganisms that produce cleaner alternatives to gasoline. Rival Amyris Biotechnologies is working on bugs that make jet fuel. Meanwhile, the genetic engineers are cooking up climate-friendly meat without feet: The first symposium on lab-grown animal flesh met in Norway in April [2008].

7. Carbon trading doesn't work. Carbon credits were a great idea, but the benefits are illusory.

What a cool idea: Instead of reducing our own carbon emissions, we'll pay other people to reduce theirs. Win-win!

Not so fast. Carbon offsets—and emissions-trading schemes, their industrial-scale sibling—are the environmental version of subprime mortgages. They both started from some admirable premises. Developing countries like China and India need to be recruited into the fight against greenhouse gases. And markets are a better mechanism for change than command and control. But when those big ideas collide with the real world, the result is hand waving at best, outright scams at worst. Moreover, they give the illusion that something constructive is being done.

A few fun facts: All the so-called clean development mechanisms authorized by the Kyoto Protocol, designed to keep 175 million tons of CO_2 out of the atmosphere by 2012, will slow the rise of carbon emissions by . . . 6.5 days. (That's according to Roger Pielke at the University of Colorado.) Depressed yet? Kyoto also forces companies in developed countries to pay China for destroying HFC-23 gas, even though Western manufacturers have been scrubbing this industrial byproduct for years without compensation. And where's the guarantee that the tree planted in Bolivia to offset ten dollars' worth of air travel, for instance, won't be chopped down long before it absorbs the requisite carbon?

Nationally managed emissions-trading schemes could do a better job than Kyoto's we-are-the-world approach by adding legal enforcement and serious oversight. But many economists favor a simpler way: a tax on fossil fuels. A carbon tax would eliminate three classes of parasites that have evolved to fill niches created by the global climate protocol: cynical marketers intent on greenwashing, blinkered bureaucrats shoveling indulgences to powerful incumbents, and deal-happy Wall Streeters looking for a shiny new billion-dollar trading toy. Back to the drawing board, please.

8. Embrace nuclear power. Face it. Nukes are the most climate-friendly industrial-scale form of energy.

Look at the environmental protection agency's CO_2-per-kilowatt-hour map of the United States and two bright patches of low-carbon happiness jump out. One is the hydro-powered Pacific Northwest. The other is Vermont, where a thirty-year-old nuclear reactor, Vermont Yankee, keeps the Ben & Jerry's cold. The darkest area corresponds to Washington, D.C., where coal-fired power plants release 520 times more atmospheric carbon per megawatt-hour than their Vermont counterpart. That's right: 520 times. Jimmy Carter was right to turn down the heat in the White House.

There's no question that nuclear power is the most climate-friendly industrial-scale energy source. You can worry about radioactive waste or proliferating weapons. You can complain about the high cost of construction and decommissioning. But the reality is that every serious effort

> How persuasive do you find the authors' ten arguments? Are some more or less persuasive than others? Which ones, and why?

> " *Electric power generates 26% of the world's greenhouse gas emissions.* "

Matt Power, Spencer Reiss, & Joanna Pearlstein, *Inconvenient Truths: 10 Green Heresies*

at carbon accounting reaches the same conclusion: Nukes win. Only wind comes close—and that's when it's blowing. A U.K. government white paper factored in everything from uranium mining to plant decommissioning and determined that nuclear power emits 2 to 6 percent of the carbon per kilowatt-hour that is emitted by natural gas, the cleanest of the fossil fuels.

Embracing the atom is key to winning the war on warming: Electric power generates 26 percent of the world's greenhouse gas emissions and 39 percent of the United States'—it's the biggest contributor to global warming. One of the Kyoto Protocol's worst features is a sop to greens that denies carbon credits to power-starved developing countries that build nukes—thereby ensuring they'll continue to depend on filthy coal.

9. Buy used cars—not hybrids. Don't buy that new Prius! Test-drive a used car instead.

In 2006, an Oregon market research firm released an incendiary 500-page report. Its claim: A Humvee (13 miles per gallon city, 16 highway) uses less energy than a Prius (48 city, 45 highway). Scientists quickly debunked the study, but the Hummer lovers got one thing right. Pound for pound, making a Prius contributes more carbon to the atmosphere than making a Hummer, largely due to the environmental cost of the thirty pounds of nickel in the hybrid's battery. Of course, the hybrid quickly erases that carbon deficit on the road, thanks to its vastly superior fuel economy.

Still, the comparison suggests a more sensible question. If a new Prius were placed head-to-head with a used car, would the Prius win? Don't bet on it. Making a Prius consumes 113 million BTUs, according to sustainability engineer Pablo Päster. A single gallon of gas contains about 113,000 BTUs, so Toyota's green wonder guzzles the equivalent of 1,000 gallons before it clocks its first mile. A used car, on the other hand, starts with a significant advantage: The first owner has already paid off its carbon debt. Buy a decade-old Toyota Tercel, which gets a respectable 35 mpg, and the Prius will have to drive 100,000 miles to catch up.

Better yet, buy a three-cylinder, 49-horsepower 1994 Geo Metro XFi, one of the most fuel-efficient cars ever built. It gets the same average mileage as a 2008 Prius, so a new hybrid would never close the carbon gap. Sure, the XFi has no A/C or airbags—but nobody said saving the planet would be comfortable, or even safe.

10. Prepare for the worst. Climate change is inevitable. Get used to it.

The awful truth is that some amount of climate change is a foregone conclusion. The Electric Power Research Institute in Palo Alto, California, calculates that even if the United States, Europe, and Japan turned off every power plant and mothballed every car today, atmospheric CO_2 would still climb from the current 380 parts per million to a perilous 450 ppm by 2070, thanks to contributions from China and India. (Do nothing and we'll get there by 2040.) In short, we're already at least lightly browned toast. It's time to think about adapting to a warmer planet.

This notion is one of the great green taboos: Climate change is a specter to be fought, not accommodated. Still, our ability to cope with global warming is far greater than our chances of stopping it entirely. Technology lets us build carbon-neutral houses seven thousand feet up in the Colorado Rockies. Monsanto and friends are engineering crops to withstand drought. For the hapless birds and bees, wildlife scientists are plotting what they call assisted migrations.

Still nervous? Then consider an even bigger taboo: geo-engineering. Invasive surgery on a planetary scale is getting attention from serious scientists, including Nobel Prize–winner Paul Crutzen and National Academy of Sciences president Ralph Cicerone. Proposals include everything from costly, low-risk efforts (lofting a giant mirror into orbit) to cheap desperation moves (adulterating the stratosphere with reflective dust).

We're in charge here. Let's get to work.

In his 1992 best seller, *Earth in the Balance*, Al Gore derided adaptation as "a kind of laziness, an arrogant faith in our ability to react in time to save our own skin." Better to take Stewart Brand's advice from the opening page of the original *Whole Earth Catalog*: "We are as gods and might as well get good at it." We're in charge here. Let's get to work.

Going Green: Ethics & Crisis

ANALYZING RHETORICAL SITUATIONS

1. Editorial. What are Alex Williams's main points? How does he back up each point? Does he convince you, overall? Why or why not?

2. Editorial. Look at the context in which Williams mentions carbon offsets. What is his attitude toward them? How can you tell?

3. Argument. Al Gore argues that global warming presents both danger and opportunity. What support does he offer for this argument?

4. Argument. How do Gore's references to Martin Luther King Jr., fascism, and Hurricane Katrina function in the excerpt from *An Inconvenient Truth*?

5. Brief arguments. How convincing do you find the ten arguments made by *Wired* coauthors Matt Power,

Spencer Reiss, and Joanna Pearlstein? Do they present enough evidence to support their claims? Are particular claims better supported than others? Explain. How do they use ethos, logos, and pathos to appeal to their readers?

6. Editorial, argument, & brief arguments. Consider the readings in this cluster together—in conversation with each other. Does Gore's idea that climate change is both a danger and an opportunity strike you differently after reading Williams's *New York Times* editorial about green consuming? How about after reading the arguments made by the *Wired* authors?

COMPOSING IN GENRES

7. Argue about buying green. Many editorials spark responses from readers. Write two responses to Williams's editorial: one that reflects concerns similar to his and one that reflects concerns different from his.

8. Research carbon offsets. The purchase of carbon offsets is a controversial way to "go green." Research carbon offsets and decide whether you think they ultimately help or hurt the environment. Present your conclusions to your class in an oral presentation.

9. Create a top 10 list. Reread the *Wired* authors' "10 Green Heresies" and rewrite that list as a David Letterman–style top 10 list. Keep in mind that Letterman's list items are short and usually ironic, playful, or humorous in some way.

10. Fact-check claims about global warming. Locate recent editorials on climate change. Consider

editorials written by people who deny or downplay global warming, such as Pete du Pont, for example. Identify the claims the writer makes in the editorial— then find sources to corroborate or refute the claims.

11. Research scholarly studies of global warming. Reflect on the issues raised in this cluster and come up with a list of research questions. For example, how is being green connected with consumerism? Or how does buying and wearing green clothing help the environment? Take at least three of the questions and compile a bibliography of scholarly articles that explore the questions. You might begin with *Environmental Communication: A Journal of Nature and Culture*; the journal *Environment, Development and Sustainability*; or the journal *Environmental Ethics*.

CORPORATE GREENING

With the growing trend toward the "greening" of industry, many manufacturers highlight positive environmental aspects of their products to appeal to environmentally conscious consumers. Bottled water producers claim to rescue us from the dangers of tap water, energy companies and car manufacturers proclaim they are working to reduce pollutants, and businesses advertise ways they are reducing their paper consumption. Corporations, through their marketing materials, often emphasize the ways they "help" the environment, but often omit facts about the pollution they contribute. Meanwhile, journalists and advertising watchdogs monitor companies' eco-claims, exposing those that are not true. The authors of the selections in this cluster provide us with a reality check for some of the claims made by various companies (Hagerman), especially the bottled water industry (Lenzer and Quraishi).

Brief Article

Eric Hagerman

Little Green Lies

Eric Hagerman is an editor for *This Old House* magazine and a freelance writer whose work has appeared in *Popular Science*, *Outside* magazine, and *Wired*, where "Little Green Lies" first appeared. In the following reading, Hagerman debunks some of the slogans companies use to position their products as environmentally friendly, asking, for example: "How does selling more H_2O in a bottle made of recycled plastic qualify as doing 'a lot of good'?" *(Wired artwork and "Little Green Lies": Copyright © 2013 Condé Nast. Eric Hagerman. All rights reserved. Originally published in* Wired Magazine. *Reprinted by permission.)*

▲ AUTHOR PHOTO **Eric Hagerman.**
By permission of Christelle Laprade.

WIRED

Subscribe

GEAR SCIENCE ENTERTAINMENT BUSINESS SECURITY DESIGN OPINION VIDEO

TECH BIZ : MEDIA

Little Green Lies—How Companies Erect an Eco-Facade

By Eric Hagerman

Company: **Comcast**

Product: **The Ecobill**

Slogan: **"PaperLESSisMORE"**

Reality check: Sparing trees is nice, but we suspect the cable behemoth's practice of carpet bombing potential customers with direct-marketing brochures—often after they've already signed up—might offset the benefits. Can't Comcast just spam people? After all, it works for those environmentally minded v1agr@ sellers.

Company: **Poland Spring**

Product: **The Eco-Shape bottle**

Slogan: **"A little natural does a lot of good."**

Reality check: How does selling more H_2O in a bottle made of recycled plastic qualify as doing "a lot of good"? Eight out of ten empties are landfilled anyway, and producing and shipping the 31.8 billion liters of water sold in the United States every year requires 17 million barrels of oil. Tap water, anyone?

Company: **Airbus Corporation**

Product: **The Airbus A380**

Slogan: **"A better environment inside and out."**

Reality check: Reducing the carbon footprint per passenger by hauling more of them at a time makes sense. But unless the aviation industry switches to some magic new fuel, it will be spewing 1.4 billion tons of CO_2 into the atmosphere per year by 2025. That's gotta make Mother Nature cry, inside and out.

Hagerman implies that we need to take companies' claims of "going green" with a grain of salt. What concerns might you have the next time you hear of a company "going green"?

Researched Essay ▼

Anna Lenzer

Spin the Bottle

Anna Lenzer is the coauthor of *Grand Illusion: The Untold Story of Rudy Giuliani and 9/11*. In "Spin the Bottle," Lenzer asks how a bottled water imported from a far-off military dictatorship became the epitome of cool. One way, she finds, is through crafty marketing that promotes a certain bottled water as eco-friendly and pure— another is through careful product placement. If environmentally minded public figures drink it, it's got to be okay, right? Ask the people of Fiji. *(Mother Jones artwork and "Fiji Water: Spin the Bottle": Reprinted with permission of* Mother Jones.*)*

▲ AUTHOR PHOTO
Anna Lenzer.
Reprinted with permission of Mother Jones.

Fiji Water: Spin the Bottle

*By **Anna Lenzer***

The Internet café in the Fijian capital, Suva, was usually open all night long. Dimly lit, with rows of sleek, modern terminals, the place was packed at all hours with teenage boys playing boisterous rounds of video games. But one day soon after I arrived, the staff told me they now had to shut down by 5:00 PM. Police orders, they shrugged: The country's military junta had declared martial law a few days before, and things were a bit tense.

I sat down and sent out a few e-mails—filling friends in on my visit to the Fiji Water bottling plant, forwarding a story about foreign journalists being kicked off the island. Then my connection died. "It will just be a few minutes," one of the clerks said.

Moments later, a pair of police officers walked in. They headed for a woman at another terminal; I turned to my screen to compose a note about how cops were even showing up in the Internet cafés. Then I saw them coming toward me. "We're going to take you in for questioning about the e-mails you've been writing," they said.

What followed, in a windowless room at the main police station, felt like a bad cop movie. "Who are you really?" the bespectacled inspector wearing a khaki uniform and a smug grin asked me over and over, as if my passport, press credentials, and stacks of notes about Fiji Water weren't sufficient clues to my identity. (My iPod, he surmised tensely, was "good for transmitting information.") I asked him to call my editors, even a UN official who could vouch for me. "Shut up!" he snapped. He rifled through my bags, read my notebooks and e-mails. "I'd hate to see a young lady like you go into a jail full of men," he averred, smiling grimly. "You know what happened to women during the 2000 coup, don't you?"

Eventually, it dawned on me that his concern wasn't just with my potentially seditious e-mails; he was worried that my reporting would taint the Fiji Water brand. "Who do you work for, another water company? It would be good to come here and try to take away Fiji Water's business, wouldn't it?" Then he switched tacks and offered to protect me—from other Fijian officials, who he said would soon be after me—by letting me go so I could leave the country. I walked out into the muggy morning, hid in a stairwell, and called a Fijian friend. Within minutes, a U.S. Embassy van was speeding toward me on the seawall.

Until that day, I hadn't fully appreciated the paranoia of Fiji's military regime. The junta had been declared unconstitutional the previous week by the country's second-highest court; in response it had abolished the judiciary, banned unauthorized public gatherings, delayed elections until 2014, and clamped down on the media. (Only the "journalism of hope" is now permitted.) The prime minister, Commodore Frank Bainimarama, promised to root out corruption and bring democracy to a country that has seen four coups in the past twenty-five years.

The slogan on Fiji Water's Web site—"And remember this—we saved you a trip to Fiji"—suddenly felt like a dark joke. Every day, more soldiers showed up on the streets. When I called the courthouse, not a single official would give me his name. Even tour guides were running scared—one told me that one of his colleagues had been picked up and beaten for talking politics with tourists. When I later asked Fiji Water spokesman Rob Six what the company thought of all this, he said the policy was not to comment on the government "unless something really affects us."

The Audacity of Branding

If you drink bottled water, you've probably drunk Fiji. Or wanted to. Even though it's shipped from the opposite end of the globe, even though it retails for nearly three times as much as your basic supermarket water, Fiji is now America's leading imported water, beating out Evian. It has spent millions pushing not only the seemingly life-changing properties of the product itself, but also the company's green cred and its charity work. Put all that together in an iconic bottle emblazoned with a cheerful hibiscus, and everybody, [including] the Obamas, is seen sipping Fiji.

That's by design. Ever since a Canadian mining and real estate mogul named David Gilmour launched Fiji Water in 1995, the company has positioned itself squarely at the nexus of pop-culture glamour and progressive politics. Fiji Water's chief marketing whiz and co-owner (with her husband, Stewart) is Lynda Resnick, a well-known liberal donor who casually name-drops her friends Arianna Huffington and Laurie David. ("Of course I know everyone in the world," Resnick told the U.K.'s *Observer*, "every mogul, every movie star.") Manhattan's trendy Carlyle hotel pours only Fiji Water in its dog bowls, and the SXSW music festival [has] featured a Fiji Water Detox Spa. "Each piece of lobster sashimi," celebrity chef Nobu Matsuhisa [once] declared, "should be dipped into Fiji Water seven to ten times."

Drinking Buds

Even as bottled water has come under attack as the embodiment of waste, Fiji seems immune. Fiji Water took out a full-page ad in *Vanity Fair*'s green issue, nestled among stories about the death of the world's water.

Nowhere in Fiji Water's glossy marketing materials will you find reference to the typhoid outbreaks that plague Fijians because of the island's faulty water supplies; the corporate entities that Fiji Water has—despite the owners' talk of financial transparency—set up in tax havens like the Cayman Islands and

Luxembourg; or the fact that its signature bottle is made from Chinese plastic in a diesel-fueled plant and hauled thousands of miles to its eco-conscious consumers. And, of course, you won't find mention of the military junta for which Fiji Water is a major source of global recognition and legitimacy. (Gilmour has described the square bottles as "little ambassadors" for the poverty-stricken nation.)

"We are Fiji," declare Fiji Water posters across the island, and the slogan is almost eerily accurate: The reality of Fiji, the country, has been eclipsed by the glistening brand of Fiji, the water.

On the map, Fiji looks as if someone dropped a fistful of confetti on the ocean. The country is made up of more than three hundred islands (one hundred inhabited) that have provided the setting for everything from *The Blue Lagoon* to *Survivor* to *Cast Away*. Suva is a bustling multicultural hub with a mix of shopping centers, colonial buildings, and curry houses; some 40 percent of the population is of Indian ancestry, descendants of indentured sugarcane workers brought in by the British in the mid-nineteenth century. (The Indian-descended and native communities have been wrangling for power ever since.) The primary industries are tourism and sugar. Fiji Water says its operations make up about 20 percent of exports and 3 percent of GDP, which stands at $3,900 per capita.

Getting to the Fiji Water factory requires a bone-jarring four-hour trek into the volcanic foothills of the Yaqara Valley. My bus's speakers blasted an earsplitting soundtrack of Fijian reggae, Bob Marley, Tupac, and Big Daddy Kane as we swerved up unpaved mountain roads linked by rickety wooden bridges. Cow pastures ringed by palm trees gave way to villages of corrugated-metal shacks and wooden homes painted in Technicolor hues. Chickens scurried past stands selling cell phone minutes. Sugarcane stalks burning in the fields sent a sweet smoke curling into the air.

Our last rest stop, half an hour from the bottling plant, was Rakiraki, a small town with a square of dusty shops and a marketplace advertising "Coffin Box for Sale—Cheapest in Town." My *Lonely Planet* guide warned that Rakiraki water "has been deemed unfit for human consumption," and groceries were stocked with Fiji Water going for ninety cents a pint—almost as much as it costs in the United States.

Rakiraki has experienced the full range of Fiji's water problems—crumbling pipes, a lack of adequate wells, dysfunctional or flooded water treatment plants, and droughts that are expected to get worse with climate change. Half the country has at times relied on emergency water supplies, with rations as low as four gallons a week per family; dirty water has led to outbreaks of typhoid and parasitic infections. Patients have reportedly had to cart their own water to hospitals, and schoolchildren complain about their pipes spewing shells, leaves, and frogs. Some Fijians have taken to smashing open fire hydrants and bribing water truck drivers for a regular supply.

> **"** Half the country has at times relied on emergency water supplies. Dirty water has led to outbreaks of typhoid and parasitic infections. **"**

The bus dropped me off at a deserted intersection, where a weather-beaten sign warning off would-be trespassers in English, Fijian, and Hindi rattled in the tropical wind. Once I reached the plant, the bucolic quiet gave way to the hum of machinery spitting out some fifty thousand square bottles (made on the spot with plastic imported from China) per hour. The production process spreads across two factory floors, blowing, filling, capping, labeling, and shrink-wrapping twenty-four hours a day, five days a week.

From here, the bottles are shipped to the four corners of the globe; the company—which, unlike most of its competitors, offers detailed carbon-footprint estimates on its Web site—insists that they travel on ships that would be making the trip anyway, and that the Fiji payload only causes them to use 2 percent more fuel. In 2007, Fiji Water announced that it planned to go carbon negative by offsetting 120 percent of emissions via conservation and energy projects starting in 2008. It has also promised to reduce its pre-offset carbon footprint by 25 percent and to use 50 percent renewable energy, in part by installing a windmill at the plant.

The offsetting effort has been the centerpiece of Fiji Water's $5 million "Fiji Green" marketing blitz, which brazenly urges consumers to drink imported water to fight climate change. The Fiji Green Web site claims that because of the 120 percent carbon offset, buying a big bottle of Fiji Water creates the same carbon reduction as walking five blocks instead of driving. Former Senior VP of Sustainable Growth Thomas Mooney noted in a *Huffington Post* blog post that "we'd be happy if anyone chose to drink nothing but Fiji Water as a means to keep the sea levels down." (Metaphorically speaking, anyway: As the online trade journal *ClimateBiz* has reported, Fiji is using a "forward crediting" model under which it takes credit now for carbon reductions that will actually happen over a few decades.)

Fiji Water has also vowed to use at least 20 percent less packaging—which shouldn't be too difficult, given its bottle's above-average heft. The company says the square shape makes Fiji Water more efficient in transport, and, hey, it looks great: Back in 2000, a top official told a trade magazine, "What Fiji Water's done is go out there with a package that clearly looks like it's worth more money, and we've gotten people to pay more for us."

Selling long-distance water to green consumers may be a contradiction in terms. But that hasn't stopped Fiji from positioning its product not just as an indulgence, but as an outright necessity for an elite that can appreciate its purity. As former Fiji Water CEO Doug Carlson once put it, "If you like Velveeta cheese, processed water is okay for you." ("All waters are not created equal" is another long-standing Fiji Water slogan.) The company has gone aggressively after its main competitor—tap water—by calling it "not a real or viable alternative" that can contain "4,000 contaminants," unlike Fiji's "living water." "You can no longer trust public or private water supplies," co-owner Lynda Resnick wrote in her book, *Rubies in the Orchard*.

> **❝** *The company has gone aggressively after its main competitor—tap water—by calling it 'not a real or viable alternative.'* **❞**

A few years back, Fiji Water canned its waterfall logo and replaced it with a picture of palm fronds and hibiscus: "Surface water!" Resnick wrote in *Rubies*. "Why would you want to suggest that Fiji came from surface water? The waterfall absolutely had to go." One company newsletter featured the findings of a salt-crystal purveyor who claimed that Fiji Water rivals the "known and significant abilities of 'Holy Healing Waters' in Lourdes, France, or Fatima, Portugal." Switching effortlessly from Catholic mysticism to sci-fi, he added that the water's "electromagnetic field frequency enables Fiji Water to stimulate our human self-regulation system."

In keeping with this rarefied vibe, Fiji Water's marketing has focused on product placement more than standard advertising; from appearances on *The Sopranos*, *24*, *The View*, and *Desperate Housewives* to sponsorship of events like the Emmy Awards, the Avon Walk for Breast Cancer, and Justin Timberlake's "Summer Love" tour, it's now "hard to find an event where our target market is present and Fiji isn't," according to Resnick. As far back as 2001, Movieline anointed it one of the "Top 10 Things Young Hollywood Can't Get through the Day Without." At the Academy Awards, E! has handed out Fiji bottles to the stars; as it happens, the complex where the Oscars is held was owned until 2004 by Fiji Water founder David Gilmour's real estate empire, Trizec (which before its acquisition by Brookfield Properties was one of the largest real estate companies in North America, with projects including everything from the Sears Tower to Enron HQ).

Gilmour told *The Times* (London) that "the world's water is being trashed day by day." He would know: Before launching Fiji Water, he cofounded Barrick Gold, now the largest gold mining enterprise in the world, with operations in hot spots from Tanzania to Pakistan. Its mines, often in parched places like Nevada and Western Australia, use billions of gallons of water to produce gold via a toxic cyanide leaching process.

In the early 1990s, Gilmour got wind of a study done by the Fijian government and aid organizations that indicated an enormous aquifer, estimated at more than seventeen miles long, near the main island's north coast. He obtained a ninety-nine-year lease on land atop the aquifer, brought a former Fijian environment minister on board, and launched an international marketing blitz inviting consumers to sample water preserved since "before the Industrial Revolution." To this day, Fiji Water has nearly exclusive access to the aquifer; the notoriously corrupt and chronically broke government has not been able to come up with the money or infrastructure to tap the water for its people.

> **❝** *The government has not been able to come up with the money or infrastructure to tap the water for its people.* **❞**

By the time Gilmour put Fiji Water up for sale in 2004, it was the fourth-most-popular imported bottled water in the United States. He found eager buyers in the Resnicks, who made their fortune with the flower delivery service Teleflora and the collectibles company Franklin Mint. The Beverly Hills–based couple are also agribusiness billionaires whose holdings include enough almond, pistachio, and pomegranate acreage to make them the biggest growers of those crops in the entire Western Hemisphere. They own a pesticide company, Suterra, and Lynda Resnick almost single-handedly created the pomegranate fad via their Pom Wonderful brand.

With the profits from their enterprises, the Resnicks have been major players on the political scene, giving more than $300,000 each over the past decade. They have supported mostly marquee Democrats—Obama, John Edwards, Hillary Clinton, Al Franken—though both also donated to the McCain campaign. They give millions to museums, environmental organizations, and other charities: Lynda is a trustee of the Aspen Institute, and Stewart is on the board of Conservation International. Fiji Water also gives to a range of conservation groups, including the Waterkeeper Alliance, Oceana, the Nature Conservancy, and Heal the Bay.

The charitable works Fiji Water brags about most often, however, are its efforts in Fiji itself—from preserving rain forests to helping fund water and sanitation projects to underwriting kindergartens. [In] January [2009], after catastrophic floods swept the main island of Viti Levu, the company also donated $500,000 to the military regime for flood relief, and gave another $450,000 to various projects [that] summer. True, some of Fiji Water's good works are more hope than reality: Though Lynda Resnick insists that "we only use biofuels," the Fiji plant runs on diesel generators, and a project to protect fifty thousand acres of rain forest—plugged on the actual bottle label—has yet to obtain a lease. Still, Resnick [says], "We do so much for these sort of forgotten people. They live in paradise, but they have a very, very hard life."

> **'We do so much for these sort of forgotten people.'**

Fiji Water may be well advised to spread a bit of its wealth around locally. During the 2000 coup, a small posse of villagers wielding spearguns and dynamite seized on the chaos to take over the bottling plant and threaten to burn it down. "The land is sacred and central to our continued existence and identity," a village spokesman told *The Fiji Times*, adding that "no Fijian should live off the breadcrumbs of past colonial injustices." Two years later, the company created the Vatukaloko Trust Fund, a charity targeting several villages surrounding its plant. It won't say how much it has given to the trust, but court proceedings indicate that it has agreed to donate 0.15 percent of its Fijian operation's net revenues; a company official testified that the total was about $100,000 in 2007. (For perspective, the trade journal *Brandweek* put Fiji Water's marketing budget at $10 million in 2008.)

Perhaps mindful of the unpleasantness of 2000, today Fiji Water executives refer constantly to the company's role in Fiji's economic life. "Our export revenue is paying for the expansion of water access at a pace that Fiji's government has never achieved," the company told the BBC. "If we did . . . cease to exist," sustainability VP Mooney told *U.S. News & World Report*, "a big chunk of the economy would be gone, the schools that we built would go away, and the water access projects would go away."

What Mooney didn't say is that though Fiji Water may fill a void in the impoverished nation, it also reaps a priceless benefit: tax-free status, granted when the company was founded in 1995. The rationale at the time, according to the company: Bottled water was a risky business with uncertain chances of success. In 2003, David Gilmour said that his ambition for Fiji Water was "to become the biggest taxpayer in the country." Yet the tax break, originally scheduled to expire in 2008, remains in effect, and neither the company nor the government will say whether or when it might end. And when Fiji has tried to wring a bit of extra revenue from the company, the response has been less than cooperative. Last year, when the government attempted to impose a new tax on water bottlers, Fiji Water called it "draconian" (a term it's never used for the regime's human rights violations) and temporarily shut down its plant in protest.

> **"** *Though Fiji Water may fill a void in the impoverished nation, it also reaps a priceless benefit: tax-free status.* **"**

At the moment, Fiji's government certainly seems in no mood to confront Fiji Water—quite the contrary. "Learning from the lessons of products, we must brand ourselves," Fiji's ambassador in Washington told a news site for diplomats, adding that he was working with the Resnicks to try to increase Fiji Water's U.S. sales. A Fiji Water bottle sits at the top of the embassy's homepage, and the government has even created a Fiji Water postage-stamp series—the three-dollar stamp features children clutching the trademark bottles.

Fiji Water, for its part, has trademarked the word "FIJI" (in capital letters) in numerous countries. (Some rejected the application, but not the United States.) It has also gone after rival Fijian bottlers daring to use their country's name for marketing. "It would have cost too much money for us to fight in court," says Mohammed Altaaf, the owner of Aqua Pacific water, which ended up taking the word "Fiji" out of its name. "It's just like branding a water America Water and denying anyone else the right to use the name 'America.'"

When such practices are criticized, Fiji Water's response is simple: "They don't have a ton of options for economic development," Mooney told *U.S. News & World Report*, "but bottled water is one of them. When someone buys a

> **"** *Without Fiji Water, 'Fiji is kind of screwed.'* **"**

bottle of Fiji, they're buying prosperity for the country." Without Fiji Water, he said, "Fiji is kind of screwed."

Additional Reading

Avni, Sheerly. SXSW dispatch: Email is for old people. *Mother Jones*. Available at https://www.motherjones.com/riff/2009/03/sxsw-dispatch-twitter-jumps-shark

Falconer, Bruce. Freedom declines for third consecutive year, report says. *Mother Jones*. Available at https://www.motherjones.com/mojo/2009/01/freedom-declines-third-consecutive-year-report-says

Moskowitz, Gary. Six celebs who almost get it. *Mother Jones*. Available at https://www.motherjones.com/environment/2008/11/six-celebs-who-almost-get-it

O'Brien, Coleen. A driving force: Arianna Huffington. *Mother Jones*. Available at http://www.motherjones.com/politics/2003/04/driving-force-arianna-huffington

Quraishi, Jen. How far did Voss and San Pellegrino travel to my Whole Foods? *Mother Jones*. Available at http://motherjones.com/politics/2009/09/how-far-did-voss-and-san-pellegrino-travel-my-whole-foods

Slade, Giles. iWaste. *Mother Jones*. Available at http://www.motherjones.com/environment/2007/03/iwaste

Witty, Julia. Your water bottle is one-quarter oil. *Mother Jones*. Available at http://www.motherjones.com/blue-marble/2009/02/your-water-bottle-one-quarter-full-oil

How does Lenzer's mix of anecdotes and research help draw her audience in and appeal to the readers' sense of pathos?

Fact Sheet ▼

Jen Quraishi

H2Uh-Oh: Dirty Facts about Bottled Water

Jen Quraishi is a San Francisco–based blogger and former assistant editor and editorial coordinator for *Mother Jones*. Her writing has appeared in *Wired*, *The Miami Herald*, and the *Contra Costa Times*. The "dirty facts about bottled water" that she describes here range from one company's dismissal of future environmental concerns to the finding that one brand of bottled water contains cancer-causing chemicals. *(Mother Jones artwork and "H2Uh-Oh": Reprinted with permission of Mother Jones.)*

▲ AUTHOR PHOTO
Jen Quraishi.
Reprinted with permission of Mother Jones.

Mother Jones

HOME   POLITICS   ENVIRONMENT   CULTURE   PHOTO ESSAYS   BLOGS

SPECIAL REPORTS

Spin the Bottle

H2Uh-Oh

From Arrowhead to Volvic, Fiji's not the only bottled water with a PR challenge.

By **Jen Quraishi**

Water brand: **Sam's Choice**
Corporation: **Wal-Mart**
[This] water comes from the Las Vegas municipal supply. A test by the Environmental Working Group found it had 200 percent of the allowable trihalomethane, a carcinogen, and included several chemicals known to cause DNA damage.

Water brand: **Dasani**

Corporation: **Coca-Cola**

Coca-Cola's bottling plant near the village of Plachimada in Kerala, India, began pumping groundwater in 2000. When wells dried up and villagers couldn't irrigate their fields, Coke offered a goodwill gesture: heavy-metal-laced sludge from the plant to use as fertilizer. After the company ignored years of protests—and two government orders to install wastewater treatment and provide drinking water to villagers—the state ordered the Coke plant to close in 2004. (Coke won the right to reopen the next year.)

Water brand: **Arrowhead**

Corporation: **Nestlé**

Nestlé is seeking a permit to pipe 65 million gallons a year from a spring in rural Colorado. When critics raised concerns about the effect of climate change on local water supplies, Nestlé said it was "illogical" to base decisions on changes "many years in the future."

Water brand: **Volvic**

Corporation: **Danone**

Last fall, Japan recalled 570,000 bottles of the French water after finding the toxic paint chemicals xylene and naphthalene in the bottles.

Water brand: **Deer Park**

Corporation: **Nestlé**

In the middle of a drought, Nestlé convinced officials to let it pump water from Florida's Madison Blue Spring State Park for fourteen years for no fee except a $230 permit (more than offset by nearly $1.7 million in tax subsidies).

Water brand: **Ice Mountain**

Corporation: **Nestlé**

Nestlé pays nothing (other than a small lease and an $85 yearly well fee) to pump from a Mecosta County, Michigan, spring. Citizens sued, saying the plant would damage nearby waterways, and prevailed. But Nestlé appealed and [in] July [2009] won the right to continue pumping up to 200 gallons per minute.

Corporate Greening

1. Researched essay. Anna Lenzer makes several claims against the Fiji brand of water. What are some of these claims? And what evidence does she use to support her claims?

2. Researched essay. Lenzer opens her essay with an account of her experience with the military junta in Fiji. How effective is this anecdote? What are some other ways she might have begun the article?

3. Fact sheet. How does Jen Quraishi's fact sheet about water serve to offer context to Lenzer's researched article about Fiji Water?

4. Brief article. Eric Hagerman debunks three corporate products with a quick "reality check." Does he provide enough evidence to convince you? Why or why not?

5. Investigate green ads. Find several advertisements for major corporations that make "green" claims. Which claims might advertising watchdogs challenge? Why? Fact-check these claims to find out how accurate they are.

6. Create a spoof ad. Create an ad that satirizes green corporate advertising. For an example, look online for spoof ads created in response to ads by oil or chemical companies.

7. Craft a memo & a PR message. Imagine that you are the head of a major corporation—one that needs to work on its image in terms of its "greenness." How would you address this in your business and marketing plans? To your workforce? To consumers? For this assignment, first, choose your industry and list its pros and cons in terms of the environment. Then, write a memo to employees that explains policies and plans regarding the

environment. Next, write a press release or blog post that conveys that message to customers.

8. Blog with Fiji Water. Go to http://www.fijiwater.com/blog/2009/08/fiji-water-responds-to-mother-jones-article/ and read Fiji Water's response to Lenzer's article. After reading the blog entry, how satisfied are you with Fiji Water's response? Create a blog entry that mixes the claims in Lenzer's piece with Fiji's response.

9. Identify more "little green lies." In "Little Green Lies," Hagerman examines some of the eco-slogans of companies. Research some other companies' slogans and the reality behind the slogans. Then create your own "Little Green Lies" piece.

10. Create a fact list. "H2Uh-Oh" lists several bottled water companies and some of their issues. Research other bottled water companies to see if they have any dirty secrets. Then create your own "H2Uh-Oh" listing.

FOOD & THE ENVIRONMENT

CLUSTER CONTENTS

In recent years, people have begun to think more critically about what they eat. Nutritional concerns and a desire to avoid obesity and diet-induced health problems are motivators, but concerns about how food production affects the environment and cultural landscapes have become important too. The authors included in this cluster study some of the factors people are taking into account as they make very personal decisions about what to eat. The cluster begins with two different viewpoints on eating meat: an essay against eating meat (Foer) and an argument in favor of eating meat (Lennon). It closes with an argument examining whether buying local is the environmental savior some claim it to be or perhaps simply a "locavore myth" (McWilliams).

Personal Essay ▼

Jonathan Safran Foer

Against Meat

Jonathan Safran Foer is the author of nonfiction, short stories, and two novels: *Everything Is Illuminated* and *Extremely Loud and Incredibly Close*. In his latest book, *Eating Animals*, Foer examines the various food choices we make and some of the inconsistencies between our relationship with animals and what we choose to eat. "Against Meat," excerpted from *Eating Animals*, originally appeared in *The New York Times Magazine*. (From Eating Animals by Jonathan Safran Foer. Copyright © 2009 Jonathan Safran Foer. Reprinted by permission of Little, Brown, and Company. All rights reserved.)

▲ AUTHOR PHOTO
Jonathan Safran Foer. *With permission from Ulf Anderson/Getty Images.*

The Fruits of Family Trees

When I was young, I would often spend the weekend at my grandmother's house. On my way in, Friday night, she would lift me from the ground in one of her fire-smothering hugs. And on the way out, Sunday afternoon, I was again taken into the air. It wasn't until years later that I realized she was weighing me.

My grandmother survived World War II barefoot, scavenging eastern Europe for other people's inedibles: rotting potatoes, discarded scraps of meat, skins, and the bits that clung to bones and pits. So she never cared if I colored outside the lines, as long as I cut coupons along the dashes. I remember hotel buffets: While the rest of us erected Golden Calves of breakfast, she would make sandwich upon sandwich to swaddle in napkins and stash in her bag for lunch. It was my grand-mother who taught me that one tea bag makes as many cups of tea as you're serving, and that every part of the apple is edible.

Her obsession with food wasn't an obsession with money. (Many of those cou-pons I clipped were for foods she would never buy.)

Her obsession wasn't with health. (She would beg me to drink Coke.)

My grandmother never set a place for herself at family dinners. Even when there was nothing more to be done—no soup bowls to be topped off, no pots to be stirred or ovens checked—she stayed in the kitchen, like a vigilant guard (or pris-oner) in a tower. As far as I could tell, the sustenance she got from the food she made didn't require her to eat it.

We thought she was the greatest chef who ever lived. My brothers and I would tell her as much several times a meal. And yet we were worldly enough kids to know that the greatest chef who ever lived would probably have more than one recipe (chicken with carrots), and that most great recipes involved more than two ingredients.

And why didn't we question her when she told us that dark food is inherently more healthful than light food, or that the bulk of the nutrients are found in the peel or crust? (The sandwiches of those weekend stays were made with the saved ends of pumpernickel loaves.) She taught us that animals that are bigger than you are very good for you, animals that are smaller than you are good for you, fish (which aren't animals) are fine for you, then tuna (which aren't fish), then vegetables, fruits, cakes, cookies, and sodas. No foods are bad for you. Sugars are great. Fats are tremen-dous. The fatter a child is, the fitter it is—especially if it's a boy. Lunch is not one meal, but three, to be eaten at 11:00, 12:30, and 3:00. You are always starving.

Jonathan Safran Foer, *Against Meat*   675

In fact, her chicken with carrots probably was the most delicious thing I've ever eaten. But that had little to do with how it was prepared, or even how it tasted. Her food was delicious because we believed it was delicious. We believed in our grandmother's cooking more fervently than we believed in God.

More stories could be told about my grandmother than about anyone else I've ever met—her otherworldly childhood, the hairline margin of her survival, the totality of her loss, her immigration and further loss, the triumph and tragedy of her assimilation—and while I will one day try to tell them to my children, we almost never told them to one another. Nor did we call her by any of the obvious and earned titles. We called her the Greatest Chef.

> ❝ The story of her relationship to food holds all of the other stories that could be told about her. ❞

The story of her relationship to food holds all of the other stories that could be told about her. Food, for her, is not food. It is terror, dignity, gratitude, vengeance, joy, humiliation, religion, history, and, of course, love. It was as if the fruits she always offered us were picked from the destroyed branches of our family tree.

Possible Again

When I was two, the heroes of all my bedtime books were animals. The first thing I can remember learning in school was how to pet a guinea pig without accidentally killing it. One summer my family fostered a cousin's dog. I kicked it. My father told me we don't kick animals. When I was seven, I mourned the death of a goldfish I'd won the previous weekend. I discovered that my father had flushed it down the toilet. I told my father—using other, less familial language—we don't flush animals down the toilet. When I was nine, I had a babysitter who didn't want to hurt anything. She put it just like that when I asked her why she wasn't having chicken with my older brother and me.

"Hurt anything?" I asked.

"You know that chicken is chicken, right?"

Frank shot me a look: Mom and Dad entrusted this stupid woman with their precious babies?

Her intention might or might not have been to convert us, but being a kid herself, she lacked whatever restraint it is that so often prevents a full telling of this particular story. Without drama or rhetoric, skipping over or euphemizing, she shared what she knew.

My brother and I looked at each other, our mouths full of hurt chickens, and had simultaneous how-in-the-world-could-I-have-never-thought-of-that-before-and-why-on-earth-didn't-someone-tell-me? moments. I put down my fork. Frank finished the meal and is probably eating a chicken as I type these words.

What our babysitter said made sense to me, not only because it seemed so self-evidently true, but also because it was the extension to food of everything my parents had taught me. We don't hurt family members. We don't hurt friends or strangers. We don't even hurt upholstered furniture. My not having thought to include farmed animals in that list didn't make them the exceptions to it. It just made me a child, ignorant of the world's workings. Until I wasn't. At which point I had to change my life.

Until I didn't. My vegetarianism, so bombastic and unyielding in the beginning, lasted a few years, sputtered, and quietly died. I never thought of a response to our babysitter's code but found ways to smudge, diminish, and ignore it. Generally speaking, I didn't cause hurt. Generally speaking, I strove to do the right thing. Generally speaking, my conscience was clear enough. Pass the chicken, I'm starving.

Mark Twain said that quitting smoking is among the easiest things you can do; he did it all the time. I would add vegetarianism to the list of easy things. In high school I became vegetarian more times than I can now remember, most often as an effort to claim a bit of identity in a world of people whose identities seemed to come effortlessly. I wanted a slogan to distinguish my mom's Volvo's bumper, a bake-sale cause to fill the self-conscious half hour of school break, an occasion to get closer to the breasts of activist women. (And I continued to think it was wrong to hurt animals.) Which isn't to say that I refrained from eating meat. Only that I refrained in public. Many dinners of those years began with my father asking, "Any dietary restrictions I need to know about tonight?"

When I went to college, I started eating meat more earnestly. Not "believing in it"—whatever that would mean—but willfully pushing the questions out of my mind. It might well have been the prevalence of vegetarianism on campus that discouraged my own—I find myself less likely to give money to a street musician whose case is overflowing with bills.

But when, at the end of my sophomore year, I became a philosophy major and started doing my first seriously pretentious thinking, I became a vegetarian again. The kind of active forgetting that I was sure meat eating required felt too paradoxical to the intellectual life I was trying to shape. I didn't know

> " When I became a philosophy major and started doing my first seriously pretentious thinking, I became a vegetarian again. "

the details of factory farming, but like most everyone, I knew the gist: It is miserable for animals, the environment, farmers, public health, biodiversity, rural communities, global poverty, and so on. I thought life could, should, and must conform to the mold of reason, period. You can imagine how annoying this made me.

When I graduated, I ate meat—lots of every kind of meat—for about two years. Why? Because it tasted good. And because more important than reason in shaping habits are the stories we tell ourselves and one another. And I told a forgiving story about myself to myself: I was only human.

Then I was set up on a blind date with the woman who would become my wife. And only a few weeks later we found ourselves talking about two surprising topics: marriage and vegetarianism.

Her history with meat was remarkably similar to mine: There were things she believed while lying in bed at night, and there were choices made at the breakfast table the next morning. There was a gnawing (if only occasional and short-lived) dread that she was participating in something deeply wrong, and there was the acceptance of complexity and fallibility. Like me, she had intuitions that were very strong, but apparently not strong enough.

People marry for many different reasons, but one that animated our decision to take that step was the prospect of explicitly marking a new beginning. Jewish ritual and symbolism strongly encourage this notion of demarcating a sharp division with what came before—the most well-known example being the smashing of the glass at the end of the wedding ceremony. Things were as they were, but they will be different now. Things will be better. We will be better.

Sounds and feels great, but better how? I could think of endless ways to make myself better (I could learn foreign languages, be more patient, work harder), but I'd already made too many such vows to trust them anymore. I could also think of ways to make "us" better, but the meaningful things we can agree on and change in a relationship are few.

Eating animals, a concern we'd both had and had both forgotten, seemed like a place to start. So much intersects there, and so much could flow from it. In the same week, we became engaged and vegetarian.

Of course our wedding wasn't vegetarian, because we persuaded ourselves that it was only fair to offer animal protein to our guests, some of whom traveled from great distances to share our joy. (Find that logic hard to follow?) And we ate fish on our honeymoon, but we were in Japan, and when in Japan. . . . And back in our new home, we did occasionally eat burgers and chicken soup and smoked salmon and tuna steaks. But only whenever we felt like it.

And that, I thought, was that. And I thought that was just fine. I assumed we'd maintain a diet of conscientious inconsistency. Why should eating be different from any of the other ethical realms of our lives? We were honest people who occasionally told lies, careful friends who sometimes acted clumsily. We were vegetarians who from time to time ate meat.

> **"** *Why should eating be different from any of the other ethical realms of our lives?* **"**

But then we decided to have a child, and that was a different story that would necessitate a different story.

About half an hour after my son was born, I went into the waiting room to tell the gathered family the good news.

"You said 'he'! So it's a boy?"

"What's his name?"

"Who does he look like?"

"Tell us everything!"

I answered their questions as quickly as I could, then went to the corner and turned on my cell phone.

"Grandma," I said. "We have a baby."

Her only phone is in the kitchen. She picked up halfway into the first ring. It was just after midnight. Had she been clipping coupons? Preparing chicken with carrots to freeze for someone else to eat at some future meal? I'd never once seen or heard her cry, but tears pushed through her words as she asked, "How much does it weigh?"

A few days after we came home from the hospital, I sent a letter to a friend, including a photo of my son and some first impressions of fatherhood. He responded, simply, "Everything is possible again." It was the perfect thing to write, because that was exactly how it felt. The world itself had another chance.

Eating Animals

Seconds after being born, my son was breast-feeding. I watched him with an awe that had no precedent in my life. Without explanation or experience, he knew what to do. Millions of years of evolution had wound the knowledge into him, as it had encoded beating into his tiny heart and expansion and contraction into his newly dry lungs.

What foods were you fed as a child? Which foods were most special? Why?

Almost four years later, he is a big brother and a remarkably sophisticated little conversationalist. Increasingly the food he eats is digested together with stories we tell. Feeding my children is not like feeding myself: It matters more. It matters because food matters (their physical health matters, the pleasure they take in eating matters), and because the stories that are served with food matter.

Some of my happiest childhood memories are of sushi "lunch dates" with my mom, and eating my dad's turkey burgers with mustard and grilled onions at backyard celebrations, and of course my grandmother's chicken with carrots.

❝ *Letting tastes fade from memory create[s] a kind of cultural loss, a forgetting.* **❞**

Those occasions simply wouldn't have been the same without those foods—and that is important. To give up the taste of sushi, turkey, or chicken is a loss that extends beyond giving up a pleasurable eating experience. Changing what we eat and letting tastes fade from memory create a kind of cultural loss, a forgetting. But perhaps this kind of forgetfulness is worth accepting—even worth cultivating (forgetting, too, can be cultivated). To remember my values, I need to lose certain tastes and find other handles for the memories that they once helped me carry.

My wife and I have chosen to bring up our children as vegetarians. In another time or place, we might have made a different decision. But the realities of our present moment compelled us to make that choice. According to an analysis of USDA data by the advocacy group Farm Forward, factory farms now produce more than 99 percent of the animals eaten in this country. And despite labels that suggest otherwise, genuine alternatives—which do exist, and make many of the ethical questions about meat moot—are very difficult for even an educated eater to find. I don't have the ability to do so with regularity and confidence. ("Free range," "cage-free," "natural," and "organic" are nearly meaningless when it comes to animal welfare.)

❝ *Factory farming has made animal agriculture the No. 1 contributor to global warming.* **❞**

According to reports by the Food and Agriculture Organization of the UN and others, factory farming has made animal agriculture the No. 1 contributor to global warming (it is significantly more destructive than transportation alone), and one of the Top 2 or 3 causes of all of the most serious environmental problems, both global and local: air and water pollution, deforestation, loss of biodiversity . . . Eating factory-farmed animals—which is to say virtually every piece of meat sold in supermarkets and prepared in restaurants—is almost certainly the single worst thing that humans do to the environment.

Every factory-farmed animal is, as a practice, treated in ways that would be illegal if it were a dog or a cat. Turkeys have been so genetically modified they are incapable of natural reproduction. To acknowledge that these things matter is not sentimental. It is a confrontation with the facts about animals and ourselves. We know these things matter.

Meat and seafood are in no way necessary for my family—unlike some in the world, we have easy access to a wide variety of other foods. And we are healthier without it. So our choices aren't constrained.

While the cultural uses of meat can be replaced—my mother and I now eat Italian, my father grills veggie burgers, my grandmother invented her own "vegetarian chopped liver"—there is still the question of pleasure. A vegetarian diet can be rich and fully enjoyable, but I couldn't honestly argue, as many vegetarians try to, that it is as rich as a diet that includes meat. (Those who eat chimpanzee look at the Western diet as sadly deficient of a great pleasure.) I love calamari, I love roasted chicken, I love a good steak. But I don't love them without limit.

To what extent is choosing vegetarianism—or adopting other food rules—related to social class and economics?

This isn't animal experimentation, where you can imagine some proportionate good at the other end of the suffering. This is what we feel like eating. Yet taste, the crudest of our senses, has been exempted from the ethical rules that govern our other senses. Why? Why doesn't a horny person have as strong a claim to raping an animal as a hungry one does to confining, killing, and eating it? It's easy to dismiss that question but hard to respond to it. Try to imagine any end other than taste for which it would be justifiable to do what we do to farmed animals.

Children confront us with our paradoxes and dishonesty, and we are exposed. You need to find an answer for every why—Why do we do this? Why don't we do that?—and often there isn't a good one. So you say, simply, because. Or you tell a story that you know isn't true. And whether or not your face reddens, you blush. The shame of parenthood—which is a good shame—is that we want our children to be more whole than we are, to have satisfactory answers. My children not only inspired me to reconsider what kind of eating animal I would be, but also shamed me into reconsideration.

> ❝ Children confront us with our paradoxes and dishonesty, and we are exposed. ❞

And then, one day, they will choose for themselves. I don't know what my reaction will be if they decide to eat meat. (I don't know what my reaction will be if they decide to renounce their Judaism, root for the Red Sox, or register Republican.) I'm not as worried about what they will choose as much as my ability to make them conscious of the choices before them. I won't measure my success as a parent by whether my children share my values, but by whether they act according to their own.

In the meantime, my choice on their behalf means they will never eat their great-grandmother's singular dish. They will never receive that unique and most direct expression of her love, will perhaps never think of her as the greatest chef who ever lived. Her primal story, our family's primal story, will have to change.

Or will it? It wasn't until I became a parent that I understood my grandmother's cooking. The greatest chef who ever lived wasn't preparing food, but humans. I'm thinking of those Saturday afternoons at her kitchen table, just the two of us—black bread in the glowing toaster, a humming refrigerator that couldn't be seen through its veil of family photographs. Over pumpernickel ends and Coke, she would tell me about her escape from Europe, the foods she had to eat and those she wouldn't. It was the story of her life—"Listen to me," she would plead—and I knew a vital lesson was being transmitted, even if I didn't know, as a child, what that lesson was. I know, now, what it was.

Listen to Me

"We weren't rich, but we always had enough. Thursday we baked bread, and challah and rolls, and they lasted the whole week. Friday we had pancakes. Shabbat we always had a chicken, and soup with noodles. You would go to the butcher and ask for a little more fat. The fattiest piece was the best piece. It wasn't like now. We didn't have refrigerators, but we had milk and cheese. We didn't have every kind of vegetable, but we had enough. The things that you have here and take for granted. . . . But we were happy. We didn't know any better. And we took what we had for granted, too.

"Then it all changed. During the war it was hell on earth, and I had nothing. I left my family, you know. I was always running, day and night, because the Germans were always right behind me. If you stopped, you died. There was never enough food. I became sicker and sicker from not eating, and I'm not just talking about being skin and bones. I had sores all over my body. It became difficult to move. I wasn't too good to eat from a garbage can. I ate the parts others wouldn't eat. If you helped yourself, you could survive. I took whatever I could find. I ate things I wouldn't tell you about.

"Even at the worst times, there were good people, too. Someone taught me to tie the ends of my pants so I could fill the legs with any potatoes I was able to steal. I walked miles and miles like that, because you never knew when you would be lucky again. Someone gave me a little rice, once, and I traveled two days to a market and traded it for some soap, and then traveled to another market and traded the soap for some beans. You had to have luck and intuition.

"The worst it got was near the end. A lot of people died right at the end, and I didn't know if I could make it another day. A farmer, a Russian, God bless him, he saw my condition, and he went into his house and came out with a piece of meat for me."

"He saved your life."

"I didn't eat it."

"You didn't eat it?"

"It was pork. I wouldn't eat pork."

"Why?"

"What do you mean why?"

"What, because it wasn't kosher?"

"Of course."

"But not even to save your life?"

"If nothing matters, there's nothing to save."

Argument ▼

Christine Lennon

Why Vegetarians Are Eating Meat

Christine Lennon is a freelance writer whose work has appeared
in *The New York Times Magazine*, *Vogue*, *Time*, and *Food & Wine*,
where the following editorial first appeared. Her writing focuses on
a variety of topics, including beauty and its relationship to going
green, fashion, interior design, and famous food caterers. In the following editorial, Lennon examines reasons why former vegetarians,
such as Mollie Katzen (author of the *Moosewood Cookbook*), have
converted to eating meat. *("Why Vegetarians Are Eating Meat" is reprinted
by permission of the author, Christine Lennon.)*

To a die-hard meat eater, there's nothing more irritating than a smug vegetarian.
I feel at liberty to say this because I am one (a steak lover) and I married the other
(a vegetarian with a pulpit). For me, "Do you now, or would you ever, eat meat?"
has always been a question on par with "Do you ever want to get married?" and
"Do you want children?" The answer to one reveals as much about a person's interior life, and our compatibility, as the response to the others. My husband Andrew's
reply to all of those questions when I asked him three years ago was, "No."

Obviously, we're now married. We had twins earlier this year. And somewhere in
between those two events, the answer to the third question was also reevaluated,
and the vegetarian soapbox was put to rest, too.

Yes, my husband has started eating meat again after a seven-year hiatus as an
ethically motivated and health-conscious vegetarian. About a year ago, we arrived at a compromise: I would eat less meat—choosing mostly beef, pork, and
poultry produced by local California ranchers without the use of hormones or
antibiotics—and he would indulge me by sharing a steak on occasion. But ar-
riving at that happy medium wasn't as straightforward as it sounds. In the three
years we've been together, several turns of events have made both of us rethink
our choices and decide that eating meat selectively is better for the planet and
our own health. And judging by the conversations we've had with friends and
acquaintances, we're not the only ones who believe this to be true.

For Andrew and about a dozen people in our circle who have recently converted from vegetarianism, eating sustainable meat purchased from small farmers is a new form of activism—a way of striking a blow against the factory farming of livestock that books like Michael Pollan's *The Omnivore's Dilemma* describe so damningly. Pollan extols the virtues of independent, small-scale food producers who raise pasture-fed livestock in a sustainable and ethical manner. In contrast, he provides a compelling critique of factory farms, which cram thousands of cows, pigs, or chickens into rows of cages in warehouses, feed them drugs to plump up their meat and fight off the illnesses caused by these inhumane conditions, and produce innumerable tons of environmentally destructive animal waste.

> ❝ *Eating sustainable meat purchased from small farmers is a new form of activism.* ❞

The terms "grass fed" and "pasture raised"—meaning that an animal was allowed to graze the old-fashioned way instead of being fed an unnatural and difficult-to-digest diet of mostly corn and other grain—have now entered the food shoppers' lexicon. But Andrew and I didn't fully understand what those phrases meant until we got to know Greg Nauta of Rocky Canyon Farms. Nauta is a small-scale rancher and farmer from Atascadero, California, who grows organic vegetables and raises about thirty-five animals on pastureland. Since we met him at the Hollywood Farmers' Market a year ago, it has become even clearer to us that supporting guys like him—by seeking out and paying a premium for sustainably raised meat—is the right thing for us to do.

Nauta's cattle graze on two hundred leased acres of pasture in central California and are fed the leftover vegetables and fruits he grows that don't sell at the farmers' market, supplemented by locally grown barley grain on occasion. "That's dessert," he says of the barley, "not a main course. That would be like us eating ice cream every day."

Three times a week, Nauta loads his truck full of coolers stocked with cattleman's steaks and handmade pork sausages and drives to the Los Angeles–area farmers' markets. Selling his vegetables and meat directly to conscientious eaters, people to whom he talks weekly about rainfall averages and organic produce, Nauta says, is "the best way small guys like me can compete." In the past several months, Nauta has noticed a handful of curious vegetarians, like Andrew, wandering over to his booth to ask questions. And they're satisfied enough with the answers to give his meat a try—and come back for more.

How does Christine Lennon's argument about eating meat compare to Jonathan Safran Foer's?

If preserving small-scale farming isn't a compelling enough reason to eat beef or pork, consider the nutritional advantages grass-fed meat has over the factory-fed kind. "One of the benefits of all-grass-fed beef, or 'beef with benefits,' as we say, is that it's lower in fat than conventionally raised beef," says Kate Clancy, who studies nutrition and sustainable agriculture and was until recently the senior scientist at the nonprofit Union of Concerned Scientists. "The other thing is that the meat and milk from grass-fed cattle will probably have higher amounts of omega-3 fatty acids, which may help reduce the risk of heart disease and strengthen people's immune systems. What's good for the environment, what's good for cattle, is also good for us."

> " 'What's good for the environment, what's good for cattle, is also good for us.' "

Combine these findings with the questions being raised about meat replacements derived from soy and wheat gluten, and the real thing seems better by the minute. "What we know about soy is that as you process it, you lose a lot of the benefits," says Ashley Koff, a Los Angeles–based registered dietician. "Any soy-based fake meat product is incredibly processed, and you have to use chemicals to get the mock flavor. Any other whole-food diet is going to be a lot better for you." Vegetarians like Andrew—he once brought a tofu sandwich to a famous Texas barbecue restaurant—may now have a harder time justifying their "healthier" dietary choices.

Former vegetarians are some of the most outspoken proponents of eating meat. "I was vegan for sixteen years, and I truly believed I was doing the right thing for my health," says the actress and model Mariel Hemingway, who is the author of *Healthy Living from the Inside Out*. "But when I was vegan, I was super-weak. I love animals, and we should not support anything but ethical ranching, but when I eat meat, I feel more grounded. I have more energy."

Even chef Mollie Katzen, author of the vegetarian bible the *Moosewood Cookbook*, is experimenting with meat again. "For about thirty years I didn't eat meat at all, just a bite of fish every once in a while, and always some dairy," she says. "Lately, I've been eating a little meat. People say, 'Ha, ha, Mollie Katzen is eating steak.' But now that cleaner, naturally fed meat is available, it's a great option for anyone who's looking to complete his diet. Somehow, it got ascribed to me that I don't want people to eat meat. I've just wanted to supply possibilities that were low on the food chain."

Recently, when responding to the invitation to her high school reunion, Katzen had to make a choice between the vegetarian and the conventional meal. She checked the nonvegetarian box. "The people who requested the vegetarian meal got fettuccine Alfredo," she says. "It's a bowl full of flour and butterfat. I'd much rather have vegetables and grains and a few bites of chicken."

For Andrew and many of our ex-vegetarian friends, the ethical reasons for eating meat, combined with the health-related ones, have been impossible to deny. "The way I see it, you've got three opportunities every day to act on your values and have an immediate effect on something you're concerned about," Andrew says. "You're probably worried about Darfur, too, but what can you do about that every single day? Write a letter? It doesn't have the same kind of impact."

Supporting ranchers we believe in, and the stores and restaurants that sell their products, has a very tangible impact that we experience firsthand all the time. But ask most vegetarians if the battle between small, sustainable ranchers and industrial farming is at the top of their list of concerns about eating meat, and you'll probably be met with a blank stare. "For people who are against eating meat because it's wrong or offensive to eat animals, even the cleanest grass-fed beef won't be good enough," Katzen says.

Convincing those people that eating meat can improve the welfare of the entire livestock population is a tough sell. But we'll keep trying. What we've discovered is that you can hover pretty close to the bottom of the food chain and still make a difference, quietly. We've found a healthy balance somewhere between the two extremes—which, come to think of it, is also a good way to approach a marriage.

When you choose what to eat, are you, as Lennon quotes Andrew, "act[ing] on your values"? Why or why not?

Argument ▼

James E. McWilliams

The Locavore Myth

James E. McWilliams teaches history at
Texas State University and is the author of
two books on food: *Just Food: Where Loca-
vores Get It Wrong and How We Can Truly Eat Responsibly* and *A
Revolution in Eating: How the Quest for Food Shaped America.* In
the following editorial for *Forbes* magazine, McWilliams argues that
eating locally grown food does not reduce our carbon footprints.
(Forbes *artwork and "The Locavore Myth," by James E. McWilliams, reprinted with
permission: from* Forbes, *7/16/2009. © 2009 Forbes. All rights reserved.)*

▲ AUTHOR PHOTO
James E. McWilliams.
© *Evan Kafka.*

The Locavore Myth

James E. McWilliams

Buy local, shrink the distance food travels, save the planet. The locavore movement has captured a lot of fans. To their credit, they are highlighting the problems
with industrialized food. But a lot of them are making a big mistake. By focusing
on transportation, they overlook other energy-hogging factors in food production.

Take lamb. A 2006 academic study (funded by the New Zealand government)
discovered that it made more environmental sense for a Londoner to buy lamb
shipped from New Zealand than to buy lamb raised in the U.K. This finding is

counterintuitive—if you're only counting food miles. But New Zealand lamb is raised on pastures with a small carbon footprint, whereas most English lamb is produced under intensive factory-like conditions with a big carbon footprint. This disparity overwhelms domestic lamb's advantage in transportation energy.

New Zealand lamb is not exceptional. Take a close look at water usage, fertilizer types, processing methods, and packaging techniques and you discover that factors other than shipping far outweigh the energy it takes to transport food. One analysis, by Rich Pirog of the Leopold Center for Sustainable Agriculture, showed that transportation accounts for only 11 percent of food's carbon footprint. A fourth of the energy required to produce food is expended in the consumer's kitchen. Still more energy is consumed per meal in a restaurant, since restaurants throw away most of their leftovers.

Locavores argue that buying local food supports an area's farmers and, in turn, strengthens the community. Fair enough. Left unacknowledged, however, is the fact that it also hurts farmers in other parts of the world. The U.K. buys most of its green beans from Kenya. While it's true that the beans almost always arrive in airplanes—the form of transportation that consumes the most energy—it's also true that a campaign to shame English consumers with small airplane stickers affixed to flown-in produce threatens the livelihood of 1.5 million sub-Saharan farmers.

Another chink in the locavores' armor involves the way food miles are calculated. To choose a locally grown apple over an apple trucked in from across the country might seem easy. But this decision ignores economies of scale. To take an extreme example, a shipper sending a truck with 2,000 apples over 2,000 miles would consume the same amount of fuel per apple as a local farmer who takes a pickup 50 miles to sell 50 apples at his stall at the green market. The critical measure here is not food miles but apples per gallon.

How well does James McWilliams use evidence to back his claims? Does he convince you? Why or why not?

The one big problem with thinking beyond food miles is that it's hard to get the information you need. Ethically concerned consumers know very little about processing practices, water availability, packaging waste, and fertilizer application. This is an opportunity for watchdog groups. They should make life-cycle carbon counts available to shoppers.

Until our food system becomes more transparent, there is one thing you can do to shrink the carbon footprint of your dinner: Take the meat off your plate. No matter how

Until our food system becomes more transparent, there is one thing you can do to shrink the carbon footprint of your dinner: Take the meat off your plate.

Reread McWilliams's argument with a focus on his writing style. How does it contribute to his persuasiveness?

you slice it, it takes more energy to bring meat, as opposed to plants, to the table. It takes 6 pounds of grain to make a pound of chicken and 10 to 16 pounds to make a pound of beef. That difference translates into big differences in inputs. It requires 2,400 liters of water to make a burger and only 13 liters to grow a tomato. A majority of the water in the American West goes toward the production of pigs, chickens, and cattle.

The average American eats 273 pounds of meat a year. Give up red meat once a week and you'll save as much energy as if the only food miles in your diet were the distance to the nearest truck farmer.

If you want to make a statement, ride your bike to the farmers' market. If you want to reduce greenhouse gases, become a vegetarian.

Food & the Environment

ANALYZING RHETORICAL SITUATIONS

1. Personal essay. What role do Jonathan Safran Foer's memories of his grandmother play in the essay? How do they help focus and structure the essay?

2. Argument. Christine Lennon argues that "eating meat selectively is better for the planet and our own health." What is her argument based on?

3. Argument. What are some of the reasons James E. McWilliams offers to support his argument about the locavore myth? How convincing is he?

4. Personal essay & argument. Compare Foer's decision to be a vegetarian with Lennon's husband's decision to eat meat. What similar goals do these men have in making conscious choices about what they eat?

5. Personal essay & arguments. In what ways do these three authors agree and disagree? How do environmental concerns and nutrition figure into each piece?

Food & the Environment

6. Fact-check Foer's claims about factory farming. According to Foer, "Eating factory-farmed animals—which is to say virtually every piece of meat sold in supermarkets and prepared in restaurants—is almost certainly the single worst thing that humans do to the environment." Research factory farming practices and how they affect the environment. Is Foer's claim accurate?

7. Create a visual argument about non-factory-farmed meat. Find out how accessible non-factory-farmed meat is in your community. Be sure to investigate the cost to consumers. Present this information in an infographic.

8. Analyze an author's techniques. Visit Christine Lennon's site to peruse some of the articles she's written. How would you describe her writing style (formal, informal, technical, literary, enthusiastic, dry, direct, clichéd)? Are there particular techniques you see her using repeatedly, such as quoting from interviews or using personal anecdotes?

9. Keep an environmentally oriented food journal. Foer, Lennon, and McWilliams are all concerned with "eating responsibly." Keep a journal for a few days of everything you eat, including where the food was procured (grocery store, restaurant, your neighbor's garden, etc.). Do some research to determine the environmental impact of your food choices on these days, and annotate your journal entries accordingly.

10. Research the Slow Food movement—and give a presentation. Another health and eco-conscious food movement is called Slow Food. Go to the Slow Food International site and read about the movement's goals and activities. Then create a survey for your classmates to find out whether they identify more with "slow food" or "fast food." You might decide to focus your questions on the role of food in their daily lives, their cooking and eating habits, their grocery-shopping habits, how food has permeated their memories, or something else.

RESEARCH EXPERIMENTS: The Environment

1. **Conduct a poster session in your class.** Conferences held by many disciplines and organizations feature discussion panels and presentations; they also include poster sessions. In a poster session, researchers present their research methods and findings on a poster that combines text and images to quickly convey information to people walking around the poster session venue. You can find examples of posters used in poster sessions at http://www.ncsu.edu/project/posters/examples/.

   a. For this project, pair up with a classmate to create a poster for a poster session on the environment. Your task will be to test a natural or organic product, such as insect repellent, lotion, cleaning solution, laundry detergent, soap, candles, or beauty products. Ultimately, you will present a poster detailing the results of your experiments to the class.

   b. Begin by choosing a natural, organic product that is for sale in your area. Many grocery stores, for example, carry cleaning products made by Seventh Generation and Mrs. Meyers. Alternatively, you may want to find a recipe online and make your own product. Web sites such as the Backyard Herbalist (http://earthnotes.tripod.com/clnrecipes.htm) and Love to Know (http://organic.lovetoknow.com/How_to_Make_Organic_House_Cleaning_Products) are good places to start. Take notes on how much the product costs to purchase or make. If you make the product, take detailed notes on how you made it and how easy or difficult it was to find the ingredients, make the product, and store the product.

   c. Next, decide what your measure of success will be for the product. For example, if you test a glass cleaner, how exactly do you determine whether the cleaner cleaned the glass? You need to know what kind of dirt was on the glass to begin with.

   d. Then, conduct your test. Take detailed notes. For example, in the case of the glass cleaner, take notes on how much glass cleaner was needed, how it smelled, what kind of wiping implement was used, how much wiping was required, and what the results were.

   e. After you've conducted your test, analyze the results and create a three-panel poster for the class poster session. In your analysis, you might consider:

      • The cost per use of the product

      • How effective the product was

      • Pros and cons of the product compared with other similar products

      • Changes you might make to your experimental protocol to get more accurate results

2. **Create an innovative response to a natural disaster.** Research a large-scale human and environmental disaster such as the BP oil spill (2010), the Haiti earthquake (2010), Hurricane Katrina (2005), the Thailand tsunami (2004), the *Exxon Valdez* oil spill (1989), the Chernobyl nuclear accident (1986), or Love Canal (1970s). Or, you might examine disasters associated with introduced/invasive species (e.g., the rabbit plague in Australia), deforestation in the Amazon, threats to coral reefs, and animal extinction due to human activity.

a. Choose one event to investigate. Your goal is to design a creative response that helps decrease the disaster's impact. For example, Brad Pitt created Make It Right (rebuilding the Lower Ninth Ward using green practices) in response to the effects of Hurricane Katrina.

b. As you research the disaster, consider the following:

- How has the disaster affected local economies?

- How has the disaster shaped legislation?

- Has tourism been affected by the disaster?

- What business practices have been developed in response to the disaster?

- What have been some innovative responses to the disaster?

c. Next, consider what innovative response you might suggest. For example, this could be a program to prevent a similar future disaster, a plan to rebuild the land, a program to eradicate the invasive species, or a campaign to make the public aware of their actions and how they contribute to the problem. Once you decide on your response, produce:

- A blueprint for the response (for example, if you were Brad Pitt, you would create drawings of the new buildings showing how they used green practices)

- An analytical researched essay that takes into account ways the disaster has affected local economies and/or tourism, and ways the disaster has spurred legislation and changes in business practices

14 HEROES & VILLAINS

CONTENTS

e For e-Pages content, visit **bedfordstmartins .com/bookofgenres.**

▲ CARTOON VILLAIN
Snidely Whiplash.

The concepts of hero and villain are woven into our lives. In popular culture, "superheroes" such as Batman, Superman, and Wonder Woman, battle "supervillains," such as the Joker, Lex Luthor, and the Nazis. In daily life, soldiers, police officers, firefighters, and others who risk their lives on the job are often considered heroes, while infamous criminals are considered villains. On local news we see stories of "everyday heroes," such as the neighbor who saves a child from drowning, or the good Samaritan who performs CPR on an accident victim. Much national news focuses on the equivalent of "everyday villains," such as corrupt politicians or Wall Street bankers cheating people out of their retirement savings.

Heroes are generally described as courageous, strong, and selfless, while villains are described as the exact opposite: cowardly, weak, and selfish. Although superheroes and supervillains tend to be one-dimensional characters in popular culture, in real life, no one is ever 100 percent heroic or 100 percent villainous. Even Mother Teresa had her detractors, including journalist Christopher Hitchens, who criticized her for glorifying suffering.

When it comes to society and politics, our definitions of *hero* and *villain* can become entangled, such as when we argue about whether taking military action is the right thing to do. Or when supporters see political leaders as heroes while opponents see them as villains, such as in the 1950s, when some viewed Senator Joseph McCarthy as a force for good who sought to rid the world of Communists, while others viewed him as a menace who conducted a witch hunt and destroyed people's lives. After the September 11, 2001, attacks, Osama bin Laden achieved hero status among al Qaeda members, while Americans, who viewed him as one of the world's most dangerous criminals, celebrated his capture and death in 2011.

In this chapter we look at examples of heroes and villains and the roles they play in our lives and culture. The first cluster, presented in the e-Pages provides definitions and examples of archetypal heroes, opening with an overview that includes Moses, King Arthur, Luke Skywalker, and Simba from *The Lion King* (Bryan Davis's slide presentation), a bird's-eye view of Odysseus's journey (Prestwick House Maps), and two views of

What is your definition of a hero? List some of your assumptions about heroes. How and why have you come to hold these assumptions?

what constitutes a Hero's Journey—one from a famous scholar (Joseph Campbell) and the other from a contemporary blogger (Lex of the blog *FANgirl*).

The second cluster takes on villains, examining some terminology and imagery associated with them, and focusing on their portrayal in film. The American Film Institute provides a list of the top one hundred greatest heroes and villains of film, including Atticus Finch from *To Kill a Mockingbird* and Dr. Hannibal Lecter from *The Silence of the Lambs*. Stuart Fischoff critiques Hollywood villains in "Villains in Film: Anemic Renderings." And writer Lee Masterson gives advice to fiction writers for creating effective villains "we love to hate."

Next, we look at a range of heroes, including well-known, iconic heroes such as Martin Luther King Jr., and lesser-known, everyday heroes, such as working people and volunteers. We present a look at Malala Yousafzai, the young Pakistani advocate for girls' education (Arbab photo), and Jason Collins, the NBA center who is the first American professional basketball player to publicly announce he's gay. A portfolio of posters includes vocational messages, followed by an *Onion* parody of the "non-hero" office worker. Concluding the cluster, Joshua Freeman of *The Nation* challenges the concept of the hero in his editorial on the visibility of workers and first responders in New York City.

We close with a collection of readings (presented in the e-Pages) that is not for the faint of heart: It's focused on murderers and serial killers. The FBI opens the cluster with a report on the traits of serial killers, followed by an argument from David Von Drehle about the relationship between narcissism disorder and killing. Next, detective Charles Montaldo presents disturbing profiles of killers Jeffrey Dahmer and Andrea Yates. The final piece is a historical document: the murder indictment of Lizzie Borden, who was accused of axing her parents over a hundred years ago.

STARTER PROJECTS: Heroes & Villains

1. **Identifying heroes & villains: Make a list.** Quickly list the traits you associate with heroes. Then make three more brief lists: a list of your favorite heroes or superheroes from TV, movies, and other popular culture; a list of your favorite heroes from history or in the news; and a list of people in your own life who are your personal heroes. Look over your lists. What do the four lists have in common? Where do they diverge? What do the last three lists you made suggest about traits you left off your first list? Now do the same thing for villains.

2. **Being a hero: Write a blurb about your fine self.** Is there anyone who might consider you a hero? Think of things you may have accomplished in your life, such as graduating from high school, maintaining a high GPA, raising a child, or doing something that got you noticed at work. Who might look up to you for these things? For example, a younger sibling or cousin might consider you a hero for having graduated from high school. How does thinking about yourself as someone else's hero change the way you see yourself? Write a two- to three-sentence description of yourself, such as those that celebrate authors on book jackets.

3. **Portrait of a villain: Collect some images.** Do a Google image search for villains in the news and in popular culture, and collect images from magazines and other media that portray bad guys/gals (real or fictional). What patterns do you notice in how villains are portrayed? What does this suggest about American society, attitudes, and prejudices?

ARCHETYPAL VILLAINS

What makes a villain a villain? Sometimes villains stand opposed to the heroes in movies and literature, playing important but often lesser roles, while other times they take a starring role, such as Hannibal Lecter in *The Silence of the Lambs*. This cluster begins with a definition (Dictionary.com) and an illustration of an iconic cartoon villain (Ward). A list of movie heroes and villains includes some of the most evil characters ever to appear on film (American Film Institute). A researched argument by a psychologist and screenwriter criticizes the lack of substance in film villains (Fischoff) and a fiction writer offers advice for how to create the perfect fictional villain (Masterson).

Definitions & Etymology ▼

Dictionary.com

"villain"

What does the word *villain* mean? Where, when, and how was the word first used? The following entries for the word are from Dictionary.com, a site that provides content from authoritative sources such as the *Random House Dictionary*, the *Collins English Dictionary*, and the *Online Etymology Dictionary*. Pay particular attention to the origins of the word. Are you surprised that the word *villain*, first used in the fourteenth century, comes from words that mean farm (or villa) worker? The *Online Etymology Dictionary* indicates that it was a derogatory term used to refer to "base or low-born rustic" working people. What does that suggest about fourteenth-century society? And how does that early meaning align with how we use the word today? *(The following entries are reprinted with permission from Dictionary.com.)*

From the *Random House Dictionary*

| Dictionary | Thesaurus | Word Dynamo | Quotes | Reference | Translator | Spanish |

Dictionary.com | villain | 🔍

vil·lain 🔊 [**vil**-*uh* n] ? Show IPA

noun

1. a cruelly malicious person who is involved in or devoted to wickedness or crime; scoundrel.

2. a character in a play, novel, or the like, who constitutes an important evil agency in the plot.

3. villein.

Origin:
1275–1325; Middle English *vilein, vilain* < Middle French < Late Latin *villānus* a farm servant. See villa, -an

Related forms
sub·vil·lain, *noun*
un·der·vil·lain, *noun*

Can be confused: **villain,** villein.

Synonyms
1. knave, rascal, rapscallion, rogue, scamp.

Dictionary.com Unabridged
Based on the Random House Dictionary, © Random House, Inc. 2013.

" Knave, rascal, rapscallion, rogue, scamp. "

From the *Collins English Dictionary*

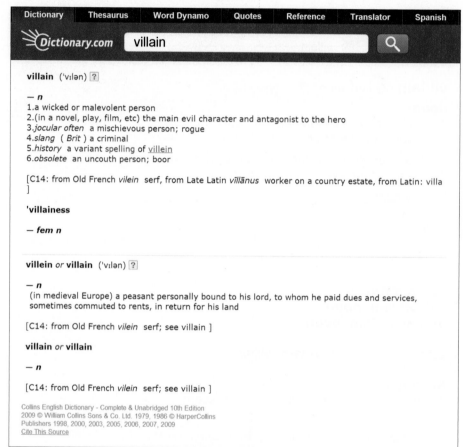

Think about words and their histories. What do those that we assign to people, places, and things have to do with our societal assumptions?

From the *Online Etymology Dictionary*

Cartoon Villain ▼

Jay Ward

Snidely Whiplash

The animated cartoon producer Jay Ward (1920–89, born J. Trop-long Ward) created the character of Snidely Whiplash as the evil enemy of Canadian Mountie Dudley Do-Right for the TV cartoon series *The Rocky and Bullwinkle Show*. Snidely is based on the mustached, black-cloaked, top-hat-wearing stock villains of early melodrama stage plays and silent movies. This stock character is sometimes an evil banker or landlord who isn't very bright, who cheats when he doesn't need to, and who ties women to train tracks if they don't pay or marry him.

▲ ARTIST PHOTO
Jay Ward.

◄ Snidely Whiplash, created by American cartoon animator Jay Ward.

How do other popular images of villains compare to Snidely Whiplash?

List ▼

American Film Institute

100 Heroes & Villains

WEB PAGE ▶
American Film Institute, "History of AFI" page.

ABOUT	TO PRESERVE	TO HONOR	TO EDUCATE	100 YEARS LISTS

History of AFI

ABOUT AFI

BOARD OF TRUSTEES

CONTACT

DIRECTIONS

PRESS

JOBS

LOUIS B. MAYER LIBRARY

AFI THEATER

The American Film Institute was founded in 1967 as a national arts organization to train filmmakers and preserve America's vanishing film heritage. The National Endowment for the Arts and Humanities recommended creating AFI as a nonprofit "to enrich and nurture the art of film in America" with initial funding from the NEA, the Motion Picture Association of America and the Ford Foundation.

"We will create an American Film Institute, bringing together leading artists of the film industry, outstanding educators and young men and women who wish to pursue the 20th century art form as their life's work," said President Lyndon B. Johnson upon signing the legislation that created AFI.

AFI's original 22-member Board of Trustees included Chair Gregory Peck and Vice Chair Sidney Poitier as well as Francis Ford Coppola, Arthur Schlesinger, Jr., Jack Valenti and other representatives from the arts and academia.

In honor of its hundredth anniversary, the American Film Institute published in 2003 a list of the top 100 greatest heroes and villains of film (that is, fifty of each). Topping the list of heroes is the character Atticus Finch (*To Kill a Mockingbird*), a lawyer who defends a wrongly accused black man, setting the example of a moral man amidst his racially intolerant fellow townspeople. Topping the list of villains is Dr. Hannibal Lecter (*The Silence of the Lambs*), a serial killer who has cannibalized his victims and has the power to psychologically manipulate people. *(American Film Institute (AFI) artwork, logo, and text reprinted with permission: Courtesy of American Film Institute.)*

ABOUT **TO PRESERVE** **TO HONOR** **TO EDUCATE** **100 YEARS LISTS**

GOOD AND EVIL RIVAL FOR TOP SPOTS IN AFI's 100 YEARS...100 HEROES & VILLAINS

SELECTION CRITERIA

The jurors were asked to consider the following criteria while making their selections:

- Feature-Length Fiction Film: The film must be in narrative format, typically more than 60 minutes in length.

- American Film: The film must be in the English language with significant creative and/or financial production elements from the United States.

- Hero: For voting purposes, a "hero" was defined as a character(s) who prevails in extreme circumstances and dramatizes a sense of morality, courage and purpose. Though they may be ambiguous or flawed, they often sacrifice themselves to show humanity at its best.

- Villain: For voting purposes, a "villain" was defined as a character(s) whose wickedness of mind, selfishness of character and will to power are sometimes masked by beauty and nobility, while others may rage unmasked. They can be horribly evil or grandiosely funny, but are ultimately tragic.

- Cultural Impact: Characters who have a made a mark on American society in matters of style and substance.

- Legacy: Characters who elicit strong reactions across time, enriching America's film heritage while continuing to inspire contemporary artists and audiences.

> " A 'hero' prevails in extreme circumstances. "

> " A 'villain' is sometimes masked by beauty and nobility. "

How are heroes and villains flawed as characters? What flaws do they share?

AFI.com

| ABOUT | TO PRESERVE | TO HONOR | TO EDUCATE | 100 YEARS LISTS |

#	HEROES	VILLAINS
1	Atticus Finch (in TO KILL A MOCKINGBIRD)	Dr. Hannibal Lecter (in THE SILENCE OF THE LAMBS)
2	Indiana Jones (in RAIDERS OF THE LOST ARK)	Norman Bates (in PSYCHO)
3	James Bond (in DR. NO)	Darth Vader (in THE EMPIRE STRIKES BACK)
4	Rick Blaine (in CASABLANCA)	The Wicked Witch of the West (in THE WIZARD OF OZ)
5	Will Kane (in HIGH NOON)	Nurse Ratched (in ONE FLEW OVER THE CUCKOO'S NEST)
6	Clarice Starling (in THE SILENCE OF THE LAMBS)	Mr. Potter (in IT'S A WONDERFUL LIFE)
7	Rocky Balboa (in ROCKY)	Alex Forrest (in FATAL ATTRACTION)
8	Ellen Ripley (in ALIENS)	Phyllis Dietrichson (in DOUBLE INDEMNITY)
9	George Bailey (in IT'S A WONDERFUL LIFE)	Regan MacNeil (in THE EXORCIST)
10	T. E. Lawrence (in LAWRENCE OF ARABIA)	The Queen (in SNOW WHITE AND THE SEVEN DWARFS)
11	Jefferson Smith (in MR. SMITH GOES TO WASHINGTON)	Michael Corleone (in THE GODFATHER: PART II)
12	Tom Joad (in THE GRAPES OF WRATH)	Alex De Large (in CLOCKWORK ORANGE)
13	Oskar Schindler (in SCHINDLER'S LIST)	HAL 9000 (in 2001: A SPACE ODYSSEY)
14	Han Solo (in STAR WARS)	The Alien (in ALIEN)
15	Norma Rae Webster (in NORMA RAE)	Amon Goeth (in SCHINDLER'S LIST)
16	Shane (in SHANE)	Noah Cross (in CHINATOWN)
17	Harry Callahan (in DIRTY HARRY)	Annie Wilkes (in MISERY)
18	Robin Hood (in THE ADVENTURES OF ROBIN HOOD)	The Shark (in JAWS)
19	Virgil Tibbs (in IN THE HEAT OF THE NIGHT)	Captain Bligh (in MUTINY ON THE BOUNTY)
20	Butch Cassidy & the Sundance Kid (in BUTCH CASSIDY & THE SUNDANCE KID)	Man (in BAMBI)
21	Mahatma Gandhi (in GANDHI)	Mrs. John Iselin (in THE MANCHURIAN CANDIDATE)
22	Spartacus (in SPARTACUS)	Terminator (in THE TERMINATOR)
23	Terry Malloy (in ON THE WATERFRONT)	Eve Harrington (in ALL ABOUT EVE)

24	Thelma Dickerson & Louise Sawyer (in THELMA & LOUISE)	Gordon Gekko (in WALL STREET)
25	Lou Gehrig (in THE PRIDE OF THE YANKEES)	Jack Torrance (in THE SHINING)
26	Superman (in SUPERMAN)	Cody Jarrett (in WHITE HEAT)
27	Bob Woodward & Carl Bernstein (in ALL THE PRESIDENT'S MEN)	Martians (in THE WAR OF THE WORLDS)
28	Juror #8 (in 12 ANGRY MEN)	Max Cady (in CAPE FEAR)
29	General George Patton (in PATTON)	Reverend Harry Powell (in THE NIGHT OF THE HUNTER)
30	Luke Jackson (in COOL HAND LUKE)	Travis Bickle (in TAXI DRIVER)
31	Erin Brockovich (in ERIN BROCKOVICH)	Mrs. Danvers (in REBECCA)
32	Philip Marlowe (in THE BIG SLEEP)	Clyde Barrow & Bonnie Parker (in BONNIE AND CLYDE)
33	Marge Gunderson (in FARGO)	Count Dracula (in DRACULA)
34	Tarzan (in TARZAN THE APE MAN)	Dr. Szell (in MARATHON MAN)
35	Alvin York (in SERGEANT YORK)	J.J. Hunsecker (in SWEET SMELL OF SUCCESS)
36	Rooster Cogburn (in TRUE GRIT)	Frank Booth (in BLUE VELVET)
37	Obi-Wan Kenobi (in STAR WARS)	Harry Lime (in THE THIRD MAN)
38	The Tramp (in CITY LIGHTS)	Caesar Enrico Bandello (in LITTLE CAESAR)
39	Lassie (in LASSIE COME HOME)	Cruella De Vil (in ONE HUNDRED AND ONE DALMATIONS)
40	Frank Serpico (in SERPICO)	Freddy Krueger (in A NIGHTMARE ON ELM STREET)
41	Arthur Chipping (in GOODBYE, MR. CHIPS)	Joan Crawford (in MOMMIE DEAREST)
42	Father Edward (in BOYS TOWN)	Tom Powers (in THE PUBLIC ENEMY)
43	Moses (in THE TEN COMMANDMENTS)	Regina Giddens (in THE LITTLE FOXES)
44	Jimmy "Popeye" Doyle (in THE FRENCH CONNECTION)	Baby Jane Hudson (in WHATEVER HAPPENED TO BABY JANE)
45	Zorro (in THE MARK OF ZORRO)	The Joker (in BATMAN)
46	Batman (in BATMAN)	Hans Gruber (in DIE HARD)
47	Karen Silkwood (in SILKWOOD)	Tony Camonte (in SCARFACE)
48	Terminator (in TERMINATOR 2: JUDGMENT DAY)	Verbal Kint (in THE USUAL SUSPECTS)
49	Andrew Beckett (in PHILADELPHIA)	Auric Goldfinger (in GOLDFINGER)
50	General Maximus Decimus Meridus (in GLADIATOR)	Alonzo Harris (in TRAINING DAY)

Researched Argument ▼

Stuart Fischoff

Villains in Film: Anemic Renderings

Stuart Fischoff is the senior editor of the *Journal of Media Psychology*; an emeritus professor at California State University, Los Angeles; a screenwriter; and a psychology consultant in the film and television industry. His critique of Hollywood villains first appeared in the peer-reviewed academic journal *Popular Culture Review*. Arguing that Hollywood filmmakers misunderstand the essence of the true villain, Fischoff points to many examples of lackluster villains whom he considers bloodless when compared to the higher-caliber villains created by Alfred Hitchcock, for example. Notice Fischoff's use of language and supporting evidence. How does this contribute to his persuasiveness? *("Villains in Film: Anemic Renderings" reprinted by permission of the author, Stuart Fischoff.)*

> *The better the villain, the better the film.*
> —Alfred Hitchcock

Hollywood filmmakers tirelessly opt for portraying villains motivationally no more complex than marionettes. These Punch and Judy villains dance through film after film jerked by a paltry clutch of overworked strings: greed, sadism, or comic book psychoticism. Movie audiences witness woodenheaded villains with substanceless form. They are what they do, moonwalking before us like so many Michael Jacksons growling "I'm bad, I'm bad." Such anemic villainous renderings purvey inaccurate and misguided stereotypes about the mentally ill (Fischoff, 1993) and about the reality of true-life criminals, denizens of dark streets and shadowed citadels of political power.

What is the typical menu of villainous images placed before us when we dine out at a movie theater? A scientist has his face deep-cleaned in a bell jar of acid to the epidermal enthusiasm of his "beauticians" (*Darkman*); a group of street thugs murder a man's wife and gang rape his daughter, giggling and cackling with erotomaniacal joy (*Death Wish*) and in another town, another decade, another sequel, their clones do it again to his maid, this time gleefully killing the man's daughter (*Death Wish II*). Perhaps all this grinning and cackling began with a sadistic Richard Widmark pushing a wheelchair-bound Mildred Dunnock down the stairs in *Kiss of Death*. But, Lord, where will it end? A quick glance at the high-concept summaries of films in production reported by *Daily Variety* suggests not soon.

Hollywood never seems to get the fundamental truth that Alfred Hitchcock so well understood about the audience appeal of ordinary people placed in extraordinary situations battling ordinary-looking antagonists: Not only is villainous character motivation important for making the darker side of reality more comprehensible for film audiences, but it generally makes for superior even memorable storytelling.

Can anyone really remember the villains of *RoboCop I* or *II* or *Die Harder*? No, of course not. They were psychological ciphers wreaking forgettable havoc in forgettable films. But we can all remember Ernest Borgnine's Fatso in *From Here to Eternity*. His was a memorable, disturbing villain because he was drawn from what we all know is real life, the real life of miserable, angry people who have a chance of elevating themselves at the expense of others in a system that is uncaring or too busy to notice.

Can anyone remember the forces of evil in Sylvester Stallone's non-sequeled *Cobra* or the death-mongers in the dreadful Bruce Willis "actioners" *Hudson Hawk* or *The Last Boy Scout*? Of course not. But John Malkovich's multilayered portrayal of the would-be presidential assassin and self-described psychological soul mate of Clint Eastwood's Secret Service agent in *In the Line of Fire* went the dramatically riveting extra mile. Malkovich played an ex-CIA operative, betrayed and targeted by "The Company" and bent on revenge. Malkovich's villain was, for many, the pulse beat of the film.

The simple truth is that what makes a villain interesting is less often what he does than why he does it. Where would *The Maltese Falcon* have been without the Sydney Greenstreets, the Peter Lorres, even the Elisha Cook Jrs.? Did any of these characters giggle maniacally when they committed some villainous act? No. Did they slaughter and slash their way through the story line? No. But, they are memorable villains. They were real, fleshed out, and motivated by something other than evil. Rutger Hauer's android leader in *Blade Runner* and Gene Hackman's Sheriff Little Bill Daggett in *Unforgiven* provide parallel indelibility.

> **"** *What makes a villain interesting is less often what he does than why he does it.* **"**

The Screenwriter's Guide to Villainy

Perhaps we can offer some reminders, some helpful facts to the architects of film villainy in the form of true-life villain verities:

Fact: True-life villains in situ do not giggle and chortle unless they are simultaneously inhaling nitrous oxide.

Fact: True-life villains do not all dabble in drug dealing or hail from South America, South Africa, or South Central L.A. Look at the S&L scandal.

Fact: True-life villains rarely look like Hollywood villains, Charles Manson and Richard Ramirez notwithstanding. Look at Jeffrey Dahmer.

Fact: True-life villains do not spring into action full blown from the head of Zeus. They had parents. They had a life.

Fact: Even villains have down time.

Fact: Villains have reasons for their actions. They rationalize like you and me.

All villainy is motivated. Psychologist Kurt Lewin (1935) provided a simple formula for understanding motivational forces: $B = f(P, E)$; Behavior is a function of Personality factors interacting with Environmental forces. Absent one part of the equation, villainous behavior lacks plausibility; it exists merely because the screenwriter wrote it that way.

Personality Forces

Assuming the environmental forces are in place, to understand the villain's mens rea, the screenwriter's guide to villainy might be viewed from one of two angles.

Angle 1: There but for the grace of God go I.

Almost two thousand years ago, the Roman playwright Terence observed, "I am a man; I consider nothing human alien to me." Given the proper nurturing, we are all capable of anything. To understand others' villainy, therefore, we need only look into ourselves at our weakest, most enraged, or most desperate and vengeful moments.

What differentiates the child-abusing from the non-child-abusing parent, for example? The normal parent restrains himself or herself; the abusive parent doesn't. It's not the angry impulse to "bash the kid" but the power of the inhibitory mechanism that makes the difference. In *Mommie Dearest*, Joan Crawford bashed away. But, we understood why. We understood her twisted values and fears. She is memorable. She is villain.

❝ *All villainy is motivated.* **❞**

In the crudely violent but curiously sensitive and poignant low-budget film *The Stepfather*, the serial murderer's psychotic longing for "the perfect family" touched a chord in the audience of psychotherapists that was invited to screen a prerelease print in Los Angeles several years ago. For the psychotherapists the stepfather cum villain's gruesome reaction to inevitable disappointments in his mythic familial quest was, in milder forms, seen endlessly in so many of their patients. Frustrated children, frustrated parents all bore witness to the anger that springs from so basic a privation. The seeds of the stepfather's villainy were very real to the audience and made an otherwise-repelling film strangely compelling and unforgettable.

Angle 2: Love me, hate me, just don't ignore me.
The other personality force for villainy may be seen in the observation by Erich Fromm (1947) that people want to have an impact on the world, something that, even momentarily, cuts them from the herd and permits them to stand alone to be counted. Fromm noted that if a person cannot create to gain attention—and if he desperately wants attention—he will most certainly destroy. The carousel of rare movies that give us glimpses into the personality infrastructure of pimps (*Street Smart*), ethnic gangs (*American Me*), drug czars (*Scarface*), all trading intimidation and death for fear-based respect and power, typifies what motivational clarity can bring to our understanding of that which both frightens and fascinates us. But for every characterologically rich *Scarface* portrait of drug czars, there are ten texturally impoverished *King of New York* drug czar cartoons.

Villainy is, in essence, behavior inspired by values that are inscrutable, aversive, or repugnant to us in our more civilized moments of reflection. We console ourselves with the thought that villains are twisted aliens. Consequently, what makes a villain truly interesting is to glimpse his or her nonalien, distinctly human rationalization of these values, much as Gordon Gekko's terse philosophizing provided in *Wall Street*. But, was Gekko a villain to Gekko?

Psychologists like Fritz Heider (1958) and Leon Festinger (1957) note that virtually no one baldly agrees that he or she is bad or evil; that he or she is wantonly destructive or rapacious. Inevitably, if only for the sake of sanity or self-concept, villains will justify every mundane or bestial act they execute with something external to themselves. Drunks blame fights on alcohol; muggers blame the establishment or addiction; corporate rapists of the environment blame their stockholders; and Nazis blamed their victims. Good filmmakers help the audience understand the proffered villain's raison d'être.

Alfred Hitchcock permitted us to understand Norman Bates in *Psycho*, which elevated it above later psychopathic slasher films. We understood his torment. We were repulsed and frightened by it, but we understood it. Contrast Norman Bates with Freddy Krueger of *Nightmare on Elm Street* infamy. Freddy is evil. He was evil before he died and evil upon his return. Revenge does not really motivate Freddy; opportunity does; opportunity to further terrorize the innocent for his own amusement. There is nothing to really understand about Freddy Krueger. That, unfortunately, makes Freddy far less interesting than Norman.

> ❝ We understood his torment. We were repulsed and frightened by it, but we understood it. ❞

Robert Louis Stevenson's *The Strange Case of Dr. Jekyll and Mr. Hyde* is classic writing precisely because of the pathos and tragedy of the villain, Hyde. Stevenson's brilliance, in part, came from his appreciating that all humans have a dark, uncivilized side. Ordinarily, we keep such dark impulses under fairly tight rein. But, that control can run amok and explode against others in psychopathologically violent and unpredictable ways.

Like so many instances of multiple personality, Hyde was monstrous because Jekyll was so repressed that he wouldn't or couldn't let out his more selfish needs. When they got out, in Hyde, it was monstrous. But, we understood the war between the selves of Jekyll. Therefore, we were both repulsed and sympathetic to Hyde. Psychologically sensitive adaptations of Stevenson's classic monster such as Victor Fleming's memorable 1941 remake starring Spencer Tracy stressed the emotional turmoil of Jekyll rather than his physical horror and garnered an Oscar for Tracy.

Anne Rice's rendering of Vampire Lestat, if faithfully brought to the screen by director Neil Jordan, would add intellectually nourishing flesh to the bones of so many pale Dracula screen incarnations. Lestat is a villain-monster with motive and self-rationalization.

Considering more realistic but equally mythic villains, what's most fascinating about Francis Ford Coppola's *Godfather* trilogy and the Mafia legend is that the Mafiosi are shown doing such villainous deeds, yet at the same time, they are shown as capable of being loving parents and grandparents, committed to certain values. We see them not as true sociopaths but as people conforming to the norms of their narrow society. They do things for reasons, for honor, for ego. But, they're not "crazy" psychopathic killers all. How can normal people live such abnormal lives? we wonder with fascination. Surely, they must be crazy . . . in some way!

Yet, according to Gordon Allport (1954), when batteries of projective and objective psychological tests were done on Nazi officers after the war, searching for truly pathological clinical profiles to explain their horrifying and brutal treatment of concentration camp victims, not much turned up. They didn't reveal the expected pathological profiles. How can that be?

The answer may lie in the other critical element of Lewin's equation—the environment.

Environmental Forces

The tiresome popularity of vicious gangs as villains in so many of today's films serves as a good lesson in motivationally dumb characters. Like other villainous retreads, our movie street gang members are violent tautologies, vicious because they are vicious. But, following Lewin's formula, we see a different confluence of determinants. A gang member (P) behaves like a normal young man when with his family ($E1$). His ongoing anger and resentment, fueled by oppression, poverty, racism—and who knows what—are contained, suppressed, or even overpowered by family values, sentiments, and the sheer presence of family. But, when he is in a group of his gang buddies ($E2$), the group postures, ventilates, activates, and accentuates rage and deadly machismo. The boys get in a car, drive to another turf. Our gang member shoots (B) rivals with righteous bloodlust.

So, the gang member's villainy potential is something he carries with him, part of his personality. But, it is only ventilated given the proper environmental encouragement, a point incisively made in Machiavelli's *The Prince* and portrayed with stunning clarity in William Golding's *Lord of the Flies*. (Drive-by shootings, it should be noted, are almost never executed by single gang members.) Martin Scorsese's *Goodfellas* and Robert De Niro's *A Bronx Tale* illustrate the seminal impact of an environment that propagates antisocial or aggressive values and behavior.

Villain Creations in Film Environments

As Sam Keen has shown in his book and documentary film *Faces of the Enemy* (1986), propaganda films from all countries contrive to show forces of good triumphing over forces of evil in many gruesome and sordid ways. Our treatment of the Japanese in war propaganda films was to set them up as vermin and then eradicate them. "How many Japs have you killed today?" was the "voice-over" in many such propaganda films. Nazi propaganda films compared Jews to rats and then showed them being exterminated. For Germans then, the villains were the Jews. For Jews, the villains were the Germans. Their respective cultural environments and reinforcement histories taught them these "truths."

Stuart Fischoff, *Villains in Film: Anemic Renderings*   711

Villain Creations in Psychological Laboratories

Phil Zimbardo's well-publicized prison study (1973) dramatically demonstrated that merely role-playing power or powerlessness in a mock prison environment converted well-functioning young men into authentic victims and villains in less than a week. Stanley Milgram's (1965) famous study of getting experimental volunteers to administer potentially lethal doses of shock to other ostensible volunteers argues the same point.

Both Zimbardo and Milgram's studies and Keen's look at propaganda films show how villainy is determined often less by personality forces than by environmental forces. Walter Mischel (1973) has persuasively argued that a strong environment can overwhelm a weak personality. And weak personalities are the most easily seduced by power that can even temporarily elevate them above others; they are the most easily seduced into the nightmare of brutality and authoritarian domination. With such power, a meek, traveling salesman for an oil company became the dreaded Adolf Eichmann.

Conclusions

Villainy is not worn on the face; it's crypted in the mind and heart. Al Pacino's portrayal of Michael Corleone in *The Godfather* saga was a virtual case study of descent into moral darkness. We watched with fascination the interplay of life forces slowly redefining the rules of Michael's life, tilting his precariously balanced morality in the corrupted direction Lord Acton* so deftly prophesied.

But, rarely are we treated to insightful filmmaking. Most Hollywood villains are mere devices to impel heroism or encourage audiences to root for their dispatch in the inevitable Armageddon in the film's closing moments. For example, to allow viewers only to hate the South Africans, our latest screen villains in this post-Soviet era (*Lethal Weapon II, A Dry White Season*), is a creatively wasteful enterprise. Audiences should understand why many Afrikaners don't want to give in and give up their system to the black majority. Audiences should also be led to understand why many Palestinians turn to violence to advance their cause instead of depicting them as dimensionless, Jihad-obsessed terrorists spouting nothing but mindless rhetoric. Without learning that screen villains are self-justifying humans,

> ❝ Most Hollywood villains are mere devices to impel heroism or encourage audiences to root for their dispatch. ❞

---

*The "prophesy" referred to here is Lord Acton's statement: "Power tends to corrupt, and absolute power corrupts absolutely."—Eds.

audiences leave the theater hating more and understanding less about the world in which they live.

To understand the motivations of others is a fundamental step toward self-understanding, as an individual or as a nation. As film increasingly becomes the literature of modern society and, along with television, the primary agent of socialization, the entertainment media become more crucial in the formation of stereotypes and explanations of life that define a culture. Shakespeare understood the dramaturgical power of a complex villain. He rendered villains whom we understand and remember—even cherish—as surely as we remember our heroes. We draw upon their portraits when we travel the landscapes of our personal lives. Iago taught us the cancerous danger of jealousy, Richard III, the evil that springs from self-loathing. Shakespeare remembered and Hollywood should never forget: Rarely do people or governments leap into villainous tyranny; they proceed one tragic, one rationalizing and self-righteous step at a time.

> Do you agree with Fischoff's argument that Hollywood heroes are flat characters created to "impel heroism"? Why or why not?

References

Allport, G. (1954). *The nature of prejudice.* New York, NY: Addison-Wesley.

Festinger, F. (1957). *A theory of cognitive dissonance.* Stanford: Stanford University Press.

Fischoff, S. (1993). A reel take on mental illness. *The Journal of the California Alliance for the Mentally Ill, 4*(1), 11–14.

Fromm, E. (1957). *Man for himself.* New York, NY: Rinehart.

Heider, F. (1958). *The psychology of interpersonal relations.* New York, NY: Wiley.

Keen, S. (1986). *Faces of the enemy.* New York, NY: Harper & Row.

Lewin, K. (1935). *A dynamic theory of personality: Selected papers.* New York, NY: McGraw-Hill.

Milgram, S. (1965). Some conditions of obedience and disobedience to authority. *Human Relations 18*(1), 57–76.

Mischel, W. (1973). Toward a cognitive social learning reconceptualization of personality. *Psychological Review 80*(4), 252–83.

Zimbardo, P., Haney, C., & Banks, C. (1973, April 8). A pirandellian prison. *The New York Times Magazine,* 38–60.

Brief Essay ▼

Lee Masterson

Creating Villains People Love to Hate

In her advice for fiction writers, Lee Masterson emphasizes that a villain needs to be as complex as a story's hero; villains, she says, must be "real, three-dimensional people." Masterson is a freelance fiction writer who has also published numerous articles and several books on writing, and an editor at *Fiction Factor*, the magazine in which the following reading first appeared. *("Creating Villains People Love to Hate" is reprinted with permission: © Lee Masterson.)*

Creating Villains People Love to Hate
by Lee Masterson

Every story has to have a bad guy. There wouldn't be much conflict for your protagonist to overcome if there was no antagonist to stir the pot.

Yours might be the evil villain who opposes everything your hero (or heroine) does. He might be the treacherous double agent from the past, or the psychotic evil scientist, or maybe just the "other woman" fighting for your hero's attention.

Whoever your villain is, making sure he is believable is far more difficult than simply creating a character who does bad things to hold up your protagonist's progress.

Your job here is to make your villains credible, logical, and believable, but not likable. You want the reader to understand what they're doing that is such a negative thing for your hero.

But it's more involved than just explaining their adverse actions. Your readers need to understand why the antagonist is doing what he does, and why he believes his actions are justified and rational.

Basically, you need your villains to be real, three-dimensional people.

Unfortunately most "bad guys" are shown as being shallow, narrow-minded creatures whose only ambition is to be as evil as possible. This approach to an antagonist loses the respect of your reader for two reasons:

1. You lose any emotional impact your story has if your readers cannot completely believe the threat to your hero is real, or threatening enough. It also lowers the reader's esteem for the hero, who they know can only beat this unthreatening villain.

2. A completely evil character equates to a totally weak character to a reader. If your villain's only motivation is evil, this does not give him enough depth of character to become real in your reader's mind. Giving your bad guy only one driving motivator is not enough—especially if you choose a lightweight surface motivator like "evil" or "greed."

Think about when you created your protagonist. Most likely you created someone you admired, a character with strength and integrity. I'm guessing you took the time to get right inside your hero's head and understand what made him tick.

Your villain is no different.

In order for your antagonist to be considered a worthy opponent, you must portray him honestly. You must be able to get inside his head, too, and learn what drives him to act the way he does.

Remember here that no one sees himself as mean or evil or bitchy or insane or stupid. Your villain won't either. To him, his actions and his logic are perfectly justifiable.

> " No one sees himself as mean or evil or bitchy or insane or stupid. Your villain won't either. "

Show your readers this side of your villain's logic and you intensify your story's suspense factor. Show that your antagonist is quite capable of winning the battle and make sure that it seems as though the outcome of your plot is uncertain.

That uncertainty doubles your suspense again, and gives you the perfect opportunity to showcase your hero's qualities as well, thus creating a stronger protagonist just by displaying the comparisons.

Put more simply, your villain has to be good about being a bad guy, but this forces your hero to be even better.

Which "bad guys" in books, comics, or film are your favorites? Why?

Your readers will be turning page after page to find out if your hero is actually good enough to overcome the monster you forced him to care about, in a twisted kind of way. Remember *The Silence of the Lambs*?

If you can actively portray your villain from his own point of view as being an intelligent, logical, complex creature with the capacity to be understanding and reasonable, who does what he does because his reasons are sound to him, then you are on your way to creating a pretty believable villain.

But when you can also show your villain's complex, devious, misguided nature from your hero's point of view, you know you've created a truly memorable bad guy, and you will have strengthened your protagonist's character and your plotline at the same time.

Archetypal Villains

1. Definitions & etymology. How does the etymology of the word *villain* connect to the present definition of the word? Are you surprised by the word's origins? Why?

2. Cartoon villain. In what ways does Jay Ward's cartoon visual of a villain reflect the dictionary definition (or not)?

3. List. Are you more familiar with the heroes or the villains on the American Film Institute's list? Are there film heroes or villains that you think should have made this list? Who are they?

4. Researched argument. According to Stuart Fischoff, what makes a well-developed film villain? Do you agree? Why or why not?

5. Brief essay. Do you think there are points Lee Masterson has left out of her instructions for creating villains? Are the instructions detailed enough to follow? If not, what revision suggestions would you make to Masterson?

6. Researched argument & brief essay. How do Masterson's points about creating villains in literature relate to Fischoff's critique of Hollywood villains?

7. Create a villainous recipe. You have been assigned the task of creating a recipe based on a film or literary villain for a cookbook titled *Villainous Delights*. Before writing your recipe, review some sample recipes to see how they are formatted. Then think of a villain that would be fitting for a recipe: maybe an apple pie for the Queen in *Snow White*, or Turkish delight for the White Witch in *The Lion, the Witch, and the Wardrobe*.

8. Review a film villain. Choose one of the fifty film villains on the American Film Institute's list. Watch the film, considering whether you would argue that the villain is an "anemic rendering" or a villain that Hollywood got right, according to Fischoff's principles. Then write an essay making your claim, integrating points from Fischoff's article to support your stance.

9. Create an illustrated dictionary entry. Using the definitions and etymology for the word *villain* as your starting point, look for photos and cartoons that could be used to illustrate each definition/etymology. Then create a visual dictionary in which each definition/etymology appears with an accompanying visual that illustrates it. Alternatively, create a matching pair of posters that makes a film hero look like a villain and a villain look like a hero.

10. Write a short-short story. Using Masterson's advice, create a short story that has a believable villain as a central character.

11. Write a complaint letter. After reviewing the American Film Institute's list of heroes and villains, think of a hero or villain that should be added to the list. Then write a letter to the AFI arguing for that hero or villain to be included. Make sure to include specific examples to help your case.

HEROES: FAMOUS & OBSCURE

A public hero is a figure who changes the world for the better, in a public and far-reaching way. This group of readings touches on a figure of the civil rights movement (King) and moves to very current public heroes: the young feminist activist Malala Yousafzai and the first professional basketball player to come out as gay, NBA player Jason Collins. This group of readings also focuses on everyday people who exemplify heroism. The posters promoting women factory workers, firefighters, and clinical trial participants, along with an editorial on New York City's working class, offer perspectives on what it means to conduct yourself like a hero in daily life—doing your best work and looking out for others. And in the spirit of the *Onion* parody of an office worker, you might even have a laugh about everyday-hero-ness.

Photo ⏷

Getty Images

Martin Luther King Jr.

This photo captures Dr. Martin Luther King Jr. after he delivered his "I Have a Dream" speech in Washington, D.C., on August 28, 1963. The occasion was the March on Washington for Jobs and Freedom, a civil rights event that called for an end to racial discrimination. In his speech, King expressed his hope: "I have a dream that one day this nation will rise up and live out the true meaning of its creed:

'We hold these truths to be self-evident, that all men are created equal.'" While there were many photographs taken that day, this one was taken by an unidentified photographer, and provided to us by Getty Images from their database of images (gettyimages.com).

Joseph Campbell wrote: "A hero is someone who has given his or her life to something bigger than oneself." For Campbell, the civil rights leader Martin Luther King Jr. (1929–68) embodied this ideal. King once said: "A man who won't die for something is not fit to live." *(Image by permission of AFP/Getty Images.)*

Getty Images, *Martin Luther King Jr.*

Photo ▼

Bilawal Arbab

Malala Yousafzai on Time *Magazine*

**How does Malala's
story connect with
the archetypal
hero's journey
(discussed in this
chapter by Bryan
Davis and Joseph
Campbell)?**

Malala Yousafzai (b. 1997) is a Pakistani student and activist for
girls' education. In October 2012, while traveling through the
Swat Valley on a bus on the way to school, she was shot in the
head by a Taliban member. After receiving medical treatment in
Britain, she recovered enough to return to school and to make appearances around the world to promote girls' rights to education.
Yousafzai, usually referred to by her first name only, has also been
nominated for the Nobel Peace Prize. She has blogged for the BBC
and communicates through social media, where she promotes
her campaign for children's right to schooling. She was featured
on the cover of *Time* magazine on April 18, 2013 and in a profile
in that issue by Chelsea Clinton, who wrote that Malala seems to
accept the "unasked-for responsibility as a synonym for courage
and champion for girls everywhere." Malala has said: "I don't mind
if I have to sit on the floor at school. All I want is an education. And
I'm afraid of no one."

The photo that follows was taken by photojournalist Bilawal Arbab,
whose work is distributed through the European Press Photo
Agency (epa) and Corbis. Arbab took the photo on April 23, 2013,
in Peshawar, Pakistan. Following is the original caption that accompanied the image.

> "A copy of *Time* magazine at a newsstand with the cover photo of a
> Pakistani girl, Malala Yousafzai, who was shot and injured by Taliban
> militants in Swat valley, in Peshawar [the capital of] Khyber Pakhtunkhwa
> province. . . . Malala Yousafzai emerged in the list of 100 most influential
> people in *Time magazine*. Malala was attacked by Taliban on October 9,
> 2012 for advocating girls' rights to education and [was] wounded along
> with two schoolmates. After initial treatment, she was sent to Britain
> where she is recovering." *(Image Reprinted by permission. © BILAWAL
> ARBAB/epa/Corbis.)*

Bilawal Arbab, *Malala Yousafzai* on Time *Magazine*

Photo ▼

Rick Friedman

Jason Collins at Boston Pride

Jason Collins has played in the NBA for eleven years, most recently for the Boston Celtics and the Washington Wizards, at center position. He wears jersey number 98, in honor of Matthew Shepard, who was killed in 1998 because he was gay. Before turning pro, Collins played for Stanford University, where he also studied alongside Chelsea Clinton. In April, 2013, Collins wrote an article for *Sports Illustrated* (sportsillustrated.cnn.com), in which he announced he is gay. He is the first professional basketball player to do so.

He wrote:

> I'm a 34 year old NBA center. I'm black. And I'm gay. I didn't set out to be the first openly gay athlete playing in a major American team sport. But since I am, I'm happy to start the conversation. . . .

I've endured years of misery and gone to enormous lengths to live a lie. I was certain that my world would fall apart if anyone knew. And yet when I acknowledged my sexuality I felt whole for the first time. I still had the same sense of humor, I still had the same mannerisms, and my friends still had my back.

This photo was taken by Rick Friedman, a Boston-based photojournalist whose work has appeared in major publications including *The New York Times*, *Time* and *Newsweek* magazines, and *The Guardian*. In this image, Jason Collins marches in the Boston Pride Parade in 2013 with his former college roommate, Congressman Joseph Kennedy III. *(Image © Rick Friedman/rickfriedman.com/Corbis.)*

❝ *I'm a 34 year old NBA center. I'm black. And I'm gay.* ❞

Parody Article ▼

The Onion

Only Guy Who Puts Paper in Copier Considers Himself a Hero

The Onion is a Web site and weekly newspaper that parodies newspapers. Founded in 1988 by two students at the University of Wisconsin, *The Onion* satirizes real news events and also presents fictional news events as if they were real. The writers create pieces that mimic the genres of real newspapers and news outlets, such as the news article, feature story, editorial, advice column, and "man on the street" interview. The following article, billed as a "human-interest story," pokes fun at the overeagerness of Americans and the media to assign the label "hero," taking aim at the local news "everyday hero" trope. (The Onion *artwork and text: Reprinted with permission of* The Onion. *Copyright © 2013 by Onion, Inc. www.theonion.com.)*

⌀ the ONION®
America's Finest News Source

VIDEO · POLITICS · SPORTS · BUSINESS · SCIENCE/TECH

Only Guy Who Puts Paper In Copier Considers Himself A Hero

BOSTON—You may not know him by name, but Eric Greeley is one of a new breed of Americans making a difference. While most employees at John Hancock Security and Financial Services just use the photocopier and walk away, Greeley considers it his duty to do the right thing: to make sure the machine is stocked and ready to go at a moment's notice.

Greeley doesn't ask for recognition, and he doesn't get it.

Though he'd never say it himself, that's just what a hero does.

"I like to think that anyone in my position would do the same thing," said Greeley. "In the end, it's such a small sacrifice for a far greater good. All you have to do is go get the paper, pop out the input tray, fill it to exactly the right level, and slide the tray carefully back in. I'm doing my part to make the world a little better, one ream at a time."

Greeley's philosophy is that a good deed is its own reward, and it seems to be paying off for the whole office: His refilling actions have single-handedly increased his department's productivity by an estimated 2.6 minutes a week.

"Is it glamorous?" Greeley asked. "No. But doing the right thing never is."

Greeley began his career inauspiciously enough in customer service in 2002, and eventually worked his way up to sales assistant in the Term Life Insurance department last year. His attention to detail was cited in his promotion, but conspicuously absent was any mention of his work with the copy machine. This omission did not seem to bother him in the least. Greeley's not in it for the glory.

"Sometimes I'll stock it up even if it's not empty," Greeley said. "Let's say it's half full. Well, nine or 10 decent-sized jobs can knock that right out, so I really have to stay on my toes, be prepared for anything. You can't wait for trouble to come to you."

Greeley doesn't ask to be thanked, saying that "the sight of a coworker receiving his or her copies smoothly and efficiently is thanks enough."

While most would stop at merely filling the copy machine, he goes above and beyond. On the frequent occasion that a coworker leaves an original document on the copier, Greeley will track down the owner. While some people might take the opportunity to deliver a lecture about being more responsible with potentially sensitive company documents, Greeley simply leaves it on the owner's desk with a Post-It note saying, "You forgot this."

"I don't have to be told what needs to be done," Greeley noted. "It's like a fireman—or a Medal Of Honor winner. They just do it. They don't ask for recognition, and neither do I."

Thankfully, Greeley is not alone. Across the country, unsung office heroes march through each workday without recognition or fanfare. Alice Gamin, an accounts executive in Utica, N.Y., has been silently changing the toner cartridge in the laser printer for three years without once receiving a thank-you. George Carlyle, a New Orleans advertising rep, consistently hangs notes on toilets that are out of order, never signing his own name.

"I have some vacation time coming up soon, but I'm thinking I might not take it," Greeley said. "I wouldn't want anyone else in the office to have to do what I do. I can't expect that from them."

Despite the tremendous sacrifice, Greeley's efforts are not discussed widely among his coworkers.

"So Eric is the one that refills the copier?" asked receptionist Frieda Bailey. "Is Eric the cleaning guy?"

It's attitudes like this that make Greeley's efforts an uphill battle. But don't call them quixotic. Greeley eventually hopes that through his tireless efforts putting single-bond paper in the copy machine, a ripple effect might occur, so that he, like the guy who always makes the fresh pot of coffee, will someday find themselves in good company.

Heroes come in all shapes and sizes, and yes, you can count Eric Greeley among them. ∅

❝ Unsung office heroes march through each workday without recognition or fanfare. ❞

Poster ▼

Westinghouse's War Production Co-ordinating Committee

We Can Do It

The poster on page 726 was created to represent American women who worked in munitions factories during World War II (1941–45). Before this time, jobs considered appropriate for women were fairly limited in number, and women were restricted to secretarial positions or teaching jobs. With so many men fighting in Asia or Europe, however, there was a serious need for women to work to make sure the country could continue producing materials needed for war. Posters such as this one, as well as the famous "Rosie the Riveter" image created by artist Norman Rockwell, were meant to encourage women to work, and to view that work as patriotic and heroic. This poster, commissioned by Westinghouse and created by the artist J. Howard Miller, was intended to boost the productivity of women laborers in the Midwest. The poster later reemerged in the 1980s when it was adopted as a symbol for feminism and women's empowerment.

Poster ▼

Jaguar Educational

I Am a Firefighter

The following poster is part of the "Everybody Is Somebody" vocational
education poster series created by Jaguar Educational. Other posters in the series include "I Am a Chef," "I Am a Scientist," "I Am a
Musician," "I Am a Mechanic," and "I Am a Computer Programmer."
All the posters feature a child wearing an adult-sized uniform or outfit
associated with the named career and the child's testimonial about
why he or she wants to pursue that career. The posters are intended to
motivate elementary school children and are marketed to elementary
school teachers and counselors as well as families that homeschool
their children. *(The "I Am a Firefighter" poster is reprinted with permission: Courtesy
of Jaguar Educational.)*

The poster reads: "I AM A FIREFIGHTER. I want to stay physically
fit, serve my community and be where the action is. It's not easy
being a firefighter, but I like a challenge. Helping keep people safe
is one of the most important things anyone can do. If I work hard
and follow my dream, someday I'll be able to save lives. **I have the
power to be somebody!**"

> ❝ *If I work hard and follow my dream,
> someday I'll be able to save lives.* ❞

Poster ▼

Center for Information & Study on Clinical Research Participation

Medical Heroes Can Be Found in Everyday Places

A stated goal of the Center for Information and Study on Clinical Research Participation (CISCRP) is to provide information to people who are thinking of participating in clinical research trials. The CISCRP "Medical Heroes" poster campaign was designed to emphasize the role that "everyday people" take in the development of new medicines and treatments by volunteering to be a part of a research program. This poster was produced in collaboration with the Food and Drug Administration and the U.S. Department of Health and Human Services. *(The following poster appears courtesy of CISCRP.)*

Medical heroes can be found in everyday places

Editorial

Joshua Freeman

Working-Class Heroes

Joshua Freeman suggests that New York's working class was largely invisible before the attacks of September 11, but because of the important role they played in the rescue efforts, New York's workers became not just more visible, but more appreciated. Freeman is a history professor specializing in labor history at the City University of New York. This article first appeared on October 25, 2001, a few weeks after the attacks, on *The Nation*'s Web site. (The Nation *artwork and "Working-Class Heroes" by Joshua Freeman: Reprinted with permission from the November 12, 2001 issue of* The Nation. *For subscription information, call 1-800-333-8536. Portions of each week's* Nation *magazine can be accessed at http://www.thenation.com.*)

THE Nation.

HOME | BLOGS | COLUMNISTS | CURRENT ISSUE | MAGAZINE ARCHIVE | MULTIMEDIA | E-BOOKS

POLITICS | WORLD | BOOKS & ARTS | ECONOMY | ENVIRONMENT | ACTIVISM | SOCIETY | LIVED HISTORY

Working-Class Heroes

Joshua Freeman

The September 11 attack on the World Trade Center led journalists and image-makers to rediscover New York's working class. In an extraordinary essay in *BusinessWeek* titled "Real Masters of the Universe," Bruce Nussbaum noted that during the rescue effort, "big, beefy working-class guys became heroes once again, replacing the telegenic financial analysts and techno-billionaires who once had held the nation in thrall." Nussbaum fulsomely praised "men and women making 40 grand a year . . . risking their own lives—to save investment bankers and traders making 10 times that amount." In *The New York Times Magazine*,

Verlyn Klinkenborg, describing the construction workers who formed the second wave of rescuers, wrote, "A city of unsoiled and unroughened hands has learned to love a class of laborers it once tried hard not to notice."

Until September 11, working-class New Yorkers had disappeared from public portrayals and mental maps of Gotham. This contrasted sharply with the more distant past. When World War II ended, New York was palpably a working-class city. Within easy walking distance of what we now call ground zero were myriad sites of blue-collar labor, from a cigarette factory on Water Street to hundreds of small printing firms, to docks where longshoremen unloaded products from around the world, to commodity markets where not only was the ownership of goods like coffee exchanged, but the products themselves were stored and processed.

> " Workers and their families helped pattern the fabric of the city with their culture, style, and worldview. "

Much of what made post–World War II New York great came from the influence of its working class. Workers and their families helped pattern the fabric of the city with their culture, style, and worldview. Through political and ethnic organizations, tenant and neighborhood associations, and, above all, unions they helped create a social-democratic polity unique in the country in its ambition and achievements. New York City became a laboratory for a social urbanism committed to an expansive welfare state, racial equality, and popular access to culture and education.

Over time, though, the influence and social presence of working-class New Yorkers faded, as manufacturing jobs disappeared, suburbanization dispersed city residents, and anti-Communism made the language of class unacceptable. Then came the fiscal crisis of the 1970s, which saw a rapid shift of power to the corporate and banking elite. When the city recovered, with an economy and culture ever more skewed toward a narrow but enormously profitable financial sector, working-class New York seemed bleached out by the white light of new money.

> " Not only were the rescuers working class, but so were most of the victims. "

The September 11 attack and the response to it have once again made working-class New Yorkers visible and appreciated. Not only were the rescuers working class, but so were most of the victims. They were part of a working class that has changed since 1945, becoming more diverse in occupation, race, and ethnicity. Killed that day, along with the fire, police, and emergency medical workers, were accountants, clerks, secretaries, restaurant employees, janitors, security guards, and electricians. Many financial firm victims, far from being mega-rich, were young traders and technicians, the grunts of the world capital markets.

The newfound appreciation of working-class New York creates an opening for insisting that decisions about rebuilding the city involve all social sectors. Whatever else it was, the World Trade Center was not a complex that grew out of a democratic city-planning process. We need to do better this time. Labor and community groups must be full partners in deciding what should be built and where, how precious public funds are allocated, and what kinds of jobs—and job standards—are promoted. Some already have begun pushing for inclusion; others should begin doing so now.

What is the class composition of your town or city? How has it changed over time? How does it compare to what Freeman says about New York City?

In the coming weeks and months, we need to rethink the economic development strategies of the past half century, which benefited many New Yorkers but did not serve others well. Might some of the recovery money be better spent on infrastructure support for local manufacturing, rather than on new office towers in lower Manhattan? And perhaps some should go to human capital investment, in schools, public health, and much-needed housing, creating a workforce and environment that would attract and sustain a variety of economic enterprises.

We need to rethink the economic strategies which benefited many New Yorkers but did not serve others well.

Winning even a modest voice for working-class New Yorkers in the reconstruction process won't be easy. Already, political and business leaders have called for appointing a rebuilding authority, empowered to circumvent zoning and environmental regulations and normal controls over public spending. The effect would be to deny ordinary citizens any role in shaping the city of the future. As the shameful airline bailout—which allocated no money to laid-off workers—so clearly demonstrated, inside operators with money and connections have the advantage in moments of confusion and urgency.

But altered perceptions of New York may change the usual calculus. On September 11, working-class New Yorkers were the heroes and the victims, giving them a strong moral claim on planning the future. Rightfully, they had that claim on September 10, too, even if few in power acknowledged it. It ought not require mass death to remind us who forms the majority of the city's population and who keeps it functioning, day after day after day.

Heroes: Famous & Obscure

ANALYZING RHETORICAL SITUATIONS

1. Photo (King). How does the photo of Martin Luther King Jr. emphasize the notion of a hero?

2. Photo (Malala). How does Chelsea Clinton characterize Malala Yousafzia? What do you find most compelling about Malala's story?

3. Photo (Collins). Why did Jason Collins choose to reveal to the public that he is gay? How and why does this make him a hero?

4. Parody article. *The Onion* is known for its satirical commentary. How does the article on the office hero meet the definition of satire? Can you find elements of satire or irony in the Freeman editorial? What similarities and differences do you see between the hero in the *Onion* article and the heroes in the Freeman editorial?

5. Posters. How does the fact that the "We Can Do It" poster does not portray a woman actually working, but rather flexing her bicep, affect how you read it?

Compare this poster to the "Medical Heroes" image. To what extent do these images correspond to or contrast with feminine beauty ideals? To what extent do these images correspond to society's ideas of women's strength and abilities?

6. Poster. In the poster headlined "I Am a Firefighter," what is the effect of the message in the headline in relation to the message of the smaller text and the photo of the boy who doesn't fill out his uniform? Considering the multiple audiences for this poster (teachers, parents, and children), why might the creators of this poster have made these choices?

7. Editorial. Joshua Freeman argues that "[t]he September 11 attack and the response to it have once again made working-class New Yorkers visible and appreciated." How does he support his claim?

Heroes: Famous & Obscure

8. Create a civil rights photo essay. Research the civil rights movement of the 1950s and 1960s. Find pictures of people and events that display heroic actions. Create an annotated photo gallery that conveys the idea of heroism and history.

9. Research women's and girls' rights & create an illustrated timeline. Research the history of women's and girls' rights in Pakistan (where Malala is from) or elsewhere, including the United States. What significant events were setbacks for women's and girls' rights? Which events were important turning points? Note these on a timeline where you also present images of each event accompanied by a brief written description and analysis.

10. Interview a basketball player about gay rights. Using the Jason Collins story as a springboard, investigate attitudes held by sports players and/or fans at your school. Why do they think it has taken so long for an NBA player to come out as gay? How do they think an openly gay player (or players) will affect the culture within the NBA? The culture surrounding the NBA? Share your findings in a presentation to your class.

11. Satirize a "non-hero." Write a satirical article modeled after the *Onion* piece, focusing on another instance of an unlikely hero.

12. Create an illustrated timeline. In 2007, singer Christina Aguilera made a video for her song "Candyman" in which she appeared as the character por-

trayed in the "We Can Do It" poster. Research other contemporary references to this iconic image. How has its presentation morphed over time, and for what purposes? Research the images and place them along a timeline. Provide contextual information and analysis of the cultural moment for each version of the figure.

13. Write a letter to fight sexism. Imagine you are the parent of a girl who wants to be a firefighter. You come across the "I Am a Firefighter" poster and are annoyed that firefighting seems to be presented only as an option for boys. Write a letter to the editor of your local paper that calls for a more inclusive vision of firefighters.

14. Research the Guardian Angels. Go to the Guardian Angels Web site (http://www.guardianangels.org) and research how they "keep it safe." In what ways can the activities the organization sponsors and encourages be seen as heroic? How do the conceptions of heroism of CISCRP and the Guardian Angels differ, and how do they overlap?

15. Create a researched slide show. Practitioners of medicine are often considered heroic. Similarly, survivors of diseases such as cancer and AIDS are often viewed as heroic. Research a high-profile cancer survivor, such as Elizabeth Edwards, or a high-profile HIV-positive person, such as Greg Louganis. Compose a slide presentation in which you explore the heroic qualities of whomever you researched.

RESEARCH EXPERIMENTS: Heroes & Villains

1. **Map a hero's (or antihero's) adventure.** Joseph Campbell's theory of the Hero's Cycle is typically applied to mythical heroes, such as Luke Skywalker and Han Solo in *Star Wars*. Trace the adventure of a real-life hero (or antihero), such as a professional athlete, a historical figure (such as Elizabeth Cady Stanton, a nineteenth-century women's rights activist), or a pioneer (such as Sonia Sotomayor, the first Hispanic Supreme Court justice).

   a. Research your hero or antihero's life to identify the challenges they've had to overcome, their "call to adventure," their mentors, allies, and enemies, etc. As you conduct your research, consider

   - Is the time or place of the person's birth a challenge he or she had to overcome?

   - What kinds of social or economic factors did he or she have to struggle against?

   - Were there specific family members, teachers, colleagues, or friends who became mentors, allies, or enemies?

   - Are there particular events or moments that seem to be "turning points" for him or her?

   b. As you research, you may want to organize your hero's journey in stages that are parallel to those that Campbell uses. You can find a list of the stages of the Hero's Journey[*] here: www.thewritersjourney.com/hero%27s_journey.htm. You may decide to use the same terms Campbell does, or you may want to critique his approach and work with your own variation of the hero's journey.

   c. Once you identify the events and relationships that you think are key to your hero or antihero's adventure, create a visual representation of the hero or antihero's adventure to share with your classmates. You might decide to create an annotated Google map, a time line, Facebook page that reflects the journey and people involved, or something else. Be sure to give credit to the sources you've used.

2. **Weigh the evidence & bulid a court case.** Sometimes a person's status as a hero or villain is called into question. For example, despite being acquitted of murdering her parents with an axe, Lizzie Borden is still widely considered guilty of the gruesome crime. On the flip side, recent research has caused many to change their opinion of Giovanni Palatucci, long considered the "Italian Schindler," from that of hero to villain.

---

[*] The list referred to is from *The Writer's Journey* site (thewritersjourney.com), edited by Brad Schreiber and Chris Vogler.

a. For this assignment, examine the record of someone—individual, organization, or company—whose status as hero or villain is controversial, such as NSA leaker Edward Snowden, the Fiji bottled water company, or Christopher Columbus. As you research, consider

- Who believes the individual, organization, or company is a hero and why?

- Who believes the individual, organization, or company is a villain and why?

- What are some of the mysteries or questions surrounding the actions of this individual, organization, or company that make it difficult to pin them down as a hero or villain?

- How reliable is the information about this individual, organization, or company?

b. After you've conducted your research, weigh the evidence and decide how you would categorize the individual, organization, or company. Then, write a "friend of the court" type brief in which you present your findings and argue your case to a hypothetical panel of judges.

Index of Genres

[e] For e-Pages content, visit **bedfordstmartins.com/bookofgenres**.

Wiki Entries

Index of Themes

[e] For e-Pages content, visit **bedfordstmartins.com/bookofgenres**.

e For e-Pages content, visit **bedfordstmartins.com/bookofgenres**.

🄴 For e-Pages content, visit **bedfordstmartins.com/bookofgenres.**

🄴 For e-Pages content, visit **bedfordstmartins.com/bookofgenres.**

🄴 For e-Pages content, visit **bedfordstmartins.com/bookofgenres.**

History

🄴 For e-Pages content, visit **bedfordstmartins.com/bookofgenres.**

e For e-Pages content, visit **bedfordstmartins.com/bookofgenres**.

e For e-Pages content, visit **bedfordstmartins.com/bookofgenres.**

e For e-Pages content, visit **bedfordstmartins.com/bookofgenres**.

Popular Culture

Protest, Civil Liberties, Social Justice

Race

---

e For e-Pages content, visit **bedfordstmartins.com/bookofgenres.**

---

e For e-Pages content, visit **bedfordstmartins.com/bookofgenres**.

Work, Job Search, Business

Index

🄴 For e-Pages content, visit **bedfordstmartins.com/bookofgenres.**

🄴 For e-Pages content, visit **bedfordstmartins.com/bookofgenres.**

 For e-Pages content, visit **bedfordstmartins.com/bookofgenres**.

Guitar, Sheet Music, and Glass (Picasso), 245–46, 251

H

I

[e] For e-Pages content, visit **bedfordstmartins.com/bookofgenres.**

ⓔ For e-Pages content, visit **bedfordstmartins.com/bookofgenres**.

🅴 For e-Pages content, visit **bedfordstmartins.com/bookofgenres**.

🅔 For e-Pages content, visit **bedfordstmartins.com/bookofgenres.**

🄴 For e-Pages content, visit **bedfordstmartins.com/bookofgenres.**

ᵉ For e-Pages content, visit **bedfordstmartins.com/bookofgenres.**

🅴 For e-Pages content, visit **bedfordstmartins.com/bookofgenres**.

Missing something? To access the online material that accompanies this text, visit **bedfordstmartins.com/bookofgenres**. Students who do not buy a new book can purchase access at this site.

Inside the Bedford Integrated Media for *The Bedford Book of Genres*

ⓔ Guided Readings

These texts, annotated by the authors of this book, highlight the rhetorical situations and genre-related choices that composers make. Each is introduced with guidelines for analysis and followed by questions and checklists for drafting.

FAIRY TALE Charles Perrault, *Little Red Riding Hood*

SHORT STORY Annie Proulx, *55 Miles to the Gas Pump*

DRAMATIC FILM George A. Romero & John A. Russo, *From Night of the Living Dead*

MAP Chris Peterson, *BurgerMap: Alaska, Kriner's Diner*

DOCUMENTARY FILM Doug Pray, *From Scratch*

BUSINESS MEMO Ellen Thibault, *Video Project*

PRESENTATION Sunni Brown, *The Doodle Revolution*

PERSONAL STATEMENT "Stay-at-Home Dad"/TopLawSchools .com, *Personal Statement for Penn Law School*

COVER LETTER & RESUME Julia Nollen, *Application for Marketing Assistant Job*

FILM REVIEW Roger Ebert, *Ratatouille: Waiter, There's a Rat in My Soup*

ⓔ Thematic Readings

These texts highlight the relationships between themes and genres, and serve as sources and models for student work.

American Identity

EDITORIAL Matthew Yglesias, *The Myth of Majority-Minority America*

SOCIAL HISTORY Ted Merwin, *What Makes the Jewish Deli Quintessentially American*

POSTER/AD CAMPAIGN Homeless Coalition of Hillsborough County, *Not Who You Expected? Shameya, Age 18; Jeff, Age 44*

Subculture Identity

WIKI ENTRY/INSTRUCTIONS eHow, *How to Become a Geek*

INTERVIEW Deborah Solomon, *Patti Smith: She Is a Punk Rocker*

Bodies 101

POEM Walt Whitman, *From "I Sing the Body Electric"*

INSTRUCTIONS University of Washington School of Medicine, *Cardiopulmonary Resuscitation (CPR)*

MEDICAL HISTORY Dr. John G. Sotos, *The Health and Medical History of President Ronald Reagan*

Cigarettes, Drugs, & Alcohol

SPOOF AD *Adbusters* Magazine, *Joe Chemo*

PORTFOLIO OF ADS Stanford School of Medicine (curators), *Vintage Cigarette Ads*

MAP & CHART John Hoffman & Susan Froemke, *Addiction Is a National Concern; Drugs and Alcohol at a Glance*

Pollution & Activism

ARTICLE Leyla Kokmen, *Environmental Justice for All*

SPEECH Barack Obama, *The BP Oil Spill*

BILLBOARD Environmental Defense Fund, *The Traffic Is Killing Me*

COMPLAINT LETTER Credo Action, *Tell the Bureau of Land Management: Ban Fracking on Federal Lands*

Plastics, Recycling, & Wildlife

OBJECT/AD Surfrider Foundation, *Catch of the Day: Plastic Surprise*

AD Oceana, *Love Flipper and His Friends?*

BROCHURE Casella Resource Solutions, *Zero-Sort: How Recycling Gets Done*

COMIC & PIE CHART Environmental Protection Agency, *From Adventures of the Garbage Gremlin; Municipal Solid Waste Chart*

Mythical Heroes

SLIDE PRESENTATION Bryan M. Davis, *Archetypes and the Hero's Journey*

MAP Prestwick House Maps, *The Journey of Odysseus*

INTERVIEW Joseph Campbell, *The Hero's Adventure*

ARGUMENT/BLOG POST Lex at FANgirl, *The Heroine's Journey: How Campbell's Model Doesn't Fit*

Serial Killers & Murderous Moms

RESEARCHED REPORT Federal Bureau of Investigation, *Common Myths and Misconceptions Regarding Serial Murder*

ARGUMENT David Von Drehle, *It's All about Him*

PROFILES Charles Montaldo, *Profiles of Jeffrey Dahmer and Andrea Yates*

MURDER INDICTMENT Commonwealth of Massachusetts, *Lizzie Borden*